This Book may be kept

FOURTEEN DAYS

Please notice the last date below. A fine of 2 CENTS will be charged for each day the book is kept after that date.

9/20 10/2	✓		
De 2 '35			
S 17 31			
APR 8 '59			
APR 29 '59			
DEC 10 '59			
NOV 30 '60			
SEP 17 '66			
OCT 29 '66			
DEC 15 '67			
FEB. 8 1990			

A SHORT HISTORY

OF THE

ENGLISH COLONIES IN AMERICA

BY

HENRY CABOT LODGE

AUTHOR OF

"THE LIFE AND LETTERS OF GEORGE CABOT" "THE LIFE OF ALEXANDER HAMILTON"
"THE LIFE OF DANIEL WEBSTER" "STUDIES IN HISTORY" ETC.

REVISED EDITION

NEW YORK AND LONDON:
HARPER & BROTHERS, PUBLISHERS,

A–R

TO

HENRY ADAMS

IN TOKEN OF GRATITUDE AND FRIENDSHIP

THIS HISTORY IS DEDICATED

H. C. L.

PREFACE.

THE history of the thirteen American colonies is at best fragmentary and provincial, and does not assume the importance and value of the history of a nation until the meeting of the Stamp Act Congress at New York in the year 1765. But who and what the people were who fought the war for Independence and founded the United States—what was their life, what their habits, thoughts, and manners—seemed to me, when I began my study of American history, questions of the deepest interest. They were questions, too, which appeared to me never to have been answered in a compact and comprehensive form; and this volume is an attempt to supply the deficiency. The chapters, therefore, which purport to describe the various colonies in and about the year 1765 represent the purpose of the book. They have been worked out, in the course of several years, from a mass of material which has been collected in all directions, and which, although wholly in print, is in many cases as generally unknown as if it still slumbered in manuscript. To these chapters I have appended notes — mere references — partly to support conclusions which I thought might be questioned, and partly to aid other students in the same field. The notes represent, however, only a portion of the books, tracts, and newspapers actually consulted. There are many titles in my note-books of works which yielded nothing, and of others again which offered matter that had to be laid aside from mere superabundance of material: only the most valuable and important figure in the notes.

When I had finished these chapters for which the work was

undertaken, and which have been in part delivered in the form of lectures before the Lowell Institute of Boston, I felt that it was essential to my purpose to give an outline of the political history of each colony, in order to present a complete picture of the various communities. These sketches are as condensed as I could make them, although they have run to a far greater length than I hoped would be necessary. They make absolutely no pretence to original research, but are merely my own presentation of facts which ought to be familiar to every one. For this reason I have thought it entirely superfluous to encumber them with notes.

The question of arrangement was not an easy one where thirteen distinct histories were involved; but, after much reflection, I decided to deal with each colony by itself, and give its complete history down to the year 1765. This plan is open to the charge of repetition; but it seemed to me better than flitting from one colony to another, and thus distracting the reader's attention more than was absolutely necessary. The three concluding chapters are added, like those which treat of the political history of each colony, merely for the sake of completeness, and aim only to be a concise outline of the events which resulted in national existence.

Many of the statistical details are, as I am only too well aware, very dry reading, and the same may be said of the political history of some of the colonies. It may be possible to make the political history of every colony in turn picturesque and exciting; but I know that in regard to certain of them, and in many portions of my history which could not be omitted, this was a task far beyond my powers. Yet at the same time I cannot but feel that the condition of the people of the American colonies in the years preceding the Revolution, however insufficiently I may have dealt with it, is a subject of deep interest and importance. I can only say that if anything I have written is of assistance to students, or helps any one to a better understanding of a nation and of a history of which we may be rightly proud, I shall feel more than repaid.

HENRY CABOT LODGE.

EAST POINT, NAHANT, 1881.

CONTENTS.

HISTORY

OF THE

ENGLISH COLONIES IN AMERICA.

CHAPTER I.

VIRGINIA FROM 1606 TO 1765.

WHEN independence was declared, Virginia stood at the head of
the English colonies in America. She was the most important politically, as she was the oldest and the most populous of the provinces.
Virginia was, moreover, the leader and representative of one of the
three great political groups which formed the thirteen colonies, and,
as such, she played a leading, and for many years a controlling, part
in the history of the United States.

The colonial history of Virginia may be divided into three periods.
The first extends from 1607–1617, and is occupied with the mere
struggle for existence. The second is a period of political and material development, covering about sixty years. The third and longest
lasted for a century—from 1677 to the outbreak of the Revolution—
and was a time of material growth and political torpor. In the last
two periods the colony closely resembled the mother country, not only
in social habits but in history. England rested after the terrible conflicts of the seventeenth century, and so did Virginia. If Walpole
could boast that during his administration England had no history,
the same remark applies with tenfold force to Virginia; for the political repose of the parent state became stagnation in the colony. But
the forces destined to convulse the world before the eighteenth century closed were even then gathering strength, and the political energies which made America foremost in that great movement were re-
cuperated during these years of slothful inaction.

1

The earliest incidents in Virginian history and in the English colonization of America carry us back to the glories of the Elizabethan era, to the days of Marlowe and Shakspeare, of Burleigh and Walsingham, of Essex and Leicester, and Francis Bacon. In that great period, the most conspicuous representative of a large class, and the typical man of action, was Walter Raleigh, whose name is inseparably connected with the first efforts of English colonization in America. There is no need to dwell upon the ill-fated attempts to found a settlement on Roanoke Island. Raleigh's first expedition was sent out in 1584, and for many subsequent years he persevered fruitlessly in his purpose of establishing a colony. These repeated failures present merely the common picture of the ill-planned, ill-managed, and disastrous endeavors of individuals in the sixteenth century to colonize the New World. Raleigh lavished money and thought upon his schemes; but he had undertaken a task beyond his strength, or that of any one man at a time when the art of colonization was unknown, and its difficulties scarcely imagined. The name Virginia bestowed upon the new colony in honor of Elizabeth is the only lasting memorial of Raleigh in America. To later times and to a new State has been reserved the privilege of naming a city for the great adventurer.

1584.

These repeated disasters did not, however, cool the zeal or diminish the confidence of those Englishmen who were interested in discovery and were the friends of colonization. Fresh voyages kindled fresh hopes. The successful cruise of Captain Gosnold, his prosperous winter in New England, and his discovery of a short northern passage, produced much excitement in London, and greatly encouraged all interested in such projects, while the fortunate voyage and favorable report of Weymouth a few years later seem to have had a decisive effect. In the following year, on the petition of certain " firm and hearty lovers " of colonization, James I. chartered two companies (the London and Plymouth) and bestowed upon them in equal portions the vast territory included in twelve degrees of latitude, and stretching from Cape Fear to Halifax. This charter and the subsequent instructions are worthy of the intelligence of the first Stuart. They are long, verbose documents, are of little historical value, and have no intrinsic merit of any kind. By virtue of them a complicated form of government was framed. For each colony separate councils, appointed by the King, were instituted in England, and these councils were in turn to name resident councillors for the colonies. Thirteen members constituted the resident council. They had

1602.

1606.

power to choose their own president, to fill vacancies in their numbers, and, a jury being required only in capital cases, to act as a court of last resort in all other causes. Religion was established in accordance with the forms and doctrines of the Church of England. The adventurers, as the members of the Company were called, had power to coin money and collect a revenue for twenty-one years from all vessels trading to their ports, and they were also freed from taxation for a term of years. One article alone, and only in the most general terms, provides for the liberty of the subject, as follows: "Who (ever) shall dwell and inhabit within every and any of said several colonies and plantations, and every of their children * * * shall have and enjoy all liberties, franchises, and immunities, within any of our other dominions, to all intents and purposes as if they had been abiding and born within this our realm of England." The good faith of this clause in the charter is somewhat shaken by the open disregard of all English rights in the instructions; but the principle contained in this provision, though little noticed in 1606, became of vital interest in 1774. The arguments of statesmen and parliaments, of patriots and colonial assemblies, turn upon the existence of this principle of citizenship and freedom conceded by James with the elaborate stupidity by which, in the same paper, he evolved a system calculated to make his colonists little more than slaves. Another clause in the instructions, as important as it was wrong and injurious, provided for community of goods.

A more awkward scheme could hardly have been devised. An arbitrary and irresponsible council in America, another almost equally so in England, the legislative powers reserved to the King, the governing body a commercial monopoly, and the chief principle of society community of property, together formed one of the most ingeniously bad systems for the government of men which could be devised. To the first settlers this frame of government and a sealed box containing the names of the resident council were confided. The men who composed the expedition cared but little for forms of government. They were imbued with the popular notions in regard to the New World. "I tell thee," says Seagull, in Marston's play of "Eastward Ho!" written in 1605, "golde is more plentifull there than copper is with us; and for as much redde copper as I can bring, I'll have thrise the weight in golde. Why, man, all their dripping-pans are pure golde, and all the chaines with which they chaine up their streets are massive golde; all the prisoners they take are fettered in golde; and for rubies and diamonds, they goes forth in holy dayes and gather

'hem by the sea-shore, to hang on their children's coates and stick in
their children's caps, as commonly as our children wear saffron-gilt
brooches and groates with holes in them." The life in the new country was to be one of ease and luxury, abounding in everything good
to eat and drink; and last, though not least, Seagull says, "There we
shall have no more law than conscience, and not too much of eyther."
This was the picture of the dramatist, and was unquestionably in its
essence the theory of the first colonists. The wild anticipations of
the gold-hunter, the spirit of the conquerors of Mexico and Peru filled
the breasts and inspired the hearts of the men who embarked with
Captain Newport late in 1606, and who were destined to lay the foundation of a great English state in the New World.

Among the leaders of the expedition were Gosnold, the voyager and
discoverer, and a prime mover in the affair; Wingfield, one of the
first-named patentees, John Smith, Ratcliffe, Martin, Kendall, and
Percy. Of these men John Smith has become famous. He has taken
a place among the founders of states, and a romantic interest has attached itself to his name. For centuries his character and deeds have
been applauded, while in late years they have become a theme for
censure and detraction. Modern investigation has relentlessly swept
away the romance, and torn in pieces many of the long accepted narratives in which Smith recorded his own achievements. Yet it was
not wholly by a false and fluent pen that Smith obtained and held
his reputation. He was something more than a plausible writer of
fiction. He was the strongest and most representative man among
the Virginian colonists. He was an adventurer of a high order in
an age of adventurers, and with all the faults of his time and class
in full measure, he had also their virtues, and it was here that he
surpassed his companions. Smith was arbitrary, jealous of power,
quarrelsome, and despotic, ready to lie audaciously to serve his own
ends, and rashly over-confident. But he was also brave, energetic,
quick-witted, and full of resource. Bewitched, no doubt, by the same
visions as his companions, and far more imaginative than any of them,
he alone of all his little company had the power of recognizing existing facts, and dealing with them as he found them. To buoyant hope
and sanguine belief in the unknown, so characteristic of the period,
Smith united the qualities of a leader, and some capacity for the
practical administration of the colony. The other principal men were
not of marked ability, and were, for the most part, of very indifferent
character. Percy united to a noble name honor, courage, and good

intentions. Gosnold had been a successful discoverer, and appears also to have been an honest and sensible man. Wingfield was, with the exception of Percy, the most important personage in point of wealth and social position, and had served for many years in the European wars, but he proved incapable of governing. The remaining leaders, and the great mass of their followers as well, were adventurers of a low type. London was swarming with such characters, who had been left idle by the cessation of the Spanish wars, and who now thronged the capital restless and dissatisfied, eager for fresh scenes in new worlds, and thirsting for the old life of freebooting and discovery. Smith concisely catalogues them as "poor gentlemen, tradesmen, serving-men, and libertines." They were certainly wretched material for the founders of a state, especially as the "poor gentlemen" were to the tradesmen and mechanics in the ratio of five to one.

With this hopeful company Newport left the Downs on the 1st of January, 1607. The worthy Richard Hakluyt sent them a **1607.** paper containing much good advice and some ingenious geographical speculations, and Drayton celebrated their departure in clumsy verses filled with high-flown compliments. The advice of the priest and the praise of the poet were alike wasted. By an arrangement ingeniously contrived to promote discord, devised probably by royal sagacity, the box containing the names of the council was not to be opened until the voyagers reached their destination. Dissension broke out almost immediately. Whatever the merits of the differences, this much is certain, that Smith was the object of the concentrated jealousy and hatred of his companions. He probably invented the story of the erection of a pair of gallows for him at the island of Mevis, "which he could not be persuaded to use;" but there is no doubt of the fact that he alone of those nominated was excluded from a seat in the council on their arrival in Virginia. His superior abilities, his arbitrary temper, and probable self-assertion, sufficiently account for this attack; but he was not long depressed by the reverse, and obtained his office within a month after the landing.

On the 13th of May, 1607, the settlers landed at Jamestown, sent out exploring parties, and began fortifications. A fortnight later, under the command of Wingfield, they repulsed an attack by the Indians; and on the 22d of June Newport sailed for England, and left them to their own resources. The prospect must have been a dreary one: nothing answered to their expectations. Instead of valuable mines, the adventurers found only a most fertile soil; instead of timid, trusting South American Indians, they encountered wild tribes of hardy, crafty, and hostile savages; instead of rich, defenceless, and barbarian cities, an easy and splendid spoil, they found a wilderness, and the necessity of hard work. From the miserable character of the settlers, dangerous factions prevailed from the first, until Smith obtained control, and maintained some sort of order—despotically, perhaps, but still effectually.

No one would work, and famine and the Indians preyed upon them mercilessly. A small fort and a few wretched huts, built after much quarrelling, represented for many months all that was accomplished. The only relief from this dark picture of incompetent men perishing, without achievement, and by their own folly, on the threshold of a great undertaking, is to be found in the conduct of Smith. Despite almost insurmountable obstacles, Smith kept the colony together for two years. He drilled the soldiers, compelled labor, repaired the fort, traded with the Indians, outwitted them and kept their friendship, and made long and daring voyages of discovery. He failed to send home a lump of gold, but he did send an excellent map of the Company's territory. He did not discover the passage to the South Sea, but he explored the great bays and rivers of Virginia. He did not find Raleigh's lost colonists, but he managed to keep his own from total destruction. The great result of all Smith's efforts was the character of permanency he gave to the settlement. Because he succeeded in maintaining an English colony for two consecutive years in America, the London Company had courage to proceed; and this is what constitutes Smith's strongest claim to the admiration and gratitude of posterity. To suppose that he had the qualities of a founder of a state is a mistake, although in some measure he did the work of one. Neither Smith's character nor the nature of his ambition fitted him for such a task; but he was a quick-witted and intelligent man, who understood, or soon discovered, the necessary conditions of successful colonization. With a strong hand, therefore, he repressed the wretched malice and ignorant folly which had ruined previous settlements; and when his opportunities and his companions are considered, it is matter for profound astonishment that Smith should have succeeded as he did. His veracity as a historian in the later years of his life has been well-nigh destroyed. But little faith can be placed in the "Generall Historie," and modern investigation has conclusively relegated to the region of legend and of fiction the dramatic story of Smith's rescue by Pocahontas. The shadow of doubt rests upon all his unsupported statements; but nothing can obscure his great services, to which the world owes the foundation of the first English colony in America. Yet, after all his struggles, Smith was severely blamed by the Company, apparently because Virginia was not Peru. In a manly letter he sets forth the defects of the colony, the need of good men with families, industrious tradesmen and farmers, not "poor gentlemen and libertines." Before, however, the actual orders came to supersede him, Smith resigned, or was forced out of the government, and returned to England. The feeble life of the colony wasted fast after his departure and during the sickness of Percy, who succeeded to the command. Matters, indeed, came to such a pass that the settlement, even after the coming of Gates and **1610.** Somers with part of the fleet, was actually abandoned, when Lord Delaware arrived as Governor and Captain-general with fresh men and supplies.

Misfortune had stimulated the London Company to fresh exertions; their charter had been extended, and powers reserved in the old one to the King were now given to the Company, which thus became thoroughly democratic in its organization. Prejudice against the colonists on account of their ill-success, and rumors that the half-starved wretches intended to parcel out Virginia, then including a large part of North America, among themselves, caused the Company, acting under the new charter, to deprive the settlers of such poor liberties as they already possessed. The Governor was in future to exercise uncontrolled authority, and he was empowered to rule, if he saw fit, by a code of martial law used in the Low Countries.

Lord Delaware, the first Governor under the new system, held office but a short time. He came surrounded by the pomp of the Old World, with a train of liveried servants, whose gorgeous dresses must have had a strange effect in the dark Virginian forests. The ostentation of his administration, which was, on the whole, a beneficial one, and the splendor of his train, show the profound ignorance of the time in regard to the necessities and conditions of colonization. Lord Delaware was soon succeeded in office by Sir Thomas Dale, to whom Virginia is more indebted than to any of her early governors. Dale administered his government in accordance with the martial code prepared for use at the Governor's discretion. By these severe and salutary laws he curbed the refractory temper of his worthless subjects, and was for five years the ruling spirit of the colony, although Gates was for a time at the head of affairs. During this period the Company improved and increased the emigration, but the advance was chiefly due to their Governor in Virginia. Taking advantage of the marriage of Pocahontas, Dale continued and strengthened his successful Indian treaties, while at the same time he extended the settlements and kept them in order. But that which did most credit to his wisdom and good sense was his initiation of a reform in the manner of holding property. He provided for the introduction of individual proprietorship, and by thus breaking down the wretched communal system imposed upon the colonists, he laid the foundations of future strength and prosperity. Dale found the colony struggling for a doubtful existence, and left it firmly established. The first period in Virginian history was terminated by this strong and wise administration.

George Yeardley, the deputy, carried on the government after Sir **1616-** Thomas Dale's departure, but was soon superseded by Samuel **1617.** Argall, who obtained the office of governor through the influence of the Court faction in the Company. Argall was a sea-captain of piratical tastes, who had been conspicuous during Dale's administration for the abduction of Pocahontas, for pillaging and burning the huts of the French fishermen in Acadia, and, as has been alleged, for bullying the Dutch traders on Manhattan. As might have been expected from his career, Argall was an active, energetic, unscrupulous man, who, placed at the head of a government administered in accordance with a military code, carried it on in the spirit of a buccaneer, and was tyrannical and extortionate. He stimulated the energy which had flagged somewhat under the mild rule of Yeardley; but he did what under the circumstances was still better, he oppressed the colonists and robbed them of their property, his especial vengeance and greed lighting on the friends of Lord Delaware. Complaints soon found their way to England. The Virginians had now awakened to the fact that they were shockingly misgoverned; that they were left at the mercy of one man's will; that their rights were unknown, and that they had no protection against the tyranny of such rufflers as Argall. The period of political development had begun.

Argall carried his oppression too far. Reports of his misrule circulating in England almost stopped emigration at a very critical period in the life of the colony. Moreover, Argall had chosen his time badly. The patriot party, who were beginning to make the London Company for Virginia a school for education in free government, found that the governorship of their colony had been stolen, and the enterprise almost ruined by the Court minority. The grievances of the Virginians obtained, therefore, a ready hearing from men upon whom the hand of majesty had already begun to press.

The fortunes of the little American settlement were caught and swept along in the political current then just beginning to run **1618.** strongly in England. The indignation aroused in London by Argall's misconduct led to the instant defeat of the Court party. Sir Edwin Sandys replaced Sir Thomas Smith as treasurer, and was in turn succeeded by another liberal, the Earl of Southampton. A mercantile company is at best a wretched sovereign; but Virginia was fortunate in falling into the hands of men who at that moment cared more for liberal principles than for anything else. The opposition was all-powerful in the Company, and they made it a battle-ground with the King. They were at last defeated; but in the mean time they conferred on Virginia a representative government, and taught the colonists the lesson of successful resistance. Thus the great political forces at work in England gave Virginia free institutions through the strange medium of a commercial monopoly. Sandys, Southampton, Digges, Selden, and the rest, using the London Company as a political engine, not only governed Virginia wisely, but, to further other ends, gave her political opportunities from which she reaped lasting benefit.

Not content with the recall of Argall, and with despatching first Lord Delaware, who died on the voyage, and then Yeardley in his stead, the Company granted a new form of political organization to the colonists. The Governor's power was in future to be limited by a council, and the assemblage of a representative body was authorized. Yeardley and the colonists immediately concurred in this measure, and the House of Burgesses met in June, 1619. **1619.** Almost their first act was to exclude the burgesses from Martin's hundred, because, by the terms of their patent, they were exempted from obedience to the laws of the colony. The burgesses prayed the Company that the clause in the charter guaranteeing equal laws might not be violated, and the maintenance of the great English principle of the equality of all men before the law dignifies the first meeting of the first representative body of America. The session was mainly occupied with the passage of sumptuary laws and police regulations. Appropriate statutes provided for the government of the clergy, and a tax on tobacco was laid for their support. The legislation of these men was as unimportant as it could well be in its general character, yet it contained the germ of that jealous resistance to the mother country and all things proceeding thence which indel-ibly marks American colonial history. Dale's firm government had imparted stability to the infant State, while Argall's galling tyranny had stimulated the latent political life. Political habits, although laid aside with difficulty, are easily resumed by all the English race. Even in this feeble Virginian settlement, among this handful of men scattered along the outskirts of the wilderness, the same spirit existed which was at that very moment making itself felt in England. Ma-terial prosperity had begun, and political development was close be-hind. With Dale's administration closes the first period in Virginian history. A year of bad government ensues, and with the meeting of the Burgesses the second stage is reached. The parasitic existence is at an end, and the colony begins to have interests and a life of its own. This year, so marked in Virginian annals by the dawn of rep-resentative government and constitutional freedom, is made still fur-ther memorable by the arrival of the first slaves in America. The landing of this ill-omened freight was probably due to the open-ing of the Virginian ports to free-trade by the London Company, al-though they may have been a legacy of Argall's piratical rule. The year was also marked by much immigration of very varied excellence. A large proportion of the immigration at this time consisted of boys and girls seized by press-gangs in the streets of London, and shipped as if they were felons condemned to transportation; yet through every difficulty growth and progress could be perceived.

When Virginia held her first Assembly, twenty-two Burgesses, rep-resenting eleven boroughs, composed that body. A few hundred sturdy, liberty-loving Englishmen, bearing up against unexampled hardships, living the rudest and most exposed lives, and striving for sudden fortune by tobacco-growing, constituted the great State of Vir-ginia in 1619. But the prospects of future success opened by the wealth which tobacco seemed to insure served to rapidly build up the colony. Immigration increased and improved. The "prudent men with families" whom Smith had sighed for began to come. The rapid growth of the colony in numbers, wealth, and commercial importance is shown by the increase of the population from six hundred to four thousand within a year after the first Assembly, and by orders in council prohibiting free-trade. So firmly was the colony established during Yeardley's administration, that the Indian outbreak, in which more than three hundred persons perished, did not destroy the settle-ments. This attack occurred in the second year of the administration

of Sir Francis Wyatt, who, when he came to Virginia as Yeardley's
1622. successor, brought a new constitution granted by the Company to their colonists. Not only were the former immunities and franchises confirmed, but definite provision was made for the regular assemblage of the representative body. This further astonishing act of generosity and wisdom on the part of a commercial monopoly was due to no efforts of the colonists. They had gone so far as to complain of Argall, and to humbly petition against unjust and unequal patents, but they had not yet thought of demanding formal securities for their rights. The permission to hold an assembly was everything to men who had only dared to hope for the recall of an obnoxious governor; but to have a regular frame of constitutional government conferred upon them by the voluntary action of the Company was something they had never even dreamed of, and their good fortune was due to far more powerful agencies than their own discontents.

The rising opposition to James and to prerogative, in favor of liberty, indicated the growth of the great movement which brought the next Stuart to the block, and the London Company for Virginia has obtained lasting fame as the first ground occupied by the patriot party in England. Under the democratic constitution of the adventurers, freedom of debate and love of independence were fostered. James, ever jealous of any invasion, real or fancied, of his prerogative, attempted interference at an early day; but the intrepid Company opposed him, and set at naught his claim to nominate their officers. James denounced the Company as "a seminary for a seditious Parliament," and said he would rather they should choose the devil as treasurer than Sir Edwin Sandys. So high did the contest run that Chamberlain, writing to Sir Dudley Carleton, says: "The factions in these two companies are grown so violent, as Guelfs and Ghibellines were not more animated one against another; and they seldom meet upon the Exchange or in the streets, but they brabble and quarrel."

From this struggle and the feelings it excited, the colonists obtained solid advantages, but the doom of the Company was sealed. James pursued them unrelentingly, the "great massacre" coming at a moment to fan discontent and encourage his schemes. Royal commissioners were thereupon sent to Virginia to gather materials for the destruction of the Company. The Virginians, however, stood by their friends. The commissioners, without producing their credentials, demanded the records of the Assembly. The Assembly declined to comply. The commissioners bribed the clerk of the House to give up the records, and the Assembly stood their clerk in the pillory and cut off his ear. But all this patriotic resistance was fruitless on the part of colonists and adventurers alike; the former learned their first lesson in resisting the royal power, and the Company lost its charter. A *quo warranto* was tried in the King's Bench, and the charters annulled. The "London" Company and the intrigues which gave it importance and led to its dissolution concern us only in their immediate connection with Virginia. In obedience to their own sentiments, and in conformity with their most cherished principles, the London adventurers endowed Virginia with free institutions, but their overthrow was none the less a distinct benefit to the colony. It not only relieved the settlers from the cumbrous, complicated, and uncertain government of a mercantile corporation, but it placed them in the same direct relation with their King as his other subjects.

Sir Francis Wyatt was continued in his office after the dissolution **1624-** of the charter, and again when Charles I. came to the throne. **1625.** Soon after the latter event he resigned the government to Yeardley, and sailed for England. The five years of Wyatt's administration are memorable for their legislative activity, for the formation of political habits, and for the first opposition to the home government which strengthened and confirmed the independent spirit of the colonists. The session of 1623–'24, the year the royal commissioners came to Virginia for assistance in ruining the Company, is marked in the Statute-book by the definition and declaration of certain guiding political principles which were never after shaken. The most important were the limitations on the Governor's power; he was not "to lay any taxes or impositions upon the colony, their lands, or other way than by the authority of the General Assembly, to be levied and employed as said Assembly shall appoint." The Governor was not to withdraw the inhabitants from their labors for his own service, and Burgesses attending the Assembly were to be privileged from arrest. These were the same great and fundamental principles for which patriotic men were then contending in England. Virginia learned and applied the best theories of English constitutional government with wonderful aptitude.

In this same session, besides a number of private acts and police regulations, monthly courts, to be held by commissioners appointed by the Governor, the commander of the place being *ex officio* of the quorum, were established in some of the more distant boroughs. One law passed at this time curiously illustrates how thoroughly English the Virginians were in the recognition of social position, and how the whole state of society was destined to be a reproduction on a small scale and in a new country of that which the colonists had left. It was enacted, "that such persons of quality as shall be found delinquent in their duties, being not fitt to undergoe corporal punishment, may notwithstanding be ymprisoned at the discretion of the commander." This delicacy in dealing with well-born malefactors shows that, though these early settlers had a hearty love of political liberty and the enforcement of law, they were by no means the sturdy young republicans they are sometimes represented. They were true Englishmen, wedded to the traditions, prejudices, and social habits of their native land.

When Charles succeeded his father he continued Wyatt, and made no mention of the liberties and franchises enjoyed by the settlers; for it probably did not occur to him that such persons needed representative government. That he discountenanced the former "popular course," is probable from the break in the meetings of the Assembly which seems to have occurred at this time. But although Virginia was a feeble colony, she produced a valuable staple. Charles wanted money, was determined to engross the profits on tobacco, and really cared very little how the men who raised the tobacco were governed. His sore need of money led him into a recognition of the Assembly. With that body he carried on his dealings, and King and burgesses haggled over their bargains with right good-will. The burgesses declined to accede to the proposed royal monopoly, although they offered Charles good terms. Meantime Wyatt departed for Ireland, and on the death of his successor the Council chose Francis West as governor, and subsequently John Pott. The latter was soon superseded by a royal **1629.** governor, Sir John Harvey, a commissioner of the King at the time of the dissolution of the Company, and between whom and the Virginians there was but little good-will. He quickly filled up the measure of unpopularity by assuming the power of granting unpatented lands, and the turbulent quarrels which ensued between governor and people show merely the former's despotic spirit and desire of encroaching upon the powers of the Assembly, and the rather ill-regulated love of liberty which then characterized the Virginians. These quarrels proved in the end to have been well timed. From complaints, the colonists soon proceeded to more active measures, and "thrust Harvey out of the government." He went to England, and laid his complaints before the King. Charles was in **1635-1636.** no mood to tolerate opposition, and reinstated the obnoxious Governor, who continued in office three years longer, followed by the bitter hatred of the colonists. But Charles was getting deeper and deeper into difficulties, which rendered harsh treatment of his colonies most unprofitable and inexpedient. He gradually relaxed his policy, and in 1639 reappointed Sir Francis Wyatt to the government of Virginia.

There were during the period of Harvey's administration two events of great importance. One was the first intercourse with another colony, that which settled Maryland in 1632 under the auspices of Lord Baltimore; the other was the rise of the Puritan party in Virginia. The former was the main cause of Harvey's trouble. Harvey was well disposed toward the new-comers, and treated them with fairness and consideration, while the Virginians swallowed their indignation at what they deemed a dismemberment of their territory, and received Calvert's colonists kindly enough. But this good-nature was of short duration. Quarrels about jurisdiction broke out almost immediately, and Harvey and the Marylanders alike suffered. Clayborne's petty wars with the Calverts excited the sympathy of Virginia, but, so far as she was concerned, repay no one's study. They served in a harsh way to accustom the Virginians to neighbors, and taught them their first lesson of forbearance for the sake of mutual advantage. The rise of the Puritans had a much more immediate and marked effect upon the fortunes of Virginia. The appearance of Puritans and Puritan principles was due to a small immigration of that class many years before, and to the increasing distrust of royalty bred by the condition of the times. Virginia had been settled before the beginning of the struggle which afterward rent England asunder, and, more strongly attached to the Established Church than to any other form of worship, the Virginians had always made it their first nominal duty to guard and support the religion of the state. They had never felt themselves injured by the Stuarts. Both James and Charles had, in the main, treated them well, and the difficulties with the latter had been only the natural disagreements of buyer and seller. Ultimate victory had crowned their resistance to Harvey; and no principle had been involved in any of these contests. Such a community was not a very promising soil for the Puritans; yet so great was the strength of their doctrines, their party had struck its roots so deep down into every part of English society, that they throve even in Virginia, although as yet the lines were not sharply drawn.

1642. After a short term of little more than two years Wyatt was replaced by Sir William Berkeley, who came furnished with abundance of mild words and fair promises from Charles, then hard pushed by his enemies. The new Governor was, of course, at the head of the Royalist interest, governed well at first, and was generally popular. The arrival of New England missionaries first aroused the dominant party, and an act was passed that "all Non-conformists shall be compelled to depart the collony with all conveniencie." The general tone of this

1642-1643. Assembly shows that the religious feeling was wholly in accordance with the moderate party of the Established Church in England. There was this act against the Puritans; but, in remembrance of Maryland, a much sterner law against Papists. The burgesses granted two houses to Berkeley, and made good his salary; but they stated distinctly in the act that it was not to be drawn into a precedent. In their revised laws they re-enacted that the Governor was not to lay taxes without leave of the Assembly, and that burgesses should be privileged; they further provided that nothing was to contravene the act of the Assembly, that every one demanding a jury had a right to one, and that appeals could be brought from county courts to the quarter courts, and thence to the Assembly. The general character of the legislation was hostile to the prerogative, and, except for the law against Non-conformists, was far more Puritan than Royalist. The first step toward federation was taken in the passage of an act ratifying and regulating commerce with Maryland.

1644. At a great distance from England, the colonists were exempt from civil war, and their prosperity increased rapidly, interrupted only by a second Indian outbreak, which Berkeley quelled with vigor and success. Yet Virginia was so exact a copy in little of the mother country, that during this period of quiet and prosperity the Puritan party grew so steadily that the restless Clayborne found it worth his while to appear as one of its leaders. The execution of the King naturally produced a violent revulsion, while the strong measures of Parliament had already aided Berkeley's party, which had been

1649. enabled to vote the Governor a guard, and to empower him to impress troops. The sorrow and indignation of the naturally loyal Virginians at the "murder" of the King put the Cavalier party in fact so completely in the ascendant that laws were passed of the very strongest nature in regard to those who dared to defend the manner of Charles's death, or to asperse his memory. The number of Independents in Virginia was trifling; and the majority of the colonists, not possessing the religious stimulus, shrank in undisguised horror from what they considered the awful crime of Cromwell and his soldiers. Virginia, therefore, went on quietly as before with a Royalist government. The last act of Charles had been a kind one in declining to restore the Company—which he did not then have the power to do—and the well-known sympathy of Virginia with the unhappy King drew many exiled Cavaliers to America, and thus increased the Royalist strength in the colonial parties.

Berkeley's invitation to Charles II. to come to Virginia was certainly made in good faith, and there is every reason to suppose that the sentiment of the colony supported the offer of the Governor; but the founders of the English Commonwealth were not the men to suffer disobedience, even in the most remote corner of their possessions. Commissioners for the colonies were appointed—among others Clayborne—and the fleet in which they sailed arrived at Jamestown in 1652. The Assembly and the commissioners very soon came to an agreement. Either the ultra-loyalism produced by Charles's execution had subsided, and the Puritan party had regained enough ground to enable it to act offensively upon the slightest external encouragement, or the loyal valor of the mass of the colonists evaporated at the sight of a fleet manned by the seamen of Blake and Ayscue. The substantial victory, at all events, rested with the Puritan party, and it is difficult to avoid the conclusion that Berkeley found himself, after all his brave talk, insufficiently supported. Colonies are proverbially selfish, and, despite their warlike preparations, the Virginians appear to have shown no overwhelming desire for bloodshed. The mildness of the terms granted accord well with the circumstances of the times. The Parliament was in no mood to make fresh enemies, especially where distance rendered them formidable; and the Puritan party in the colony, upon whom the home government had to rely, probably set the safety and prosperity of Virginia far above all other considerations. The ascendancy of the Puritan element, however, was secured in Virginia, and their leaders administered the affairs of the colony until the Restoration. Nothing could have been more free and independent than the government established and maintained under the auspices of Cromwell. The Protector did not appoint one of the three Puritan governors—

Bennet, Digges, and Matthews; they were all chosen by the Assembly, and derived their power entirely from the representatives of the people. The same was true of the Council, and at no period did Virginia enjoy so large a measure of self-government as under the Protectorate. The Parliamentary commissioners, headed by the active Clayborne, occupied themselves chiefly with the affairs of Maryland, and with settling boundaries; while the Assembly defined the powers of the Governor and Council, and asserted the popular rights in their fullest extent. Indeed, in their difficulty with Matthews, they removed and re-elected him, and succeeded perfectly in all their claims to the supreme power in the state. They followed the principles and example of the great Parliament in England, but acted with more moderation and fairness, and they fortunately met no provincial Cromwell ready and able to tear power from their grasp. That Virginia prospered during the period of the Protectorate is not surprising; for, under the guidance of the Puritan party, the liberties of the people were quietly, legally, and successfully affirmed and established, while their interests were prudently protected.

But Puritanism left a more enduring mark upon the English colonial policy than a passing alteration of particular governments. When Berkeley was first sent to Virginia, he brought with him royal instructions regulating trade, and requiring that all Virginian products should be shipped to English ports alone. This was the dawn of the famous restrictive policy; but it was reserved to Cromwell to put this policy into an enduring shape by means of the Navigation Act passed as a war measure by the Long Parliament, the first of the famous series which led ultimately to the revolt of the colonies. This act was not observed in Virginia, despite the equivalents granted by Parliament in the treaty, and no attempt was then made to enforce it.

The government of the colony during the term of the Puritan ascendancy was not only wise but strong. Clayborne and Bennet, at the head of a victorious party, were not the men to forget their former difficulties and defeats in Maryland; and backed by the Virginian strength, and in the name of the Commonwealth, they subdued and governed their Catholic neighbor. The theory of repressed loyalty in Virginia can be safely abandoned. Satisfied with the triumph of his party and its leaders, Cromwell left the colony to take care of itself. On the other hand, his party, strong in the Protector's support, governed wisely and well, oppressing no one, and making the colony prosperous at home and respected abroad. The death of Oliver and the accession of Richard were received in Virginia, as in England, without an outbreak of any kind, and Richard was universally acknowledged. When Samuel Matthews died, shortly after, Virginia was left without a Governor, and the abdication of Richard left England without a recognized Government. The Virginian Assembly, with all the power of the state in its hands, determined to await the arrival of commissioners, and in the mean time re-elected **1660.** Berkeley. This fatal reversion to the head of the old party is not easy to understand. It indicates an absence of party-spirit, and apparently a lack of leading men on the Puritan side, and was certainly a mistake which led to many troubles subsequently. During the Protectorate Virginia enjoyed peace, prosperity, and good government, and at the time of the Restoration possessed free-trade, universal suffrage, and religious freedom. There was no reason for her craving a return to the old government. The mildness of parties, however, permitted the feeble Royalist reaction to go on unchecked. The general sentiment of Virginia was undoubtedly Royalist, but not extreme; and, in obedience to what was at best a sentiment, the people suffered the King's party to recover without a struggle their power in the colony. Some of the old leaders of the Puritan party were dead, and the survivors were neither active nor decided. They and their followers yielded at a moment when self-assertion would have been all-sufficient, and afterward resisted in a way and at a time when utter overthrow was alone possible for them. Hope made the Royalists active, while the Puritans were inert; and the former, aided no doubt by the general human desire of being on the winning side, carried with them the unresisting mass of the people. This want of foresight and firmness at a critical moment afterward cost the Virginians dear. An opportunity for the establishment of liberal and independent government was lost, which no amount of subsequent turbulence and rebellion could retrieve. During the period of the Commonwealth another great political question had shown itself for the first time. Treaties had been begun with New England and New York, and the bonds connecting Virginia and Maryland had been drawn closer. This more general intercourse is the first faint indication of the confederating spirit, and was largely due to the rule of Cromwell, under which most of the colonies enjoyed the greatest measure of freedom they ever obtained while in a state of subjection to the parent country.

Berkeley, on his second accession, was at first disposed to obey the

Assembly, and govern after the manner of his Puritan predecessors; but the news of the Restoration put the public mind into the same transport of Royalist zeal and repentance which was manifested in England. This new popular feeling at once threw all the power into the hands of the old Royalist faction, who were weak enough and foolish enough to at once push their advantages to dangerous extremes.

1661. The Commonwealth men disappeared from the new Assembly, and Royalists took their place. An address was voted to the King, and a munificent outfit was granted to Berkeley, who went to England to protest against the enforcement of the Navigation Act. Berkeley, on his return, brought back advantageous patents for himself, but nothing for the colony; and Clayborne, the last of the Puritan leaders, was displaced from his office of Secretary. The power of taxation was put into the hands of the Governor and Council for three years. The Church of England was re-established, and severe laws were passed against Dissenters. Worst of all, the royal government at home proceeded to enforce the Navigation Act; and as a consequence of this last step, tobacco fell to a low price, and imports rose. The persecutions of the Dissenters, who had so recently been all-powerful,

1663. and the navigation laws could lead only to trouble. The first outbreak came as early as 1663, when the celebrations of the blessed Restoration were still fresh in every one's memory. Public feeling, however, was not yet ripe; the plot, conducted by a few obscure extremists of the Puritan faction, failed miserably, and some of the ringleaders were hung. No heed was taken of this warning. The profligate government of Charles II. cared only for the money to be squeezed from Virginia, and enforced the Navigation Act, until the trade of the plantation was almost extinguished. Charles even went farther, and granted to Lords Arlington and Culpepper the whole of Virginia. Thus the colonists saw themselves deprived not only of their trade, but of the very titles to the land they owned, and the vile government in England did not in the colony lack petty imitators of their feeble policy, or of their gross corruptions and oppressions. The justices levied taxes for their own emolument, and a wretched policy of severity was pursued toward the Indians, which exasperated without subduing them. The Church, in whose behalf the government persecuted Dissenters, fell into contempt. The priests were licentious and incompetent, and corruption and extortion prevailed. Frontier forts were established, many of which were useless grievances. In 1674 a second revolt was on the point of breaking forth; but there were no leaders, and the people, unable to lead themselves, were induced by some partial reforms to remain quiet. There had been **1674.** no election of burgesses since the Restoration, the ultra-royalist Assembly then elected having been continued from year to year by prorogation; and the mere existence of such an Assembly was a constant reminder to the people of the liberties they had lost and of the rights which were infringed. Everything was in a combustible condition. An immediate grievance and a popular leader were alone required to produce rebellion, and neither was long wanting. The Indian policy led to an Indian war, and for some unexplained reason Berkeley disbanded the forces gathered to repress it.

We are left to suppose that Berkeley regarded Indian troubles as a wholesome antidote to domestic ones; but in murders by Indians the colonists had a sharp, pressing grievance, and in Nathaniel Bacon they found a leader. Bacon was a young Englishman who had been but a short time in the colony; but he was one of the Council, and of so great a popularity that he not improbably excited the jealousy of Berkeley. He was brave, rich, eloquent, well-meaning, apparently ambitious, and certainly far from wise. It seems probable that the real movers in the business were two planters named Drummond and Lawrence, who used Bacon and his popularity to advance their own ends, and to accomplish changes more important than the punishment of Indian hostilities. Drummond and Lawrence, the latter especially, evidently intended a general reform of all the great abuses, and probably used the pretext of the Indian wars for this object. Bacon, in response to the popular call, after having in vain applied for a commission, marched at the head of a few men against the savages, and in the mean time Berkeley proclaimed Bacon and his men rebels, and pursued them vainly with troops. While Berkeley was absent the revolt became general, breaking out in the lower counties, and he was obliged to retreat. The Governor, at last aware of the rising storm, had issued writs for a new Assembly, to which Bacon was elected. On his way thither Berkeley arrested him, but soon released him on parole; and when the Assembly met, Bacon read at the bar a written confession and apology, and was thereupon pardoned and readmitted to the Council. Shortly after this submission Bacon fled on suspicion of a plot against his life, and returned to Jamestown with a large force. After scenes of much excitement, he appealed, not without a show of violence, to the Assembly, who made him their general, vindicated his course, and sent a letter approving him to England. The

Assembly also endeavored to reform abuses, and were resisted by Berkeley, who, in his turn, wrote a letter to England for aid. The Assembly, now entirely committed to Bacon, were persisting in their redress of grievances when Berkeley dissolved them. Bacon, powerful both by the support of the Assembly and the troops, extorted the necessary commissions from the Governor, and marched against the Indians. As soon as he was gone Berkeley once more proclaimed him a rebel. Bacon, on hearing this news, in the midst of a successful campaign, retraced his steps; and Berkeley, deserted by his troops, fled to Accomac. Bacon was now supreme. He summoned a convention of all the principal men at the Middle Plantation to replace the Assembly, and pledged them to his support, and to resistance, even to England, if their wrongs were not redressed. He then marched once more against the Indians; but in his absence the fleet which he had sent to capture Berkeley was betrayed, and the Governor returned to Jamestown at the head of his would-be captors. The Baconians in Jamestown at once made peace with Berkeley, and Bacon once more returned. After a mere travesty of a siege, Berkeley, again deserted by his men, fled to Accomac; and Bacon, entering Jamestown in triumph, burned the town. Shortly after, Bacon died from a fever contracted in the marshes, and his followers scattered at once, to be caught in detail and executed by Berkeley. So ended the Virginia rebellion. Nothing was gained; the political energies of the people were exhausted, and they sank back into apathy for the next century. Yet every circumstance was favorable to the popular cause. The grievances were intolerable, the whole people were ripe for revolt, and their oppressor, Berkeley, was a narrow-minded and tyrannical man of the old Cavalier school, whose pristine popularity had totally disappeared. As between Bacon and Berkeley there can be but one decision. The former was brave, impetuous, and honest; the latter acted with consistent bad faith from the outset. Yet Bacon was utterly incompetent for the task before him. He lacked discretion, and when placed in a position too trying for his powers wasted his opportunities, so that his death threw the whole game into Berkeley's hands. But the real causes of the failure of this ill-starred insurrection lay deeper. The people were dependent entirely on leaders, or, rather, on a leading class, and could not manage for themselves. Their sympathies were with Bacon, and when he appeared he carried everything with him by sheer force, courage, and readiness to bear responsibility. The whole movement rested on Bacon and his personal popularity. When Bacon was absent, the people fell back

helplessly into the hands of Berkeley, the only other man ready to
take a determined lead.   But the life of a single man was but a slender staff to support a successful revolution, and when it broke everything went to immediate wreck.   The people, much as they hated
Berkeley and longed for reform, had no cohesion, no definiteness of
aim, and no persistence.   The prominent gentlemen at their head having failed them, the Virginians could bring none from their own midst
to supply their places.   With as good a cause and as general a sympathy as any popular movement ever had, or ever could have, Bacon's
rebellion came to nothing, and left no impress on the state, because
the people themselves were not fit to conduct their own affairs in trying times.   In Virginia, while there was plenty of courage, love of
freedom, and good English pluck, there was not enough of that dogged
persistence and quiet sagacity which wrung victory from the Stuarts
in Old and New England.   In Virginia resistance became turbulence,
and revolution degenerated into rebellion.   The nature of the immigration, the occupations of the people, their mode of life, and the general
structure of society all led to this result.   An aristocracy governed the
country ; but in the time of Bacon it was a timid and half-grown aristocracy, and when the pinch came it failed.   The people, deprived of
the natural leaders which circumstances gave them, had no substi-
tutes to put in their place, for the powerful aristocracy of 1776 was in
its youth a century earlier, and in no condition to head, control, and
lead to a successful issue a great popular movement.   Society in Virginia was so constituted that without strong leaders in the ruling class
the people were helpless.

This rebellion, however, was the legitimate result of the great
movement which had just convulsed England, and which was destined, before it had spent its force, to remove another Stuart from
the English throne.   The strength of the movement in Virginia resided in the Puritan party, which had grown up there during the
Protectorate.   Its weakness lay in the latent royalism of the people,
in their inability to conduct a slow but persistent resistance, and in
the failure of the aristocracy.   As a result, mismanagement was able
to waste the power of the movement, and to accelerate the reaction
which threw Virginia into a state of torpor for nearly a century, and
long arrested the progress of political development.   With the failure
of Bacon's rebellion the second period in Virginian history comes to
an end.

Shortly after Bacon's death arrived an English regiment and royal commissioners. The King was disposed to be merciful, and had issued a proclamation of pardon, but it came too late. Berkeley had already butchered a number of influential men, including Drummond, and in some cases had confiscated their estates to his own use. The Assembly repealed all Bacon's laws, although they afterward re-enacted some of the most salutary, and proved themselves thoroughly subservient to Berkeley in attainting and condemning whomever he desired, although they finally succeeded in checking the executions and mitigating the punishments of the captured insurgents. At last Berkeley was recalled, and died soon after his arrival in England, embittered in his last moments, according to a most probable story, by the well-earned gibe which the amiable Charles flung at him.

1677. Colonel Herbert Jeffreys succeeded Berkeley, and ruled for about a year, until his death in 1678. He was succeeded by Sir Henry Chicheley, Berkeley's Deputy-governor, and he in turn by Lord Culpepper, one of the ornaments of Charles's Court and councils, upon whom the Governorship of Virginia had been bestowed for life in 1675. The bad effects arising from the failure of the popular movement were soon perceived. The new charter which the agents of Virginia had been urgently asking, and with a fair prospect of success, was quickly consigned to oblivion. The Assembly was to be summoned but once in two years, and was then to have the right **1680.** of sitting for only fourteen days. Culpepper, on his arrival, found Virginia tranquil. Jeffreys had made peace with the Indians, and the people were disposed to grant anything to the dispenser of royal pardons. Culpepper's sole object, however, was extortion, which he freely practised. During his absence in England in the following summer, the turbulence of the Virginians broke out in renewed disturbances, caused by the low price of tobacco and the legislative establishment of ports of shipment. Culpepper, on his return, renewed the demand of the commissioners of James I. to examine, in behalf of the King, the records of the Assembly—a claim the Assembly always resisted. After hanging the leaders in the plant-cutting riot, therefore, Culpepper turned his attention to the Assembly, and Robert Beverley, the clerk of the House, and a former adherent of Berkeley, who refused to give up the records, was persecuted almost to death by the exasperated and arbitrary Governor. Culpepper's administration was, as a whole, one of simple greed and violent exactions, varied by an extensive swindle in raising and lowering the value of the coin. By continued absence from his post he soon forfeited his patent, and Lord Howard of Effingham succeeded to the government of Virginia.   He, too, came to make his fortune, and neglected no means to further that laudable end.   He shared the clerks'

1686-1687. perquisites, established a new and oppressive Court, cheated the Assembly by means of a new seal, and carried out in a petty way the stupid tyranny of James II.   By royal wisdom printing was abolished in Virginia, the prisoners taken in Monmouth's rebellion were sent out as convicts, the Navigation Act was enforced, the appointment of all small local officers was absorbed by the Governor, and Virginia did not flourish.   The Governor became richer, the province poorer, and the people more discontented, while voluntary immigration almost ceased.   The unregulated love of independence and the turbulence which the Virginians mistook for political opposition were once more displayed.   Censures, imprisonment, and general servility were the first effects; then more oppressions, riots, and impending insurrection, until Effingham finally embarked for England, only to find on his arrival that James had been driven from the throne.   Thus ended the Stuart domination.   The reigns of Charles and James, the one contemptible for its meanness and sordid corruption, the other for its weak and stupid oppression, are the greatest blots on the history of the English race.   Bad enough at home, they were even meaner, more oppressive, and more corrupt in the provinces, for the people there were more helpless.   Like master like man: Charles debauched and debased England, and Culpepper and Effingham degraded their governments and almost ruined Virginia.   In the whole range of American colonial history there are to be found no administrations at once so contemptible, so sordid, and so injurious as those inflicted upon Virginia by the noble governors appointed by Charles II.

One event but little noticed at the time rises above the sorry details of this period.   In 1684 Virginia sent delegates to Albany to meet the agents of Massachusetts and the Governor of New York, in order to discuss the Indian troubles, and thus another uncertain step was taken on the road to confederation.   Every event of this nature, no matter how trifling, acquires importance in marking the slow stages by which the principle of union rose by external pressure from the jarring interests of separate colonies.

But little immediate benefit accrued to Virginia from the English revolution.   Her energies had been wasted in 1675 instead of being reserved for 1689, when she could have taken advantage of the times, and made solid political gains. Effingham, in England, continued to be Governor, and Sir Francis Nicholson, lately expelled by a **1690.** popular rising from New York, came out as deputy. Nicholson tried to endear himself to the people by the common arts of a demagogue, while he obeyed his patron in refusing to call an Assembly until absolutely forced to by popular discontent. The only **1692.** event of his administration was the grant of the charter of William and Mary College to James Blair, who was for many years a noted character in Virginia. An active, energetic Scotchman, brimming over with the controversial spirit, more of a politician than a clergyman, yet zealous in both capacities, James Blair played an important part in the colony. He was the head of the college and the head of the Church; and the latter position brought him into constant collision with the Governor on ecclesiastical matters, until finally he became the leader, and often the successful leader, of the opposition party. His success was marred by his disputatious temperament, his readiness to quarrel, and his stubbornness of opinion. But his sturdy good sense, official position, courage, and high character made him a serviceable man to Virginia in days when competent party leaders were rarely to be found in the colony.

Virginia at this time seems to have been selected as a resting-place for all unpopular governors. Sir Edmund Andros, fresh from his unlucky New England government, succeeded Nicholson. He appears to have been somewhat sobered by the treatment of Massachusetts, and to have considerably softened his arbitrary tastes. His administration was, on the whole, a good one; but he gave offence by enforcing the Navigation Act, and fell into the great error of a quarrel with the commissary, Blair. After a term of six years, he was succeeded by Sir Francis Nicholson, commissioned this time as **1698.** Governor-in-chief. Nicholson brawled on through his second administration for nearly seven years, making many stupid speeches, and quarrelling with various persons on a variety of subjects, public and private, and ultimately with Dr. Blair, who, after a prolonged struggle, defeated him, and drove him from the colony. Although arbitrary, Nicholson was not corrupt; and had he been less violent, and not tasked a by no means powerful mind with extended schemes for the general defence and government of the colonies, he might have made a respectable Governor. As it was, he effected nothing, and the most remarkable event of his administration was the control which the Assembly succeeded in obtaining over the treasury. By Nicholson's

neglect or indifference, the burgesses made the treasurer of the colony
an officer of their own, which was a valuable gain at the time, and of
the highest importance in the future when the purse was the great
weapon of the Assembly against the Governor.

1704. In 1704 the Earl of Orkney was made titular Governor of Virginia,
a sinecure which he held for forty years at an annual profit of
£1200.   Edward Nott was the first deputy under this new arrangement, and died in office, after an uneventful administration of
two years.   Robert Hunter was appointed his successor; but the ship in
which he sailed was captured, and on his return to England he received
another government in lieu of that of Virginia.   Connection with one
of the greatest Englishmen of the day has given to Hunter's name a
peculiar interest.   Jonathan Swift was his friend, and desired to go
out with him as Bishop of Virginia.   The plan was seriously discussed
between the two, and there are several allusions to it in Swift's journals and letters; but for some unexplained reason the scheme came
to nothing.   The incident lies outside the path of Virginian history.
It concerns a Governor who never arrived, and a man who rarely referred to the American colonies except as the abodes of malefactors.
Yet when the name of Swift indirectly and faintly touches the theme
of Virginian history, we cannot but turn aside to speculate on the possible results to the colonies and to the world if that dark and mighty
genius of the reign of Anne had been transferred to America as the
head of the English Church in the young West.

1706. The history of Virginia at this time becomes little more than a list
of governors, well-meaning men of ordinary abilities, who for
the most part conducted their governments in a lumbering,
quiet fashion, treating the people pretty well, and, as a rule, doing little to improve the methods of administration or develop the resources
of the country.   On the other hand, the nagging resistance of the
burgesses to the Governor, simply because he was a Governor, and
therefore made to quarrel with, now begins.   Yet it was this snarling,
and often unreasonable and factious but ever persistent and watchful
opposition, which slowly trained the people, accustomed them to Parliamentary and constitutional principles, and gradually raised their
political thought to the level of 1776.   In this period of rest, too, the
various social elements which had gathered in Virginia during the
stormy years of the seventeenth century crystallized.   It was then
that the social fabric which we find in existence when the English
colonies entered upon their career as a nation was built up and con-

solidated. Politically barren as the eighteenth century is in Virginian, and, indeed, in all the colonial history, it is socially the most important period. From those times we can learn who and what the people were who fought the Revolution and founded the United States.

In the interval which ensued after the death of Nott, natives of the province, all Virginian grandees, were at the head of affairs as Presidents of the Council, until at last a new Governor came to them **1710.** in the person of Alexander Spotswood, a Scotchman and a soldier, active and energetic—the best of the eighteenth century governors—and possessed of some imagination and of enlarged views. Spotswood brought with him the grant of the writ of *Habeas Corpus*, and, thus provided, made friends with his first Assembly. He was highly pleased with his prospects, and his description of the colony reflects very accurately the grateful political lethargy into which Virginia had sunk. Spotswood says: "This government is in perfect peace and tranquillity, under a due obedience to the royal authority, and a gentlemanly conformity to the Church of England." The political apathy of the times was deep enough, but it was not such absolute torpor as the new Governor supposed, and he was soon rudely undeceived on this point, for the next year we find him wrangling with his burgesses.

Spotswood, however, proved himself very superior to the ordinary run of colonial governors. His enterprise and his liberal opinions, indeed, became the causes of his recall by the Home Government, who did not at that period admire too great a display of such qualities; but while in office Spotswood did much for the colony. He subdued an insurrection in North Carolina; fought and finally made peace with the Indians; and endeavored sedulously, but in vain, to improve the condition of the Church. His attempts at ecclesiastical reforms only led him into fresh difficulties, a final collision with Commissary Blair, and ultimate defeat at the hands of the vestries. Spotswood also, at his own expense, sought to carry out various benevolent schemes for the civilization of the savages, and established schools for them at outlying posts, where he placed competent teachers. The principal school was at Christanna, where he had at one time over seventy Indian children in regular attendance. The years of peace with the Indians, obtained by Spotswood's policy, gave opportunity for extending the settlements, for a great development of material prosperity, and for the growth and consolidation of an aristocracy capable of furnishing leaders to the people of Virginia. The Gov-

ernor's activity also brought about friendly relations with the colonists of the Carolinas, whom the Virginians assisted against the Indians as well as in their domestic difficulties, and thus began to knit
the bonds which afterward held together the Southern group of colonies. Spotswood also directed his energies to exploration, and led a
party in person across the Blue Ridge—an expedition which made no
little noise in its day. He strove to organize the militia and put it
in good condition for service, and he strenuously urged the home
government to build a line of forts on the western frontier, to guard
against Indian attacks and possible French encroachments. The
events of the French war fully justified the soundness and wise foresight of this advice, but at the moment it only served to hasten the
recall of the over-zealous governor who had devised it. Spotswood
was a vigorous administrator, but, like many other men of the same
type of mind, he lacked capacity to deal successfully with those who
differed from him. He could originate and command, but he could
neither manage nor conciliate. He wrangled with the Assembly
throughout his administration, and the burgesses found him a difficult man to control. Taxes were, of course, the chief bone of contention; and as the Governor was able and determined, while the burgesses were factious and obstinate, the course of public affairs seldom
ran very smoothly.

Spotswood was replaced by Hugh Drysdale, a great contrast to
1722. his bustling predecessor, and a mild, inoffensive man, who
at once made peace with the opposition, and died after four
years of tranquil rule. He was succeeded by William Gooch, an-
1727. other Scotchman and soldier, who came in with George II.
at the moment when Walpole had just obtained a fresh lease
of power. By his own shrewdness, which led him to form a coali-
tion with the Council, in which the royal quit-rents alone were sacrificed, and by the flourishing condition of the colony, now reaping
the benefits of Spotswood's administration, Gooch ruled Virginia
acceptably and well for twenty-two years. This long term was the
most uneventful period in the annals of the province. The Governor
was moderate and sensible, and the usual contentions were in great
measure avoided. The most important event of all these years was
the co-operation of Virginia and her sister colonies with the mother
1740. country in the fruitless expedition against Carthagena, which
served merely as one more step in the development of union.
Wealth and population increased rapidly while Gooch was ruling

the province so quietly. Printing was introduced, education began to be slowly diffused, and its improving effects felt among the upper classes of society. The close of Gooch's otherwise calm administration was disturbed by religious difficulties. The loose and often licentious character of the clergy made the Established Church but a feeble bulwark against the tide of religious enthusiasm which swept in with Whitefield, and the old cry was therefore raised against dissenters by those who found the Established Church in conformity with their habits and valuable to their worldly interests, if not beneficial to their souls. In submission to this feeling, Gooch attempted to suppress heterodox opinions by all the powers of the State, and there was a good deal of petty persecution, which left the Church weaker and more unpopular even than before.

After Gooch's departure there was a short interval of Presidents of the Council as acting governors, and then a successor from England, Robert Dinwiddie, whose administration was the dawn **1749.** of a new era in Virginia. The long repose was broken, and **1752.** the forces that had been gathering strength began to come in play. Dinwiddie started with a large amount of unpopularity, which he had incurred when surveyor of customs in the colony; and this dislike of the new Governor was not diminished by his announcement of the royal dissent to several bills which had received the approbation of Gooch. He also interfered oppressively with the ordinary method of acquiring land by a simple warrant of survey, and demanded instead a formal patent, accompanied by a fee for the official seal. In **1753.** 1753 the Assembly remonstrated against this extortion and injustice; and remonstrance now had deep meaning, for the colony was no longer poor and weak as at the time of Bacon's rebellion. Once more, after a long interval of quiet, Virginia found herself opposed to her Governor on a question of principle. But times had greatly changed since she had last occupied this hostile attitude. Her revenues were good, her population had increased and consolidated, and there was a large, wealthy, united, and patriotic aristocracy ready to lead the people intelligently and well. In this first instance of resistance the Assembly sent Peyton Randolph to England, with a handsome salary, to protest against the Governor's action, and they denounced any one who should submit to the exactions of the new patents. The current of parliamentary resistance in Virginia began to flow in those channels which have always led either to redress or revolution. At the next session the burgesses refused sup-

plies, on the ground that their privileges were in danger. These were
ominous words, and might well have recalled to Dinwiddie the language of another English Assembly a hundred years before. At the
next meeting, in January, 1754, they voted £10,000, but clog-

1754. ged the bill with various provisos against invasions by prerogative.

But events were near which were destined to throw power still
more into the hands of the representatives of the people. America
was on the eve of great changes, in which Virginia was to take a
prominent part. While the long repose which the policy of Walpole
gave to England and her dependencies had allowed the political energies of the people to gather once more the force which had been
expended in the conflicts of the seventeenth century, a new and important element in colonial questions had come into existence. Another nation had gradually assumed a position which made it a
weighty factor in the development of the English empire in America.
The French had extended their power by means of their influence
with the Indians, and having slowly worked their way to the valley
of the Ohio, now planned to connect by a chain of forts their possessions in Canada and Louisiana, and thus hem in the English colonies and prevent their progress toward the West. It was a grand
though impracticable scheme, and its overthrow was to cost the blood
and treasure of a world-wide war.

In London, about this time, an Ohio company had been formed,
in which Dinwiddie and many prominent Virginians were interested. Thus colonization was to be favored and extended, and
it was now inevitable that French and English should soon come
into collision. When they did so, the first effect was to throw the
power in the colonies into the hands of those who laid taxes. In
this way the Virginian Assembly, working on Dinwiddie's necessities,
and aided by their control of the finances through the medium of
the treasurer, affirmed and established their supremacy in the State.
That the substantial victory remained with the Assembly is shown
by the fact that in 1754 they granted £20,000 without limitations,
despite their quarrels about granting half that amount a few months
before. Thus the burgesses gained their first victory; but the war
had two other important results, which greatly affected the future
march of events. It removed the hostile power which had served to
bind them to the powerful protection of the mother country, and it
taught the colonists the force and value of united strength.

To trace the history of Virginia during this great conflict is to follow the career of one man. The long period of dependent life is over; the dead level of colonial history is at an end; the monotonous average of provincial respectability is broken, and great men rise up whose characters and abilities have shed an enduring lustre upon the land which gave them birth. The time had come when Virginia would produce great leaders in abundance. The most illustrious of all these distinguished men was the first to step upon the stage of public affairs, and as we follow the early life of George Washington we are borne on through all the swaying fortunes of his native State in the long and bitter struggles of the old French war.

Washington sprang from a good English stock, and from one of the best families in Virginia. As a boy he was fond of out-door life and athletic sports; but the most striking fact, except his very meagre education, about his early years, is the soberness of mind and solidity of judgment which he displayed from the first. We can hardly imagine Washington destitute of some heavy responsibility. As a lad of sixteen, surveying in the wilds of West Virginia, he manifested the prudence and discretion which marked his subsequent career. In the care of his brother's estate he showed the same unselfishness and fidelity as when he filled the Presidential chair, and was trusted by a nation. His early mission to the French brought out in the strongest way his habits of mind and great moral qualities. An Adjutant-general and Major in the Virginian militia at the age of nineteen, Washington was selected by Dinwiddie to negotiate with the Indians and the French at Fort Du Quesne. His minute journal of that expedition has been preserved, and reads like the account of an experienced man well past middle life. Not only is there none of the fun, but there is none of the exuberance of youth. The narrative is clear, condensed, and vigorous; but there is throughout the all-pervading sense of responsibility, and the truthful, forcible simplicity which gave to all Washington's writings that gray soberness of thought and expression which commands the deepest respect and most implicit confidence, even if it does not excite our imagination. In every event of this dangerous journey we see the unerring judgment, the deep sagacity, and the marvellous foresight which made Washington a king of men. The conduct of this perilous mission was in every way characteristic. Dangers were met and overcome; hardships were endured; crafty savages were outwitted and timid ones encouraged, and neither hostile Indians nor courteous and deceitful Frenchmen could divert Washington from his object, or mislead his understanding for a moment. All the success possible under the circumstances was obtained, and this early mission and the journal which preserves its history reflect alike those qualities of mind and character with which the world has become familiar.

On his return, Washington was appointed to the second place in the little Virginian army, and soon after marched with a small troop in advance of the main body against the enemy. At the Little Meadows he surprised a party of French and Indians. A skirmish ensued, and M. de Jumonville, a young French officer, was killed. Thus was shed the first blood in a war which spread over the whole globe, and the results of which were a principal factor in the American Revolution. The death of De Jumonville is one of the trifling events in history which gain from accidental circumstances a startling dramatic effect. It reveals Washington as the leading figure in a petty affray which was the signal for a world-wide conflict, the prologue to that great revolutionary drama which, opening in a Massachusetts village, rolled on for nearly half a century, involving all the civilized nations of the earth in its progress, and closed at last upon the plains of Waterloo. Thus the greatest man of the great revolutionary period was present at the obscure beginning of those mighty changes which convulsed the world, and conducted the petty action which was the nominal cause of a long and devastating war.

On leaving the Little Meadows, Washington was joined by the main body of the army, and the death of his colonel soon after left him in command. He pushed on, and passed the Great Meadows, to which, however, he was soon forced to return, pursued by a large body of the enemy. Throwing himself into the stockade fort which he had built at the Meadows, he prepared to defend himself; but he was greatly outnumbered, and relief was hopeless. Rather than prolong a useless contest, he therefore surrendered on honorable terms, and returned to Virginia, where his services and misfortunes were understood, and where he was received with all honor. He soon after stood forward as the champion of the provincial officers by refusing to submit to the degradation in rank which they were forced to undergo when associated with those who bore the royal commission. Rather than suffer such an indignity and injustice, Washington resigned; but stirring times were at hand, and a man of his talents and reputation, filled with longing for a military career, could not remain in retirement. From the feeble and inauspicious beginning of a handful of provincials, the war had begun to assume vast dimensions. Edward **1755.** Braddock, general and commander-in-chief of all the forces in America, was sent out by the British Government, together with a fine body of veteran troops. His arrival created a great sensation in Virginia, which looked with admiration on the splendid soldiery of Europe. Almost his first act, and the wisest one of his brief career in America, was to invite Washington to enter his military family—an invitation which was at once accepted. If all Braddock's actions had been as sensible as this, he would have met with a very different fate; but he had all the ignorance and arrogance of an Englishman of that period in regard to America. He came prepared to despise the provincials, and he was profoundly irritated by the apathy of the legislatures and the difficulty of supplying his requirements; but as his contempt increased, so did his unpopularity. The more he raged and stormed, the more sullen and uncomplying became the temper of all about him. Washington expostulated, but in vain; and if it had not been for the exertions of Benjamin Franklin, Braddock might have waited a lifetime before he would have obtained the necessary means of transportation. At last the army, counting about two thousand effective men, of whom one-half were regulars, started from Will's Creek early in June. They pushed on slowly toward Fort Du Quesne, encountering every sort of difficulty, and making but little headway. Washington offered a great deal of good advice, which was sometimes taken, but much oftener rejected; until at last Braddock's provincial mentor was struck down by a fever, and obliged to see the army march on without him. He managed to overtake it, however, before the culmination of the campaign, and in season to be present at the disastrous fight near Fort Du Quesne. Braddock, relying on discipline alone, and guided only by European experience, marched straight into an ambush, was surprised by a motley crowd of French and Indians, insisted on fighting in platoons and according to recognized principles, and saw his men picked off by an invisible enemy without being able to return a single effective shot. The result was ruin and massacre. In that scene of carnage Washington displayed the highest courage and efficiency, and finally brought off the wounded and dying general and the shattered remnants of the army. The fame of this ill-starred expedition is a good proof of its importance; but this importance consists not so much in the comparative magnitude of the expedition, or the suddenness of its destruction, as in the lessons which it taught. Braddock and his army were typical of British arrogance, courage, and obstinacy. They offered to the colonists the spectacle of the finest troops in the world butchered by savages because of their own unconquerable ignorance and unwillingness to learn. They showed conclusively, also, that the Englishman, as such, was not necessarily braver than the American, while the latter understood the exigencies of American warfare far better. The awe inspired by the British arms was broken, and the British army was no longer a name to conjure with.

On his return from Braddock's expedition, Washington was put in command of all the Virginian troops. During the years of war which followed this appointment he occupied a position curiously like that which he filled in the war for Independence. The Assembly was friendly and well meaning, but as incompetent in execution as most legislative bodies. The Governor, Dinwiddie, was more competent, perhaps, in administration than the Burgesses; but he was unreasonable and headstrong, domineering, and at times insulting. Washington, generally beloved and popular with all classes, was in a position where he was expected to accomplish wonders, without means being provided to effect anything. Doing the best under the circumstances, writing bold, urgent letters to the Assembly and the Governor, planning radical remedies, and putting up with temporary expedients, responsible for everything, and supported in nothing, Washington appears at this time in an attitude which was typical of almost his whole military career. But while Washington was thus contending with difficulties, the war was running its course. Frenchmen and Indians were ravaging the frontier, the inhabitants were massacred, and the back settlements broken up. The whole country was in alarm and constantly pillaged, yet nothing was done. There **1756.** is a famous passage in one of Washington's letters which brings all this suffering and wretchedness vividly before us: "The supplicating tears of the women," he writes to Dinwiddie, "and moving petitions of the men, melt me into such deadly sorrow, that I solemnly declare, if I know my own mind, I could offer myself a willing sacrifice to the butchering enemy, provided that would contribute to the people's ease." There are here revealed not only the miseries of the country and the trials of Washington's situation, but that keen sense of responsibility and public duty in which no other man ever equalled him. The pathos of the sentence comes from the passionate force of that strong reserved nature, moved at last to open expression. For the moment it was all in vain. Lord Loudon

came and went as commander-in-chief, left his name to a Virginian county — which was all the province that he never visited, obtained from him as Governor and successor to Dinwiddie—and did nothing. The weary struggle dragged on, and even Washington, worn out with vexation and fatigue, retired for a time. But at
1757. last Mr. Pitt came to the head of affairs in England, and all was altered. Francis Fauquier, ruined at the gaming-table, but fascinating and high-bred, a gentleman and scholar, a charming companion and a popular Governor, came to rule over Virginia; but this was the least and most unimportant of the changes. Under Mr. Pitt men came to America to serve England; armies and fleets were sent, and money was poured out in all directions. All were imbued with the spirit of the great commoner. General Forbes, who was in command in Virginia, was able to gather a numerous and excellent army. Slowly and carefully, rather stupidly perhaps, Forbes pushed on for Fort Du Quesne, not at all in the way in which Colonel Washington, who was in command of the advance, desired. The capital mistakes of Braddock, however, were not repeated, although the French surprised and nearly destroyed a large detachment sent forward under Grant. But this was not enough to check the English. The French stronghold, owing largely to the efforts of Mr. Pitt and the British navy, was doomed, and the brave garrison, deserting their hopeless post, permitted Forbes to march in unmolested, and name
1758. his conquest Fort Pitt. This practically closed the war so far as Virginia was concerned, and Colonel Washington was able to withdraw to Mount Vernon, and remain there with the wife he had
1759. just married. In the North the war went on for two years longer. Wolfe took Quebec the first summer, and the next
1760. saw Montreal and Canada in the hands of the British. Two years now passed by. Pitt was driven from office, and peace was concluded under the auspices of Bute, while Frederick of Prussia soon followed England's example. The map of Europe was not changed, but the destiny of America was determined. England retained Canada, the Floridas, and the Great West as far as the Mississippi.
1763. Henceforth the English race was to rule unquestioned upon the North American continent. But these vast changes were only preliminary to still greater ones. The French war had cleared the way for the momentous questions involved in the future relations of the English colonies with the mother country. The thirteen provinces were disclosed to the eyes of England in all their immense and

hitherto unnoticed value. Territories so vast, a people so numerous, so wealthy, and so enterprising, could no longer be neglected. The old, slow, let-alone policy of Walpole was clearly insufficient, and must be abandoned. These were the thoughts which filled the minds of English statesmen when the clouds of war which had so long enveloped the world rolled slowly away. But if the lessons of the war were just, their practical application became fatal in the hands of the men to whom it was committed.

The teaching of the war, so much considered in England, was not lost upon the colonies. With the close of the French war the whole current of American history changes. Not only did that struggle bring the colonies together in a common cause, but it destroyed the power of France in America. Fear of France no longer bound the colonies to the parent State. Their loyalty in the future depended on the policy of England alone.

For Virginia these years had been especially useful. She had learned that the King's troops were not invincible; she had tested her own resources, and she had proved the strength and independence of her Assembly. While Washington was neglected on the frontier, and even before Dinwiddie and the Assembly quarrelled, the Governor had discovered that without great assistance from England he was sure to be worsted in every encounter. Whatever right there was in the questions then at issue was probably with Dinwiddie, who had to carry on a defensive war; but none the less did the Assembly put him down and assert their own independence. As the war drifted away from her borders, Virginia, under the genial rule of Fauquier, took breath after her exertions and hailed with delight the peace which marked the triumphs of England. But the lull was only momentary. Now that the terrible fear which hung over the Western border was removed, men began to watch the progress of their domestic affairs more closely, and to scrutinize most narrowly every incident in their relations with the mother country. The past had shown that things never went smoothly unless the policy of non-intervention, except in a beneficent manner, was adhered to by England. Virginians were thoroughly loyal, but they liked to manage their own affairs in their own way; and now that they began to be conscious of their strength, and to know their own importance, they were very quick to detect any meddling, and equally ready to resent it. Interference on the part of England was certain, sooner or later, especially when ministers had come to the conclusion that America was not governed enough, and only the most delicate and judicious treatment could avert the worst results. The rejoicings which greeted the return of peace had not died away when the inevitable collision came. This first conflict was brief and comparatively unimportant; but it acquires an immense significance as an exponent of the new spirit which was abroad, and was the forerunner of revolution.

In 1755 the Assembly passed, under the pressure of war and general distress, a relief act providing that for the next ten months all debts due in tobacco (the standard of value in the colony) might be paid either in kind or in money, at the rate of twopence per pound of tobacco. The year was one of great scarcity, and tobacco rose to sixpence per pound. The result of the act, therefore, was a virtual repudiation of about sixty-six per cent. of all existing debts; and as the State and the great mass of the people were debtors, the act seems to have met with general acceptance, and to have encountered but little opposition. So satisfactory, indeed, did the act prove to the majority of the voters, that in 1758, in anticipation of another short crop of tobacco, another relief act, determining anew the rate for tobacco in the payment of all debts, was passed. There was one class in the community whose salary was fixed by law at 16,000 pounds of tobacco, and upon whom this forced reduction of debts seemed therefore to weigh with peculiar severity. This was the clergy. Deriving some benefit, probably, from the operation of the first act, the ministers had contented themselves with petitioning the Assembly for a more liberal maintenance; but the second act fell upon them with full force, and although there was no apparent intention of especially abridging their income, they now broke out into violent opposition. A bitter controversy ensued which drew down the utmost popular odium upon the ministers. At last the clergy appealed to the King in Council, and Sherlock, the Bishop of London, denounced the act as hostile to the prerogative, and tending to withdraw the allegiance of the people from the Crown. On the other side, Colonel Bland defended the act as justified by its most salutary end, the preservation of the people. This he boldly put forward as the highest duty, and one which took precedence of every other, and rendered treason impossible. The King, however, denounced the act as a usurpation, and declared it null and void. The clergy thereupon brought suits to recover the unpaid salary, and the Court of Hanover County, in a test case, decided the point of law in favor of the plaintiff, the Rev. James Maury, holding that the royal disapprobation made the act void *ab initio*.

They ordered that the plaintiff should go before a jury to determine the amount of damages, which, after their decision, appeared a merely formal matter. The counsel for the defendants, who were the collectors of the county, retired from the case. It was, indeed, a forlorn-hope, and the defendants were obliged to employ a briefless young lawyer who, after six months' study, had just been admitted to the Bar. But this young lawyer was Patrick Henry, and the argument he was about to make was the second eloquent appeal, as that of Otis on the writs of assistance had been the first, to the independence of America from the domination of the English Crown. The son of respectable parents, and connected with the aristocracy of Virginia, Henry was utterly unknown, except to his immediate circle, and even there very unfavorably. As he stood before the magistrates in the little Virginia court-house in November, 1763, to defend a desperate cause, the gentlemen on the bench could hardly have regarded him with partial eyes. Uncouth in form and rugged in feature, as he stumbled over the first sentences of his speech, his father's friends and neighbors, who filled the court-room, probably expected that one more failure was to be added to the record of an unsuccessful career. Although well-born, Henry appeared to those about him as the boy who had early left school but half-educated, to devote himself to fishing and hunting, to indolent hours of dreaming in the woods and by the banks of streams, and to the violin and the dances of the Virginian plantation. His serious occupations had been even worse than his idle amusements. An unsuccessful farmer, a broken tradesman, a tavern-keeper, earning a precarious living, and now a hastily prepared lawyer who had barely gained admission to the Bar, this thriftless fellow and jolly companion seemed hardly likely to sustain a failing cause before all the respectability of his native county.

But the hour had come and the man. As Henry broke through the trammels of hesitation and embarrassment the words began to come, the deep-set gray eyes began to flash, and the great orator stood forth before the astonished eyes of the planters, farmers, and clergymen who had gathered in the Hanover Court-house. Of all that brilliant rhetoric and savage invective not a word remains, but the theme which drew it out is as distinct in every contemporary record as the person of the orator himself. Henry brushed aside all legal points—he knew little of them, and cared less; and, moreover, the law was utterly against him. With the intuitive perception of the great advocate, he seized the one point on which he knew he could move his countrymen. He left the narrow field of the law for the broad ground of political principle. He did not strive to convince men's reason, but he appealed to their innate convictions, their passions, their emotions. He declared that a king who annulled good laws dissolved his compact with the people, and was a tyrant; that, unless the jury were disposed to rivet the chains of bondage, they would sustain the authority of the representatives of the people. Henry's eloquence was irresistible, his arguments appealed to the heart of every man present, the jury awarded merely nominal damages, and the orator was borne from the court-house upon the shoulders of his excited auditors. Henry became from that moment a great popular leader; but the importance of the event does not lie in the fact that a famous orator then made his first success or won a hopeless case. "The Parson's Cause" deserves lasting remembrance, because Henry then gave utterance to the latent feeling of the community. He owed much of his greatness to being the first in Virginia, and the second in America, to express in words what every one was thinking more or less indistinctly. Henry's whole speech resolves itself into one proposition: "The Colony of Virginia must manage her own affairs in her own way, and she cannot brook outside interference." Henry's voice was the voice of the people, and its warning note sounds clearly enough now across the chasm of a century. But in 1763 it was lost in a multitude of confused ephemeral noises, and passed by unheard. Perhaps England, if she had heard, would not have stopped to listen and to understand; but the next time he spoke she heard him, and attended, although she failed to learn the great truths of which he was the exponent. Other signs, however, were not wanting, and they all pointed in the same direction. Some were of little importance; others, as, for example, the appointment of a Bishop, and the enforcement of the laws of trade, excited the bitterest resistance. But all alike announced in unmistakable language that Englishmen in America were too powerful and too many not to govern themselves freely through their own representatives. Unfortunately the theory that America was not enough governed, and that she did not contribute enough to the expenses of the mother country, had taken deep root in the minds of English statesmen. Pitt, with his high and generous policy and enlarged views, had gone from office, and his successors were just clever enough to see the defects in the colonial system without having the wisdom to grasp all the conditions of the case and apply the proper remedies. The chief objects of the new ministers were to maintain a standing army, to enforce the navigation laws, and to lay taxes upon the colonists in order to exact their proper contribution to the financial burdens of the Empire. The execution of these plans by means of the Stamp Act and revenue laws led to the first Congress, to the union of the colonies, to resistance to England, and finally to war. Virginia was the first to sound the alarm against the Stamp Act in the famous resolutions of May, 1765, introduced by Henry and advocated by him in the celebrated speech which compared George III. to Cæsar and Charles I. Fauquier's management prevented the choice of delegates, and Virginia was not represented at the Congress in New York, but she warmly supported its action, and sent to England a declaration of similar principles. With the Congress of 1765, and the measures which led to and succeeded it, the thirteen provinces began to live a national life, and the history of Virginia unites with the great current of the history of the United States.

Chapter II.

VIRGINIA IN 1765.

WITHOUT a knowledge of her social, economical, and political condition, the great part played by Virginia in the history of the United States is almost unintelligible. The always difficult task of reconstructing on paper a past society is enhanced in the case of Virginia by the almost total want of contemporary literature; and this want is not supplied by private correspondence, for if intelligent letters or journals were written, they have not come down to us. In the middle of the eighteenth century Virginian society was not much given to literary pursuits of any sort; and when the correspondence of the great leaders of the Revolution begins, the stern interests of war and politics drove from men's minds and from their letters the simple details of every-day life. To summon up the past in Virginia, we must turn to the dry narratives of travellers, the gossiping histories of families and churches, and the yellow pages of old newspapers.

Virginia has altered as little probably as any State in the Union; but in this country of rapid changes, and after a century of hurried progress and unexampled development, closing with a civil war which utterly wrecked the social system of the South, it may be safely said that nothing now remains of the ancient Dominion of the year 1765. The great physical features of the country are of course the same. There are still the rich soil, the genial climate, the noble rivers, the safe and capacious harbors, which greeted the eyes of John Smith and his companions. The face of the country, moreover, is but little changed since the middle of the last century. More territory has been cleared and utilized, but great tracts of wild land still remain untouched. Where a hundred years ago there were a few scattered villages, there are now some respectable towns; but no great cities, in obedience to the laws of modern civilization, have sprung up upon Virginian soil. Yet the whole fabric of society has been radically altered. Even in 1822, long before the far-reaching changes effected by the extinction of slavery, John Randolph of Roanoke could say with truth: "Traces of the same manners could be found some years subsequent to the adoption of the Federal Constitution—say to the end of the century. At this time not a vestige remains. We are a new people."

To draw an accurate picture of the vanished society lamented by Randolph, it is first necessary to ascertain the numbers of the people. Accurate government statistics had then no existence, and we are forced to rely upon the estimates of individuals. The figures generally accepted, therefore, are at best only approximately true. For the year 1650 a contemporary tract gives fifteen thousand whites and three hundred negroes as the population of Virginia. It is worth while to pause a moment here in order to get a general notion of Virginia in the middle of the seventeenth century, for we are thus enabled to see the germs of the subsequent development. From the scanty material which the time affords, a rough sketch can be made of the first colony planted by Englishmen in America fifty years after its foundation. The race had then finally taken root in its new home, and the lines of social and political development were already marked out. The results seem at first sight small, but they represent stability of existence, the first great prize wrung from the wilderness. From the tract just referred to, other statistics than those of population may be gathered. Imported cattle, as well as horses, swine, goats, and fowls, had thriven in Virginia. The flocks and herds, sure signs of permanency and well-being, had increased and multiplied, and become a source of wealth to their owners. Agriculture had taken a firm hold, and was the main support of the people. Tobacco, the source of Virginian wealth, was then as always the great staple; but the more familiar products of English soil were not lacking. Wheat and corn were raised in sufficient quantities to supply the plantations. Hops were successfully cultivated, and good beer brewed, to the satisfaction, doubtless, of the colonists, who had not left their tastes and habits behind them. Vines were indigenous, and grapes plentiful, while imported fruit-trees took so kindly to the new soil that fine orchards had already become a part of every plantation. Trade had grown up with the other colonies and the West India Islands, as well as with the mother country. Small vessels for the coasting trade and for fishing had been built, and pitch, potashes, furs, and lumber were exported in considerable quantities. Other industries showed but feeble signs of life. Efforts had been made to establish iron-works and introduce silk culture, but with little success.

Colonel Norwood, a Royalist refugee, who was wrecked on the American coast, left a journal recounting his adventures, and among other incidents his first reception by a Virginia farmer. From his brief account it may be gathered that the circumstances of this planter, although rough and simple, were not uncomfortable. The table to which the shipwrecked traveller was welcomed seems to have been plentifully supplied with the fine game of the country and the wholesome products of the plantation. The host was dressed in coarse, strong homespun, and would seem to have been contented. This was probably the condition of most of the planters at that period. They had comfortable houses of wood or brick in the midst of large estates, which yielded all crops in profusion. They lived in comparative solitude, scattered along the banks of rivers and isolated in the great forests, holding little intercourse with each other or with the outside world. Almost the only highways were the great natural watercourses; and the annual ship from England, laden with goods to pay for tobacco, was the great event in their lives. Except for the little village of Jamestown, there was nothing even resembling a town. Alone on the edge of the ocean, it seemed as if the wilderness behind must, by the sheer force of its vast desolation, drive the colonists into the sea. Strange stories were current of marvellous and abnormal races of men beyond the mountains, which were supposed to be washed on the other side by the waves of the Indian Ocean.[1] Nothing but the sturdy and unimaginative nature of the Anglo-Saxon race could have enabled the Virginians to support their solitary life in the seventeenth century.

Their political instincts were as keen as in the mother country, whose customs and laws they had brought with them. Except for the brief period of the Protectorate, the suffrage was carefully limited, and class distinctions were always maintained. The Established Church was supreme, and dissent met with harsh and intolerant treatment. The planters exercised their political faculties as sharply in the little Assembly at Jamestown as did their English cousins in London. Slavery was as yet trifling in its influence; but the convicts and indented servants formed a servile class, and helped forward the aristocratic system which had been founded. The professions of law

---

[1] Discoveries of John Lederer, 1671.

and medicine hardly had an existence, and merchants, as such, were unknown. There were only two classes—landlords and servants. Neither arts nor letters flourished. Every man taught his children according to his ability, and the Royalist Governor Berkeley thanked God that there were no free schools.[1]   The Virginians were Royalist in their sympathies, and firm supporters of Church and State. In the rude outlines of the seventeenth century can be seen all the great forces which attained a vigorous life and full development in the eighteenth.   The hard life, the isolation, the great estates, and the servile class, added to the inborn conservatism of the race, were moulding an aristocratic system as distinct and powerful as that which had been left behind.

In 1671 the population, according to Berkeley,[2] had risen to forty thousand souls, two thousand of whom were negroes. This was probably a large estimate ; but the troubles toward the end of the century and dangers from the Indians checked the growth of the colony, which does not seem to have numbered much more than forty thousand inhabitants in 1700.   The period of quiet which then ensued, and the vigorous Indian policy of Spotswood, gave repose, while the general tranquillity of all the British dominions after the accession of the House of Brunswick contributed to the same result.   In the first fifty years of the eighteenth century the white population increased from less than sixty to more than two hundred and fifty thousand, and the handful of negro slaves had grown to such a point that it more than equalled the whites in numbers, and raised the total population to over half a million.[3]

It is an easier matter to determine with accuracy the Virginian revenues and taxes and their sources than to estimate the population. Campbell, relying on the contemporary account usually attributed to Lord Culpepper, enumerates four sources of revenue at the close of the seventeenth century.   First come the quit-rents, amounting to about eight hundred pounds per annum, and paid to the King; second, the export duty of two shillings per hogshead on tobacco, and the port duties of fifteen pence per ton on vessels arriving, averaging three thousand pounds a year; third, a duty of one penny in the pound on all tobacco exported to the other colonies, amounting to one hundred pounds a year, and paid to William and Mary College, under the

---

[1] Foote's Sketches of Virginia, ii., 1671.
[2] Ibid., i., 10.   [3] J. F. D. Smyth's Travels, i., 72.

grant of 1692; fourth, any money-duty raised by the Assembly. There were also three levies: the parish levy, assessed by the vestries; the county levy, assessed by the justices of the peace; and the public levy, assessed by the Assembly. All these three levies were paid in tobacco, collected by the sheriff, assessed on the whole number of persons in the parish, county, or colony, and divided by the number of tithables. The tax so collected amounted to about one hundred pounds of tobacco for each tithable person, and yielded between eight and nine thousand pounds sterling annually. This system was continued with little change, except natural increase, until the French war. The Governors and the Assembly were in the habit of wrangling on the question of taxes; but all power in the matter rested with the burgesses, and, until the royal government interfered, they easily mastered their Governors. This system of taxation was of the simplest and most direct kind, levied principally upon real estate and negroes.[1] Its moderation alone made it tolerable, and the burdens created by the French war soon caused bitter complaints of its inequality and injustice.[2] In that great conflict a debt of four hundred thousand pounds was contracted, and heavy taxes were laid to sink it, while gold and silver were banished from circulation and replaced by a depreciated paper currency. The hardships produced by this change in the standard were so severe that a law to fix the rate of exchange was passed.[3]

Despite the defective methods of taxation, however, the colony rapidly recovered from its financial difficulties, which were caused solely by the exigencies of war. There were no great sources of expenditure in time of peace, and the most costly public luxuries, an army and a navy, were wholly wanting. The only defenders of the country were the militia, supposed to include every able-bodied freeman between the ages of sixteen and sixty.[4] The organization of this militia, however, was extremely loose and imperfect.[5] They were called out in time of war by the Governor and Assembly, who also had power to raise colonial troops. Washington's difficulties, when in command during the French war, give a startling picture of the wretched military arrangements of the province. The commander

---

[1] White women working in fields were also held to be tithable, Beverly, p. 224; and Foote, ii., 208. As to taxation generally, Burke, ii., 137; Rochefoucauld, ii., 47; Hening, 1644, 1645, 1657, 1769.

[2] Burnaby's Travels, p. 39.   [3] Ibid., pp. 39, 40.

[4] Beverly, p. 224.   [5] Smyth, ii., 160.

had no voice in the choice of officers, there was no proper system of military regulations, and the pay was irregular and uncertain. Even when these faults had been remedied, Washington found himself without any martial code by which he could check insubordination, desertion, or the natural perverseness of his raw levies. The militia system, as then constituted, was thoroughly insufficient except in peace. Men were to be called out to repel invasion; but there were no powers to effect this, or to control them when in actual service. There was, besides, the annoying question of rank. Every officer in the royal army claimed to outrank every provincial officer, and this led to continual jealousies and difficulties. In one case Washington refused to serve; in another, a man who had in the last war held an English commission of captain, refused to obey Washington, then in command of all the Virginian troops. The frontiersmen, of course, made good soldiers, and the young Virginians of good family were just the stuff to make dashing and gallant officers; but the mass of the people, though brave and ready to fight, could not at once bear the severe strain of a prolonged and exhausting war. Moreover, the majority of Virginians at the time of the French war had never seen or known any fighting; for Bacon's rebellion and the great wars with the savages were then little more than traditions.

With the other branch of public defence it was even worse. There was, of course, no navy whatever, nor were there even merchant-ships to be turned into privateers. The Virginians were in no respect a seafaring race, and did not even furnish material to man a possible navy in the future. Other public expenses were small. The Governor's salary, charged on the export duties, was twelve hundred pounds for the nominal, and seventeen hundred for the real Governor. Three hundred and fifty pounds were distributed among the councillors. The other expenses for clerks, courts, etc., were all trifling. Salaries were small, but the income in money of even the richest Virginians was not large. So much was afforded by a great plantation and numerous slaves that comparatively little ready money served to procure every luxury; yet, if a small sum had to be suddenly provided, the wealthiest were often obliged to seriously burden their estates. These circumstances gave to the offices the rare attraction of yielding a sure income in cash. The government was upon the familiar British model of King and Parliament. The Governor represented the Crown, and was a most important and very powerful personage. He was not only the executive officer, the commander of the militia, and the admiral of the navy, but he was also lord chancellor, chief-justice, and practically the bishop of the province, and the dispenser of pardons, except in capital cases. He possessed the veto power as to all legislation, and could convoke, prorogue, and dissolve the Assembly. He was nominally under the control of his Council; but the councillors were really his creatures, appointed by him, and liable to suspension at his hands. His patronage was another element of strength. All offices, except those of Treasurer and Speaker of the House, and even including the clerks of the Assembly, were in his gift. He appointed also the sheriffs and coroners, and through the former often exerted a decisive influence upon the elections. His power in the House of burgesses itself was very great; and he added largely to his salary, as well as to his political weight, by farming the quit-rents, disposing of unpatented lands, and profiting by the exchange of public money. This matter of fees, especially in regard to land, was a fruitful cause of contention with the Assembly, as well as a valuable source of income to the Governor.[1]

The Council came in for a goodly share of the spoils of the Executive department, and a seat in this body was much sought after by the leading men of the colony. In 1680 they had ceased to sit with the burgesses, and had become an upper house;[2] and in process of time they obtained an almost equal share of legislative power. They were twelve in number,[3] and by virtue of their position as councillors were exempt from taxation, became judges, colonels of counties, naval officers clearing all vessels, collectors of the revenue, and farmers of quit-rents.[4]

After Governor and Council had been thus liberally provided for, there was little left in the way of offices for the burgesses. Under the Commonwealth (1653) they had successfully asserted their right to elect their own Speaker,[5] and at the beginning of the next century they wrested from Nicholson the election of the Treasurer, thus obtaining complete control of the finances, and supplementing the power of laying taxes, which resided wholly with them.[6] This single but all-sufficient weapon armed them for their conflicts with the

---

[1] This account of the Governor's powers is drawn chiefly from Hartwell, Blair, and Chilton's Present State of Virginia, 1729. But see also Beverly and Burnaby, p. 23.

[2] Beverly.   [3] Burnaby, p. 22.

[4] Present State of Virginia, Hartwell, Blair, and Chilton; Hening, 1637.

[5] Burke, ii., 95.   [6] Burke, ii., 145; as to Privileges, Hening, 1657.

executive, and was the great safeguard of the people. There were, in the year 1760, one hundred and ten burgesses, two from each county, and one from Jamestown, Williamsburg, Norfolk, and the college respectively.[1] They received[2] one hundred and twenty pounds of tobacco, or about twelve shillings a day, and were elected by the freeholders, who were alone entitled to vote.[3] No act could become law without the assent of both Houses and of the Governor, besides the ratification of the King in Council.[4] Such was the government of Virginia; English and practical, but very far from being symmetrical or theoretically perfect.

Still further removed from either symmetry or perfection was the judicial and legal system which had grown up during the hundred and fifty years of the colony's existence. The machinery of the law had been constructed to meet definite wants, and had been amended and added to from time to time, as necessity demanded. Provision for a judiciary followed closely the political emancipation effected by the establishment of the House of Burgesses. Until the year 1621, all cases were tried by the Governor and Council at Jamestown, whenever it was convenient. This system was awkward and unsatisfactory, and quarter-sessions were established; and in the following year inferior courts were erected.[5] These two courts formed the essence of the judicial system, and continued with sundry additions of jurisdiction and changes in the number of sessions practically unaltered until the Revolution. In the year 1765 there were inferior courts, known as county courts, sitting once a month at the county town, and the general court, composed of the Governor and Council, which sat twice a year at Jamestown as a court of oyer and terminer, and to hear appeals.[6] Quarter-sessions were also held at the county towns by members of the quorum, and by those of the general court on the circuit.[7] The county courts were composed of the gentlemen of the county, appointed as judges by the Governor. They were eight in number, and, as finally arranged, superseded the private courts held by individual planters in the early part of the seventeenth century.[8] Four judges sufficed to constitute a quorum, and the bench of the county court was thus filled by country gentle-

---

[1] Burnaby, p. 22.
[2] These figures are of 1729.
[3] Beverly.
[4] Burnaby, p. 22.
[5] Burke, i., 162; ii., 31.
[6] Burnaby, p. 21; Smyth's Travels, i., 19, 20.
[7] Hening, 1661-'62.
[8] Hening, ibid.

men or planters, "able and judicious persons," in the language of the statute,[1] but wholly innocent of any legal training. With the natural aptitude of their race, however, they administered substantial justice between man and man, and were respected and obeyed by their neighbors as the best, wisest, and wealthiest men among them. They had criminal jurisdiction in all but capital cases, and had final jurisdiction in all civil causes involving less than twenty pounds.[2] The county courts were also made at an early day courts of probate, although administrations were later recorded in the office of the Secretary of the colony.[3] In cases involving more than twenty pounds there was an appeal to the general court, composed of the Governor and five members of the Council. The judges of this, the highest court, which presented the odd combination of the executive and judiciary united in one body, knew as little law as their brethren of the lower jurisdiction; but they were a much stronger body. Their court was not commissioned, but was the growth of custom; they heard all causes involving more than twenty pounds, as well as all appeals from the county courts, and held two sessions as a court of oyer and terminer. In addition to all this, the general court sat in chancery, the Governor being chancellor, and was a court of admiralty and a spiritual court. There was an appeal from them to the King in Council for all causes involving more than five hundred pounds; but such appeals were so expensive that the decision of the general court was practically final.[4]

The right of trial by jury, after some vicissitudes in the early days of the colony, was thoroughly established. A jury was required only in criminal cases, but was given to all demanding it.[5] The jury was selected arbitrarily by the sheriff, without a panel. Six jurors were required from the vicinage, and the sheriff summoned always the "best gentlemen" of the neighborhood.[6] A late law required that a juror should be a freeholder, and possessed of real and personal estate of more than one hundred pounds in value.[7] Practice was simple. Writs ran not in the name of the King, but as simple justice's warrants, and were published at the door of the parish church.[8] There were no writs of error, but appeals only, allowing no new matter, and

---

[1] Hening, 1661–'62. [2] Burnaby, p. 21; Smyth, i., 20.
[3] Hening, 1657, 1661. [4] Burnaby, p. 21.
[5] Hening, 1643; Present State of Virginia, Hartwell, 1729; Burke, ii., 30.
[6] Beverly, App. [7] Hening, 1748–'55.
[8] Present State of Virginia, Hartwell, 1729; Beverly, App.

as late as 1729 there was no formal pleading.[1] This legal system indicates unmistakably the absence of a strong class of professional
lawyers. Lawyers were, in fact, only just beginning to flourish and
gain importance as a class in the years immediately preceding the
Revolution. In the early times there appears to have been a number
of sharp and unscrupulous attorneys, probably adventurers from England, whose existence called forth much hostile legislation. In 1643,
on account of the heavy fees, attorneys were compelled to take out a
license, could plead only in general court and one county court, and
fees were limited. Two years later "mercenary" attorneys were to be
expelled; and in 1646, all fees were prohibited, and the court appointed some one from the people to help the suitors, but without fees. A
few years later these enactments were repealed; and after many fluctuations between no attorneys on the one hand, and no regulations for
practitioners on the other, the system of licenses and examinations was,
on account of the grievances arising from ignorant lawyers, revived
and enforced, and fees were regulated by the court.[2] The growing importance of the lawyers as a class is shown about the middle of the
eighteenth century by the distinction carefully made in the statutes
between barristers and attorneys.[3] Such was the judicial and legal
system of Virginia. It was in many respects rude and imperfect;
but it seems to have worked well, and to have served the ends of
justice. The courts were trusted and obeyed by the people, and the
general organization, as well as the lawyers, and the knowledge of
law, kept pace with the development of the community. As in all
the colonies, the common law was adopted and followed, except in
so far as it was modified by acts of Parliament or the local statutes.

The distribution of the population which lived under the system of
government and laws which have just been described was an important
factor in the social and political condition of Virginia. One great
element of modern life was wholly wanting. There were practically
no towns and no centres of population. The people were widely
scattered over the whole face of the country. This diffusion had begun at an early day, and the habit of dispersion became strongly
rooted before efforts were made to remedy the evils which it produced.
The want of trade, the loss incurred by dependence upon foreign merchants, and the difficulties of transportation, first led to legislative action

---

[1] Present State of Virginia, Hartwell.
[2] Hening, 1643-'45, 1646-'51, 1657-1742, 1745.   [3] Ibid., 1748-'55.

in 1661–'62,[1] when an act was passed for the benefit of Jamestown, where each county was required to build a house. More strenuous measures were, however, found to be necessary, and in Lord Culpepper's time an act known as the Cohabitation Act was passed, ordering towns to be built at certain specified points, for the benefit of trade and manufactures.[2] The most eminent of the dissenting clergymen supported this policy in a tract called a "Perswasive to Towns and Cohabitation," urging the loss of trade, the helpless dependence upon England and the other colonies, as arguments for the scheme;[3] but the act was inoperative. Ten years later there were still no towns, but only paltry villages; and the legislative towns generally consisted of one house with a store and office for the transaction of a small retail business.[4] The government, however, persisted. The "paper" towns, as they were called, were made the only ports of entry; privileges were offered to tradesmen who would settle in them;[5] and it was further enacted that every town should have a fair and market.[6] Everything failed alike—not only laws, but the much stronger influences of diminishing trade, heavy losses through payments to small retailers, and the powerful support of the Governor and of the Crown.[7] In 1716 Jamestown consisted of a church, court-house, and three or four brick houses,[8] and it was even worse with the "paper" towns. Colonel Byrd, in 1732, writes of Fredericksburg, that "besides Colonel Willis, who is the top man of the place, there are only one merchant, a tailor, a smith, an ordinary keeper, and a lady who acts both as doctress and coffee-house keeper;" he adds that Richmond and Petersburg existed only on paper.[9] Between this period and the Revolution there was little change. At the close of the French war, Norfolk, with about seven thousand inhabitants, was the only considerable town in Virginia.[10] Williamsburg, the gay capital and the seat of the university, was a straggling village of about two hundred houses. Burnaby, who visited Virginia in 1759, describes it as a pleasant little town, with wooden houses and unpaved streets.[11] At one end was the college,

---

[1] Hening, 1661–'62.   [2] Ibid., 1680.   [3] Makemie's "Perswasive to Towns," etc.
[4] Foote, i., 9.   [5] Maxwell's Hist. Register, i., 166.
[6] Hening, 1705.
[7] Collections of Mass. Hist. Soc., 1st series, v., 124, account of Virginia; Burke, ii., 124.
[8] Huguenot Family in Virginia, p. 271.   [9] Byrd MSS., ii., 9, 72.
[10] Smyth, i., 11; Rochefoucauld, i., 6; Abbé Robin, p. 107.
[11] Burnaby, p. 6.

said by Mr. Jefferson to have looked like a brickkiln with a roof,[1]
and at the other the Governor's palace, as it was affectedly called, likewise of brick, and apparently the handsomest structure in Virginia.
An indifferent church and some insignificant public buildings completed the architectural glories of the capital. A dozen families of
the gentry lived in the town, and the rest of the inhabitants were
tradesmen. Such life as there was in Williamsburg was due solely to
its selection as the seat of government.[2] Jamestown, the old capital,
was utterly effaced, and the only substantial sources of growth to the
legislative towns were the Government warehouses for the inspection
of tobacco. This system had been established in the earliest times,[3]
and after a long period had built up Petersburg, Fredericksburg, and
Alexandria;[4] but these places were, after all, mere unpaved, straggling villages, with no business outside the tobacco-houses, and inhabited chiefly by liquor-dealers, small shopkeepers, and smaller lawyers,
who preyed upon the country people of the neighborhood.[5] It fared
no better with the county seats established by law in each county for
the better administration of justice. These towns, planted in many
cases in the midst of the forest, usually consisted of the court-house,
the prison, and its accompaniments of stocks, pillory, whipping-post,
and ducking-stool, with one miserable inn, where the judges lodged
when they came to hold court.[6] Usually, too, the parish church flanked
the court-house;[7] but this was not universal. The Sunday services or
the sessions of the court called all the people to the county seat; but
when these were over the town relapsed into the quiet of the wilderness. The explanation of this strange state of affairs lay in the character of the population and their pursuits. Colonel Byrd, one of the
wealthiest of Virginian planters, who wrote against the legal ports of
entry, argued that the system of life, the country, and the popular
habits, were all opposed to them.[8] Writers on the other side admit
that the popular aversion to towns was very strong; but they con-
tend that this was due to indolence, jealousy, and the desire of every

[1] Weld's Travels, p. 127.
[2] For descriptions of Williamsburg, see Burnaby, p. 6; Rochefoucauld, i., 24–
27; Smyth, i., 17; Weld, p. 127; Abbé Robin, p. 107; Georgia Hist. Coll., IV.,
Itin. Observations, 1745, p. 48.   [3] Hening, 1633.
[4] Smyth, i., 62, 152, 201; Burnaby, p. 43; Brissot, p. 367.
[5] Rochefoucauld, i., 21.
[6] Ibid., i., 65; Hening, 1661–'62, p. 2; Byrd MSS., i., 72.
[7] Meade's Old Churches, ii., 68.   [8] Byrd MSS., ii., 162.

planter to have the port of entry at his own door.[1] These reasons undoubtedly explain the opposition to towns, and the fact of their remaining small and insignificant villages; but the cause of this opposition is to be found in the occupations of the people, which, until fixed and endeared by habit, were, of course, merely the result of circumstances at the foundation of the settlement.

What the pursuits and occupations of Virginians were at the period preceding the revolution it is not difficult to discover, for they were few and simple to the last degree. The legal profession, as has been shown by the course of legislation against attorneys, was not held in high repute, and lawyers, as a class, were only just beginning to assume importance in the years immediately before the Revolution. In early days there were evidently plenty of attorneys, so called, but they were for the most part pettifoggers and sharpers, broken adventurers from London, and indented servants, who, having been convicts, chose on their release the profession which, in a rude state of society, gave them the best opportunity of fleecing the community. The only man who appears to have attained an honorable eminence in the seventeenth century simply as a lawyer was William Fitzhugh, the defender of Beverly in his gallant struggle with Lord Culpepper.[2] In 1734 two lawyers are mentioned who had displayed ability and achieved legitimate success in their profession, although one of them was a broken-down London practitioner.[3] Sir John Randolph, for many years attorney-general, was a conspicuous and learned advocate. But the rarity of such cases shows as clearly as the course of legislation the low standing of the legal profession. The increase of wealth and civilization effected finally a change in this respect; but it is only at the close of the colonial period that we find men of high position and real talents devoting themselves to the law, and only just in season to play an important and leading part in the conflict with the mother country. It was at this period that such men as Patrick Henry, Jefferson, George Mason, and Wythe studied law, and were admitted to the bar, which found its crowning glory in John Marshall, the greatest name of all those that have adorned the legal profession in America.

The profession of medicine, which nowhere enjoyed in the eighteenth century the consideration that it now deservedly possesses, was

---

[1] Makemie, "Perswasive to Towns;" Coll. of Mass. Hist. Soc., I., v., 124.
[2] Maxwell, Hist. Register, i., 165.   [3] Ibid., i., 119.

especially low in Virginia. Almost all the knowledge we have of the medical profession is from the statutes relating to it, and this is in itself a significant fact. In 1657 laws were passed to regulate surgeons, and the power to settle fees was given to the courts. A few years later bills of surgeons were made pleadable against the estate of a deceased person, which indicates the precarious, half-recognition extended to the profession. In the next century elaborate laws were passed in regard to physicians, because " surgeons, apothecaries, and unskilful apprentices, who exacted unreasonable fees, and loaded their patients with medicine," took up the practice of the healing art, to the detriment probably of the good people of Virginia. Fees were fixed by this statute, one shilling per mile being the rate, and all medicines were to be set forth in the bill. Two pounds was to be the price of attending a common fracture, and twice as much for a compound one. Those physicians who held university degrees were allowed to make a double charge;[1] and there were undoubtedly a few of this last class in Virginia, men of position and family, who had been educated abroad, and were a credit to their profession.[2] But their number was very small, and it cannot be doubted that the dispenser of drugs, the rude village surgeon and barber, or the unskilful apprentice, were the representatives of medicine in Virginia, and were not held in high esteem. The profession offered little attraction to the best part of the community, was, as a rule, merely a means to more or less ignorant men of making a living, and had neither social nor political influence.

As the army and navy had no existence in Virginia, only one profession now remains to be accounted for. The clergy formed the only professedly learned class in the community.[3] They possessed considerable influence, and they were a picturesque element in society —more, it must be admitted, from their failings than their virtues. But they represented also a great institution which had an important effect upon the people of Virginia, and to understand them and the Church which they served involves a discussion of the whole religious system.

John Smith and his followers brought with them a worthy minister of the Established Church, which from that time onward was protected and fostered by the government of Virginia. During the

---

[1] Hening, 1657–'60, 1661–'62, 1666, and 1736.   [2] Meade, i., 407.

[3] Foote, i., 149.

seventeenth century the Puritan spirit, which leavened the whole of English society, was felt in Virginia, and showed itself strongly in the Church. Elaborate measures for the maintenance of the Church and the clergy, and for the propagation of the true faith, were passed by the early Assemblies, and re-enacted and extended by all their successors in turn.[1] Severe laws against Sabbath-breaking exhibit still more strongly the puritanical spirit which pervaded the Virginian establishment. Work, sport, and travel were prohibited on Sunday, and heavy penalties were paid for absence from divine service.[2] One man was formally excommunicated for wearing his hat in church.[3] The same stern quality of the times was manifested in the most rigid laws for conformity.[4] Separatist meetings were broken up, a fine of five thousand pounds of tobacco was exacted from the participants, and Non-conformists were expelled from the colony. Under the Commonwealth there was some relaxation, but both Churchmen and Puritans persecuted Papists and Quakers. The former were disabled from office; the latter were thrown into prison without bail, banished, and adjudged to be felons if they returned a second time. Those who brought in or entertained Quakers were liable to heavy fines.[5] With the Restoration, the Established Church again asserted its supremacy, and all dissenters came under the ban, and were pilloried and fined.[6] The first sect to make head against the prevailing intolerance was the Presbyterian. The conflict was carried on by the Rev. Francis Makemie, and was supported by the presence of a large and useful body of Scotch-Irish settlers. Yet pastor and people suffered alike from the laws, and even the emigrants from Londonderry could not obtain recognition, but were compelled to pay tithes, and forced out to the frontier. The Toleration Act of William and Mary obtained only the barest sufferance for Makemie and his followers in Virginia.[7] The superstitious side of religion at this period was not without vitality, for, as late as the year 1705, Grace Sherwood was ducked for witchcraft.[8]

But with the beginning of the eighteenth century the vigorous, zealous, intolerant spirit began to decline, and the Church rapidly

---

[1] Hening, *e.g.*, 1623-'24, 1632, 1660.   [2] Ibid., 1629, 1632, 1643, 1691, 1705.
[3] Ibid., 1640.   [4] Ibid., 1623, 1645-'46; Foote, i., 23.
[5] Foote, i., 35; Hening, 1643, 1659, 1661-'63.
[6] Ibid.; see also Anderson's History of Colonial Church, ii., 27; Burke, ii., 131; and Meade, i., 283, 384.
[7] Foote, i., 35.   [8] Howe's Virginia.

lost ground among the people. In 1699 there were few dissenters in Virginia, and three or four Presbyterian meeting-houses and a Quaker conventicle were the only places of worship outside the pale of the Church.[1] At the time of the Revolution more than half the population were dissenters, and in the shock of war the old Establishment went helplessly and hopelessly to pieces, unregretted, apparently, by any one. The course and reasons of the change can be readily followed. The reaction which ensued after the intense spiritual excitement of the seventeenth century produced a species of religious lethargy in the eighteenth. Frigid morality, a well-bred abhorrence of anything like zeal, and a worldly indifference, characterized the English clergymen of the latter period, and their Virginian brethren as well. The colonial ministers were as a class ruder and narrower than those of the mother country, and their coldness and indifference to great religious principles showed themselves more plainly and coarsely; but the essential spirit of both the imperial and the provincial Church was the same. The results, too, were identical. Religion declined, and "paganism, atheism, and sectaries" began to prevail.[2] "Quakers," says Colonel Byrd, "prevail in Nansemond County, for the want of ministers to pilot people a better way to heaven." Clergymen would not go there because the tobacco, in which their salaries were paid, was bad; and the honest colonel, who retained the old spirit, and would not have permitted on Sunday any work but that of charity, self-preservation, or necessity, wonders rather grimly that Jesuits and Puritans have not seized on so promising a field.[3]

Although the Jesuit and the Puritan did not come, the religious revival which swept over England with Wesley broke out with great force in the province. But the Virginians dealt with this movement in more simple and vigorous fashion than did their English cousins. Not long before, the Presbyterians, who had taken the field more than half a century earlier, supported by a strong and growing element of the population, had wrested from Governor Gooch promises of toleration to those of their faith who were pushing the settlements on the western frontier.[4] Immediate advantage was taken of this relaxation, and some of the leading clergymen, eloquent and earnest men, began an active proselyting,[5] which soon aroused the latent hostility

---

[1] Mass. Hist. Soc. Collections, 1st series, v., 124.
[2] Tyler's Hist. of American Literature, i., 80; Campbell, p. 382.
[3] Byrd MSS., i., 42, 153.   [4] Foote, ii., 84, 164.   [5] Ibid., p. 104.

of the ruling Church; and the Presbyterians, who had borne for so many years the brunt of the battle in behalf of the rights of conscience, were the first to feel the wrath aroused by their renewed activity. Gooch joined in the resistance to the new doctrines, and indictments were found against the Presbyterian clergy for their unlicensed preaching.[1] But the character and respectability of the Presbyterians saved them from the savage attacks made upon the humbler and more energetic sects which sprang up with the revival. The Moravians, New Lights, and Baptists were denounced by Gooch in 1745 in a charge to the grand-jury, and in the following year their meetings were forbidden.[2] The Baptists suffered most severely. Their meetings were broken up by rough crowds, their preachers were thrown into prison, and treated with the utmost ignominy, and the mob invaded their baptismal services, and abused and assaulted the participants, who were beaten and maltreated in every way.[3] This antiquated method of dealing with religious differences of opinion was due not to zeal, but to interest. The Established Church was one of the appendages of the Virginian aristocracy. They controlled the vestries and the ministers, and the parish church stood not infrequently on the estate of the great planter who had built and managed it.[4] The ruling class, therefore, regarded the revival as an attack upon property and vested rights, and as an assault upon one of the bulwarks of society. It was the conservative opposed to the innovating spirit. The conservative element had the political power, and they put down the innovators with a high hand. In all attacks upon the Baptists, the magistrates, who were of the ruling class in the province, were the most active,[5] and Peyton Randolph, bearing the first name in Virginia, headed the opposition to giving licenses to the Presbyterians.[6]

Such a policy could have but one result. The dissenting sects were full of vitality, and they grew apace, while the Established Church, maintained simply as part of a social system, declined with proportionate rapidity. Good judges estimated the number of dissenters at the time of the Revolution as comprising two-thirds of the population.[7] The intolerance and persecution of the ruling class

---

[1] Foote, ii., 133, 135.   [2] Burke, iii., 119, 125.

[3] Semple's Hist. of the Baptists, pp. 7, 15, 17, 23 ; Hening, 1759; Tyler's Hist. of American Literature, i., 90.

[4] Foote, i., 23.   [5] Burke, iii., 121.   [6] Foote, ii., 171.

[7] Foote, ii., 319, citing Jefferson and Burke ; see contra, Burnaby, p. 23.

awakened the active indignation of the coming leaders in the new era of political development. The gentle nature of young James Madison was deeply stirred by the harsh treatment of the sectaries, and he exerted himself strongly against their oppressors.[1] The powerful human sympathies and liberal views of Thomas Jefferson brought him to similar conclusions, which rapidly gained ground among the revolutionary leaders. The shock of war precipitated the inevitable result, for the dissenters to a man almost were on the patriotic side,[2] and public opinion could not consistently overlook religious freedom in a struggle for political liberty. After a short, sharp conflict the privileges of the old Established Church were swept away, and all faiths became equal before the law.[3] The fall of the Church revealed painfully its low condition; the substance had gone, and nothing remained but the husks. As soon as the State support was withdrawn, the whole edifice of the Church went to pieces, for it had no genuine religious strength. Religious indifference was found to prevail everywhere; the people seemed to have no religious sense; the churches fell into ruin and neglect; the service of the Church was abandoned, not only in outlying parishes, but in many of the towns, and the legacy of irreligion was all that the Church of England bequeathed to Virginia.[4]

This religious indifference had of course existed for many years, but it was covered up by forms and by the strong shelter of the State. The organization of the Church had real power and meaning, although the spiritual force had decayed. At the close of the French war there were in Virginia sixty or seventy parishes of the Established Church, and these were governed by the vestries, which were very important and active bodies. They represented all the local and municipal government there was in Virginia, and had attained, moreover, a commanding position in Church affairs. At an early day secular functions were assigned to them by the Burgesses. They were to make returns of births, marriages, and deaths, present for crimes under the statutes against vice, command the sheriff to hold the election for Burgesses, and assist the county courts in building workhouses. To the vestry belonged the duty of "processioning the land" once in four

---

[1] Rives's Life of Madison, i., 42–44.
[2] Semple, p. 23; Foote, ii., 171.　　　　　　　　　　　　　[3] Burke, iv., 377.
[4] Weld's Travels, pp. 107, 133; Rochefoucauld, i., 50–56, 101. As to the general condition of the Church, see Letter of Bishop of London in vol. iii. Doc. Rel. to Col. Hist. of New York.

years, and upon them devolved the care of roads and ferries.[1] Thus far they corresponded to the English vestries and the New England town-meeting; and, as might be imagined, became in time of revolution a nucleus of opposition.[2] Their ecclesiastical powers were more extended. In the time of the Commonwealth, and under Bacon's brief rule, they obtained rights which were never wrung from them.[3] The most important was the power of raising the salary of the minister, and they also made good their claim to the right of controlling the induction, after bitter contests with the Governor and Commissary. They were able to hire their ministers from year to year, and thus kept their pastors entirely at their mercy, crippling the Governor's power of inducting for life completely, and not infrequently they handled their spiritual guides very roughly.[4] By a law of the Commonwealth period all affairs of the vestry and Church were assigned to the control of the members of the parish, and the Restoration simply obliged the vestry to take the oaths of supremacy, allegiance, and conformity to the Church of England, but did not revoke their right of settling the minister's salary.[5] At the time of the Revolution the vestries, consisting of twelve of the parish, were chosen by the heads of families, and were in the hands of the ruling class.[6] Washington, Henry, the Randolphs, and the Lees fairly represent the kind of men who sat at these local boards, and thus controlled the sources of political power.[7]

The head of the Church was the royal Governor, to whom belonged, nominally at least, the right of induction, while the supervision of ecclesiastical matters was intrusted to a commissary appointed by the Bishop of London and paid from the royal quit-rents.[8] Attempts were made to substitute a bishop for the commissary; but, though often renewed, they never succeeded, and invariably aroused a most bitter resistance. Among the many causes of hostility to England was the dread of a bishop, and the efforts to bring about such an appointment did much to injure the Church and render unpopular the

---

[1] Hening, 1632–'45, 1646–'57, 1659–'60, 1668–'76, 1696, 1727, 1748; Foote, i., 23.
[2] Rives's Madison, i., 49; Meade, i., 151, 163.
[3] Hening, 1646, 1657, 1676.
[4] Anderson's Hist. of Col. Church, i., 350, 377; Present State of Virginia, Hartwell; Present State of Virginia, Jones.
[5] Hening, 1660.   [6] Present State of Virginia, Hartwell.
[7] Rives's Madison, i., 49; Meade, p. 151–160.
[8] Present State of Virginia, Hartwell; Burnaby, p. 25.

clergymen who advocated it.[1] This office of commissary and that of president of the college, which, except in one case, always went with it, was a high and important one, uniting, when in the hands of a strong man like James Blair, much political as well as religious power.[2] But, although the commissaries were often able to successfully resist the Governor and maintain their own independence, they were not able to keep up the character of the clergy.

The ministers of the Church were an important class in Virginia. By a law of 1696 their salary was fixed at 16,000 pounds of tobacco, and this stipend was largely increased by legal fees for marriages, funerals, and christenings.[3] They were also given by law a glebe and a parsonage, supplied by the vestry at the cost of the parish. In the seventeenth century, although there were undoubtedly many adventurers and scapegraces from England[4] among the clergy, the body of the profession appear to have been honest and zealous men, not highly educated, but faithful and sufficient in their discharge of duty. During the eighteenth century they rapidly declined in character, although to the last they formed an important and picturesque element in Virginian life. The overpowering influence of the vestries, the transatlantic patronage which filled the ministry, and the foreign extraction of many of the incumbents of livings did much toward the degeneracy of the clergy. But the main cause was to be found in the cold and worldly spirit which characterized the Church of England at this time, both at home and abroad. With some exceptions, the Virginian clergy aped the manners and habits of the laity. Most of them were men who cultivated their glebes like other planters, preaching once a week, and performing the other services of the Church for the sake of an addition to their income. Their morals were loose, and the general tone of the profession was low. Here and there might be found a man of exemplary life and high character ; but the average parson was coarse and rough, and his parishioners might be thankful if he was not also a drunkard and a gambler. They hunted the fox and raced horses, they played cards, turned marriages, christenings, and funerals alike into revels, and sat out the stoutest planter after dinner, to finally accompany him under the table. One reverend gentleman bawled to his church-warden during communion, " Here, George, this

[1] Anderson, ii., 358 ; iii., 153 ; Meade, i., 170, 171.
[2] Meade, i., 94, 150 ; Foote, ii., 153 ; Tyler's Hist. of Am. Literature, i., 90.
[3] Hening, 1696 ; Foote, ii., 148.   1743, fees fixed by law.
[4] Foote, i., 23 ; Mrs. Behn, The Widow Ranter, iv., 115.

bread is not fit for a dog." Another commemorated his church and office by fighting a duel in the graveyard. Another received a regular stipend for preaching four sermons annually against atheism, gambling, racing, and swearing, although he was notorious as a gambler, swearer, and horse-racer. Still another, of great physical strength, thrashed his vestry soundly, and then added insult to injury by preaching to them next day from the text, "And I contended with them, and cursed them, and smote certain of them, and plucked off their hair."[1] One married a wealthy widow, although he had a wife living in England. Another was brought before the magistrate, a fellow-clergyman, for drinking and carousing on Christmas-eve; and yet another is remembered who, after dinner every Sunday with the great planter of the neighborhood, was tied in his chaise and sent home with a servant. At every race-course and cock-pit might be seen reverend divines betting on the contending birds or horses.[2] The petty tradesmen would not trust them beyond their salary, and extorted one hundred and fifty per cent. for interest. They were both extravagant and poor,[3] and the list of clerical exploits in card-playing, horse-racing, fox-hunting, and drinking might be extended indefinitely. Worthy Bishop Meade, who recounts their doings with much sorrow, says "There was not only defective preaching but, as might be expected, most evil living among the clergy." The natural result, already described, followed, and the revival of the eighteenth century, headed by the Baptists, Wesleyans, Moravians, and "New Lights," broke down the old clergy and their abuses together. Then came the ill-advised struggle for salaries, famous as "The Parson's Cause," the fatuous effort to procure a bishop, and a fatal indecision and lukewarmness in the contest with England. The Revolution was a finishing-stroke, and the old Church of Virginia perished with as much justice, and as completely, as did the English Catholic Church under Henry VIII.

If it fared ill with the learned professions in Virginia, the case was no better in regard to trade and industry, which have risen to such commanding positions in modern times. The representatives of these important interests did not even attain to the dignity of a class. There were a few merchants in Norfolk; but the tradesmen were merely small shopkeepers, scattered about among the little towns. Other

---

[1] Meade, i., 18, 162, 231, 250, 275, 361, 387, 470; ii., 179.
[2] Foote, ii., 371. [3] Byrd MSS., i., 46.

petty retailers were established at the county seats, where they kept the one store of the neighborhood, which formed, with the inn and court-house, the county town.[1] Others, again, travelled about the country, exchanging their goods for tobacco, and pushing even beyond the mountains to traffic with the frontiersmen and Indians for furs, the savages offering an inviting and lucrative market, in which even the great planters were not ashamed to share.[2] These small traders carried on a thriving business, preying upon the necessities of the planters and clergy, and extorting ruinous interest whenever they gave credit. There was, indeed, but little encouragement for a mercantile class. The merchants fared best; but were obliged to give long credit, and take their pay in tobacco, on which, from its fluctuation, there were often serious losses. The tradesmen had no markets, and had either to raise corn and stock themselves, or take them in payment. All exchange was slow and cumbrous, and business dragged heavily. It was, in fact, essentially petty, for almost everything of necessity, and all manufactured articles were imported by the planters direct from England,[3] and the shipping was entirely in the hands of English merchants and natives of the other colonies.[4] Descending a step lower, we find that, except in the immediate neighborhood of Norfolk and the sea-coast,[5] there were few or no mechanics.[6] The ruder and most necessary arts were practised on every plantation by slaves trained for the purpose, and each landlord had in this way his own workmen.[7] All articles requiring any skill in manufacture, and even many of the simplest in domestic use, were brought ready-made from England.[8] Such mechanics as there were had to gain, in many cases, a precarious livelihood by travelling about among the plantations, obtaining the odd bits of work for which the slaves were incompetent.[9]

The condition of the tradesmen, merchants, and mechanics implies great lack of variety in natural products, and a very low state of industries of all sorts. Indeed, no successful attempts had been made to utilize the resources of the country. Good cattle and horses abounded, and the exportation of wheat had risen to five hundred thousand bushels;[10] but other exports, which included pork, cider,

---

[1] Anburey, ii., 318.   [2] Byrd MSS., i., 180.
[3] Foote, i., 9 ; Rives's Life of Madison, i., 543.
[4] Beverly.   [5] Rochefoucauld, ii., 13.
[6] Hening, 1633. Early law forbidding mechanics to plant shows the tendency.
[7] Rochefoucauld, ii., 80.   [8] Hening, 1659.   [9] Mass. Hist. Coll., I., v., 124.
[10] Smyth, ii., 140 ; Burnaby, p. 19.

bar-iron, and indigo, together with beef and lumber from Norfolk to the West Indies, were trifling in amount.[1] The valuable fisheries, from which at first much had been expected, were wholly neglected.[2] In the earliest times great results had been anticipated from vineyards and silk culture, and legislative encouragement had been freely given.[3] But neither of these industries ever came to anything. We hear of isolated cases where wine was successfully made,[4] and hopes of raising silk were never entirely abandoned. Here and there silk was made and woven, and there is an account of a silk suit made by a young Virginian girl for Washington,[5] but this was all. Other and more useful manufactures fared little better. In the seventeenth century an act of the Legislature obliged the counties to set up and maintain looms, and employ a weaver, but even this violent legislation had little effect.[6] Cotton was grown in small quantities before the Revolution; and a coarse fabric used by the lower classes, and known as Virginia cloth, was woven on the plantations.[7] Early encouragement had been given by the Assembly to the manufacture of linen; but as late as the year 1730 it was found necessary to offer premiums for its production, which, even with this artificial stimulus, remained very trifling, and had little more than a bare existence.[8] So great was the lack of capital and enterprise that even the grist-mills were few and poor, and the advantage of grinding their own corn was resigned by the Virginians to other colonies.[9] Nothing shows more strikingly the absolute dearth of manufactures and the industrial dependence of the country than Beverly's lament, in 1720, over the shiftlessness and indolence of his countrymen. Chairs, tables, stools, chests, boxes, cart-wheels, and even bowls and birchen brooms, were imported.[10]

The great mineral wealth of the country was likewise wholly undeveloped,[11] except as to iron, of which there was an insignificant production. Governor Spotswood and some of his friends had opened

---

[1] Burnaby, p. 21; Byrd MSS., i., 19.   [2] Burnaby, p. 15; Smyth, i., 57.
[3] Force's Hist. Tracts, The Silkworm in Virginia; Hening, 1628, 1657.
[4] Huguenot Family in Virginia, p. 265 (1715); Rochefoucauld, i., 87.
[5] Soldier and Pioneer; Anderson.
[6] Hening, 1666.
[7] Burnaby, p. 21; Abbé Robin, p. 107; Anburey, ii., 378.
[8] Maxwell's Hist. Reg., i., 167; Burnaby, p. 21; Hening, 1682, 1730.
[9] Rochefoucauld, i., 9.
[10] Beverly, book iv., 58; compare Hening, 1759.
[11] Present State of Virginia, Hartwell; Burnaby, p. 16.

iron mines, and built forges at Germanna, and others had been started in various parts of the province by individual planters.[1] The industry reached the dignity of exportation, but it was depressed and almost ruined by English duties and management; and, although always receiving legislative aid, its existence was so feeble that in the eighteenth century the Assembly exempted all persons employed in the iron-works from taxation and militia duty.[2] Most of the forges, and, indeed, most of the manufacturing of all sorts was carried on by the Germans and Irish, who had settled in the West, beyond the mountains.[3]

The explanation of the condition of trade and industry is to be found in the absorption of the population in the cultivation of tobacco.[4] There has never been a community, probably, in which any one great staple has played such a part as in Virginia. Tobacco founded the colony and gave it wealth. It was the currency of Virginia; as bad a one as could be devised, and fluctuating with every crop; yet it retained its place as circulating medium despite the most strenuous efforts to introduce specie.[5] The clergy were paid and taxes were levied by the Burgesses in tobacco. The whole prosperity of the colony rested upon it for more than a century, and it was not until the period of the Revolution that other crops began to come in and replace it.[6] The fluctuations in tobacco caused the first conflict with England, brought on by the violence of the clergy, and paved the way for resistance.[7] In tobacco the Virginian estimated his income and the value of everything he possessed; and in its various functions, as well as in its method of cultivation, it had a strong effect upon the character of the people.

As early as the year 1614 tobacco had become the staple, and plants were growing in the streets of Jamestown. Sudden wealth, over-production, famine,[8] laws to limit planting and to enforce the sowing of corn, and quarrels with England, were the first-fruits of the new crop. Then followed more over-production, falling prices, financial ruin, attempts to raise prices artificially, and occasional plant-cutting riots of a desperate character.[9] Every interest centred in the

---

[1] Byrd MSS., ii., 59; Smyth, i., 28, 57; ii., 177.
[2] Byrd MSS., ii., 53; Hening, 1727, 1748.   [3] Smyth, ii., 258.
[4] Foote, i., 9; Abbé Robin, p. 110.   [5] Foote, i., 8.
[6] Raynal, Rev. in America, p. 90; Weld, p. 116; Rochefoucauld, i., 57.
[7] Burnaby, p. 25.   [8] Burke, i., 1614.
[9] Burke, ii., 134; Foote, i., 7; Hening, 1629, 1632; Hist. Coll. of South Carolina; Young's Letters; see also Campbell.

great staple as it rose and fell with each ensuing year, while its use as
money never failed to give an unhealthy incentive to its lavish and
exclusive production. It was, too, always a sore subject with England; and the "Case of the Planters of Tobacco," in 1733, presents
a sad picture of the losses inflicted by the mother country by extortionate duties, and, what was much worse, by fraud, corruption, clip-
ping, and favoritism of all sorts in the custom-house.[1] Tobacco-
planting made slaves necessary and profitable, and fastened slavery
upon the province. The method of cultivation, requiring intense labor and watching for a short period, and permitting complete idleness for the rest of the year, fostered habits which alternated between
feverish exertion and languid indolence.[2] The immense returns, and
the fact of staking the year's income on the result of a short period,
as well as the rude practice of growing the plants until the land was
exhausted, and then letting it go wild again, and clearing fresh acres,
all tended to produce extravagance, recklessness, improvidence, and a
spirit of speculation among the people.[3] As the whole commercial existence of the State rested on obtaining a market for tobacco, the government took every measure to maintain a high standard in respect
to quality. Warehouses were established at an early period, and a
system of inspection organized which was both severe and thorough.[4]
Just before the Revolution the exportation of tobacco, including a
small quantity from North Carolina, had risen from sixty thousand,
in 1759, to one hundred thousand hogsheads, was worth nearly a
million pounds sterling, and employed about three hundred vessels.[5]
From the distant plantations the tobacco was floated down on canoes
lashed together, and carrying eight or nine hogsheads, as far as the
head of navigation, where there was a warehouse, and a small town
springing up around it; but the trade was chiefly carried on by the
planters themselves.[6] The vessels from England worked their way
up the river, delivered their manufactured articles, and loaded with

---

[1] The Case of the Planters of Tobacco in Virginia, Pamphlet, 1733.
[2] Massachusetts Hist. Coll., I., v., 124; Present State of Virginia, Hartwell.
[3] In regard to the mode of cultivating tobacco in the last century, see full accounts in Anburey, ii., 344; Brissot, p. 375; Weld, pp. 116–'17; Rochefoucauld, i.,
80; Smyth, i., 59.
[4] Rochefoucauld, i., 35; Byrd MSS., ii., 9; Anburey, ii., 314.
[5] Smyth, ii., 139; Burnaby, p. 21; Abbé Robin, p. 110; Brissot, p. 375; Jefferson's Virginia.
[6] Huguenot Family in Virginia, p. 388; Smyth i., 33.

tobacco at the planter's own wharf, picking up a full cargo by a succession of such visits. This simple and lordly system had begun to decline slightly, but it was still maintained very generally at the period of the Revolution.[1]

By a gradual process of elimination we have seen that, with the exception of the clergy and the lawyers—the latter just rising into prominence about the middle of the eighteenth century—both numerically small classes, the people of Virginia were wholly agricultural, and further, that they were devoted to the production of a single great staple. It only remains to trace the origin of the planters to classify them, and become acquainted with their education, amusements, opinions, and daily lives and occupations, in order to understand thoroughly the Virginia of the last century.

When Smith and his companions landed at Jamestown, the art of colonization was but little understood. The first settlers were for the most part idle and dissolute adventurers, attracted solely by the hope of speedy fortune; and they were not improved by the sweepings of the London streets, sent out to people the colony and act as indented servants, nor by the convicts, whose transportation to America was a bitter grievance against the mother country, down even to the Revolution.[2] It would be wholly wrong, however, to suppose that immigrants of this sort were a controlling element, or even one which had a marked effect on the quality of the population. The Virginians sprang from a fine English stock. Many younger sons of wealthy or noble families, many of the yeomanry, and many of the merchant-class came to Virginia. The Cavalier element predominated after the great rebellion; but there was also an infusion of Puritans with their characteristic qualities of strength and tenacity. There was, in addition, a small Huguenot immigration, wholly good in its results, and which was rapidly fused with the dominant race.[3] At the beginning of the eighteenth century a large number of Scotch-Irish Presbyterians came out,[4] who, with Germans from the middle colonies, pushed out to the frontier, and did much to open up the western country.[5] Even in the aggregate, however, the foreign elements were small, and without effect on the people, who may be accurately described as thoroughly and essentially English.

---

[1] Sparks's Life of Washington; Rives's Life of Madison, i., 543.
[2] Hening, 1670.   [3] Foote, i., 156.
[4] Smyth, i., 156; De Haas, Early Settlement of West Virginia, p. 36.
[5] Burnaby, p. 55; Smyth, ii., 257–'58.

With no towns, no diversity of pursuits, no important learned professions, scarcely any opportunity for constant and liberalizing social friction, and with a comparatively small population scattered over a large area, much of which was still a wilderness, the structure of Virginian society was, as might be expected, very simple. There were four classes in the community. The African slaves, who formed nearly one-half of the population, were the lowest element; then, divided from the negroes by the impassable gulf of race and blood, came the indented servants and poor whites; then the middle class of small farmers and planters; and then at the top the great landlords, who ruled and represented Virginia. These divisions were supported and maintained by a strong belief in social distinctions, and they increased in power and meaning as they descended.[1]

Beginning at the bottom of the social scale, we find the African slaves, although far from being, as they afterward became, the one decisive influence in the conduct of Virginia, a numerous body, important to the material interests of the province, and by their very existence producing deep and lasting effects upon the character of the whole population. For fifty years after the first ill-omened cargo of human beings had been landed at Jamestown, but few slaves seem to have been imported, and the sparse legislation in regard to them shows that they formed neither an important nor formidable element.[2] The only severe legislation was directed to the prevention of illicit intercourse between the races, which was punished by public whipping and penance in church inflicted upon the guilty white man.[3] In the year 1667 it was declared that baptism did not exempt from bondage;[4] and after this period legislation becomes rapidly more stringent, servile rebellion begins to cast its shadow over the country, and a tone of dread is perceptible in the acts of the Assembly, to all of which the negro insurrection on the Northern Neck in 1687 gave terrible meaning. From that time forth the slave laws have but one quality, that of ferocity engendered by fear.[5] It is only possible to give a bare outline of this legislation, which filled many pages of the statute-book; but it may be summed up in a few words. The slaves

---

[1] In regard to classes in Virginia, see Wirt's Life of Patrick Henry, p. 32; Anburey, ii., 330; Rochefoucauld, i., 69; Smyth, i., 65; Rives's Life of Madison, i., 49, 78, 79; compare also Wirt's description of tenants in the British Spy.

[2] Burke, ii., 300; Hening, 1640, 1661–'62, 1668; Foote, ii., 155; 1671—2000 negroes in the colony.

[3] Hening, 1629, 1646.   [4] Ibid., 1667.   [5] Burke, ii., 300.

had no rights which any white man was bound to respect. They could not gather at feasts or burials,[1] and if found away from their plantation without a certificate they received twenty lashes at the public expense, and thirty if they raised their hand against a Christian.[2] If a master killed a resisting slave, it was no felony, for no man could be presumed to have any "malice prepense" in destroying his own property.[3] It was no felony to kill a slave while correcting him,[4] and slaves were debarred from giving evidence except at the trial of one of their own race for a capital offence.[5] If they fled from servitude they were proclaimed by the Assembly to be outlaws, and could then be killed at sight by any one, a reward being sometimes offered, or castrated at the pleasure of the sheriff. The public purse reimbursed the owner if the slave was slain, and the surgeon in the second case was liable in damages if his patient died from the effects of the operation.[6] They were not allowed to carry arms, or even to have dogs, and the officers of militia were ordered to search all negro huts for concealed weapons. Even the free negroes who served in the militia were finally deprived of this privilege, and confined to servile employments when on military duty.[7] Every one was deterred from aiding or harboring runaways by the severest penalties. Stealing a slave was felony without benefit of clergy, and was ranked among crimes as equivalent to the murder of a friendly Indian.[8] Great importance was attached to keeping the races separate, and the dominant class pure in blood. Any white man, bond or free, marrying a negress, was to be banished, and at a later period was thrown into prison and fined, while the officiating clergyman paid a penalty of ten thousand pounds of tobacco, nearly a whole year's salary.[9] The doctrine of *partus sequitur ventrem,* rigidly enforced against both bastards and legitimate children, had the same dividing tendency.[10] Emancipation was hampered; being in England was no discharge, and the condition of free negroes was little better than that of the slaves.[11] They were simply property in the eyes of the law, and, as such, were taxed, passed as chattels, and could be annexed to the land by the tenant in tail.[12] But they were a very perilous sort of property, and their increase was very rapid and very alarming,

[1] Hening, 1680.   [2] Ibid.   [3] Ibid., 1669, 1723; Foote, i., 23.
[4] Hening, 1705.   [5] Ibid., 1732, 1744.   [6] Ibid., 1701, 1705, 1723.
[7] Ibid., 1723, 1738, 1752, 1757.   [8] Ibid., 1670, 1732, 1748.
[9] Ibid., 1691, 1753.   [10] Ibid., 1661–'62, 1748; Foote, i., 23.
[11] Hening, 1668, 1691, 1748, 1762.   [12] Ibid., 1682, 1726, 1727, 1732.

especially toward the middle of the eighteenth century.[1] The anxiety thus stimulated was first expressed in renewed legislation of the most frightful character, which may be exemplified by a single clause providing that slaves found abroad at night without a license should be dismembered.[2] This repressive movement was replaced by a desire to check importation, and a wish to ameliorate the condition of the negroes. Some of the most barbarous penalties were curtailed, better opportunity of obtaining justice in the courts was given, and slight modifications were everywhere apparent.[3] The movement in this direction went so far that the slave-trade became one of the grievances against England, embodied in the original draft of the Declaration of Independence; and the ideas of the Revolution even led to projects of emancipation, and the foundation of societies for that purpose. But even at this time the life of a black was held very cheap. Juries would not convict for the murder of a slave, and the interest in emancipation, which was languid at best, after the close of the war rapidly died away. It was impossible to overcome the love of luxury and the commercial value of slavery.[4] The ferocity of Virginian slave legislation shows only too clearly the manner in which the wretched negroes were regarded, as well as the tone and temper of the ruling class, and the atmosphere in which they lived; but it is far from giving a just notion of the treatment of the slaves in everyday practice. Here comes in the broad distinction in this respect between Virginia and the more southern colonies. There can be no question that Virginian slaves were almost universally well and mildly treated. They were fairly clothed and fed. Many of them had gardens and poultry; and, as they were carefully kept in a state of the densest ignorance, it is not going too far to say that they were tolerably happy and contented. They were not overworked, and both the climate and the methods of cultivating tobacco favored their well-being.[5] It is in its effect upon the character and habits of the white population that slavery in colonial Virginia becomes of the first importance as a factor, both in politics and society.

Slave laws, at first infrequent and unimportant, increased, as has been seen, in number and stringency as the colony grew, until they occupied a principal place in the statute-book. With indented white

---

[1] Huguenot Family in Virginia, p. 346.   [2] Hening, 1748.   [3] Ibid., 1769, 1772.
[4] Burnaby, p. 31; Brissot, p. 237, 249; Rochefoucauld, i., 43.
[5] Present State of Virginia, Jones; Brissot, p. 240; Weld, p. 114; Abbé Robin, p. 112.

servants the case was exactly reversed; they were in the beginning
the only servile and the principal laboring class. The influx of negroes reduced them to insignificance, although their numbers do not
appear to have proportionately diminished. As early as the year
1623 laws were framed to compel obedience to masters,[1] and for the
next fifty years there was much severe legislation to regulate the servants. They were not allowed to marry without leave of their masters; if they ran away, additional service was the punishment, and for
a second offence, branding on the cheek, while those who harbored
them were subjected to heavy penalties.[2] If they came without indentures, they were to serve four years, and years of service were added
for an assault on their master, for engaging in trade, refusing to
work, or, in the case of women, for having a bastard, unless the father
was also the master, as well as for running away.[3] These provisions
of the law enabled grasping masters to greatly protract the period of
servitude, and rendered the condition of the servants miserable in the
extreme. The only protection afforded them was the right of public burial, and if their death was under suspicious circumstances the
neighbors were to view the body.[4] Although the legislation in regard to servants disappears almost entirely after the middle of the
seventeenth century, the existing laws remained in force. An act
passed in 1748 provided that when a free person was liable to a fine,
a servant should be whipped; and this illustrates their position as well
as possible in the years prior to the Revolution.[5] Their condition
was little better than that of slaves. Loose indentures and harsh
laws put them at the mercy of their masters. They were coarsely
clothed, and fed upon meal and water sweetened with molasses,[6] and
were frequently punished with great barbarity. They were, as a class,
of very poor character, for the most part transported convicts and
the scum of the London streets. Many were kidnapped as children,
as the traffic was lucrative; and in some cases, like that of James Annesley, who afterward established his claim to the Anglesea peerage,
they were shipped to Virginia to be put out of the way, and die on a
remote plantation.[7] In the seventeenth century they formed a picturesque and important element in society, and were considered in

---

[1] Hening, 1623–'24.   [2] Ibid., 1643, 1657–1659.
[3] Ibid., 1643–'57, 1696–1705, 1726, 1753.
[4] Ibid., 1661–'62.   [5] Ibid., 1748.
[6] Anglesea Peerage Case, Howell's State Trials, xvii., 1447.
[7] Howell's State Trials; Maxwell, Hist. Register, i., 166.

England as typical Virginians. In this way they figured on the London stage, and served as leading characters in the novels of Defoe, who seized upon the rough life of Virginia as a welcome aid in his portrayal of low and criminal adventures.[1] In fiction the indented servant, either by superior virtue or superior vice, usually by the latter, commonly rises from the most menial offices to fortune and estate, carries off rich widows, becomes a successful and unscrupulous attorney, a magistrate, perhaps a clergyman, always a prominent member of colonial society.[2] There were, no doubt, enough instances of such careers to justify their use in romance; but in the great majority of cases, when the period of servitude expired the indented servants became what were known as poor whites, and thus formed, whether bond or free, the lowest class in the community. They were illiterate, degraded, and despised even by the negroes. The presence of an inferior and servile race made them idle, shiftless, and unenterprising. They never worked except to obtain a bare subsistence, and on the frontier they were actually barbarous.[3] These poor whites and the free negroes formed the criminal class;[4] and crime, from their existence, and owing to the unequal division of property, seems to have been more common in Virginia than in the other colonies, where it was exceptional and sporadic, and not so directly attributable to any particular portion of the community.[5] Criminal offences and misdemeanors were punished in Virginia, as elsewhere during that period, in a rude and simple fashion. Murder, rape, arson, and robbery were capital crimes; while smaller offences, from swearing upward, were expiated by fines, lashes, exposure in the pillory or stocks, imprisonment, and the ducking-stool; and every county court was required to provide the appurtenances necessary for these punishments.[6] In a society where slavery made labor a mark of shame, and where the poor-law required those receiving public relief to wear a badge of bright color, denoting that the possessor was a pauper,[7] the lowest white class naturally gained a livelihood by dubious and dishonest as well as precarious methods. Besides these darker qualities of ignorance and crime

---

[1] Mrs. Behn, the Widow Ranter; Defoe, Moll Flanders and Captain Jack.

[2] Ibid.; and see also "The Life and Character of a Monster lately arrived in London," Tract, 1726.

[3] Anburey, ii., 309–333; Meade, i., 366; Memoirs of Count Fersen, i., 63; Rochefoucauld, i., 69.

[4] Meade, i., 366. [5] Brissot, p. 374. [6] Hening, 1671, 1705, 1727, 1745, 1748.

[7] Ibid., 1755; compare as to poor-laws at a later time, Rochefoucauld, i., 27.

these people were also illiberal, narrow-minded, prying, and inquisitive.[1] Their only good qualities seem to have been an easy temper, and much real good-nature and hospitable feeling. They were fortunately few in number, and were perfectly unimportant both socially and politically. They were the turbulent element of Virginian life, and figured prominently in the crowds which gathered at the horse-race, the hustings, or the sessions of the county court. They hung about the taverns drinking and gambling, and on all festive occasions engaged in single combats, and sometimes general battles.[2] Their fighting was not simply with the fists, but included the brutal practice of "gouging." A northern man entering Virginia from Maryland rescued a fellow-traveller from the hands of a native who had sworn he would "try the strength of his eye-strings." When he reached Hanover Court-house, he found an election in progress, and the usual crowd assembled. He was immediately invited to "swap horses and watches," narrowly escaped a fight, and had the pleasure of witnessing a gouging-match. One of the combatants succeeded in getting a twist in the side-locks of his adversary, and then pressed his thumb against the eyeball of his opponent, who bawled out "King's cruse" (enough), and the pleasing match terminated without mutilation, although so tame an ending was by no means the rule.[3] This is a fair picture of the lowest class of Virginians—rude, noisy, brawling, drinking fellows, very lazy, and sometimes criminal; but with a redeeming dash of generous and hospitable good-nature.[4]

It is not easy to distinguish between the two remaining classes in Virginian society. The middle class, beginning with the tradesmen and merchants, rose gradually through the farmers and small planters, until it merged imperceptibly in the ranks of the great landholders. The differences between the middle and upper classes were of degree, not of kind. Both were of sound English stock. Both were landholders and slave-owners in a greater or less degree,[5] and marriages served constantly to unite them more closely by the ties of blood. This does not apply to the trading portion of the middle class, who were regarded with great contempt by the owners of lands and slaves, who esteemed trade a mark of inferiority, and an occupation unsuited

---

[1] Smyth, i., 71; Michaux's Travels, p. 194; Anburey, ii., 333.

[2] Anburey, ibid.; Weld, p. 142.

[3] Memoirs of Elkanah Watson, 1777, p. 32; see also the excellent description of similar scenes in Rochefoucauld, i., 64.

[4] Smyth, i., 68.   [5] Rochefoucauld, i., 69.

to a man of birth and position.[1]   The majority, however, of the middle class were yeomen and farmers.   A writer long resident in the country describes their daily life as follows : " A man in this line rises in the morning about six o'clock ; he then drinks a julep made of rum, water, and sugar, but very strong ; then he walks, or more generally rides, round his plantation, views all his stock and all his crops, breakfasts about ten o'clock, on cold turkey, cold meat, fried hominy, toast, and cyder, ham, bread-and-butter, tea, coffee, or chocolate, which last, however, is seldom tasted but by the women ; the rest of the day he spends much in the same manner as a man of the first rank, only cyder supplies the place of wine at dinner, and he eats no supper ; they never even think of it."[2]

This was the daily life of the men who formed the great mass of the white population of Virginia.   They were good specimens of the nationality to which they belonged, and were a fine, sturdy, manly race, aristocratic in feeling, and from the ownership of slaves despotic in temper ; but they were earnest in the maintenance of English liberty. They lacked polish of manner, and were sadly deficient in education and knowledge of the world, but were without exception generous and hospitable.   Their families were less ancient and respectable than those of the first rank ; but they often acquired large fortunes, and the successful ones worked their way to the top in the course of a few generations.   They were attached to gaming and all sorts of rude sports, and roughness was in them always oddly mingled with gentler qualities.[3]   Such was the vigorous class of genuine English stock which gave strength, support, and political power to the great planters who ruled and represented Virginia, and imparted tone and color to the whole of her society.

This upper class was Virginia, and the rest of the people were merely modifications of the type or simple appendages.   These great planters were country gentlemen, not in the modern sense, but in that of the eighteenth century.   Many of them, no doubt, closely resembled the famous Squire Western of Fielding, and none of them differed in any essential particular, except a more intense pride, from the English country gentlemen of the same period.   Their origin has already been described, and the next step is to understand their education, and the influences which surrounded them in boyhood and youth.

The means of education were sadly deficient.   In the early days

---

[1] Soldier and Pioneer, Anderson.   [2] Smyth, i., 41.   [3] Ibid., pp. 66, 67.

worthy people in England had been profoundly impressed with the necessity of Christianizing the Indians, and under this impulse money was subscribed for a college in Henrico parish, an institution which was actually started, when the great massacre swept it out of existence. The East India school was started at the same time, under similar auspices, and met the same fate.[1] In the year 1660 there was a movement in favor of a college, owing to the low condition of the clergy; and in the following year provision was made for such an institution, and land was set apart by the Assembly. This solitary attempt came to nothing, and the fate of like efforts on the part of public-spirited individuals was equally unfortunate.[2] It is probable that there was little or no education of any sort at that period in Virginia. An old tract refers vaguely to "a free school and petty schools," but they must have been of the rudest kind. The government was generally lukewarm toward education, and the Stuart governors were distinctly hostile.[3] Sir William Berkeley, in 1671, declared that every man instructed his children according to his ability, and gave thanks to God that there were no free schools in Virginia, and no probability of any for a hundred years to come.[4] This amiable prediction was substantially verified. The untiring exertions and manly persistence of Blair succeeded in obtaining a charter for the college of William and Mary in 1692, and in establishing it on a firm foundation, despite the friendly remark of Seymour, the attorney-general, who said to the Virginian applicants for a charter, when they urged, as a reason for the higher education, the salvation of souls by the clergy, "Souls! Damn your souls, grow tobacco." But the college was all. There is no indication in the statutes of any desire to provide education, and no system of public schools was even attempted before 1776.[5]

In the years prior to the Revolution education in Virginia was at as low an ebb as can well be imagined. In childhood the young Virginian was brought up among the slaves and their offspring, which had the worst possible effect upon both speech and manners,[6] and the

[1] Meade, i., 84.

[2] Ibid.; Foote, i., 11; Jones, Present State of Virginia. There were renewed efforts at a much later time. Hening, 1753–'56.

[3] Tyler's Hist. of American Literature, i., 90. [4] Foote, i., 11.

[5] Hening; and see also Rochefoucauld, i., 48.

[6] Life of Arthur Lee, i., 11, 12; Georgia Hist. Coll., Itinerant Observations, 1745, p. 48.

only resource for the first years of education was in the grammar or country schools conducted by the parish minister, or by a freed servant.[1] The principal branches of study were English grammar, algebra, surveying, and navigation; but the quality of the instruction was poor in the extreme, and the schools themselves were scarce.[2] In some of the more fortunate parishes the clergyman possessed real attainments and a classical library, and received, as tutor, the sons of the wealthy planters.[3] In many instances, too, the boys studied at home; but it is to be feared that in all cases the discipline was slack, and that many young Virginians resembled Patrick Henry in giving more time to hunting and fishing than to their books.[4] The meagre schooling received by Washington was a not uncommon example of the education of young men even of good family. In the middle and lower classes only the barest rudiments were taught, and those very badly. Early in the eighteenth century the Bishop of London addressed a series of questions to the Virginian clergy. One of them was, "Are there any schools in your parish?" The uniform answer, with but two exceptions, was, "None." Another question was, "Is there any parish library?" All the clergy replied, "None," except one, who answered, "We have the Book of Homilies, the Whole Duty of Man, and the Singing Psalms."[5]

After such preliminary training as these trifling opportunities offered, the young Virginian, when his parents could afford it, was sent to William and Mary, or to England, to complete his education. The college founded by Blair prospered for many years under his energetic rule as president, and did much good; but during the eighteenth century it steadily degenerated, falling under the same evil influences which ruined the Church. The officers were a president and six professors, all poorly paid, and there was a library of some three thousand volumes (a large collection for that day), and a cabinet for experiments with philosophical apparatus. The Indian department had proved an utter failure. Courses were given in the classics, moral philosophy, metaphysics, mathematics, and divinity.[6] At the close of the old French war instruction had fallen to a low point. The pro-

---

[1] Maxwell, Hist. Reg., iii., 142; Georgia Hist. Coll., Itinerant Observations, 1745, p. 48.

[2] Jones, Present State of Virginia; Meade, ii., 90; Rochefoucauld, i., 105.

[3] Foote, i., 55.   [4] Soldier and Pioneer, Anderson.   [5] Meade, i., 190.

[6] Burnaby, p. 30; Smyth, p. 65; Abbé Robin, p. 107; Maxwell, Hist. Reg., p. 67; Georgia Hist. Coll., p. 48.

fessors were incompetent, and, in some cases, of dissolute lives. The students were unrestrained and disorderly, and the vicious transatlantic patronage, and the old useless endowments were ruinous in their effects.[1]   At the time of the Revolution the college was little more than a poor grammar-school, sustained by an occasional professor who chanced to be worthy of his place.

Many rich Virginians, especially younger sons who desired a professional training, went to England; but they fared little better than their brothers who stayed at home, and brought back quite as much vice as book-learning.   The viciousness of foreign education became, indeed, so well recognized that planters were deterred from sending their sons abroad.[2]   There were, of course, men like Colonel Byrd of Westover, who was educated in England, was a friend of Charles Boyle, Earl of Orrery, was admitted to the bar in the Middle Temple, and, having travelled in the Low Countries and figured at the Court of France, came back to make the most of all the advantages of his European training.[3]   Byrd was, as it happened, a man of real talent, and left the only writings produced in colonial Virginia which have genuine literary merit and skill.   But there were others, like Arthur Lee, who profited greatly by study at English and Scotch universities, and it cannot be doubted that there were many members of the ruling class who were liberally educated, and showed the results in their reading and tastes.[4]   Still these were the exceptions.   The mass of Virginians were not well educated, and depended much more on mother-wit, of which they had an abundant portion, than on any acquired advantages for their success in life.[5]

To the recipients of this education the one serious occupation of existence, after school and college had been passed, was the care of their estates.   To promote the growth of tobacco, to attend to the sale of his crop, to import the necessary implements and the desired luxuries, and to bring up a sufficient number of his negroes to useful trades, were the chief employments of the Virginian gentleman.   His public duties were to act as vestryman and justice of the peace, to hold court, and sit in the House of Burgesses, and in some cases to serve in the militia, or as an officer of the Crown in the civil service.

---

[1] Meade, i., 175, note, and ff.; Rochefoucauld, i., 25; Life of Jefferson, Parton, or Randall.

[2] Governor Page was kept at home on this account; Meade, i., 147, 190; ii., 90; Maxwell, Hist. Reg., iii., 142.   [3] Byrd MSS., i., 11.   [4] Smyth, i., 65.

[5] Jones, Present State of Virginia; Dawson's Hist. Mag., iv., 218.

To such lives were the sons bred up; while the mother and daughters of the household were entirely occupied with domestic affairs. Endless needle-work, the training of negro maids, and the charge of the house, filled the days of Virginian women.

The style of living was one of reckless profusion and indiscriminate hospitality. The latter quality was fostered by circumstances. Even in the seventeenth century the custom of receiving strangers was so prevalent that it became a subject of legislation. "They shall be reputed to entertayne those of curtesie," says the statute, "with whom they make not a certain agreement,"[1] and the habit grew with the colony. Gentlemen were wont to send to the neighboring tavern and invite any stranger home to stay as long as he pleased,[2] and no traveller described his wanderings without recording his obligations to the generous hospitality of the Virginian planters.[3]

This unstinted welcome to strangers was due in some measure to the isolation and monotony of life. The early settlers spread themselves over the land, clearing plantations here and there in the wilderness, and this custom was always adhered to. The plantations followed the rivers, which formed for many years the only means of communication with the outer world. This was slow and circuitous at best; but, although ferries, bridges, and bridle-paths were established at an early period,[4] travel was difficult, and even dangerous, all through the eighteenth century.[5] Roads winding along the rivers were gradually opened, and were sufficiently good in fair weather; but they passed through dense forests broken only at intervals of four or five miles by a plantation,[6] and wayfarers were frequently lost and obliged to pass the night in the woods, even in the most settled parts of the country and in the immediate neighborhood of towns.[7] Bridges were scarce, and the deep and frequent rivers were crossed usually in rickety boats, or by swimming, which resulted in fatigue and danger to the travellers, and great loss of horses swept away in the current.[8] Public coaches and post-chaises were unknown. Every one travelled

---

[1] Foote, i., 10; Hening, 1661–'62, 1667.   [2] Rochefoucauld, ii., 70.

[3] Huguenot Family, p. 271; Rochefoucauld, ii., 117; Smyth, i., 65.

[4] Hening, 1643; Foote, i., 10.

[5] Present State of Virginia, Hartwell.

[6] Jones, Present State of Virginia; Beverly; Anburey, ii., 300; Rochefoucauld, ii., 121; Smyth, i., 15; Georgia Hist. Coll., Itinerant Observations, 1745.

[7] Weld, p. 77.

[8] Ibid., p. 128; Huguenot Family, p. 271.

on horseback or in small sulkies, while the middle classes contented themselves with the cart and farm horses.[1]

The difficulty of travel, and the hospitality of the planters to the few who journeyed through the country, prevented any improvement in the taverns, or ordinaries, as they were commonly called. Here and there in the towns a good inn could be found; but in the country, and especially in the back districts, the public-houses were wretched, often mere huts, affording only a shelter from the weather.[2] There were plenty of them, however, such as they were; but they were used not by travellers, but by the natives as places of resort for drinking and gaming, and had such a bad effect that many acts were passed for the restraint of " tippling-houses," as the Burgesses saw fit to style them.[3]

The taverns, however, were probably the most uncomfortable habitations in the province. The homes of the Virginians, varying greatly with the social position of the occupant, were, as a rule, comfortable. In the towns the houses were of wood for the poorer classes, while the better ones were large, and built of brick.[4] In Norfolk they were commonly built of Dutch brick, with thick walls and large chimneys at each end, and the more expensive structures were handsomely wainscoted within in hard woods.[5] In the country wood prevailed in building. The homes of the lower classes were mean and small.[6] Those of the middle classes and small farmers, likewise of wood, were larger and more convenient. They were all low, generally of one story, with a loft-roof, and invariably built with two enormous chimneys, one at either end, and outside the house, which gave a picturesque appearance to these simple and even rude dwellings. The poorer ones were neither lathed nor plastered, had wooden chimneys lined with clay, and wooden shutters alone to protect the openings for light and air. The better sort were plastered and painted, and possessed brick chimneys and glass windows, but the furniture was simple. The beds were good, but uncurtained; and homely wooden stools took the place of cane chairs.[7]

The houses of the ruling and representative class were very different from those of the great majority of Virginians. When the trav-

[1] Meade, i., 19 ; Anburey, ii., 63 ; Smyth, i., 59.
[2] Anburey, ii., 303 ; Rochefoucauld, ii., 93 ; Smyth, i., 16, 50.
[3] Georgia Hist. Coll., Itinerant Observations, 1745 ; Hening, 1644, 1668, 1748.
[4] Jones, Present State of Virginia.
[5] Forrest, Historical and Descriptive Sketches of Norfolk.
[6] Rochefoucauld, ii., 23.   [7] Smyth, i., 49 ; Huguenot Family, p. 265.

eller came to one of the widely separated gaps in the forest and found himself upon the borders of a great plantation, the estate presented the appearance of a small village. In the centre stood the house of the planter, around which were clustered the offices, all separate from the main building, the tobacco-houses, and the numerous huts of the negro quarters. In the fields the slaves were seen sawing wood and making clearings, or cultivating tobacco. Not far away the herds of cattle were at pasture, and the whole scene recalled an English farm.[1]

The houses of the planters varied, of course, greatly with the taste of the occupants. Some were of wood, with massive timbers, and the typical outside chimney.[2] Many were of brick, and others still of cut stone. Some were low and picturesque, while others piled one story upon another as in the great Page house at Rosewell, and towered above the trees in bare and tasteless masses. All, however, were spacious, with large, low rooms, panelled and wainscoted in hard woods, and rejoicing in great fireplaces, where wood fires blazed, and over which were sometimes carved the armorial bearings of the family. These great houses, with their narrow windows, diamond panes, and tall chimneys, rising in the midst of estates of great natural beauty, strongly resembled the manor-houses of England, and were often furnished with a substantial elegance not unworthy of the mother country.[3]

The houses indicate fairly enough the extravagance and profusion of the Virginia planter, induced by the easily acquired wealth resulting from the sale of tobacco raised by low-priced slaves. The constant fluctuations in the price of the great staple tended to increase extravagance of living, and give a tone of reckless speculation to all affairs of business and money-making. An amount of style was maintained strangely at variance with the ignorance of the people, and the isolated and commonly solitary lives of the planters. The most marked display was in carriages and horses, due, in some measure, no doubt, to the fact that there were no other means of getting from place to place; but owing still more to the fondness for show and the love of

[1] Anburey, ii., 287; Weld, p. 114; Beverly; Smyth, i., 15; Chateaubriand, Œuvres, tom. vii., Voyage en Amérique, 1791, p. 16.

[2] Anderson, Soldier and Pioneer; Weld, p. 119.

[3] "My Ride to the Barbecue," Description of Gates's House; Beverly; Meade, i., 331, Rosewell; Anburey, ii., 319, Randolph House at Tuckahoe; Weld, p. 113, 119; Smyth, i., 15, Country-seats on the James River; p. 27, Carter Estate at Shirley Hundred; p. 146, Estates on Potomac; Byrd MSS., ii., 59, Spotswood House at Germanna.

horse-racing. Coaches, chariots, and chaises were all in common use.[1] In the year 1739 Colonel Spotswood advertises for sale " his coach, chariot, chaise, and coach-horses ;" and the chariot is described as having been "looked upon as one of the best made, handsomest, and easiest chariots in London." Every planter had his stud, including fine coach-horses, hunters, and racers ; many had famous stallions, and great attention was paid to breeding.[2] In every great house there was a handsome service of plate, and the table was bountiful, although chiefly supplied by the products of the plantation.[3] All articles of apparel were imported and costly ; but, nevertheless, both men and women dressed handsomely, and in the height of the English fashion.

A good deal of this splendor was crude and rough. "It is a miserable luxury," said Brissot, the famous Girondin ; "they wear silk stockings and boots ;" and again he says, speaking of the showy dresses of the women, " It is a poor luxury of high prices."[4] In many houses, where the tables were bountifully spread, and masses of old plate graced the sideboards, there were windows broken ten years before, and still unmended, buildings out of repair, and only the stables in good condition.[5] Even the fine coach-horses, on which they prided themselves, were not always carefully matched.[6] The planters lived on their noble estates, and kept open house with the splendor and affluence of nabobs,[7] in the midst of retinues of slaves and studs of horses ; but their magnificence had a certain barbaric element, was unfinished and incomplete, and showed here and there ragged edges and coarse linen beneath its brocaded silks. Ready money was, moreover, very scarce, despite the apparent wealth, and luxuries had to be paid for. The result was debt ; and it seems as if the leading families must have gone through bankruptcy once in a generation. The folly of building great houses brought many estates to the hammer.[8] High living and play ruined others ; and many young heirs were forced to the frontier to begin a new career.[9] Legislation favored the debtor class. During a "stint" in the tobacco crop debtors were to pay only two-thirds of their debts, a little later it was enacted that money debts were not recoverable ; and as early as the year 1657 an approach was made to a

---

[1] Hening, 1720, 1762.　　[2] Anburey, ii., 320 ; Brissot, p. 373 ; Smyth, i., 21, 66.
[3] Smyth, ibid. ; Burnaby, p. 43 ; Anburey, ii., 293 ; Burke, iii., 265 ; Hist. Doc. relating to South Carolina, Young's Letters ; Huguenot Family, p. 265.
[4] Brissot, pp. 367, 373 ; Georgia Hist. Coll., Itinerant Observations, 1745, p. 48.
[5] Rochefoucauld, i., 117 ; Smyth, i., 27.　　[6] Georgia Hist. Coll., p. 48.
[7] Memoirs of Elkanah Watson, p. 32.　　[8] Meade, i., 332.　　[9] Foote, i., 149.

bankruptcy act by relieving poor debtors on a surrender of their property.[1] As time went on the habit of running in debt increased. Physicians could not collect their fees; a lawsuit was necessary for tradesmen to recover payment for their goods. Lands were declared by law not liable to seizure, and in regard to slaves and personal property the creditor was easily evaded. In an agricultural community, headed by a small body of land-owning country gentlemen, the financial integrity so essential to the very existence of a trading people was almost unknown.[2] And so the extravagance and ostentation, the generous hospitality, and the high living and running in debt, went on, and the Virginians, for the most part, lived in a chronic state of insolvency, and borrowed money at most extortionate rates of interest, and were withal very happy, and jovial, and contented.[3]

The home life of the Virginian gentleman was one of easy monotony. An observant traveller has left a detailed account of their everyday existence and habits.

"The gentleman of fortune rises about nine o'clock; he may, perhaps, make an excursion to walk as far as his stable to see his horses, which is seldom more than fifty yards from his house; he returns to breakfast between nine and ten, which is generally tea or coffee, bread-and-butter, and very thin slices of venison, ham, or hung-beef. He then lies down on a pallet on the floor, in the coolest room in the house, in his shirt and trousers only, with a negro at his head and another at his feet, to fan him and keep off the flies; between twelve and one he takes a draught of bombo, or toddy, a liquor composed of water, sugar, rum, and nutmeg, which is made weak and kept cool; he dines between two and three, and at every table, whatever else there may be, a ham and greens, or cabbage, is always a standing dish. At dinner he drinks cider, toddy, punch, port, claret, and madeira, which is generally excellent here; having drank some few glasses of wine after dinner, he returns to his pallet, with his two blacks to fan him, and continues to drink toddy, or sangaree, all the afternoon; he does not always drink tea. Between nine and ten in the evening he eats a light supper of milk and fruit, or wine, sugar, and fruit, etc., and almost immediately retires to bed for the night.

"This is his general way of living in his family, when he has no

---

[1] Hening, 1640, 1643, 1645, 1657.   [2] Rochefoucauld, ii., 39.
[3] Burnaby, pp. 31, 33.

company. No doubt many differ from it, some in one respect, some in another; but more follow it than do not."[1]

This description may have been drawn from an extreme case; but the author had abundant opportunities and is supported by sober Burnaby, who remarks with surprise that he had seen a man in the full vigor of life lying on a couch with a negress standing by to keep off the flies.[2] That they were self-indulgent in other ways, high livers, and often hard drinkers, is the testimony of all the contemporary authorities, native and foreign.[3] The plantations were managed, as a rule, by overseers,[4] and, except a brief and feverish interest in the tobacco crop, there was nothing in their occupations to break the indolent tranquillity of existence.

The domestic life of the Virginian lady was more monotonous, even if her time was better employed, than that of the men. A letter quoted by Bishop Meade[5] says, " Let us repair to the old lady's room (Mrs. Washington's), which is precisely in the style of our good old aunt's— that is, nicely fixed for all sorts of work. On one side sits the chamber-maid with her knitting; on the other, a little colored pet, learning to sew. An old decent woman is there with her table and shears, cutting out the negroes' winter clothes, while the old lady directs them all, incessantly knitting herself." In these pursuits, managing the house, training the servants, and working for the benefit of the whole establishment, the lives of Virginian women were passed. They were notable house-keepers, and good wives and mothers. They were both virtuous and agreeable,[6] and intrigues and love affairs seem never to have been in vogue. We hear of slave mistresses,[7] but never of the gallantries then in fashion in Europe. Burnaby has left an account of the life of the Virginian ladies which, although very much colored by English prejudices, is not without interest.

"The women (of Virginia) are, upon the whole, rather handsome, though not to be compared with our fair countrywomen in England. They have but few advantages, and consequently are seldom accomplished; this makes them reserved and unequal to any interesting or refined conversation. They are immoderately fond of dancing, and, indeed, it is almost the only amusement they partake of; but even in

[1] Smyth, i., 41.   [2] Burnaby, p. 156.
[3] Burnaby, pp. 31, 43; Jones, Pres. State of Virginia; Anburey, ii., 293; Burke, iii., 265; Memoirs of Count Fersen, i., 63; Hist. Doc. relating to South Carolina, Young's Letters; and compare account of John Bolling in Dawson's Hist. Mag., iv., 218.
[4] Weld, p. 114.   [5] i., 98.   [6] Rochefoucauld, i., 117.   [7] Anburey, ii., 342.

this they discover great want of taste and elegance, and seldom appear with that gracefulness and ease which these movements are so calculated to display. Toward the close of an evening, when the company are pretty well tired with country-dances, it is usual to dance jigs; a practice originally borrowed, I am informed, from the negroes. The Virginian ladies, excepting these amusements, and now and then a party of pleasure into the woods to partake of a barbacue, chiefly spend their time in sewing and taking care of their families."[1]

This description gives us a glimpse of the simple amusements which served to break the level of daily life. A dance in the evening, when some young neighbor, possibly Patrick Henry, or Thomas Jefferson, came to the hospitable house, ready to play on the violin, or, perhaps, a picnic in the woods, were the best diversions afforded in the solitude of the country. The great event was the annual visit on business or pleasure, or both, to Williamsburg. Once a year, when the House of Burgesses met, and the Supreme Court was in session, the great coaches were brought out on the plantations, the six horses were harnessed, and the leading families drove in state to the capital. There the fashionable world of Virginia assembled. They spoke of their annual gathering with all the simple and ludicrous pride of a provincial aristocracy as rivalling the Court of St. James and the society of London. Sources of interest and excitement were not lacking during the season. If politics ran high, as in the years when revolution was preparing, society could gather at the capitol and listen to the classic oratory of Richard Henry Lee, or the fervid speeches of Patrick Henry, dressed in his suit of peach-blossom velvet, and defying King George, to the great alarm of the conservative land-owning gentry.[2] Perhaps the event of the year was the inauguration of a new governor; and glowing accounts are extant of the pomp and parade which greeted Lord Botetourt, and of the feasting and the loyalty which hailed his entry into office.[3] At all times the season at Williamsburg was gay. English fashions prevailed, and the officers of the Crown did much to promote social enjoyment. The Governor gave balls in his palace, as it was the fashion to term his house, and the birthnights of majesty were celebrated with great rejoicing. There were regular assemblies, and two sets of races for subscription purses were given annually.[4] In the gayeties of Williamsburg both sexes

[1] Burnaby, p. 36.   [2] Wirt's Life of Patrick Henry, p. 90.
[3] Burke, iii., 342.   [4] Jones, Present State of Virginia; Smyth, i., 20.

shared; but the season was short, and the ladies relapsed into the routine of daily plantation existence after a brief holiday. The men were more fortunate, and made up for their indolence in regard to work by a surprising activity in play. Their amusements were such as might be expected in a rural society of considerable wealth and comparatively slight education. Horse-racing and race balls were the events, and fox-hunting, cock-fighting, drinking, and card-playing the regular pastimes. A contemporary sermonizer, with some severity, says of the Virginians, " To eat and drink delicately and freely ; to feast, and dance, and riot ; to pamper cocks and horses ; to observe the anxious, important, interesting event which of two horses can run fastest, or which of two cocks can flutter and spur most dexterously ; these are the grand affairs that almost engross the attention of some of our great men, and little low-lived sinners imitate them to the utmost of their power. The low-born sinner can leave a needy family to starve at home, and add one to a rabble at a horse-race or a cock-fight. He can get drunk, and turn himself into a beast with the lowest as well as his betters with more delicate liquors.''[1] Even the partial Burke admits, that " The character of the people for hospitality and excess, and those of the land proprietors, particularly on the banks of rivers, enabled them to indulge their passions even to profusion and excess. Drinking parties were then fashionable, in which the strongest head or stomach gained the victory. The moments that could be spared from the bottle were devoted to cards. Cock-fighting was also fashionable. I find, in 1747, a main of cocks advertised to be fought between Gloucester and James River. The cocks on one side were called ' Bacon's Thunder-bolts,' after the celebrated rebel of 1676.''[2] But fortunately there has been preserved an exact account of the sports in which all classes then indulged.

In the *Virginia Gazette* for October, 1737, we read : " We have advice from Hanover County, that on St. Andrew's Day there are to be Horse Races and several other Diversions, for the entertainment of the Gentlemen and Ladies, at the Old Field, near Captain John Bickerton's, in that county (if permitted by the Hon. Wm. Byrd, Esquire, Proprietor of said land), the substance. of which is as follows, viz. : ' It is proposed that 20 Horses or Mares do run round a three miles' course for a prize of five pounds.

" 'That a Hat of the value of 20s. be cudgelled for, and that after

---

[1] Campbell, p. 495.   [2] Burke, iii., 402.

the first challenge made the Drums are to beat every Quarter of an hour for three challenges round the Ring, and none to play with their Left hand.

" ' That a violin be played for by 20 Fiddlers; no person to have the liberty of playing unless he bring a fiddle with him. After the prize is won they are all to play together, and each a different tune, and to be treated by the company.

" ' That 12 Boys of 12 years of age do run 112 yards for a Hat of the cost of 12 shillings.

" ' That a Flag be flying on said Day 30 feet high.

" ' That a handsome entertainment be provided for the subscribers and their wives; and such of them as are not so happy as to have wives may treat any other lady.

" ' That Drums, Trumpets, Hautboys, &c., be provided to play at said entertainment.

" ' That after dinner the Royal Health, His Honor the Governor's, &c., are to be drunk.

" ' That a Quire of ballads be sung for by a number of Songsters, all of them to have liquor sufficient to clear their Wind Pipes.

" ' That a pair of Silver Buckles be wrestled for by a number of brisk young men.

" ' That a pair of handsome Shoes be danced for.

" ' That a pair of handsome silk Stockings of one Pistole value be given to the handsomest young country maid that appears in the Field. With many other Whimsical and Comical Diversions too numerous to mention.

" ' And as this mirth is designed to be purely innocent and void of offence, all persons resorting there are desired to behave themselves with decency and sobriety; the subscribers being resolved to discountenance all immorality with the utmost rigor.' "[1]

These were rough, honest English sports, whose very names sound strange now, but much better than the card-playing and cock-fighting. Such amusements prevailed everywhere. At Norfolk a fair was held at regular intervals in the market-place, accompanied by sack and hogshead races, greased poles, and bull-baiting.[2] At Assateague the great event of the year was the horse-penning, when the wild colts were driven in, and the whole country-side flocked to see the show, and

---

[1] Quoted in Rives's Life of Madison, i., 87.
[2] Forrest's Hist. Sketches.

join in the expected barbecue and dancing.[1]   Public events in England were commemorated in Virginia with vast show and much loyal effusion.   The battle of Culloden was celebrated by processions, carrying a child in a warming-pan, hanging and burning the Pretender in effigy, and by public balls and illuminations.[2]   In fine weather barbecues in the woods, when oxen, pigs, and sturgeon were roasted, were frequent, and much enjoyed by all, ending usually, among the lower classes, with much intoxication.[3]   Another great source of delight was the cock-fight.   The pit was placed in the centre of the square formed by the two or three houses of the nearest village, and at an early hour the road was alive with carriages and pedestrians on their way to see the match.   All classes crowded eagerly together about the pit, where the fine cocks gave great sport.[4]   It was the same at races and fox-hunts.   The isolation of their daily lives drove men to seek every occasion for meeting.   The small farmers assembled at the nearest tavern to play billiards and drink.[5]   The session of the court filled the county towns once a month with a large and miscellaneous crowd, whose great topics of conversation were horses and lawsuits, and a day of conviviality generally ended with fights of a rather savage character.[6]   Duelling does not seem to have been common, and was probably rendered fashionable by our French allies.[7]   In colonial times differences were usually settled by the more primitive fist.   The evil of all these meetings, and the bane of Virginian society, was drinking and gaming, especially the latter, which was carried to a frightful extent by all classes.   We can trace the growth of this evil in the laws.   Statutes were passed against gaming; and a penalty was exacted from innkeepers who permitted it; it was forbidden on race-fields; gambling debts were declared void, and private lotteries were suppressed as harmful to the morals of the people.[8]   But legislation was vain.   The genial, dissolute, free-thinking Fauquier, who gathered about his table the rising genius of Virginia — Jefferson, Wythe, Mason, and the like—was a devotee, and a ruined one, to high play.   The great Byrd fortune was probably but one of many dissipated at the gaming-table.   Gambling was rife among all ranks of society, and was the fascination and excitement on every occasion.[9]

---

[1] Howe's Virginia.   [2] Forrest's Hist. Sketches; Howe's Virginia.
[3] Weld, p. 140.   [4] Memoirs of Elkanah Watson, 1787.
[5] Rochefoucauld, ii., 21.   [6] Michaux, p. 194; Anburey, ii., 333.
[7] Abbé Robin, p. 182.   [8] Hening, 1744, 1748, 1769.
[9] Anburey, ii., 328; Brissot, p. 373; Burke, iii., 333; Weld, p. 142; Rochefoucauld, ii., 39; Michaux, p. 194; Byrd MSS., ii., 77.

In a society so constituted, and so much addicted to the amusements just described, intellectual pursuits of any kind found little room. Fauquier, with all his gambling and high living, was a patron of arts and literature, but he found little of either to encourage in Virginia.[1] There were no arts, and the literature was next to nothing. During the whole colonial period only three books were produced by natives of the country which rose above the level of statistical or political tracts and occasional sermons. Robert Beverly beguiled the leisure of a country gentleman by writing an inaccurate but not uninteresting history of the province, and the Rev. William Stith followed his example with an exact and very dull account of the early years of the settlement. The third Virginian author was Colonel Byrd, whose rambling memoirs and journal of his doings as a commissioner to run the North Carolina boundary-line exhibit strong powers of observation, great humor, and possess genuine literary merit. Such was the literature of Virginia. That it was so very meagre is not to be wondered at when we remember that it was after the Restoration that the Cavalier Berkeley gave thanks to God, not only that there were no schools, but that there was no printing-press in Virginia, and no prospect of any. It was not until 1736 that the first newspaper, the *Virginia Gazette*, appeared, and this remained for many years the only journal in the colony.[2] The first theatre was opened at Williamsburg in 1752, for a company of New York comedians; so that the drama at the period of the Revolution was of very recent date.[3] Intercourse with the outer world was extremely limited. The first general post-office was established in 1692–'93; but it was local in its operation and very expensive.[4] Its sphere was gradually enlarged; yet even in the middle of the eighteenth century a mail from the North a fortnight old, and a post to the South once a month, both conducted by individuals, were considered expeditious and very convenient.[5]

English classics and a few of the standard authors of the day formed the resources of those who read. Blair's "Sermons," Sterne's works, *The Spectator*, the "Whole Duty of Man," and Tillotson's "Sermons," were the books most in use.[6] In a private library at Yorktown were found the "History of England," a collection of charters and bills, the works of Pope, Essays of Montaigne, "Gil Blas," and an essay on Women by "Mr. Thomas," which last, we are told,

---

[1] Burke, iii., 401. [2] Ibid., iii., 125. [3] Ibid.
[4] Hening, 1692–'93. [5] Maxwell's Hist. Register, i., 67. [6] Meade, i., 25,

had a great popularity in all the colonies.[1] Such reading was good
so far as it went, but it was not extensive, and it is to be feared that
the Virginians were not much given to reading, nor to the sister art of
writing. Governor Spotswood, who was not slow to take every advantage of the Burgesses in their many controversies, remarked on one occasion, in an official reply to some remonstrance: " I observe that the
grand ruling party in your House has not furnished chairmen of two
of your standing committees who can spell English or write com-
mon-sense, as the grievances under their own handwriting will man-
ifest."[2]   Matters no doubt improved in this respect during the
eighteenth century ; but, even in the years prior to the Revolution,
Virginians, as a rule, read little and studied less,[3] if we except the
young and rising men who belonged to the new period then just beginning.

Although the intellectual resources were slender, the Virginian gentlemen had, apart from merely physical amusements, one subject of
abiding interest. As has already been mentioned, they absorbed all
the appointed offices of the State, and they also participated actively
and steadily in current politics. After some fluctuations during the
period of the English Commonwealth, the suffrage had been restricted
to freeholders, and finally to those owning fifty acres of land.[4]   Immigrants were naturalized at first, after a term of years, on taking the
oaths of allegiance and supremacy ; then by act of the Assembly ;
then by the Governor on application ; and, finally, by the Assembly
on petition.[5]   The suffrage, therefore, was enough of a privilege to be
desired, and its exercise was further enforced by law.[6] Voting was
oral, and if the poll was not concluded on the first day, it was adjourned by the sheriff.[7] The leading planters usually stood for the House,
and election day was one of the great occasions similar to court day ;
all the people poured into the polling-place, where there was the customary drinking and gaming, and many rough scenes. The candidates were obliged on this day of the year to unbend and mingle
with the crowd. They were compelled to treat their constituents,
and sometimes walked about with a can of grog, asking the free and

[1] Abbé Robin, p. 142 ; compare also Burke, iii., 400.
[2] Tyler's Hist. of Amer. Literature, 1715–'80, i., 88 ; Campbell, p. 395.
[3] Jones's Present State of Virginia.
[4] Burke, ii., 108 ; Foote, i., 13 ; Hening, 1655, 1762.
[5] Hening, 1667, 1670–'80, 1705 ; and see petitions of later years.
[6] Hening, 1769.   [7] Ibid., 1646, 1769.

independent electors to drink with them.[1] It was a good school of practical politics, even if somewhat rough, and the excitement, rude as it must have been, was not without zest to the participants.

The society which was organized in this way, and lived after this fashion, gave little opportunity for the growth of the democratic sentiment. There was none of the friction and stimulus afforded by large towns. There was no intercourse with the outside world through the channels of commerce. The people were scattered, and wholly agricultural. The large number of convicts, of bonded servants, and of negroes helped to brand very deeply the lines of demarcation between the different members of the community. The solitary life on a great plantation in the midst of inferiors and slaves, the system of primogeniture, and the importance attached to landed estates as the only form of wealth, all contributed powerfully to one result. Theoretically, an aristocracy should have been developed, and it is easy to show that it existed as really as if the members had been distinguished by titles. In a word, Virginian society developed into an aristocracy of commoners, but none the less into a genuine aristocracy. The most powerful support was given by the system of entail. No estate tail over two hundred pounds was defeasible without an act of the Assembly, and the entailed estate passed, of course, invariably to the eldest sons, while the younger ones were brought up to professions. In some cases land was settled on the younger children, but the bulk of the property went to the oldest son. In the middle of the eighteenth century legislation was largely concerned with land, and was strongly in the land-holding interest; but the drift of public opinion then began to set against it, the business of docking entails increased rapidly, and, finally, the whole system fell during the Revolution beneath the attacks headed by Jefferson.[2] Prior to that time, however, it flourished in full force, and formed, as primogeniture and entail always must, the surest foundation of a strong and permanent aristocracy.

Scattered allusions also curiously illustrate the purely aristocratic society of Virginia, of which the existence is proved by the law of entail. The early law in regard to well-born persons has already been adverted to, but there is much stronger and later evidence. A letter

---

[1] Rives's Life of Madison, i., 179; Foote, ii., 177.
[2] Howe's Virginia; Maxwell's Hist. Register, iii., 142; Hening, 1727, 1748; and from 1764 to 1773 for the business of docking entails.

is preserved, by Bishop Meade, from one Mr. Thompson, a clergyman of the best sort, who desired to marry the widow of Governor Spotswood. The family objected on the score of inferiority of social position. The letter begins as follows: "Madam,—By diligently perusing your letter I perceive there is a material argument, which I ought to have answered, upon which your strongest objection against completing my happiness would seem to depend, viz., that you would incur the censures of the world for marrying a person of my station and character. By which I understand that you think it a diminution of your honor and the dignity of your family to marry a person in the station of a clergyman." Then follows a curious piece of reasoning to show the social equality of clergy and gentry.[1]

The social distinctions were most rigidly observed in the churches, where all classes of necessity met together. One vestryman was publicly thanked for displacing an unworthy woman who had ventured to sit above her degree.[2] The great families occupied the principal pews, generally in the galleries, while the floor was common to all.[3] In some of the churches certain pews were set apart, and marked "Magistrates" and "Magistrates' Ladies."[4] It is related of the Carter family that they built the parish church, reserving a large pew near the chancel, and that on Sunday the congregation waited outside until the family arrived, and then followed them in.[5] A member of a similar family " was buried, according to her own directions, beneath the pavement of the aisle of that wing of the church which was occupied by the poor. She directed this to be done as an act of self-abasement for the pride she had manifested and the contempt she had exhibited toward the common people during her life, alleging that she wished them to trample upon her when she was dead."[6] The old records abound also in examples of the state kept by the old families. A servile class rendered labor a shame, and trade was despised. It was esteemed a disgrace for a young man to enter the counting-house of the first merchant in Virginia.[7] The planters looked upon themselves as of different clay from the rest of the community. One of them drives his sword into a billiard-marker, but no notice is taken of it, although the man barely escapes death.[8] One foreign traveller says that every proprietor would be a lord, and that they had every

---

[1] Meade, ii., 79 ; see p. 13. [2] Ibid., i., 366. [3] Ibid, i., 210; ii., 375.
[4] Maxwell, Hist. Register, v., 38. [5] Meade, ii., 116. [6] Ibid., ii., 412.
[7] Fersen, i., 63 ; Anderson, Soldier and Pioneer ; Anburey, ii., 293.
[8] Rochefoucauld, ii., 40.

aristocratic principle. They took great pride "in his majestie's ancient and great colony and dominion of Virginia;"[1] and one of them declares that "Virginia may be justly esteemed the happy retreat of true Britons and true Churchmen."[2] But, although they held all the offices, their fortunes were not wrapped up in the royal government. Their loyalty was as independent as it was zealous, but with no tinge of inferiority; and they would not even suffer any attempt to introduce an etiquette other than their own.[3] There were few Tories among them, and while they gave freely to government, they chafed at the duties and restrictions on trade.[4]

They had the vices and the virtues of an aristocracy. They were indolent, vain, and imperious; politically haughty, and sensitive to any restraint.[5] They were neither enterprising nor inventive, but their address was excellent; they spoke well and fluently; had excellent sense, and much shrewdness in matters of business.[6] Many of them were men of liberal sentiments, enlightened understanding, and knowledge of the world.[7]

Leading a life which alternated between intense bodily activity and the most profound indolence, addicted to coarse indulgences and rough sports, without the opportunity or desire for mental effort, the Virginian gentleman was still essentially a patrician. As proud of his acres, and as haughty among his dependents as the greatest English lords, the Virginian was as sensitive in regard to his rights and as jealous of his political position as any Puritan of New England. A rigid code of honor was scrupulously preserved, and every gentleman was accountable under it for his actions. The Virginian planter was proud of his descent. He knew by heart his own genealogy and that of all his neighbors. No peer of the realm more fully believed himself to be of a different stuff from other mortals than the Virginian. Burke's famous sentence describes them exactly: "Those who had been accustomed to command were the last who would consent to obey." Despite the indolent life, the boorish amusements, and the too prevalent illiteracy, the natural genius of the great planters was strong and sound. They looked on themselves as the governing class, as the natural leaders of the people, and they possessed an unquestioned supremacy. When the shock came, they proved themselves fine

---

[1] Hening, 1699.   [2] Jones, Present State of Virginia.   [3] Burke, iii., 376.
[4] Howe's Virginia; Burnaby, p. 35.   [5] Burnaby, pp. 31, 35.
[6] Jones, Present State of Virginia; Abbé Robin, p. 205–'6.   [7] Smyth, i., 65.

soldiers, sagacious politicians, great lawyers, and statesmen. Out of this apparently inert aristocracy, steeped as it would seem in pride and sloth, came a set of leaders who have done the greatest honor to the American name. All the stress of oppression and of war was required to rouse the latent life; but at the great period in our history, the Virginian aristocracy proved themselves worthy of the foremost places. The ruling class was small numerically; but a body which produced in one generation George Washington, John Marshall, Thomas Jefferson, Patrick Henry, and James Madison, to say nothing of the Lees, the Randolphs, the Pendletons, Wythe, Mason, and the rest, is one which deserves a great position not only in the history of the United States, but in that of the English race and of the world.

Chapter III.

MARYLAND FROM 1632 TO 1765.

THE colonial history of Maryland offers two points of especial interest. Maryland was the first proprietary government in America, and she lays claim to the distinction of having been the first state where religious toleration not only prevailed in practice, but was established by law. These two facts, their causes and results, and the questions growing out of them, not only form the staple of her colonial history, but give it all the interest it possesses. From their nature, too, they are closely connected with the characters and careers of the founder of the settlement and his successors. They present, also, the first instance in America of a colony upon which the influence of an individual left an abiding mark, and did much to shape its future history.

George Calvert, Baron of Baltimore, began his public career under the patronage of Robert Cecil. His talents and industry united with a quiet moderation of character and a wise discreetness to raise him, under James I., to the office of Secretary of State, and to the position of a leader of the government forces in the House of Commons. In an evil hour he resisted Buckingham, or was, at least, unlucky enough to stand in the way of the all-powerful favorite. George Calvert was too prudent a man to persist in such an opposition, and, proclaiming himself a Catholic, he resigned his office. For this loss of place he was consoled by a peerage and a fee of £6000, paid him by his successor. Like most of the men in James's Court, Calvert had a taste for money-getting, without being troubled by unfashionable scruples; but he differed from his fellow-courtiers in his ability to keep the riches he acquired. From an early period Calvert had been interested in schemes of colonization, and in a purely commercial way. He was one of the patentees of the Virginia Company, and subsequently received a large grant of territory in Newfoundland. His religious opinions, or rather the period of his conversion to Catholicism, have been matters of warm discussion; but the most recent investigations make it probable that Calvert was either born a Catholic, or became one at an early period of his life. The old and generally accepted story that he resigned the secretaryship on account of scruples of conscience, arising from his recent conversion to Rome, can no longer

1625. be sustained. Whatever else is doubtful, it is certain that Calvert was forced out of office by Buckingham; and the avowal of the religion he had long secretly professed served as a convenient cloak to the real reasons for his retreat. That Calvert concealed his religious opinions for a long number of years, is in perfect keeping with his character and career. The court of James I. was not the place for a sternly religious man of hostile faith to obtain worldly success. When Calvert, now Lord Baltimore, found himself deprived of office, he turned his thoughts to his colony of Ferryland, in the province of Avalon, in Newfoundland, whither he soon after proceeded with his family. In that inhospitable region he quickly

1628. perceived the impossibility of successful colonization, and in 1628, therefore, he sailed to the South, and landed in Virginia. His purpose was an obvious one—the foundation of a settlement in a country blessed with a more genial climate than that which he had left. The Virginians tendered to him, on his arrival among them, the oath of allegiance, which he took, and the oath of supremacy, which he refused; and he was then requested to depart the colony, as he would not acknowledge the King's prerogatives. The objects of Lord Baltimore were as plain to the Virginians as they are to us. He was no ordinary colonist, nor were his schemes those of even the richest planters. He came to found a state, and to be its ruler. The Virginians had gone too far, and were too numerous to pass under his control, nor would they voluntarily permit the erection of an *imperium in imperio*. Courteously but firmly they dismissed Lord Baltimore, and hastened his departure. He returned to England and again visited Ferryland, where he did good service against the French; but the remembrance of the Virginian country did not leave him,

1632. and in 1632 he drew a charter for the signature of Charles I., granting to himself and his heirs all the country included in the present State of Maryland, and a large part of what is now the State of Delaware. Before this charter passed the seals Lord Baltimore died. From what is known of his career, it appears that in politics he was a friend of high prerogative, and a complaisant courtier in a corrupt court; that in religion he was a moderate Catholic, and in general character a shrewd, discreet man of the world. Of such a man worldly wisdom and good management in both public and private affairs could be safely predicated; but it was not from such persons that liberal views emanated in the reign of James I. Subservient to the slightest wishes of the King and to the will of Buckingham, Calvert was not the man to have far-sighted plans and high-minded, enlightened views of religious toleration. As a Catholic, he appreciated fully the bitter English hostility to Rome, and there can be little doubt that he desired his provinces to be peopled with men of his own belief, and to become in a certain sense an asylum for English Papists. But his primary object was commercial and financial success, and he well knew that nothing papistical could thrive under English auspices. The merest whisper of Catholic domination would have wrecked his enterprise at the start. The Catholics were oppressed and down-trodden, and if they happened to possess political power in any dependency of England, there was but one course compatible with existence open to them—an avowed policy of religious toleration. There can be little doubt that such were the views of the first Lord Baltimore, and this opinion is confirmed by the government he erected, and by the subsequent history of the colony.

The charter drawn by Lord Baltimore was granted to his eldest son, Cecilius. By this charter a government was framed on feudal principles, and modelled on that of the Durham Palatinate. The object was to found an English barony, and the lord proprietary was also invested with regal rights. The only reservation is in the annual payment of two Indian arrows by the lord of the province to the Crown, which was a mere recognition of the duty of allegiance, and of the title of the King to the land as lord paramount. There is a saving clause of the allegiance of the inhabitants, and a guarantee to the colonists of the rights and immunities of Englishmen. The government set up was a copy of the English form, or, rather, of the form of English government as it ought to have been in the opinion of George Calvert. An Assembly of Burgesses filled the place of the Parliament, and the lord proprietary that of the King. The constitution was exactly such a one as a high prerogative courtier in the reign of James would be likely to draw if left to himself. The lord proprietary was to have the right to make laws, not repugnant to those of England, when the freeholders and Burgesses could not be brought together, and he was further to have the power of granting titles and erecting manors and courts baron. Exemption from taxation was also granted. Much of it was merely a wild scheme to transplant decaying feudalism to the virgin soil of America. But all this paraphernalia of a dying system proved as worthless in the face of the strong tide of progress as the paper on which it was engrossed. Certain other provisions, however, deserve attention from their connection with the vexed question of toleration.

In the second article occurs the usual formula, expressing, as the reason for the grant, " a laudable and pious zeal for extending the Christian religion." In the fourth article the right of advowsons and patronage in the Church, as well as the license to erect chapels, churches, etc., are granted to the lord proprietary. But these sacred buildings were to be " dedicated and consecrated according to the ecclesiastical laws of our kingdom of England." In the twenty-second article, which gives to the lord proprietary the right to have all disputed points in the charter decided in his favor, occurs this clause, " Provided always, that no interpretation thereof be made whereby God's holy and true Christian religion, or the allegiance due to us, our heirs and successors, may in anywise suffer by change, prejudice, or diminution." These three passages contain all the references to religion in the charter. The first is purely formal, and occurs in all the colonial charters. The second puts the control of the Church in the hands of the lord proprietary. That the head of the Church in the province should be a Roman Catholic was not at variance with English habits. Catholic noblemen in England could present Protestant clergymen to livings of the Established Church down to the reign of William and Mary. The Church thus given away in the charter was the Established Church of England, and no other, and whatever may be claimed for the English Church in the seventeenth century, it was certainly not marked by a wise spirit of toleration. The last passage goes even further, and provides for the exclusive maintenance of the English Church. " God's true and holy religion," in 1632, was in England the religion of Charles and Laud, as distinguished from that of Rome or Calvin. Other forms of Christian belief were not considered or then recognized in England by law as " true" or " holy." To say that this clause simply meant the religion of Maryland was not to be Turkish, Jewish, or pagan, is absurd. No sane man, or body of men, would have enacted a law against the substitution of the Koran for the Bible, the abolition of the New Testament, or the worship of an Indian Okee for the regulation of an English colony. Under the Maryland charter there was to be but one Church recognized by the State, the Church of England. The religion of Calvert and of Calvert's followers was connived at, but it was not safe to recognize even in a colonial charter the followers of him whom Englishmen generally regarded as the Antichrist. Nor was it characteristic of Charles to extend a beneficent toleration to Protestant sects opposed to his own. In a word, there is no toleration about the Maryland charter. George Calvert was too astute a man, and had led too worldly a life, to risk a great enterprise by any talk about toleration. He believed in toleration, because men of his creed were oppressed; but that he believed in it as a great general principle, is to give the lie to his whole life and to the age in which he lived. A man who had fostered the dark intrigues of the Spanish marriage, and had been the close friend of Gondomar, was not likely to be the apostle of toleration in a bitterly intolerant age. Yet there can be no doubt of the fact of religious toleration in Maryland at the outset, and there were two very good reasons for its existence. The all-powerful lord proprietary and the principal men in Maryland were Catholics, and Catholicism was oppressed and hated in England. To oppress Catholics would have been gross folly on the part of the Protestant colonists, and to oppress Protestants would have been ruin to the proprietary. Religious toleration in Maryland must be attributed solely to the very commonplace law of self-interest; and that this theory is the correct one the subsequent history of the colony amply proves.

On the 29th of October, 1633, Hawkins, the searcher of vessels for London, administered the oath of allegiance to one hundred and twenty-eight persons on board the *Ark* at Gravesend. Over three hundred persons sailed in the *Ark* and *Dove* for Maryland. At the Isle of Wight two Jesuit priests, White and Altham, were smuggled on board. During the voyage twelve of the emigrants died, and of these only two were confessed by the Jesuits, and acknowledged themselves Catholics. Lord Baltimore, writing to his father's friend, Thomas Wentworth, describes the expedition as consisting of "his two brothers, with very near twenty other gentlemen of very good fashion, and three hundred laboring men, well provided in all things." From the number who took the oath of allegiance, and from the faith of those who died, together with Lord Baltimore's own account, it is a fair presumption that a majority of the settlers were

1633.

7

Protestants. The "twenty gentlemen of good fashion" and their immediate followers were probably the only Catholics. In such a case, when a Catholic lord was the ruler of a colony largely composed of Protestants, religious toleration was the only possible policy. Any other would have been madness.

The ships reached the mouth of the Potomac in March, 1634. In **1634.** the previous year a petition had been sent to the King by the Virginians, remonstrating against the encroachments of the Baltimore patent, and the question had been referred by the King to the Council, who had decided that Lord Baltimore should be left to his patent, and the Virginians to the course of law. At the mouth of the river they encountered the Virginians, who, in obedience to the King's written orders, received the new-comers kindly, and furnished necessary supplies. Here, too, they met William Clayborne, who spread ugly rumors among them of Indian hostility. Leonard Calvert, in his turn, informed Clayborne that his trading settlement on Kent Island was within the jurisdiction of the Baltimore patent. Clayborne was the person most aggrieved by the Maryland charter. Under a general license from Charles I. to trade, he had established a lucrative post on Kent Island. The King, as he had an unquestioned right to do under the theory of English law, granted to Lord Baltimore a certain tract of wild land, including Kent Island. Clayborne had no legal right there except as the subject of Baltimore; but, since his real injuries coincided with the fancied ones of the Virginians generally, his claim assumed importance. Calvert planted his colony on a bluff near the mouth of the Potomac, and named the settlement St. Mary's. Experience had taught men now the art of colonization. The emigrants were of the right sort, and Lord Baltimore's wise munificence, and the near neighborhood of an established colony, freed the Maryland settlement from the privations which marked the first years of the earlier colonies. The savages, moreover, through the influence of the Jesuits, were treated sensibly and honestly; land was from the first granted to individuals in fee-simple, and the little colony prospered. A visit from Governor Harvey assured Calvert that Clayborne could not hope for official support, however well off he might be in the way of popular sympathy. There was, however, so strong a feeling in favor of Clayborne in Virginia, that he was soon able to send an armed pinnace up the **1635.** Chesapeake to defend his invaded rights at Kent Island, but the expedition was unfortunate. Governor Calvert, after a sharp encounter, captured Clayborne's pinnace, and proclaimed its owner a rebel. Calvert then demanded that the author of this trouble should be given up by Virginia; but Harvey, who had been in difficulties himself on account of his lukewarmness toward Clayborne, refused to comply, and the rebel solved the problem in his own way by going at once to England to attack his enemies in their stronghold. The same year an assembly of the freeholders was held in Maryland, and many laws were enacted, all of which Lord Baltimore refused to sign, on the broad ground that his colonists had no right to initiate legislation. Among these laws was one providing that all felonies should be tried by English law, and there is a tradition of a bill of attainder against William Clayborne, who at least left a distinct mark upon early Maryland legislation—if not in 1635, soon after, and for many succeeding years.

For the next three years the colony progressed peacefully, established order upon Kent Island, and was only anxious about the Indians, whom Clayborne had remembered to inflame by various ingenious fabrications as to the character and objects of the new settlers. Immigration increased, and the Protestant interest in the colony grew with the population, and gained additional strength from the acquisition of Kent Island, whose settlers were not only hostile to the Calvert government in politics, but in religion as well. When the Assembly next **1638.** was called together, they retaliated upon Lord Baltimore his own action of three years before. The freemen rejected the code of laws prepared by the proprietary, and prepared others themselves, taking their stand on the broad ground that the initiation of legislation belonged to them, and to them alone. This point they eventually carried, and the lord proprietary was forced to content himself with a free exercise of the veto power in rejecting all the Assembly's laws. They did not at this session forget to pass bills of attainder against Clayborne's followers, nor had Clayborne, on his part, been unmindful of them. On his arrival in England he had presented a petition to the King, and by adroitly working on the cupidity of Charles, not only came near recovering Kent Island, but almost obtained a large grant besides. After involving Lord Baltimore in a good deal of litigation, Clayborne was obliged, by an adverse decision of the Lords Commissioners of Plantations, to abandon all hopes in England, and therefore withdrew to Virginia, to wait for better times.

For some years Maryland throve, undisturbed except by slight Indian outbreaks. The wise policy of toleration and the liberal land grants increased immigration, and men of all creeds sought the peaceful government of the Calverts. Religious toleration, however, not only induced persecuted Catholics, but oppressed Puritans as well, to come to the colony; and English Protestants soon wearied of liberality when practised by men of a hated faith and less political strength than their own. The rapid rise of the Puritan party in England fanned this discontent, and prepared the way for radical changes. An insight into the real purposes of the proprietary is afforded by a letter written to Governor Calvert in 1642. Lord Baltimore **1642.** therein directed "that no ecclesiastic in the province ought to expect, nor is Lord Baltimore, nor any of his officers, although they are Roman Catholics, obliged in conscience to allow such ecclesiastics any more, or other privileges, exemptions, or immunities for their persons, lands, or goods, than is allowed by his majesty or other officers to like persons in England." The reason for this course was "the dependence of the State of Maryland on the State of England, unto which it must, as near as may, be conformable." Lord Baltimore was a true son of his father, discreet and not over-zealous. He was glad to control this policy in favor of the Catholics as long as he could; but if that policy endangered the success of his colony, the Catholics had to go to the wall. Leonard Calvert, apparently unable to comprehend the course of his shrewder brother in the troubled times now beginning, sailed to England for instructions. He found Lord Baltimore **1643.** more trying hard to keep on good terms with both parties in England; but dexterous as he was, this was an impossible task. Although anxious to preserve the favor of Parliament, he still adhered to the King, and was commissioned by Charles to seize any Parliament ships in Maryland. Unluckily, Brent, the Deputy-governor, saw fit to execute the order, and seized the ship of one Richard Ingle, who was also strongly suspected of piracy. The Puritan party was roused by this step, and by the course of public affairs, to active hostility. Clayborne's opportunity had come, and he was not slow to take advantage of it. He easily obtained possession of Kent **1645.** Island, and shortly after Ingle, eager to revenge the loss of his ship, broke into the Assembly convened by Governor Calvert at St. Mary's at the head of an armed band, and made himself master of the government. Leonard Calvert, just returned from England, was forced to fly to Virginia. Clayborne and Ingle, acting in the name of the Parliament, made Hill, a Virginian, governor; but their power was badly used, their party was weak, and their rule was of short duration. The Catholics were too numerous and too active to submit to a government of force in the hands of the small Puritan faction, while the majority of the Protestants seem to have remained neutral throughout; and Ingle, who appears to have been more of a buccaneer than politician, filled his ship with goods and departed. Further resistance by Clayborne and his followers became impossible. Calvert returned from Virginia at the head of considerable forces, took possession of the government, and quiet was restored. Soon after Calvert died—a wise, prudent man, and a good governor after the fashion of his family. He appointed as his successor Thomas Greene, who was a Catholic, a Royalist, and the head of both interests in the colony. He seems to have continued the judicious government of his predecessor, and ruled peaceably, except for the customary wrangling with the Assembly, this time on the matter of informality in the summons. The wounds of the late rebellion were healed by a general amnesty, from which Ingle alone was excepted. This desirable quiet did not long endure, for the struggle in England was too mighty to permit the smallest colony to escape its influence. The triumph of Parliament compelled Lord Baltimore, always keenly alive to the value of his colony and his own interests, to abandon the policy of Catholic rule accompanied by general toleration; but with his wonted shrewdness, he perceived that only by timely and genuine concessions could he hope to save his possessions and render the province of a Roman Catholic nobleman acceptable to the Puritan party of England. Acting upon this opinion, he removed Greene, and appointed in his stead William Stone, a Virginian, a Protestant and a strong supporter of the terrible Long Parliament. A Protestant secretary and Protestant councillors were also appointed. Stone's commission forbade him to meddle with religion, and his oath of office bound him not to discountenance any persons who professed to believe in Jesus Christ, nor, in particular, any Catholic. Lord Baltimore, by the appointment of Protestants, endeavored to secure from attacks in England his own interests in Maryland, while by the commission and oath he sought to protect his Catholic subjects against Protestant persecution. The first Assembly called by Governor Stone passed the now famous "toleration act." The mixture of sects in the colony, due to the previous policy of religious toleration, and the presence of a small but united body of Puritans who had been driven from Virginia, made such a measure an absolute necessity unless the proprietary was prepared to face an immediate insurrection,

1646.

1647.

1649.

formidable in itself, and irresistible when supported, as it would be by the dominant party in England. The "toleration act" was probably due to Lord Baltimore's influence; but it was passed by a Protestant governor and Protestant councillors, while the lower house, on the other hand, had, apparently, a majority of Catholic members. Lord Baltimore was bound by his religion to persecute heretics, and probably thought the tenet in the abstract a good one; but he knew that such a course would be fatal to any Catholic who attempted it, whether in England or the colonies. For the sake of self-interest and the protection of fellow-believers, Lord Baltimore got his Council and Assembly to agree not to persecute Catholics. This is what the famous act of toleration amounted to. Religious toleration really exists only when the strong tolerate the weak, and not when the weak by fortuitous circumstances are enabled to present the appearance of tolerating the strong. The largest measure of toleration can exist, moreover, only when Church and State are disunited; but the terms of the Maryland charter provided for an Established Church, and the Assembly seems never to have doubted its right to interfere oppressively or otherwise in matters of conscience.

But to whatever causes this toleration was due, it worked well in populating Maryland. There was an influx of immigration, composed in part of the Puritans driven from Virginia by Berkeley. These people, although refusing the oath of fidelity, settled at Providence, near the site of Annapolis. Not merely the Protestant but the Puritan interest was now predominant in Maryland, and in the next Assembly the Puritan faction had control. They elected one of **1650.** their leaders Speaker, and expelled a Catholic who refused to take an oath requiring secrecy on the part of the Burgesses. Even if most of the Protestant party were members of the English Church, the Puritans were clearly the controlling element, and the objectionable clauses were expunged from the oath of fidelity. Yet they passed stringent laws against Clayborne, and an act reciting their affection for Lord Baltimore, who had so vivid an idea of their power that he deemed it best to assent to sumptuary laws of a typically Puritan character. The Assembly appears to have acknowledged the supremacy of Parliament, while their proprietary went so far in the same direction that his loyalty was doubted, and Charles II. afterward appointed Sir William Davenant in his place to govern Maryland. This discreet conduct on the part of Lord Baltimore served, however, as a protection neither to the colonists nor to the proprietary rights.

To the next Assembly the Puritans at Providence refused to send delegates, evidently expecting a dissolution of the proprietary government, and the consequent supremacy of their faction. Nor were they deceived. Such had been the prudence of the Assembly and of Lord Baltimore, that Maryland was not expressly named in the Parliamentary commission for the "reducement" of the colonies, but, unfortunately, Clayborne was the ruling spirit among the Parliamentary commissioners, and he was not the man to let any informality of wording in a document stand between him and his revenge. In vain did Governor Stone lend assistance to the commissioners in Virginian matters. Clayborne and Richard Bennet, one of the Providence settlers, and also a commissioner, soon gave their undivided

1652. attention to Maryland. They proceeded to St. Mary's, required of the Governor and Council a test called the "engagement," which was thereupon subscribed to, and they also demanded that writs, etc., should be issued in the name of the Commonwealth, which was refused. Stone was then displaced; but at the expiration of a year Clayborne and Bennet, requiring the aid of his popularity, reinstated him. Stone, however, appears to have yielded to their terms, and to have definitely sided with the Puritan party. The Council was entirely composed of the Providence settlers, who were now, as they anticipated, supreme. Stone, who seems to have been torn between his wish to serve Lord Baltimore faithfully, and his desire to stand well with the commissioners, soon swung back to the old proprietary rule, under which writs again ran with Calvert's name upon them; but he endeavored to trim at a time when trimming was impossible. Naturally he suited no one, and, although seemingly a very well-meaning man, he got only hard knocks from one side and harsh words from the other. Stone's second change, however, was a decided one. Although he proclaimed Cromwell as Lord-Protector, he carried on the government exclusively in Baltimore's interest, ejected the Puritans, recalled the Catholic Councillors, and issued a proclamation against the inhabitants of Providence as factious and seditious. A flagrant attempt

1655. to convert a young girl to Catholicism added fuel to the flames. Moderation was at an end. Clayborne and Bennet, backed by Virginia, returned and called an Assembly, from which Catholics were to be excluded. In Maryland, as in England, the extreme wing of the Puritan party was now in the ascendant, and exercised its power oppressively and relentlessly. Stone took arms and marched against the Puritans. A battle was fought at Providence, in which the Puritans, who, whatever their other failings, were always ready in a fray, were completely victorious. A few executions and some sequestrations followed, and severe laws against the Catholics were passed. The policy of the Puritans was not toleration, and they certainly never believed in it. Nevertheless, Lord Baltimore kept his patent, and the Puritans did not receive in England the warm sympathy they had expected. Cromwell, now all-powerful, cared less than ever for useless fighting or unnecessary extremities. He listened to the explanations of Bennet and Mathews, said he had not intended, by his previous proclamation in favor of Lord Baltimore, to abridge their powers, and gave his decision in favor of the government of the commissioners. Thus the Puritan government was established in Maryland. But Cromwell's support was too lukewarm to be at once decisive. Although the commissioners of the Puritans were in nominal as well as actual control at Providence, yet Baltimore removed Stone, and appointed Fendall as Governor, to whom the Catholic population of St. Mary's adhered. This state of dissension injured greatly the prosperity of the colony, until at last Lord Baltimore on the one side, and Bennet and Mathews on the other, came to terms, which were carried out in the province. The proprietary government was to be re-established and recognized, and a general act of oblivion and indemnity was to be passed. Fendall was continued as Governor, and the Assembly ratified the agreement. The results of all this turbulence were the right to carry arms, the practical assertion of the right to make laws and lay taxes, relief from the oath of fealty with the obnoxious clauses, and the breakdown of the Catholic interest in Maryland politics. Toleration was wisely restored. The solid advantages were gained by the Puritan minority at the expense of the lord proprietary. In the interregnum which ensued on the abdication of Richard Cromwell, the Assembly met and claimed supreme authority in the province, and denied their responsibility to any one but the sovereign in England. Fendall, a weak man of the agitator species, acceded to the claims of the Assembly ; but Baltimore removed Fendall, and kept the power which the Assembly had attempted to take away. This action of the representative body simply shows the decided political advance made in Maryland, as in all the British dominions, under the impulse of the Great Rebellion. Maryland did not suffer by the Restoration, as was the case with her sister colonies, but gained many solid advantages. The factious strife of years was at last allayed, and order, peace, and

1657.

1660.

stability of government supervened. Philip Calvert, an illegitimate son of the first proprietary, was governor for nearly two years, and **1661.** was then succeeded by his nephew, Charles, the oldest son of Lord Baltimore, whose administration lasted for fourteen. It would have been difficult to find at that time better governors than these Calverts proved themselves. Moderate and just, they administered the affairs of Maryland sensibly and well. Population increased, and the immigration of Quakers and foreigners, and of the oppressed of all nations, was greatly stimulated by a renewal of the old policy of religious toleration. The prosperity of the colony was marked, and its only difficulties were due principally to external causes. The overgrowth of tobacco, and a corresponding scarcity of corn, were sources of anxiety to both people and rulers. Vain attempts were made to remedy these evils by law and by agreements with Virginia; but these economical problems, questions of boundary with Dutch and English, a few trifling troubles with the Indians, and Fendall's "seditious practices" alone disturbed Maryland's internal tranquillity during the mild rule of the Calverts. The Assembly, unmolested in their possession of the law-making and taxing power, were quiet and reasonable, and granted the proprietary an annual allowance from the export duty on tobacco.

In 1675 Charles Calvert, the Governor, became lord proprietary by **1675.** the death of his father, Cecilius. He instituted a thorough revision of the laws, for which his new position and presence in the colony gave peculiar advantages, and then, having appointed Thomas Notly Deputy-governor, he sailed for England. His departure was the signal for a renewal of the old dissensions from which the colony had been so long exempt. As had happened twenty years before, a minority in the colony, in sympathy with the dominant party in England, wished to obtain control in matters of religion, and, backed by the home government, renew a policy of intolerance in their own interests. Now, of course, this minority was composed of Protestants of the Established Church, instead of the Puritans, as in **1676.** the days of the Commonwealth. The first attack came from the Episcopalian clergy, who complained of the bad condition of the Church in the province, and urged Lord Baltimore to support it with the power of government. This Lord Baltimore refused to do. The condition of the Established Church was no doubt very bad, but, as the lord proprietary wisely pointed out, they already had received some assistance from the government, and the improvement of their

Church must rest with themselves. The old policy of toleration was thus maintained for the time, at least; but there was great laxness in religious matters in the province, which gave opportunities for complaints on the one hand, and the rapid propagation of new sects on the other. Quakerism, then just beginning its career, took strong hold in Maryland, and was for many years a vigorous and good influence socially and politically. But the complaints of the Episcopal clergy, though unsuccessful with Lord Baltimore, marked the beginning of a struggle between the Protestants of the Established Church on the one side, and the Quakers and Roman Catholics on the other. The latter appeared as the defenders of the toleration policy, which the former aimed to subvert and replace with the Church and State system then in vogue in England. Thus supported by an active party, Lord Baltimore had nothing to fear in the province; but in England the course of public affairs proved most unfavorable to his fortunes. The excitement produced by the Popish plot and the

1681. consequent proceedings in Parliament compelled Lord Baltimore to fill all the Maryland offices with Protestants, and served also as a signal for numerous accusations against the proprietary of partiality to his fellow-believers. These attacks Lord Baltimore easily repelled; but there were others also forth-coming which seriously imperilled his possessions, inasmuch as they concerned the royal coffers. Almost the only real grievance of the Maryland colonists was the enforcement of the Navigation Act, and the levying of customs for the benefit of the Crown. In true colonial fashion the former was avoided, and the latter both resisted and eluded. Lord Baltimore, ever watchful of his own interests and of those of his colony, had undoubtedly connived at these practices. The government of Charles II., touched by such conduct in its tenderest point, threatened a *quo warranto*, and the Duke of York granted to William Penn lands lying within the Maryland boundaries; while a limitation of the right of suffrage afforded a new and advantageous battle-ground for the discontented elements in the province, so that, although the colonists throve, the poor proprietary was beset with difficulties. The accession of James II. brought no relief to Lord Baltimore. Instead of sympathy from a fellow-Catholic, he met only with oppression. The grant to Penn, dismembering his province, was confirmed, and a fresh writ of *quo warranto* was issued against his charter. In the province itself the Protestants, who chafed at the spectacle of toleration, which they knew need not exist if the proprietary power were overthrown, at last rose in arms. This time, of course, members of the Established Church controlled the insurrection, and only a very subordinate part was taken by the Puritan element. An old supporter and friend of Fendall, one John Coode, appeared at the head of the "Association for the defence of the Protestant religion." The crisis came, as in all the other colonies, at the moment of the Revolution in England, and this gave force and strength to these provincial insurrections which, in Maryland at least, they could never have acquired otherwise. The President of the Council, Joseph, demanded an oath of fidelity from the Assembly, and hesitated to proclaim William and Mary. This gave the insurgents their opportunity, and they took arms to assert the rights of William and the Protestant religion, neither of which had

1689. been infringed. The efforts of the "Associators" were crowned with success. They called a convention, and forwarded an address to William, who responded by creating a royal government—

1692. the proprietary being excluded by the new laws against Catholics—and sending out Sir Lionel Copley as Governor. The pecuniary benefits accruing to Lord Baltimore from his province were alone left untouched. Never did an insurrection and successful revolution arise so absolutely without apparent cause. The government of Maryland as administered by the Calverts was, according to modern notions, the best, probably, at that day in existence. There was nothing in the least resembling oppression; and although the feudal nature of the government was an anomaly, it did not injure the people, and the powers of the proprietary were suffering constant diminution. According even to the address of the rebels, not one real grievance existed. The causes of the revolution in Maryland were due to two facts—the policy of toleration, for which the popular mind was not yet prepared, and the condition of affairs in England. Toleration was even then little more than a speculative principle, and its practice in Maryland gave a peculiar religious aspect to her whole history : indeed, religion was at the root of all the troubles. The tolerated party in the State was the one possessing the support of the mother country. They therefore found themselves the objects of toleration, when, if they could once obtain control, no such thing need exist. The result of this was that there was always a large faction in Maryland hostile to the proprietary government, because it would not permit them to indulge their bigotry. Every revolution in England was sure to produce one in Maryland, from the existence of a class of men discontented in religious matters, and anxious to make their faith the religion of the State, and have it enforced as such. Lord Baltimore suffered because he wisely persevered in the only policy compatible with his interests and his religion, and because James II. insisted on misgoverning England.

The new royal government went on with little apparent change, except that the King's name was substituted for that of Lord Baltimore in the writs. The remaining proprietary rights were protected by the government against the attacks of the Assembly. The Church of England was established, and taxes laid for its support.

1692-1694. Other Protestant sects were practically tolerated, but Catholics were made the subject of persecution. The public exercise of their religion was forbidden, and their immigration was prevented by stringent laws. In furtherance of this anti-Catholic policy the capital was removed from St. Mary's to Annapolis, the site of the old Puritan settlement. The period of royal government in Maryland was one of steady decline. The establishment of a Church of which only a minority of the population were members, and the general taxes laid for its support, caused deep and ever-increasing dissatisfaction, and the new religious policy fostered also a dislike of the external power which alone made it possible. It bred a coolness and distrust in regard to England, and wholly alienated large classes of the community from the mother country. The Roman Catholics were persecuted, and the Quakers discountenanced, and thus the two best elements in the State lost all influence, and were forced into a bitter opposition. The course of the provincial government of Maryland sowed the seeds, and the establishment of the English Church prepared the soil for the hostile feelings which ripened so readily in 1776. The effects of the royal government and of its policy were soon apparent. Prosperity declined, the tone of society was lowered, and a general spirit of resistance to the administration in the matter of the charter and of taxes was developed. Royal requisitions at the time of the French wars were made on the colony, and were sometimes complied with, but were much oftener sullenly refused. At last the proprietary,

1714.1715. Benedict Leonard Calvert, the son of Charles, changed his religion, and, dying soon after his recognition as proprietary, the province devolved upon his infant heir, Charles Calvert, and the old government was firmly re-established. At the restoration of Lord Baltimore, fresh efforts were made in England for an abrogation of the charter, but, like those in the time of the royal governors, these attempts were defeated. The resistance of both people and proprietary was crowned with success, and forty years of perfect tranquillity ensued under the restored government of the barons of Baltimore. Insignificant conflicts with the Indians, a share in the Carthagena expedition, and disputes with Pennsylvania and Virginia about boundaries, constitute Maryland's external history during this long period. The course of domestic affairs was hardly more eventful. The same features were presented in Maryland as in Virginia during the first half of the eighteenth century. A general political indifference, followed by petty and harassing quarrels between Governor and Assembly, were the political characteristics of both colonies at this time. The first conflict arose about the introduction of English laws. The Assembly desired them, because they would be beneficial to the people; the proprietary opposed them as **1732.** infringements on his rights, and after ten years of rambling argument and discussion, the Assembly prevailed. The next discussion found its origin in that ever-fruitful source of trouble, taxa-

1739. tion. The Assembly came to the conclusion that the duties levied by the proprietary were oppressive and unjust, and they protested also against the Governor's power of fixing official fees by proclamation, and of creating, without the consent of the Assembly, new offices and new perquisites. They finally prevailed, in a measure, on all these points, but the tobacco and tonnage duties remained an ever-recurring annoyance.

Maryland never displayed much readiness to join with the other colonies in times of difficulty and danger, and when events suggested the necessity of union, she usually manifested great indifference. When the French war came, Maryland held aloof; and although commissioners were sent to Albany, they refused to agree to the plan of union presented by Franklin, and adopted by the Con-

1754. vention. In the actual operations of the war Maryland had but a small share. She suffered from the results of Braddock's defeat, and panic and terror spread through the province, yet nothing effectual was done to check the tide of Indian invasion. Fort Cumberland, the only Maryland outpost, had been built on the western frontier, in a position where it served principally as a source of contention with Virginia. The chief exploit of the Marylanders, and the one certainly which will be longest held in remembrance, was performed by the commander of this fort, one Dagworthy, who had held at one time a royal commission as captain. On this ground he claimed to outrank Washington, then in command on the border.

Trouble ensued, and finally Washington went to Boston, laid the case before Shirley, the commander-in-chief, received his support, and Dagworthy was reduced to the rank of a provincial captain.

As the war progressed the Indians ravaged the western part of the colony, the back settlements were driven in, and one effort after another to repel them failed. Maryland believed that all these misfortunes were due to her union with the other colonies, and she thereupon resolved to devote all her strength to the defence of her own borders. Meantime Governor Sharpe got into a dispute with the Assembly about garrisoning Fort Cumberland. As usual, the Assembly carried their point; but the capture of Fort Du Quesne relieved Maryland from further anxiety, and put a stop to this particular source of contention.

Were it not for the question of toleration, the history of Maryland would be one of the most uninteresting, although not the least instructive, of the colonial histories. The proprietary government was unusually mild and well administered, even though it involved the incongruity of a third person intervening between subject and sovereign. Nothing but the moderation of the Calverts preserved to them their province. Their popularity mitigated the attacks of the Assemblies, and their high character as rulers was a barrier against assaults in England. Yet the anomalous nature of the government led to constant troubles, which would otherwise have had no existence. There was, however, no government in America which was, on the whole, milder, and, except for a few years of disorder, less checkered by either oppression or turbulence. The very lack of incident and of disputed principles, although fatal to the interest of history, and indicative perhaps of a stagnation of the intellectual forces, is the best proof that the people were contented, and the government well and prudently administered. Apart, therefore, from religion, Maryland history is almost perfectly featureless. The period of settlement was undistinguished by hardships or perils; the period of revolution was accompanied with comparatively little injury, and was, on the whole, productive of good results, while the period of political quiet preceding the French war was more uneventful even than in the other colonies. Yet in the history of this small and peaceful province can be seen unmistakable indications that the very same forces were gathering there as in Virginia and Massachusetts. There is the same disposition on the part of the Assembly to assert itself and to encroach on the powers of the Governor. The same half-expressed desire on the part of the people for complete control which is manifested by the same persistent wrangling with the authorities, who excite jealousy merely from their being sustained by an external power of whose influence they are the living evidence. Despite the French war and the consequent losses, the people were prosperous, and frugality and industry prevailed to a greater extent than in Virginia, ready to heal the wounds of war. The spirit of resistance to taxation by England showed itself at an early day. The Stamp Act was bitterly attacked through the Press, **1763-** and the opposition concentrated, although the Assembly was **1765.** not in session. Thus Maryland drifts into the current of national life. In no colony had the government been gentler or more peaceable; yet geographical isolation, the struggle for existence in a new country, the absence of traditions, the sturdy independence of character and love of local self-government innate in the English race, did their work as surely in Maryland as among her more powerful and more turbulent neighbors.

Chapter IV.

MARYLAND IN 1765.

The materials existing for a picture of Maryland in the last century are, as in the case of Virginia, and for the same reasons, extremely meagre.[1] Everything, however, which relates to the latter can be applied more or less directly to the former, and a standard of comparison is thus furnished which is of great assistance. Maryland differed but slightly from the great State out of which her territory was originally taken. The modifications were due to the more northern situation of the younger province, and the consequent influence of the Middle States, and to the causes which led to the first settlement. Maryland was the northern member of the group of colonies of which Virginia was the head, and to all of which she gave a lasting impression. In climate and natural conformation the two colonies were, of course, practically identical. There were the same fine harbors and rivers, the same fertile soil and boundless forests in both, and in both the land rose gradually from the level of the coast until the spurs of the Alleghanies were reached.

The customary policy of religious toleration, and the mild and sensible government of the Calverts after the troubled period of the Great Rebellion, were highly favorable to the growth of population. In 1660 the number of inhabitants was estimated at 16,000, and had increased to 20,000 in 1688.[2] The best authorities put the pop-

---

[1] Some months after this chapter was written Mr. Scharf's History of Maryland was published. The first chapter of the second volume gives a full account of the condition of Maryland in 1755. Mr. Scharf has used the same materials that I have used in this chapter, and has drawn conclusions, in the main, the same as my own. But as he deals with only one colony, and I with thirteen, his work is fuller and more elaborate, and therefore better than mine. It is to be hoped that the same service may be rendered to the history of every colony which Mr. Scharf has rendered to that of Maryland.

[2] M'Mahon's Hist. View; M'Sherry, Hist. of Maryland, p. 83; Neill, Terra Mariæ, p. 138.

ulation in the year 1756 at 154,000.[1] At the time of the Revolution there were probably 250,000 people in the province, and of this number eighty to one hundred thousand were negroes.[2]

The character of the immigration to Maryland had been excellent, if we except a large number of transported convicts. English gentlemen, farmers and yeomen, had followed Leonard Calvert, and founded the colony. Many of the early settlers came from Virginia,[3] and were chiefly Puritans. The mass of the population at the time of the Revolution were of English race, and drawn from the great middle classes of the mother country.[4] The only foreign element of importance were the Germans, who had built up some of the towns, and who, as in Virginia, were to be chiefly found upon the western frontier.[5] But, although the English race prevailed so strongly, the religious freedom of Maryland had attracted the victims of persecution from all countries, and the foreign races made up in variety what they lacked in numbers. In the poorest quarter of Baltimore a large body of the luckless Acadians obtained a resting-place and employment as sailors;[6] while in other parts of the province were to be found Irish, Scotch, Dutch, Bohemian, Spanish, and Italian settlers.[7]

The government of this population was upon the usual English model common to all the colonies, differing only in respect to the proprietary, who interposed between the people and the Crown. The shrewdly-drawn charter of George and Cecil Calvert assured nearly regal powers to their successors. The proprietary held the title to

---

[1] M'Mahon ; M'Sherry, p. 115.

[2] The following figures are the evidence for this estimate, and will also serve to show the difficulty of coming to any exact conclusion, and the vagueness of the computations in regard to population in the colonies: Neill, Terra Mariæ, p. 204, 211, 1719—55,000 whites, 25,500 blacks; 1752—107,000 whites, 45,000 blacks; M'Sherry, p. 115, 1761—114,000 whites, 50,000 blacks; Burnaby, p. 67, 1759—58,000 whites, 32,000 blacks; Smyth, ii., 187, 1770 — 275,000, one-half to two-thirds negroes; Maryland Hist. Soc., vol. i., Allen's " Who were the early Settlers of Maryland;" 1758, return to Governor Sharp, 200,000 total population. I have relied principally upon the return to Governor Sharp, and have calculated the proportion of negroes, and the yearly increase of the whole population, from a comparison of the other estimates.

[3] Maryland Hist. Soc., i., Allen.   [4] Ibid.

[5] Eddis, Letters from America ; Smyth, ii., 187.

[6] Journal of Claude Blanchard, p. 171 ; Abbé Robin, p. 98.

[7] Maryland Hist. Soc., i., Allen ; Smyth, ii., 187 ; Eddis, Letters from America ; Georgia Hist. Coll., IV., Itin. Observations.

all the land, was captain-general, and head of the Church. All patronage, lay and clerical, amounting to fourteen or fifteen thousand pounds a year—from the Governor, with a salary of fifteen hundred and fifty pounds, down to the naval officers and sheriffs—was in his hands. He had a negative upon all laws, and the power of pardon. To the proprietary belonged the quit-rents, the tobacco and tonnage duties, and the legal fines and forfeitures, although the Assembly vigorously resisted this last source of emolument. The net yearly income of the proprietary was over twelve thousand pounds.[1] To the Governor, who was appointed by the proprietary, the exercise of all these sovereign powers was, as a rule, intrusted. The Governor represented the proprietary in the province, summoned, prorogued, and dissolved the Assembly, and assented to laws. He also claimed a veto on legislation; but this right was not admitted by the Burgesses. He made all appointments to office, issued pardons, signed the warrants for execution, and exercised great political influence.[2] The legislative body consisted of the Council and the Burgesses, who were divided into separate Houses in the year 1650. The Council, consisting of twelve members, was nominated by the Governor, and was wholly in the proprietary interest. They received nine shillings a day for their services, and were men of wealth and position.[3] The Burgesses were elected by the people. There were sixteen counties, eight on the eastern, and eight on the western shore, the two geographical divisions being always carefully balanced. Each county was entitled to elect four Burgesses, and two were chosen in Annapolis. Elections were triennial; the suffrage, as in Virginia, was restricted by a property qualification; and the Burgesses, " good ordinary householders " in the early days, were, at the time of the Revolution, in almost all cases the leading men of the province. They had succeeded in wringing from the proprietary the entire law-making power, and limited the exercise of the patronage by the regulation of fees. They held the purse-strings, and, as they were extremely jealous of their liberties, were nearly always at variance with their governors, carrying their opposition to such an extent as to sometimes hamper the government completely, and, at the time of the French war, they

---

[1] Burnaby, pp. 67, 68 ; M'Mahon, Hist.View ; Neill, Terra Mariæ, pp. 216, 217, note; Eddis, Letters from America ; Mass. Hist. Soc. Coll., I., vii., 202 ; A Relation of Maryland, Tract.

[2] Burnaby, pp. 67, 68 ; Neill, Terra Mariæ, p. 217 ; Eddis, Letters.

[3] Burnaby, ibid. ; M'Mahon ; Eddis ; Kalm's Travels, ii., 28 ; Bozman.

reduced it to a state of almost entire inaction.[1] In forms of government, and in political training, therefore, Maryland differed but little from her sister colonies.

The legal system of Maryland was simpler and better than that of Virginia. There were county courts holding quarterly sessions, with a bench of magistrates appointed by the Governor from among the leading gentlemen, removable at pleasure, and competent to try cases involving not more than forty shillings. No legal knowledge seems to have been required from the members of these courts, whose principal occupation was to mete out punishment to refractory servants.[2] The important legal business of the colony was transacted by the provincial court, which sat twice a year at Annapolis. The judges of this higher court were also appointed by the Governor, but with a due consideration for legal attainments. In early times, a general court of assize had existed, but had been dropped as useless. There was also a high court of appeals, and a court of chancery, both composed of the Governor, who was chancellor of the province, and his Council, with an appeal to the King in Council.[3] The common and statute law of England prevailed when the provincial law was silent, although there was a chronic battle as to the statute law, despite the provision in the charter that no laws should be passed repugnant to those of the mother country.[4]

The business of the provincial court was large, for the people were of a litigious spirit, and this operated in favor of the creation of a much better class of lawyers than in Virginia. Few lawyers were regularly called to the bar, but there were many of deserved eminence. There were, of course, where the regulations were so loose, many adventurers also who found a profit in legal pursuits through the defective land-titles which abounded in all the colonies, and which they bought up and defended; but this element did not seriously affect the good standing of the profession, which drew to its ranks many men of ability and position.[5]

The government was inexpensive and taxation light, the only complaint being in regard to quit-rents and Church dues, both of which

---

[1] Burnaby, pp. 67, 68; Alsop; M'Mahon, Hist. View; Eddis, Letters; Bacon, Laws of Maryland; Smyth, ii., 182.

[2] Sot-Weed Factor, p. 15.

[3] Burnaby, pp. 68, 69; Eddis; Maryland Hist. Soc. Coll., vol. ii., Brown's Civil Liberty; Kalm's Travels, ii., 28; Bozman.

[4] M'Mahon, Hist. View.   [5] Eddis; Georgia Hist. Coll., Itin. Observations.

were considered high.[1] The exemption from taxation granted by the charter existed only until commerce became valuable, and in 1661 revenue was raised for the Crown by customs duties. These restrictions helped to cripple trade, but did not weigh with great direct severity upon the people.[2] The currency was in a wretched condition. Although a mint had been established as early as the year 1662, tobacco was the common medium of exchange; and in the eighteenth century the loss of specie induced large emissions of paper money, which at once depreciated, and was of a value so uncertain that it was not received in the western counties. In 1733 the state of affairs was so bad in this respect that it was found necessary to declare tobacco a legal tender.[3]

The principal burdens of government—an army and navy—were, as elsewhere, entirely wanting. There was a great love of military titles; but the militia was inefficient, badly organized, and ill-armed.[4]

With the exception of the legal profession, the possible occupations in Maryland were almost wholly agricultural, and in this respect the example of Virginia was closely copied. In the seventeenth century nothing was raised for export but tobacco, and the over-cultivation of this staple was so great that the King attempted to check it. Even royal interference was fruitless. Tobacco continued to be the great interest, and brought in its train the usual difficulties of speculation and enormous profits, alternating with over-production and low prices, which caused conspiracies to destroy the crop, and thus restore artificially the value of the staple.[5] Despite the injurious effects of the cultivation of tobacco, it remained the only solid staple until the close of the French war. The average annual export amounted to thirty thousand hogsheads, and was worth one hundred and forty thousand pounds, and at the time of the Revolution it had risen to nearly fifty thousand hogsheads.[6] Prior to that period, however, an important change had set in. Taught by their losses, by the low state of agriculture, by the exhaustion of their land, and by the example of their northern neighbors, the planters began to turn from tobacco to grain. The improvement was rapid and marked. When the contest

[1] Georgia Hist. Coll., ibid., Itin. Observations.   [2] M'Mahon's Hist. View.

[3] Ibid.; M'Sherry, p. 117; Georgia Hist. Coll., ibid.

[4] Georgia Hist. Coll., ibid.

[5] M'Mahon, Hist. View; Alsop; M'Sherry, p. 87; Neill, p. 204; Gentleman's Magazine for 1732.

[6] Smyth, ii., 140; Burnaby, p. 68; M'Sherry, p. 117.

with England opened, Maryland exported six hundred thousand bushels of wheat—a larger amount than that sent from the great State of Virginia. A large foreign trade in wheat and flour sprang up in Baltimore, and, in addition to the other exports, which were similar to those of Virginia, speedily reduced the importance of tobacco.[1]

The evil results of this absorption in the growth and sale of tobacco were conspicuous, as in Virginia, by the dearth of manufactures. Fruitless efforts had been made to establish them in the seventeenth century; but at the time of the Revolution petty household industries were all that had grown up, and the people of Maryland were clothed almost entirely in English stuffs, and obtained from the mother country almost every article of either luxury or necessity which could not be actually grown on the plantations.[2] A few vineyards were successfully cultivated, but were of interest chiefly as experiments.[3] Copper-mines were opened in the year 1742; but the only important industry which was not purely agricultural was the mining and smelting of iron, which toward the close of the colonial period had become large and valuable. Many forges were then in operation, and the annual production had risen to twenty-five thousand tons of pig, and five hundred tons of bar, iron.[4]

The lack of industries and the narrowly limited occupations of the people had, during most of the colonial period, the same depressing and dwarfing influence upon traffic, and all methods of trade, which was so marked a feature in Virginia. There was no foreign commerce conducted in the usual way by merchants and factors. There were a few shopkeepers in the towns, the familiar store-keeper in the little villages which sprang up at the county seats, and strolling peddlers and mechanics. All this was, of course, very petty and insignificant. The commerce was wholly carried on by the planters themselves, who all transacted business on their own individual account. On the great plantations, which were villages in themselves, the landlord usually kept a store, from which he and his servants were supplied. All the plantations on the rivers had their little wharves, and constituted small ports, where the English merchantmen touched to gather a cargo and

---

[1] Smyth, ii., 110, 112, 128, 140, 186; Eddis, Grain raised by Germans; Georgia Hist. Soc., ibid.; Rochefoucauld, ii., 355.
[2] Burnaby, p. 68; M'Mahon, Hist. View; M'Sherry, p. 116; Magazine of Amer. Hist., ii., 104. [3] Burnaby, p. 70.
[4] M'Mahon, Hist. View; Abbé Robin, p. 98; M'Sherry, p. 151.

leave the manufactures of the Old World. Tobacco was brought down from the interior by mules attached to an axle run through the hogshead. This isolated system of trade left the planters very much at the mercy of their English correspondents; but it suited their lordly tastes, so they clung to it for more than a century, and successfully prevented any innovation.[1]

Notwithstanding this conservatism, however, a change came at last in the period prior to the Revolution, and was due, as in the case of the grain exports, to the example of the Middle States. The alteration showed itself in the growth of towns, which had no existence so long as the rude system of solitary barter was successfully maintained. The first town, so called, was the little village of St. Mary's, founded in 1634, as the capital of the colony, by Leonard Calvert.[2] Fifteen years later the Puritan exiles from Virginia founded Providence. At the period of the Restoration there were still no towns. St. Mary's had fifty or sixty houses, and Providence was a still smaller village.[3] The revolution of 1689 altered at once the fate of the two settlements. The capital was transferred to Providence, soon rechristened Annapolis, and as the town of the Puritans rose with the aid of official standing, the little village of the Roman Catholics declined, was deserted, and finally relapsed into the silence of the wilderness.[4] At the new capital a state-house, court-house, armory, and academy were soon built; and in the year 1708 Annapolis was made a city.[5] All this, however, was artificial at best, and the town showed no real vitality until the middle of the eighteenth century, when a small trade, carried on by two or three vessels, sprang up. Thus Annapolis became a centre of trade as well as fashion, grew more rapidly, and at the time of the Revolution, although still small, had become one of the prettiest and pleasantest towns in America. The new public buildings were handsome, particularly the state-house, although endless quarrels with the Assembly brought the Governor's palace, designed on a scale of great magnificence for a province, to an untimely end. The unpaved streets radiated from the Province House, among

---

[1] Burnaby, p. 66; M'Mahon, Hist. View; Neill, pp. 199, 200; Georgia Hist. Coll., Itinerant Observations; Magazine of Amer. Hist., ii., 104.

[2] Relation of the Successful Beginnings in Maryland.

[3] Ridgely, Annals of Annapolis; M'Mahon's Hist. View; M'Sherry, p. 83; Georgia Hist. Coll., Itin. Observations.

[4] Ridgely, Annals of Annapolis; Neill, pp. 200, 206, 207.

[5] Ridgely, Annals of Annapolis.

well-built houses standing in the midst of handsome gardens, with here and there an open field.[1]

The ill effects of having no towns had attracted, of course, general notice, and an effort was made to remedy it by legislative enactment. Owing to more efficient natural causes, the attempt met in some instances with success. Several small and thriving villages grew up at different points; and one of the paper towns, called Baltimore, in compliment to the proprietary, and founded in 1729, developed with such rapidity that it held, forty years later, the first place in the province, and was one of the half-dozen considerable towns on the continent. In 1774 Baltimore had a population of between fifteen and twenty thousand inhabitants, was the centre of an important trade in wheat and flour, and drew by the rivers from the back districts of Pennsylvania the products of the Middle States for exports. Commerce and prosperity induced the erection of new and handsome houses; but the rapid growth made the appearance of the town rough and crude. There was no pavement, and no police or street lighting until after the Revolution; there were pools of stagnant water in the heart of the town, and in autumn and spring the mud rendered the main streets almost impassable.[2] Here, however, was the source of a prosperity and a form of interest and of occupation quite at variance with the Virginian system, and introducing a small but important element of northern existence into the midst of the great planters. The immediate effect upon the colony was not striking, but it was widespread and important when the province became a State.

Only one great interest and pursuit remain now to be considered— religion and the clergy. In religious matters the origin of Maryland led, as has already been said, to the existence of peculiar features, which are essential to an understanding of her social condition. From the time when Leonard Calvert took possession of the country in the name of our Saviour,[3] the history of Maryland consisted of strenuous efforts on the part of the Roman Catholic founders, backed by the influence of the proprietary, to maintain themselves against the attacks of the more numerous Protestants. As a minority they advocated, and when in power carried out, a policy of toleration. In the

---

[1] Smyth, ii., 185; Burnaby, p. 66; Neill, p. 205; Eddis; Penn. Hist. Mag., i., Journal of William Black.

[2] Griffiths, Annals of Balt.; Smyth, ii., 186; Brissot, p. 365; M'Sherry, p. 112; Eddis; Rochefoucauld, ii., 129.

[3] A Relation of Maryland.

dark days of the Commonwealth they fell beneath the iron hand of the Puritans. The return of the Stuarts brought back the old policy, and instead of Puritans, the Catholics had now to face a new opposition, composed of real or pretended members of the Church of England. The triumph of William and Mary brought permanent supremacy to the Protestant party, and the establishment of the English Church. The Catholics lost all political power. They were made ineligible to office, disfranchised, and obliged to pay a double land-tax, in addition to tithes for the support of the Church of England.[1] The day had gone by for direct religious persecution; and although public worship in forms of the Roman Church was rigidly suppressed, and the powerful and rich organizations of Jesuits dissolved, there was no interference with private chapels built and maintained by wealthy planters of the proscribed faith.[2] Oppressed by taxes, hostile to the Church of England, and galled by the disfavor shown to their religion by government, the Catholics of Maryland were by no means a loyal body of subjects. Many, no doubt, like the father of Charles Carroll, thought seriously of retirement to the dominions of France. At the time of the French war rumors were rife that the Papists intended to rise, and many of them certainly rejoiced at the defeat of Braddock. As may be supposed, they all strongly espoused the patriotic side when the difficulties began with the mother country.[3] At the period of the Revolution the Catholics, who had founded the colony, formed a comparatively small minority of the whole population, but were still a numerous and respectable body, comprising many of the oldest, best, and most important families in the province.[4]

The Church which finally drove Catholicism to the wall was, perhaps, as contemptible an ecclesiastical organization as history can show. It had all the vices of the Virginian Church, without one of

---

[1] Neill, Terra Mariæ, p. 215 ; Eddis.

[2] Magazine of Amer. Hist. ii., 104 ; Smyth, ii., 180.

[3] Neill, p. 215 ; Maryland Hist. Soc. Coll., i., Allen's Who were the early Settlers of Maryland.

[4] The authorities are very conflicting in regard to the number and quality of the Catholics. Official reports and official and Church writers represent them as insignificant in numbers, property, and position. Outside observers, on the other hand, speak of the Catholics as numerous and highly respectable. For the former view, see Hammond, in Force's Hist. Tracts ; Anderson's Hist. of Col. Church, ii., 412 ; Eddis ; Maryland Hist. Soc., i., Allen's thorough and elaborate paper on the early settlers of Maryland. For the latter view, see Smyth, ii., 180; Burnaby, p. 69 ; Abbé Robin, p. 101.

its safeguards or redeeming qualities. From the early days, when a Jamestown minister came to Kent Island, it had always maintained itself in a small but safe way.[1] Before the revolution of 1688, the Rev. John Yeo addressed to the Archbishop of Canterbury the following "rude and undigested lines," to acquaint his grace "with the deplorable estate and condition of the province of Maryland for want of an established ministry. Here are in this province ten or twelve counties, and in them at least twenty thousand soules, and but three Protestant ministers of us that are conformable to the doctrine and discipline of the Church of England. Others there are (I must confess) that runne before they are sent, and pretend they are ministers of the Gospell, that never had a legall call or ordination to such an holy office; neither (indeed) are they qualified for it, being, for the most part, such as never understood anything of learning, and yet take upon them to be dispensers of the Word, and to administer the Sacrament of Baptisme; and sow seeds of division amongst the people, and no law provided for the suppression of such in this province. Society here is in great necessitie of able and learned men to confute the gainsayers, especially having soe many profest enemies as the Popish priests and Jesuits are, who are incouraged and provided for. And the Quaker takes care and provides for those that are speakers in their conventicles; but noe care is taken or provision made for the building-up Christians in the Protestant religion, by means whereof not only many dayly fall away either to Popery, Quakerisme, or Phanaticisme, but also the Lord's day is prophaned, religion despised, and all notorious vices committed, so that it is become a Sodom of uncleannesse and a pest-house of iniquity."[2] The whole matter was referred to Lord Baltimore, who pointed to the toleration acts of 1649 and 1676, said that provision had been made for four clergymen of the English Church, and declined further interference.[3] It was this Church—which had not in itself enough force or enough popular support to cure such a condition of affairs—that finally took advantage of the strong arm of the government to overthrow the toleration policy, and establish itself as part of the state upon its ruins. An act was passed to establish the Church, fixing the marriage fees, and laying a tax of forty pounds of tobacco per poll for the support of ministers.[4]

[1] Allen, Maryland Hist. Soc., i.

[2] Anderson, Hist. Col. Church, gives this letter in full, ii., 395; see also Neill, Terra Mariæ, p. 138.   [3] Neill, p. 138.

[4] Trott's Laws of Col. Church, p. 172; Georgia Hist. Coll., Itin. Observations.

Brick parsonages were afterward built for the new pastors, and the worthy Bray came out at once as commissary. He struggled with every kind of difficulty; strove manfully to correct the evil living of the clergy; had his powers questioned at every point, and went back to England, leaving only the memory of his example.[1] The increase of power and profit thus obtained by the Church did not improve its morals or general character. A clergyman, writing in 1714, describes the disregard of holy things as universal; the Sacraments as neglected, and sometimes not celebrated at all; the manners of all classes as dissolute; and the laws of marriage despised. Another says the clergy were ill paid, and had to travel great distances to perform service in various parishes, while Colonel Hart, the Governor, reported that some of the ministers were a scandal to their profession.[2] The Church had no government of any kind. Presentation and induction were in the hands of the proprietary, or his representative, the Governor.[3] The commissary had merely an advisory power in regard to licenses, and his remonstrances were unheeded, while, as a rule, the Governor would not let him even enter the province.[4] The Assembly made various efforts to remedy the evils by establishing a spiritual court of laymen; but the opposition of the clergy prevented the assent of the Crown, on the ground that it would result in Presbyterianism.[5] The clergy, on their side, petitioned for a bishop, and the Bishop of London directed them to choose one of their own number for the position. They thereupon selected one Colebatch, upon whom a writ of *ne exeat regno* was immediately served, so that he could not leave the province.[6] Not only was the influence of the commissary, so valuable in Virginia, wholly lacking, but even the rude check afforded by the power of the Virginian vestries was wanting. In Maryland, the vestry, consisting of twelve members, besides the wardens, was utterly powerless.[7] A clergyman once inducted in a living could not be removed, nor even controlled, no matter how abominable his conduct might be.[8]

---

[1] Anderson, ii., 412; Neill, Terra Mariæ, p. 188.

[2] Anderson, iii., 181, 182.

[3] Burnaby, p. 69; M'Mahon, Hist. View; Neill, p. 213; Eddis; Massachusetts Hist. Soc. Coll., I., vii., 202; Anderson, iii., 178.

[4] Anderson, iii., 178, 190; Burnaby, p. 69.

[5] Anderson, iii., 180 and ff.; Massachusetts Hist. Coll., ibid.

[6] Anderson, iii., 182, 190.   [7] Burnaby, p. 70.

[8] Neill, p. 217, note; Massachusetts Hist. Soc. Coll., ibid.

Maryland, like Virginia, had also the misfortune of not receiving ministers through the Society for the Propagation of the Gospel. The patronage was badly administered, unworthy men were frequently appointed, and the whole organization closely resembled a corrupt civil service.[1] In the year 1753 a visiting clergyman wrote to the Bishop of London that "the general character of the clergy is wretchedly bad. It is readily confessed that there are some in the province whose behavior is unexceptionable and exemplary; but their number seems to be very small in comparison—they appearing here and there like lights shining in a dark place. It would really, my lord, make the ears of a sober heathen tingle to hear the stories that were told me by many serious persons of several clergymen in the neighborhood of the parish where I visited; but I still hope that some abatement may be fairly made on account of the prejudices of those who related them."[2] It is not easy to conceive the utter degradation of the mass of the Maryland clergy. Secure in their houses and glebes, with a tax settled by law, and collected by the sheriffs[3] for their benefit, they set decency and public opinion at defiance. They hunted, raced horses, drank, gambled, and were the parasites and boon companions of the wealthy planters. A common jest was the question:

"Who is a monster of the first renown?"
"A lettered sot, a drunkard in a gown."[4]

They extorted marriage fees from the poor by breaking off in the middle of the service, and refusing to continue until they were paid.[5] They became a by-word in the other colonies, and every itinerant clergyman who was a low fellow and a disgrace to his profession passed under the cant name of a "Maryland parson."[6]

The first and the only beneficial result of this contemptible clergy was the spread of the dissenting sects. In the year 1657 the Quakers first appeared, and fell at once beneath the relentless rule of the Puritans then in power. In the simple language of the law, they

[1] Meade's Old Churches of Virginia, ii., 351; Anderson, iii., 178.
[2] Meade, ibid., p. 352; Bishop Meade entirely concurs with this statement from Dr. Chandler's letter.
[3] Eddis; Burnaby, p. 69; M'Sherry, p. 117; Neill, p. 217.
[4] Neill, p. 213; Coke's Sermon in Baltimore, 1784, published in London; Allen's Sketches in Sprague's Episcopal Clergy.
[5] Kalm's Travels, 1748–'52, ii., 28.
[6] Grayson, Memoirs of a Life passed chiefly in Pennsylvania, p. 102.

were "to be whipped from constable to constable, out of the province." Those who received them were fined and whipped. They held up against persecution, however, and the Restoration brought relief. The first general meeting was held under the auspices of Fox in 1672; congregations were gathered, and the Quakers increased and throve. They formed an excellent element in the population, encouraged trade, and were thrifty and industrious citizens. In 1711 their general meetings, under the stimulus of the Established Church, had become so large that laws were passed to suppress drinking at them; and they finally grew to be a kind of annual market or exchange, and places of popular resort.[1] The same spread and progress, in a less degree, attended the other sects. Scotch-Irish Presbyterians began to come toward the close of the seventeenth century; at a later period Methodism met with great success and acceptance; and in every county dissenters abounded.[2]

How much harm was directly caused by the pernicious example of the clergy cannot, of course, be exactly estimated, but there is no doubt that it was the origin of the religious laxity and indifference which prevailed extensively.[3] The ministers of the Church were not only despised, but they were bitterly disliked. Early in the century the Assembly did all in its power to reduce their emoluments, and the occasional regulations of tobacco debts led to clerical resistance, secret appeals to England, and additional unpopularity in consequence.[4] A majority of the population belonged to other sects, and hated the Church and clergymen for whose support they were taxed. The efforts to obtain a bishop formed another grievance, in which all laymen of every denomination shared. In all these matters the clergy displayed a short-sighted indifference to public feeling. They and the officials of the proprietary were the only Tories almost in the province; and their conduct, and the condition of the Established Church, were the principal causes of coldness toward the mother country, and rendered the people ready to join in any opposition to English rule.[5]

---

[1] Maryland Hist. Soc. Coll., ii., Norris, Early Friends in Maryland; Neill, Terra Mariæ, p. 138.

[2] Neill, Terra Mariæ, p. 219; Maryland Hist. Soc., i., Allen.

[3] Neill, pp. 213, 220; Eddis.   [4] Anderson, iii., 185, 191.

[5] Neill, p. 215; Georgia Hist. Coll., Itin. Observations. Eddis, who was of the official class, describes the clergy as fair, with no pluralities, and no altercation about tithes; but the testimony on the other side is overwhelming, and all one way, and even Eddis admits the unpopularity of bishops.

The structure of Maryland society was simple, and similar to that of Virginia. There were the upper and middle classes, composed of planters, farmers, and merchants, the poor whites and freedmen, and the servile class.[1] This last class comprised four grades — African slaves, convicts, indented servants, and what were called "free-willers."[2] Slavery in Virginia is the type of that which existed in all the colonies. It was modified and softened as one travelled northward, until it practically disappeared in New England, while in the southern colonies its worst features were intensified. The condition of the slaves deteriorated as their numbers increased. In Maryland the Virginian type was but little changed. The slaves were less numerous in proportion to the whole population; but they were introduced at an early day, and increased so rapidly and to such an extent as to cause great anxiety, so that their importation came to an end before the Revolution.[3] The legislation in regard to them had the same savage character as in Virginia; yet, although there was, of course, more or less cruelty, their condition and treatment were good, on the whole. They appear to have led generally an easy life, and to have enjoyed a good deal of individual liberty, and met with reasonable justice in the courts.[4] The distinction of race was carefully maintained, and marriages between low white women and negroes caused, in the year 1663, the passage of a law making such women and their children slaves.[5] The value of slaves in growing tobacco, and the luxury of their service, led to their being owned in large numbers, and the whites made them their chief investments; but slavery was not well adapted to Maryland, and its evils were strongly felt, so that even before the Revolution public opinion began to tell upon the system.[6]

Next to the slaves, but separated from them by the insurmountable barrier of race, came the convicts. The forced immigration of these undesirable settlers began early, assumed large proportions, and continued long after it had been stopped in the other colonies.[7] They worked on the roads in gangs, loaded with irons, and were extensively employed in building the houses of the great planters.[8] The indented servants differed but little from the transported criminals,

---

[1] Neill, p. 211, 1763.　　[2] Eddis.　　[3] Neill, p. 201; Eddis.

[4] Neill, p. 201; Georgia Hist. Coll., Itin. Observations; Eddis; Rochefoucauld, ii., 282.　　[5] Neill, p. 203.

[6] Ibid.; Rochefoucauld, ii., 290, 355, 357.　　[7] M'Mahon; Eddis.

[8] Rochefoucauld, i., 129; Memoir of Col. Thomas White.

and were, in fact, chiefly convicts and paupers. Some of them were kidnapped as children in England, and sold in Maryland. They were regarded as little above the negroes; were ill-treated; punished for offences by additional years of servitude; and, if they escaped, were sometimes sentenced to work in the iron mines.[1] The women of this class—sometimes kidnapped, but usually of doubtful character—fared little better than the men, and were often forced to work in the fields.[2] The condition of the "free-willers," who sold themselves, was hardly superior to that of the indented servants. They were usually deceived in their contracts, and suffered all the miseries of serfdom.[3]

When the term of servitude expired for these various classes of white servants, some raised themselves by their own exertions to a respectable position, and were absorbed in the middle class. Others returned to England. Very few turned out well, and the majority remained where they found themselves, and formed the class known as "poor whites."[4] This class was shiftless, ignorant, idle, and improvident, as was painfully demonstrated by the poor-houses in every county, and with the freedmen, who were numerous in the province, composed the criminal portion of the community. There was less crime in Maryland than in Virginia, but more than in the northern colonies, from the fact of the existence of such a class as has just been described. Murder was rare, but robberies were numerous; there were highwaymen in the thinly-settled counties, and all offences were punished severely, after the fashion of the day, by hanging, stripes and exposure in the pillory or stocks, and more rarely by imprisonment.[5] The better sort of "poor whites," galled by the inferiority which was the badge of work in a slave-holding community, were constantly leaving the coast region and pushing out upon the frontier, where there was hope of improving their fortunes. This lowest class of freemen was at no time an important portion of society, and had no influence of any sort. They were simply the outcome of a servile system of labor.[6]

The upper and middle classes differed little from each other, or from the same classes in Virginia. The former was less compact, less strong in every way, less distinctively marked, and less representative

---

[1] Neill, p. 201 and ff.; Eddis.   [2] Sot-Weed Factor, p. 7
[3] Eddis.   [4] Ibid.
[5] Huguenot Family in Virginia, p. 303; Rochefoucauld, ii., 281, 282.
[6] Rochefoucauld, ii., 355.

than its prototype in the older and larger colony; and there was also in Maryland a small but respectable body of enterprising merchants, some of whom were wealthy, who ranked with the great planters, and increased in numbers and consideration with the development of Baltimore. With these exceptions, the social system of the two higher and governing classes was almost identical with that of Virginia. Any general description, therefore, applies to all alike, if allowance is made for the differences of fortune which entailed modifications of an unessential sort, and of degree only.

The people of Maryland were practically all planters. Their plantations were scattered through the forests, generally along the banks of the rivers, which formed the principal means of communication. Passengers for England were picked up by the passing vessel at the plantation wharves, and all trade was carried on by water.[1] The fate of those who journeyed by land was much less agreeable. The roads, which were none of the best, wound through thick woods; rivers were crossed by ferries of a rude and often unsafe kind; and the inns were mere stopping-places or shelters, dirty, uncomfortable, and with most wretched living.[2] The method of getting from place to place was usually on horseback; but Maryland was not so absolutely deficient as Virginia in this respect, and post-chaises, with horses and servants, could be hired.[3] At the best, however, travelling was difficult and slow, and rarely indulged in except as a matter of necessity.

The plantations, isolated and scattered, were generally large, and closely resembled a village. The family mansion stood in the centre, flanked by numerous out-buildings and storehouses, and surrounded by the straggling quarters of the negroes.[4] The houses were commonly of wood, but the parsonages were always of brick, while on the great plantations the manor-houses were usually of brick or stone. These last were large, sometimes of great size, with heavy walls. They covered a great deal of ground, and were, as a rule, not more than two stories in height. The exterior was often bare and tasteless; but in many instances the roof was broken with gables, and these, with the deeply sunk and mullioned windows, presented a very picturesque appearance. Near Annapolis were many pretty villas, with handsome grounds and gardens. The interiors were attractive

---

[1] Neill, Terra Mariæ, p. 207.
[2] Ibid., p. 208; Journal of Witham Marshe; Eddis.
[3] Burnaby, p. 73.
[4] Abbé Robin, p. 103; Rochefoucauld, ii., 128; Neill, p. 199.

and spacious. Large, low rooms, wide panelled halls, sometimes hung with portraits, wainscots everywhere of rare hard woods, and convenient chambers, were common to all. Handsome furniture, imported from England, great open fireplaces, and sconces with candles made from the wax of myrtle-berries, gave an air of comfort and luxury. Pewter was in common use for the table; but there was always a state service of plate, sometimes of great beauty and value.[1]

Despite the isolation of their lives, and the rough state of society, much style was maintained. The table was spread with a rude abundance, and the cheapness of provisions was one efficient cause of the lack of economy.[2] Hospitality was universal and excessive, for the usual solitude made the rare company of strangers an object of competition, and they were welcomed without much discrimination as to whether they were from jail or college.[3]

Both men and women dressed expensively, in the latest English fashions, held the French barber in high estimation, had their slaves richly clothed, drove light and handsome carriages, kept innumerable horses, and lived well in every way.[4] The extravagant expenditure, unstinted hospitality, and free living did much to impair the fortunes of the planters. The laws show the prevalence of bankruptcy, and great land-owners were often obliged to fly from their English creditors, and leave their estates to fall into the hands of overseers and indented servants.[5]

The people were, as a rule, industrious, prosperous, shrewd, and penetrating, and the general morals were good; but the wealthier planters were very indolent. They spoke English well; there was a singular uniformity of speech and absence of dialects, except in the more remote and thinly settled counties, despite the mixture of races, and in manners they were frequently easy and well-bred.[6]

Life in the back districts was, of course, much rougher than in the region near the coast. On the frontier and in the thinly settled counties the houses were built of logs, with only two rooms, and the

---

[1] For this description of the great houses and their furniture, see Abbé Robin, p. 103; Eddis; Memoir of Colonel Thomas White; and Magazine of Amer. Hist., ii., 104.　　　　　[2] Neill, p. 206; Eddis.

[3] Neill, ibid.; Georgia Hist. Soc. Coll., Itin. Observations; Sot-Weed Factor, pp. 4, 5; Ridgely, Annals of Annapolis.

[4] Ridgely, ibid.; Abbé Robin, p. 104; Neill, p. 205; Eddis.

[5] Neill, p. 204; Eddis.

[6] Alsop; Neill, ibid.; Eddis; Rochefoucauld, ii., 360.

food was usually Indian meal.[1] All the magnificence of the planters, too, had its unfinished side, and the imitation of English vices and follies was often of a very poor sort.[2]

The amusements were the same as in Virginia, and made up in quantity what they lacked in quality. The young men were devoted to fox-hunting and horse-racing, while cock-fighting and gaming were universally popular; and there was much card-playing and many dances, sometimes of a very wild kind, at the country houses. The great day for meeting was when the county court was in session. The little county town was then filled with a large crowd, who drank freely at the inn, gamed and betted, and wound up their day's pleasure by fighting.[3]

The gayety and fashion of the colony centred at Annapolis, where the government officials lived and the Assembly met. Many of the wealthy planters and merchants had both a town and country house; and in autumn the great coach, imported from London, made of mahogany, and leather topped, was brought out, the family was packed in, the coachman and footman mounted the high box, and they drove down to the capital.[4] Here there was no lack of amusements. There was a jockey club and annual races, a South River club, with a club-house for fishing-parties and picnics. There were assemblies once in a fortnight, grand balls given by the Governor on the birthnight of the King and the Proprietary, and when some victory, such as Culloden, occurred, there was general feasting and merry-making, illuminations and processions, in which all joined, with a Punch-and-Judy show for the populace. At all parties there was card-playing as well as dancing, and elaborate suppers. Excursions down the bay were a favorite diversion; and at Christmas society assembled at the nearest country-seats and celebrated the season in the wonted English fashion. The Virginia comedians appeared in 1752; and in 1760 a theatre was opened, which, with the company, was under the especial patronage of the Governor. The patron saint-days of the various races were carefully observed, and the tutelary divinity, Saint Tamina, had a society, founded in her honor, which gave balls and masquerades. Marriages were always celebrated at the house, and were succeeded invariably by dancing, supper, and cards.[5]

---

[1] Eddis.   [2] Neill, p. 205; Sot-Weed Factor, p. 7.
[3] Sot-Weed Factor, p. 15; Neill, pp. 210, 212; Journal of Witham Marshe; Rochefoucauld, ii., 294.   [4] Magazine of Amer. Hist., ii., 104.
[5] Ridgely, Annals of Annapolis; Smyth, ii., 185; Eddis; Magazine of Amer. Hist., ii., 104.

One of the Virginian commissioners who came with Governor Gooch to Annapolis in the year 1744 has left a detailed account of fashionable life in the little provincial capital. He and his party were, of course, entertained first by the Governor. Punch was served before dinner, which was of great plenty and variety, with wines of every description, and strawberries and ice-cream as rarities. This entertainment was followed by a series of dinners of a similar character at all the principal houses. The dinner was at an early hour in the afternoon, and when it was concluded the company sat about conversing and drinking wine until supper was served. This was succeeded by dancing, singing, and card-playing. The guests, for the most part, retired at ten o'clock; but the dancers would keep it up until after midnight, when each gentleman escorted his partner home. This agreeable duty was sometimes varied, in the case of strangers, by the young lady running away and leaving her admirer to grope his way home; and the diarist tells of one unlucky cavalier who concluded his evening's entertainment by wandering into a swamp.[1] The gayety of Annapolis, although imitated from the great English capital, had a primitive and colonial tinge, but was none the less enjoyable, probably, to the pleasure-loving planters of Maryland.

More intellectual amusements than those just described were totally wanting, and the planters had but little taste for them even had they existed. Education had never been an object of interest or solicitude. There was no college, and King William's academy and library, founded at Annapolis toward the close of the seventeenth century, was the only substitute, and probably not much better than an ordinary high-school.[2] In the year 1728, free schools were established by law in every county; but they were in the interest and under the evil influence of the Church, and neither grew nor prospered.[3] Education among the mass of the people was almost entirely neglected, and two-thirds of what little there was, was obtained from convicts and indented servants, who were regularly advertised for sale as teachers.[4] The wealthy sent their children abroad, and some of the Baltimore merchants sent their sons to Pennsylvania for an education; but the effect upon them when they returned to take up their life in an uneducated

---

[1] Pennsylvania Hist. Mag., i., Journal of William Black.
[2] Ridgely, Annals of Annapolis; Burnaby, p. 70; M'Sherry, p. 101.
[3] Burnaby, p. 70; M'Sherry, p. 117; Neill, p. 188.
[4] Neill, p. 212; Letter of Boucher, and advertisements in newspapers; Burnaby, ibid.

society, and among inferiors and slaves, was often to make them only more haughty and intemperate.[1] Literary pursuits were scarcely known.[2] A press for public printing was established in 1689; another for general work in 1726; and the *Maryland Gazette* was first issued in 1745.[3] The only literature, if it may be so termed, consisted of the Sot-Weed Factor, a rough, strong satire, by "Eben Cooke, gentleman," an unknown author; poetical effusions and Addisonian essays in the newspaper, and occasional political tracts and sermons.[4] Private libraries were rare; and although a post to Philadelphia was started in 1695, communication was slow, tidings of fashions in dress and amusement were more eagerly sought for than books, and even the newspapers were but little read.[5]

In spite of the life of indolence, pleasure, coarse amusements, and much illiteracy, the people were sensible and intelligent, with the typical keenness of their race in all relating to public affairs. In the eighteenth century a large majority of the people were natives, and neither knew nor cared much about royalty. In the year 1722, the Assembly declared that whoever said they had lost any of their English liberties was an ill-wisher to the country.[6] The independent spirit characteristic of a new and distant country, and of an often rough and adventurous life, was, in this instance, powerfully aided by the hostility engendered by the Church and clergy. The great planters cannot, as a class, bear comparison with their Virginian brethren, either in the power they possessed or the talent they produced; but the whole body of the upper and middle classes was sound and vigorous, and when the stress of Revolution came, able leaders of the stamp of Charles Carroll and Samuel Chase were not lacking.

---

[1] Griffiths, Annals of Baltimore; Neill, ibid. [2] Neill, p. 214.
[3] M'Mahon, Hist. View; M'Sherry, p. 111.
[4] Neill, p. 214; Tyler's Hist. of Amer. Literature.
[5] M'Sherry, p. 101; Rochefoucauld, ii., 360. [6] Neill, p. 215.

CHAPTER V.

NORTH CAROLINA FROM 1663 TO 1765.

NORTH CAROLINA occupies in the southern group of colonies much the same position that Rhode Island filled in the history of New England. The former was an offshoot, in large measure, of the great colony of Virginia; the latter of the vigorous commonwealth of Massachusetts. Both became places of refuge for the lawless, the adventurous, and the often thriftless population, which was discontented and restless beneath the strong and well-ordered governments of their powerful neighbors. The early history of Rhode Island is full of faction and turbulence; while her southern prototype exhibited these qualities constantly until the Revolution, and even after the adoption of the Constitution occasionally broke out into disorder and license. There is, moreover, a marked absence of individuality in the history of North Carolina; and she was sadly deficient in men of great abilities and commanding character, such as made Virginia illustrious. Yet it was owing only to the natural conformation of her coast that the foundations of a great State were not laid upon the banks of the Roanoke instead of by the waters of the James. To North Carolina came the **1584.** first important English expedition sent forth by Raleigh, and led by Amidas and Barlow. On her shores Raleigh's successive colonies settled, and here their author lavished his money and crippled his fortune. All these first English settlements in America, of which North Carolina was the scene, perished, and history has only to record their failure. Many years elapsed before the territory of North Carolina was again even thought of for purposes of colonization. As early as 1609 Virginian planters were on the Nansemond river, and here and there must have pushed their way into Carolina. In 1622 John Pory, an adventurer and traveller of the early Virginian type, and secretary of the colony, made his way as far south as the Chowan, and was favorably impressed with the country. But North

Carolina did not become the subject of royal gift until 1629, when Charles I. granted it to his attorney-general, Sir Robert Heath, " as the province of Carolana," and upon condition that he should colonize it within a reasonable time. The condition was not fulfilled by Heath, nor by Lord Maltravers, to whom Heath afterward transferred his patent. An abortive attempt at colonization was made in 1639, and a titular governor appeared in Virginia; but this, and a number of conflicting claims originating in this patent, and sufficiently troublesome to the proprietaries of a later time, were the only results of the grant of Charles I. This action on the part of the Crown, and the official information received, did not, however, suffice to prevent the Virginia Assembly lending itself to a scheme by which possession might be obtained of the neighboring territory, or at least substantial

1643. benefits realized therefrom by their constituents. With this object, they made grants to a trading company, which led, however, only to exploration and traffic. Other grants of a similar

1653. nature followed for the next ten years, at the expiration of which a company of Virginians made their way from Nansemond to Albemarle, and established a settlement there. The Virginian Burgesses granted them lands, and promised further grants to all who would extend these settlements to the southward. Emigration from Virginia began. Settlers, singly and in companies, crossed the border, and made scattered and solitary clearings within the wilds of North Carolina. Many of these people were mere adventurers; but some of them were of more substantial stuff, and founded permanent settlements on the Chowan and elsewhere. Other eyes, however, as watchful as those of the Virginians, were also turned to the rich regions of the South. New England enterprise explored the American coast from one end to the other, in search of lucrative trade

1660- 1661. and new resting-places, and after a long acquaintance with the North Carolina coast, they bought land of the Indians, near the mouth of Cape Fear river, and settled there. For some unexplained cause—possibly on account of the wild and dangerous character of the scattered inhabitants, who had already drifted thither from Virginia, possibly from the reason which they themselves gave—the New England colonists abandoned their settlement and departed, leaving a written opinion of the poor character of the country expressed in very plain language and pinned to a post. Here it was found by some wanderers from Barbadoes, who were of a different opinion from the New Englanders as to the appearance of things; and they according-

ly repurchased the land from the Indians and began a settlement. At
this date, therefore, there was in North Carolina this infant
1663. settlement of the Barbadoes men, on the extreme south-east-
ern point of the present State, and in the north-eastern corner the
Virginia settlers scattered about, with here a solitary plantation, and
there a little group of farms, but always a restless van of adventurers
working their way down the coast and into the interior.   The older
colonies had not as yet done much for North Carolina; but a beginning had at least been made, and this handful of dispersed, unsocial,
lawless, and ungoverned men would in time have laid the foundations
of one more English commonwealth.   But this slow progress was now
to receive a sudden impulse.   Whatever rights the North Carolina
settlers may have had in the eyes of the Virginians, who had granted
them land, or in those of the Indians who had sold it, they had none
recognized by the English King, who claimed to own all that vast region.   It may be doubted whether anything was known of these early
colonists in England; and their existence was certainly not regarded in
the least when Charles II. lavished their territory, and much besides, upon
a band of his courtiers and ministers.   There were many men then in
England who had deserved well of Charles Stuart, and when he was
on the throne meant to have their reward.   Many men were looking
carefully about to see what they could get from the Crown, now that
the King had his own again.   Among the royal possessions were vast
tracts of wild lands in America, where innumerable States could be
parcelled out, and whose natural resources had all the charm of the
unknown.   Charles's followers desired money above all things, and
here was a field not only for a speculation of immense possibilities,
but a certainty of glory incident to the proprietors of provinces, even
if those provinces were uninhabited forests.   That the gift was held
in high esteem, is shown by the fact that it fell to the share of those
who were highest in place and power under the government of the
Restoration.   Great names stand in the list of those to whom was
granted a territory covering more than eight degrees south of the
thirty-sixth parallel, and stretching in the other direction from the
Atlantic to the South Sea, in accordance with the charter issued in
March, 1663.   Edward, Earl of Clarendon, and George, Duke of Albemarle, were the first two of the grantees, among whom may be found
the well-known Royalist names of Berkeley and Carteret; while near
the end occurs the name of him who was the moving and guiding
spirit of the whole enterprise, Lord Ashley, better known a few years

before as Sir Anthony Cooper, and who has come down to posterity by his later title of the Earl of Shaftesbury. The charter had scarcely been issued when the Duke of Norfolk and Sir Robert Greenfield's heirs started up as claimants under the old Heath grant. Their claim was soon disposed of by a declaration from the King in Council that the Heath charter was null and void. Before this claim was quieted another was raised by the New Englanders, through their friends in England, for the lands purchased from the Indians at Cape Fear, and this the proprietors found it for their interest to deal with gently. In May the proprietaries organized, formed a joint-stock company, decided on the general principles of the government to be founded, divided their territory into two counties, Albemarle and Clarendon, and prepared for colonization. They first turned their attention to the beginnings already made in the new province. The Virginian settlements about the Chowan had reached a considerable importance, having grown largely by additions from the non-conformists of Virginia and the badly treated sectaries of Massachusetts. Governor Berkeley, of Virginia, himself a proprietary, was instructed in September to settle the government of the North Carolina colony. This he did by severing their connection with Virginia, appointing William Drummond, afterward a leader in Bacon's rebellion, Governor, instituting an Assembly, simple forms of law, and an easy tenure of land, and then leaving the people to shift for themselves. The New Englanders were treated in a similar spirit, and were offered by the proprietaries every inducement to return to or remain under their government.

1664. To Sir John Yeamans, who led a company from the Barbadoes, they said, " Make things easy for the people of New England; from thence the greatest supplies are expected." This emigration from Barbadoes was the third and most successful of the purely colonial attempts. The emigrants settled near the mouth of the Cape Fear river were joined by such New Englanders as may have remained there, established a considerable lumber trade, and throve apace.

But while the proprietaries were encouraging other provincials to settle their new territory and become their subjects, without expense to the rulers, they were also engaged in examining the geography of the region where their possessions lay. Their cupidity was excited. They determined to enlarge their bounds, and obtained a new charter, which granted to them the southern half of what is now the United States as far west as the Pacific. That this charter utterly disregarded the rights of Virginia on the north, and of Spain on the south, was a matter of small moment. Charles gave liberally when it cost him nothing; and the terms of the charter, wholly in favor of the proprietaries, reserved but little in the interests of either Crown or colonists. Fresh efforts signalized these new acquisitions. Agents were sent into all parts of the British dominions to solicit emigration. Yeamans was made Governor of the southern county. People from the Bermudas settled on the Pasquotank, and New Englanders came to swell the number of settlers on the Chowan. William Sayle explored

1667. the coast, and his description of the Bahamas led the proprietaries to ask and obtain those islands in addition to their already vast territory. In the same year Samuel Stephens was appointed to succeed Drummond as Governor of Albemarle. He was assisted by a council of twelve, one-half of whom he appointed, while the remainder were chosen by the Assembly, consisting of twelve delegates elected

1669. by the people. This first legislature soon met. They enacted laws, chiefly with a view to populate the country, and their principal and most characteristic measure was to make North Carolina a safe refuge for insolvent debtors. The proprietaries assented to these laws, and also ordered that lands should be held in Albemarle on the same tenure as in Virginia. Under these simple forms of government the colony progressed peaceably and rapidly; but such a system was not at all in keeping with the imperial ideas of the proprietaries.

In the seven years which had elapsed since the first grant, the proprietaries had done little toward colonization; but they now began to take more active measures for the settlement of their territory. Besides sending out an expedition, which landed in South Carolina, they established an elaborate system of government, known as the "fundamental constitutions." The leader among the proprietaries throughout was Shaftesbury, and the new activity now displayed by them was due to his restless energy. At this time, too, Shaftesbury drew to his service John Locke, who engaged in the task of colonizing the Carolinas, and who labored assiduously for some years as unofficial secretary to the proprietaries for the advancement of their projects. The first practical politician and the first philosopher of England united their abilities to give a system of government to Carolina, and the result was a simple absurdity. The "fundamental constitutions," amended somewhat by the proprietaries, and revised and corrected by Shaftesbury, were drafted by John Locke. For those who are interested in the character, career, and mental development of Locke or Shaftesbury these constitutions possess an interest. To the student of American history they are valueless, except as one explanation of the turbulence and faction which prevailed in the Carolinas. The system was a clumsy and complicated form of aristocratic government, tricked out in the rags of feudalism. There were to be seigniories, baronies, and manors, and there were to be four estates of the realm—proprietaries, landgraves, caciques, and commons. The chief power in the state was vested in a nobility which had no existence, and in a landed aristocracy which the future was to create. What remained was given to the people—a handful of rude settlers—who could not comprehend the system imposed upon them, and only felt instinctively that it was unsuitable, and probably oppressive. There were elaborate arrangements for the government of every division and subdivision of the provinces, and a scheme for a judiciary. The only provision showing foresight and judgment was that which guaranteed religious freedom. This was due to the wisdom of Locke; but it was marred by the clause which engrafted upon religious toleration the establishment of the English Church as that of the State.

Delighted with their work, and having decreed that the constitutions should stand forever, the proprietaries organized under the new system, and sent directions to Governor Stephens to put it in force among the settlers on the Chowan. Naturally enough Stephens failed to carry out the commands of his masters, despite the most earnest efforts. The only result of the attempt was to shake severely the existing government then naturally developing in Carolina in accordance with the wishes of the people and with their conditions of life. The lawless spirit of the settlers was still further strengthened by the ill-judged efforts of the proprietaries to regulate and limit trade. Religion gained a foothold, it is true, soon after, but it came through Quaker missionaries, and not at all in conformity to the well-bred schemes of the proprietaries. The first results of the famous constitutions in North Carolina were the lasting injury of the existing government, the increase of turbulence and faction, and the establishment of a despised and persecuted faith. The great and varied abilities of Locke and Shaftesbury bore strange fruit in America.

When Stephens died, the Assembly chose Carteret, their speaker, to succeed him. The new Governor had as little success as the old in introducing the constitutions, and utterly failed to preserve order. He soon departed to lay before the proprietaries the state of the country, and the Assembly sent their new speaker, East-

1674.

church, after him to present their side of the story. The proprie
1676. taries sensibly enough appointed Eastchurch Governor, with a
new set of instructions; but they sent with him one Miller,
who had recently been expelled from the province by the popular
1677. party. While Eastchurch lingered in the West Indies to woo
and win a bride, Miller proceeded on his way, and took possession of the government in the triple capacity of president, secretary, and collector of the customs. He found himself surrounded by
difficulties. The generous laws of the province had drawn thither
large numbers of debtors and other lawless and adventurous characters. North Carolina had already become a thorn in the side of
Virginia, who complained bitterly of her sister colony as a refuge for
bankrupts and criminals of every sort. There was, too, a strong element of adventurous and trading New Englanders, who had little affection for the Royalist proprietaries, and carried on a large illicit
traffic with great profit both to themselves and the tobacco planters.
With such a people Miller rashly endeavored not only to set up a
strong government and enforce its laws, but to carry out the Navigation Act and collect revenue, which went largely into his own pocket.
The Carolinians stood it longer than might have been expected. At
last, however, they accused Miller of interfering with the freedom of
elections, with levying taxes for his own behoof, and, worst of all, with
interfering with their trade. This last grievance was decisive. An
insurrection, headed by John Culpepper, an adventurer from the
southern province, broke out, and the insurgents, getting possession
of a large sum of money in the public treasury, made themselves mas-
1678. ters of the government, which they arranged to suit themselves. Miller escaped; Eastchurch was refused admittance;
and soon after Culpepper was sent to England to negotiate. Cul-
1679. pepper found Miller already in the field, and, though the proprietaries treated him sufficiently well, he was arrested just as
he was about to set sail, and tried soon after for high-treason, because
he had illegally acted as collector and embezzled the King's money.
Shaftesbury, who probably felt a sympathy for a successful rebel, interfered decisively, however, at this point, and Culpepper was acquitted. In the mean time the proprietaries had selected one of their
own number, Seth Sothel, to go out as Governor and settle the affairs
of the troubled province. Sothel was captured on his voyage by
pirates, and the government went on for some years under temporary rulers, who were too feeble to establish order, and sufficiently

strong to quarrel with their subjects. At last, however, Sothel arrived. He found the colony, of course, in its normal condition of anarchy, but he was the last man to quell it, for he was **1683.** a choice specimen of the greedy, petty, and tyrannical officials who flourished in all parts of America under the benign auspices of Charles and James. He robbed the people and the proprietaries alike with perfect indifference, and devoted himself wholly to extortion and theft for his own benefit. For some unexplained reason the colonists bore with him for five years before they rose in arms and **1688.** drove him from power. Condemned by the Assembly, Sothel was stripped of the government and exiled from the province.

Philip Ludwell, of Virginia, was appointed his successor. He gave out that he was prepared to redress all grievances, and **1689.** remedy, so far as possible, the misery inflicted by his predecessor; but he resided chiefly in Virginia, and although the people were not oppressed as before, disorder and license continued to prevail, and the colony did not prosper. The population diminished to such an extent that in 1694 it was not more than half as large as at the time of Miller's arrival and Culpepper's insurrection. **1693.** Ludwell, after four years of ineffective service, was succeeded by Lillington, and then by Thomas Harvey as Deputy-governor. At this time, under pressure of the revolt in South Carolina, and of the continuing turbulence in both the northern and southern provinces, the proprietaries abandoned the constitutions framed for eternal duration, and determined to allow the colonists to govern themselves according to the terms of the charter of Charles II. Thus, at the expiration of twenty-three years, the work of Locke and Shaftesbury wholly perished. Almost ludicrous in conception, the defunct system had borne bitter fruit in broils and factions, which went on unchecked by inefficient rulers until the proprietaries, resolving that the best talent was needed in their possessions, sent out John Archdale—a Quaker, and one of their own number—to administer **1695.** the government of both colonies. Archdale was firm, judicious, and wise—the first Governor of ability the province had been blessed with. The southern colony chiefly occupied his attention, but he met with quicker success in North Carolina, where the population was scattered, and where many of the leading men were of his own religious faith. Under Archdale's guidance the questions most productive of ill-feeling, and the long-standing quarrels, were settled in the Assembly by suitable legislation. Order was restored, contentment diffused, population again began to increase, and the government **1696.** went on peaceably, after Archdale's departure, under Harvey, who had, a year previously, proved so incompetent. Upon **1699.** Harvey's death, Henderson Walker, the President of the Council, succeeded to the government. During the five years of Walker's administration order and tranquillity prevailed in North Carolina, broken only by the depredations of the pirates. The impulse given by Archdale to the affairs of the colony, and the discreet poli- **1704.** cy of his successors, came, however, to an end upon the death of Walker.

Governor Johnson, of South Carolina, now in control of both the provinces, sent Robert Daniel to be President of the Council, rule in the northern province, and establish there, as he had done in the south, the Church of England. Daniel carried out his instructions faithfully. The Church was established, and taxes laid for its support. The immediate result was a union of all the dissenters with those of South Carolina in opposition to the lord proprietaries, while the old spirit of faction and discord was again let loose. The wild, adventurous, and ill-educated settlers of North Carolina needed a strong, firm government, whose policy was to interfere as little as possible. Instead of that, they were burdened anew with one which was not **1705.** only weak, but meddling and aggravating. Thomas Cary succeeded Daniel, being appointed Deputy-governor, but the proprietaries disapproved the choice, and the Council elected Glover. The whole province was immediately plunged into a state of anarchy, produced by the struggles of the contending factions. Many fled to Virginia, and at last the proprietaries removed Cary, and sent **1710.** out Edward Hyde to be Lieutenant-governor. He was well received by both parties, and everything proceeded quietly until the elections were held, when Cary, being defeated, put himself at the head of an open insurrection. His complete selfishness of purpose, and the limited amount of plunder he was able to offer, prevented his finding much popular support. But, on the other hand, nobody came to the assistance of Governor Hyde—the people apparently regarding the conflict with that perfect indifference which is the offspring of a normal condition of political disorder and license. Governor Hyde, however, managed to hold Cary at bay until Governor Spotswood, of Virginia, interfered with decisive effect, dispersing the rebels with his troops, seizing Cary, who fled to Virginia, and finally sending him a prisoner in a man-of-war to England.

Hardly had civil commotion begun to subside, when the unlucky colony was visited by the scourge of Indian war. There had been from time to time Indian outbreaks, and the North Carolina settlers were not of a disposition to conciliate the savages; but at last the troubles culminated in a union of the tribes and a general **1711.** massacre of the borderers, from which the Palatines and Swiss alone partially escaped by a treaty of neutrality. Assistance was received from South Carolina, the North Carolina militia refusing very generally to obey the requisition of the Governor. The South Carolinians inflicted one defeat upon the Indians, and then withdrew.

Soon after Hyde died, and was succeeded by Thomas Pollock, **1712.** who was made President of the Council. President Pollock draws a black picture of the condition of affairs when he assumed the government, and it was but little better when the new Gov- **1714.** ernor, Charles Eden, arrived. The Indian war still raged, and fresh assistance had to be asked from both South Carolina and Virginia. Aid was readily given by both, the power of the Tuscaroras was broken, and in 1715 peace was finally made with the other tribes; but intestine struggles, Indian wars, incompetent or corrupt officials, and depreciated currency had reduced North Carolina to a low point. Nothing gives a more striking impression of the difficulties which had beset the colony than a comparison of the numbers of the people in 1676 and 1717. In the former year there were fourteen hundred tithable; and after forty years of immigration, settlement, and growth, there were only six hundred more.

Better prospects seemed to open with the new administration. The laws were revised and ordered to be printed; more bills of credit were issued; the establishment of the Church of England was confirmed; but toleration was secured, and a variety of useful measures of police were enacted. Much of this legislation was bad, no doubt; but it at least showed a settled policy on the part of the government. Still, the old factions were far from extinct. The former partisans of Cary controlled the lower house, and opposed every species of resistance to the Governor. In this, unfortunately, they were much aided by Eden's complicity with Teach, the most noted of the pirates who then infested the coast. The secretary of the provinces, one Knight, was undoubtedly an ally of the buccaneers, and the Governor was somewhat involved. At last Virginia **1718.** interfered once more in the affairs of her troublesome neighbor with decisive effect. The pirate vessel was captured, Teach was killed in the fight, and four of his comrades were hung. Piracy was at last sharply checked in North Carolina, but the corrupt practices of the administration did not tend to keep political factions in order. The leaders of the opposition headed a riot, broke into the secretary's office, and seized all the records of the State. The administration proved strong enough to put down the incipient rebellion, and throw the ringleaders into prison; but such affairs as these and that of the pirates indicate a low and rude state of society. The only good sign was that the government had gained sufficient strength to maintain itself. After this the colony rested, and Eden ruled in peace until his death. Two Presidents then governed in succession until the arrival of the new Governor, George Burrington, who appears to have been a mere adventurer and common brawler. He held office for little more than a year, when he was removed, and his place filled by Sir Richard Everard. The event of the new administration was the settlement of the long-pending boundary dispute with Virginia. Everard himself was an improvement on Burrington; but he was far from being a good Governor. He paid little attention to the Assembly, did not try to remedy gross grievances, quarrelled with the Council, and effected but slight improvement in the affairs of the colony.

1722.

1724.

1725.

At last, despairing of success, and justly censured for their bad officers, the proprietaries abandoned their attempt to rule a province. Their authority had been for some time practically at an end in South Carolina, and they now—with the exception of Lord Carteret—sold all their rights to the Crown. To abolish the clumsy form of proprietary government, with all its attendant evils, was a step in the right direction; but the first move on the part of the Crown was a sadly mistaken one. Burrington, appointed previously by royal favor, was reinstated, and returned to the province for a much longer period of ill-doing than on the prior occasion. He began his administration by a quarrel with the Council, excited general resentment by the appointment of assistant judges, for whom he claimed large powers, and concluded by an open breach with the Assembly, who wished to inquire into the abuses connected with official fees. The representatives of the people, however, began at last to gather strength, and learn the art of parliamentary government. They impeached and removed a judge, who was one of the worst of the officials with whom the proprietaries had cursed North Carolina; and they evinced in other ways an intelligent conception of the popular

1731.

grievances. Burrington continued in his old courses, scandalous in private life, and unwise in public conduct, whether he aimed sincerely at reform or merely oppressed those who thwarted him. At last **1734.** complaints were sent to England, and Burrington soon followed them, unwilling to await the result, although his principal opponent, the chief-justice, was little better than himself.

A new Governor, Gabriel Johnston, was immediately appointed, and was an improvement upon his predecessor, though by no means an ideal officer. But he had definite views, real capacity for business, and held office long enough to carry out a policy. To his first Legislature he recommended the establishment of fixed salaries; to his second, the necessity of public education, of patronizing religion, of new jails and sufficient execution of penal laws, and called attention to the great defects in the methods of acquiring land. Wise as these suggestions were, the Legislature stubbornly resisted the Governor, and passed no bills. This was not an auspicious beginning; but, nevertheless, in the course of Governor Johnston's long administration of eighteen years many substantial advances were made. The boundary-line was run between North and South Carolina, the laws were revised and amended, and something was done in the matters of education, religion, and land titles. A vain attempt was made to purify the bench by driving Smith, Burrington's old enemy, from office, but the chief-justice was protected by the Governor, and by a packed majority of the Assembly. Johnston also tried, for his own purposes, to change the system of representation, but failed. He appeared to more advantage in his persistent though fruitless efforts to check the issue of a depreciated currency; and he effected a change in the site of the capital after prolonged wranglings with the Assembly. During Johnston's term of office the colony had its share in the Spanish war, sending its quota to the West India expedition, and giving aid to Oglethorpe in his Florida campaigns. Johnston's rule was, on the whole, prudent, and it was certainly beneficial. Population increased rapidly, trade flourished, new lands were brought under cultivation, the judicial system was extended, and was enabled to reach the scattered and lawless inhabitants of the back counties.

When Governor Johnston died, the Assembly took advantage of **1752.** the lax rule of native presidents to issue more currency, although their resources were soon to be strained to the uttermost by the impending French war. The successor of Johnston, Arthur Dobbs, an Irishman, a friend of Swift, and a man of letters, although of slender abilities for business, found himself on his arrival confronted by the difficulties which beset every American colony in the great conflict which was to have so deep an effect upon the destinies of the continent. North Carolina was not within immediate reach of the French arms, but she felt that the dangers of Virginia nearly concerned her, and she furnished men and money for the war in the neighboring colony and in the northern provinces. She had troubles of her own, too, with the Indians of the Carolinas, who seized the opportunity to break out into open and devastating hostility, which was only checked after much hard fighting.

These various forms of war put a severe strain upon the province, and in North Carolina, as elsewhere, led to political struggles over civil matters between the representatives of the people and those of the Crown, foreshadowing the dissensions which opened the way for Independence. Like his immediate predecessor, Governor Dobbs made a vigorous attempt to reduce the representation, and model it in such a manner as to secure to himself the control of legislation. After proceeding quite far in the execution of this project, he was checked and ultimately defeated by the determined resistance of the Assembly; and he was undoubtedly overawed by the riots and violence which broke out, as they always did in North Carolina whenever the spirit of opposition to the laws was aroused. The only result of this contest was a clause requiring special and new charters for the establishment of counties and boroughs—a device which put many large fees into the pocket of the Governor, and which subsequently led to much ill-feeling. The next conflict was about the old question of the currency. Here the Governor and Council appear, as usual, in the best attitude, resisting further issues of depreciated paper; but in all other respects the administration put itself in the wrong. Affairs in the province were in a bad condition. The old judiciary act had been repealed, and there had been no courts for eight months. There had been much turbulence, rioting, and bloodshed. The sheriffs failed to collect the taxes properly, and the treasurers gave no satisfactory accounts. The Assembly endeavored to meet the difficulties by inserting a clause in the aid bill, compelling the treasurers to account, and by establishing courts, where the judges were to hold office during good behavior; but to these measures the Governor would not assent. Matters went from bad to worse. It was the old story: no reforms, no money. Then came addresses and petitions to the King against the Governor, and the appointment of an agent in Eng-

1760.

land in the interest of the Assembly. The next session the Governor gave way, and assented to the court bill on condition of the subsequent royal consent. Dobbs, however, learned nothing from this experience. Fees were a fruitful source of trouble among the lawless people of the back counties, and the extortion of Lord Granville's agent in regard to land patents led to riotous outbreaks. The Governor, instead of trying to mitigate the evil of unjust fees, created and exacted new and more burdensome ones. One dissension led to another. The Governor and the Assembly quarrelled about paper-money, about the position of the capital, about the appointment of an agent, about public accounts, and in all the passage of the aid bill **1762.** was made the means of coercing the executive. The disallowance of the court laws did not tend to mend matters, and of course the full weight of popular displeasure fell upon the Governor, now loaded with the blunders of the home government as well as his own. A prolonged wrangle ensued between the two Houses over **1763.** a new judiciary act, which finally passed after much amendment. The discontent with Dobbs rapidly increased. He even quarrelled about the appointment of a printer and the correction of a private bill, and complaints poured in against him in England. **1765.** Thus beset, he asked for leave of absence; but, before he could take advantage of it, died at his country-seat in North Carolina.

His successor, William Tryon, was a conspicuous example of those ill-starred selections for high provincial office by which England did so much to precipitate revolution. He came to North Carolina at a time when the Assembly was fresh from their altercations with his predecessor, when riots upon one account or another were breaking out everywhere, and when the Stamp Act was about to be enforced. He carried matters with a high hand when it was too late to be of any use; and although he met with apparent success, the ultimate result of his policy was to embitter the hostile feelings of the colonists, and prepare the way for separation. He first took measures to establish the Church, and then prorogued the Assembly, to avoid legislative resistance to the Stamp Act. In this he was successful. No delegates were chosen, and North Carolina was not represented in the Stamp Act Congress. The public indignation and the general hostility to the measures of Parliament found utterance in meetings, addresses, and pamphlets; but there was no concerted action, and the colony, as a whole, was not involved. Thus Tryon avoided a conflict with the old

10

Assembly, but he made no attempt to land the stamped paper, which he knew would be resisted; and when he met his new Assembly he was able to announce to them the repeal of the hated law. From a general feeling of gratitude, the members voted five thousand pounds to build the Governor's palace, a fresh imposition which came at an unlucky moment. The people of the back counties—poor, ignorant, and lawless—suffered greatly from the extortionate fees exacted by all the petty officers of the courts and land-offices. Tryon showed no more real disposition than his predecessors to reform the fees, and the cost of the new palace, greatly exaggerated by report, still further incensed the settlers of the interior. Associations were formed and known as " Regulators," who rapidly advanced to open violence, in accordance with the prevailing habit of the country. Courts were closed; unpopular attorneys and Crown officers treated with brutality; and, finally, payment of taxes was refused. Rioting had grown to rebellion. Tryon, at the outset, took measures to repress the troubles, and arrested two of the ringleaders; but he was forced to release them, and concession proved of no avail. Success had turned the heads of the insurgents. One violent act succeeded another; illegal combinations extended; to the abolition of fees was now added that of all debts, and terror and anarchy prevailed in the back counties. Husbands, the leader of the rebellion, had been chosen to the new Assembly, and was expelled from that body as soon as it came together. The Assembly also took measures to enforce the laws by the ordinary machinery of the courts, but this was manifestly too feeble, and Tryon determined to bring matters to a final decision. He called out the militia, marched into the most disturbed county, saved his army by his energy and activity, and utterly routed a force of insurgents three times as large as his own. Some of the insurgents were hung, others fled, and the majority took advantage of Tryon's proclamation of indemnity, and submitted. If Tryon had been as good an administrator as he was a general, much might now have been done to remedy the evil state into which North Carolina had fallen; but he was not fit for the task, and only increased the hostility to the government in the body of the people.

1766.

1770.

His successor, Josiah Martin, was a change for the worse. The admiration of Tryon by the usual supporters of the government disgusted Martin, who strove to curry favor with the Regulators and the most turbulent of the population. In this task he suc-

1771.

ceeded so well that he led them into armed opposition to the Revolution; but he did nothing to remedy the evils, legal, financial, and social, which beset the province. He quarrelled bitterly with the Assembly, who, to defeat him, encouraged popular license and disorder by advising evasion of taxes, and who themselves resisted the establishment of proper courts. In such a colony, and among such a people, lawless, and inflamed against all government, there was abundant material for the Revolution, and local quarrels fostered those of national significance. In Governor Tryon's time strong resolutions had passed the Assembly, denying generally the right of England to tax the colonies; and when the Virginian resolutions of March, 1773, were laid before them, they approved at once the action of their neighbor, and appointed a Committee of Correspondence. This done, angry domestic broils over the old subjects of taxes, fees, courts, and the powers of the Assembly once more supervened, and the great issues involving the fate of a continent were again lost sight of. But when the summons to a Congress came from Massachusetts, North Carolina at once responded, by choosing delegates in a popular convention. Colonial and provincial days were over, and the history of North Carolina became part of that of the United States.

Dec., 1773.

1774.

Chapter VI.

NORTH CAROLINA IN 1765.

NORTH CAROLINA was, with perhaps the exception of the recently settled Georgia, the least important of the southern group of colonies. It was scarcely more than an uncivilized reproduction of Virginia, with little individuality or force of any kind. Unsettled government, turbulent, and even riotous politics, and the character of the population, had so weakened every bond, and rendered society so unstable and loose, that it had hardly an existence.

The coast of the province was hemmed in by sand-banks, and almost wholly deficient in safe and commodious harbors. Near the sea the soil was light and sandy, and great tracts of swamp and pine barrens offered neither a profitable nor a wholesome region for colonization.[1] In the interior the soil became richer, and the country improved greatly as it gradually rose to the summit of the southern portion of the Alleghany Range.

The population at the time of the Revolution was not far from two hundred thousand, of which one-fourth to one-half were slaves.[2] The white population was recruited from various sources. The controlling element was of English origin, and composed in large measure of adventurers and exiles from Virginia and the other colonies, supplemented by emigrants from the mother country. There were also French Huguenots, Moravians, Palatines who came under the leadership of Graffenried, and some Swiss and Scotch in the hill country. These foreign elements were not numerous, but they were of better quality

---

[1] Smyth, i., 234; ii., 94; Raynal, Engl. Ed., 1766; Williamson, ii., 174.

[2] The statistics of North Carolina are so hopelessly vague that the roughest approximation is alone possible in any estimate: Smyth, i., 270, puts the population at 270,000, with one-half slaves; Martin, ii., 395, 1770, says 150,000, and one-fifth slaves.

than many of the English settlers, and, as a rule, more thrifty and industrious.[1]

The government under Locke's constitutions consisted of a general court, held by the chief-magistrate, and was composed of a proprietary, two assistants, and deputies chosen by the people.[2] This was afterward converted into the familiar form of Governor, Council, and Deputies. A qualification of property in land was required to hold office, and only freeholders could vote. This system was ingrafted on the constitution adopted when North Carolina became a State, and by which senators were obliged to own three hundred acres of land, and representatives one hundred, while the suffrage was restricted to freeholders of fifty acres.[3]

For the administration of justice the province was divided into six districts and thirty - two counties. There were two courts — the supreme court, with very large jurisdiction, which sat twice annually at each district town; and the county or monthly courts, which met at the county towns, and were limited to small causes, and the punishment of slaves and servants. The bench of the county courts was of very inferior quality, and that of the supreme court was little better.[4] There was also a court of chancery and admiralty, composed of the Governor and Council. The county courts were charged with the care of orphans, to save expense to the usually small estates, and both these and the supreme courts were required to sit once a year for probate and administration.[5] The whole legal system was very lax and badly conducted. The terse phrase of Bancroft, "that there were no laws and no lawyers," describes not unfairly the administration of justice in North Carolina.[6] The laws were not even printed, but only read in the market-place, and the assemblies and courts met here and there in private houses or taverns.[7]

Revenue was raised for the Crown from quit-rents, tonnage duties, and duties on rum and wine;[8] while the expenses of the province were met by simple and direct taxation of polls, tithables, free negroes and their intermarriage, and by an excise on spirits.[9] There were, in ac-

---

[1] Lawson's Description of North Carolina, p. 79; Martin, i., 233; Smyth, i., 162, 216.   [2] Martin, ii., 205.

[3] Iredell, Laws of North Carolina; Constitution of State.

[4] Smyth, i., 234; Iredell, 1722, 1766; Martin, ii., 205.   [5] Iredell, 1762.

[6] Bancroft's History of the United States, ii., 164.

[7] Bancroft, ibid.; Williamson, i., 162.

[8] Iredell, 1738, 1749, 1756.   [9] Ibid., 1723, 1734, 1738.

cordance with the Virginian fashion, public, county, and parish levies, collected by the sheriffs.[1] Taxation was light; but it was sedulously avoided by the people, who were clearly of opinion that all taxes were an evil, and was only enforced with the greatest difficulty; so much so that the government found it necessary to get a portion of its revenue by compelling the inhabitants to work on the roads, and keep the streets of the towns clean.[2]

There was an almost total absence of professions. There was no army and no navy, and no physicians, except a few surgeons and apothecaries in the towns, so unskilled that one traveller affirms that neither medical attendance nor nursing could be obtained in case of illness.[3] Lawyers were equally rare, except in the towns, where there were some attorneys of poor standing and attainments. The lack of lawyers is shown by the rapid rise of such a man as Henderson, who became a popular leader and successful man simply by his oratory at the bar.[4]

The case was equally bad with the clergy, and the condition of religion, and everything connected with it, strongly illustrates the extreme rudeness of society in North Carolina. The first minister was settled in 1703; the Church of England established in 1704; and the first church built in 1705.[5] There were no sects, says one authority,[6] and the people certainly appear to have been indifferent to theological doctrines. When the Quakers appeared no objection was raised, and the North Carolinians beguiled the hours of silent prayer by smoking, but they indulged in no persecution.[7] To them one sect was as good as another, except the Established Church, to which they had a rooted objection, because taxes were required for its support. Twenty years and more after the establishment of the Church but little religious progress had been made. Colonel Byrd notes in his journal that, for "want of men in holy orders," justices of the peace and members of the Council were empowered to marry those who would not take each others' word; that marriage was a lay contract, and christening wholly a matter of chance. He also remarks that there was no church in Edenton; that the efforts of the Society for the Propagation of the Gospel had been failures; and that the people paid no tribute either to God or Cæsar.[8] This condition of affairs was in some degree at-

[1] Iredell, 1756.   [2] Ibid., 1738.   [3] Smyth, i., 98, 130.
[4] Ibid., i., 98, 124, 127.   [5] Bancroft, ii., 164; Williamson, i., 162.
[6] Bancroft, ibid.   [7] Martin, i., 155.
[8] Byrd MSS., i., 44, 46, 59, 60, 65; as to lack of professions and general condition of North Carolina, see Autobiog. of William Few, Mag. Am. Hist., Nov., 1881, p. 344.

tributable to the early political conflicts;[1] but when they ceased, and the government turned its attention to the religious establishment, its efforts were marked neither by wisdom nor success.

In the year after Colonel Byrd penned his observations, an act was passed for the regulation and inspection of vestries and church-wardens.[2] Ten years later, although justices of the peace were to marry, the preference was to be given to the minister, under a heavy penalty, and fines were exacted for marriages either within or without the church without a license. At the same time, Sunday laws were passed against swearing, work, and profanity on the Lord's-day, and these, as well as the act against illicit intercourse and in regard to bas-tards, were directed to be read in all the churches. The vestries were to be encouraged by having certain powers of local government con-ferred upon them.[3] The futility of these attempts is clearly shown by the continual legislation from this time on in behalf of the Church.[4] Commissioners were appointed to build churches, wardens and vestries were appointed to encourage an orthodox clergy, pastors were to have glebes, money was raised to complete churches, and sheriffs were to compel collectors to apply and account for their taxes.[5] Harsh ex-perience even taught the supporters of the State Church the need of a little liberality for the benefit of religion in general. Quakers were given the custody of children of their own faith, although neither they nor the Catholics could be appointed guardians by others.[6] A few years later, Presbyterian ministers, but no others, were given the right to marry by license, and all previous marriages of any kind were declared legal.[7] Still later, all marriages by dissenters were legalized through the efforts of Governor Tryon. But all legislation, wise and unwise, on this subject was fruitless, for the simple reason that the people paid no heed to it. It was in vain to direct that the freeholders should meet and choose vestries to lay taxes for the support of Church and clergy, when none of the freeholders wanted them, and when in the back counties such laws were rendered null and void by obstinate inaction.[8] There is "very little of the Gospel in all that colony," says one contemporary, with more truth than kindness.[9] At the time of the Revolution, although ministers were nominally estab-

---

[1] Williamson, i., 162. [2] Iredell, Laws, 1729. [3] Ibed, 1741.
[4] Iredell, 1743, and ff. [5] Ibed., 1749, 1754, 1759, 1760, 1770.
[6] Iredell, 1762. [7] Ibed., 1766.
[8] Ibed., 1761; Williamson, ii., 116.
[9] Huguenot Family in Virginia, 1754, p. 344.

lished in every parish, there were actually only six of the English Church in the colony. The Presbyterians had as many, and the Moravians had the same number, although their followers did not number more than five hundred. The Quakers were the most numerous and extended. Besides these there were no regular denominations, but many itinerant preachers; Baptists, Methodists, and New Lights wandered through the colony, and their ardent discourses seem to have met with general acceptance. The great majority of the people were dissenters, and in the frontier region without any religion at all. There is no evidence that this arose from any deeply grounded and well conceived opinions, but it is perfectly clear that the peculiar antipathy of the North Carolinians to taxes had much to do with their dislike of the State Church.[1]

The lack of professional pursuits was not made good by any variety in other occupations. Everybody was either a planter or a store-keeper, and in the western counties a hunter. In the towns there were a few mechanics, shopkeepers, and innkeepers, the latter an influential and popular class. All branches of trade and manufacture were in the hands of the store-keepers, who sold everything, and supplied the planters and farmers.[2] The people were, as a rule, wholly agricultural, and there was a much greater variety of production than in Virginia. Yet the agriculture was the lowest in all the English colonies. Land was cleared by girdling trees, thus entailing loss of life and property from conflagrations and falling timber. Crops were then raised, until the land was exhausted; when another clearing was made and the old process repeated, and the fallow acres remitted to trees and underbrush.[3] In the northern counties the Virginian example, it is true, was followed, and tobacco was the great staple; but in the southern portion rice and indigo were grown, and cotton was raised of good quality, while in the interior farm products were the principal interest.[4] Throughout the province lumber, tar, and turpentine were produced, and returned great profits to those engaged in the industry.[5] Cereal and grass crops were trifling, only sufficient for home consumption.[6] There were also immense herds of cattle and hogs, which ran wild, and could be identified only by brands, which it was made

---

[1] Smyth, i., 102, 132; Williamson, ii., 180; Martin, ii., 395.

[2] Smyth, i., 98, 99, 114.

[3] Ibid., ii., 94, 96; Martin, ii., 395; Rochefoucauld, i., 638.

[4] Smyth, i., 84; ii., 97.   [5] Martin, ii., 395.   [6] Byrd MSS., i., 31.

penal to alter.[1] There were valuable fisheries, but they were little developed, nor were the opportunities for a lucrative trade with the Indians improved.[2]

There were no manufactures of any kind. The efforts even of the Assembly in this direction had not gone beyond acts to encourage leather tanning and grist-mills.[3] Every manufactured article, without exception, was imported from the mother country or from the other colonies.[4] At the Moravian towns, where whites worked, there were some profitable industries and good farms, but they were so few as hardly to form an exception. The province depended wholly on the North for workmen and sailors.[5] The same lack of enterprise characterized the commerce which was necessary to carry the products of the colony to the markets of the world, and this commerce was by no means unimportant. The exports amounted to over one hundred thousand, and the imports to nearly two hundred thousand pounds.[6] The carrying trade was, however, in a great measure lost. Much of it "was engrossed by the saints of New England, who carry off a great deal of tobacco without troubling themselves with paying that impertinent duty of a penny a pound."[7] All foreign commerce was characterized by evasion of the laws of the land, and of trade as well. The tobacco sold was largely of a bad kind and inferior quality, and nothing was done to improve this or other exports by government inspection until after the middle of the eighteenth century.[8] Much of the commerce was diverted from the colony altogether, and found vent at Norfolk on the one side, and Charleston on the other.[9] None of the harbors admitted ships of large burden, yet nothing was done to improve either harbors or rivers. The act establishing ports was repealed, because it was found that by taking away the free trade of North Carolina it might benefit the Virginians. Small vessels cruised up the navigable rivers, and picked up a cargo where they could.[10] All business transactions were further hampered by the scarcity of

---

[1] Iredell, 1715, 1748 ; Byrd MSS., i., 32 ; Smyth, i., 144.

[2] Smyth, i., 90 ; Lawson, Description, p. 86.

[3] Iredell, 1727, 1748, 1758.   [4] Lawson, p. 86.

[5] Smyth, i., 216 ; Rochefoucauld, ii., 13 ; Memoirs of Elkanah Watson, p. 39.

[6] Smyth, ii., 98 ; Martin, ii., 395.

[7] Byrd MSS., i., 23.

[8] Ibid., p. 50 ; Iredell, 1755, 1758, 1759.

[9] Williamson, ii., 174 ; Rochefoucauld, ii., 7 ; Lawson, p. 86.

[10] Iredell, 1743 ; Williamson, ii., 174 ; Rochefoucauld, i., 638.

money, which induced payments in kind, and large emissions of depreciated paper currency.[1]

It is needless to say that with trade in such a condition, and with such occupations as have been described, there were no towns in North Carolina. There were only three, when Independence was declared, which could by any stretch of the imagination be dignified by such a name. These were Wilmington, Edenton, and Newbern, sufficiently pretty little villages, each of which had been in turn the capital, and the largest of which had a population of about six hundred inhabitants.[2] The legislature had erected many villages into towns and townships, and ordered fairs to be held in them; but they remained villages still, with a few scattered houses, and, except among the Moravians, mere centres of resort on court and election days.[3]

The structure of society was of course, as the condition of the professions, of religion and of trade, indicates, loose and simple. At the bottom of the social scale was a large body of African slaves and a small number of indented white servants. The slaves were in sufficient numbers to cause the usual fear-inspired and ferocious legislation. Heavy fines were exacted from both minister and culprit for the intermarriage of whites with either negroes or Indians, and also from those who harbored runaways. Fugitives were whipped by order of the county courts, and could be outlawed. Slaves were forbidden to leave the plantations or to raise cattle.[4] They were not allowed to carry guns, and their quarters were regularly searched for concealed weapons.[5] They could receive freedom only as a reward for meritorious service. They were kept in a state of the densest and most barbarous ignorance; and when the Quakers first appeared, and they were admitted to the meetings, the slaves said, "They had always been kept in ignorance, and disregarded as people who were not to expect anything from the Lord."[6] As in Virginia, however, their general treatment was said to have been mild.[7]

The condition of the indented servants, although sufficiently wretched, was, on account of their greater resemblance to the rest of the community, better, and their rights were, in appearance at least, more protected than in the northern colonies. No "imported Christian" was

[1] Williamson, ii., 174.
[2] Smyth, i., 84, 234; ii., 87, 89, 93; Byrd MSS., i., 59; Martin, ii., 395; Rochefoucauld, i., 638.
[3] Smyth, i., 266; Iredell, 1738, 1749.   [4] Ibid., 1741.
[5] Ibid., 1753.   [6] Life of Thomas Story.   [7] Rochefoucauld, i., 638.

to be a servant without an indenture; they had to be brought before the magistrate for corporal punishment, and could complain to the courts if they were wronged. If they ran away they had to serve a double term, and they could not marry without leave of their masters and the payment of lawful fees. If a woman servant gave birth to an illegitimate child she had to serve an additional term; and if the master was the father, then she was sold by the church-wardens for the public benefit.[1]

The bulk of the population above the servile classes consisted of "poor whites" and small farmers. There were but few large planters; but such as there were closely resembled those of Virginia, and were often agreeable and intelligent men.[2] These men, however, were exceptional. The mass of the population were small land-owners of varying degrees of ignorance and poverty.[3] The turbulent and unsettled character of the colony attracted many adventurers of the worst class from the other provinces, and the coast was the favorite resort of pirates, with whom the people had strong sympathies. North Carolina was the refuge of all the slaves, criminals, and debtors who fled from Virginia, and found shelter and protection from her southern neighbors.[4] There was a general dread, when the boundary-line was run, of falling within the Virginian limits, because there some order and government existed. In North Carolina every one did what was right in his own eyes.[5] "A girl of good fortune and reputation," says one Virginian, no doubt with a good deal of wholesome prejudice, "is a thing somewhat scarce in those parts, as they have no established laws and very little of the Gospel."[6]

From the want of commerce even the best plantations afforded little more than a coarse subsistence which was cheap and plenty. For everything else the planters ran in debt at the country store, paying in tobacco, and contriving to be generally a twelvemonth in arrear.[7] This indifference to financial obligations was another effect of the want of trades, and in the early years caused the passage of a law to prevent the exportation of debtors without security being given.[8] The general feeling on the subject of debts was better reflected, however, by later legislation, which provided amply for the relief of debtors.[9]

The genial climate, the ease of obtaining a subsistence, and the

---

[1] Iredell, 1741. [2] Smyth, i., 103. [3] Ibid. [4] Byrd MSS., i., 34.
[5] Ibid., i., 34, 46. [6] Huguenot Family in Virginia, p. 344, 1754.
[7] Smyth, i., 99; Byrd MSS., i., 31. [8] Iredell, 1715. [9] Ibid., 1762, 1773.

cheapness and plenty of provisions, led to early marriages and large
families, and, joined with the contempt for labor inspired by the presence of a servile class, made the men slothful and lazy to the last degree.[1]   While the men lolled in bed or idled about the farm, most of
the work was done by the women, who were generally superior to their
husbands.   They wove homespun to clothe the family, could handle
a canoe, and were ready to help in planting.   They managed the accounts, and the girls were brought up to the affairs of the farm.[2]

Daily existence was solitary in the extreme.   The farmers and planters saw no one outside of their families and slaves, except at long intervals.   There was very little intercourse, and communication between
different parts of the province was extremely difficult.[3]   They were,
too, almost wholly cut off from the world.   A mail from Virginia and
the North passed through the coast towns once in a month; but nothing was done to encourage a local postal service before the year 1770.[4]
Travelling was almost impossible.   Roads were hardly known in the
interior, such bridges as there were were dangerous, and the ferries
were few, and owned by individuals.   To journey from one point to
another the traveller had to force his way through dense forests, losing
himself constantly at night in the woods and swamps.   Provisions had
to be carried, for there were no inns, except near the coast, and those
wretchedly bad.[5]

To a people so isolated in their lives, the infrequent stranger was
a welcome guest.   The poor whites had an ignorant dread of them;
but at the plantations the traveller stopped as a matter of course, and
was always received with a good deal of rude state and a thoroughly
generous hospitality.[6]   The profound solitude in which most of the
settlers dwelt is strongly shown by the law providing that before
burial on a plantation the corpse, whether the deceased were bond or
free, should be seen by two or three of the neighbors.[7]

There was, of course, great dearth of amusements.   The only meetings were, on court and election days, at the court-house in the midst
of the forest.[8]   On these occasions there was much drinking and
gaming, and rough fighting, but the young men were, nevertheless,
owing to narrow means and early marriages, neither dissolute nor

[1] Smyth, i., 162; Byrd MSS., i., 56; Lawson, p. 79, 86.
[2] Smyth, i., 132; Lawson, p. 84.   [3] Smyth, i., 110.   [4] Iredell, 1770.
[5] Smyth, i., 102, 103, 112, 173, 238; ii., 100; Memoirs of E. Watson, p. 39.
[6] Smyth, i., 90, 99; Watson, p. 39.   [7] Iredell, 1715.   [8] Watson, p. 39.

prodigal.[1] The passion for gambling, the only form of excitement, was probably excessive, as is shown by repeated laws against it ; but this seems to have been the only prevalent vice, and even that could find but rare opportunities.[2]

There was scarcely any means of education, and no literature whatever. Printing was not introduced until 1764 ; and at the time of the Revolution there were only two schools, lately incorporated at Newbern and Edenton, in the whole province. An act of the year 1770, to endow Queen's College at Charlotte, was repealed by proclamation ; and even after the war for Independence, with the exception of a feeble academy at Hillsborough, in all relating to education North Carolina was far behind the other States.[3]

The existence of slavery made the whites an aristocracy in fact and feeling, and drew the distinction of rank strongly at the color line ; but among the whites themselves the democratic sentiment prevailed. The law was entirely hostile to the system of entail, and among the settlers of the back districts there was an absolute hatred for the word servant.[4]

Society in North Carolina was that of Virginia on a much smaller and ruder scale, and with many of the most striking features of the older colony lacking. The people were very lawless, and averse to order and government,[5] although they had a keen perception of their own rights, as is shown by the passage of an act to secure the *Habeas Corpus* as early as the year 1715.[6] They fell in eagerly with the movement against England ; but there was also a numerous and active body of Tories, so that fierce internal dissensions were added to the miseries of civil war.

It is not to be wondered at that such a population and such a society produced no great leaders in the Revolution, or that the State, like its northern counterpart, Rhode Island, lagged behind the others in the adoption of the Constitution. But it is a strong proof of the vigor and soundness of the English race that this lawless, apathetic people finally raised themselves in the scale of civilization, and built up a strong and prosperous State.

---

[1] Watson, 1715 ; Lawson, p. 79.   [2] Iredell, 1764, 1766, 1770.
[3] Ibid., 1770 ; Bancroft, ii., 164 ; Martin, ii., 395 ; Memoirs of E. Watson, 1784.
[4] Iredell, 1715, Act for Intestate Estates ; also 1749, 1757.
[5] Crévecœur, p. 67 ; Smyth, i., 132 ; Byrd, i., 65 ; Iredell, Act against Sedition, etc., 1715.   [6] Iredell, 1715.

CHAPTER VII.

SOUTH CAROLINA FROM 1663 TO 1765.

As the coast of North Carolina was the scene of the first ill-starred attempts of Englishmen to settle in America, that of South Carolina was the scene of the first failures of the French to colonize the New World.   In the year 1562 Jean Ribault sailed with two ships,
1562.   under the auspices of Coligny, to explore the lately discovered regions of the West, and find if possible a spot where the foundation of a Huguenot state could be laid.   Ribault cruised along the coast of Florida, landing here and there, and finally left a company of thirty men at Beaufort, in South Carolina.   The men thus left behind were mere adventurers, soldiers of fortune, who erected a fort, but planted no corn ; who hoped to find treasures of gold and silver and sudden wealth, but had no capacity to found a state.   They quarrelled among themselves while they waited helplessly for supplies from France.   Ribault had not forgotten them ; but civil war made it impossible to attend to the small and distant colony, and at last the little band of settlers, half-starved, and having effected nothing, built a pinnace, ventured out to sea, and were picked up by an English vessel.   Before they could reach home, a fresh expedition had been determined upon, which sailed in 1564, commanded by René de
1564.   Laudonniere, an old companion of Ribault.   On the St. John's River they founded their settlement, and the old story was at once renewed.   They built a fort, and then their exertions ceased.   They longed to find masses of gold and silver, and listened eagerly to the flattering tales of the Indians.   Their spirit was that of the time— a mere lust for gold—and the usual consequences followed in quick succession ; quarrels among themselves, treachery toward the Indians, and war with them, and then famine, disease, and despair.   Just as they were losing all hope, Sir John Hawkins came in with his slavers, gave them relief, and sold them one of his ships.   They were pre-

paring to leave their settlement, when the long-expected fleet from
France arrived, commanded by Ribault. It would have seemed that
their trials were now at an end; but the worst enemy of all was still
to come in men of their own race inspired with burning religious
hatred. Within a week after the arrival of the fleet, Pedro Menendez
appeared at the mouth of the river Mary, with Spanish ships and
Spanish soldiers, to rid the New World of the heretic Huguenots.
Part of the French fleet got to sea, part was at Fort Caroline. Menendez marched overland to the fort and captured it; and then came
treachery and massacre of prisoners, the arrival of the French ships
and more treachery, more butchery of helpless prisoners, and thus the
extirpation of the Huguenots. The Spaniards followed up this bloody
beginning by founding St. Augustine, the first permanent settlement
of Europeans in the United States. France took no steps to avenge
1568. this awful wrong; but in 1568 retribution came at the hands
of Dominique de Gourgues, a gallant adventurer of the type
peculiar to the time, who landed in Florida, surprised the forts, and
put the Spaniards to the sword with as little mercy as they had shown
to his countrymen. The Spanish settlement survived the shock, and
struggled on, but never grew nor spread, nor came to any good. The
French efforts, however, had failed; and South Carolina, the scene of
their first attempt, relapsed into the wilderness, where savages wandered undisturbed. A century passed away before a new trial was made;
but this time the men were of another nation, one which had learned
the art of colonization, and had the natural talent of ruling races, for
founding new states, and governing distant provinces.

South Carolina was part of the magnificent territory which Charles
II. gave to Clarendon and Albemarle and others of his followers, and
for which Shaftesbury and Locke devised their famous constitution
—a monument of brilliant and futile theorizing. Several years passed away after the charter was granted before the lord proprietors did
anything more than contemplate the orders of nobility, and the elaborate system of government which Locke had produced. In 1667
William Sayle visited the coast, and his report was so favorable that
he was sent out two years later prepared to colonize. After landing
1670. at Beaufort, Sayle made his way northward, and finally fixed
his head-quarters on the Ashley river, while a settlement was
also started lower down, at the confluence of the Ashley and Cooper
rivers—the point to which the capital was subsequently removed, and
where the present city of Charleston was founded. Sayle soon

died, and was succeeded by Sir John Yeamans, one of the landgraves of the Locke constitutions, who ruled over the languishing colony for about four years, with little profit to anybody except himself.   Re-

1674.   turning to the Barbadoes in the year 1674, he was succeeded by Joseph West, the commercial agent of the proprietaries, under whose direction the first Assembly was called, and government organized on the practical English model, and without the least regard to Locke's beautiful and symmetrical scheme.   The early settlers were, as usual, for the most part broken-down adventurers and other vicious characters from London, with a sprinkling of sturdy colonists from the North, and some restless dissenters from the mother country.   The first necessity was order, and this West maintained, playing the same part in South Carolina that Dale had played in Virginia, and giving the settlement the opportunity to strike root and acquire permanence.   West was a shrewd, competent man, not over-scrupulous, but able to govern with a strong hand the disorderly elements about him.   He found the colony loaded with debt, and embroiled with the proprietaries; but he held it together, and steered through all difficulties, moving the capital, and fighting an Indian war, which he made profitable as well as successful by selling the prisoners into slavery.   This rather savage traffic, and his leaning to the dissenters, brought West into disfavor with the proprietaries, and he was removed,

1683.   to be replaced by Joseph Moreton, who called another Parliament or Assembly, which led to an outbreak of factious contention, and to the usurpation of all legislative power by the people of Charleston.   This new Parliament passed a law to prevent the prosecution of foreign debts, which so enraged the proprietaries that they removed Moreton, and West again came in for a brief term. The disorderly elements in South Carolina had now fairly got beyond control, and the factious turbulence which ensued would have wrecked the colony if it had not been for the years of comparative quiet during West's first term.   Besides the troubles arising from the character of the early settlers, there were many special subjects of conflict.   The religious controversies of the mother country were transferred to the colony, the only difference being that the dissenters, who were crushed at home, were here in a majority.   The Cavalier and Church party was favored by the proprietaries, and endeavored to keep all government in their own hands, but they were overborne by the dissenters, upon whom West appears to have leaned.   His removal and the supremacy of the Church party only led to still fiercer conflicts. Another subject of quarrel was the distribution of representation, which resulted finally in a seizure of all legislative power by the Charleston district, and the practical disfranchisement of the other counties. Still another struggle was caused by the immigration of the Huguenots—people of most excellent character, who settled chiefly in Craven county. The English settlers refused to give them representation or political rights, and excluded them for a time from the Assembly, although their cause was strenuously supported by the proprietaries. Still another source of trouble was found in the pirates infesting the coasts, and making their head-quarters at Charleston, where they were popular and well received because they spent money, and brought thither their ill-gotten gains to enrich the colony. These buccaneers preyed on Spanish commerce and Spanish possessions; the Spaniards retaliated naturally on the English settlements, and the South Carolinians prepared to invade Florida, and were only stopped by the proprietaries, who had no wish to see their enterprise bring on a war between Spain and England. Attempts were made by the government to stop this piracy; but the pirates were acquitted by the Charleston courts, and nothing effectual was done until the general suppression of piracy under William III. In the midst of all these contentions, it is almost impossible to describe the parties. Each new quarrel begot new factions. The body of the dissenters was sound, and so were those who supported the government; but between these was the old vicious and dissolute band of adventurers of broken fortunes, active and unscrupulous, opposed to every form of government and order, in league with the pirates, and ready to take advantage of every fresh conflict. In all this confusion governors came and went with extraordinary rapidity. West, Moreton, Kyle, Quarry,

1686. and Colleton succeeded each other within two years. Colleton called a Parliament on his accession, which resisted him to the utmost, and sent laws for approval to the proprietaries, which were indignantly rejected. At last parties began to crystallize into that of the proprietaries, and that of opposition to their rule. The latter prevailed. In the next Parliament they attacked Colleton more fiercely than ever, and he unwisely undertook to declare martial law. Open revolt followed. Sothel, fresh from his exploits in North Carolina, whence he had been driven out, appeared on the scene and usurped

1690. the government in his quality of Palatine. He resorted at once to his old extortion, corruption, and oppression, lost the confidence of the people, over whom he tyrannized, and was finally

11

obliged to withdraw and hide in Albemarle by the orders of the proprietaries, now thoroughly alive to his character. He was succeeded by Philip Ludwell, of Virginia, the first general Governor of both Carolinas. Ludwell proved incompetent, unable to deal with piracy, or to resist the popular factions, and was soon removed to make

1692. room for Thomas Smith, one of the leading planters. Smith did little better than his predecessor, but his term of office was marked by the introduction of rice—the future source of wealth to the colony—and by the abandonment of the attempt to establish the "Grand Model" of Locke. The Parliament became an Assembly, and Locke's fine scheme was at an end. Faction and disorder did not cease, however, and on Smith's representation that only a proprietor would suffice as Governor, Joseph Archdale, a Quaker, and one of the proprietaries, came out and assumed the government.

The party of the proprietaries, including the officials and the Churchmen, and the opposition, comprising the dissenters and the great majority of the settlers, were now fairly face to face, and feeling ran very high, particularly in regard to the quit-rents, which the colonists refused to pay, and which were a standing grievance and a constant cause of conflicts whenever efforts were made to collect

1695. them. Archdale was a good appointment. He was not only a dissenter, and therefore in sympathy with the colonists, but he was a wise, firm, and prudent man, and a good administrator. He came with almost unlimited powers, and set to work at once to allay dissensions. He conciliated the Assembly; appointed popular men to the Council; remitted arrears of quit-rents; examined grievances of all sorts; made peace with the Indians; and provided for the defence of the colony. So well did he do his work during his year of

1696. office, that his successor, Joseph Blake, a nephew of the great admiral, was able to rule peaceably in South Carolina for the rest of the century, and the colony gained a much needed breathing space, and time to give attention to the development of the great material resources of the country. Even under Blake, however, the colonists refused, in Assembly, to accept laws sent out by the proprietaries; but they adopted a liberal policy toward the French refugees, who were secured in their lands and rights, and rapidly assimilated with the English, as the Huguenots did in all the colonies. At the same time, religious toleration was assured to all Christians except Papists.

As the century opened, Blake's peaceful rule was closed by his

death, and James Moore became Governor. Political strife had already
1700. been renewed. The lower House, under the lead of Nicholas
Trott, an active and capable popular leader, denied to the
Governor and Council the right of appointing public officers, and refused to recognize their appointees. Governor Moore, a needy and
adventurous man who had pushed himself into office, found this quarrel on his hands, and matters were further complicated by the instructions of Lord Granville, the Palatine, to introduce the Established Church. To this the Assembly, controlled by the dissenters, opposed a stubborn and successful resistance, and they now regretted
that they had voted a salary to the rector of the Episcopal church.
Moore, however, was bent on gain, not on religion. He renewed the
infamous traffic in Indian slaves, and attempted to pass a bill giving
to himself the control of the Indian trade. This last measure was
defeated in Assembly, and Moore then threw himself into party politics. Nicholas Trott was brought over to government by the office
of attorney-general, and the elections were carried for the Governor
by force and fraud. The rupture between Spain and England, however, led Moore to turn his attention to another quarter. He invaded
Florida; but the expedition failed, and the only result was a crippling
public debt. An Indian war in which Moore next engaged was more
successful, and the tribes were routed and beaten.

Moore had hardly concluded his Indian war when Sir Nathaniel
1703. Johnson came out as his successor. The new Governor was
an incompetent and narrow-minded man, devoted to the interests of the Church. Backed by the officials, among whom Moore
and Trott were prominent, Johnson procured the passage of an act
excluding those who denied the authority of the Bible from the Assembly, and followed it up by another law excluding all who were
not members of the Church of England. The struggle now broke
forth with bitterness; the proprietaries, appealed to by both sides, under the lead of Granville, and, despite the remonstrance of Archdale,
supported the Governor, who, encouraged by his success, proceeded
to take steps for building churches, providing pastors, and for the
appointment of a commission of his own choosing to govern the
Church. The dissenters, numbering two-thirds of the population,
now went further, and took an appeal to the House of Lords. There
the exclusion of the dissenters and the act relating to religious worship were condemned, and the Queen ordered steps to be taken for
the revocation of the charter. While these matters were pending,

Johnson had an opportunity to show himself in a better light by successfully repulsing a French attack upon Charleston.   As the
legal proceedings were dragging along, Lord Granville died,
and was succeeded by Lord Craven, a moderate man, who sent out
Colonel Edward Tynte as Governor, with instructions so conciliatory that it seemed as if all differences might be healed;
but quiet had hardly been restored when Tynte unfortunately died,
and a factious and corrupt contest, resulting in the election of
Robert Gibbes, took place for the governorship.   Gibbes was,
however, soon displaced by the proprietaries, who appointed Charles
Craven, brother of Lord Craven, and a representative of his
moderate policy, Governor; and under his temperate and
wise rule the colony obtained a brief respite from domestic discord.
His administration was marked, however, by two Indian wars — one
with the Tuscaroras for the relief of North Carolina, and the other
and more extensive one with the Yamasees.   In both conflicts Craven was successful, and the South Carolinians, officers and men, behaved well; but the result was to sink the province still further in debt, and render the paper currency and the raising of
money to meet obligations burning political questions.   Craven returned to England after a term of four years, leaving Robert
Daniel in charge of the province until Robert Johnson, the
son of the former Governor of that name, arrived.

1706.

1708.

1710.

1712.

1716.

1717.

Johnson, unlike his father, was a good governor and competent man,
besides possessing a genuine popularity.   But no amount of popularity or ability was sufficient to enable any man to deal successfully with
public affairs in South Carolina.   The proprietary government was
radically vicious, and, whether its policy was good or bad, it invariably
ran counter to the wishes of the people, and there was nothing to sustain it against the effects of popular resentment.   The attempts of the
proprietaries to force the Established Church upon the colonists had
produced a conflict of which the effects were still felt, and Johnson
came out hampered with instructions which seemed designed to take
all power from the Assembly.   Not only did the King disapprove the
law for duty on imports, the only means of sinking the debt, but the
proprietaries asserted the right to repeal all acts of the Assembly, and
did repeal two, generally and rightly esteemed of great value—one to
regulate elections, and another to regulate the Indian trade.   This sort
of interference was bad enough; but there were other and worse grievances.   The proprietaries encouraged every oppressive scheme put for-

ward by the officials, and strove to wring all possible revenue from the province, while they utterly neglected it, and declined to give any help in the Indian wars. This refusal to aid the colonists led them, of course, to appeal to the Crown, and to look more and more to the strong arm of the sovereign for shelter and protection. Lands won by the sword from the Indians, and thrown open to immigrants by the Assembly, were torn from the settlers, and distributed in baronies and seigniories among the proprietors. Another and still worse grievance was to be found in the condition of the courts. Nicholas Trott, the popular leader of early days, had improved his opportunities since he had been bought by the attorney-generalship, and had risen to be chief-justice. By visiting England, he had obtained the confidence of the proprietaries, and control of their secretary, to whom the management of affairs was very largely intrusted. In this way Trott became not only chief-justice, judge of the vice-admiralty court, president of the Council, and sometimes acting Governor, but he was mainly instrumental in causing the ruinous policy of the proprietaries.

With matters in this unpromising state, new burdens were thrust upon South Carolina. The pirates, who in earlier days had been welcomed in Charleston, now ruined the commerce of the city, and sapped the prosperity of the province. They were under the lead of Teach, "Black Beard," whose head-quarters were in North Carolina. Determined efforts were at last necessary to suppress them; and Johnson opened the way by sending out Rhett, who captured one of the principal captains, and by going himself in pursuit of another, who was finally seized after a bloody fight. Johnson's personal bravery and enterprise won for him great popularity; but these expeditions produced more debt, and required more taxation, and thus led to renewed and bitter controversy. The conduct of Trott, too, had finally become so outrageous, and the courts so bad, that the Assembly and the bar sent out one of the Council, Francis Yonge, to remonstrate with the proprietaries. Their appeal was treated with contempt, and brought fresh instructions to Johnson to enforce the rights and prerogatives of the proprietaries, and persist in every way in the policy already entered upon.

This brought matters to a point where a trifle would cause revolution, and the needed impulse came from the dread of a Spanish invasion. Johnson wished to put the province in a state of defence, and asked for money. The Assembly pointed to the tax on imports, and were told it was repealed. They declared they would enforce it, and

Trott swore that the courts would sustain those who refused to pay. The members of the Assembly now formed associations; and when Johnson called out the militia, to prepare for the Spaniards, the troops revolted and went over to the Assembly, which became a convention, elected James Moore Governor, chose a council, and made themselves masters of the government. The practical deposi-

1719. tion of Johnson, although he tried to maintain himself for a year or two longer, and even ventured a futile attack on Charleston, attracted, of course, immediate attention in England, where the action of the colonists harmonized too well with the general policy of converting all charter and proprietary provinces into royal governments, to be neglected. The Crown interfered; the old inquiry of Anne's time was revived, and the attorney-general ordered to look into the affairs of the proprietaries and find out the extent of their misgovernment. If everything else failed, the omission of the proprietaries to spread the Christian religion among the savages could be used for the abrogation of the charter, of which proselyting the heathen was nominally,

1721. at least, a main object. In the mean time, Sir Francis Nicholson was sent out as provisional Governor. Whatever Nicholson's faults and failings had been in the other colonies over which he had ruled—and they had been neither few nor small—he was now, at least, a man of wide experience in colonial administration, and he had learned many lessons. Coming, as he did, backed with the vast power of the Crown, to South Carolina, which had hardly known anything but turbulence and insurrection, he was received with joy, and with a deep sense of relief. The proprietary party sank out of sight, and Nicholson, free to turn his attention to the general good, treated successfully with the Indians, did much for religion and the Church, and even made vigorous exertions to introduce some sort of public education. He withdrew after a term of four years, leaving the government in the hands of Arthur Middleton. On this change the proprietary party immediately revived in the province, and in England claimed the right first of appointing a Governor, although the writ of *quo warranto* was actually issued, and then demanded the right of consenting to the nomination by the Crown. Fortunately for South Caro-

1729. lina, the contest was too unequal and too hopeless to be persisted in, and after a year or two the proprietaries sold both Carolinas to the Crown.

In pursuance of Nicholson's policy, Sir Alexander Cumming was sent to push further negotiations with the Indians. Returning to

England, he brought six chiefs with him, who went back in the fol-
1731. lowing year with Sir Robert Johnson, the first royal Governor, who, now that he was freed from his duty to the proprietaries, was received with enthusiasm by the colonists, whose favor he
had retained through all his conflicts with them. With the establishment of the royal government the whole condition of public affairs in South Carolina underwent a marked change. The form of
government was that common in the royal provinces—of Governor,
Council, and Assembly—the former appointed, the latter elected. But
the sense of permanence and security given by the Crown was the chief
advantage derived by the colony. The restraint upon the exportation
of rice was removed, and a bounty on hemp allowed by Parliament.
The arrears of quit-rents were remitted, and the bills of credit were
continued. Cannon were sent out, forts were built, troops were stationed at Charleston, and ships-of-war were granted to defend their
commerce. These measures and the strength of the new government
drew the attention of English merchants to the province, and trade
increased with great rapidity, while large bodies of immigrants, including Scotch, Irish, and Swiss, came out to settle. Land, now easily
obtainable, rose quickly in value, and was taken up by the planters in
large tracts, too large, indeed, for the general prosperity. The establishment of the colony of Georgia did much to increase the safety of
the colony by beginning a line of settlements on the southern frontier, where the attacks of the Spaniards and Indians had hitherto been
a constant danger.

Although the fall of the weak and ill-conducted government of the
proprietaries had put a stop to the bitter and violent factions of South
Carolina, parties were by no means extinct, and the opposition to government, which had achieved a substantial victory by the transfer of
the province to the Crown, soon became active. The too rapid taking of lands received the royal veto, and the Assembly were soon engaged in a vigorous contest with the courts and the law officers of the
Crown, and even refused to allow the writ of *Habeas Corpus* in favor
of those whom they committed for resistance to their will. The Assembly also insisted on voting the salary of the Governor annually,
1735. which caused a steady conflict with that officer. Even Johnson's popularity could not prevail here, although when he died
the Assembly erected a handsome monument to his memory.

Johnson was succeeded by Thomas Broughton — one of the old
leaders against the proprietaries—and the popular party was now in

full possession, and under his rather weak rule they still further in-
flated the currency by the issue of one hundred thousand pounds in
bills of credit. The unchecked sway of the Assembly seemed, indeed,
to threaten a recurrence of the old factions, and a consequent diminution in the prosperity of the colony. But Broughton's term
1737-
1738. of office was not prolonged. He died after two years of service, and Samuel Horsley, who was appointed to succeed him,
died before leaving England; so that the government devolved on
William Bull, President of the Council, and Lieutenant-governor.
Other events of a more serious nature also intervened to turn the
attention of the colonists from political questions. Oglethorpe invaded Florida, and South Carolina troops were sent to join him.
The expedition failed; the friendly relations with Georgia changed to
dislike and suspicion; and while the colony was thus harassed by the
danger from the Spaniards, a desperate negro insurrection oc-
1740. curred, which was only suppressed after much bloodshed; and
this was in turn followed by a fire in Charleston, which laid a large
part of the city in ashes. Despite these drawbacks, and the great increase of debt, the colony throve, and grew rich from the rice trade,
and from the production of indigo, which had been lately introduced.
Many of the planters made large fortunes, or rather large incomes,
and money began to be freely spent, and great luxury displayed at
Charleston.

The Spanish war was still a cause of anxiety, and a descent on the
coast was much feared. Oglethorpe, however, succeeded in repulsing
the Spaniards at Frederica, and the dread of invasion and of
1742. negro revolt gradually diminished. In the mean time, the controversy regarding the Crown-lands had gone on with increasing acrimony. The agent of the Crown, sent out by the government to investigate the matter, had been thwarted and foiled by the Governor;
and the popular party was supposed to be encouraged by James Glen,
a South Carolina proprietor who had been appointed Governor, but
had lingered in England to care for the interests of the province. At
last Glen arrived at Charleston, where he was warmly received
1743. as a friend of the colony. He was reproached in England
with betraying the interests of the Crown; but notwithstanding all
this, so ineradicable was the hostility between the Assembly and their
Governor, that Glen soon found occasion to complain of the encroachments of the Council, and the levelling principles of the popular representatives. Glen was, however, a good Governor, and his contests

with the Assembly do not appear to have interfered for many years with the interests of the province. He cemented and extended the Indian treaties, and obtained additional troops from England to secure the colony from Spanish invasion and negro insurrection. The development of the colony now progressed steadily and rapidly, and settlements were extended in all directions. The prosperity was unchecked; and the only trouble of importance arose from the illicit trade which sprang up here as elsewhere under the fostering influence of the oppressive laws.

This happy condition of affairs, however, began to be darkened after the middle of the century by the growth of the French power, and by the extension of the French posts on the west and south. Distant as South Carolina was from Canada, the danger caused by the French system of Indian alliances began to be felt even there. Governor Glen, with wise prevision, went in person among the Cherokees, strengthened the old treaties, made new ones, and obtained the cession of a large tract of territory, of which he took advantage **1753.** by erecting forts on the frontier in the immediate neighborhood of the Indians, and well adapted to protect the outlying settlements. When, however, he went a step farther, and attempted to raise money in support of the war between England and France, his normal quarrel with the Assembly reached such a height that the grant of supplies was refused; and South Carolina, as was only too common in the American colonies during the whole of the war, remained entirely inactive. In the following year, however, Glen retired, and a new governor, William Lyttelton, came out from **1756.** England. He succeeded in soothing the Assembly, obtained a grant, enlisted men, and got additional troops from the other provinces.

For a time these preparations seemed needless; and distance from the seat of war and Glen's treaties appeared sufficient to save the province. But at last this good fortune terminated. The Cherokees, in accordance with their treaties, had followed Forbes in his expedition to Fort Du Quesne. On their return, they became involved in a quarrel with the backwoods settlers of Virginia and of the Carolinas, whose horses they stole, and several men were killed on both sides. Their chiefs, however, desired peace, but were roughly treated by Lyttelton, who marched against them; and, having thoroughly exas- **1760.** perated them, and made a worthless peace, returned to Charleston with his army broken by disease. The Cherokees, maddened

by this treatment, and by the murder of some hostages, and instigated by French emissaries, began a general war, ravaged the frontier, and threw the whole province into a state of terror. At this
juncture Lyttelton, promoted to the governorship of Jamaica, departed; and the government devolved on his lieutenant, William Bull,
a son of the former Governor of that name, who was a man of position, talent, and education, and who continued, except during the
brief administrations of Thomas Boone, Lord Charles Montague, and
Lord William Campbell, at the head of affairs until the Revolution.

The provincial levies were at once united with some royal troops
sent by Amherst, and a bloody but indecisive campaign followed.
Soon after the royal troops were withdrawn to the North, and the
province was again left to face the scourge of Indian warfare alone.
The Cherokees succeeded in capturing one of the forts, and butchered most of the prisoners. This led to renewed application for
troops, which were sent under Colonel Grant, who, aided by fresh provincial levies, devastated the Indian country, and succeeded at last
in bringing them to terms. The war was an unnecessary and
1761. injurious one, resulting in great loss of life and property, and
might have been avoided by a more moderate conduct on the part of
Lyttelton. Although peace was made, the friendship of the Cherokees was lost, and the smouldering embers blazed forth again when
revolution came.

Relieved from the stress of war, South Carolina, one of the richest
of the colonies, through her staples of rice and indigo, made rapid
strides. Her agriculture and trade alike increased, while immigration
was strenuously encouraged, and new settlements were pushed rapidly
to the westward. Among these settlers in the back country were
many loose characters, who harassed the farmers and planters by horse-
stealing and other depredations. All the courts sat in Charleston, and
the local justices were either inefficient or in league with the thieves.
This state of affairs led the most respectable of the inhabitants to
form associations known as Regulators, who took the law into
1764. their own hands, and a good deal of rough-and-ready justice,
and much complaint, were the results. To settle matters, Lord Charles
Montague, then acting Governor, sent one Scovil out to deal
1766. with the difficulties. Scovil undertook to treat the Regulators
as rioters, and arrested two of them, whom he sent to Charleston.
This injudicious course came very near causing civil war, and both
parties were ready to appeal to arms. They fortunately refrained,

however, and the establishment of district or circuit courts by the Assembly gave the Regulators an opportunity, of which they availed themselves, to bring criminals to justice in the ordinary way. The controversy, however, engendered much bitterness of feeling, which found vent during the Revolution, when the Regulators espoused the patriotic side, and the former followers of Scovil became Tories.

1767.

With this exception, peace reigned in South Carolina after the French war. The colony was more closely connected by her trade with the mother country than many of the others, and the general spirit was one of loyalty to the Crown and attachment to the constitution. But as their whole history shows, the people of South Carolina were extremly jealous of any interference with their affairs, of any manifestation of external power, and of anything like oppression. They had, moreover, the usual grievances arising from the laws of trade and the restrictions on industry. The plan of taxing America, therefore, excited great alarm among them, and the Stamp Act aroused deep hostility, especially among the Regulators of the back country then engaged in a sharp conflict with the government. The deep feeling awakened by the new policy soon found expression. The Assembly was in session when the Massachusetts Circular arrived, and after a prolonged debate responded to the call. Two of the future leaders of the Revolution appeared at New York in the Stamp Act Congress—Christopher Gadsden and John Rutledge. The prompt action of the Assembly was a decisive measure in bringing about that Congress, and in founding the union of States, of which South Carolina then became a part.

1765.

Chapter VIII.

SOUTH CAROLINA IN 1765.

In South Carolina we pass beyond the last traces of northern influence, and the Virginian type of manners and society becomes wholly southern, while all the essential peculiarities of the Virginian group of colonies are intensified, and are here not only predominant but reign alone.

The general configuration of the province did not differ greatly from that of North Carolina. The coast was low and sandy, and the land near the sea of inferior quality, while the interior was covered with vast forests intersected with many fine rivers, and broken by swamps and savannas. The low lands along the river bottoms were extremely rich, and the soil of the whole province, except for the stretches of pine barrens, was of good quality, and improved steadily as it rose with a gradual ascent from the sea-coast to the mountains on the western frontier. The climate, although very variable, and exhibiting great extremes of heat and cold, was distinctly tropical in character, usually intensely warm, and marked by violent thunder-storms and wild hurricanes.[1]

The population, consisting of a few thousands at the beginning of the century, had risen at the time of the Revolution to between one hundred and fifty and two hundred thousand. The increase was largely due to the constant importations of African slaves at the rate of three thousand yearly, so that the blacks were to the whites in the proportion of two or three to one—a circumstance which had a deep effect upon the social condition as well as the political future of the colony.[2]

---

[1] For contemporary accounts of soil, climate, etc., see Smyth's Tour, i., 202; ii., 70, 73, 74; and Glen's Answers to the Lords of Trade, 1749, in Doc. relating to South Carolina, Weston, pp. 69, 71, 79.

[2] The estimates of population in South Carolina vary greatly, and the statement given above is the result of a careful comparison of the different and differing au-

The dominant element among the whites was English; but it was neither so strong nor so numerous as in the other colonies, and the foreign elements were not only many and varied, but one or two of them almost equalled the English in power, and contributed many of the political and social leaders. In the early days, writes Governor Archdale, "many dissenters went over, men of estates, as also many whom the variety of fortune had engaged to seek their fortunes in the New World. * * * The most desperate fortunes first ventured over to break the ice, being generally the ill-livers of the pretended Churchmen."[1] The wretched government of the charter checked immigration, which revived under Archdale, and brought people from New England and Scotland, and dissenters from all parts of the English dominions.[2] At a very early period an inconsiderable number of Dutch settlers came from New York, and a few years later the immigration of French Protestants began, which increased after the revocation of the Edict of Nantes, in the year 1685, to large proportions. This Huguenot element was larger in South Carolina than elsewhere, and by their standing and success attracted many of their brethren from the northern colonies. They formed an excellent and influential part of the population, were wealthy, and of high social position, and their descendants were conspicuous in the history of the State.[3] In the year 1696 a congregation came from Dorchester, Massachusetts, under the leadership of the Rev. Joseph Lord; and there was always more or less emigration from Virginia, Pennsylvania, and North Carolina, which strengthened and improved the colony. The policy of religious toleration, finally adopted, offered strong inducements for settlement to dissenters of all nations, and there was, in consequence, a large German immigration, principally composed of Palatines, which continued until it was stopped by Frederick the Great. These Germans were thrifty and industrious, and a good population, although they clung for a long time to their own speech, and although among the Palatines there was much ignorance and superstition. After the

---

thorities. The fullest data are given in Mills's Statistics of South Carolina, p. 173, and ff. Other estimates may be found in Smyth, i., 207; The Case of the Dissenters in South Carolina, 1703; Glen's Report to the Lords of Trade, Hist. Coll., Weston; Glen's Description of South Carolina; Milligan's Account of South Carolina, in Carroll's Hist. Coll., ii., 24; Purry's Account of South Carolina, in Carroll's Hist. Coll., ii., 128; Von Reck's Journal, and Bolzius.

[1] Archdale's Description of South Carolina, Carroll, ii., 100.   [2] Ibid.
[3] Letter from South Carolina, p. 41, in Bishop Kennett's Tracts.

risings of 1715 and 1745, bodies of Highlanders came out and settled in the back districts, chiefly as small farmers and Indian traders. The largest and most steady immigration, however, came from the north of Ireland. These English or Scotch-Irish, with English names, and of the Presbyterian sect, were, like the Huguenots, a strong and flourishing element in the community. They founded some of the most important families, and produced some of the most brilliant leaders of South Carolina.[1]

From this brief enumeration of the varied sources from which the population of South Carolina was drawn, it may be readily inferred that the great majority of her people dissented in religious belief from the Church of England. The establishment of the English Church, therefore, and the general religious policy and condition of religion, form a most curious chapter in the history of the province.

The charter of 1669, providing for the support of the English Church by the govenment, also guaranteed to the colonists religious toleration. More settlers were attracted by the latter clause than the former; and political power remained with the dissenters. No clergy of the English Church came to the colony for many years after its foundation; and it was not until 1681 that an Episcopal church was built in Charleston by private benevolence.[2] Jealousy of the growth and prosperity of the Huguenot population induced an intolerance toward them, and a restraint of their freedom, which led to complaints on their part, and thence, in 1697, to an act securing liberty of worship to all Protestant sects,[3] while in the following year a grant was made by the Assembly for the maintenance of the single Episcopal church, the ruling dissenters, under the lead of Governor Blake, cheerfully giving their support to the act.[4] This policy of a true and broad toleration met with general acquiescence, but it was of short duration. The question of religion became involved in the bitter, turbulent, and factious political struggles of the time. Although two-thirds of the people, and those the richest and most commercial, were dissenters, a small and corrupt set of officials, sustained by a faction of High-Churchmen, succeeded by means of high-handed measures, and by frauds and riots at the elections, in securing to them-

[1] In regard to the elements of population in South Carolina, see Doc. relating to South Carolina, Weston, Glen's Report, p. 82, 166 ; Mills's Statistics, p. 173, and ff.; O'Neall's Annals of Newbury, pp. 27, 32.

[2] Anderson's Hist. of Colonial Church, ii., 328, 461.   [3] Ibid., 465.

[4] Case of the Dissenters in Carolina, p. 11 ; Mills, p. 216.

selves control of the government. They at once used their power to
effect the political ruin of the dissenters; and in the year 1704 passed
acts for the organization of the Church, vesting the governing power
in the hands of a lay commission, for the exclusion or disfranchisement of dissenters, and against occasional conformity. This policy
pleased no one. The members of the Church disliked the lay commission; the dissenters were, of course, outraged beyond endurance,
and opposition also found vent among the London merchants, who saw
their trade deeply injured by this intolerance. The dissenters at once
sent an agent to England, who laid the case before Parliament. The
House of Lords passed resolutions condemning all the acts, the Queen,
on address, declared them null and void, and in 1706 they were repealed by the Assembly.[1]

Even during this brief period of absolute rule the dominant spirit
in religious matters seems to have been of a Puritanic cast. A strong
law was passed against blasphemy; and any one denying the Trinity,
the truth of religion, or the Scriptures, was disfranchised for the first
offence, and outlawed for the second.[2] The Sunday laws of a later
time partook of the same character, and showed at the same time the
real weakness of the Church party. Attendance upon some church
was required under a penalty; trade, work, and sports, as well as
drunkenness, were prohibited on the Sabbath; innkeepers were forbidden to entertain any but genuine travellers, and no writ or process
could be legally served.[3]

The obnoxious legislation of 1704 did not strengthen the Established Church, which had for many years but a feeble growth. It
retained, however, its organization and unquestioned recognition as
the State Church, and its ascendency was maintained for the next
seventy years. The province was divided politically into parishes,
and in each there was nominally at least a vestry and church-wardens
to whom certain functions of local government were assigned. They
had charge of the poor, assessed and collected the poor rates, and
also superintended the elections.[4] All the clergy, dissenting and conforming, were elected by the people, and were men of excellent character. The latter were paid by the Assembly by funds raised from
the custom duties, and were sent out by the society for the propa-

[1] Party Tyranny in South Carolina, 1705; Case of the Dissenters of Carolina,
1704; Mills, p. 216; Grimke, Laws of South Carolina, 1703; Archdale's Description of South Carolina, Carroll, ii., 117; Anderson, iii., 478.

[2] Grimke, 1703–'4. [3] Ibid., 1712. [4] Ibid., 1712, 1721, 1722.

gation of the Gospel. They were hard-working men, who taught schools, and labored also among the negroes; and the respect they inspired is shown by the funds bequeathed to them by benevolent persons for educational and religious purposes. A general spirit of toleration prevailed after the early conflicts, and its good effects were seen in the spread of religion, and in the high character of the ministry.

In the middle of the eighteenth century Governor Glen estimated the members of the Established Church as forming nearly one-half the population; but this is probably an official exaggeration, and there can be little question that the dissenting sects were much the most numerous. In Charleston the Established Church had two handsome brick churches, while there were six meeting-houses of dissenting sects, besides an assembly of Quakers and another of Jews. In the year 1749 the ministers were paid by the Assembly, but there were sixteen parishes, and these notoriously incomplete. The State Church was, in fact, but a small sect, controlling probably not a fifth of the population. The largest dissenting sect was the Presbyterian, supported by the Scotch-Irish immigration. The Quakers, who played an important part at the beginning, gradually dwindled, and finally became extinct, owing to their disowning slave-holders, and to their courageous opposition to slavery. The clergy of the Established Church, differing widely from those of Virginia and Maryland in their zeal, character, and steady work, were no less distinct in their politics. Not one-quarter of the Virginian or Maryland ministers, who were almost all bitter Tories, espoused the patriot side; while in South Carolina the case was exactly reversed, and her excellent ministers, as a rule, sided with the opposition to England. They thus retained their hold upon the affections of the people, and preserved their organization through the Revolution. The clergy of all sects in South Carolina formed the principal, if not the only, learned class; their position in society was respectable; and they confined themselves to their professional duties, leaving to laymen the conduct of pleasure and business.[1]

The early government was under the charter of Charles II., and nominally, at least, in conformity with the famous constitutions drawn

---

[1] For this account of Church and sects in South Carolina, see Doc. relating to South Carolina, Weston, Glen's Report, pp. 80, 178; De Brahm, ibid., p. 178; Mills, p. 216; Glen's Description, p. 78; Missionaries sent to Carolina, Humphreys, in Carroll, ii.; O'Neall, Annals of Newbury, p. 32.

by Shaftesbury. The rule of the proprietaries was generally bad and unpopular, and at one time it was found necessary to pass a law to punish any one speaking against the lords proprietary;[1] but the bad government went on, the people became more and more discontented, and remonstrated more and more frequently.[2] At last the colony was turned over to the King, and the government assumed the form usual in the Crown provinces. It consisted of a Governor and Council of twelve, constituting the Upper House, appointed by the King, and an Assembly, chosen by the people. The Governor was much less powerful than was commonly the case; and although Glen, who held the office, wished for more power, he felt obliged to confess that on general grounds it was very well as it was. The Governor, of course, represented the Crown, and could convoke, prorogue, and dissolve the Assembly. He also had the power of reprieve, until instructions could be received in the case from England. His weakness was due to his slender patronage, which extended only to justices of the peace and officers of the militia. The important offices were granted by the Crown, and included, besides the Council, the judiciary, the secretary of the province, the attorney, and the surveyor-general, and some lesser but more lucrative offices, such as the provost marshal and clerk of the Crown and Pleas—sinecures held at one time by the dramatist, Richard Cumberland, who made various attempts to capitalize them by sale to the Assembly.

The Assembly was chosen by the freeholders voting by ballot, and the members were required to own five hundred acres of land and ten slaves, or be worth one thousand pounds in land, houses, and other property. They represented the parishes in theory according to a proportional system, but the parishes were very unequally divided; some towns which were entitled to representation had none; and the Charleston precinct returned a majority of the delegates, and absorbed the lion's share of the political power. The Assembly held the purse-strings, and possessed the patronage of all the financial offices, such as the public treasurer, the county controllers, the powder receiver, and Indian commissioner.[3]

Revenue was raised chiefly from general duties on everything but the manufactures of Great Britain, and from exported deer-skins.

---

[1] Grimke, 1691.   [2] Party Tyranny in Carolina, 1705.

[3] In regard to organization of government, see Doc. relating to South Carolina; Glen's Report, pp. 80, 105, 127; Grimke, 1721; Milligan's Account, 1763, Carroll, ii., 465.

There was also a direct tax on realty and personalty. The quit-rents, when they could be collected, were paid to the Crown, to which the duties on imported negroes and liquors were likewise granted by the Assembly. The salaries and ordinary expenses of government absorbed the revenue; but both were insignificant, and taxation was, as a rule, very light and little felt.[1]

The judiciary was arranged in a rough way upon the English model, but without any attention to legal acquirements on the part of the judges. There was a court of chancery, consisting of the Governor and Council, and an admiralty court, appointed by the Lords Commissioners of Admiralty. There was also a court of common pleas, holding quarter-sessions in the districts, and sitting once a year as a court of oyer and terminer. The judges of this court were appointed by the Crown, and transacted most of the legal business of the colony, sitting in Charleston exclusively until within a few years of the Revolution. There were also small county or justices' courts, to try petty causes, and attend to the punishment of slaves and servants. These inferior courts meted out justice in a very rough fashion, it is said, especially in the back districts. The power of punishment for contempt appears to have been freely exercised, and a fine of five pounds inflicted upon the judge and county attorney for a personal encounter in the court-room gives a curious idea of the backwoods administration of justice.[2]

The common law prevailed, and at an early day an act was passed for the *Habeas Corpus*, and certain English statutes, beginning with Magna Charta, were declared to be in force by the Assembly. The criminal laws were very severe, and crime was on the increase, owing chiefly, in all probability, to the savage ignorance of the negroes. Criminals were punished in the simple fashion of the day—by whipping, stocks, and pillory—and any form of restraint, indeed, was probably out of the question, if we may judge from the stories of the prisoners breaking out of the court-room and fighting in the yard.[3]

There was much litigation; and as the administration of justice was centred at Charleston, a good class of lawyers began to grow up in the years preceding the Revolution, and the profession was both re-

---

[1] Glen's Report, p. 98; Grimke, 1731; Glen's Description.

[2] Smyth, i., 206, 207; Glen's Report, p. 80; De Brahm, p. 178; Mills, p. 192; Grimke, 1721, 1736; O'Neall, Annals of Newbury, p. 18.

[3] Grimke, 1712; Rochefoucauld, i., 563, 565; O'Neall, p. 18.

spectable and promising, although still numerically small.[1] Other professions fared less well than those of law and divinity. We hear of no physicians, and the practice of medicine was probably, for the most part, in rude and unskilled hands. There was no navy and no regular army; but, owing to the dread of negro insurrection, the militia, numbering eight thousand, were efficient, well-drilled, and well-armed.[2]

The occupations of the great body of the inhabitants were agricultural. Almost all the whites were planters or farmers. The country was roughly but effectually cleared by cutting or burning the trees, the former being the most common and profitable, as the lumber was exported. The chief product was rice, introduced about the year 1694. Its cultivation rapidly increased, owing to the great profits— one slave raising more than his own value in a year; but by the middle of the century the staple was over-planted, the zenith of great prosperity had passed, and low prices ruled. The loss of income thus occasioned was made good at the time, however, by the introduction of indigo, which soon nearly equalled rice in value and importance. Corn and cotton were also raised in large quantities, and cattle multiplied with great rapidity. Many planters had herds of two or three thousand head, which ran wild, and were penned and counted yearly; and owing to this inexpensive mode of grazing, large quantities of beef were exported with great profit to the West Indies.[3]

The prosperity consequent upon these productions was of late date. Under the rule of the proprietaries, not only the evils incident to a new settlement—such as disease, fires, and Indian wars—had to be encountered, but the wretched and corrupt condition of the government, and the violent and factious divisions of party, as well as the pirates, who infested the coast, ruined trade, and were connived at by government officials, retarded all progress. Yet even then those of the colonists who were not given up to dissipation rapidly accumulated property.[4] After the establishment of the firm and well-ordered royal government, rapid growth and prosperity ensued. The

---

[1] Rochefoucauld, i., 563.

[2] De Brahm, Doc. relating to South Carolina, Weston; Dr. Milligan's Account of South Carolina, Carroll, ii., 465.

[3] Smyth, ii., 53, 70, 78, 79; Doc. relating to South Carolina, Glen's Report; De Brahm, ibid.; Mills, p. 160; Glen's Description, p. 95; Stephens's Journal, ii., 129.

[4] Purry's Account of South Carolina, Carroll, ii., 128; Proceedings of South Carolina in 1719, ibid., p. 146; Mills, p. 160; Grimke, 1685, 1703; Archdale's Description of Carolina, Carroll, ii.

pirates were broken up, and the rice trade began. In the decade from 1730 to 1740 exports and imports doubled; and, although there was some falling off after the decline in rice set in, they amounted at the period of the Revolution to six or seven hundred thousand pounds annually, and employed between one hundred and fifty and two hundred vessels. Much of this was due to the better system of trade in South Carolina than in the other members of the southern group. Some few planters attempted to save money by exporting directly; but the great majority sold their products to the Charleston merchants, who shipped them to England, the northern colonies, Europe, and the West Indies. This made trade much sounder than in Virginia and Maryland, but did not rid South Carolina of the evils of depreciated currency—dating back to Queen Anne's wars—or of the total lack of industries. Not only every luxury and every manufactured article was brought from England, but even objects of prime necessity were imported. During a large part of the colonial period the province was dependent on New York and Philadelphia for flour and bacon. Every form of skilled labor was high-priced, and mechanics were in great demand; and the carrying trade was wholly in the hands of British and New England merchants. There were, in fact, absolutely no industries of any kind, except those of agriculture and a profitable traffic with the Indians, carried on by the Charleston merchants, who transported their goods to the West on pack-horses.[1] These merchants, who did so much for the well-being of the state, were generally rich men, who did not speculate, but bought from the planters, and carried on a strictly legitimate trade.[2] Yet they were regarded as an inferior class by the planters, who formed the bulk of the population, and absolutely controlled the state.[3] There were, indeed, but two classes in South Carolina—the planters and the slaves—forming as pure and despotic an aristocracy as could well be imagined. With the exception of the Scotch Highlanders, who farmed in the back districts, small landholders and poor whites were few in number, and the indented servants were not numerous.

---

[1] Smyth, i., 208; ii., 53, 66, 70, 84, 86; Doc. relating to South Carolina, Glen, pp. 71, 82, 190; De Brahm, ibid.; Mills, p. 160; Grimke, 1721, 1746, 1759; Glen's Description, for account of currency, and also, p. 80, for labor; Purry's Account, Carroll, ii.; Proceedings of South Carolina, 1719, ibid., p. 146, as to frauds in currency; also Von Reck's Journal, 1733, and Bolzius.

[2] Rochefoucauld, i., 577; Glen's Description, p. 78, and summary of occupations.

[3] Ibid., ii., 175.

The condition of this last class did not differ essentially from that in the other colonies. They were generally "redemptioners," who paid their passage to America by selling themselves into service for a term of years. Their masters were at liberty to whip them; they were punished with additional years of servitude if they ran away; no one could trade with them; and their travel was strictly limited. At the expiration of this degraded servitude they received a certificate of freedom, and were soon lost among the poor whites and small farmers.[1]

Far more important was the still lower class of African slaves. They greatly outnumbered all other elements of population, and were the foundation and support of the whole industrial and economical system. They numbered more than one hundred thousand, of whom about eighty per cent. were employed on plantations, and the remainder as house servants, and in various menial capacities. They performed all the hard work of the colony. They cost about forty pounds each; and as they produced in one year more rice or indigo than sufficed to pay their entire value, the profit upon them was very large, and the temptation to get all the work possible out of them very great. The culture of both rice and indigo was sickly, and this, joined to unremitting toil, wore them down rapidly, so that they became prematurely old and shrivelled, presenting a marked contrast to the slaves of Virginia. The slave legislation of South Carolina resembles, in a general way, that of the northern colonies; but a close examination reveals some very characteristic differences. Mixture of races was prevented, and the taint of black blood rendered hopeless by laws making all negro, mulatto, or mestizo children follow the condition of the mother, unless freed before the court. Slaves could be baptized, were not to be beaten without cause, and excessive punishments were prohibited, and the hours of labor fixed—limitations which show very forcibly the habits of the masters. No slave could be absent from his plantation without a ticket, and any white person was authorized to stop a slave, examine and beat him, and, if he resisted, could lawfully kill him. All persons were empowered to disperse meetings of blacks, and those hurt in the common cause—the pursuit of fugitive slaves—were to be rewarded at public expense. A justice and two freeholders could try a slave for any offence, and, against slaves and free negroes, the evidence of other slaves and of Indians was

---

[1] Grimke, 1744.

admissible. Heavy penalties were exacted from them for all crimes, and especially for conspiracy. They could neither buy, nor sell, nor hire horses, nor travel in companies of more than seven, and were forbidden to learn to write. The wilful murder of a slave was expiated by a fine of seven hundred pounds, and manslaughter by one of three hundred and fifty. Those who harbored fugitives were heavily fined; while enticing a slave away was, until a late period of the colony, punished by death, which remained the penalty for stealing them. No planter was allowed to leave his plantation except in charge of a white, and the law required that slaves should never be left alone. All whites were obliged to go armed to church, and patrols from the militia were constantly on duty to search for arms, and give all stray negroes whom they met twenty lashes.[1] This legislation shows in every line the atmosphere of terror in which the planters lived, and there is a careful ferocity and well-planned barbarity which is wholly wanting to the northward. But the grounds for this fear-inspired code were only too real. The negroes were hopelessly degraded. They were rarely baptized or married, but lived, like animals, in a state of promiscuous intercourse. After six days of incessant labor for their masters, they were permitted on the seventh to work for themselves. Their condition, therefore, was one of almost complete barbarism, and they retained some of the savage bravery and independence which a kinder dispensation had almost obliterated in their Virginian brethren. The planters were always haunted by the dread of a West Indian rising and massacre. Combinations and conspiracies were constant sources of anxiety. It was believed that the slaves were ever ready to run away and form frontier communities, which would menace the safety of the province, and it is certain that the negroes were dangerous, discontented, hated the whites, and were always ripe for revolt. Insurrections, involving more or less bloodshed, did, in fact, break out during the eighteenth century.[2] In South Carolina, too, there was none of the distinction between theory and practice which prevailed elsewhere. The slaves were harshly and cruelly treated, and grievously overworked. A clergyman who ventured to preach in regard to the savage treatment of the slaves was

---

[1] Grimke, 1712, 1740, 1743, 1746, 1751, 1754. There is a summary of this legislation in Rochefoucauld, i., 564.

[2] As to slavery in South Carolina, see Smyth, i., 205; ii., 68, 70; Doc. relating to South Carolina, Glen's Report; De Brahm, ibid.; Milligan, Carroll, ii., 465; Von Reck's Journal; Bolzius's Journal; Stephens's Journal, i., 399; ii., 129.

sharply reproved by his congregation. "Sir," they said, "we pay you a genteel salary to read to us the prayers of the liturgy, and to explain to us such parts of the Gospel as the rule of the Church directs; but we do not want you to teach us what to do with our blacks." The unlucky pastor was completely silenced.[1] A traveller records the spectacle of a negro exposed alive in a cage to die of hunger and thirst. The miserable wretch was torn by birds, and his eyes had been picked out. His crime was the murder of an overseer, and the argument in favor of this ghastly punishment was the defence of society.[2] Such extreme barbarity was probably not common, but it vividly illustrates the state of a society which required such a defence.

The planters who lived in the midst of such a slavery, and sustained it, were not only an overwhelming majority among the whites, but practically owned and governed the province. Approaching them as masters, we see the worst side of South Carolinian society, but we also clearly appreciate the fact that it was an aristocracy of the most marked kind. Lords and slaves formed the community. The former maintained an anxious and grinding despotism, and were, as a class, brave, imperious, hot-tempered, and too often fierce and cruel.

The plantations were, as elsewhere, scattered through the forests and along the banks of rivers; but the planters did not live on their estates unless they were in the neighborhood of Charleston, but left them in charge of overseers. They all had houses in Charleston, and there the whole life of the colony — social, political, legal, and commercial—centred. The town stood low, near the mouths of the Cooper and Ashley rivers, and contained, at the time of the Revolution, rather more than fifteen thousand inhabitants. The streets were well laid out, although unpaved and sandy; and the public buildings and churches were handsome for the time, with some architectural pretensions. The houses were nearly all of brick, with broad verandas, and contrived always with a view to mitigate the intense heat. Although the population seems small to modern notions of cities, it was by no means so insignificant in the eighteenth century; and the peculiar structure of society made the wealthy and fashionable classes much more numerous proportionally than they ever would be in a northern or in an English town of the same size. All labor was performed exclusively by negroes, who formed half the population; while the rest of the inhabitants, with the exception of a few shopkeepers, were

---

[1] Crévecœur, p. 224.   [2] Ibid., p. 234.

officials, wealthy planters and merchants, or the best professional men
in the colony. The centralization thus effected was something quite
uncommon in the English provinces. Charleston had no rivals—the
other towns being small—and absorbed and drew to itself every interest of the province.[1] In the immediate vicinity of Charleston the
plantations were occupied by their owners, and were well maintained.
The negro huts, of course clustered about the house, gave the usual
village-like look; but there were handsome gardens and fine avenues,
showing the effects of a close contact with society, instead of the Virginian isolation.[2] The town produced the same effect upon facilities
for travel. Although the roads were often sandy and heavy, they
were well laid out. Causeways were built over marshes, and private
roads were as good as those built by the public. This was true only
of the great roads leading north and south, and of those near Charleston and the sea-coast. In the interior travel was difficult, and the
roads little more than woodland paths.[3]

Many planters lived in Charleston all the year round; and all of
them, as well as many invalids from the West Indies, gathered there
in summer, for the relief afforded by the sea-breeze.[4] This constant
social contact and town life had of course a marked effect. The
South Carolinians were at bottom the same country gentlemen as
those of Virginia; but they were more polished, more men of the
world, and more refined in manners and habits of life. There was all
the gayety of a fashionable watering-place in Charleston. In winter
assemblies were held every fortnight, with "a brilliant appearance"
of well-dressed women, besides frequent dinners, balls, supper-parties,
and amateur concerts. There was also "a genteel play-house, and a
tolerable set of actors." In summer no amusements except riding
and driving were possible; but in winter there were field-sports of
every description, such as fox-hunting and horse-racing, foot-ball, bear
and bull baiting, and entertainments described in the laws as "inter-
ludes and common plays." Nothing began until after four in the afternoon; and besides the more innocent pleasures just described, the
gambling-houses were crowded, and high play prevailed.[5]

---

[1] For contemporary accounts of Charleston, see Michaux's Travels, p. 7 ; Smyth,
i., 202; ii., 82; Glen's Answers, in Doc. relating to South Carolina ; De Brahm, ibid.,
p. 178; Milligan, Carroll, ii., 465 ; Von Reck's Journal ; Rochefoucauld, i., 556.

[2] Memoirs of Elkanah Watson.

[3] De Brahm, p. 178 ; Rochefoucauld, i., 588.   [4] Crévecœur, p. 214.

[5] For amusements, see Crévecœur, p. 214 ; Grimke, 1712 ; Milligan, Carroll, ii.,
465 ; Rochefoucauld, i., 558.

The men led a rather wild and dissipated life, and drank deeply—an intemperance which in that climate carried them off very early, and their mortality was so marked, that the women, who contented themselves with the brackish water of the coast, always married two or three times. These fortunate ladies were much in society, but modest, attractive, and accomplished. Many of them played upon the harp, and sang well. The climate caused them to fade early; and it is said they looked old at thirty.[1] The life of both sexes was one of greater luxury than in any other American colony, and was sensual, self-indulgent, and indolent. Women never walked, and men but rarely. No family had less than twenty slaves as house-servants, and extravagance, although there were few very large fortunes, was the rule. All had handsome equipages and horses, and kept open house. They were extremely hospitable, and the negroes were directed in the country to ask in any passing stranger. The effect of slavery and of the warm climate was perceptible in the slovenliness which showed itself even in the most extensive establishments; but the general characteristics were luxury and comfort.[2]

In the back country life was much ruder, and the people of a lower class; but except near Cape Fear, where the inhabitants, after the North Carolina fashion, avoided taxes and quit-rents, law and order prevailed, although the planters usually ruled with a high hand. Thanks to the absence of freed servants and poor whites, there was little or no poverty. All who were not rich planters were small and self-supporting farmers and Indian traders or hunters.[3]

General education could hardly be said to exist even after the Revolution; there were no free and scarcely any paid schools, and there was no college. The very excellent clergy did what they could to remedy the prevailing ignorance, even among the blacks, and both they and laymen left bequests for the foundation of schools. But this general illiteracy did not obtain among the numerous and powerful body of planters.[4] The sons of the rich were all educated in Europe,

---

[1] Smyth, ii., 54; Crévecœur, p. 214; Milligan, Carroll, ii., 465; Purry, ibid., p. 178.

[2] Smyth, ii., 83; Glen's Answers, p. 82; Milligan, Carroll, ii., 465; Memoirs of Elkanah Watson; Rochefoucauld, i., 555, 574, 591; De Brahm, p. 178.

[3] Smyth, i., 205; ii., 80; Glen's Answers, p. 67; O'Neall, Annals of Newbury, p. 18.

[4] Mills's Statistics of South Carolina, p. 216; Milligan, Carroll, ii., 465; O'Neall, generally, and especially, pp. 86, 111, 249; Anderson's Hist. Col. Church, iii., 488; Rochefoucauld, i., 580.

and in Charleston, besides a society for the promotion of literature, there was also a library society, promoted by Governor Bull, which imported many valuable books and gave them circulation; yet despite these societies and the comparatively high education of the upper classes, there was no native literature of any sort. The Rev. Alexander Garden produced some controversial tracts under the stimulus of Whitefield, and a few sermons found their way into print; but this was all. Intellectual development, except in politics and trade, did not go farther in South Carolina than in the other southern colonies.

In all connected with these two subjects of politics and commerce, there was no lack of acuteness and experience, nor of love of independence. The utter dependence both in exports and imports drew South Carolina closer to England than the other provinces, and the result was seen in the active existence of a powerful and bitter Tory party when the Revolution came. But the strongest and best among the planters adopted the patriot cause, and carried the State safely through the stress of war. We find in South Carolina that the northern qualities perceptible in Virginia have wholly disappeared, while all the southern elements have been intensified. Her close slave-holding aristocracy produced many leaders of ability, who rendered great services to the cause of the united colonies, and afterward gave their State a strong position in the country, and a place second only to that of Virginia in the southern group.

CHAPTER IX.

GEORGIA FROM 1732 TO 1765.

THE settlement of South Carolina, and the danger to which the inhabitants were exposed of incursions from the Spaniards and Indians, drew early attention to the fertile region lying between the Savannah River and the boundaries of Florida. Nothing, however, was done to occupy this territory until after the Carolinas had formally passed into the possession of the Crown, and that portion of the new provinces which afterward became Georgia was retained by the King when the governments of the Carolinas were settled.

The Atlantic coast of the United States was from the time of its discovery the field for many experiments. Some were Utopias designed for the regeneration of mankind, which never got farther than the paper on which they were described, while others failed when put to the hard tests of life in a new country. Even the colonies actually founded present every variety of origin and motive, from the highest and most far-reaching purposes of politics and religion to the small beginnings of posts for the better prosecution of the fur trade. Among all these, Georgia was the only one to owe its foundation to charity. The benevolent scheme, out of which a state was finally developed, would be dull enough historically, were it not for one or two of the principal personages who figured in the history of the youngest of the American colonies.

Among those who led the English race into the wilds of North America, and who there won noble places in the world's records as founders of states and of a nation, were many strong men of striking character and marked ability. In this goodly company there is hardly one who is more conspicuous or more interesting than the gallant soldier who founded Georgia. Some of them may have been actuated by more important principles of politics or religion; but there is not one who displayed greater devotion to duty or greater unselfishness, or to whom any colony from its inception owed more than Georgia did to James Oglethorpe.

The colonization of Georgia is naturally the achievement by which Oglethorpe is best known, and upon which his fame rests; but his career was in every way a remarkable one. His active life covered more than three-quarters of a century. He sprang from an ancient family, and one which had sacrificed both life and fortune in the cause of the Stuarts. By inheritance he was a Jacobite, and was always a high Tory; but his loyalty to the reigning house was unstained, and he proved his devotion by his service against the Pretender in "forty-five." Born just at the close of the reign of James II., Ogle-
1688. thorpe entered the army at an early age. He served with Marlborough in the Low Countries, was with Peterborough in his Italian embassy, and then, as aide-de-camp to Prince Eugene, went through all the battles fought by that commander with the Turks, and was present at Petrawardin and the siege of Belgrade. His long life extending to 1785, during which his powers of mind and body remained unimpaired, connects him with every period of the eighteenth century. An officer with Marlborough and Eugene, the defender of Atterbury, and immortalized in the familiar lines of Pope, his sayings are also recorded by Boswell, he was the friend of Johnson, was sneered at by Walpole, after his death, for not living longer, and is even united to our own times by his appearance in the diary of Samuel Rogers, to whom he described the days when he had shot snipe in what is now Conduit Street in London. Such a life and such a career deserve a better relation than scanty materials have permitted; but even with what remains, the brave soldier, and the honest, upright, kind-hearted gentleman, stands out clearly; and in the early history of Georgia there is an abundance of information which exhibits him not only as a soldier, but as a strong leader and wise administrator. That Oglethorpe made mistakes is not only probable, but was inevitable; for, in addition to all that may be set down to human fallibility under difficult circumstances, was the fact that he did his work under an impracticable system, and to further a generous but probably impossible experiment. Yet, after every deduction has been made, he is a man whom any state might regard with reverence and admiration as its founder, first ruler, and defender.

After his return from campaigning against the Turks with Prince Eugene, Oglethorpe was chosen to Parliament. He was a use-
1722. ful and active member, a sensible and straightforward speaker, and was especially interested in what would now be called domestic reform. He did much for the relief of abuses, and his attention was

at last drawn to the condition of the debtors' prisons. He obtained the appointment of a special committee, and their investigations brought to light a state of affairs which was simply frightful. Prosecutions and legislation followed; but Oglethorpe, not satisfied with this, devised a scheme for settling members of the debtor class in America, in the hope of giving these unfortunates an opportunity to redeem their past, and at the same time relieve England from the burden of their support. An association was formed, with a Board of Trustees, to serve without pay, and was incorporated for twenty-one years under a charter giving them all the territory between the Savannah and the Altamaha. Upon these Trustees the power was conferred to raise money by subscription, govern and defend the colony, make laws, and establish courts. The liberties, franchises, and immunities of citizens of Great Britain were guaranteed to the colonists, as well as liberty of conscience to all except Papists. The promoters of this benevolent scheme hoped to accomplish much by their enterprise. South Carolina was to be protected by the barrier of new settlements; the improvident debtor was to be converted into a producing and profitable subject; other oppressed people were to be invited to this haven of rest and prosperity; independent settlers were to come over and form a class of large landholders, and bring servants with them; Christianity was to be spread among the Indians, and silk, wine, oil, and dyestuffs were to be produced, which would vastly increase the wealth and aid the manufactures of the mother country. With such projects, visionary though they were, and with free passage and a gratuity of tools and lands, the Trustees had no lack of volunteers from whom to choose colonists. Thirty-five of the best and soberest families were selected, and under the charge of Oglethorpe, who had been made Governor and General, with full powers but no pay, they sailed from England in November, 1732, and reached Charleston in the middle of the following January.

The emigrants were warmly received in South Carolina, both by government and people; and Oglethorpe at once made a journey to the south and selected a site for the settlement. There, to a chosen spot, a bluff overlooking the river, Oglethorpe brought his company and founded the future city of Savannah. Under his energetic guidance rapid progress was made. Houses were built, supplies and money obtained, treaties made with the Indians, the town laid out in wards and tithings, courts established, and the land divided into lots.

Ample provision was made for defence, and Fort Argyle was built on the Ogeechee as an outlying post. Fresh colonists arrived, among them Jews, to whom the Trustees made objection—the first indication of their narrow views. Money was voted by Parliament; and in the following year came a ship-load of the oppressed and exiled Salzburgers, who, under the lead of Oglethorpe, founded another town, to which they gave the name of Ebenezer. Everything had **1734.** prospered with the new colony, and in May Oglethorpe returned to England, taking with him the Indian chief, Tomochichi.

In the following year Oglethorpe returned at the head of what is known as the "grand emigration." The news of the success-**1735-** ful beginnings of the colony had spread, and settlers came from **1736.** among the Salzburgers and Moravians, as well as from England, many being of a better class than were the first beneficiaries of the Trustees. In this second emigration, also, came two more of those marked characters which have given a peculiar personal interest and animation to the early history of Georgia. Charles Wesley came out as Oglethorpe's secretary, and John Wesley as missionary to the Indians. The former made trouble by slandering Oglethorpe, and by injudicious and factious meddling, while the latter embroiled the whole settlement by a love affair in which he was disappointed, and by his zealous religious intolerance. The stay of the brothers in Georgia was brief, however, and their departure was a relief to the colony in which they had only made trouble. Their doings and sayings, and their contentions, form an interesting chapter in their biographies, and relieve the monotony of the early settlement; but they had no lasting influence or effect, and their sojourn in America was to them and to Georgia simply an episode, neither creditable nor important. John Wesley left the colony with an indictment for libel hanging over his head, and was replaced by an equally distinguished leader in the great religious movement of the century. This was George Whitefield, who succeeded far better than his predecessor, and did much more as missionary and preacher; but he, too, came and went without leaving any enduring impress.

Annoying as the Wesleys were, Oglethorpe brought two far more prolific sources of trouble than the future reformers. Parliament had seen fit to pass two acts, one excluding rum, the other slaves, from the new colony. The theory of these restrictions was sound enough; but one was in its nature impossible, and the other was impracticable, not only because South Carolina employed slaves, but because it was universally believed that Georgia could not be cultivated except by negro labor. Rum came in from the neighboring province as freely as ever, and evasion of the law was added to drunkenness. Slaves, too, were smuggled in now and then, and the prohibition of slavery formed a normal grievance and subject of controversy, which became more and more serious as time went on.

Oglethorpe found the colony much extended and improved, and set himself at once to work with his accustomed energy to still further strengthen and spread the settlements. He superintended the removal of the Salzburgers to a new place, extended and confirmed the Indian treaties, established a trading-post at Augusta, and strengthened the Scotch colony at Darien. His principal work, however, was to found Frederica, and establish there a portion of his new emigrants. This was a task of considerable difficulty, and while the new settlement was in its infancy Oglethorpe was in constant fear of a Spanish attack, which would have ruined the colony and cost him his life. By a mixture of strategy and audacity, however, he succeeded in warding off the danger. He had an indecisive interview with the Spanish commissioner, upon whom he imposed by a show of force, and gained time to form some defences; and after settling a variety of vexatious disputes at Savannah, he again returned to England in order to obtain troops, for he plainly perceived that the colony, in its weak state, would quickly fall before a Spanish invasion.

On his arrival in England, he found abundance to do in dealing with the question of the Indian trade, which had come to an issue between South Carolina and Georgia, and which was mixed up with seizures of South Carolina rum by the Savannah magistrates. He had also to repel the calumnies spread against him by opponents in the colony, and settle the difficulties raised by the Wesleys. He steadily persevered, too, in his main purpose of procuring aid to defend the colony, and was appointed General for Georgia by the King, and given authority to raise a regiment. This he at once proceeded to do, and, besides some regular troops sent from Gibraltar, he raised a force of six hundred men, with which he returned to Georgia. These **1738.** troops were allowed to take their families, in order to induce them to settle in the province, and there were, besides a number of officers, young volunteers of good family.

These re-enforcements came none too soon, for the relations between England and Spain had become very strained, and a rupture was imminent. Oglethorpe immediately strengthened his posts everywhere, and opened a road from Frederica to the sea-forts, where he shrewdly perceived the decisive struggle would come. He then passed some time at Savannah, where there was much disorder and faction. He removed the Company's store-keeper, who had been corrupt and extravagant, retrenched expenditures, and reorganized the militia. His most important act, however, was a visit to the Creeks and Cherokees, for he succeeded in checking Spanish intrigues, and in gaining great influence over these tribes, which he never lost, and in binding them firmly to the English alliance. The next effort of the Spaniards was to stir up a negro insurrection in South Carolina which proved very formidable, but was finally put down by the exertions of the government, and by Oglethorpe's activity in stopping the runaways. This attack and the murders of soldiers at outlying posts, as well as the news from England, decided Oglethorpe that the time had **1739.** come for energetic measures, and he accordingly made a solemn declaration of war at Savannah.

The winter passed in raising and disposing troops, preparing forts, summoning Indians, and in an occasional incursion into Florida, until in the spring Admiral Vernon appeared with the English fleet. Some ships were detached, and a combined attack was made under Oglethorpe on St. Augustine. After a few slight successes everything went wrong; the Indians deserted, some of the troops were cut off, ships got in and relieved the town, and Oglethorpe had finally to withdraw, and bear the loud censure of the naval officers, and **1740.** of the South Carolinians, who were chiefly to blame by their delays. This unlucky expedition, considering the undoubted military abilities of the commander, can only be explained by a lack of cohesion among the troops, and an apparent failure on the part of Oglethorpe, despite strenuous exertions and great gallantry, to show his usual foresight. The invasion, although a failure, had one good result, for it put the Spaniards on the defensive, and gave the colony peace for two years. In this interval Oglethorpe had time to regulate the internal affairs of his government, which were loose and disordered, as they always became except when under his immediate supervision. The plan of a colony as a charitable institution did not, in fact, work well; the rule of the Trustees was feeble and injudicious, and the settlements did not grow as they would have done under a firmer government.

Having regulated matters at Savannah, Oglethorpe returned to Frederica, now a neatly and strongly built town of about a thousand inhabitants; and here he established his head-quarters, and devoted himself to further improvements in the defences. He suffered continual annoyance from the factions at Savannah, who took advantage of the unpopularity of the slave and liquor laws to violate them, and to intrigue against and abuse the Governor; and he was still further troubled by the schemes and quarrels of Whitefield, who, both by his preaching and by his orphan asylum, succeeded in keeping the colony in a state of ferment. Oglethorpe carried himself and his government through these difficulties with a steady hand, and remained at his post preparing for the Spanish attack which he foresaw would be attempted.

At last news began to come of the preparations of the Spaniards, and Oglethorpe sent to South Carolina and to Admiral Vernon for aid. No help came; but in the summer of 1742 the Spaniards, with five thousand men from Florida and Havana, and a fleet of thirty vessels, appeared off St. Simon's Island, and threatened Frederica. Oglethorpe called in all his troops, but could only muster eight hundred men, and with these he determined to defend himself to the last extremity. His first feat was to carry relief to one of the sea-forts, forcing his way in two galleys through the Spanish fleet, sinking four of their galleys, and returning in safety. This exploit greatly encouraged the troops, and a stubborn resistance was made to the passage of the sound by a few vessels, and by the shore batteries. When the Spaniards at last got through, Oglethorpe fell back in good order on Frederica, and his carefully planned defences now stood him in good stead. The Spaniards, unable to reach the town by sea, landed troops, and advanced on the road cut by Oglethorpe. The English troops fled at the Spanish advance; but a detachment of Highlanders and Indians, concealing themselves in the woods, fell upon the Spaniards in the rear as they were resting, and routed them with terrible slaughter, Oglethorpe appearing with the other troops, which he had rallied, just at the moment of victory. This disaster caused dissensions among the Spaniards, and Oglethorpe, assuming the aggressive, harassed them without mercy, and finally, by a well-conceived stratagem, and by the fortunate appearance of some English vessels, deceived them into the belief that heavy re-enforcements were at hand, and had the satisfaction of seeing them take to their ships in a panic and sail away. Thus Oglethorpe saved two provinces to England by as gallant fighting and shrewd generalship as the whole history of the American colonies can show. In the following year he again assumed the offensive, and carried the war into

Florida with his faithful Indians and Highlanders, even to the walls of
St. Augustine, reducing the Spaniards to a state of timorous
1743. defence. He soon after left Georgia, never to return; and
on his arrival in England, having refuted various calumnious charges
made against him by one of his officers, and by the South Carolinians, who had used him very badly, he was promoted to be a lieuten-
ant-general. Thus closed Oglethorpe's career in America; and few
men have ever rendered better service to their own country, or to the
commonwealths they have founded.

The colony, however, in spite of Oglethorpe's exertions, had not
thriven. The policy of the Trustees had been a narrow and mistaken
one. The Rum Act had been a constant source of trouble, discontent,
and corruption on the part of the magistrates, and was at last repealed
in 1742. The tenure of land had been made that of tail-male, with
close restrictions on alienation, and this had led to much discontent,
to opposition, petitions, and resistance, until a more liberal tenure was
granted in 1739. In the matter of slaves, the course of events was
somewhat similar. The Highlanders and Salzburgers were opposed to
the introduction of negroes, but the landholders and planters at Savannah were most eager for them. Petitions for the introduction of slaves
began to come in 1735; but, although the Trustees had no objection
to modified white slavery in the way of indented servants, they held
firm against negroes. On this subject feeling soon ran high, and all
the elements of opposition united against the Trustees with a bitter
and factious hostility, which gave Oglethorpe great trouble, and finally reached such a point that the quarrel became the subject of Parliamentary investigation. Parliament exonerated the Trustees, ordered
the repeal of the Rum Act, but refused to meddle with that against
slavery. The struggle was then renewed both in Georgia and England, and became so bitter as to threaten the very existence of the
colony. At last, in 1749, in the face of the popular demand and of
the constant violation of the law, the Trustees gave way and admitted slaves, but under humane restrictions. The system of government
by bailiffs, magistrates, and town courts proved a failure also, after
causing much bickering and faction, and was changed to government
by a President and assistants.

On Oglethorpe's departure, William Stephens, the secretary, was
made President, and continued in office until 1751, when he
1751. was succeeded by Henry Parker. The colony, when Stephens
came into office, comprised about fifteen hundred persons. It was al-

most at a stand-still. The brilliant prospects of the early days were dissipated, and immigration had ceased, thanks to the narrow policy and feeble government of the Trustees. An Indian rising, in 1749, headed by Mary Musgrove, Oglethorpe's Indian interpreter, and her husband, one Bosomworth, who laid claim to the whole country, came near causing the destruction of the colony, and was only repressed by much negotiation and lavish bribes.

The colony, thus feeble and threatened, struggled on, until it was relieved from danger from the Indians and from the restrictive laws, and encouraged by the appointment of Parker, and the establishment of a representative government. This produced a turn in the affairs of Georgia. Trade revived, immigration was renewed, and everything began to wear again a more hopeful look. Just at this time, however, the original trust was on the point of expiring by limitation. There was a party in the colony who desired a renewal of the charter ; but the Trustees felt that their scheme had failed in every way, except perhaps as a defence to South Carolina, and when the limit of **1752.** the charter was reached, they turned the colony over to the Crown. Georgia then passed from the stage of philanthropic experiment into the normal condition of a Crown province, after the fashion of most of the American colonies, and according to the laws which had governed the development of all the British possessions in America, no matter what their origin had been.

A form of government was established similar to those of the other **1754.** royal provinces, and Captain John Reynolds was sent out as the first Governor, and was joyfully received by the inhabitants. The new Governor was somewhat dismayed at the wretched appearance of the colony, but set to work to survey and improve the forts and other defences, established a judicial system, and called together an Assembly. This last act was the signal for immediate contention. In the first Assembly the trouble was caused by a faction ; and the quarrel which concerned the Indian trade almost reached the dimensions of a revolt. After this, matters went from bad to worse, the fault now being on the side of the Governor, who fell under the influence of the secretary, a corrupt and intriguing politician ; and this resulted in so much oppression and extortion, and the complaints of the colonists became so repeated and loud, that Reynolds **1757.** was at last recalled, and succeeded by Henry Ellis as Lieutenant-governor. The change proved fortunate, and brought rest to the colony. Ellis ruled peaceably and with general respect

for more than two years, and was then promoted to the governor-
 1760. ship of Nova Scotia. In the same year his successor arrived
at Savannah, in the person of James Wright, who continued
to govern the province until it was severed from England by the
Revolution.

The feebleness of Georgia had prevented her taking part in the
union of the colonies, and she was not represented in the Congress at
Albany. Georgia also escaped the ravages of the French war, partly
by her distant situation, and partly by the prudence of Governor Ellis;
and the conclusion of that war gave Florida to England, and relieved
the colony from the continual menace of Spanish aggression. A great
Congress of southern Governors and Indian chiefs followed, in which
1763. Wright, more active than his predecessor, took a prominent
part. Under his energetic and firm rule, the colony began
to prosper greatly, and trade increased rapidly; but the Governor
gained at the same time so much influence, and was a man of so much
address, that he not only held the colony down at the time of the
Stamp Act, but seriously hampered its action in the years which led
to revolution. When the circular from Massachusetts arrived regarding the Stamp Act Congress, it met with general favor in the Assembly and among the people; for there was deep and bitter opposition here as elsewhere to the new policy of taxation. Wright, how-
1765. ever, succeeded in preventing the sending of delegates to New
York, and crippled the action of Georgia, reducing it to a mere
expression of good intentions. In the months of excitement which
ensued, great disorder prevailed; armed bands appeared at various
points; there were mobs in Savannah, and serious attacks meditated
upon the fort and the Governor's house; but Wright proved equal to
the emergency. With a mere handful of troops, he kept the peace,
avoided bloodshed, and although obliged to remove the stamps to the
British man-of-war in the river, he compelled their use in clearing
vessels, a proceeding which caused deep indignation in South Carolina and elsewhere. The repeal of the Stamp Act brought a temporary calm; but Georgia, although unrepresented at New York, and
although the youngest and weakest of the provinces, was drawn into
1768. the general current, and when the next circular letter came
from Massachusetts, was prepared to enter into conflict with
her adroit Governor, and take a part in the history of the united colonies and in the national movement.

Chapter X.

GEORGIA IN 1765.

THE late settlement of Georgia, and its use as a field for the trial of philanthropic experiments, rendered society there, at the time of the Revolution, extremely crude and unformed, and in the country districts rude and wild. It was on the South Carolina model, but had neither the stability nor the well-defined features of its older and stronger neighbor.

So long as the province continued in the hands of the Trustees its progress was extremely slow, and sometimes totally arrested. The population, when Georgia passed to the Crown, did not amount to five thousand whites, and slaves had been excluded by the policy of the Trustees. With the establishment of the royal government, and especially after the treaty of Paris, slaves were imported in great numbers, and the white immigration assumed large proportions. Just previous to the Revolution the population had risen to over fifty thousand souls, of whom one-half at least were slaves.[1] The character of the white population was not so good as in many of the other colonies. Among the first settlers there were, of course, some men of good substance, who came out at their own expense, but the great body of immigrants were taken from the debtors' prisons in accordance with the humane objects of the Trustees. Some of the persons thus released made the best of their opportunities, and did well in their new home; but many were either vitiated by the prison life, or were by nature shiftless, bankrupt adventurers, who were an injury to any society, and especially to one just founded and struggling for existence. The servants, too, were the scum of the London streets, and, unrestrained by the severe laws in vogue elsewhere, ran away to South Carolina and Florida, or lurked in the woods and on the boun-

---

[1] Bancroft, iv., 127, note; Smyth, ii., 45; Georgia Hist. Soc. Coll., iii., Sir James Wright's Account.

dary-lines, and preyed upon society. Gradually better elements began to come. There were Scotch settlements at Darien and Frederica; some thriving villages of Salzburgers, and later, descendants of the Puritans, who had settled in South Carolina in 1697; while a Jewish immigration, which began with promise, was checked by the Trustees. After the establishment of the royal government, immigration increased and improved. A large body of Quakers came in 1763, besides the usual and valuable settlers always attracted by the profits promised in agriculture and trade.[1]

The government founded by the Trustees was one in name alone. There was in reality no general government. The towns either had no government at all, or were organized according to the taste of the inhabitants. Savannah had bailiffs and recorder, and her government was thoroughly bad. The Salzburgers had in their villages a semi-religious system, with large tracts of communal land held by the Church, while at Sunbury the government was on the New England model. The legislation of the Trustees was chiefly concerned with matters of police, and had a general character of philanthropic meddling. Their policy of prohibiting rum and negroes, based on moral views, and on the scheme of making the colony a sort of half military outpost, was highly distasteful to their subjects, who grumbled that the loss of the former destroyed their trade, and the want of the latter made agriculture impossible. In this way the Trustees became terribly unpopular. Their cattle were killed, their laws evaded, and their high quit-rents avoided. A war of pamphlets ensued, political faction ran high, all progress was stayed; until at last the Trustees, in disgust, handed over their charter to the Crown, and Georgia entered upon a career of prosperity.[2]

The first Assembly, which met at Savannah in the year 1751, seems to have been little more than a grand-jury elected to make presentations of grievances to the Council; but a few years later the government of the Crown was organized on the usual model. There was a Governor possessing the customary powers, a Council which sat as an

---

[1] Smyth, ii., 41; Jones, Dead Towns of Georgia; Moore's Voyage to Georgia, p. 24; Georgia Hist. Soc. Coll., Stephens's State of the Province; Ibid., A Brief Account, p. 97; Lee's History of Savannah; Rochefoucauld, i., 604; Graham's United States, iv., 135.

[2] Jones, Dead Towns of Georgia, pp. 23, 145; Georgia Hist. Coll., i., Brief Account, p. 97; Ibid., True and Hist. Narratives, p. 195; Ibid., Trustees' Account; Lee's Savannah, p. 8, 1734; Stephens's Journal, i., 169.

Upper House, and an Assembly. All executive and judicial officers were appointed by the Crown, and paid fixed salaries by the British government. The delegates were required to own five hundred acres of land, and were chosen by the freeholders, the suffrage being confined to those who were proprietors of fifty acres or a town lot.[1]

The Governor was chancellor, and sat with the Council as a court of chancery and of admiralty. There was also a general court of common-pleas, county courts, and local justices' courts. An appeal could be carried to the Governor if involving more than three hundred, and to the King in Council if more than five hundred pounds.[2]

The militia of the colony, owing to its exposed situation, was effective, and included all males between sixteen and sixty. Taxation was light. Quit-rents were paid to the King, and revenues raised on rum, negroes, and West India produce, supplemented by a small direct tax on lands, houses, and slaves. The salaries were few and small, and the necessary charges of government not above four thousand pounds, while the militia were thriftily required to furnish themselves with arms and clothing.[3]

The philanthropy of the Trustees had an effect upon the material growth of the colony no less depressing than upon its political development. They wished to achieve the impossible, to form a community, and establish methods and habits wholly at variance with the conditions of climate and soil. They sought to build up a society living in towns, and consisting of small freeholders, after the New England fashion in the tropical region of Georgia. To prevent the formation of large estates, they made grants of only fifty acres and a town lot to each settler in tail-male, with reversion to the Trustees, and a special license was further required for the alienation of any estate in land. This arrangement led to frauds and dissatisfaction, crippled the activity, and cooled the interest of the colonists, and was finally abandoned by its projectors.[4] In the same spirit they interfered with the natural course of agriculture and industry. They obliged the Salzburgers to maintain the culture of silk, considerable quantities of which were made and exported, and which was sustained at Ebenezer even down to the

---

[1] Georgia Hist. Soc. Coll., iii., Sir James Wright's Account; Lee's Hist. of Savannah; Hildreth, ii., 454.

[2] Sir James Wright, ibid.; Hildreth, ii., 454.   [3] Sir James Wright, ibid.

[4] Georgia Hist. Soc. Coll., i., 25; Ibid., Impartial Inquiry, p. 165; Ibid., ii., 92, A Brief Account; Ibid., Trustees' Account; Moore's Voyage to Georgia, p. 24; Jones, Dead Towns of Georgia, p. 145.

Revolution by bounties. But the manufacture was carried on at a loss, and when state aid was withdrawn this always languishing industry speedily expired. In a similar way they strove to enforce the planting of vineyards and the production of oil, and not wholly without success; but both ultimately shared the fate of the silk-worm, and were too artificial to have any real prosperity.[1] For moral purposes they prohibited the importation of negroes, whose labor was essential in that latitude, and of rum, which injured the trade with the West Indies. Both prohibitions were evaded by encouraging and receiving runaways from South Carolina, and by the open sale of the forbidden liquor, and thus a contempt for law was engendered as well as general discontent.[2] The general result of this whole system was that trade stagnated, and the small plantations failed.[3]

Under the royal government these restrictions disappeared, rapid progress began, and at the time of the Revolution the exports and imports were worth one hundred and fifty thousand pounds.[4] The trade was principally with Great Britain, but there was also a fair traffic with the West Indies. The land was being rapidly cleared and occupied, and the colony had settled down to the production of rice, indigo, lumber, and skins obtained by a lucrative and active trade with the Indians. Cattle had become numerous and valuable, and cheese and butter were made, instead of being imported from the north. They still depended on the Middle States for flour, which drained them of specie; and although they grew cotton, only a small portion was spun by the Scotch settlers for domestic use. They had no manufactures of any sort, but were wholly dependent on the mother country —a misfortune common to all the southern group—and no mines had been opened. Despite these drawbacks, however, and an agriculture much lower than that of South Carolina, Georgia was prosperous, and the employment of over two hundred vessels, of which thirty-six were owned in the colony, was a sure sign of active and profitable commerce.[5]

The towns were, of course, insignificant, although Savannah gave

---

[1] Jones, Dead Towns of Georgia, p. 23 ; Stephens's Journal, iii., 186 ; Hist. Coll., i., 25.

[2] Hist. Coll., i., p. 25 ; Ibid., ii., True and Hist. Narrative ; Stephens's Journal, i., 169, 273.   [3] Jones, Dead Towns of Georgia, pp. 23, 145.

[4] Smyth, ii., 50 ; Hist. Coll., iii., Sir James Wright's Account.

[5] Bartram's Travels, p. 19 ; Smyth, ii., 44, 45, 53 ; Jones, Dead Towns of Georgia, pp. 23, 145 ; Rochefoucauld, i., 609 ; Hist. Coll., iii., Sir James Wright's Account ; Lee's History of Savannah.

promise of growth and importance. At the time of the Revolution it was a pretty country town of some twelve hundred inhabitants, with large, cool houses, built of wood, and separated by open spaces of garden or field. Sunbury, founded by the New England immigrants, came next, with about a thousand inhabitants, and a good share of the commerce; but it had already begun to decline in importance, although it still retained its character for a polite and educated society of wealthy planters and farmers. Augusta, above Savannah, at the head of navigation, was a straggling but thriving village, where the Indian trade centred. The chief seat of the Salzburgers at Ebenezer was a mere hamlet; and the Scotch settlement at Frederica, a neat, busy little town in the early days, when it was an outpost, had been almost deserted after the withdrawal of the troops.[1]

It is obvious that there was nothing in Georgia which could be properly called town life. Almost every one was a small farmer or planter, and large estates were comparatively rare. In the neighborhood of Savannah and along the coasts were many pretty plantations, some of which possessed large houses, and displayed the Virginian magnificence, but on all the owners led an easy, tranquil existence. In the back districts, then being rapidly settled, the life was much ruder, more isolated, and, owing to the proximity of Spaniards and Indians, very dangerous. Men went to church armed, and a trip to Savannah was a great event, as the only mode of travel was on horseback, whether for business or pleasure. Gigs were not introduced until after the Revolution, and the infrequent mail was carried through the province by riders. Among the planters of the better sort much time was given to the simple amusements of fishing, sailing, hunting, and riding; while as early as the year 1748 horse-races were established at Savannah, betting began, and a club was founded. The gambling, once started, took a strong hold upon the people, if we may judge from the laws against betting, gaming, and lotteries. Gambling brawls were common, and there was not only a good deal of fighting whenever any gathering occurred, but the brutal practice of gouging was so much indulged in that it was found necessary to make the pillory and lashes the punishment for the first, and death the penalty for the second offence.[2]

---

[1] Smyth, ii., 44; Moore's Voyage, p. 24; Jones, Dead Towns of Georgia, p. 23; Hist. Coll., iv., Itinerant Observations, p. 18; Lee's History of Savannah.

[2] Jones, Dead Towns of Georgia, pp. 23, 145; Georgia Laws, 1764, 1770, 1777, 1787; Stephens's Journal, i., 329; ii., 421; Memoirs of Elkanah Watson.

Among the whites of Georgia there were no well-defined classes. The great majority of the inhabitants belonged probably to the middle class—as known in Virginia—and were not distinctive or peculiar in any way. The system they had founded was unfinished and crude, but it was essentially aristocratic in theory, and could develop only into an aristocracy. This was, of course, determined by the introduction of slavery under the royal government. As soon as the blacks became numerous and important, legislation was framed upon the ferocious model of South Carolina, the code of Georgia being little more than a repetition of that of the older colony. Patrols were established to search the negro quarters for arms, beat stray blacks, and break up their meetings. Slaves could not leave the plantations without a ticket, nor travel in companies of more than seven ; and any one who ventured to teach them to write incurred a heavy penalty. The punishment for striking a white, if it was a second offence, was death. Slavery was said to be milder in Georgia than in South Carolina, but the theory of their position was the same, and they probably fared little better, on the whole. It is certain that they were wretchedly fed, clothed, and housed.[1] The indented servants, after the royal government came in, differed in no respect from those of the other colonies.[2] These servile elements furnished the criminal class, which was numerous and dangerous, out of proportion to the size of the colony, being augmented by runaway servants and slaves from the other provinces, who escaped into Spanish territory, mingled with the Indians, and were a source of constant peril and fear to the outlying plantations. These vagabonds, when captured, received a full allowance of whipping, branding, and pillory for their robberies and cattle liftings ; but the situation of Georgia, at the extremity of a line of slave states, made even the worst punishments ineffective in reducing the number of criminals or the frequency of crime.[3]

The youth and unsettled condition of the colony had, of course, been unfavorable to religion and education. The religious sects varied from the little spiritual tyranny of the Salzburgers to the English Church, and the early history of religion in Georgia is one of utter confusion and pointless wrangling. Members of every known sect almost—Roman Catholics alone excepted—when they arrived found

---

[1] Georgia Laws, 1765, 1778 ; Rochefoucauld, i., 609 ; Memoirs of Elkanah Watson.

[2] Georgia Laws, 1762 ; Stephens's Journal, i., 389.

[3] Georgia Laws, 1778 ; Stephens's Journal, i., 357, 436.

themselves confronted by Wesley, with his dictatorial ways and bitter hostility to dissenters. The royal government produced a certain calm, and the Church of England was duly erected, vestries formed, and taxes authorized for the support of the clergy ; and in the toleration toward all faiths, as well as in the general tone of ecclesiastical legislation, we see both the numerical strength of the dissenters and the influence of the Puritan element. All persons were compelled to attend church ; work and play were forbidden ; taverns were closed on the Sabbath ; and the constables, in true New England fashion, were directed to patrol the town on Sunday morning, and see that these laws were enforced and all delinquents punished. The Church went on smoothly enough until the Revolution, and then was abandoned as a state institution.[1] Unimportant as were the clergy, and wholly devoid of influence, the case in regard to education was even worse. Itinerant school-masters, who never stayed in any one place more than three months, were loose characters, and habitually and proverbially drunk, had a monopoly of teaching, and nothing else was offered by state or individuals in the cause of education.[2] After the Revolution a state university was established, and the New England spirit, still lingering among the settlers, founded the Sunbury Academy ; but, in the colonial period, the illiteracy in Georgia was necessarily extreme, and few persons were wealthy enough to relieve the general ignorance by obtaining for their sons a foreign education. There was no literature whatever, except the spicy and vigorous pamphlets called out in the early days by the Oglethorpe controversy, when none of the writers were natives. A printing-press and the *Georgia Gazette* were established at Savannah in the year 1763, but this was all that was effected for the diffusion of knowledge.[3]

The general political tendencies of the colonists did not differ much from those of their neighbors ; but there was more loyalty and dependence upon the Crown than elsewhere, on account of the weakness caused by recent settlement. The movement against Great Britain started with the New England element at Sunbury, in St. John's parish ; and this small faction finally succeeded in breaking down the control so long maintained by Sir James Wright, and in carrying the

---

[1] Georgia Laws, 1758, 1762, 1778 ; Hist. Coll., ii., 92, Brief Account ; Ibid., True and Historical Narrative, p. 195 ; Stephens's Journal, iii., 101.

[2] Miller's Bar and Bench of Georgia, i., 356.

[3] Tyler's American Literature ; Lee's History of Savannah.

colony over to the patriot cause.[1] But there was much lukewarmness among the people. The Germans were generally on the patriotic side, but they were not enthusiastic, and a vigorous Tory party was developed as the war progressed. The withdrawal of the strong hand of England, and the conquest of independence, showed at once the crude and unformed state of society, and that Georgia had not fairly emerged from the first stage of settlement. For many years the government was ill-regulated and unsettled, and there was much faction and disorder; while the back settlers were rough and lawless, and made continual inroads upon Florida.[2] From this social and political immaturity, Georgia played but an insignificant part either in Congress or in the war, and produced but few able men. It was long before she reached the position or gained the weight to which she was entitled by her extensive territory and great natural resources.

[1] Jones, Dead Towns of Georgia.   [2] Rochefoucauld, i., 604.

CHAPTER XI.

DELAWARE FROM 1609 TO 1682.

THREE kindred people from the north of Europe contended for the possession of the noble bay and river of Delaware, and of the great region which is now occupied by three States. The Dutch were the first discoverers, and they were also the first settlers, when a portion of the company which came out with May landed about four miles below the present city of Philadelphia. This post, established, as all

1623. the early Dutch settlements were, for trade, languished, and the North River proved more profitable than the South. On the establishment of the Patroons, private enterprise made another attempt to found a colony upon the Delaware, Heyes acting for the Patroons.

1631. The settlement of Swaanendael was begun, and a fort built near the site of the present town of Lewiston; but the destruction of a tin plate, bearing the arms of Holland, led to a foolish quarrel with the Indians; the colonists were massacred, and the settlement destroyed. When De Vries came out the following year with

1632. additional men and supplies, he found only ruins and skeletons. He sadly concluded a peace with the murderers of his colonists, and set about retrieving his fortunes by trade and whale-fishery. De Vries went also to the original settlement at Fort Nassau, now deserted and neglected, and, after a visit to Virginia, abandoned his whale-fishery and sailed away. After his departure, a pause ensued in Dutch colonization on the Delaware; but the efforts were soon renewed. A house was ordered to be built at Fort Nassau, and soon after the Company bought out the Patroons, and took possession of the South River. Their hold, however, was nominal and precarious. Already the future masters of the continent had turned their eyes to the region of the Delaware, and a party from Virginia seized the vacant

1635. Dutch fort. They were speedily expelled by its rightful owners, who continued in possession until a third nation sent forth its colonists to share in the vast country held by Holland.

The great Swedish king had perceived, many years before, the necessity and value of colonies in the New World, and, per-

1624-1626. suaded by the Amsterdam merchant Usselincx, founded, after the Dutch fashion, a Swedish West Indian Company. But greater matters required the attention of the Northern races. The battles of Protestantism were to be fought upon the plains of Germany, and when Gustavus Adolphus fell at Lutzen, Swedish colonization in America was still unrealized. Oxenstiern, the heir of the pol-

1633. icy of Gustavus, if not of his throne, revived the scheme soon after his master's death, and invited the co-operation of Germany, but nothing was effected; and it was not until four years had

1637. passed that Peter Minuit, ex-director of the Dutch West Indian Company, headed the first Swedish expedition to America. A settlement was made on the Minquas, near the present site of

1638. Wilmington, and Fort Christina was built, while the Dutch, through the mouth of Governor Kieft, protested, after their usual fashion. They had watched their South River territory, although they had not used it; but they confined themselves to protests, for it was at that time neither desirable nor safe to meddle with Sweden, governed by statesmen and generals who had been trained by Gustavus Adolphus. The Swedes, meantime, treated the Indians well, and relied upon deeds from them as their only title to possession. Although the governing power was in the hands of a commercial monopoly, and under government patronage, the colonists were well treated. Minuit started a lively trade in furs and other products of the country, and after a winter of privation, fresh settlers, including

1641. many Dutchmen, arrived, and the colony prospered and grew strong. Minuit died not long after the establishment of his colony, and was succeeded by a Swede, one Hollandaere, who was fol-

1643. lowed by the most noted of the Swedish Governors, John Printz, renowned for his violent temper, his great bulk, and his fighting propensities.

During Hollandaere's administration came the first intimation to the South River colony of the existence of the race destined to become their rulers, and the owners of their territory. The restless people of New England, though hardly yet fixed in their own homes, had already begun to cast longing eyes abroad. They had ruined the

1641. Dutch on the Connecticut, and they now prepared to get a share in the trade and lands of the Middle States. An expedition from New Haven sailed up the South River, and founded two settlements. Instinctively aware that these intruders were a common foe, Dutch and Swedes united and broke up the English posts. The confederated colonies of New England remonstrated, and fresh trading parties issued from Connecticut; but Printz, who had arrived in the mean time, and built a fort, besides a fine house for himself—"Printz Hall"—and founded a new settlement at Tinicum, twelve miles below Philadelphia, was not the man to stand such intrusion. The New England ships were fired on, and their crews imprisoned. Again the Confederacy remonstrated, only to be met with a denial of violence from Printz. Englishmen were driven from Delaware, for the time at least.

Printz was, however, as determined and aggressive toward the Dutch as he had been to the New Englanders, and his perpetual interference with the Dutch at Fort Nassau led at last to an open breach between the nations. The Swedes, however, were in the ascendant, and controlled the trade of the river. The power of the Dutch was at a low point, and their Scandinavian rivals threatened to become the possessors of the great regions of the Delaware. This state of affairs lasted for some years, and the only settlement possible was by force of arms. Stuyvesant, who succeeded Kieft, was of a very different temper from his predecessor, and determined to vindicate Dutch authority everywhere; so as soon as he could find time from the pressing affairs of New Amsterdam, he turned his attention to the South River, and built below the Swedish forts Fort Casimir, thus gaining control of navigation, and disposing effectually of foreign interference. Printz, perplexed by the gathering difficulties, and unpopular from his stern rule and violent temper, returned to Sweden, leaving the government with his son-in-law, John Pappegoia. Soon after came a Swedish vessel-of-war, commanded by John Rysingh, who landed near Fort Casimir, made himself master of the place, and expelled the Dutch without bloodshed. Rysingh then assumed the government of the colony, and set about extending and consolidating the Swedish power, now in appearance stronger than ever before. But the appearance was deceptive and short-lived. Stuyvesant seized a vessel laden with stores for Sweden, quietly prepared an overwhelming force for the reduction of the South River settlements, and in early autumn sailed from New York with an army of six or seven hundred men. Fort Casimir capitulated at once at sight of the Dutch, and Stuyvesant, marching on, compelled Rysingh to surrender Fort Chris-

1646.

1651.

1653.

1654.

1655.

tina. The Swedes were outnumbered and overawed. There was no
bloodshed; private property was respected, and the inhabitants were
merely required to swear allegiance to the States-General. Thus fell
the Swedish empire in America. Holland was supreme upon the Delaware and upon the Hudson. One of the Northern races had been
conquered, and only two remained to contest the dominion of the
continent. Sweden complained, as Holland had done years before;
but the positions of the two nations were now reversed. Complaints
were not listened to at the Hague, and Sweden henceforth could do
no more for her colonists than send out faithful ministers to encourage them in the maintenance of their religion.

A year after the conquest, the West India Company sold the Delaware region to the city of Amsterdam. The municipality at
1656. once took possession of their property, sent out a governor
and a body of emigrants, who, on arrival, named Fort Casimir New
Amstel, and took possession of it, while the Company retained
1657. Fort Christina and the northern settlement on the Delaware.
At first the new colony planted by the Amsterdam burghers flourished; but sickness and bad crops came, and, despite fresh immigration, the new settlement had a hard struggle for existence. Harsh
measures on the part of the city, suspicion and desertion among the
inhabitants, combined with outbursts of famine and disease, gave the
fertile region an evil name, and brought New Amstel to a low point;
while their difficulties were still further aggravated by troubles with
Maryland. Boundaries too were sources of disturbance, and rumors
came of armed English invasion. Stuyvesant sent troops, and negotiated successfully; but the external pressure was a fresh cause of
1660. alarm, and the new director, Hinoyossa, of discontent, while the
proposed retransfer to the Company gave good ground for renewed popular distrust. Matters went on in this way, with the colony
thriving at last, and trade increasing, but with the director constantly
quarrelling with the Company's agent, until at last the whole South
1663. River territory was surrendered to the city. This needed
change had hardly been accomplished, when the whole fabric of
government was overthrown by the English. The rule of the Dutch
had been sufficiently uneasy, but the Swedes were fully avenged when
Robert Carr, one of the royal commissioners, appeared in the South
River to complete the seizure of the Dutch possessions in the name
of the Duke of York. The burghers and planters capitulated after a
brief delay, but the Governor and soldiers refused to assent. The

English stormed the fort; a few of the Dutch were slain; and Carr, master of the settlements, proceeded at once to display the mean cruelty and greedy rapacity which seemed inseparable from the rule of Charles Stuart and his followers.

The Swedish government roused for a moment to revive its claim, but it was hopeless. The Delaware settlements gave way tranquilly to the English rule, Dutch and Swedes both prospering under their new masters; and being of a practical turn of mind, do not appear to have repined much at their fate. After the first brutality of Sir Robert Carr, the government went on peaceably enough, and the inhabitants, having at least as much liberty as they had been wont to enjoy under the Company or the city, were contented. One outbreak is recorded which was headed by a Swede; but, on the whole, Delaware, as an appendage of New York, prospered under English rule, and the English Governor at New York dealt so much more effectively with the encroachments from Maryland than the Dutch had been able to do, that the agents of Lord Baltimore were held in check.

With the reconquest of New York by the Dutch, Delaware came quietly again under the rule of Holland, and in little more **1673-1674.** than a year was handed back as quietly to England by the treaty of Westminster. Thus fell the power of the second Northern race which had contested the dominion of America with the English. Always an appendage of New York, Delaware had passed from the control of one nation to that of another, and her whole history had been made up of these changes. Henceforth the ruling nation in Delaware remained unaltered, but the colony went on for some years longer in the old way of shifting masters. The only difference now was that the contending rulers were all English. The first attempt came from the New Jersey settlers, led by Fenwick, who landed and established himself at Salem, the El**1675-1676.** singburg of the Swedes. Andros objected. Fenwick resisted, but was finally seized by the Duke's agents in Delaware and taken to Newcastle, and thence to New York. In the following year Fenwick was at Salem, again carrying himself as an inde**1677-1678.** pendent proprietor. He was again arrested and sent to New York, and his colony at Salem placed under the government at Newcastle. The first Quaker effort on the Delaware failed. The second was more successful. The great province of Pennsylvania was granted to William Penn, who soon found that he needed access to the ocean, and rights sufficient to prevent the encroachments of

14

his Maryland neighbors. Penn's influence prevailed at court. He obtained a grant of all the Duke's interest within twelve miles of Newcastle, and as far south as Cape Henlopen. On his ar- 1682. rival, the Duke's agents met him at Newcastle, when they surrendered to him the South River settlements; and thus Delaware was finally separated from New York, passed under the government of Penn, and formed part of his province.

The people received Penn with gladness, and, under his mild and free government, the condition of the colony rapidly improved. Population increased, while trade and agriculture revived and flourished, and the colonial history of Delaware was merged in that of Pennsylvania.

Chapter XII.

PENNSYLVANIA FROM 1681 TO 1765.

The history of the settlement of Pennsylvania is closely interwoven with that of the man whose name was given to the new province. Into the life of William Penn it is not necessary to enter. The story is a familiar one, and has been spread and maintained by the once powerful sect of which he was the most eminent leader. Penn was, too, of all the men who founded states in America, the most celebrated in the mother country. He was a very conspicuous figure in England during the period of the Restoration and the closing years of the seventeenth century. Every one knows how the son and heir of a wealthy, worldly, and successful sailor and courtier became the zealous and persecuted leader of a despised sect; and how his influence and power steadily increased, until he became the favorite and adviser of James. His character is a curious mingling of dissimilar qualities. He was at once a saint and a courtier, a religious fanatic and a shrewd man of affairs and of the world. With the controversies awakened by Macaulay's sweeping charges we have here nothing to do. Penn appears in American history simply as the wise founder of a state, the prudent and just magistrate, the liberal-minded law-giver and ruler. His attention was first drawn to colonization by the misfortunes of New Jersey, in which Quakers had become interested, and in which he himself finally took part in hopes of ordering and regulating the confused affairs of that province; but he had, besides, two strong motives impelling him in the same direction. He had a large inherited claim against the government, which he could only hope to have paid in wild American lands; and he was the guide and protector of a numerous, industrious, and persecuted people, admirably fitted for colonization, and eager for the peace denied them in England.

At last, after some difficulty before the Lords of Trade, Penn's petition was granted, and he received a deed from the Crown of forty

thousand square miles of territory, which was christened by the King
"Pennsylvania." Penn then issued an address setting forth
1681. his scheme. The government was to be a just and righteous
government, in conformity with Quaker principles. It was to be a
government of law, and the people were to be a party to it, while the
great principle that governments depend upon men, not men upon
governments, was clearly and emphatically expressed. Perfect liberty
of conscience was guaranteed to all. Capital punishment was to be
inflicted only for murder and treason; and other penalties were to be
imposed on the theory of reformation, and not of retaliation. Trial
by jury was assured not only to white men but to Indians. The
whole document was statesman-like in tone, and broad and liberal in
principle. Penn offered land at forty shillings for a hundred acres,
subject only to a small quit-rent; and even servants were to be allowed
to hold fifty acres in fee-simple.

The effect of these proposals was great and immediate. Quakers
from all parts of England pressed forward to join the emigration,
while Penn's fame drew other settlers from all over Europe, and notably from Germany, where a company was formed, under the lead of
Franz Pastorius, which took fifteen thousand acres. The first year
three ships went out filled with emigrants, who established themselves
in caves and huts on the banks of the Delaware. The following
1682. year Penn himself, with a company of a hundred, went over
and landed at Newcastle, where he was heartily welcomed by
his Dutch and Swedish subjects, whom he naturalized, and confirmed
in their property and offices. He then proceeded up the river to
Chester, where the first Assembly of delegates, chosen by the commissioners whom Penn had sent before him, was held, and the government was organized. Acts of settlement and union with the old
Delaware colonies were passed, and a body of law adopted in conformity with the principles laid down in the advertisement. He
then put in execution his Indian policy, involving a great departure
from that pursued in the other colonies. Under the famous tree at
Shackamaxon, Penn made a treaty of peace with the Indians, winning their confidence, and obtaining their land by fair purchase; although, as walking was the method adopted for measurement, the
trained English pedestrians had much the same advantage over the Indians that the Carthaginians obtained by means of the famous ox-hide.
External relations being thus settled, Penn selected the broad peninsula
between the Delaware and the Schuylkill, and there founded the city

of Philadelphia. He also ordered two handsome houses to be built for himself—one in Philadelphia, and one at his manor of Pennsbury.

The auspicious beginning was followed by an emigration and a growth of population unequalled, except in Massachusetts, in American colonial history. In one year seven thousand settlers are said to have arrived; and before the century closed the colonists numbered more than twenty thousand, and Philadelphia had grown to be a thriving town. After two busy years, in which he had organized and established a government and courts of justice, made firm alliances **1684.** with the Indians, and founded a city, Penn returned to England. Everything had gone smoothly thus far. The charter provisions had been modified to suit the people, and the Assembly had granted money to the proprietary. It seemed an opportune moment for Penn to visit England, revive his influence at court, and combat Lord Baltimore on the question of boundaries. On his departure, he left the government in the hands of Thomas Lloyd, president, Colonel Markham, secretary, and a Council composed of the judges and other provincial officers.

Penn hardly had time to reach England before the troubles common to proprietary governments broke out in Pennsylvania. The first conflict arose between the ruling or Quaker party and some of the more prominent men who were not of their sect. Nicholas Moore, the chief-justice, was impeached and expelled the Assembly for violence, partiality, and negligence; and the clerk of the provincial court was arrested because he refused to produce his minutes. Other troubles also broke out in the form of disorder, while immorality and looseness prevailed in the caves of the Delaware. The need of the proprietary was sorely felt, and yet Penn found reason to complain of the treatment he received; for the impost granted him was imperfectly collected, and the people let the quit-rents fall into arrears and resisted payment.

With matters in this unsatisfactory condition, Thomas Lloyd resigned; and Penn, in the hopes of quieting the province, appointed **1688.** one Blackwell, an outsider and stranger, his deputy. Blackwell quarrelled at once with everybody. He succeeded in breaking up the Assembly, and was then involved in a conflict with the Council. After nine months of stormy and high-handed rule, he withdrew, leaving the government once more with Thomas Lloyd. The disorders of Blackwell's administration had, as their chief result, the production of a new and able popular leader in the per-

son of David Lloyd—Penn's attorney-general. Blackwell had hardly been removed when a fresh contest arose between the province
and the Delaware territories, caused by jealousies in regard to offices; and after much bickering and negotiation, the union was
1691. dissolved. Lloyd remained at the head of the province, and
Markham, as Lieutenant-governor, with a separate legislature, took
charge of Delaware. Hard upon these political dissensions came religious strife. George Keith, an active, unscrupulous, and violent zeal-
ot, brought about a serious schism among the Quakers, and caused so
much irritation by his attacks, that the secular power was called in,
and he was arrested and thrown into prison. Then was heard the cry
of religious intolerance in the State devoted to liberty of conscience,
and complaints rapidly found their way to England. These accumulated troubles came upon Penn at an evil hour. He had gone home
to rise to the greatest height of favor and influence under James, and
had been cast down and covered with suspicion and dislike by the
Revolution. In vain had he striven to prevent the disunion of the
province and the territories, to allay the political bitterness, and stifle
the schism in his sect. The conflict aroused by Keith had its dreaded
result. Religious controversy and intolerance offered a sufficient excuse
to rulers by whom Penn was regarded with disfavor. The government
was taken from him, and intrusted by royal commission to
1693. a royal Governor—Benjamin Fletcher. To Fletcher the government was surrendered, at Philadelphia, without resistance; and the
new Governor, without regard to charter or laws, or to the separation
of Pennsylvania and Delaware, summoned a general Assembly from
both province and territories, and a Council on his own model, and
demanded assistance for the war with France upon the northern frontiers. Instead of giving money, the Assembly entered into a controversy with Fletcher as to his powers and their rights under the old
charter; and, after a fruitless wrangle, the new Governor returned to
New York, to which he threatened to annex the province of the re-
calcitrant Quakers. The next year Markham was left as deputy, while
Fletcher contented himself with sending letters asking for money and
supplies, which he did not obtain.

Meanwhile Penn had gained a hearing, and a prompt acquittal of
disloyalty, and the restoration of his government followed.
1694. Unable to leave England at that moment, he continued Markham in the office of deputy. Markham, assuming that the old charter and laws had been abrogated by the suspension of the proprietary,

convened the Assembly without regard to them. The Assembly had no objection to this theory, for they aimed, under the able leadership of Lloyd, to change the frame of government to suit themselves; and this, **1696.** after a short struggle with Markham, and by voting money for the war, they effected. The Assembly was to sit on its own adjournments, originate bills, and be indissoluble during the term for which it was elected. The Assembly was also to be elected annually, the Council biennially, and all offices were carefully defined. The rest of Markham's term was quiet, except for the pirates, who infested the coast here as elsewhere, and received enough sympathy to bring the province into disrepute. Markham, supported by the Assembly, took steps to remedy this evil, which, however, was destined for a long time to injure and disgrace the province.

As the century closed, Penn, freed at last from affairs which had **1699.** kept him in England, came out with his family and resumed control of the province, where he intended to pass the rest of his life. Without regard to the constitution already enacted, he called the Assembly together, and took steps to form a new charter and laws, while he also attempted to check the slave-trade, and succeeded in having a law passed regulating the treatment and punishment of the negroes. His Indian policy, which involved further restrictions on the intercourse of whites and Indians, and aimed also at a spread of the Gospel among the savages, met with no support. The money demanded by the Crown for the war was not given by the Assembly, on account of religious scruples; and in the midst of his labors Penn received news that the policy of changing the proprietary to royal governments was again revived. He was obliged, therefore, to push through the charters of Philadelphia and Pennsylvania, which he was ready to grant, and which, in view of his probable loss of the province, he was willing to make liberal. The city charter was easily adopted, but the Assembly made a contest, and tried to extort the last possible concession from their proprietary. The government, as finally established, differed but little from that created previously by the Assembly, and was in accordance with the general principles laid down in Penn's original scheme. All power was vested in the Assembly, to whose discretion the creation of courts was also given. The Council was to be merely an advisory and executive body, and not an upper house, and the union of the province and territories was again to be dissolved if the people so desired, as was probable from the grumbling and discontent once more apparent in Delaware. When this important work

was done, Penn sailed for England, never to return.   He left Andrew
Hamilton, of New Jersey, as his deputy, and James Logan as
1701.   secretary.   To Logan was also confided the management of
the proprietary estates; and the secretary thus became the representative of Penn and his family, the leader of his party, and, as he was a
shrewd and able man, the power behind the throne, and the principal
person in the province for many years.

Hamilton's administration was short and unfortunate.   He was constantly at war with the Assembly and the popular party, headed by
Lloyd; and during this time a High-Church or Crown party, small but
active, grew up under the direction of Colonel Quarry, the judge of
admiralty.   This royal party delayed the confirmation of Hamilton,
and used the failure of the pacific Quakers to provide for defence as
an argument in England for the destruction of the proprietary government.   At the same period, too, the territories again became restive, and the province, which by this time had had enough of them,
shook them off, and let them have a legislature of their own, thus
finally severing the union.

In the year 1703 Hamilton died, and was succeeded by John
Evans, a young Welshman, who put himself wholly under Lo-
1703.   gan's direction.   Failing in his first scheme, which was to re-
unite the province and territories, Evans at once came to blows with
the Assembly on the matter of prorogation, which the popular party
denied to the Governor.   Not content with a stubborn opposition to
Evans, the Assembly sent a memorial to Penn, abusing him, and his
officers and government, most violently.   The forces were now fairly
engaged, Lloyd leading on one side, Logan on the other; the Assembly against the Council and the officers.   At first the Assembly prevailed; but the memorial to Penn caused a reaction, and Penn's reply
1705.   and strong support of the Governor gave the victory at last to
Logan, whose party triumphed in the elections, and returned
a House which devoted itself to passing necessary laws.   Evans,
meantime, rapidly lost the ground he had gained by setting himself
against the pacific policy of the Quakers, and trying to get support
for the war.   To arouse them, he caused a false alarm of invasion to
1706.   be given—a scheme in which Logan was said to be involved,
and which only resulted in profound disgust, and a return of
the popular party to power at the next election.   There was now a
new and important subject of dispute before them.   The bill drawn
by Lloyd to establish a judiciary had been rejected by the privy

council through proprietary influence, and the whole question was again open. Evans, threatening to establish a judiciary by preroga-tive, would come to no terms with the Assembly, who were deter-mined the Council should not be a court of chancery; and an in-terview between the Governor and Assembly led to a personal quarrel with Lloyd, who was now back again as Speaker. The Assembly, baffled and angry, voted to impeach Logan of every misdemeanor in the calendar. The Governor denied their power. The Assembly then drew up a remonstrance, accusing the Governor and Logan of every form of wrong-doing, from excluding Quakers from offices to stopping the judiciary bill, and sent this remonstrance to Penn and to the Board of Trade. The next Assembly came together in a similar temper, and Evans again negatived the judiciary bill, and de-clared he would do nothing until he heard from the Board of Trade. The affair had now reached a dead-lock. The Assembly would grant nothing to the proprietary; the Governor would not establish courts. Pirates infested the Delaware, and disgraced the colony; but when Evans appealed for aid, the Assembly, after the manner of colo-nial legislatures, refused to give anything, alleging the most disingenu-ous reasons, and striving to gain a political advantage from the neces-sities of the State. The controversy had not been helped by the char-acter of Evans, who was loose in his morals, haughty, headstrong, and imperious. Guided by Logan, he had made a strong fight; but the remonstrance of the Assembly obliged Penn to remove him, and send out Charles Gookin as his successor.

1708.

1709.

The Assembly at once attacked the new Governor on a number of small points, and refused to give aid for the war, now urgent in its demands; and they were still further exasperated by instructions which forbade the Governor to act without the assent of the Council, or, as they naturally interpreted it, of Logan. This re-newed the war between Lloyd and the secretary. The latter ac-cused the former of grave misdemeanors; but as he was unable to sustain them, they were pronounced by the Assembly false and libel-lous. Logan then in a most insulting fashion asked them to try him on the impeachment. The Assembly arrested him, and the Governor released him. He then sailed for England, and thus gave the finishing stroke to the long controversy by inducing Penn to write a letter re-proving the Assembly, and threatening an immediate cession to the Crown, which at once brought the popular party to terms, and in the next Assembly everything went smoothly. The right to sit

1710.

on their own adjournment was conceded; the judiciary established without a court of equity, and the expenses of the government were cheerfully voted. The following year two thousand pounds were given to the Crown in aid of the war, and Gookin's administration moved easily. The government was regulated, and the importation of slaves restrained.

This relief seemed to have come too late for Penn. With his prov-
1712. ince mortgaged and harassed by creditors, he decided to sell his rights to the Crown for twelve thousand pounds; but before the sale was consummated, a stroke of apoplexy enfeebled his mind, and put a stop to business. The province was relieved by the failure of this scheme, for they were attached to the easy and simple forms of the proprietary rule, and harmony continued to subsist until
1714. the Governor, irritated by constant irregularity of payment, quarrelled with the Assembly about his meagre salary. Once started, he rapidly lost the ground he had gained. He insisted that the statutes should be construed so as to make all affirmations illegal, which tended to throw all the legal and official business of the province into disorder, for almost every one of importance was a Quaker, and it also awakened the strong animosity of religious feeling. Still, not content, the Governor, whose mind was probably impaired, proceeded to assail Norris, the Speaker of the Assembly, and Logan, the
1717. two chief men of the province. This produced an organized movement for his recall, which was effectual, and Sir William Keith came out as his successor. The new Governor was hardly established when the distinguished man who had founded the
1718. colony died; but his death made no change in the condition of his province, which passed, after a protracted lawsuit, to the children of his second wife.

Sir William Keith, who came to the head of affairs just as the great Quaker was passing away, had been surveyor of the customs for the southern provinces, and was familiar with the affairs of Pennsylvania. He was an adroit man, insincere, and with a good deal of the demagogue in his disposition. He succeeded in obtaining the confidence of the people, put himself at the head of the popular party, and, by conceding everything desired by the Assembly, he raised his own influence to such a point that he gained all he wished for himself. He freed himself from the control of the Council, for which there was no constitutional ground, and thus shackled Logan, who, however, remained quietly at his post as secretary, and bided his time.

Keith also succeeded in establishing the obnoxious court of equity, with himself as chancellor. His Indian policy was wise and successful, and preserved the peace of the province; but his financial policy, when the fiscal affairs were in a very tangled state, was, though popular, thoroughly bad. He introduced and carried through the issue of bills of credit, saddling Pennsylvania with the curse of a depreciated paper currency. The same year there came to Philadelphia a young man who soon became and continued the central figure in Pennsylvanian provincial history. This was Benjamin Franklin, who was almost immediately brought in contact with the Governor. The story of their connection is familiar, and Keith has the almost unique honor of having overreached and deceived Franklin.

1723.

Misled by the strength of his position, Keith, in the midst of his successes, determined to rid himself of his enemies, and on very slight provocation removed Logan from the Council and the office of secretary. This was the false step for which Logan had waited. He at once sailed for England, and his journey soon bore fruit in letters from Hannah Penn and the Trustees, accusing Keith of neglect of the proprietary interest and disregard of the Council, and reproving him severely for his issue of paper-money. Keith replied, asserting his right to act independently, and indiscreetly laid Mrs. Penn's letter before the Assembly, who still had great regard for the wishes of the proprietary. Lloyd, now chief-justice, roused at the new controversy, and easily overthrew Logan's argument in favor of the powers of the Council; but neither he nor Keith could destroy Logan's influence in England, by which the latter was removed, and replaced by Patrick Gordon, who, having been appointed by the family, and confirmed, came out the following year and took possession of the government. Keith, after his deposition, entered the Assembly, and strove to oppose and break down the new Governor; but his influence and popularity rapidly waned, and he soon after disappears from the history of the province.

1726.

Gordon's administration partook of the uneventfulness characteristic of the Walpole period in England. The Governor and the Assembly got on very well together, and without any serious dissensions. The court of equity erected by Keith was abolished, and Pennsylvania plunged still deeper into the ruin of depreciated and popular paper-money by an additional issue of thirty thousand pounds. Trade flourished, and population increased rapidly, especially the German immigration, which was so large as to cause

1729.

serious alarm both in the province and England ; but the Germans
proved, as a rule, excellent citizens.   This growing population, however, pushing out on the frontier, came in contact with the Indians,
and there was from time to time a fear of Indian war.   During this
period, too, we first perceive in Pennsylvania a vague anxiety in regard to the spread of the French power, which began to cast its shadow, dark with savage war, over the future of the colonies.   There was
also a moment of brief suspicion and dread of the Roman Catholics,
and some agitation against them ; but in the land of religious toleration nothing was done, and the only break in the quiet of the time
was a bitter and rather turbulent contest with Maryland on the matter of boundaries.

After a peaceful administration of ten years, Governor Gordon died,
and was succeeded by James Logan, who, as President of the
1736. Council, ruled the province in which he had so long been the
master-spirit for two uneventful years, when he was superseded by
George Thomas, a planter of Antigua, who was sent out as Governor.
Soon after the arrival of Thomas, the Maryland dispute was
1738. finally settled, leaving Delaware intact, and arranging the other differences on the general theory of *uti possidetis.*   The new Governor had some trouble at the outset in regard to issuing warrants
for proprietary lands, which had been suspended during the minority
of the Penn heirs, and was revived with considerable opposition, especially from those who, during the interval, had taken up lands without the formality of a warrant.   With this exception, everything
promised to proceed as harmoniously as under the previous Govern-
or ; but these pleasant appearances were, unfortunately, soon dissipated
by the war between Spain and England.   Thomas, instead
1739. of using a little management, attempted to argue down the
Quaker principles in regard to fighting, and the Assembly, nettled at
the attack, refused supplies.   The next year came peremptory demands from England, and great pressure, not only from the proprietaries, but from a portion of the people.   Thus pushed, the Assembly, after much delay, granted money, but under such conditions as
to almost nullify their action.   They based their renewed opposition on the fact that the Governor, in raising militia, had, by enlisting
bond-servants, invaded the rights of property ; and supported by the
people, although the merchants remonstrated, the Assembly continued
to thwart and oppose every measure of the Governor for the defence
of the province, and in aid of the Crown, while they put the usual

pressure on the Governor by withholding his salary. The Quaker party was less strong than in the early days, and that of the Governor more vigorous, and better supported by the wealthy inhabitants, especially in Philadelphia. The conflict became excited and bitter, and at last resulted in a violent election riot in Philadelphia, in which the forces of the Governor were routed. This led to fresh quarrels; and finally the Governor, harassed by lack of salary, made advances of a conciliatory nature, gave way as to certain bills, and was paid in full. There had been no difficulty in raising men, but the narrow and selfish policy of the Assembly had reduced Pennsylvania to insignificance, impotence, and unpopularity during the war.

When war with France was added to the existing complications, **1744.** Thomas again went actively to work to raise men; and as he was powerfully aided by Franklin, and supported by Logan, the Quaker Assembly were obliged to content themselves with mere apathy. Volunteers were enrolled, and a fort was built by means of a lottery; but the Assembly, uninfluenced by all this, refused, on one frivolous excuse and another, to take any part in the Louisburg expedition, and were only forced by royal command at the last moment to grudgingly give money for supplies. Thus, by their continued selfishness, they lost all share in the glory won by the provincials in the capture of Louisburg. They took no part, either, in the subsequent Canada expedition which was attempted by the other colonies, and the only gain made by the province was through the troops raised by Thomas, which enabled him to carry out a firm Indian policy, and prevent a border war. Soon after these events, **1746.** Thomas resigned, and was succeeded by Anthony Palmer, President of the Council, who persisted successfully in maintaining and renewing the Indian treaties, withdrawing the tribes from **1748.** French influence, and thus held them in check until peace was declared. The quarrels between the Council and the Assembly continued undiminished on the subject of the ravages of the defenceless coasts and shipping by privateers, and the efforts of the executive to ward off these attacks.

A new Governor, James Hamilton, the son of Andrew Hamilton, the eminent lawyer and Speaker of the House, found that he had inherited not only the dignities and duties, but the quarrels, of his predecessors. The peace of Aix-la-Chapelle did not stop the extension of French influence, nor check the dangerous schemes of that power. The policy of making treaties with the Indians and holding them to their alliance had to be persevered in closely; and this policy had now become a heavy burden to the State. This burden the Assembly justly felt ought to be shared by the proprietaries, whose wild lands were more benefited by peace than those of any others, and they therefore demanded that the proprietary estates should be taxed. The proprietaries replied feebly and offensively, and the Assembly had much the better of the argument. They had, too, the **1750.** advantage of a great leader in the person of Franklin, who from being clerk had become a member of the Assembly, and who managed the whole of the discussion. The first encounter was without result; but the controversy was destined to grow, and to last many years.

Under the lead of Franklin, too, they entered upon another conflict, in which they were as much in the wrong as they had been in the right in the matter of the proprietary estates. Money was scarce, and the Assembly wished to issue more depreciated paper. The Governor wisely and firmly opposed this scheme, although he attempted a compromise by fixing means of redemption, and by referring to the Crown. Both proposals were rejected. The real secret of the difference was that the Governor was required to keep all the interest of loans within the control of the proprietaries, and forbidden to countenance **1754.** issues of paper. The outbreak of war and the defeat of Washington on the frontier made the need of money imperative. The Assembly voted thirty-five thousand pounds, fifteen of which were for the use of the King in bills of credit; but the Governor still refused to assent, and soon after gave up his office, which he had resigned some time before.

He was succeeded by Robert Hunter Morris, son of Lewis Morris, of New Jersey, who brought urgent instructions that Pennsylvania should unite with the other colonies and contribute to the war. The result was a vote of forty thousand pounds in bills of credit, twenty thousand being intended for the Crown. The Governor demanded that they should be made redeemable in five years. The Assembly refused; and a dispute began which lasted for two years, and utterly crippled the province. As the bitter, useless quarrel progressed, Braddock could get no assistance except from the personal exertions of Franklin, and then went to defeat and death on the frontier. The rout of Braddock laid the whole border bare to the wasting and cruel ravages of the Indians. In vain did the cry of distress go up from the hunted people of the interior; the wrangle at Philadelphia still went on. The Assembly receded from its first position, and took up their opposition on the ground that the proprietary estates ought to be taxed; and at this point another dead-lock ensued. Gradually the terrible distress of the province forced them to dole out money to help Massachusetts and the other eastern and northern colonies. Under great pressure they passed a volunteer militia bill, and, inadequate as this was, Franklin succeeded in bringing about the enlistment of a considerable number of troops, and, although he was no soldier, went at their head to the interior, producing a good effect upon the Indian tribes. The Governor, from time to time, extorted a little money; but his salary remained unpaid. The Indians were again on the frontier, carrying war in all directions; and again came a **1756.** dead-lock on the proprietary estates. The controversy was about to be renewed in all its senseless stages, when Morris was superseded by Governor Denny.

The new Governor was received with great joy, which speedily cooled when it was found that he could not assent to any bill which did not give him a share in disposing of any issue of bills or money raised by revenue; that he could not permit the issue of more than forty thousand pounds in bills; and that he was only to allow a partial taxation of the proprietary estates. The struggle was at once renewed over a bill to lay an excise; and the position of the Assembly was defended with acute ability by Franklin. Meantime, of course, devastation proceeded; and, urged by commands from England, provincial troops were raised, but with no supplies. An expedition, planned by Morris and led by Armstrong, inflicted a severe defeat upon the Indians at Kittanning, and was the first gleam of light in the darkness of the time. Stimulated by this success, the Assembly granted one hundred thousand pounds, and, giving way on the proprietary estates, sent Franklin and Norris to England to lay their grievances before the King. Matters, however, did not mend. Everything sank beneath the imbecile rule of Loudon, in command of all the colonial forces, and affairs went from bad to worse, until the victo- **1757.** ries of Montcalm roused even Pennsylvania to authorize troops for the protection of the frontier. Yet even at this moment of general danger, the Assembly and the Governor took occasion to have another quarrel over a judge, attacked by the former and protected by the latter. The strength of the Assembly in all this weary contest rested on the Quaker and German voters, who were utterly opposed to taxes and war.

At last even Pennsylvania was aroused by the ringing, commanding voice of the "Great Commoner." Loudoun and the rest disappeared. New men came out full of energy and vigor, and the letters of Pitt brought the Assembly to a sense of the needs of the time. The Governor, foreseeing the result of Franklin's mission, offered to have the proprietary estates taxed by special assessors; but the Assembly disdained the compromise, and voted one hundred thousand pounds, without including the proprietaries. A quarrel, of course, broke out, and went on between the commissioners of the Assembly and the Governor; but this time men and money were forthcoming, and the province appeared to better advantage than before. Fort Du Quesne was taken, the border of Pennsylvania was safe, Indian treaties were once more successfully negotiated, and the next year came the succession of victories in the North, and the overthrow of the French power in America. In the mean time Franklin had been fighting adroitly and forcibly the battle of the Assembly in England. The proprietaries addressed a long letter to the Assembly, who refused to recede, and the Governor at last gave way, and assented to a bill taxing the proprietary estates. This bill the proprietaries carried to the Privy Council, and, after a sharp contest, it received the royal approbation on the engagement of Franklin that the Governor should have a share in the disposal of the funds, and that the quit-rents should not be paid in bills of credit. Thus the Assembly finally carried their point; but in the conflict they had sacrificed the honor and welfare of the province during a long and trying war. They took advantage of war and danger to defeat the government; and although, with the exception of their paper-money schemes, and their refusal to provide for redemption, they were right in principle, their conduct was narrow, selfish, and unpatriotic. They put the safety of the country in peril to carry a political point, and hamper the executive. The controversy should have been postponed, for the end did not justify the means.

Governor Denny obtained his salary by finally assenting to the money bills; but he lost the favor of the proprietaries, and was replaced by James Hamilton, the former Governor, who was reappointed. The Canadian victories, meanwhile, relieved the middle colonies of all dangers; the forces of Pennsylvania were disbanded; and the Assembly undertook, despite Franklin's engagement, to retain the disposal of the funds granted by Parliament. The old contest was thus renewed, and when a requisition came from the Crown to main-

1758.

1759.

1761.

tain two-thirds of the troops on a war footing, the Assembly flatly refused; and, in their quarrel with the Governor, all the supply bills fell to the ground. The war with Spain brought a return of reason, however, and the parliamentary allotment of 1759 was devoted to the defences of Philadelphia. From this new strain they were soon re-lieved by the peace; but their relief was of short duration. A desolating Indian war broke out; the settlements were again driven back, and the frontier forts were in danger. Individual citizens came forward with money; but the everlasting conflict between the Governor and Assembly rendered the government impotent. Fortunately for the people, Colonel Bouquet, with the royal troops, defeated the Indians by great skill and bravery, and restored safety to the province; but his victory was followed by a rising of the people, and the wanton massacre of large bodies of friendly Indians at Lancaster and Paxton. This was the natural outcome of the senseless struggle for power, in a time of war, between Governor and Assembly. The insurgents marched on Philadelphia, where the Assembly passed a riot act, and the Governor helplessly lost his head. The exertions of Franklin, and the spirited conduct of the people of Philadelphia, alone saved the province, and put an end to this wretch-ed business of massacre and insurrection.

1762.

1763.

While the Indian war was still fitfully raging on the frontier, John Penn, one of the proprietaries, came out as the successor of Hamilton. After another struggle and much remonstrance, the Assembly granted money, and then started a movement to separate the government and the proprietary estates, or, in other words, to obtain a royal government for Pennsylvania. Petitions for the change poured in, and were sent to the English agent, with orders to push the business. The next election, after a sharp contest, left the power in the hands of those who favored a change, and who were led by Franklin and Galloway, and opposed by Dickinson; but while this was pending, a much graver question came before all the colonies, and ab-sorbed the attention of every one. The little matter of taxing pro-prietary estates was forgotten in the plan of the British ministry to tax the colonies. The Assembly instructed their agent, Mr. Mauduit, to ask a repeal of the Sugar Act, and oppose taxation; and they fol-lowed this up by sending Franklin again to England to represent them. The circular of Massachusetts was not laid before the Assem-bly, but as many members as could be brought together were sum-moned, and a committee was chosen. The opposition to the Stamp

1764.

15

Act was universal and deep-seated. John Hughes, the collector, was forced to sign a pledge that he would not execute his office, and the stamps were not allowed to be landed, and were not used. When the **1765.** Stamp Act Congress met in New York, the Pennsylvania committee was among the delegates, and the history of Pennsylvania becomes part of that of the United Colonies.

CHAPTER XIII.

PENNSYLVANIA AND DELAWARE, 1765.

THE social atmosphere changes completely as we pass from Maryland—the last of the southern group—into Delaware and Pennsylvania. These two provinces may be treated together; for their practical union under one government, and the circumstances of their settlement, had effaced any distinctions that might otherwise have existed. The older and smaller colony was a mere strip of land at the mouth of the noble river from which it takes its name, while the great province of Pennsylvania, alone among the thirteen colonies, had no coast, and only indirect communication with the ocean. On the eastern boundary the rich farming land began, and stretched away — rolling and broken, but always fertile—until the region rich in hidden iron and coal, and, finally, the steep slopes of the Alleghany range, were reached. The climate typified the geographical and political position of the middle colonies. It was temperate in the main, but displayed the extremes of both heat and cold, characteristic of the southern and northern groups; and, as Penn said, the "weather often changeth without notice, and is constant almost in its inconstancy."[1]

Bancroft estimates the population of the two colonies possessing this large and rich territory at one hundred and ninety-five thousand in the year 1755.[2] At the time of the Revolution it had increased probably to more than four hundred thousand, of whom one-quarter to a third were negroes.[3] The first-comers in this large and rapidly-

---

[1] Watson's Annals of Philadelphia, ii., 1683.   [2] Bancroft, iv., 129.

[3] The contemporary estimates are, as usual, very wild, and differ hopelessly: Board of Trade, 1755—220,000, see Bancroft, iv., 129, note; Smyth, ii., 309—320,000, one-third blacks; Brissot, p. 279, Payers of Capitation tax, 1760—31,000; 1770—39,000; 1779—45,000; 1786—66,000; Burnaby, p. 80, 400,000 to 500,000, one-fifth Quakers, few negroes; Watson's Annals, ii., Franklin's estimate, 1766—160,000 whites, one-third Quakers, one-third Germans; État Présent de la Pennsylvanie, 1756—250,000 whites; Colonial Records, vii., 448, Peters's estimate, 200,000, one-eighth Quakers; Hazard, Pennsylvania Archives, 1773—300,000 whites, 200,000 blacks.

growing community were the Swedes, a simple, agricultural people, peaceable alike with Dutch, English, and Indians.   At the close of the seventeenth century they were still numerous and powerful in the Delaware settlements, and retained their mother tongue; but after that time they were rapidly absorbed by the new population which surrounded them, and, unaided by fresh arrivals, lost their distinctive qualities.   They were a strong, sturdy race, and a valuable element among the people.[1]   The Dutch, who superseded them, left but few settlers to survive the rush of English immigration, which, begun by the Quakers, consisted almost exclusively of families drawn from the middle classes of tradesmen, shopkeepers, and small farmers, with an infusion, by no means trifling, of convicts, indented servants, and wandering adventurers.   Many Welsh also came to Pennsylvania, and seem to have been a valuable addition.   The two foreign elements, however, which together outnumbered the English, and gave to Pennsylvania a character wholly different from that of any other colony, were the Germans and Irish.   The former began to come immediately upon the foundation of the colony, and settled at Germantown. These first-comers were drawn thither on account of religion, and included Quakers and Palatines, and, later, Ridge Hermits, Dunkards, Mennonists, and Pietists.   Afterward the immigration thus started grew from natural causes, until, at the time of the Revolution, they formed nearly a third of the population, and occupied exclusively large districts of western Pennsylvania.   They were chiefly farmers, thrifty, saving, and industrious, but stubborn, ignorant, and unreliable in times of war.   Their numerical importance is shown by the effect they had upon the language, producing a well-defined dialect known familiarly as Pennsylvania Dutch.   The Irish immigration began in the year 1719, and assumed such large proportions as to demand legislation ten years later.   A large part of these settlers were Scotch - Irish Presbyterians, valuable and good colonists; but there were also many others of Irish race, who were, as a rule, a very undesirable addition at that period.   Scarcely more than a third of the latter succeeded as farmers; and they were a hard-drinking, idle, quarrelsome, and disorderly class, always at odds with the government, and did much to give to that government and to politics the character for weakness and turbulence, which, beginning before the Revolution, has broken out at intervals down to the present day.   This brief outline

---

[1] Pennsylvania Hist. Coll., iii., Holme's History.

of the population shows the great mixture of races, and in a rough way the qualities of the principal elements, which had a marked effect upon the society of the colony and the later history of the State.[1]

The people of Pennsylvania and Delaware relied chiefly upon agriculture for support, and the great mass of them were tillers and cultivators of the soil. But there were many merchants and tradesmen as well, besides shopkeepers and mechanics. The radical difference between the middle and southern colonies is nowhere better shown than in the economical contrast. The single staple of Virginia was here replaced by varied products, and the commerce of Pennsylvania was a fruitful source of wealth. The exports and imports were worth at the period of the Revolution more than a million pounds; and trade, legal and illicit, extending not only to England, but to Lisbon, Madeira, and the West Indies, employed nearly five hundred vessels and over seven thousand seamen.[2] The exports embraced many natural products. Penn had at an early day set his face against the cultivation of tobacco, and although some was grown in the more southern districts, the great Virginian staple was superseded. The principal exports were grain and flour; but timber and every kind of farm produce were sold in large quantities, and there was an extensive and valuable fur trade, founded by Penn himself. The imports, besides wines and sugar, consisted, of course, mainly of manufactured articles. There could hardly be said to be any manufactures as yet in Pennsylvania; but the germs were there, and the first experiments were in progress; the coarser articles were made in considerable quantities, and these indications, as well as the mining industries, clearly showed the bent of the people. Saw-mills and grist-mills were numerous, and employed, not only by the Pennsylvanians, but by their less enterprising neighbors of the south; and ships were built at the Philadelphia docks, and used by the traders of the province. As early as the end of the seventeenth century the manufacture of paper and of glass was tried by the Germans at Germantown and Mannheim, as well as

---

[1] Michaux's Travels, p. 31; Smyth's Tour, ii., 279, 309; Brissot, p. 290; Kalm, i., 58, 216; Foote, Sketches of Virginia, i., 99; Watson's Annals, ii.; Crévecœur, p. 48, and in regard to Irish, p. 78; Coll. Hist. Soc., v., Braddock's Exped., Sargent, Convicts, etc.

[2] Smyth, ii., 307; Wallace, Inaugural Address to Hist. Soc., 1872; Watson's Annals of Philadelphia, ii.; État Present de la Pennsylvanie; Huguenot Family in Virginia, p. 30; Burnaby, p. 80; Colonial Rec., i., 1697; Hist. Soc. Coll., ix., 1702, Customs on goods from Pennsylvania.

that of druggets, crapes, and stockings, the last forming a thriving and profitable industry. Some of the Irish made linen of good quality, and homespun was in general domestic use. Vines and silk were also tried under government auspices, as in the other colonies, and with a like lack of success. The most marked development was seen in the iron industry. The first furnace was started in the year 1720, and in 1750 three thousand tons of pig-iron were exported. The industry had reached such proportions as to attract the notice of Parliament, and led to an act to suppress rolling and slitting mills, and to encourage the exportation of the raw material only for the benefit of the mother country. The establishment of a fire-insurance company, and, later, of one for life insurance, together with steps taken to secure patents of new processes of weaving and for cleansing corn, all indicate the existence of an active and enterprising business community. The produce of the farms was floated down the rivers from the interior, or brought in sacks on the backs of horses, and shipped from Philadelphia. The farms were, as a rule, well managed, and the agriculture was, as compared with that of the other colonies, high and thrifty. A hasty survey of the trade and industries of Pennsylvania gives at once an insight into the character of the people, and displays a rich and growing prosperity, and a thrift in management wholly different from the south, which stamps the middle colonies with a peculiar character.[1]

The governments of Pennsylvania and Delaware consisted of a single executive for both provinces, with a legislature for each; and it is sufficient to describe the system of the former to understand both. The government of Pennsylvania differed in some important respects from those of the other colonies. With the exception of Maryland and, of course, Delaware, it was the only proprietary government, and the descendants of William Penn stood in a relation of quasi sover-

---

[1] As to trade and industry in Pennsylvania, see Huguenot Family in Virginia, p. 30; Crévecœur, p. 46; Smyth, ii., 303, 307, 308; Kalm, i., 52, 102, 160; ii. 139; Burnaby, pp. 78, 80, 82; Coll. Hist. Soc., i., 197; Ibid., Republ., Watson's Annals of Buckingham County, etc., as to late development of coal; Watson's Annals of Philadelphia, ii., 1768; Description of Pennsylvania by Gabriel Thomas; Wallace, Inaug. Address, Hist. Soc., 1872; Hist. Coll., ix., Penn and fur trade; Pennsylvania Hist. Mag., i., 68; Watson's Annals of Philadelphia, ii.; Col. Records, iii., 1717; iv., 1736; v., 1750; Hazard, Pennsylvania Archives, 1750, Smuggling, 1775; Rochefoucauld, i., 32; Pennsylvania Laws, 1700, 1730; and in 1759, Laws for inspection of lumber for protection of Province, common to all great articles of export; for Delaware, Brissot, p. 362; Pennsylvania Hist. Soc. Coll., xi., Acrelius; Rochefoucauld, ii., 272

eignty, and drew a large revenue from the great colony which bore their name. The executive department was composed of the Governor and his Council, who were simply advisory, and did not sit as an Upper House, the entire legislative power being vested in a single body of delegates chosen by the people. The deputy or acting Governor was appointed by the proprietary to serve in his absence, and was subject to the royal approval. As in all colonies where the people were not opposed by the power of the Crown, the Governor was of little importance. The sheriffs and coroners were elected by the people, and all officers whose duties were financial were chosen either by the people or the Assembly. The only appointments of importance in the hands of the Governor were judicial, and his only valuable prerogative was the power to pardon in all cases but those of murder and treason, where he might grant a reprieve, subject to the approval of the Crown. The Assembly also held the purse-strings, excluded the Governor from Indian affairs, and, going much further than elsewhere, sat on their own adjournment, and denied successfully the right of the Governor to either dissolve or prorogue, although admitting his power to summon them by writ. The confusion and faction of an earlier period, when Logan was wont to advise a surrender to the Crown, had resulted in the supremacy of the Assembly. The representatives had a property qualification, and were voted for by the tax-paying freemen, a more liberal suffrage than that in vogue elsewhere, while naturalization was, as usual, obtained by petition, examined by the Governor, and recommended to the House. The only check upon legislation was the right of repeal reserved to the King in council.[1]

The proprietary drew his income from the quit-rents reserved in all deeds, and which could be collected by distress, and from his great manors, the taxation of which was such a fruitful source of contention. Salaries were small, and taxation light. The net revenue, raised by direct taxes, excise, and light customs, amounted to eight thousand pounds, and one thousand pounds was derived from the tonnage duties for the benefit of light-houses. There was no navy, and the militia, established with difficulty on account of the hostility of the Quakers, was small, no expense to the public, and wretchedly

[1] Smyth, ii., 303; Burnaby, pp. 82, 84; for Delaware, p. 74; Pennsylvania Laws, 1705, 1750; Col. Rec., iii., 1729; iv., 1745; vii., 1757; Hazard, Pennsylvania Archives, 1775, Answer to Hillsborough; Watson's Annals of Philadelphia, i., 25.

inefficient, except in Delaware, where it was established by law, and where all men between eighteen and fifty were required to serve.[1]

The judicial system was above the colonial standard, both as regards bench and bar. The early Quaker scheme of peace-makers to act as arbitrators and prevent lawsuits seems to have met with little success;[2] and at the time of the Revolution there was an adequate and efficient organization for the administration of the common law, which prevailed in Pennsylvania as elsewhere, except when modified by statutes, imperial or provincial. All judges were appointed by the Governor. The lowest court was that of the local magistrate or justice of the peace, competent to try cases involving less than forty shillings. The next was the county court, or court of quarter-sessions, composed of three justices, who sat by special commission as a court of common pleas; while the highest tribunal was the supreme court, consisting of a chief-justice and three puisne judges, with general appellate jurisdiction, and combining the functions of the English courts of common pleas, king's bench, and exchequer. They held two terms, and were also empowered to sit as a court of oyer and terminer, and hold a general jail delivery, a power rarely exercised. Causes involving more than fifty pounds could be carried up from the supreme court to the King in council. There was no court of chancery. Keith had succeeded in establishing one, with himself as chancellor, under the charter; but after his rule it was suppressed, and such equity jurisdiction as was required was exercised by the common-law courts. There was a register-general of probate and administration at Philadelphia, and recorders of deeds appointed at an early period in each county. There was also an English court of vice-admiralty, from which there was an appeal to England; but this court was so unpopular that the judge at one time complained that he could not perform the duties of his office. The judiciary of Delaware was similar in arrangement, but formed an independent organization.

The bar in Pennsylvania was exceptionally good, and had always received full recognition. Practice was simple, and attorneys were admitted by the justices after slight examination; but the law, as a profession, had many excellent representatives in the colony, and drew to its ranks many men of learning and ability. Andrew Ham-

---

[1] Burnaby, p. 89; Watson's Annals, i., 25; État Présent de la Pennsylvanie; Col. Rec., vii., 1757, Militia; ix., 1767, Letter from J. Penn to Shelburne; Hazard, Pennsylvania Archives, 1753.

[2] Hist. Soc. Coll., iii., Hist. of Bristol Borough, 1683; Col. Rec., ii., 1709.

ilton, who defended Zenger, was the first American lawyer who gained more than a local reputation, and the only one who did so in colonial times.[1]

The religious system of Pennsylvania was peculiar to that province, and was the most important feature of her public policy, for it was the system of Pennsylvania which received the sanction of the revolutionary Congress and of the Convention of 1789, and which now prevails throughout the United States. There was, with one trifling exception due to secular causes, genuine religious freedom from the beginning. The oppression of New England and Virginia, of Congregationalist and Episcopalian, was unknown, and toleration did not rest on the narrow foundation of expediency to which it owed its early adoption in Maryland. The Quakers in power were true to the tenets which they had preached when persecuted. Penn's followers were, however, a religious people, and, although they promised to all Christians perfect toleration, a strong tone of religion pervades the "nervous proclamation" against vice, and the early laws of the same character.[2] Yet there was but little Sabbatarian legislation such as we find upon the statute-book of both Virginia and Massachusetts, although an unfortunate barber was presented by the grand-jury of an early period for "trimming on the first day."[3] There is, however, no indication that Sunday was less observed, or that the morals of the people were worse on this account, and the same may be said in regard to the recognition of marriages solemnized in any religious society whatever. The generous toleration thus afforded attracted all forms and creeds to Pennsylvania, and at the time of the Revolution the facts especially noticed by all observers are the universal toleration, and the number and mixture of sects. One writer asserts that religious indifference was a characteristic of the people owing to this mingling of sects, and his opinion would seem to be borne out by the religious laxity indicated by the prevalence of church lotteries.[4] The forms were certainly less rigid than elsewhere; but the piety was as genuine and religion as wholesome and wide-spread as in any colony.

---

[1] As to the courts and the bar in Pennsylvania, see Burnaby, pp. 83, 84; for Delaware, p. 74; Laws of Pennsylvania, 1705, 1713, 1715, 1722; Jud. Act, 1752, 1767; Col. Rec., iii., 1720; Hazard, Pennsylvania Archives, 1727; Watson's Annals, i.

[2] Hist. Coll., ix., 12, Penn to Logan, "Prepare a nervous proclamation against vice."   [3] Watson's Annals, i., 1703.

[4] Crévecœur, p. 62; Pennsylvania Laws, 1765, 1767, 1768; Memoirs of a Life passed chiefly in Pennsylvania, p. 6.

The oldest church in the two provinces was that founded by the first settlers, who were Swedish Lutherans, and this sect maintained itself for more than a century, forming the only connecting link between the worshippers and their mother country. The ministers came from Sweden until the year 1786, when a petition for their discontinuance was sent, because their speech was no longer intelligible.[1] But though the distinctions of race were effaced, the creed survived, was adopted by the Dutch, and extended by the German immigrants of like faith. The Quakers were, of course, much stronger than any other single sect, although they speedily sank from controlling numbers to a minority of the whole population. They had much more religious energy than any other denomination, more fondness for their forms, and maintained with greater solicitude their connection with the parent societies. The English Church, although founded at an early period, never flourished. It served as a cry to the "Hot Church party," which was headed by Colonel Quarry, to oppose Penn and favor a royal government; but it never obtained any importance, and was sustained only by the gifts of the Society for the Propagation of the Gospel. Weak as it was, however, it was the only one of the churches which might some day be raised above the others by the strong arm of government; and when the Bishop of London proposed to present a minister his right was resisted and denied by the people, and claimed for the proprietary and Governor.

The most important sects next to the Quakers were the Lutherans and Presbyterians, the latter supported by the Irish and Scotch settlers, and with an active, able, and energetic ministry, who spread their doctrines with much success through the province. There were also respectable bodies of Dutch Calvinists, Baptists, Anabaptists, and Moravians. There were, too, many of the strange sects and mystical societies whose members came from Germany in search of the peace and toleration offered by the Quakers. Among these, besides the Moravians, were Dunkards, dressed like Dominican friars, Mennonists, Pietists, and Ridge Hermits. Last of all come the Roman Catholics, a small body, principally composed of Irish and Germans, which was certainly insignificant, and would have remained contented and unmolested but for the coming of the hapless Acadians, and the fact of the old French war. The possible danger of Indian

[1] Hist. Soc. Coll., xi., Acrelius, Hist.; Pennsylvania Hist. Mag., p. 1, Black's Journal; Col. Records, ix., 1765.

inroads, conducted by Frenchmen, was enough to rouse the two strongest hatreds of which a man of English race was at that time capable. Frenchmen and Papists could mean nothing but harm to any community. The Acadians were both; and some of the Irish and Germans were the latter. In the year 1755 three Frenchmen were arrested for poisoning wells, and the excitement was at its height. The Acadians, by the interposition of certain Huguenot Quakers, were provided for by the Assembly; but they were dispersed among the counties, and, broken by misfortune, sank into poverty, and rapidly disappeared. It was also said that Irish priests stirred up the people at the mass-houses to join the French; and as a consequence of this union, Roman Catholics were disarmed, and their houses searched; they were exempted from the militia, and compelled to pay fines. Their number in Philadelphia was not at this time over two thousand, and they were the poorest and most ignorant of the population. Their persecution was, however, only passing, and was due, not to religious bigotry, but to the wave of fear which swept over the English colonies when France let loose her savages upon their borders.[1] With this single exception, the religious system of Pennsylvania was one of perfect toleration, and the condition of religious affairs differed in no essential respect, either social or political, from that which is common to all the United States to-day. With this simple policy of tolerance to all, religion in Pennsylvania plays no conspicuous part in her history. There was little ostentation connected with the varied worships. The churches or meeting-houses were, as a rule, small and plain, but neat buildings, and the clergy a respected and respectable class, honored in their calling, but neither a picturesque body, as in Virginia, nor one of great social and political influence, as in Massachusetts.

The standing of the lawyers and the clergy are indications of the great differences existing between the middle and southern colonies. Another similar and even more striking illustration is to be found

---

[1] As to Religion in Pennsylvania, see Crévecœur, p. 62; Abbé Robin, p. 93; Kalm, i., 36; Burnaby, p. 84; Hist. Soc., i., 62, Procl. of Evans; Ibid., iii., History of Bristol Borough Episcopal Church, 1683; Ibid., vi., as to Acadians; Pennsylvania Laws, 1700, 1705, 1724, 1725, 1756; Watson's Annals, i. and ii., as to English Church and German Sects; Col. Rec., vii., 448, 1757; ix., 1755, 1756, 1757, 1765; Hist. Soc. Coll., xi., Acrelius, as to Ephrata and Herrenhutters; Huguenot Family in Virginia, p. 301; Chateaubriand, vii., 18; Anderson's History of Colonial Church, ii., 435; Chambers, A Tribute to the Irish and Scotch settlers; Rochefoucauld, i., 26.

in the third great profession — that of medicine. As has been remarked, in the colonies to the south, medical men, as a class, were in themselves of little merit, and socially and politically had no importance, whereas in Pennsylvania the case was exactly reversed. Although Gabriel Thomas asserts, in mentioning the attractions of the colony, that it had neither lawyers nor doctors, and was therefore both peaceable and healthy, yet there is no doubt that two physicians of good reputation came out with Penn, and that from that time on the profession was respected, and was always extending its influence and its services. The country physicians, except in the back districts, where the practice was of the rudest sort, were apparently men of good repute, eking out a slender professional income by farming or shopkeeping; but the most eminent of the profession were gathered, of course, in Philadelphia. There were certain marks of simplicity about them which seem odd to-day, but were then either the fashion everywhere, or qualities incident to a new country. Although there were regular druggists, yet even the best doctors were expected to be apothecaries as well, and dispense medicines to their patients. They almost invariably walked in making their round of visits in the towns, and in the country rode on horseback. Midwifery was given up exclusively to women. The profession, as a whole, was of remarkably good quality, and it is said that in all Philadelphia there were not more than two or three quacks. The services rendered to the progress of medical science by the profession in Pennsylvania were as great, if not greater, than in any other colony, and were in themselves very considerable. Inoculation was successfully introduced in the year 1731, although not without the usual hard contest with existing prejudices. Three years later Dr. Thomas Cadwalader, a graduate of the London schools, published an essay upon the "Iliac Passion"—the first medical book produced in Pennsylvania, and one of the earliest which appeared in the colonies. About the middle of the century he began to lecture upon anatomy, and was the pioneer in this branch of medical instruction. He was also one of the first physicians appointed to the hospital founded in Philadelphia in the year 1750. Ten years later Dr. William Shippen began a course of anatomical lectures in a private house, and by these small beginnings he and his friend, Dr. Morgan, succeeded in starting the medical college which in the year 1765 was ingrafted upon the University of Pennsylvania. Dr. Shippen subsequently did much to raise the practice of midwifery from the rule of thumb methods of the old women, who had a monopoly of this department.

These energetic and able men—among whom Dr. Rush, famous also by his controversy with Cobbett, held a leading place—were fair examples of their profession. They were men of family, position, and wealth, were educated abroad, and were adherents of the English school. They not only did much to advance medical science in America, but they helped to break the old tradition of barbers and apothecaries, which even now weighs upon medicine in England, and to put the profession, one of the noblest to which a man can devote himself, in its true position, and to render it attractive, honorable, and desirable to men of all ranks and of the highest attainments.[1]

Variety of pursuits and a membership representing all classes of the community was not confined to the learned professions. In Philadelphia there were great merchants, many busy shopkeepers, and not a few ingenious artisans and mechanics.[2] In the smaller towns there were the petty store-keepers and the restless Indian traders, who roamed from the sea-coast to the Alleghanies and to the fertile region of the Ohio in search of furs for the European market.[3] There were others of the people, too, engaged in the infant manufactures, and in the mining industries just coming into life. Thus, although the bulk of the population consisted of farmers, there was an active and important element of tradesmen, great and small, which made its influence felt throughout the entire community, while, in addition, the learned professions were eagerly sought and successfully practised by the best men in the province. Variety of interest and of occupation was not, therefore, wanting in Pennsylvania, and it caused liberality and enterprise among the people, and a rapid material development which was even then in progress.

In a community with so large an interest in trade and shopkeeping, there was, of course, from the outset the usual tendency to concentrate for the better prosecution of business. Philadelphia throve from the beginning, was in the year 1750 second only to Boston in size and importance, and by the time of the Revolution had become the first city in America in population. The inhabitants of the city

---

[1] As to medicine in Pennsylvania, see Wickes, Hist. of Medicine in New Jersey, pt. i.; Raynal, Eng. ed., p. 120; Brissot, p. 301; Gabriel Thomas's Descript. of Pennsylvania; Pennsylvania Laws, 1724, 1750; Wallace's Inaugural Address, 1872; Hist. Soc. Coll. Republ., i., Watson's Account of Buckingham County, etc., Med. Hist. of Pennsylvania; Hist. of University of Pennsylvania, iii.; Watson's Annals of Philadelphia, ii.; Rochefoucauld, i., 8.

[2] Kalm, i., 58.   [3] Gabriel Thomas's Description.

proper numbered more than twenty-five thousand, and those of the
suburbs carried the total above thirty thousand.[1]

The city was laid out on the imbecile checker-board pattern now
almost universal in the United States, and the High Street running
through the centre of the town was the great promenade for the citizens. From the very outset good building was the rule; the houses
were chiefly of brick, some of stone, and but few of wood. The public buildings were comely and useful structures, and considered in their
day imposing and handsome. The churches were small and unpretentious, but neat. The open squares, long rows of poplars, and large
gardens and orchards about the houses of the better sort, gave some
relief to the rigid lines of the streets. In the matter of police regulations, more had been done in Philadelphia at that time than in
most cities in any part of the world, and this was chiefly due to the
genius and the quiet energy of Franklin. At his arrival the town
was filthy, and unpaved, unlighted, and guarded only by half a dozen
constables drawn from the citizens. When the Continental Congress assembled, the crossings everywhere were paved, as well as the
principal streets; there was a regular watch to patrol the town,
cleaning was performed by contract, instead of inefficiently by convicts, and the streets were dimly lighted. By Franklin's exertions
the city had come to be the pride of the province, and there was
abundant legislation for its benefit. The well-built houses, sometimes
rising over shops and store-houses, sometimes surrounded by gardens,
were generally in the English style of the eighteenth century. They
all had broad porches and projecting roofs and windows. Many were
adorned with balconies, and the old dials set in the walls served in large
measure as time-keepers to a race ignorant of steam-engines. The most
characteristic feature of the town was the sidewalks, marked off from
the roadway by posts at short intervals, and by pumps, surmounted
by lamps, and thirty yards apart. Within these posts foot-passengers
found protection from vehicles; and convivial gentlemen, groping their

[1] Magazine of Amer. Hist., i., 231, Narr. of Prince de Broglie, 30,000; Elkanah
Watson, 1784, 6000 houses, 50,000 people; État Présent de la Pennsylvanie, 1756,
12,000; Michaux, 1749, 11,000; 1785, 40,000: Smyth, ii., 304, 35,000; Abbé Robin, pp. 88, 93, 1781, 20,000; Brissot, p. 120, 1766, 20,000; Kalm, i., 31, Philadelphia
second to Boston only, p. 57, 1746, 10,000; quadruples nearly in twenty years:
Burnaby, p. 76, 1759, 3000 houses, 18,000 to 20,000 people; Watson's Annals, ii.,
in Philadelphia and suburbs, 1753, 2300 houses; 1762, 2969; 1769, 3300; 1777,
4474; 25,000 to 30,000 people.

way home through the faintly lighted streets, butted against them, and were thus kept in the foot-path and out of the gutter. Houses and sidewalks were scrupulously clean, and even the large and commodious market at the end of the High Street, filled every morning with a busy crowd, was neat, quiet, and orderly. All the foreign commerce of the province centred in Philadelphia, and the quays along the river were the scene of bustle and activity inseparable from thriving trade. Great fairs brought in the country people, and these, with the seamen and strangers, gave life and variety to the streets and squares. High rents indicated the growth and business importance of the town, which, small as it appears in comparison with modern cities, was large by any standard of the eighteenth century. To Chateaubriand Philadelphia seemed *triste*, and he comments on the similarity of the houses, and the dull, monotonous aspect of the town. To Jefferson, on the other hand, the impression of the neat, well-built, and prosperous, yet simple Quaker city, after the slovenly little villages of Virginia, was never lost, and he wrote, many years later, that he thought Philadelphia handsomer than either London or Paris. The truth lies probably somewhere between. Philadelphia before the Revolution was a genuine English country town of the best sort, well-kept and thrifty, with unmistakable signs of the well-being of its inhabitants.[1]

The forces which had built up Philadelphia were not without effect elsewhere in the province. Germantown, with its infant manufactures, was a prosperous village. The houses were less good than in the capital, and here and there were to be seen the little dwellings of the early settlers, with gabled ends toward the streets, low rooms, and projecting eaves. Other towns were rapidly springing up at a greater distance from Philadelphia. Reading, in the year 1749, had only one house, and two years later had one hundred and thirty; while Lancaster, with a German and Irish population of nearly ten thousand, was the largest inland town in the colonies, and York did not fall far behind it. The little town of Bristol, a fair type of the Pennsylvania village, has been described by one who was born and lived there in the late

---

[1] For Philadelphia, see Huguenot Family in Virginia, pp. 301–2; Michaux, p. 20; Smyth, ii., 303, 304, 307–9; Abbé Robin, p. 93; Brissot, pp. 204, 207; Raynal, pp. 119, 120; Journal of Claude Blanchard, p. 135; Kalm, i., 34, 35, 44, 45, 57; Burnaby, pp. 76, 78; Wansey's Tour, p. 184; Gabriel Thomas's Description, 1698; Pennsylvania Laws, 1761, 1768, 1771; Pennsylvania Hist. Mag., i., Black's Journal; Watson's Annals of Philadelphia, i., ii., generally; Memoirs of Elkanah Watson, 1784; Chateaubriand, vii., 17.

provincial times. The great road to New York "formed the principal and, indeed, the only street marked by anything like a continuity of building. A few side streets were opened from this mainroad, on which, here and there, stood an humble, solitary dwelling. At a corner of two of these lanes was a Quaker meeting-house; and on a still more retired spot stood a small Episcopal church, whose lonely graveyard, with its surrounding woody scenery, might have furnished an appropriate theme for such a muse as Gray's. These, together with an old brick jail (Bristol having once been the county town of Bucks), constituted all the public edifices."[1]

In Delaware, Newcastle, the capital of the lower counties, was an ill-built and unattractive place; but Wilmington, with an active population of merchants and mechanics, was growing rapidly. The houses were generally of brick, and many of the quaint buildings of the Swedes still remained. It had fairs and a good trade, and is spoken of by all the travellers of the time as a neat, pretty, and prosperous town. The town life, the constant association of many members of the community with their fellow-beings, had, of course, a marked effect upon society, and found its fullest expression in Philadelphia.[2]

The well-defined classes, and simple but strongly marked social and political system of the southern States, are lost in Pennsylvania. There was, as in all the colonies, an aristocracy composed of the descendants of Penn's principal followers, many of whom were landed gentry, owning great estates from which they drew their revenues, and of wealthy farmers and successful merchants; but this aristocracy was neither distinctly marked nor homogeneous and compact. Its members received a certain recognition, and were often leaders in the province, but they were not politically or socially powerful. Indeed, they were so ill-defined as a class, that one careful observer, who lived long in Pennsylvania, declares that there was no aristocracy in existence.[3] This weakness arose in great measure from the absence of primogeniture, excluded by Penn's hostility,[4] from the supineness of the upper classes themselves, and from the character and pursuits of the mass of the population; for there is no indication that there was any levelling

---

[1] Memoirs of a Life passed chiefly in Pennsylvania, p. 4.

[2] For small towns in Pennsylvania and Delaware, see Smyth, ii., 278, 279; Burnaby, pp. 73, 75, 80; Hist. Soc. Coll., i., Republ. Conynham's Hist. Notes; Watson's Annals, ii.; Brissot, p. 362; Kalm, i., 89, 157; Pennsylvania Hist. Mag., i., Black's Journal; Ferris's Original Settlements on the Delaware; Elkanah Watson's Memoirs, 1784.   [3] Crévecœur, p. 46.   [4] Watson, i.

spirit in Pennsylvania, or any of the vigorous democratic theories which prevailed in New England. But, however weak and ill-defined the aristocracy may have been, there is no doubt of its existence, nor of that of the aristocratic spirit which must always be found when any portion of the community is in a state of enforced servitude. Free labor was the rule in Pennsylvania, and there was also free service; but there were, besides, bond-servants and slaves.

African slaves were brought to Pennsylvania as to the other colonies soon after the settlement, but they never became very numerous. They were employed generally as house servants, and in Delaware as field hands, but do not appear to have been much used on the Pennsylvania farms, and not at all in iron-works or any other of the industries. They gathered principally at Philadelphia, and in the eastern counties. Their insignificance as a class, and the feebleness of slavery as an institution, were due to a variety of causes, of which the first and most important was the supremacy of free labor, and the consequent presence of large bodies of white men who worked themselves. The climate was too severe for the negroes fresh from Africa or the West Indies, and they were expensive and precarious property, while the bond-servants were cheap and plentiful. The Quakers, as a sect—although many of them came to hold slaves with indifference—displayed toward slavery an unwavering hostility very bitter at the outset, and while under Penn's immediate influence, but always persistent and active. They used the arguments of religion to bring about manumission by members of the meeting; and such men as Woolman and Benezet devoted their lives to warfare upon slavery. This spirit was strongly manifested in the slave legislation of the province, although there were, of course, harsh clauses. Blacks received lashes for all misdemeanors for which whites were fined. Intermarriage of the races was prohibited under heavy penalties: the maxim *partus sequitur ventrem* was rigidly enforced, and the negroes were buried in separate graveyards outside the towns. The rights of property in slaves were scrupulously guarded by the government; but the general character of the laws was mild, and slaves had some security for life and limb. The murder of a slave was punishable with death, although public sentiment would not sustain the infliction upon a master of such a penalty. Whippings were generally administered by public officers at the jails, on the request of the owners. More important than anything else were the steady efforts of the Assembly during the eighteenth century to stop the importation of slaves by means of a prohibitory duty, and they per-

16

242 242 HISTORY OF THE

sisted in this policy, despite the opposition of England, until they finally obtained complete success. Slaves were still sold in open market,
and driven in gangs to the southward; but cargoes of human beings
ceased to be landed in Philadelphia some years before the Revolution,
and the general treatment of slaves was, in everyday practice, mild and
humane. The constant manumission by individuals either by will or
during their life increased the class of free blacks, to whom the laws
gave ample and adequate protection. They were better than the same
class in the southern States, and in a few exceptional cases were men
of ability; but as a rule they were idle and shiftless, sometimes disorderly and turbulent, and it was usual for the masters to pension
their freedmen in order to prevent their becoming a burden upon the
community.[1]

The indented white servants in Pennsylvania formed a much larger
and more important portion of the population than the slaves, whom
they assisted in driving out by their own greater cheapness. They
were chiefly Irish and German redemptioners, who sold themselves
to pay their passage, and transported convicts, who at last became so
numerous and troublesome that laws were passed to prevent their importation. There were also among these bond-servants many waifs
from the London streets—children sold by their parents, and unhappy beings who had been kidnapped and exported sometimes to further criminal schemes. Lord Altham was of this latter description,
and romances were written by convicts and personations attempted of
those who had been wrongfully forced into servitude, as the easiest
method of disposing of them. The condition of indented servants
was unenviable enough; but it was better in Pennsylvania than in
the southern colonies. They were more humanely treated, and better fed and clothed, and the laws did not leave them utterly at their
master's mercy. They could not be sold out of the province without their own consent; and they could not be sold at all except before a justice of the peace. The term of servitude was four years;
and if they had been faithful they were entitled not only to a

---

[1] As to slavery in Pennsylvania, see Kalm, i., 44, 387, and ff.; Hist. Soc. Coll.,
i., 262; Pennsylvania Laws, 1700, 1710, 1724, 1761, 1771, 1773; Hist. Soc. Coll.,
Republ., i., Bettle, Negro Slavery in Pennsylvania; Watson's Annals, i., 201, and
ii.; Smith, Hist. of Delaware County, 1750; Col. Records, i., 1707; xi., 1779; Magazine Amer. Hist., i., 231. In Delaware; Acrelius; Rochefoucauld, ii., 272; Brissot, Free Blacks, 238; Kalm, i., 394; Hist. Soc. Coll., ii., pt. ii., Watson, Country
Towns, Wilmington.

full discharge, but to a suit of clothes and some agricultural tools. They received five days additional servitude for every day's absence by flight, and were whipped for theft at the cart-tail. There was a severe penalty inflicted if they married without their master's consent; and women having bastard children were punished by additional servitude. Any one who concealed a runaway servant, or who traded with them, was liable to a heavy fine. Many of them turned out well after emancipation, owing to the mildness of their treatment. The free servants who engaged by the year were a respectable class, and were sufficiently well paid to lay up money for a wedding outfit. They formed a comparatively small body, but were numerous enough to remove in some measure the disgrace attendant upon service of any kind in the purely slave provinces.[1]

From these classes, or rather from the first two, the criminals and paupers were recruited. Crime was probably no more common in Pennsylvania than in the other colonies, but pauperism certainly was; and both subjects were better understood and more thoughtfully dealt with than elsewhere in America. In almost every English colony some new scheme of social regeneration was attempted, and even the sober-minded Quakers were touched with the infection of Utopian theories, and believed that they could overcome crime by fine, restitution, and imprisonment, without resort to the methods then in vogue. This was the system founded by Penn, under which murder was the only capital offence, and it was so far in advance of its time, and in details, indeed, of what was practicable, that failure was inevitable from the outset. It is sad as well as instructive to see how this benevolent plan went to pieces under the harsh pressure of circumstances. The liberal spirit of the founders which drew settlers was in itself a chief cause of its downfall, for many of the new-comers were of a very low class, and brought crime and poverty with them. The curse of pirates and smugglers, who infested the American coasts, fell heavily, also, upon Pennsylvania. These outlaws brought trade and specie to the struggling colonists, whose virtue was not proof against the temptation. The pirate Evans owned land in Philadelphia, and the famous Blackbeard traded in its shops; while even the family of Penn's deputy, Markham, was mixed up with these illicit dealings. The scandal and

[1] As to indented servants and free blacks, see Kalm, i., 29, 387, and ff.; Pennsylvania Laws, 1700, 1701, 1705, 1722; Hist. Soc. Coll., v., Sargent, Braddock's Expedition, Introd.; Watson, i. and ii.; Smith, Hist. of Delaware County; Col. Records, xi., 1777.

injury which this caused to the province led finally to strenuous measures on the part of the Assembly, and piracy was suppressed, but not
wholly until twenty-five years'[1] had elapsed.

Besides this particular evil, vice in general increased under the influence of a large immigration and the growth of towns.   The Quakers
attempted to meet the difficulty by proclamations and laws against vice
and every form of immorality, from murder down to scolding, smoking in the streets, and working on Sunday, thereby trying to reach a
class of offences which legislation cannot deal with directly.   Their own
morals, too, began to relax in the second generation.   William Penn,
the younger, not only went over to the Church of England, but, after
the fashion of young gentlemen in London, raised a riot in the quiet
Philadelphia streets, wrenched off knockers, beat the watch, and was
finally arrested and brought into court, where the matter was hushed
up and the watch reprimanded.   At last the new theory of criminal legislation was abandoned, in the year 1718.   Workhouses and jails were
established, the number of capital offences was increased from one to
fourteen ; every felony, except larceny, was made capital on a second
offence, and matters went on in Pennsylvania in the ordinary fashion
of that day.[2]

At the time of the Revolution, while, as compared with England, the
amount of crime was trifling, it was as compared with the other colonies very considerable ; and although infrequent, there was much variety.   About the middle of the century there was a good deal of hanging for house-breaking, horse-stealing, and counterfeiting.   Highway
robbery was not unknown, and informers were tarred and feathered in
the back counties by a population loyal to the cause of untaxed liquors.
In Philadelphia the disorders inaugurated by young Penn broke out
at short intervals, assuming not infrequently the proportions of a dangerous riot.   After the French war the town was thrown into a state
of alarm by assaults with knives upon women who ventured out after
dark.   The habit of rioting spread to the other towns, and the brutal
massacre by the Scotch-Irish " Paxton boys " of the Indians at Cones-

---

[1] Pirates ; Hist. Soc. Coll., iv., 1702 ; Watson's Annals, i., 120, and ii. ; Smith, Hist.
of Delaware County, 1700 ; Col. Records, ii., 1700 ; iii., 1717, 1718, 1732 ; Hist. Rec.
of Pennsylvania.

[2] Hist. Soc. Coll., i., 62, 260, 262 ; Pennsylvania Laws, 1700, 1701, 1705, 1718 ;
Hist. Soc., iv., 1704, Affair of W. Penn, Junior ; Watson, i., 1705 ; Col. Rec., i.,
1697, Letter from W. Penn, 1704, W. Penn, Junior's, case ; Smith, Hist. of Delaware County, decrease of morality in Quakers of second generation.

toga was the most notorious result of this turbulent disposition. The rioters and the criminals were almost wholly Irish. Not one native or Englishman was found in any ten of the inmates of jails, and the unfortunate prominence of Pennsylvania in this respect was attributable to the character of a large portion of her immigrants.

Rough and disorderly as were the back counties, they did not develop the immorality which grew up in Philadelphia as one of the almost inseparable concomitants of town life. Drinking was the curse of every part of the province; but in Philadelphia duelling, although strongly discountenanced, was more or less practised even by the clergy, and there is record of one reverend gentleman who was killed by a cornet of horse. Lotteries, at first frowned upon, came to be the regular and recognized method of raising money for churches and public improvements, afforded an ample opportunity for general gambling, and offered apparently the principal if not the only occasion for this sort of dissipation. In no respect were the Quakers more active than in their efforts to suppress all offences of a sexual nature. The early laws regulating marriage were detailed and strict in the extreme, and sharp measures were taken against all "lewd women." This legislation appears to have been effective. Prostitutes there were, of course, in Philadelphia; but they were only to be found along the wharves and in the sailors' dens. The policy was, in fact, supported by public opinion. In the country a couple whose child was born too soon after marriage were forced to stand at the whipping-post; and in the Scotch-Irish communities those detected in illicit intercourse were compelled to make public confession of their sin in church, concluding with the words:

"For my own game have done this shame,
Pray restore me to my lands again."

The system of punishments conforming to the common theory of the day relied principally upon "lashes well laid on." Men and women were whipped for stealing, for bastards, and for all small offences. The stripes were inflicted upon the market-day, and in the market-place, where stood the whipping-post, which was a great source of interest to the crowd, but fell far short of the pillory as a popular amusement. The wretched criminals were placed in the pillory, the populace gathered round, the price of eggs rose, and they were pelted and abused from morning till night; while simple vagrants were turned loose and pelted and hunted out of town. Criminals who could not pay fines were sold as servants for the public benefit. As late as the

year 1731 a woman was burnt at the stake for the murder of her husband, and death was the penalty for many comparatively trifling offences.   In 1772 even, the punishment for burning the State-house was
death, and for breaking into it the pillory, lashes, and imprisonment.
The result of the constant infliction of the death penalty led gradually to its evasion, as it did in England, and to its ultimate abolition.
But, although the early schemes of the Quakers had no effect upon
penalties, they bore good fruit in the matter of prisons and prison
discipline.   In the year 1732 prisoners were kept in filthy cells—
usually under the court-house—naked, and covered with vermin.   At
the period of the Revolution the prisons of Philadelphia and the system of management were, on the testimony of foreign observers, the
best in the world.   In this direction genuine progress had been made,
and it was due wholly to the humane principles of the Quakers.[1]

The immigration to Pennsylvania was more fruitful of pauperism
than crime, and the laws are full of attempts to stop by legislation the
coming of " poor and impotent persons " into the province.   The unlimited opportunities of the new land did much to check the spread
of pauperism, and in the country districts there was little or none.
Such as there was in the province was concentrated in Philadelphia and
its immediate neighborhood, and the government endeavored to deal
with it systematically and thoroughly.   In Philadelphia overseers of
the poor were to be appointed by the mayor and two justices, and in
the borough to be elected by the freeholders.   These overseers were
to lay rates to be levied like taxes; poor children were to be bound
out to service by the workhouse managers; and no person was to be
entered upon the poor-books without an order from two magistrates.
The settlement laws, modelled on those of England, were extremely
strict, and paupers were obliged to wear a large badge on their shoul-
der to denote their condition; but the whole amount of pauperism

---

[1] As to crime, punishments, and prisons in Pennsylvania, see Crévecœur, pp. 40,
67; Brissot, p. 317; Abbé Robin, p. 95; Hist. Soc. Coll., i., 262, 1744; Pennsylvania Laws, 1701, 1705, 1745, 1767, 1772; Hist. Soc. Coll., ii., pt. ii., Watson's Country Towns; Ibid., iii., Hist. of Bristol Borough; Ibid., iv., 322; Watson's Annals,
i., 25, 103, and ff., generally, 1731, 1750, 1760, 1761; ii., 1693; and generally for
crimes, lotteries, duelling, etc.; Rupp, Hist. Lancaster County, 1739; Smith, Hist.
Delaware County, 1690, 1693, 1743; Chambers, A Tribute to Irish and Scotch
Settlers; The Quaker Unmasked; Col. Rec., iii., 1726; vii., 1756, 1762; ix., 1765;
Hazard, Pennsylvania Archives, 1737, 1773; Rochefoucauld, ii., 336, 377; Pennsylvania Hist. Mag., i., Black's Journal, Wilmington; Wansey, p. 157.

was comparatively trifling, and the system shows a progressive public opinion.[1]

Another matter of morals, more directly connected, perhaps, with the condition of trade than anything else, was the standard of financial honesty, and here we find a marked departure from the loose dealing and indiscriminate debts of the southern provinces. There were on the statute-book the customary laws to regulate interest, and acts characteristic of the American colonies, which released debtors on a full assignment of their property. The colony was also cursed heavily with the paper-money delusion, of which large amounts were emitted; but in other respects the commercial spirit was predominant, and the standard of business morality sound. Creditors' rights were fully protected, and careful provision was made to prevent fraud under the acts for the relief of debtors. The aristocratic tendency cropped out curiously in a law of the year 1724, which permitted freeholders of fifty pounds to be arrested only on suit of the King, or on refusal to give security.[2] The people were honest; the general tone was sound in matters of morals; there was no sympathy with crime or frauds on creditors; and failures were a matter of deep and general regret.

The enlightened spirit of the Quakers in matters of social economy and improvement was strongly shown in their efforts to better the condition of the sick and insane by private as well as public benevolence. In Philadelphia was the only lunatic asylum in America, where an attempt at least was made to alleviate the condition of this unhappy class, rendered doubly miserable by the treatment they usually were subjected to at that period; and in this respect, as in prison management, Pennsylvania was more advanced than Europe. Outside of Philadelphia there was also a large brick hospital for men and women, to which was attached a reform school. Efforts were made, too, to combat, by proper sanitary regulations, the introduction of infectious diseases. There was a good soldiers' home, and various societies existed for the furtherance of philanthropic objects, and for the care of the poor, aged, and infirm. All these matters of public health and morals show in Pennsylvania a much greater progress in

---

[1] As to pauperism, see Pennsylvania Laws, 1738, 1743, 1765, 1771; Poor Law, cited in text, Watson, ii., 1719; Col. Rec., iv., 1738; Rochefoucauld, i., 8; ii., 272; Michaux, p. 20.

[2] Pennsylvania Laws, 1700, 1705, 1723, 1724, 1730, 1731; Watson, i., 174 and ff.; Ibid., ii., Paper Money, 1773; Burnaby, p. 90.

questions of social science than can be found in any of her sister colonies.[1]

The life, habits, and manners of the people varied greatly. Between the inhabitants of the frontier and those of Philadelphia great differences necessarily existed; and between these extremes were the different classes of farmers, ranging from the pioneer settlers of the backwoods to the great landholders of the eastern counties. The life of the backwoodsmen, contrasting strongly with that of the denizens of the capital, was rude and simple in the extreme. The pioneers cleared a little tract in the forest, began to farm in a rough sort of fashion, and hunted, and traded with the Indians. A log-house of the simplest construction gave shelter to the settler and his family. The men dressed in hunting-shirts and leggings, the women in bedgowns and linsey petticoats, while young and old went barefoot in warm weather. The two bare rooms were festooned with the garments of the family; the utensils were of pewter; china, glass, and silver were unknown, and the furniture was all of home manufacture. "Hog and hominy" were the principal articles of food, varied, when the chase proved fortunate, by roast venison. The amusements were as rude as the appliances of comfort. There was much drinking on all occasions, wild dancing, and rough sports; but the great event was a marriage. The widely scattered neighbors then gathered from all sides to fell trees, shape logs, and build the one room, called by a stretch of courtesy the house of the young couple. Then followed the house-warming, with unlimited drinking and dancing. The newly-married pair withdrew at an early hour from the scene to the attic, where pork and cabbage were liberally supplied to them by the company below, who kept up the festivities with enduring zeal. At all public meetings there was a good deal of pretty savage fighting, and the border conflicts between the Irish and Germans make a dark chapter in the colonial annals of Pennsylvania. At one time the former, under the lead of Cresap, endeavored systematically to drive their more thrifty and industrious rivals from the western country; and another bloody struggle, extending over twenty years, was caused by the efforts of Connecticut men to settle in Wyoming. This came at times to open and regular war with the government, and resulted in the victory of the hardy intruders, and the estab-

---

[1] Smyth, ii., 309; Abbé Robin, p. 96; Brissot, pp. 167, 176; Burnaby, pp. 77, 95; Pennsylvania Laws, 1770; Col. Records, iv., 1741, 1742; Rochefoucauld, ii., 377.

lishment of the democratic government of the New England township.[1]

Passing from the rude outposts of civilization toward the east, we come upon the great farming class which, in all its varieties, formed the bulk and the strength of the Pennsylvanian population. The farms near the border partook to a certain extent of the character of backwoods clearings, and their occupants were rather rough in life and habits. This was the region where the continual contest went on with the " accursed Irish," as their German opponents styled them. Here, too, the Irish brought on themselves the hostility of the government, which forbade them to settle in York or Lancaster, and attempted to remove them to the west. From this field they carried their quarrels to the Assembly, and divided the legislature into two parties—on one side the Quakers and Germans, on the other the rest of the English and the Irish, who succeeded, usually, in obtaining the upperhand.[2]

But these outlying settlements, with their feuds and struggles, were not the types of the agricultural population. The Pennsylvania farmers belonged, as a rule, to the substantial, permanent, and best class of freeholders. They were, for the period, scientific and economical farmers, and thoroughly well off, which was especially the case with the Germans, who were thrifty, temperate, never in debt, and whose women-folk labored in the fields. The farms, worked for the most part by bond-servants or hired laborers who received high wages, were rich, and yielded good crops. The owners were themselves practical farmers, working in the fields with their men, and superintending everything. A Russian traveller, going to visit John Bartram, found the eminent botanist in the fields with his farm-hands. The style of living was not infrequently marked by a patriarchal simplicity. Master and men all dined together in one large room, where, at the lower end of the table, sat the negroes; then came the white servants and the hired men; and then the master and his family. Food was everywhere plentiful and simple; and the dress, generally consisting of leather breeches and hempen jackets, was coarse and substantial. In

---

[1] Backwoods Life; Michaux, p. 29; The Olden Time, p. 141; Hist. Soc. Coll., v., Sargent's Hist. of Braddock's Exped., Introd. Memoir; Rupp, Hist. of Lancaster County; Stone's Hist. of Wyoming.

[2] Watson, ii., 1743; Rupp, Hist. of Lancaster County; Ibid., Hist. of Northampton, etc.; Chambers, Defence of Scotch and Irish; État Présent de la Pennsylvanie.

the eastern counties were the Quaker farms, models of neatness and well-being, where the houses were usually of brick, thoroughly built, and plastered and papered; the furniture heavy and well made; the linen white, and the glass and china of good quality. On every farm honey was made and cattle raised, while large orchards clustered about the houses, protected only by hurdles, and open to the wayfarers, who plucked the fruit unmolested. In the east there were also gardens, abounding in every sort of vegetable; and the estates, not only of the wealthy but of the prosperous farmers, had each their fish-pond.[1] The farms were scattered through the forest—here a group of two or three, and then again a single clearing, but never at great distances from each other in the older settlements. Near Philadelphia the farmhouses changed to handsome villas, and here and there were great manors, of which the most famous was Penn's seat at Pennsbury, with a large mansion-house richly furnished. Keith's house, which was another of the same class, was sixty feet front, wainscoted throughout, with large rooms and a broad oak staircase. Baron Stiegel's house at Mannheim was built of imported brick, and had a private chapel, while over the high wainscots landscapes were painted or tapestry hung on the walls, and the fireplaces were decked with porcelain tiles. Other leading men, like Logan, had great estates, and fine houses of a similar character.

The farming class was throughout one of great prosperity. Marriage was young, and very fruitful. Sons were easily provided for, and daughters soon married. The people were temperate and healthy, infant mortality not large, and the increase of population rapid. Tradesmen in the small towns made money quickly, and would insure fortune to industrious children by establishing them on a farm in the neighborhood. The rapid material development of Pennsylvania may be measured by the growth of means of transportation from rude sleds of the early days to nine thousand wagons employed in the farm service at the close of the French war.[2]

Luxury was almost unknown, although solid comfort abounded.

---

[1] Crévecœur, pp. 1 and ff., 110; Brissot, pp. 154, 287; Kalm, i., 70, 87, 124, 149, 216, 307; Memoirs of Elkanah Watson, p. 31; Rochefoucauld, i., 8; Hist. Soc. Coll., ii., pt. ii., Watson, Country Towns; Ibid., xi., Acrelius; Ibid, i., Watson's Account of Bucks, etc.

[2] Burnaby, pp. 75, 86; Hist. Soc. Coll., i., Mooreland, pp. 197 and ff.; Ibid., Republication, Keith's House; Ibid., ix., Penn's House; Pennsylvania Hist. Mag., i., 68, Stiegel's House; Watson's Annals, i., 19; ii.; Rochefoucauld, i., 29, 32.

The daily life and habits remained primitive until the middle of the eighteenth century, when a marked change began. Tea and coffee were then introduced, and many of the worthy country people boiled the leaves of the former and ate them with butter. Straw carpets, too, began to make their appearance, but were strongly opposed by old house-keepers, who protested that they gathered dust, and that the bare sanded floor alone was decent. The Swedish beer, the English ale, and the brandy of the early settlers were gradually replaced by punch, liquors, and wines of every variety, and the same changes made themselves felt in their amusements. In early times the great festivals were the weddings. Then the rare finery was put on, and there was a great deal too much drinking, and "vain practice" of firing guns, condemned at Quaker meeting, and games and dances of a very loose sort, presenting scenes apparently not unlike the famous "Kermesse" of Rubens. Gradually this sobered down. Weddings came to be held generally at the house, and only the poor were married and proclaimed in church; while the riotous feasting diminished and disappeared, or drifted away to the borders of the province. With the last ceremonies of death the same rule held true. The bodies were still borne out through the woods on men's shoulders, and laid quietly and simply in mother earth, but the subsequent eating and drinking declined.

Other customs held their own better. The rare events of country life were seized upon in the recurring seasons and enjoyed to the full. Seed-time and harvest, husking and cider-pressing, house-raising and vendues, shooting-matches, sleighing, and Christmas sports, were always the occasions of social gatherings. There was a good deal of drinking, and still more dancing, and in every hamlet the fiddler was an important personage. Vendues and fairs, legal and illicit, drew all the youth of both sexes to the little towns for a day of boisterous fun, terminating frequently in fist fights of a rather brutal character.

In such a community, simple in tastes and habits, equal in fortune and never idle, there was little place for a strong aristocracy; and yet the aristocratic principle prevailed in gentle fashion in all the older settlements, and there was a simple, conservative, country respect for superiors everywhere apparent. Each village had its "squire," the local magnate and magistrate, looked up to by all, who rode or walked about with cocked hat and powdered wig, broad ruffles and gold-headed cane, or who sat at the nearest inn, where he tried the petty offenders of the neighborhood and dispensed substantial

justice.[1] The people were eminently social, and, despite the hard travelling, visited each other continually.   Almost all journeys, great and
small, were made on horseback.   Men and women rode to church and
to market.   The bride went to the wedding on a pillion behind her
father, and returned seated on another behind her husband.   Some time
before the Revolution chaises began to come into use ; but the roads
were so bad, even in the neighborhood of Philadelphia, that it was
pleasanter to ride for seven days to Pittsburgh than to go to the same
place on wheels.   In the eastern counties stage lines were established,
in 1756, to go to New York in three days ; and ten years later another, known as the " Flying Machine," was advertised to perform the
distance in two days.   Other lines of coaches to Baltimore and to
Germantown sprang from this, and the post-chaise soon ceased to
be unknown ; but although Pennsylvania was imbued with the spirit
of trade, which did something to facilitate travel, the inns remained
deplorably bad, except in Philadelphia ; and even there most of them
were simply ale-houses.   Over these taverns swung the signs of the
last century, with heads of king and generals upon them, and doggerel
verses beneath—an English custom long since extinct.   The fare afforded by these inns was far from good ; and although travellers speak
of cleanliness as a virtue highly prized in America, yet the colonial
landlords were unable to understand why Europeans should object to
dining with the landlord — usually a leading man in the village, or
sleeping two in a bed, or should desire such luxuries as fresh sheets.
But if the inns were poor, their deficiencies were more than made up
by the genuine and universal hospitality of the country people.   The
traveller might stop at the first farm he came to, and be sure of as
hearty a welcome nearly as he would have had at home.   The determination of the people to travel and move from place to place, and
the restless spirit of trade, did much more than any rude facilities to
prevent the isolation which formed so marked a feature in Virginian
life.[2]

---

[1] Hist. Soc. Coll., i., Mooreland, p. 197 and ff. ; Ibid., Republ., Watson's Account
of Buckingham, etc., and ii., pt. ii., Country Towns ; Watson's Annals, i., 19 ; ii., Local Magistrates, etc. ; Smith's Hist. of Delaware County ; Hist. Col., iii., Holm's
Hist. ; xi., Acrelius ; Ferris, Original Settlements on the Delaware.
    [2] Travelling, etc. ; Observations of John Bartram, p. 11 ; Rochefoucauld, i., 68,
140 ; Narr. of Prince de Broglie, Magazine Amer. Hist., i., 231 ; Hist. Soc. Coll., i.,
Mooreland, p. 197 and ff. ; ii., Watson's Country Towns ; Huguenot Family in Virginia, p. 302 ; Michaux, p. 29 ; Crévecœur, p. 72 ; Chateaubriand, vii., 17 ; Brissot,

Despite all these liberalizing and enlightening habits and opportunities, there was, owing to the strong infusion of foreign blood, more superstitious ignorance among the country people of Pennsylvania than among those of any other colony. The earliest instance appeared in a trial for witchcraft in the year 1683. One Margaret Matson was tried, on perfectly trivial evidence, for bewitching cows and geese, and appearing at the foot of the accuser's bed. Penn and his Council had the good sense to find the woman not guilty according to the terms of the indictment, but guilty of common fame as a witch; and they bound her in the sum of one hundred pounds to good behavior.[1] This was the only genuine witch case under the mild Quaker rule; but the statute of James I. was in force, was recognized by the Assembly, and received the formal approval of George II. and his Council.[2] The belief in witchcraft, however, manifested itself in other forms. About the year 1693 presentations were made by the grand-jury against astrology, necromancy, geomancy, and divining-rods.[3] But the law was powerless, and superstition flourished, especially among the Germans, down to the time of the Revolution. Red ribbons were tied on the horns of cattle to guard against conjurations; divining-rods were in high repute; dogs were burnt to drive away witches; love-spells, charms, rings, herbs, and the like, were widely used; and when the lightning-rod appeared it was strongly resisted, and even proscribed by some sects. Second-sight found many believers, and haunted spots and ghost-ridden houses were common to every hamlet. So fertile a field produced the usual crop of impostors and swindlers, who professed, after the manner of modern quacks and spiritualists, to be possessed of devils and spirits, to see ghosts, to cure diseases, discover hidden treasures, and reveal the places where the pirates buried their ill-gotten gold. Most of these magicians were of German extraction, and in the early times there were some connected with the fanatical sects who were not without learning. One Dr. Witt flourished as late as the year 1765, and as astrologer and Rosicrucian did a thriving business. This prevalent superstition shows a weak element among the people of Pennsylvania, and was one which

---

pp. 219, 362; Wansey, p. 175; Pennsylvania Laws, 1710; Hist. Soc., iii., Hist. Bristol Borough; Watson's Annals, i. and ii.; Stage-coaches and Taverns, Col. Rec., i., 1697; vii., 1756.

[1] Hist. Soc. Coll., iii., Hist. of Bristol Borough, p. 8, note; Col. Records, ii., 1700.
[2] Watson's Annals, i.
[3] Smith, Hist. of Delaware County; Watson's Annals, i.

it took years of civilization to wholly eradicate.[1] It indicates, also, a very general ignorance, which was singularly great in a population so largely composed of the English middle and dissenting class, but which, like the superstition, was due undoubtedly to the foreign immigration. The Germans as a rule were far behind the English in point of information, although they produced some distinguished men, like Rittenhouse and Muhlenburg; and the same held true of the Swedes and Dutch, and in a less degree of the Irish. The German and Swedish pastors made great efforts to remedy this state of affairs by establishing schools in connection with the churches, but they met with little success. The Scotch and Irish Presbyterian clergy, more active and more zealous, fared better, and did good work with their country schools, known at this time as "log colleges." But the general condition of education in the rural districts was wretched in the extreme. School-houses were few and small, and rudely built of logs, and even these did not begin to appear much before the middle of the eighteenth century. The barest rudiments only were taught, and those badly, and for small fees. There was little learning, loose order, and much whipping everywhere. There was no public system of schools, and education was almost wholly in the hands of itinerant masters, who were frequently convicts and foreigners; and even they generally abandoned a profession where the fee of a scholar was only five shillings a quarter. The case was a little better in the towns, such as Wilmington; but the educational efforts of the English, who were the governing race, seem, except in the case of private schools kept by individual clergymen, to have been confined to the capital.[2]

In Philadelphia there was much activity and progress in education from the earliest years of the settlement. In the year 1683, Enoch Flower, assisted by the municipal government, opened the first school; and this was followed six years later by a public school, which was sustained by the Quakers, and finally chartered by Penn in 1711. In the year 1743 the energy of Franklin produced a plan for a university, which was abandoned at the time, but revived six years later, when an academy, where Latin, English, and mathematics were taught, was

---

[1] Watson's Annals, i. and ii.; Hist. Soc., Mooreland, i., 197 and ff.; v., Sargent's Braddock's Expedition, Introd. Memoir.

[2] Brissot, p. 290; Hist. Coll., i., Mooreland, p. 197 and ff.; Ibid., i., Republ., Watson's Country Towns; Rupp, Hist. of Northampton County; Chambers, A Tribute to the Scotch and Irish; Rochefoucauld, i., 98; Ferris, Original Settlements on the Delaware; Hist. Soc., xi., Acrelius.

opened, together with charity-schools. The institution prospered, was chartered in the year 1755, and a college was added, with tolerably extensive courses of study. So great was the need that within seven years there were four hundred students in all the departments; dormitories were built, subscriptions raised in England as well as in the province, and professors of good character and sufficient learning were employed. This was the foundation of the University of Pennsylvania, considered at the time one of the best, if not the very best, in the colonies, and drawing its students from the whole province.[1]

Philadelphia was not only the centre of education in the province, but also of literature, arts, and science. The first two were, of course, still in their infancy, but they had an existence and the promise of a good future, while in science the great name of Franklin not only placed Pennsylvania at the head of the colonies, but gave her a high position in the scientific world. The influence of that remarkable man was felt, not only in his great discoveries, in politics, and in every form of public improvement, but it leavened and stimulated the whole intellectual development of the province. The early literary efforts here, as elsewhere in America, were devoted to descriptions of the country, and controversial pamphlets and sermons; but even then was to be found a promise of better things. James Logan, the leading man in the province, was not only a politician, but a scholar versed in many languages, and the author of a translation from Cicero's De Senectute. Then came Andrew Bradford, the first printer, and the editor of the first newspaper, with a large book-store and bindery, where he published almanacs, the popular literature of the day, and sold, besides Bibles, dictionaries, and grammars, Virgil, the *Spectator, Tatler, Guardian,* and Fénelon. His newspaper was at once a source of fame and trouble, for liberty of the press was no better understood in the colonies than in the mother country at that period. A very harmless paragraph about the finances in the year 1721 brought Bradford before the Council, whence he escaped with an apology and a severe reprimand. A few years later he was again in custody for letters which he had allowed to appear in the *Mercury.* This time he stood firm, was thrown into prison, refused to retract, the case against him was dropped, and he gained a substantial victory as a defender of the

---

[1] Hist. Soc. Coll., iii., Hist. of University; Smyth, p. 308; Raynal, p. 120; Memoirs of a Life in Pennsylvania, p. 16; Kalm, i., 45; Burnaby, p. 85; Wallace, Hist. Address, 1872; Watson's Annals, i. and ii.

liberty of the press. During Bradford's career Franklin came upon the scene, and began the publication which first made him famous. Around him gathered a number of young men, members of his club, and literary Bohemians for the most part, who wrote verses of all degrees of merit, essays and political disquisitions, and gave to the young press a liveliness and originality which could not be found in any other colony. This literary activity was believed to give promise of a great literary future, and it certainly led to more extended reading and more ambitious efforts at authorship. The Letters of Junius were read in the province as widely as in England, and called up a crowd of imitators, while satires and epigrams were much in vogue, and many fair translations from ancient writers found their way into print. But among and outside of the imitators of Pope, of the poetasters, and satirists, and writers of political tracts and squibs, were men who did real service to their kind, and who gained and deserved enduring fame. At the head of all stands Benjamin Franklin, versatile, subtle, acute, in some respects the greatest intellect the New World has yet produced. There is no need to dwell upon his acts or to recall his writings. From "Poor Richard" and the lightning-rod, down to the fire company and the iron stove, they are all as familiar as household words. But among Franklin's friends, and even outside his circle, were men who did good work in the world.

Thomas Godfrey, the glazier, a self-taught mathematician, invented the quadrant, while his son produced the first American drama, Artabanus and Evanthe, and, later, the Prince of Parthia, modelled on Dryden's Oriental plays, and not far short of their very mediocre originals in merit. John Bartram, the simple Quaker farmer, with deep love of nature, careful observation, and patient study, won a European reputation as a botanist; and his son, William, followed in his footsteps with considerable credit. In the year 1732 Rittenhouse was born, and in 1768 completed his first orrery. Public encouragement was not lacking, for at the same time the Assembly voted one hundred pounds for a telescope, and a year later the Philosophical Society erected a platform for the observation of the transit of Venus. In the year 1771 Rittenhouse received three hundred pounds for his orrery. Much, too, was done by the medical profession in the way of public instruction; and the lectures of Dr. Spencer on the eye, and on light and color, accompanied by experiments with the microscope, were the fashionable entertainments of the day. The desire for knowledge ran strongly in the upper classes. There were many private libraries, small, but furnished with the classics of the time — Goldsmith, Fielding, Don Quixote, Gil Blas; and the taste of the community is strongly shown by the publication of Blackstone, Robertson's Charles V., and Ferguson's Essays; great enterprises for the time, and carried through by the local publishers. Booksellers usually eked out their income by the sale of more material articles, but the character of their stock of books is the important feature in this connection. Besides the taste for reading, music and painting were also cultivated by those who had leisure, and not without success. Philadelphia, says the historian of American literature, was a literary centre of more activity than any except Boston.

This is apparent also in the public press. Not only newspapers were set on foot, but magazines and reviews were attempted. At the time of the Revolution there were two English newspapers and one German in the colony. They had the latest and most accurate foreign intelligence in detail, little local news, and a correspondence supplying the place filled now by editorials, which was not without merit. Philadelphia, not only as a great port, but from its geographical position, was the centre of news on the continent. A post was first established by Penn as soon as he had founded his colony, which ran at great expense, and the delay of which for six weeks by snow caused the inhabitants "to pass the time very melancholy." In the year 1717 mail-lines were opened to Virginia and Maryland, and letters were carried to the south at enormous rates of payment. Here, too, was subsequently the head of the whole continental postal system, which it was one of Franklin's greatest achievements to make not only efficient but profitable. The city stood alone in possessing two public libraries—the one founded by Franklin, the other by Logan. Both had good collections of standard English works, besides some in French and Latin; and Franklin's contained also mathematical and physical instruments. Thus Philadelphia had many advantages to offer. As the great news centre, she was in constant contact with the world beyond the sea, whose thoughts and feelings were carried to her doors by each succeeding packet; while the scientific exploits of Franklin brought pre-eminence in one great field, and the literary activity and budding arts showed a disposition to enter upon others.[1]

[1] Literature, etc., in Pennsylvania, see Raynal, p. 120; Brissot, p. 273; Kalm, i., 44, 56; Burnaby, p. 76; Hist. Soc., i., 196, 423; Wallace, Hist. Address, 1872; Phil-

Such intellectual development indicates a social life and habits, and manners far more advanced than those of the country districts or of the southern States. The Philadelphians were a trading community; the large land-owners, supported by the revenues of their estates, forming but a small fraction of the upper classes, which were composed in the main of rich merchants, carrying on an extensive trade, and of professional men. The middle classes were made up of small traders and shopkeepers, and the lowest of the laborers, and those who followed the sea. There was also a large suburban and floating population, who came in daily to business, or flocked in twice a week to the bustling market, and crowded the town, filling it with life and movement when the great fairs were held.

Most of the citizens lived in rooms over their shops, which were tended by their wives and daughters; and their daily life was as sober, monotonous, and respectable as their Quaker garb. They still preserved the customs and traditions of their founder, which were rapidly giving way before the accumulation of wealth, the increase of luxury, and the presence of ever-increasing sects, whose leading tenets were not simplicity of dress or manners. But the traders and shopkeepers differed only in degree from the upper classes, whose mode of life has been preserved for us in many ways. The old style of living was one of extreme simplicity, but luxury began to come in rapidly after the middle of the eighteenth century, when tea and coffee came into general use, the bare floors began to be carpeted, and the bare walls papered. There was in every way plenty of substantial comfort. The houses were large, broad, with dormer-windows and balconies, and usually in the midst of pretty gardens. The rooms were low and spacious, with heavy wainscots and large open fireplaces; while the furniture and silver were plain and massive, but handsome, and often rich.

The luxury which began to show itself in the houses appeared much sooner in the matter of dress. Philadelphia was the social centre, and the English fashions came early, and were carried to a great height. Old men carried gold-headed canes and gold snuffboxes, and had huge silver buttons on their richly-laced drab coats as a mark of distinction, while men of all ages wore vast wigs, and many rich velvet

adelphia Hist. Soc., Annual Discourse, 1869; Hist. Soc. Coll., i., Republ. Prov. Lit.; Hist. Soc., ii., pt. ii.; ix., 1769, 1704, Letters from Norris to Zachary; Hist. Mag., i., Black's Journal; Watson's Annals, i., ii., Libraries and Newspapers; Tyler, Hist. of American Literature.

and silk. The young men of fashion wore swords and laced hats and coats, for which red cloth was common even among boys. The amount of color in men's dress, according to the fashion of the times, is now almost inconceivable. A lady, struck with the appearance of some gay fellow at a ball, addressed him in the following lines:

> "Mine a tall youth shall at a ball be seen,
> Whose legs are like the spring, all clothed in green;
> A yellow ribbon ties his long cravat,
> And a large knot of yellow cocks his hat."

The women dressed in the extreme of the fashion. Flowered stuffs of every variety—brocades, satins, velvets, and silks—were much in vogue, and hours were spent in the construction of tall head-dresses and mounds of hair. They wore masks in cold weather, and carried fans of ivory with pictured sides. Even the Quakers gave way; and, while the stricter members wore plain but rich materials, a portion of the sect, known as Wet Quakers, yielded to the fascinations of powder, silver buckles, and bright colors.

The men of Philadelphia—young and old—were regularly occupied with business and trade; while the women of the family in the middle classes tended the shop; and those of higher rank cared for the house, played the spinet, walked a great deal, and worked endless pieces of embroidery, covered with impossible landscapes. Although the life of a trading town and the constant presence of strangers chilled the hospitality which was so marked in the country districts, there was a constant social intercourse, and an unfailing round of amusements for both sexes. Fishing-clubs with pleasant houses on the river, glutton clubs for the consumption of turtle and madeira, and social clubs abounded. In winter there was sleighing and skating, besides dancing parties and assemblies, where the social line was strictly drawn, as in the case of a young lady of good position, who, having married a jeweller, was forthwith excommunicated. In summer there were great fairs, with amusements like bear and bull baiting, and oxen roasted whole, in which all ranks joined, and for the wealthy there were fishing and sailing parties and picnics. To theatres there was a strong opposition. The first company, composed of natives, was suppressed in the year 1749 by the magistrates; but five years later an English company was licensed, on condition that their plays contained nothing indecent or immoral, and they seem to have met with success, and to have drawn fashionable audiences. In the year 1758 a theatre was built outside the city limits, despite the relentless opposition of both Quakers and Presbyterians, who took the matter into the courts, where permission was obtained for the performances which thus became thoroughly established. As a rule, however, the spirit of the Quakers and of the community generally was very liberal in respect to all forms of amusement, although one of our French allies, M. Claude Blanchard, murmured because his landlady objected to cards on Sunday.

There was evidently abundance of comfort and good-living, although manners were in many respects curiously primitive. In summer the young ladies always put on full dress for the evenings, and sat in the porches of the houses, while the young men strolled about from house to house and made visits. Dinner, and even fashionable dinner-parties, were at twelve o'clock, and in the afternoon calls were made, and there was much tea-drinking, and at sundown supper was served. If there were no balls, the men then went to their clubs, which were quite numerous, and which met at the taverns, where there was more supper, a great consumption of wine, and a plentiful flow of discussion, chiefly of a political nature. Marriages, especially among the Quakers, were always occasions of great festivity. The banns were pronounced at two successive meetings, and on each occurrence there was a reception; while the wedding entertainment sometimes extended over two days, during which time there was open house kept for all comers. The marriages, however, were outdone by the funerals, which were attended with immense pomp and parade. The body was borne from the house by friends, and was followed to the grave by a long procession, generally on horseback, and sometimes numbering several thousands. Then ensued the usual eating and drinking, and distribution of scarfs and rings. The expense and extravagance became so great in this respect that a strong effort, following the example of Boston and New York, was made to stop the outlay at funerals.

From what can now be gathered, it is evident that society was agreeable in Philadelphia, and manners, if not easy, pleasant, and good-natured. "They are as far behind us in etiquette," says the Abbé Robin, "as they are ahead of us in legislation;" and the statement is probably correct. However good manners may have been, they were tinged with provincialism, and were not highly polished. This was equally true of the women, who were agreeable, good-looking, well-bred, and often accomplished, but who lacked the grace and ease of Europe. But however much elegance and refinement of manner may have been wanting, the wholesome virtue of a simple society was still retained; adultery was unknown, and gallantry and intrigue had no existence. The women prided themselves on their fidelity to their husbands and their devotion to their children; and the Frenchmen of the Revolution, who paraded their mistresses in the streets, were regarded with unfeigned disgust. Marriages were wholly from inclination, and there was but little parental control in such matters. This simplicity, as has been said, did not reach dress or amusements, nor the general style of living among the wealthy. Besides hackney-coaches and other conveniences of that sort, there were many handsome private carriages and fine equipages. There were numerous slaves and servants in every rich family, generally in livery, and large studs of horses were maintained. In the suburbs were extensive tea-gardens, places of great popular resort, where there were fireworks, billiards, and bowling-greens, and where much time was spent in the season of pleasant weather. The whole mode of life was that of a rich, comfortable, and rather self-indulgent trading community, which grew apace, and where fortunes were easily acquired.[1]

The political habits and modes of thought differed widely in some respects from those of the southern and eastern groups, and were typical of the middle provinces; for narrow as were the domestic politics of all the colonies, they were especially contracted in Pennsylvania, which was due principally to the Quakers, who as a sect struggled hard to retain their supremacy. The usual quarrels with the governors, always pushed far in the stress of war, were carried to great extremes when fortified by the peace principles of the Friends. In the French war the selfish supineness and indifference of Pennsylvania seem almost inconceivable when we remember the savage warfare which raged upon the borders, and how the other colonies fought their own and England's battles. The Quakers, who were mainly responsible, retained their power by playing off the Germans, with whom they were allied, against the rest of the English and the Scotch and

---

[1] For manners, customs, and amusements, Watson's Annals of Philadelphia furnish an inexhaustible store; see also Smyth, i., 308; Abbé Robin, pp. 89, 94; Chateaubriand, vii., 17, 19; Brissot, pp. 160, 270, 271, 272, 276, 303, 324, 344; Raynal, i., 116; Blanchard's Journal, p. 183; Memoirs of a Life in Pennsylvania, pp. 24, 45, 105; Kalm, i., 29, 43, 54, 103; Burnaby, pp. 77, 86, 87; Wansey, p. 127; Memoirs of Schuylkill Fishing Club; Hist. Soc., i., Mooreland, p. 197 and ff., 367; Bent. Hist. Soc., Address Wash. House; Wallace, ibid., 1872; Hist. Soc. Coll., ix.; Pennsylvania Hist. Mag., i., Black's Journal for Daily Life; also for same, Shippen Papers, edited by Thomas Balch; Hazard, Archives of Pennsylvania, 1754; Elkanah Watson, Memoirs; Mag. of Amer. Hist., i., 231, Narr. of Prince de Broglie; Rochefoucauld, ii., 381, 384, 388; Hist. Soc., ii., pt. ii., Watson, Country Towns.

Irish, who furnished a turbulent element, which formed a strong contrast to the peaceable politics of their opponents. Election riots were
by no means uncommon, and in the disposal of offices there appears
to have been a good deal of intrigue and corruption of the sort then
familiar in England.[1]

In regard to the mother country, the people, Franklin said, were
"docile, and led by a thread;" and that the colony was warmly attached to England, there is here, as elsewhere, every evidence, as in the
loyal addresses called forth by the death of the Prince of Wales and
the defeat of the Pretender; but there were also the usual grievances,
such as the injurious laws of trade, and the attempts at impressment,
while the large number of foreigners did much to weaken the bonds.
All this was enhanced by the conduct of the British, who behaved
with their customary short-sighted arrogance to the "Mohairs," as
they contemptuously termed the Americans, by whom they were always treated with regard and respect. But there was nothing strong
or aggressive in the attitude of Pennsylvania, and the Quakers were
eminently conservative and slow in action.[2] The sense of being a colony, and not born to the soil, was apparently very marked. "Cette
société," says Chateaubriand, "sans aieux et sans souvenirs;"[3] and
this was to a large extent true, not only on account of the foreign
element, but because of the origin and character of the people. The
memory of great hardships, of difficulties overcome, of efforts for
great principles, which gave force and character to Virginia and Massachusetts, were lacking to the middle provinces. The Pennsylvanians were essentially shopkeepers and traders, prosperous and contented, with a loose social system and a heterogeneous population. Their
politics and their character were conservative and at times timid; and
when independence was at stake, they were a weight upon the action
of Virginia and Massachusetts, who dragged them forward irresistibly
on the inevitable path. At the period of the adoption of the constitution their conservative tendencies again came into play, and were
of vast importance; and thus they continued the uncertain balance
between the great contending forces, social and political, of their
southern and northern brethren.

---

[1] Hist. Soc. Coll., xi., Acrelius; Watson's Annals, i., ii.; Quakers Unmasked;
État Présent de la Pennsylvanie; Answer to a Brief Statement; Col. Records, iv.,
1742; v., 1750; Shippen Papers, ed. by Balch.

[2] Memoirs of a Life in Pennsylvania; Kalm, i., 52; Burnaby, p. 86; Watson's
Annals, i.; Col. Records, v., 1751; Hazard, Pennsylvania Archives, 1743.

[3] Chateaubriand, vii., 18.

Chapter XIV.

NEW JERSEY FROM 1664 TO 1765.

1617. The Dutch from New York were the first to settle within the borders of New Jersey, as early, it is said, as in the first quarter of the seventeenth century; but their settlements never grew or reached an importance sufficient to give them a place in history; and it was not until after the capture of New Netherlands by the English, and the grant by the Duke of York to Lord Berkeley and **1664.** Sir George Carteret, that the province then named New Jersey begins to play a part in American history. Gradually the conquering race swept in—Protestants from New York, Quakers from the mother country, Puritans from New England—and a new state was added to the British dominions.

Berkeley and Carteret first established a form of government by an instrument known as the "Concessions." This scheme was a liberal one, assuring religious toleration, and a government composed of Governor and Council appointed by the proprietaries, and a general Assembly chosen by the people. The concessions were speedily followed by the appointment of Philip Carteret as Governor, **1665.** who went out at once with a body of emigrants. There was some opposition from Nicolls, Governor of New York, which proved the source of much future trouble; but the Duke had gone too far to retreat, and Nicolls was obliged to reluctantly admit the newcomers, who at once proceeded to allot the land at Elizabeth, and found their towns and colony. There was some difficulty, also, with the old settlers, but their claims were compromised, everything went smoothly, and immigrants began to come in companies from New England. Towns rapidly sprang up, and it was soon found necessary to call the representatives of the people together. The first **1668.** Assembly was brief and harmonious, and in the criminal law we see the unmistakable work of Puritans, who at once began to impress themselves upon the colony. At the very next session came the inevitable quarrel between Assembly and executive; in this instance because the Council insisted on sitting as a separate House, instead of with the Assembly, where they could be outvoted. The contest had no result, and the Assembly adjourned, not to meet again for seven years.

The controversy, however, took another shape, and passed to the towns—independent corporations, and full of the New England **1670.** spirit, whose inhabitants objected to paying quit-rents. This was sustained by the old settlers, who had paid for their lands, and had grants from Nicolls; and, finally, the disaffected towns held an Assembly, and chose a new Governor, James Carteret, an ille**1672.** gitimate son of the lord proprietary. The last vestige of power having gone, Philip Carteret, leaving John Berry as his deputy, betook himself to England, where the proprietaries, backed by the Duke of York, sustained their officers, and sent out letters extending the executive power, declaring the old grants void, and deferring for a short time the payment of quit-rents. This was ef**1673.** fective, and James Carteret sailed for Virginia; but the trouble proved sufficient to frighten Lord Berkeley, and make him part with all his right and title in the province. Meantime, the efforts of the proprietaries to settle the difficulties of their province were cut short by the Dutch reconquest of New York. The inhabitants of New Jersey submitted quietly to the Dutch, in the autumn of 1673, on receiving sufficient promises of protection and liberty, and went back as quietly under the English rule the following year, when peace was made. This passing change of masters had the effect of leaving in doubt the validity of the old grant to the Duke of York, and this grant was, therefore, made again, and the Duke commissioned Andros as Governor of the whole territory. Charles, however, recognized Carteret's government, and the Duke was obliged, in turn, to renew his former conveyance, which was now made separately to Carteret, and included East New Jersey, nothing being said about the portion alienated by Berkeley. Philip Carteret again came out as Governor, and **1675.** was well received, and everything went quietly in the Assembly which he called in the following year.

Lord Berkeley, in the mean time, had sold his share to John Fenwick, in trust for Edward Byllinge, both Quakers. A controversy arose, and one-tenth was awarded by Penn, as arbitrator, to Fenwick, and nine-tenths to Byllinge. Soon after Byllinge failed in business, and his nine-tenths were assigned to trustees, with Penn at their head, for the benefit of his creditors; while Fenwick also mortgaged his share, and, having sold some lands, came out with a number of emigrants, and settled at Salem, near the Delaware. This had hardly been done when Andros, despite the Duke's original grant, and his own recognition of the concessions, sent down officers, stopped the trade of the Quakers, and finally arrested Fenwick and sent him to New York, where he was soon released; but afterward returned, and was again released on parole. In the mean time the trustees of Byllinge and the mortgagees of Fenwick had combined, and effected an agreement with Carteret, by which the province was divided into East and West New Jersey. The Quakers then framed a government of extreme liberality, providing for toleration in religion, for a representative Assembly, and for an executive composed of commissioners to be chosen by the freeholders. Commissioners were at once appointed, and sailed with a large number of settlers. They were detained at New York by Andros, who denied their authority, and who only allowed them to proceed on taking a warrant from him. This done, they entered upon their work, allotted lands, and founded towns; but in the midst of their labors Fenwick appeared, released from New York, and set up a government of his own at Salem. The commissioners forbore to meddle with Fenwick, but Andros was not so gentle; and, on the former's refusal to pay customs to the Duke's officers, arrested him again, and took him once more to New York. Andros then went further, and undertook to enforce the customs upon the other settlements, which were growing rapidly; but this produced complaints, and the proprietors had the whole question referred to Sir William Jones as arbitrator. After elaborate arguments, Sir William Jones decided that the Duke had no right to customs; and a new grant was then made by the Duke to the proprietors, which, however, complicated matters still further, by reserving the powers of government to Edward Byllinge.

1676.

1677.

1678.

1680.

Meanwhile the same policy had been attempted by the Duke's officers against East New Jersey, where everything was moving peaceably, and where Carteret, anxious to encourage commerce, had opened Elizabeth as a free port, which was strenuously resisted by Andros, who demanded duties. Carteret refused, and Andros, with this quarrel rapidly ripening, went to England, where he received instructions to exact the duties for three years more. On his return he paid a visit to Carteret, who, backed by the Assembly, declined to submit;

and soon after an armed force was sent out by Andros, and Carteret was surprised, arrested, and taken to New York. There Carteret was tried, and, although acquitted by the jury, was still detained as a prisoner, while Andros tried to seize the New Jersey government, and was baffled by the firm resistance of the Assembly. Instructions came from the widow of Sir George Carteret, who died at this juncture, to refuse submission to the Governor of New York; and the Duke soon after executed a release to the heirs of Carteret, and recalled Andros. The deputy, Brockholst, made one more attempt to carry out the high-handed policy of his superior and predecessor, but was success-
1681. fully opposed by Carteret, who had been reinstated, and the protracted contest came to an end.

Not long after the Carteret heirs sold out their property to Wil-liam Penn and others, who obtained still another release from
1682. the slippery Duke, and formed an association of twenty-four proprietors for the government of East New Jersey. Robert Barclay, one of the principal leaders of the Quakers, was appointed Governor, and Thomas Rudyard was sent out as his deputy. Much practical legislation was enacted by the new Governor and the Assembly; counties were laid out, courts erected, and the penal code revised. Soon after, the government was reorganized, Barclay made Govern-or for life, and Gawen Lawrie, one of the founders of West New Jer-sey, appointed deputy. Lawrie came out the year after his appoint-
1684. ment with some new concessions, which provided for the choice of the Governor by the proprietors, for a representative Assem-bly, religious toleration, and other less important matters, and which aroused considerable opposition in the province owing to the favor-itism shown the Quakers, who were but a small minority of the in-habitants. Lawrie also became involved in a contest with Governor Dongan, who renewed the efforts of Andros, and attempted, with the aid of the royal collector, to force all ships to enter at New York; and when the proprietors remonstrated, Dongan's defence made it evident that he aimed at the annexation of the province. This amiable policy reached success by the accession of James, who, once on the throne, threw aside the underhand frauds by which he had tried to control the Jerseys, and by the issue of a writ of *quo warranto* forced the proprietors of East New Jersey to surren-
1688. der their province, on condition that they should retain the ownership of the soil. The fate of West New Jersey was sim-ilar. This province had increased rapidly in population and prosper-

ity, while its proprietors wrangled and quarrelled, and wound themselves up in every form of legal and business complication. When, however, they saw the *quo warranto* suspended over East New Jersey, they followed the example of their sister province and surrendered to the King, on the same condition of retaining the ownership of the soil.

Andros, now Governor-general of New England and New York, took charge of the government and administered it in irresponsible fashion, but mainly through the old officers; and when the Revolution came, there was too little harmony or sympathy between people and proprietaries, and too little affection for the old governments to lead to any active measures. Governors were appointed, and resisted by the people; and, finally, Andrew Hamilton, who had been deputy at the time of the surrender, came out as Governor, and succeeded in carrying on an administration. He was also made Governor of West New Jersey, which had passed through various hands into the possession of a society. Thus the two divisions of New Jersey came together gradually, and the arrangement was continued under Hamilton's successor, Jeremiah Basse. Under the new Governor the old trouble with New York once more broke out, and the question of customs again came before eminent lawyers, and was again decided in favor of the proprietors. At last the seizure of a vessel brought the matter to the courts, and East Jersey won again. In the mean time Basse had lost the confidence of both people and proprietors, and was recalled. The proprietaries wished to reappoint Hamilton, and he came out as Governor of West Jersey, but for East Jersey the royal approbation could not be obtained. The people of East Jersey petitioned the Crown against the proprietors, whose title was also contested by the King, and the Council of proprietors, now become an unwieldy body, was itself divided. Some of them urged an immediate surrender, others sought to make terms, and, after much bickering and bargaining, the surrender was finally made. West Jersey followed in the same course, although there was less faction among the people, and joined in the surrender to Queen Anne, soon after the death of King William. The rights of the proprietors in the land were sufficiently protected, and a form of government satisfactory to all was promised.

This new constitution was embodied in the instructions of Lord Cornbury, who was appointed Governor of both New York and the Jerseys, now consolidated into one province. The form of govern-

1689.

1692.

1698.

1699.

1702.

ment thus established provided for a Governor and Council appointed by the Crown, and was on the common model of the royal provincial governments of the eighteenth century. It put an end to the wretched jarring and confused political arrangements from which New Jersey had suffered for nearly half a century at the hands of the proprietors, and introduced permanence and order. The proprietors, secure in their rights of property, were simply deprived of government which they could not carry on, while the people lost much of the entire liberty which they had practically enjoyed under the feeble rule of the proprietors. There were the seeds for many future controversies in such a condition of affairs, and before long they produced a plentiful harvest.

Lord Cornbury was well received on his arrival, and addressed the Assembly in gracious terms, so that formal business was rapidly transacted; but when the settlement of proprietary rights and the raising supplies were reached, there was a pause, and the Assembly was dissolved. At the next session matters were even **1704.** worse. The Assembly, after much hesitation, granted a sum of money which the Governor thought lamentably insufficient, and would do nothing for a military force. The result was a dissolution, and a struggle at the elections, in which the government was beaten. Cornbury, who was one of the most worthless of the many bad colonial governors, then unseated three members, and, having packed the House, got through the supply and militia bills which he desired, and made himself master of the province. For two years he retained this ill-gotten power, troubled only by contests with some of the proprietors about lands; but the spirit of discontent spread rapidly, and **1707.** at the next Assembly he found himself facing a determined opposition, ably led by Samuel Jenings and Lewis Morris. The Assembly drew up a memorial to the Queen and a remonstrance to the Governor, setting forth their grievances in the failure of justice, the establishment of fees, the prohibition of land grants by the proprietors, and finally the invasion of their liberties by the removal of the three members. Then ensued the usual conflict—replies from **1708.** the Governor, refusal of supplies, repeated dissolutions, and at last the removal of Cornbury, against whom complaints went up from every part of the region unfortunate enough to be governed by him.

His successor, Lovelace, was welcomed in the province, but did not live long enough to deal with the restrictions which the Assembly put on the money bill; and his death left the government in the hands of Ingoldsby, the Lieutenant-governor, and a tool of **1709.** Cornbury, against whom the Assembly had already addressed the Queen. The Assembly, however, cheerfully voted three thousand pounds in aid of the war against Canada, enlisted men, and entered upon the favorite colonial system of paper-money by issuing bills of credit for this purpose. They then turned their attention to domestic affairs, and had little to do with Ingoldsby, who succeeded in forming a party in the Council hostile to the representatives of the people; but his universal unpopularity and the complaints **1710.** against his government soon led to his removal, and he was succeeded by General Hunter, who made a favorable impression, and gave promise of a good administration. The quarrel went on between the Assembly and the Ingoldsby party in the Council in regard to the attacks of the latter, the disabilities of Quakers refusing to take an oath, and the qualification of jurors. The popular grievances were laid before Hunter, who, after an impartial consideration, removed the obnoxious members of the Council from office, which so restored the confidence of the Assembly that at their next session they authorized the raising of volunteers, and gave cheerfully five thousand pounds for the war in bills of credit. The next Assembly, which did not meet until two years later, con**1713.** tinued to act in harmony with the Governor, voted supplies, removed the disabilities of the Quakers, settled the qualifications of jurors, and regulated slavery. An interval of three years elapsed before another Assembly was summoned, and then came the first contest with Hunter, who had been instructed to remove the capital from Burlington to Amboy. This produced a factious opposition, but Hunter's instructions were so plain that submission was alone possible. The hostile faction undertook to break up the Assembly, but the majority stood by the Governor, and the members who absented themselves were expelled, and not allowed to sit again in the House. After this conclusion the attention of the Assembly was turned to the finances of the province, which were much involved. They tried to meet their deficiencies by more bills of credit, and did **1719.** their best to furnish proper salaries and supplies to the government; but the close of Hunter's administration left them still in trouble, and when his successor, William Burnet, who arrived in the following year, met the Assembly, matters had not much improved, and the province was still encumbered with debt. Burnet entered at once upon the domineering, meddling policy which he adhered to with such pertinacity during his whole career in America, and in all his governments. He not only demanded the settlement of a lasting revenue and an increase of salary from the impoverished province, but he rebuked the Assembly for the length of its sessions, questioned the validity of laws regulating the qualifications of members, and interfered in every way with the rights and privileges of the representatives. This awakened a stubborn resistance and refusal of supplies, and sudden dissolutions followed each other in the usual fashion for two years. Then the Governor abated somewhat his preten-

1723. sions, the Assembly voted salaries smaller than before, made appropriations for five years, passed laws against the Papists, and dealt with the debt by authorizing the emission of forty thousand pounds in bills of credit, which were legal tender and bore interest, and by the establishment of a loan-office. There were contests on the judiciary and other questions; but the measures which were passed enabled the government to go on smoothly enough until the year 1727, when the people began to be restive on account of the protracted existence of the Assembly and the long intervals between the sessions. A new Assembly was therefore convened, but nothing was done, and soon after Burnet was transferred to Massachusetts.

1728. Burnet's successor, John Montgomerie, ruled quietly and acceptably. A strong effort was made for a separation from New York, but the movement effected nothing. On the death of

1731. Montgomerie, Lewis Morris, as President of the Council, was at the head of the government until the arrival of William Cosby, in the following year, with a commission as Governor of New York and New Jersey. The Assembly passed a bill providing for triennial elections, and calling an Assembly at least once in three years at Amboy and Burlington alternately, which received the assent of the Governor, but was disallowed by the King, and, together with the similar fate of bills regulating legal matters, caused much discontent. Cosby was not over-popular, and the Assembly complained of his selections for the Council; but, on the whole, his administration

1736-1738. was peaceful; and at the time of his death, the petition for a separation from New York being finally granted, Lewis Morris was appointed Governor of New Jersey.

This excellent and needed change, which brought a man identified with New Jersey to the head of affairs, produced some alterations in the form of government. The Council was made a separate branch of the legislature, and the Governor no longer presided at their meetings. After an exchange of courtesies and congratulations, the Assembly got to work, and found that the former leader of the popular party was no more manageable than his predecessors. The old quarrel over fixing elections and shortening lawsuits was renewed, and the supply bill and salaries, passed after much delay, were so highly unsatisfactory that the Governor dissolved the Assembly in disgust. The next Assembly, despite a sharp lecture from the Governor, was no

1740. better; the old subjects of contention were brought forward, and matters were still further complicated by the Spanish war. Morris refused to adjourn the House until they had given aid to the war, and this led to the passage of a bill which opened up the question of the disposal of the revenue, and to which the Assembly adhered, despite the opposition of the Governor. The controversy thus begun rapidly developed. Every possible subject of dispute was drawn in, including fees, salaries, and meetings of the Assembly; and the House refused to pass supply bills until their other measures received the Governor's assent. They also came to an open breach with the Council, accusing them of an improper union of offices; there was a further contest about a militia bill, there was no money, government was at a standstill, and at this juncture Morris, from whose adminis-

1746. tration so much had been expected, died, and left the government in the hands of John Hamilton, the senior member of the Council.

The death of Morris softened the bitterness of parties, and the Assembly passed bills for raising men, and issued ten thousand pounds for the war, in accordance with the royal instructions sent to

1747. Hamilton. Shortly after Hamilton died, the government devolved on John Reading, another councillor, and then passed to Jonathan Belcher, who came out as Governor. The peace of Aix-la-Chapelle relieved the province from the burdens of war; and Bel-

1748. cher, a shrewd, wary man of long political experience, put an end to the quarrels of his predecessors, humored the Assembly as far as possible, assented to several bills which Morris had stoutly resisted, and never opposed the popular wishes, except when his instructions left him no choice, and then the Assembly were obliged to yield. This insured a quiet, peaceful, and prosperous administration, of which the province stood much in need. The only break was caused by riots arising from the knotty questions of land titles, and directed against the courts and the old proprietors. The Assembly, sympathizing with the rioters, prevented the employment of force, and the insurrection finally subsided.

The French war affected New Jersey but little, owing to her protected situation — shut in by the great colonies of New York and Pennsylvania. While professing their readiness to resist French encroachment, New Jersey, having no interest in the Indians or the Indian trade, declined to meet the commissioners of the other colonies at Albany in 1754, and promptly refused to ratify Franklin's constitution, which was proposed by that meeting to all the American provinces. During the war New Jersey did little. The Assembly generally complied with the requisitions made upon them, but they would refuse or modify at their own discretion, with the exercise of which neither Belcher nor his successors seem to have interfered. Belcher's **1757.** judicious rule was closed by his death, and the government devolved again upon Reading. Then followed several Governors for very short terms : Francis Bernard, who was active in Indian affairs ; Thomas Boone, soon transferred to South Carolina ; Josiah Hardy ; **1762.** and, finally, William Franklin, who was appointed through the influence of Lord Bute, and held office until driven out by revolution.

The concord and good feeling produced by the great victories of the French war, and by its successful close, were soon disturbed by the new policy of taxation. New Jersey had been as ready as any colony, during the war, to oppose anything like taxation by England, so that the Stamp Act aroused general discontent ; and, when it came to the point, the stamp-collector resigned, without an attempt to perform his duties. The circular of Massachusetts found the Assembly on the eve of adjournment ; and, owing to this and to the efforts of Franklin, an evasive reply was returned. This produced general dissatisfaction ; so marked, indeed, that the Speaker called a convention of the members, denounced violently by Franklin, and delegates were **1765.** appointed, who met with those from the other provinces at New York, and thus placed New Jersey among the united colonies, and bound up her interests with theirs.

Chapter XV.

NEW JERSEY IN 1765.

THE province of New Jersey, stretching along the Atlantic, with low, sandy shore, and a wide extent of low, flat country, rising gradually toward the west and south, and intersected with noble rivers, occupied a position wholly different from any other American colony. New Jersey alone never had a border on the wilderness. She was shut in by the great provinces of New York and Pennsylvania, and, from the time the settlements were fairly founded, never knew the dangers which haunted the frontier settlers of the other colonies, except in the case of Connecticut and Rhode Island, down even to the period of the Revolution.

Except for internal dissensions, and the troubles with the government of New York, there was nothing from the outset to check the quiet and prosperous growth of the province. The population numbered seventy-five thousand at the period of the French war, and about one hundred thousand at the time of the Revolution. The number of negroes was, as in Pennsylvania, comparatively small.[1] There was little diversity of race among the New Jersey people. The trifling Swedish and Dutch elements had been completely absorbed, and there were some German settlements; but with these exceptions the population was of pure English stock. West New Jersey was settled by Quakers chiefly, of whom a few had gone also to East New Jersey, which was occupied principally by New England men and by some Scotch Presbyterians. These were good materials, and the colony benefited from the purity, vigor, and homogeneousness of her population.[2]

"They are a very rustical people," said Governor Belcher, "and deficient in learning." A "rustical people" they certainly were, for near-

---

[1] Sussex Centenary, Edsall's Address; Burnaby, p. 101; Board of Trade Estimates, Bancroft, iv., 127, 129; Hildreth, ii., 419.

[2] Murray, Notes on Elizabeth; Kalm, i., 228; ii., 123; Sussex Centenary, Edsall's Address; Barber's Hist. Coll. of New Jersey.

ly the whole community was absorbed in farming. Wheat and provisions were the staples, and the chief articles of commerce, and there was also some bar-iron exported, a small traffic in fur, tar, and timber, and large herds of cattle; but the trade of New Jersey with England and Europe went out through New York and Philadelphia, and only a small coasting and river traffic was kept up in the local ports.[1] The towns were small, comely villages. Some, like Trenton, were built on the line of travel between New York and Philadelphia, which gave them support. A long street, down which Washington rode one famous December night to turn the wavering scale of Revolution, ran through the centre of the town, and was flanked by comfortable houses close to the highway, with large gardens stretching out behind them. Other villages were simply the centres of the farming district for which they furnished supplies; while others, again, were merely straggling collections of two or three farms, of which the pasture-land was held in common. So insignificant were the towns, that in early times legislation was necessary to compel them to have "ordinaries" for passing strangers. Some of the houses in the New Jersey villages were of wood, but brick was the most usual material. They were lightly but well built, with high stoops, where their occupants gathered in the summer twilight to gossip with their neighbors.[2] The great majority of the inhabitants were farmers, and lived in brick or wooden farm-houses, scattered over the whole province, and deriving a plentiful subsistence from their land. One writer, about the middle of the eighteenth century, who probably had but slight acquaintance with the back districts of Pennsylvania or with any of the southern States, says, "Farms in New Jersey, in thick woods, resemble the face of the sky after a tempest when the clouds are breaking away." Yet New Jersey was the most thickly settled of any of the colonies, except, perhaps, the coast region of New England. The intervals of forest between the clearings were not long; one farm often ran into another, and little hamlets were passed frequently by the traveller. The farms were given up to the plainest kinds of country prod

---

[1] Huguenot Family in Virginia, p. 301; Smyth, ii., 396, 400; Burnaby, p. 101; Gabriel Thomas, Hist. of West New Jersey; Leaming and Spicer, Laws of New Jersey, 1676.

[2] Huguenot Family in Virginia, pp. 300, 301; Smith, ii., 397; Abbé Robin, p. 82; C. Blanchard's Journal, p. 134; Kalm, i., 220, 228; Burnaby, p. 96; Wansey, p. 195; Gabriel Thomas, History of West New Jersey; Barber's Hist. Coll. of New Jersey, Early Legislation; Rochefoucauld, i., 546.

uce. There was little or no fencing, and no walls, except to protect the apple, peach, and cherry trees, the only fruits grown. The agriculture was low, as in most of the other colonies, and few improvements were attempted.[1] The contemporary letter-writer, just quoted, says, " It is as well cultivated as any of the colonies, yet is much in dishabille, or at least seems so to one that has not seen late settled places." There was no foreign trade, and the manufactures were trifling.[2]

Society and social life, under such conditions, were both simple. There was a mild recognition of social distinctions, and an acknowledged aristocracy of gentlemen farmers without great political influence. The underlying and strongest principles were those of democracy, brought in by the New England immigrants, and which found in New Jersey a favorable soil. All persons above slaves and indented servants were, with the exception of the few small traders and shopkeepers in the towns, and of those who added a profession to agriculture, farmers of one sort or another, and the differences existing among them were only of degree, not of kind, while the various grades melted so imperceptibly into each other that it was not easy to mark the various stages in the descent from the large gentleman-farmer to the small freeholder. One reason for this slackness in class distinctions and for the shadowy cast of the aristocratic system was the very small number of slaves and the comparative scarcity of indented servants. The servile classes in New Jersey seem to have been socially as well as numerically insignificant. They were usually employed in domestic service, and the laws in regard to them were severe, like the southern codes upon which they were modelled. The penalties for receiving or trading with runaways were heavy, and the slaves and servants were severely whipped for these offences. They were forbidden to carry arms, and were burnt at the stake for murder, all their fellow-servants being summoned to witness the horrid spectacle. The general treatment of the slaves was extremely mild, and the spirit of the colony was, as a rule, so far hostile to slavery that it was stoutly and successfully resisted by the Quakers in the southern counties, and laws were passed by the Assembly in 1762 and 1766 to check the importation by means of duties. But despite all this, and the small numbers of the negroes, there was a constant fear of insurrection; and this uneasiness was justified by occasional risings which were either carried out or attempted, and

---

[1] Smyth, ii., 397; C. Blanchard's Journal, p. 133; Kalm, i., 222; ii., 25, 195; Letter from New Jersey, 1745–1756.   [2] Burnaby, p. 101.

which resulted in the execution of several negroes. At the time of the excitement caused by the negro-plot in New York, in the year 1741, the panic spread to New Jersey, and two or three wretched blacks were burnt at the stake.[1] The indented servants were not more numerous than the slaves, and their condition did not differ much from that of the same class in other colonies. They were, too, of a somewhat better sort, as the jail-birds went generally to the southern provinces, where they were strictly indented and harshly used.[2]

These servile classes furnished, probably, as elsewhere, the paupers and criminals; but there appear to have been few of either in New Jersey. In the towns settled by New Englanders paupers were sold at auction, and farmed out on the simple Puritan plan; but there was no other means taken of dealing with them, and their numbers were very trifling. In regard to the much more serious evil, it may be said that, practically, there was no crime in New Jersey. Houses were left unfastened at night; thefts and robberies were uncommon; pick-pockets were unknown; and the roads were uninfested and secure. The failing of the population seems to have been in illicit sexual connections, which were severely punished, after the New England fashion, by fines and whipping. Adultery was expiated by heavy fines and many lashes; and the whole code, in its severity against drinking, swearing, challenges, and wearing swords, shows the New England origin of the laws. Punishments were simple and severe. A woman received twenty lashes, in the year 1732, for larceny; and small offences were ordinarily dealt with by the whipping-post, stocks, and pillory. For capital crimes, of which there were thirteen in East, and none under the early and mild Quakers in West New Jersey, white men were hung, and negroes were sometimes sent to the gallows and sometimes to the stake. The methods of meeting the difficulties of pauperism and crime were utterly rude and unimproved, and in the fashion of the period. But, with a pure English people and plenty of good farming land, neither of these social evils was either pressing or important.[3]

---

[1] Hist. of Salem, in West New Jersey; Hatfield, Hist. of Elizabeth; Barber's Hist. Coll.; Leaming and Spicer, Laws of New Jersey, 1682, 1686, 1693; Rochefoucauld, i., 544.

[2] Leaming and Spicer, Laws, 1682, 1686; Letter from New Jersey, 1745–1756.

[3] Hist. of Salem, in West New Jersey; Leaming and Spicer, Laws, 1675, 1682, 1686, 1698; Letter from New Jersey; Hist. Coll., iii., Field, Prov. Courts; vi., Records of Newark.

Above the servile classes came the various grades of farmers. The highest were gentlemen farmers, who lived on their own estates, and worked them with great profit. Some of their country seats were very handsome, bordering on the rivers, and running far back into the country, like the New York manors; and the owners not infrequently displayed in their houses a good deal of elegance. We hear of Vandycks and other fine Dutch paintings in these country houses, and there is even mention of a park, belonging to Peter Schuyler, with tropical plants and deer. But such estates were exceptional, and on most of them a primitive simplicity prevailed. The houses were of wood or brick, spacious and comfortable. Through the centre ran a wide hall, and here the wife and daughters sat at work, in the words of a contemporary, "like Minerva and her nymphs, without head-dress, gown, shoes, or stockings." In all classes a rude plenty reigned; the table was abundant and plain; cider, which had replaced the beer of the Dutch, was the customary drink, and every farm produced the necessaries of life, including clothing, soap, and tobacco. Even the poorest farmers lived well, and their numerous children found ready employment. In the interior, and off the line of travel between New York and Philadelphia, the mode of life was ruder, and the dwellings often mere log-huts, with unstopped chinks and no shutters, and so cold that, as Kalm, the Swedish traveller, relates, the ink would freeze in the pen and in the inkstand.

There was a striking lack of amusements. The primitive Swedish customs had been driven out, and the Puritan theory of existence held sway. The early laws were sharp against all forms of indulgence; "stage-plays, games, masques, revels, bull-baitings, and cock-fighting, which excite the people to rudeness, cruelty, and irreligion, were to be discouraged and punished;" and men were indicted for suffering cards to be played in their houses; while at a much later period church lotteries were rigorously suppressed. The laws died out, but their spirit survived, and the only relaxation of the New Jersey farmer was to meet with his neighbors at the club in the village tavern to drink, and perhaps witness a horse-race, or to hang about the court-house in the crowd which gathered there on the court day, or go to the fairs in the small towns, once disorderly, but now quiet by the prohibition of liquor-selling. They were a hard-headed, prosperous, thrifty people, despite the absence of foreign trade and the customary depreciated currency. They were good-natured, friendly, and hospitable, with little superstition, and a strong respect for law, order,

and vested rights.   They recognized also the social distinctions, after
the New England fashion, and seats were held in church according to
office, age, estate, infirmity, desert, and parentage.   They were sociable
too, and, especially in the winter-time, made many visits to each others' houses.   The only extravagance was in the way of funerals, when
the neighbors gathered at the house of mourning to follow the body
to the graveyard attached to each farm, and always retained by the
original family.   Even this was reformed when the general movement
against lavish display at funerals was made in 1764.   Marriages were
quiet, by banns with the poor, and by license among the more prosperous.   The daughter of the average farmer was considered to be
well dowered if she was given a cow and a side-saddle, although the
connection between these articles is not at first apparent.[1]   The side-
saddle, however, finds its explanation in the common mode of travel,
which was on horseback.   Local stages appeared as early as the year
1732, were then extended to New York, and were finally replaced by
the through lines from Philadelphia.   The roads were good or bad,
according to the nature of the soil, for the people were careless about
mending them, and found it easier to go round a fallen tree than to
remove it.   The fact that New Jersey became a sort of highway made
inns a necessity, and they seem to have been generally very good
and comfortable, while the constant passage of travellers did much
to remove the isolation and break the solitary existence so common
in the American colonies.[2]

Thus far only the agricultural and farming population, which constituted the larger portion of the New Jersey people, has been mentioned, but the professions, although small, were respectable, and their
members active and influential.   The churches were of every Protestant denomination, and from the time of the "Concessions" liberality in religion, except during Lord Cornbury's rule, was the consistent policy of the State.   The Church of England had a nominal but
no real establishment.   It started in Lord Cornbury's time with laws

[1] Kalm, ii., 25, 49, 123 ; Burnaby, pp. 96, 98, 99, 103 ; Gabriel Thomas, West New
Jersey ; Murray, Notes on Elizabeth ; Hist. of Salem, in West New Jersey ; Sussex
Centenary, Edsall's Address ; Mickle's Old Gloucester ; Hatfield, Hist. of Elizabeth,
Description of a Funeral ; Barber's Hist. Coll. of New Jersey, Early Legislation ;
Leaming and Spicer, Laws, 1682 ; Letter from New Jersey, 1745–1756 ; Hist. Soc.
Proc., pp. 3, 4, Journal of Spicer ; vi., Rec. of Newark ; Rochefoucauld, i. 548.
[2] Journal of Claude Blanchard, p. 134 ; Kalm, ii., 24, 25 ; Mickle's Old Glouces-
ter ; Barber's Hist. Coll. ; Letter from New Jersey, 1745–1756.

compelling the reading of the Book of Common Prayer, and a report to the Bishop of London of all dissenting ministers—a repressive policy from the effects of which it never recovered; nor did it ever gain a hold among the people. By the middle of the eighteenth century, according to the reports furnished the Society for the Propagation of the Gospel, the Church was in a bad, unsettled way; the people were going over to the dissenters; the country abounded with Anabaptists and Quakers; children were not baptized; godfathers and godmothers were held in contempt; and the church buildings were out of repair. There were, in fact, few regular clergymen, although the Gospel Society maintained six missionaries, who did good work. The Governor was the head of the Church, the representative of the Bishop of London, and entitled to hold a prerogative court; but his office and his duties in this respect must have been almost wholly nominal. There were, of course, Episcopalians in New Jersey; but they formed only a fraction of the population, and had little zeal. The most marked effect of the Established Church here, as in most of the other colonies, was the dislike it aroused against England, which was heightened by the conduct of the clergy, who were, as a rule, Tories, sided with the mother country, and saw their churches closed in consequence during the Revolution. The Quakers were numerous and influential in the early days; but the energetic and powerful sects were the Scotch Presbyterians and the New England Congregationalists, led by active and earnest ministers of good character and no little learning, both as divines and physicians. Their influence is seen in the earliest legislation and in the strict Sunday laws, which forbade, under pain of stocks, imprisonment, and lashes, any work, travelling, or recreation on the Lord's day. These acts were somewhat modified in Lord Cornbury's time, but they remained substantially in force down to the period of the Revolution. The ministers were not well paid, their fees were small, and even the revenues which they derived from retailing licenses, through the New England custom of civil marriage, were cut down by the justices of the peace, who were "great marriage-mongers, and tied the knot very rapidly." Yet, despite these drawbacks, the dissenting clergy remained an excellent and active body.[1]

[1] Anderson's Col. Church, ii., 441; Kalm, i., 228; ii., 25; Murray, Notes on Elizabeth; Hist. of Salem, in West New Jersey; Henderson, The Days of Old; Barber's Hist. Coll.; Leaming and Spicer, Laws, 1693; Letter from New Jersey, 1745–1756; Rev. Thomas Thompson's Journey; Hist. Soc. Coll., vii., Elmer's Constitutional Government of New Jersey; Burnaby, pp. 102, 103.

To these two sects of Presbyterians and Congregationalists New Jersey owed the great debt of such education as she possessed. As it was, schools were few at the time of the Revolution, and school-masters poorly paid; but such as there were, were due to no public system, but to the New England practice of throwing the burden of education upon the towns, and requiring the election of three men to lay and levy taxes for the support of a school-master. Thus, in the towns of New England origin, schools were maintained; and at a later period a good grammar school was opened by private enterprise in Elizabeth, and was well attended. There seems, too, to have been a general readiness among the people to avail themselves of any oppor-tunities of instruction that came in their way.[1] The greatest service, however, to the cause of education was that rendered by the Pres-byterians, who first brought forward in their synod a plan for a college, which they afterward founded in the year 1746, and removed to Princeton, where Nassau Hall was built ten years later. Here, at the close of the old French war, in school and college were eighty students, taught by a provost and two professors. The provost re-ceived two hundred pounds a year, and the professors fifty each; while the annual expenses of each student amounted to about twenty-five pounds. The instruction was of good quality so far as it went; there were the germs of a library and some philosophical instruments, and the college was promising and wisely administered.[2]

In the field of general literature New Jersey had little to show. The first press was established by James Parker in the year 1751, at Woodbridge, where, in 1758, a magazine was issued, which had a brief existence of two years; but the first newspaper, the *New Jersey Gazette*, did not appear until the Revolution had fairly begun. No books by native authors were published; but some of the leading men, like Governor Morris, wrote well, and had fine imported libra-ries, which indicated classical and general learning, while others con-tributed fair verses, and essays, political and otherwise, to the ga-zettes of the neighboring capitals. The geographical position of the province gave the inhabitants opportunities for knowledge of the out-side world, and for news from the journals of New York and Phila-delphia. The first mails—once a week in summer, and once a fort-

---

[1] Sussex Centenary, Edsall's Address; Hatfield, Hist. of Elizabeth; Leaming and Spicer, Laws, 1682–1693; Hist. Coll., iii., Prov. Courts, Field; Rochefoucauld, ii., 433.

[2] Abbé Robin, p. 82; Claude Blanchard, p. 134; Murray, Notes on Elizabeth.

night in winter—were carried on horseback in the year 1729; and in 1754 Franklin provided the colony with three mails a week. Thus New Jersey, although herself behindhand in literary development and in outside connections, had the benefit of everything done in this direction by her great neighbors on the north and west.[1]

The two other professions of civil life did not fall behind the clergy in character and competency. Indeed, in medicine, when it is remembered that there was nothing but country practice, the standing of New Jersey is remarkably good. Here, as in Pennsylvania, the Quakers brought physicians with them, who eked out a slender income by trade and farming. Few of their successors had a European training. Most of them acquired their education by an apprenticeship, involving care of the shop and many menial services, with some older practitioner, whose daughter the student, after the apprentice fashion, would not infrequently marry, and then succeed to his father-in-law's business. There were, of course, many quacks; and no improvements were effected until they were forced upon the profession by the demand for surgeons in the French war. In the year 1766 a medical society was founded, most intricate tables of small fees for every conceivable case were adopted, and physicians had to pass an examination at the hands of established practitioners and before the court; receiving, if successful, a testimonial signed by the judge. This led to a great advance in the character of the profession, which rose into importance only in the years preceding the Revolution. The practice was rough and unscientific, but in the fashion of the day, and the life was a hard one. The doctor had to ride long distances, sometimes across country, with his saddle-bags stuffed with drugs, and usually consumed a fortnight in a round of visits. Midwifery continued in the hands of women; but the physicians, as a class, were a respectable and efficient body.[2]

The lawyers also appear to have been men of ability and character. They formed at first no regular class, and attorneys were not in good repute. The Quakers in West New Jersey forbade any pleading for money; but in the year 1694 an act was passed regulating attorneys; soon after they were required to have a license from the Governor, and as early as the year 1733 seven years' study was required to prac-

---

[1] Barber, Hist. Coll. of New Jersey; Hist. Soc. Coll., iv., Morris Papers; Tyler's Amer. Literature.

[2] Wickes, History of Medicine in New Jersey.

tise as an attorney, which indicates a desire to maintain a proper efficiency; yet, notwithstanding these efforts, the profession and the courts at a later time seem to have excited the popular resentment in a manner which recalls the Regulators of North Carolina. Where the fault lay is not easy to determine; but the lawyers were, as a rule, respectable. Most of them espoused the popular side in the troubles with England, the leaders of the bar, who were Tories, and later refugees, forming the most marked exceptions.[1]

The early system of courts was simple in the extreme. Monthly or town courts, and county courts with elected judges, were established where the New England influence prevailed, and in the Quaker region this example was followed. The Scotch immigrants added a court of common right, with both law and equity jurisdiction. Then came a court of appeals, consisting of a member of the council and justices of the peace, and a court of oyer and terminer, with justices and one appointed judge. This loose system was simply regulated by the royal government, which took to itself all judicial appointments. All cases of debt and trespass, under forty shillings, were to be tried by justices of the peace, with an appeal to the court of sessions or the court of common pleas, which replaced the county courts. From them there was an appeal, in all cases involving more than ten pounds, to the supreme court of the province, composed of appointed judges, and combining the jurisdiction of the English Common Pleas, King's Bench, and Exchequer; and from this supreme court an appeal in error could be taken to the Governor and Council, and over two hundred pounds, to the King in Council. The court of chancery, as first established, consisted of the Governor and three councillors; but Hunter, in the year 1718, made good his claim to act alone as chancellor, and this system, together with the fees fixed by Burnet, which led to much abuse and extortion, remained in force until the year 1770, when the court was enlarged and improved by William Franklin. Neither this court, however, nor that of vice-admiralty, also pertaining to the Governor, had great importance, and some of the governors did not care to take the trouble to act as chancellors. The common law, of course, prevailed, and there was always a great deal of litigation, often of a very frivolous and petty character. The simplicity of the early days, when Thomas Olive, the Quaker Governor, sat on a stump in his meadow and dispensed justice, disappeared when the province came to the Crown. In

---

[1] Hist. Soc. Coll., iii., Field, Provincial Courts.

provincial times the judges wore red gowns, with black velvet trimming, and bag wigs, and in summer black silk gowns, which were also worn by the members of the bar. This excellent practice of an appropriate dress went out with the Revolution, and all subsequent efforts to revive it failed. The general administration of justice was good and effective, and the judges of the supreme court, though too apt to be under the influence of the Governor, were, as a rule, trained and capable lawyers.[1]

The government of New Jersey, at first proprietary, was transferred to the Crown as early as the year 1702. It consisted of a Governor appointed by the Crown; a Council of twelve members, in theory appointed by the Crown, in reality by the Governor, who took six from East and six from West New Jersey; and an Assembly elected by the freeholders. The Governor could veto, prorogue, dissolve, and convene; the Council formed the Upper House, and each House had a veto. The Governor and Council made all appointments by writ of privy seal and in the name of the Crown, and issued patents for land, from which the fees were considerable. The system, as a whole, differed in no essential respect from the ordinary royal governments in America. There was the usual jealousy of the Governor common to all the colonies, which found vent on all occasions, and never hesitated to gratify itself even at the expense of the public welfare. The absence of trade narrowed the grievances against the mother country to the protection extended to naval deserters, for desertion was followed by the press-gang, and the press by fights, lawsuits, and ill-feeling. The general tone of the people, however, was very loyal, as is illustrated by a curious passage in an old record, where it appears that one "Richard Duddy was prosecuted for damning his Grace the Duke of Cumberland." There was, indeed, no good ground for anything but loyalty. Taxes, chiefly levied on land, were light, and although the militia included in theory every man between sixteen and sixty, the law was not very rigidly enforced, and New Jersey was saved by her protected situation from the scourge of French and Indian war.[2]

---

[1] A detailed account of Bench and Bar in New Jersey may be found in Hist. Soc., iii., Field, Provincial Courts; see also Burnaby, p. 102; Gabriel Thomas; Leaming and Spicer, New Jersey Laws, 1675, 1682; Hist. Soc. Coll., vii., Elmer's Const. Government in New Jersey.

[2] Burnaby, pp. 96, 101, 102; Murray, Notes on Elizabeth; Leaming and Spicer, Laws, 1675; Sussex Centenary, Edsall's Address; Hist. Soc. Coll., iv., Morris Papers; vii., Elmer's Const. Government in New Jersey.

The people were, as a whole, a conservative, thrifty community of English farmers. They were pure in race, and differed in this respect from the other colonies of the middle group; but they nevertheless strongly partook, socially and politically, of the peculiar qualities which distinguish New York and Pennsylvania.

Chapter XVI.

NEW YORK FROM 1609 TO 1765.

In New York was made the only settlement which seemed at any time seriously to threaten the dominion of the English race in America. An Englishman, the famous Henry Hudson, in the **1609.** pay of Holland, first discovered and explored the noble river which bears his name, and one of the earliest permanent settlements of Europeans in the New World was the result. Adventure brought men to Virginia; politics and religion to New England; philanthropy to Georgia; but New York was founded by trade and for trade, and for nothing else. The settlement on the island of Manhattan was due to the active spirit of Dutch commerce. The shrewd merchants of Amsterdam saw great profit in the cheap furs to be obtained of the Indians, and their vessels began to come in numbers, and make repeated voyages to the Hudson soon after the discovery of the river. A post, consisting of a few small houses or huts, sprang up on Manhattan, and the hardy Dutch captains and seamen began to push out in all directions, extending their trade and exploring the bays and rivers of all the adjacent coasts. Christiaensen worked his way up the river, built a fort, and founded another post, near the present site of Al- **1614.** bany. Adrian Block explored Long Island Sound and the coasts of New England, while May had been to the southward as far as the cape which bears his name.

The profits of the fur-trade were so great that others began to turn their eyes to the new region; and the original adventurers among the **1615.** merchants hastily formed the New Netherland Company, and obtained a monopoly of the trade for three years. During that period everything went on prosperously. A post was established on the South or Delaware river, and the Dutch ships went so far, both to the north and south, that they threatened interference with the English of Plymouth and Virginia alike. But while trade was thus advanced in all directions nothing was done for colonization. The

States-general, however, gained a knowledge of the value of their new possessions, and when the charter of the New Netherland Company expired, they refused charters to the small merchants, and frowned upon their trade. After an interval of uncertainty, the problem was solved by the establishment of the great West India

1621. Company, similar to the immense monopoly of the East; and to the Amsterdam chamber of this new company the New Netherlands were intrusted. They formally took possession, proceeded to stop the small private traders, and, after a year's delay, sent

1623. out a body of Walloons, who had been driven from their homes by Spanish persecution, to settle in the new territories of Holland. These first immigrants were planted near Albany, while others who followed settled on the South river, on Long Island, and some on Manhattan. The settlements prospered; the people were thrifty and industrious, and a lively traffic sprang up with the

1624- 1626. Indians everywhere. During this time May first acted as Director; then William Verhulst; and, lastly, Peter Minuit, who united all the settlements under one government, bought the island of Manhattan from the natives, extended the settlement there, and withdrew from Fort Orange all but a small garrison, on account of Indian troubles. The Company built warehouses, Fort Amsterdam was begun, and relations were opened with Plymouth of a friendly character, al-

1628. though even then Bradford questioned the right of the Dutch to their possessions. Mills were also erected, and trade rapidly increased; but it was all trade, and colonization did not prosper nor agriculture develop.

The Company met this difficulty by the creation of what was intended to be a powerful and noble class. A charter was agreed

1629. to, which gave any member of the Company founding a colony of fifty persons the right to an estate with a river frontage of sixteen miles, and of otherwise indefinite extent, while with these estates went every sort of feudal right, including manorial courts and the privilege of trading within the dominions of the Company. Leading directors promptly took advantage of this great opportunity. Godyn and Blommaert secured the region of the South river; Kiliaen Van Rensselaer that about Albany; and Michael Pauw that of Hoboken. These purchases, which were of enormous extent, alarmed the Company, who ordered the patroons to take partners—a command they easily evaded by taking each other in that capacity. Colonization speedily followed. Rensselaer established Rensselaerswyck, near Fort

Orange; and Godyn and Blommaert, with De Vries and others, the **1631.** village of Swaanendael, on the South river. Not content with their landed possessions, the patroons proceeded to absorb all the trade of these vast regions; but this was more than the Company could bear. An angry order was passed forbidding all trade except that of the Company, and insuring a plentiful supply of quarrels; **1632.** while Minuit, who was thought to favor the patroons, was recalled. On his way home he was seized by the English, on account of trading in their dominions, and was only released after a long correspondence. Difficulties seemed now to beset the Dutch. The Indians tore down the arms of Holland on the South river, and this led to a war, a massacre of the settlers, and the destruction of Swaanendael; so that when De Vries, the patroon, and the best of all the Dutch leaders, came out, he met with nothing but the ruins of his village; and, **1633.** after a visit to Virginia, made his way to the north. There he found, at Manhattan, a new Governor, Wouter Van Twiller, a wretched clerk from the Company's office, appointed by Van Rensselaer's influence, and as miserably incompetent as a man could well be for his post. His first feat was to bluster at and threaten an English vessel, which sailed up the river despite his threats, and which was only brought back with difficulty by a force sent out for the purpose. His next exploit was to refuse permission to a vessel belonging to De Vries to sail down the Sound, and he actually brought the cannon of the fort to bear upon her; but De Vries taunted him with the affair with the English, and the vessel proceeded unmolested on her voyage. These acts were fair examples of Van Twiller's miserable and ludicrous administration.

Nothing, however, could damp the spirit of trade. Corssen established a post on the Schuylkill; and Van Curler, following up the traders in the east, built Fort Good Hope, on the Connecticut. Down came the Plymouth people and built another post, and the foundations of a fine contention were securely laid. The Virginians also pushed up the South river; but Van Twiller, in this instance, mustered enough energy to repel the intruders. The English difficulties were carried to Europe, too, in the case of the ship expelled from the Hudson, and a lively correspondence ensued between the home Governments, which, after the fashion of colonial squabbles, came to nothing. Meanwhile the town on Manhattan grew slowly. New houses and a substantial church were built, while the "staple right" brought a revenue to the town from every passing vessel. Still the colony did not thrive. The patroon system kept settlers away, and the paternal government of a trading corporation checked all vigorous and independent growth, while Van Twiller went steadily from bad to worse. He engaged in childish quarrels with every one, from the minister down, and finally sent home Van Dincklagen, the schout, one of the few really competent men in the town. This utter misgovernment led at last to Van Twiller's removal. He retired in possession of large tracts of land, which he had succeeded in acquiring, and was replaced by William Kieft, a bankrupt merchant of bad reputation. Kieft practically abolished the Council, and got all power into his own hands; but he had some sense of order. His first report showed that Van Twiller had allowed the property of the Company, both buildings and vessels, to go to ruin, and that the lawless crews of the trading-vessels smuggled goods, cheated, and ran riot in the town. Kieft made a series of laws which checked these abuses; but, despite his improvements, the place remained a mere trading-post, and would not develop into a colony. The patroons were the curse of the scheme, and too powerful to be overthrown; so they proposed, as a remedy for the existing evils, that their powers and privileges should be greatly enlarged. The Company had bought back some of the lands; but they were still helpless, and the State would do nothing for them. In this crisis they had a return of good sense, and solved the problem by destroying their stifling monopoly. They threw the trade to New Netherlands open to all comers, and promised the absolute ownership of land on the payment of a small quit-rent. The gates were open at last, and the tide of emigration swept in. De Vries, who had bought land on Staten Island, came out with a company; while ship followed ship filled with colonists, and English came from Virginia, and still more from New England. Men of property and standing began to turn their attention to the New Netherlands; fine well-stocked farms rapidly covered Manhattan, and healthy progress had at last begun. Thus strengthened, the Company restricted the patroons to a water-front of one mile and a depth of two, but left them their feudal privileges, benefits which practically accrued to Van Rensselaer, whose colony at Beverwyck had alone, among the manors, thriven and grown at the expense of the Company.

The opening of trade proved in one respect a disaster. The cautious policy of the Company was abandoned, and greedy traders who had already begun the business, and were now wholly unrestrained, hastened to make their fortunes by selling arms to the Indians in return for almost unlimited quantities of furs. Thus the Mohawks obtained guns enough to threaten both the Dutch and all the surrounding tribes, and this perilous condition was made infinitely worse by the mad policy of Kieft. He first tried to exact tribute from the Indians near Manhattan, then offered a price for the head of any of the Raritans who had destroyed the settlement of De Vries; and, when a young man was murdered by a Weckquaesgeek, the Governor planned immediate war. In all this he had no sympathy from the people, who realizing their weakness, had no wish to fight, and the popular feeling rose so high, even among the phlegmatic Dutchmen, that Kieft was obliged to call a public meeting, at which twelve select-men were chosen to advise the Governor. The "twelve" counselled peace, a demand for compensation for the murder, and that the Governor should put himself at the head of the troops. Kieft thanked them for their advice, and issued a proclamation forbidding popular meetings; but the people of New Amsterdam could not undo the work of the traders. The Mohawks, armed by the Dutch, swept down from the north, driving the river tribes before them. The fugitives sought refuge in the Dutch settlements, and were well received, especially by De Vries, who sought to give them every protection; but the helpless condition of his former enemies only aroused Kieft to fury. Two or three of the "twelve," who had been dissolved, met and presented a petition to the Governor that the Indians should be attacked. Acting on this illegal and fraudulent petition, Kieft, despite the remonstrances of De Vries, ordered out the troops, and sent them across the river to Pavonia and Corlaer's Hook, where most of the runaway Indians were assembled. The wretched fugitives, surprised by their supposed protectors, were butchered, in the dead of a winter's night, without mercy, and the bloody soldiers returned in the morning to Manhattan, where they were warmly welcomed by Kieft. This massacre lighted up at once the flames of war among all the neighboring tribes of Algonquins. All the outlying farms were laid waste, and their owners murdered, while the smaller settlements were destroyed. Vriesendael alone was spared. A peace, patched up by De Vries, gave a respite until summer, and then the war raged more fiercely than before, the Indians burning and destroying in every direction, while trade was broken up, and the crews of the vessels slaughtered.

Popular feeling now ran so high against Kieft that his life was in danger; and although he tried to put down resistance with a high

1641.

1643.

hand, he was overborne and compelled to call a meeting of the
people. "Eight men" were chosen, who this time seized the government, organized a force of English and Dutch, under the command of
John Underhill, of Pequod fame, and, this done, addressed letters to
the Company, setting forth their miserable condition and the need of
relief to save the colony. The winter dragged heavily along, until an
1644. appeal from the English on Long Island led to an expedition
which sacked two Indian villages, and killed a hundred warriors, and this was followed by another campaign directed by Underhill.
The principal Indian town in Connecticut was taken, where seven hundred warriors were gathered; the feeble defences were stormed; the
wigwams fired, and all the savages were put to the sword. This terrible slaughter crippled the Eastern tribes, and put an end to their ravages; but the river tribes still continued hostile, and kept the colonists
shut up in Manhattan. The "eight men" desired further vigorous measures, and the employment of a hundred and fifty soldiers who had arrived from Curaçoa; but there was no money, the Company was bankrupt, and Kieft made a bad matter worse by attempting to raise a revenue from a tax on beer. Thus the government blundered on without
a single useful measure, until at last the "eight men" addressed another letter to the Company, demanding flatly the recall of Kieft, and
the right of choosing local officers, who should send deputies to confer with the Governor and Council. This definite request produced
an immediate effect upon the bankrupt Company in Holland, who determined upon the recall of Kieft and the appointment of Stuyvesant;
but a long delay ensued before the change was actually made, and in
1645. the interval the Indian tribes, weary at last of war, came in and
made peace. Kieft continued his quarrels; but his power was
gone, and he was hated as the principal cause of all the misfortunes
of the colony.

The results of his miserable administration were certainly disastrous
enough. Sixteen hundred Indians had perished in the war; but all
the outlying Dutch settlements and farms had been destroyed, and the
prosperity of the colony had received a check from which it recovered
very slowly. In Connecticut the English had left the Dutch merely
a nominal hold, and had really destroyed their power in the East. On
the South river the Swedes had settled, and, disregarding Kieft's blustering proclamations, had founded strong and growing colonies. The
restless New Englanders had come to the same region; but these adventurers, Kieft first, and then the Swedes, had successfully expelled.

Still the power of Holland sank before that of Sweden, and the energetic Printz bullied and abused the Dutch commanders at Fort Nassau, and made himself master of the Delaware. The interests of Holland were at a low ebb when Peter Stuyvesant, of uncertain **1647.** reputation, imperious, high-tempered, energetic, and persistent, landed at Manhattan amid the shouts of the delighted people, and took under his protection his beaten and hated predecessor, who was reviled by his enemies, even at the moment of surrendering his office. The matter, however, did not stop here. Kuyter and Melyn, two of the "eight men," and citizens of good standing, demanded a rigid investigation of Kieft's administration. Stuyvesant's arrogant and tyrannical temper at once broke out. He refused to recognize Kuyter and Melyn officially, and with his subservient Council dismissed the complaint. Kieft then turned on his assailants, accused them of getting up the appeal to Holland, and of disturbing the peace; and Kuyter and Melyn were at once convicted, heavily fined, and banished, Stuyvesant grumbling because he could not have Melyn put to death. Kieft soon after sailed, master of an ample fortune, and taking his two foes with him as prisoners. The vessel was wrecked on the English coast, Kieft was drowned, and Kuyter and Melyn, who were saved, hastened to Amsterdam to demand relief and reparation.

This violence and injustice were fit precursors of Stuyvesant's rule. Personally honest and very energetic, he gained the hatred of every one by the rough-and-ready manner in which he attempted to improve public affairs, raise money by taxation, and regulate trade. The taxes were ill-judged, burdensome, and slowly paid; while the Governor was accused of illicit trade in his efforts to stop smuggling. Prosperity diminished, the colony languished, there was no revenue, and Stuyvesant was at last compelled to order the towns to elect representatives, from whom a board of nine men was to be chosen. This board had merely advisory powers, and some judicial duties; six were to go out annually, and their places were to be filled by appointment. This close corporation was the best substitute for popular representation obtainable, and the only defence of the popular rights which Stuyvesant utterly disregarded. The director adopted the same treatment for foreign opponents that he did for the colonists. The agent of Lady Stirling was promptly ousted from Long Island, and Stuyvesant soon after seized a ship at New Haven for trading without license. At this the New Englanders broke out into fierce remonstrance, and sheltered runaway servants, while Stuyvesant retaliated by offering a refuge to all fugitives, criminal or otherwise, from New Haven; and thus the foundation for a bitter quarrel was solidly laid. In the same spirit he attempted to control the property of the Van Rensselaers; but their agent kept him off, and he had only the pleasure of issuing blustering proclamations. Matters went from bad to worse, and discontent grew beneath oppression, foreign quarrels, and increased taxation.

1649. The first board of nine became intractable, and a new one was appointed, which at once set about sending a delegation to Holland. Stuyvesant denied them the right of popular meeting, and threw the leader, Van der Donck, into prison; while Melyn's return, with a reversal of his sentence, and a mandamus to Stuyvesant to appear and defend himself, added fuel to the flames, and led to an actual brawl at a public meeting. The popular clamor at last reached such a pitch that Stuyvesant was forced to allow Van der Donck and two others to proceed to Holland; sending his secretary, Van Tienhoven, to defend him. The petitioners demanded burgher government; that Holland should take the colony; and the recall of Stuyvesant, who was ably defended by his secretary. The States-general passed some good measures for the government of the colony, and ordered Stuyvesant to return; but the Company did not accede, and Stuyvesant went on in the old way. He refused to fill vacancies in the "nine men," thus dissolving the board; drove Melyn out of the town, and compelled him to fortify himself in his manor on Staten Island; and went about whipping and imprisoning all who dared to oppose him.

1650. In all his contests thus far Stuyvesant seems to have relied upon his English subjects on Long Island, and he appointed two of them boundary commissioners, who speedily concluded a treaty with their kinsmen, by which the Dutch lost half Long Island and the whole of Connecticut and Rhode Island. This led to fresh complaints from the popular party; and soon after, the States-general **1652.** decreeing the establishment of burgher government, including courts and modifications of trade laws, the Company gave way, and Van der Donck returned with this decree as the fruit of his toil. Stuyvesant, in view of pending war with England, was not recalled, and he boldly evaded the decree of the States-general by appointing all the officers in the new government, including the obnoxious Van Tienhoven as schout. Even this meagre concession was eagerly accepted by the people, and they cheerfully aided Stuyvesant in improving defences against the threatened war, which, fortunately for the Dutch, never came to anything. The English of Connecticut were eager to fight, but Massachusetts would not move. Rhode Island, unfettered by the confederation, entered upon a ludicrous war upon her own account; and under her standard Underhill, who had already been twice arrested for raising riots on Long Island, marched with twenty men, and formally took possession of the empty Dutch fort on the Connecticut; selling the land twice over for his own benefit, and finally effacing the last vestiges of Dutch ownership in New England. Rhode Island vessels preyed with rare impartiality, in a small way, upon the commerce of both Holland and England, but this was all. There were rumors of Indian wars started by Dutch influence, and the towns of Connecticut became much excited; but still **1654.** Massachusetts held back. At last Cromwell took the matter in hand, and sent out a fleet and soldiers; but there were more delays, and peace relieved the New Netherlands from danger.

It was a welcome deliverance to the Dutch; for after the first alarm of war discontent had again sprung up in New Amsterdam, and the officers of the burgher government headed the opposition, which received a powerful addition from the English of Long Island—Stuyvesant's quondam allies. A convention of delegates from the towns was called, in which the English—far better political agitators than their kinsmen of Holland—took the lead, and a sharp memorial was drawn up by Baxter against Stuyvesant, who denied their right to meet, and, after much discussion, the convention sent an agent to Holland. The news of peace, which freed the Dutch from the imminent peril of Cromwell's soldiers and sailors, was accompanied with letters from the Company strongly supporting the Director; and thus strengthened, Stuyvesant arrested Baxter and Hubbard, who were raising a new rebellion on their own account in the Long Island towns, and threw them into prison. In appearance, at least, the Governor was stronger than ever. During this troubled period Stuyvesant had found time to look into the affairs of the South river, where the Dutch power, confined to Fort Nassau, was at low ebb. The Dutch were helpless among the **1651.** Swedes, and treated as mere trespassers. Stuyvesant's first act was to abandon Fort Nassau, and build, below the Swedish posts, Fort Casimir, thus commanding navigation. Printz protested; but both parties were afraid of the English and their claims, and nothing was done beyond the despatch of messengers to Sweden to complain of the invasion. Printz's successor, Rysingh, coming out with a force of three hundred men two years later, immediately captured Fort Casimir, and subjected the Dutch to Swedish rule, which caused a burst of indignation in New Netherlands and in the Company; and after much delay Stuyvesant sailed with seven ships and more than six hundred men—a powerful force, which made all hope of resistance impossible. The Swedes surrendered, and the Swedish power was finally overthrown. The bankrupt Company was, however, burdened with its conquest, so they gave part of it to the city of Amsterdam; New Amstel was founded, and emigrants came out. But the colony did not thrive; disease was rife, and complete possession seemed worse than doubtful ownership of the Delaware.

1655.

While Stuyvesant was conquering the Swedes an Indian war broke out in the neighborhood of Manhattan; and, in the absence of troops, the savages massacred the inhabitants of Pavonia, and harried Long Island. Stuyvesant, summoned back in haste, by his bravery and vigor checked the war, and soon after obtained peace; but there was now a fresh danger to New Netherlands in the advances of the French, and only the shrewd and peaceful policy pursued by the patroon's people at Beverwyck kept the Mohawks neutral, and saved the settlements from utter destruction during a second Indian war, which began with a massacre at Esopus, and went on, intermittently, for more than five years. Relieved, however, from his most serious troubles, Stuyvesant turned his energy into a new channel, and undertook to enforce religious uniformity by a relentless persecution of Lutherans and Quakers. He arrested and imprisoned the former, refused them a meeting-house, and drove their ministers from the colony, while the Quakers suffered still more; they were arrested, tried, and imprisoned; beaten, hung up by their hands, forced to hard labor, and subjected to every form of abuse and punishment. This policy had little result, except to create ill feeling, and found no sympathy among a people who were profoundly indifferent on such matters; neither did it interfere with the prosperity and growth of New Netherlands, which seemed at last to have reached firm ground, and was steadily advancing in wealth and population.

1658.

In these years of prosperity, however, the end of the Dutch power drew on. The danger did not come from the Indians, nor from the French, but from the kindred race which was destined to rule the continent. At the north, Massachusetts threatened to settle upon the banks of the Hudson; on Long Island, the English of Connecticut pressed hard upon the boundary lines; on the South river, New Englanders traded in defiance of Dutch laws and Dutch forts; and the southern English began to encroach upon Dutch territory. Lord Baltimore renewed his claim to the whole South river region; and his agents demanding a surrender of the province, bade fair to wrest it from the Dutch as the latter had from the Swedes. By skilful and pro-

1660. tracted negotiation, the Dutch warded off this attack, and transferred the controversy to Europe. At the same time they turned over the whole province to the city of Amsterdam; but the effort was vain; the colony of the south continued feeble and languishing, and the temporary success against Lord Baltimore was soon clouded by events at the north. In the charter which Winthrop obtained from

1662. Charles II., Connecticut and New Haven were consolidated, and all Long Island and the northern New Netherlands were declared within the Connecticut boundaries. Thereupon the independent towns on Long Island fell off, and Connecticut men appeared not only in Westchester, but among the Dutch towns of Long Island, which they renamed, and proclaimed to be under English jurisdiction. Stuyvesant, with an empty treasury and a breaking province, was helpless and desperate, and a new turn of affairs only made matters worse. One John Scott, an adventurer well known in that region, came out with a commission, in which Maverick and Baxter were joined, from the committee on trade and plantations. He obtained aid from Connecticut, and then announced that all Long Island had been granted to the Duke of York. The English then united in support of the new dispensation; Scott was declared president, and, making himself master of the Dutch towns, threatened to invade New Amsterdam. This roused Stuyvesant to a last despairing effort. He raised money and men, after much altercation, renewed the defences, and defied Scott, who was brought to terms, and agreed to leave the Dutch towns unmolested for a year. The lull was deceitful. The commissioners of the King of England—Nicolls, Carr, Cartwright, and Maverick—soon arrived at Boston to regulate New England and

1664. conquer the Dutch. They could get no troops from Massachusetts, but they did from Connecticut; and in August, 1664, while the Director was at Fort Orange, appeared off the Narrows, and, before he could return, the whole squadron was assembled. Stuyvesant strove to prepare for an energetic defence; but the citizens were panic-stricken, and the soldiers mutinous; so that the favorable offers of Nicolls were only too readily listened to. Stuyvesant raged and swore, and wished to make a desperate fight in his indefensible and terrified town; but his struggle was vain. Nicolls guaranteed protection of life and property, religious liberty, freedom of

trade and emigration, and representative government. Stuyvesant was forced to ratify the treaty of surrender, and on the 8th of September marched out at the head of his soldiers and embarked them for Holland, and New Amsterdam became New York; while Fort Orange was taken by Cartwright and christened Albany. Carr reduced Fort Casimir and the South river settlements, and the Dutch power in America perished.

The English carefully observed the terms of the surrender, and everything proceeded quietly and with little apparent change, except in the new English names. Nicolls was Governor, with an English secretary and English councillors to assist him; but the former Dutch officers were consulted, and nothing was done to wound the feelings of the people. An oath of allegiance to the Duke was exacted, and taken without much opposition. Nicolls's first trouble came from his grants in New Jersey, which were interfered with by **1665.** the Duke's gift to Carteret and Berkeley. He was compelled to admit the new-comers, but at the same time wrote complainingly to the Duke, and thus began the long and discreditable attempt to recover what had once been given away. There were differences, too, with Connecticut, which were finally amicably settled. New York obtained the whole of Long Island; and Connecticut secured the main-land west of the Connecticut River, by a boundary which was defined very shrewdly in the Connecticut interest, was never confirmed, and became the source of future controversy. A code known as the Duke's laws was drawn up, and promulgated at first on Long Island, where there was more interest in matters of government, and afterward in New York. This code, with little regard for popular representation, provided for a court of assizes annually at New York, for courts of sessions and county officers, and for town overseers. Land grants were to be confirmed, trade was regulated, crimes and penalties were defined, and religious liberty assured. There was some grumbling over English names in the municipal government of New York, but the offices were fairly distributed between the two races. The war in Europe did not disturb the peace, but Nicolls took every precaution against the French, who contented themselves with first fighting and then making peace with the Mohawks—an event of ill omen to the English. The only political agitation was on Long Island, among the English, in regard to quit-rents, fees, and land **1668.** grants, but Nicolls, with quiet firmness, prevailed. The news of peace, which restored an interrupted commerce, was hailed with delight; and soon after Nicolls, wise, just, and an excellent Governor, left the province, regretted by all.

Under his successor, Francis Lovelace, matters went on quietly and in the same way. English energy and activity began to make themselves felt in New York; but the easy Dutch customs still prevailed, and there was peace and comfort everywhere, except on Long Island, where there were again disturbances on account of taxes. All this quiet, however, was threatened and finally broken up by the second war between Holland and England. Lovelace was ordered to make every preparation, and did what was in his power; but as nothing happened, the old feeling of security returned, and while Lovelace was absent from the city the dreaded Dutch fleet appeared. The English were now as helpless as their predecessors, with rotten fortifications, a feeble garrison, and a hostile population. Manning, the lieutenant of Lovelace, tried to protract negotiation; but the Dutch grew impatient, opened fire on the fort, which was returned, landed soldiers, and **1673.** the town capitulated. The people of English blood quietly submitted, the Dutch colonists rejoiced, and again there was little change except in names. Anthony Colve was appointed Governor, and took active measures to prepare against an invasion from New England, which was both alarmed and enraged by the Dutch triumph. Just as Colve, however, had brought all the province under Dutch authority, the treaty of Westminster ceded New Netherlands to the dominions of England. The Dutch colonists were furious, but there was nothing to be done. English frigates appeared, and Colve turned over the province to Sir Edmund Andros; it seemed as if the gov- **1674.** ernment of Nicolls and Lovelace had hardly been disturbed, and the Dutch power, after this last returning gleam, finally disappeared from America.

With the arrival of Andros, English energy and activity, which were interrupted by the war, came in again on all sides, and began to develop rapidly the wonderful resources of the province, which, under the long years of Dutch supremacy, had gathered only some seven thousand inhabitants against the hundred and twenty thousand of their New England neighbors. The rule of Andros, although despotic, was, within the bounds of his province, on the whole, wise and strong. He quarrelled with the people about the arbitrary customs duties imposed by the Dutch; but he also began and carried on the sound and essential policy of detaching the Five Nations from the French and fastening them to the English interests. He strove in every way to thwart and check the French power at the north, and endeavored to develop Albany, and secure for the town the monopoly of the great Indian trade, of which it was the natural centre. His foreign contrasted strongly with his domestic policy. He felt the insignificance of his place, and to him more than to any one was due the scheme, finally adopted when James reached the throne, of uniting under one government all the northern colonies, and he even endeavored to give effect to this policy during his own administration. He claimed all the western portion of Connecticut; but when he landed at Saybrook to enforce his demands he was driven off by a troop of New England soldiers, and was hardly permitted to read his patent. In Maine he established a fort at Pemaquid, as a sign of his master's ownership; but it was an expensive and unprofitable experiment. His chief effort was in New Jersey, where he carried on an aggressive and violent contest to regain the province. He strove to raise duties, seized ships and goods, arrested Fenwick several times, and followed this up by arresting Carteret and trying him in New York, refusing to free him, even after the jury had acquitted him. This quarrel in East New Jersey, although it did **1680.** not displease the Duke of York, aroused a hostility in England before which Andros had to succumb, and he was recalled.

Anthony Brockholst succeeded him, and after a brief term, distinguished only by a violent quarrel with the merchants about duties, which resulted in the arrest of Dyre, the collector of customs, **1683.** and by a last attempt to domineer over East Jersey, he was in turn succeeded by Colonel Thomas Dongan, who brought with him a charter of liberties, which gave New York her first taste of representative government, and which was as liberal as most of the colonial charters. It provided for a general Assembly of eighteen, who, with the Governor and Council, were to constitute the government of the colony. The Duke was to grant lands and establish custom-houses; but no tax was to be levied without the assent of the Assembly. Trial by jury was assured, together with religious toleration; but no act was to become law without the assent of **1685.** the Duke, and as he gave his assent to no act, and revoked the charter as soon as he came to the throne, the gleam of popular government was short-lived. Dongan was sent out largely because he was a Roman Catholic, and was therefore fitted to forward the religious schemes of James; but, unfortunately, the principal events of his administration were the struggles to maintain the Iroquois alliance, and ward off both the armed assaults of the French upon the Five Nations, and their scarcely less dangerous efforts to draw them away by means of intriguing, proselyting Jesuits. James in many ways did everything to hamper Dongan, and help the French, on account of his bigoted love of every Catholic; but the Governor remained true to the interests of the province. He persisted in the policy of Andros, supported the Iroquois with success, and did all in his power to check the French. He continued, too, like Andros, to urge the annexation of Connecticut, although he settled the much-disputed boundary with that colony. He also advocated the absorption of Pennsylvania and New Jersey, but he effected nothing; and while incurring the displeasure of his master by his wise Indian policy, he gave great vitality to the dread of Papists, always strong among a people who had known French massacres and feared Jesuit intrigues. There was therefore **1688.** but little regret when he was removed, although the manner in which it was done by annexing New York to New England under the rule of Andros was far from popular.

Andros was, nevertheless, well received in New York when he returned there with enlarged powers. He visited the Iroquois, and cemented their alliance, and then departed, leaving the now absolute government in the hands of the appointed Council and of Francis Nicholson, the Lieutenant-governor. This government, in appearance so fairly begun, was of short duration. In February it was known that William had landed in England, in April that the Bostonians had cast Andros into prison. Everything was prepared for an outbreak in New York. The strong popular dread of the Papists, inflamed by Dongan's open Catholicism and Nicholson's doubtful Protestantism, the Dutch admiration for the Prince of Orange, and the general hatred of Stuart government, common to all the colonies, furnished the elements for insurrection. Nicholson and his Council seem to have been paralyzed. They renewed the fortifications, and, calling together the militia, gave the alarm of French invasion, but would not proclaim William; and soon after, Nicholson laid down his government, and prepared to sail. The power, dropped in this nerveless way, was seized, of course, by the men in arms, the militia, under the lead of Jacob Leisler, a merchant, and captain of a train-band. An agreement was signed, the fort taken, the Prince of Orange proclaimed; and Leisler, who was at the head of the government, got the benefit of the confirmation of all Protestant officers, which came from William to Nicholson. The remnant of the Council was opposed to Leisler, who proceeded to put down all opposition with a high hand.

He was arbitrary, inexperienced, and hot-headed. He crushed out his enemies, and managed the affairs of the province despotically, taking to himself all authority and instructions only from England. In outside matters he appeared to better advantage. War had been declared with France, and Frontenac, the ablest and most daring of the French governors, was in command in Canada. In the dead of winter his war **1690.** parties swooped down upon Schenectady, fired the village, and slaughtered the inhabitants. The whole frontier was in danger, and a merciless Indian war had come. Leisler called upon the other colonies to send representatives to New York; and in response seven delegates appeared, chiefly from New England. An expedition was arranged and quotas agreed upon; but the expedition was a failure, although Leisler's military administration was vigorous and spirited. He not only helped the expedition, but rebuilt the fort, and sent out privateers to attack French cruisers. Still harsher vigor in the province did not increase his popularity, and embittered his enemies, whose opportu- **1691.** nity was now at hand. Major Richard Ingoldsby arrived from England with a company of grenadiers and demanded the surrender of the fort; which, as he had no commission, Leisler refused. Firing ensued on both sides; but the unlucky Leisler was shooting at royal troops. At last Sloughter, a worthless fellow, appointed Governor more than a year before, reached New York, and Leisler was obliged to surrender; when he and his friends were at once thrown into prison, tried for murder and treason, found guilty, and sentenced to death. Sloughter reprieved the prisoners until the King's pleasure could be known, and then, as he was ordered, called an Assembly, which, in the excitement of the times, was secured by the party of the old councillors—Leisler's bitter enemies. With this influence, and backed by petitions, they persuaded Sloughter, during a drinking bout, to sign Leisler's death-warrant, and he, together with his son-in-law and chief-abettor, Milborne, were immediately executed. Perhaps Leisler was technically guilty. He was a man thrown to the surface, and strong enough to grasp power in a time of popular convulsion, ill led, and based on no definite principles, and he had certainly acted illegally and arbitrarily. But his death was a revengeful political murder. It was as foolish as it was cruel and unnecessary, it created two bitter parties in New York, and left a lasting mark on **1692.** her provincial histoty. The insurrection itself was a passing thing, and was otherwise without result. Sloughter himself died soon after, when Ingoldsby held power for a short time, and then Benjamin Fletcher came out as Governor, with a royal commission.

He brought instructions involving no change from the policy of James, except in the recognition of the Assembly. The Governor was to have a salary from the revenue, the Council was to be appointed, all laws approved, and the Book of Common Prayer was to be introduced. He was also ordered to take command of the Connecticut militia, which involved a quarrel with Governor Phips of Massachusetts, who had received a similar order, and took Fletcher to Hartford, where he found the general court in session. Tradition says that the militia were drawn up to receive him, and that, when he attempted to read his commission, the drums were beaten, and the voice of the reader drowned. It is certain that the resistance in Connecticut was so determined and formidable that Fletcher retired to New York humiliated and baffled. He fared better in the war with the French, who

1693. were again on the frontier. They were driven off by Peter Schuyler, after destroying the Mohawk villages, and the rest of Frontenac's campaign came to nothing. This was the only creditable event of Fletcher's administration. He was one of the leavings of the Stuart period, as worthless a man as Sloughter, but not without ability, and thoroughly corrupt. He was in league with the pirates who infested the coast, openly sold them licenses, and is even said to have shared their spoils; while at the same time he plundered the revenue, and connived at smuggling and every sort of illicit trade. The province was torn with the dissensions of the Leislerian and anti-Leislerian factions; and, instead of trying to allay them, Fletcher devoted himself

1698. to intriguing and quarrelling with his Assemblies for money. At last his evil doing led to his recall, and the Earl of Bellomont came out as his successor.

The old policy of consolidation had been lately revived, and Bellomont received the government not only of New York, but of Massachusetts and New Hampshire. He came with excellent intentions, purposing to cure the evils of Fletcher's rule, stop frauds, and provide for an honest collection of the revenue; and, above all, suppress piracy. In these objects he succeeded in large measure. He had been chiefly instrumental in sending out Kidd to break up piracy, and was personally interested in bringing him to justice, now that he had become the terror of the seas. This he accomplished, and he gave a severe check to piracy everywhere. He brought the government of New York back to order and decency, and obtained from the

Assembly an act of indemnity for Leisler, whose body, with that of Milborne's, he caused to be taken up and buried with public observance. His efforts to remedy the injustice of his predecessors gave him the full support and confidence of the popular party, so **1701.** that his death, which occurred three years after his arrival, was much regretted.

The old party of the Council, headed by Bayard and Livingston, took advantage of the opportunity thus afforded, and made a desperate attempt to regain power; but were thwarted by Nanfan, the Lieutenant-governor, and the popular party. Livingston, the collector, was declared a defaulter, and his property confiscated; while Bayard, for complaining of Nanfan, was tried for disturbing the peace, found guilty, and would have been punished had it not been for the **1702.** arrival of the new Governor in the person of Lord Cornbury, a wretched profligate and bankrupt spendthrift, for whom his royal kinswoman made provision by thrusting him into a colonial government. His first idea was to get rich, and he opened his administration by stealing some fifteen hundred pounds which the Assembly had voted for fortifications; a freak which led to the appointment of a treasurer by the Assembly to stop further thefts—a course of action very disgusting to the Governor. He sought the support of the old anti-Leislerian faction, thus alienating the majority of the people; and finally lost the support of all parties by his misconduct. He was as zealous in religion as in vice, and endeavored to enforce the worship of the Church of England by attacking all dissenting sects, and especially the Presbyterians, whose churches, parsonages, and glebes he seized and gave to the Established Church. He incurred the bitter enmity in this way of the mass of the people, roused an enduring hatred of the English Church, and established a controversy and a grievance which were only appeased by the Revolution. While he thus gained general hatred, he also won universal contempt by his debaucheries and excesses, by his debts, and by his habit of dressing as a woman. He was plunged in one long quarrel with his Assemblies, both in New York and New Jersey, plotted with Dudley, of Massachusetts, to destroy the free-charter governments of Connecticut and Rhode Island, and at last excited such loud and **1708.** strenuous opposition that he was recalled, but could not return to England until his accession to the Earldom of Clarendon released him from prison, into which he had been thrown for debt.

His immediate and warmly welcomed successor, Lord Lovelace, died soon after his accession, and the government fell into the hands of In-

1709. goldsby, as Lieutenant-governor, the friend of Sloughter and Fletcher, and the tool of Cornbury. He made a wretched Governor, and was soon removed, the only event of his administration being the first issue of bills of credit in aid of an invasion of Canada, which failed miserably through the miscarriage of the English fleet. The long, protracted war between France and England, and the continual attacks from the north, excited in the colonists an eager desire to conquer Canada, and several futile attempts were made. Peter Schuyler took five Iroquois chiefs to England to raise an interest in the mat-

1710. ter, and by the greatest efforts the combined English forces succeeded in capturing Port Royal and getting possession of Nova Scotia. Before this, however, Robert Hunter, a soldier and courtier, and the friend of Swift and Addison, came out as Governor. He surrounded himself with the aristocratic party of the Council, which thus came again to power, and at once was in conflict with his Assembly on the question of salaries and supplies; for the representatives, with Cornbury in their minds, were naturally suspicious, and in no mood to turn over the public funds to any Governor. They all managed, however, to unite in support of the war and a grand expedition against Canada. New York issued ten thousand pounds in bills of credit; there was a

1711. congress of Governors, and the colonies raised four thousand men to march under the command of Nicholson against Montreal; but all the great hopes raised by these preparations came to nothing. The British fleet and forces, under the command of Admiral Walker and General Hill, miscarried stupidly and miserably in the St. Lawrence, and withdrew, and Nicholson was thereby forced to retreat. This disastrous result caused great depression and fear at New York, which found expression in the discovery of a supposed "negro plot,"

1713. and the consequent execution of nineteen wretched blacks. The peace of Utrecht relieved the colony from war, but it found itself encumbered with debt, and in no very good humor with the Governor, who persisted in fighting for salaries and revenue. He also erected a court of chancery, with himself as chancellor—a measure which produced a violent and lasting opposition. Hunter, however, was sustained in England, and the court of chancery remained, and became a standing grievance; but after this conflict matters set-

1719. tled down, and the peaceful Walpole era began. Hunter got the upperhand in the Assembly, and ruled wisely and judiciously; so that he was able, when he left the province, to justly congratulate the Assembly on increased prosperity, and upon the improved condition of public affairs.

His successor was William Burnet, the son of the bishop, an active, imperious, energetic man, with high notions of his office, and a **1720.** determination to carry out his schemes at all costs. He resolved on an active policy against France, and obtained the passage of an act forbidding all trade with Canada; thus arousing a powerful and interested opposition on account of the interference with a profitable trade, which went on despite the law. This resistance was strengthened by a fresh opposition to the unpopular court of chancery; and Burnet, hot-tempered and the reverse of conciliatory, plunged along from one quarrel to another—from courts to salaries and fees and supplies—until, despite his success in cementing and extending the **1727.** Indian alliances, and establishing a trading post at Oswego, he found himself in a hopeless minority in the Assembly, and was transferred to Massachusetts, where still worse contests awaited him.

He was succeeded in the following year by John Montgomerie, who **1731.** died after a brief and uneventful rule of three years. For a few months Rip Van Dam, the president of the Council, was at the head of affairs, and then Colonel Cosby came out from England **1732.** as Governor. Cosby was a money-getter, like most of the royal Governors; and, as he had been appointed nearly a year before his arrival, he demanded that Van Dam, who had held sway in the interval, should divide with him his salary and perquisites. Van Dam naturally declining, there was a great equity suit, and the whole matter drifted into politics, Van Dam being supported on general principles by the popular, and Cosby by the aristocratic party, so that the struggle soon became bitter and violent. This contest formed the principal feature of Cosby's administration; and although he was unpopular, and had the usual wrangles with the Assembly about money, and interference with land grants and titles, nothing else happened of importance. Out of this controversy, however, between Van Dam and the Governor grew another suit, which was of abiding interest. Peter Zenger published the *New York Weekly Journal;* and as he used it in behalf of the opposition, his paper was ordered to be burned, and he was thrown into prison and brought to trial for libel. He was defended by Andrew Hamilton, of Pennsylvania—born in England, and there bred to the bar—who was the first lawyer to win great professional fame in America. In Zenger's case, he admitted the publishing and printing, but took the ground that the truth was a justification, and that the words were neither false, scandalous, nor seditious; and after listening to his masterly speech, the jury returned a verdict of not guilty. Hamilton was presented with the freedom of the city in **1736.** a gold box, and departed amid the firing of salutes in his honor. Soon after this victory of the popular party Cosby died, and the contest assumed a new form. Van Dam claimed the place of acting-Governor as the oldest member of the Council; but that body held that he had been removed, and declared George Clarke to be the oldest member, and Lieutenant-governor. Van Dam had the popular support; Clarke, who was disliked as the lineal successor of Cosby's policy, had that of the Council and the aristocracy. Both men assumed to hold the office and to act; and while Clarke seized the fort, the populace rallied about Van Dam. Feeling began to run very high, and it looked as if there would be a resort to arms; but a royal commission arrived confirming Clarke in his office, and quiet was restored. Clarke, although a native of England, had been long in the province, and was a shrewd and successful local politician; so that for seven years he contrived to prevent his being superseded by the arrival of a Governor, and during that time, despite a never-dying controversy with the Assembly, he managed to rule peacefully by yielding to the popular party on all important points, and confining himself to remonstrances. He farther mitigated the opposition to his administration by offers of office to the popular leaders, thus dividing and distracting them. The only great event of his term was the dark misfortune of the negro **1741.** plot, with its resulting panic and judicial slaughter. This matter is discussed elsewhere; but it may be said here that the government generally, including De Lancey, the chief-justice, on one side, and Clarke on the other, fell in readily with the popular terror, and supported the steps taken for the punishment of the supposed criminals.

Two years after this event a new Governor was appointed—Admi- **1743.** ral Clinton, the second son of the Earl of Lincoln—who fell into the hands of De Lancey, the leader of the popular party, and was by him persuaded to confirm the concessions of Clarke, from whom the Assembly had extorted the right to fix the Governor's salary annually, a claim which had been successfully denied by Hunter, and strenuously resisted by his successors, until Clarke had given way. Not content with their triumph on this point, De Lancey induced the Governor to assent to an appropriation bill, which named the officers to whom salaries were to be paid, thus practically putting the control

20

of appointments in the hands of the Assembly.   At last Clinton was
awakened to the effects of his acts, and the rest of his term of office was one prolonged struggle to regain lost ground, and re-establish
his enfeebled prerogatives.   He quarrelled with De Lancey, and selected Cadwallader Colden as his chief adviser, which merely added
the hostility of the Council to that of the Assembly.   He complained
bitterly to the ministers; but even there he found no sympathy, and
was obliged to convey to De Lancey, after much delay, the commission of Lieutenant-governor.   The struggle began just as war with
France was declared, and the Assembly proved thoroughly intractable, and would not make provision for defence.   They finally gave
1745.   three thousand pounds for the Louisburg expedition, but raised
no men, and had no farther share in the matter.   A new Assembly proved no more compliant, and although they voted more
money for the Louisburg expedition, would do nothing for the Governor.   That winter the Indians were on the frontier and destroyed
Saratoga; and the next year preparations were made for a grand
expedition against them, which failed through inaction and delay,
while the Assembly persisted in their refusal to pay the troops, both
branches uniting against the Governor.   William Johnson, a friend of
the Governor and the famous agent among the Indians, failed to take
Crown Point; the troops mutinied and began to disperse, and this
1748.   miserable condition was only relieved by the peace of Aix-
la-Chapelle, which, however, gave full opportunity for political
warfare.   The fight was made on the well-worn subject of permanent
supply for the government, and public feeling was still further inflamed by attempts at impressment and by the overbearing conduct of
British officers.   A dead-lock ensued which lasted nearly two years,
when the Governor gave way, and signed the obnoxious bills making
annual appropriations; and after this decisive defeat, matters went on
1753.   more smoothly until the close of his term.   He was succeeded
by Sir Danvers Osborn, who committed suicide a few days after his arrival, and Clinton was thus forced to turn the government
over to his enemy, De Lancey, and return to England with such comfort as he could derive from the handsome fortune which he had
amassed during his administration.   Under De Lancey political harmony was restored.   The Assembly amused themselves by bringing
heavy charges against Clinton, whom they accused of every sort of
pecuniary misdeed; but they did not gain a hearing from the Board
of Trade.   Meanwhile the slowly gathering war with France began,

and De Lancey had the honor of presiding at the Albany Congress, where he opposed Franklin's scheme of union, which provided **1754.** for a general government, with certain specified powers, chiefly relating to war, Indians, and lands, and was to be composed of a President and Council appointed by the Crown, and a House of Representatives elected by the colonial Assemblies. The scheme was rejected both in England and America, by ministry and people, and De Lancey's opposition had plenty of support.

In the following year the war became general and active, and in the great conflict which followed New York was not only the scene **1755.** of many important battles, but played herself an important part. At the outset Braddock was to march against Fort Du Quesne, Shirley, with American troops, against the French at Niagara, and the northern forces were to attack Crown Point. The story of Braddock's expedition and his crushing defeat belongs to the history of Virginia, whose soldiers shared in the losses and did most of the fighting, and does not need repetition here. To the northward the English fared better, and Nova Scotia was reduced by Winslow. Shirley gathered troops at Oswego, but advanced no farther, stopped, apparently, by rumors of superior forces, and by the depression and dismay caused by Braddock's defeat. The other northern expedition was put under the command of Johnson, the Indian agent. He left troops at the Hudson, where defences were thrown up, which afterward took the name of Fort Edward, and then moved northward to the southern extremity of Lake George, where he proceeded to intrench himself and make a base for his movement against Crown Point, and where he heard that Baron Dieskau, with an army of French and Indians, was rapidly pushing southward. Dieskau's first plan was to attack Fort Edward; but he was deterred by the Indian dread of cannon, and turned against Johnson. He surprised and routed a heavy detachment sent out by Johnson, and the English retreated in haste to Fort George. A quarter of an hour gave the English time to recover themselves; so that when Dieskau advanced the cannon opened fire, and the provincials, gradually gathering their senses disordered by the sight of regular troops, began to pick off the French soldiers. The battle soon raged furiously. Johnson was wounded, but his place was well filled by Lyman, of Connecticut. Repeated charges were made by the French; but all were repulsed. Dieskau was badly wounded. The provincials rushed over the works, and with clubbed muskets beat down the French regulars, while the Indians and Canadians fled in disorder.   The remnant of the French army, surprised on their retreat by the garrison of Fort Edward, was broken, and suffered heavily, and lost their baggage and ammunition.   Johnson, however, did not follow up his victory, but remained at Fort George and strengthened his defences.   He was made a baronet, and received five thousand pounds for his services, while the brave Lyman, whom he slighted in his despatches, got nothing.   This success did something to relieve the gloom of Braddock's overthrow.

The same autumn a new Governor, Admiral Sir Charles Hardy, came out to New York; but as he suffered himself to be guided by De Lancey, matters went on as before.   The winter was passed in **1756.** futile scheming, and Shirley was removed to make room for Lord Loudon, who summoned the colonial Governors, made great plans, scolded the colonies, and did nothing.   The English government, both at home and abroad, seemed to be in its dotage.   With the French it was very different.   In Montcalm they had an able, energetic leader, and a bold and enterprising general.   They were beaten back by Bradstreet, in northern New York, in several small affairs; but while Loudon lingered at Albany, Montcalm came down with all his forces and captured Oswego.   Loudon thereupon gave up his Canadian expeditions, went into winter-quarters, and devoted himself to strengthening Fort William Henry, at the foot of Lake George, and **1757.** Fort Edward.   Soon after Hardy departed to take command of a fleet, after urging upon the Assembly the necessity of prosecuting the war, and left the government once more with De Lancey.   In the following spring Loudon again summoned the Governors, rated the colonies, and laid great schemes.   The colonies again responded, men were furnished, and then scattered in detached bodies on the frontier, while Loudon, with the other British officers, gave their attention to an attack on Louisburg; and as they were making up their minds that this attempt would be hopeless, Montcalm came down Lake Champlain and Lake George with all his forces, and captured Fort William Henry and two thousand men.   Many of the prisoners were butchered by the Indians; and during the siege Webb, at Fort Edward, with four thousand soldiers, was deaf to the entreaties of the provincials, and refused to move to the relief of Fort William Henry.   This utter and disgraceful defeat converted the campaign into one of weak defence; and Loudon took occasion to quarrel still further with the colonies, and almost produced riots by his methods of distributing and quartering soldiers.

1758. This reign of palsied incompetence had, however, now reached an end. Pitt had control, Loudon was removed, the spirit of the "Great Commoner" was felt everywhere, and men and money were readily furnished for another campaign, and in larger measure than ever before. In June, Boscawen with his fleet, and Amherst and Wolfe with the land-forces, took Louisburg, and large bodies of troops were gathered to attack the French at every point. The principal expedition was directed against Ticonderoga, consisted of ten thousand provincials and seven thousand regulars, fully equipped, and was commanded by General Abercrombie and Lord Howe. This large army advanced full of confidence; but in the first skirmish the advance-guard was surprised, and Lord Howe killed. A desperate attack was then made upon the French defences, and was kept up until two thousand men had fallen, when a retreat was ordered, which turned into a precipitate flight. The dispirited and beaten army was rallied at Fort William Henry; but nothing was done to retrieve the disaster which had befallen them, except by Colonel Bradstreet, who induced Abercrombie to let him have three thousand men and some cannon. With this force he reduced Fort Frontenac, on Lake Ontario, and fortified Oswego, restoring safety to the northern frontier of New York, and holding the Indians in check. Forbes, meanwhile, had captured Fort Du Quesne, and thus, despite the terrible disaster to Abercrombie, the balance in the campaign was decidedly in favor of the English. This was strongly felt in America, and, incited by Pitt, New York and the other northern colonies made greater efforts than ever for the coming campaign, which was destined to be one of great and unalloyed triumphs. Expeditions were planned for every assailable point, and, fortunately, all succeeded. Wolfe captured Quebec, and, by one of the great battles of history, decided the fate of the empire of France in the New World. Stanwix succeeded on the Ohio. Prideaux, who had been sent against Fort Niagara, was killed by the bursting of a cohorn early in the siege; and the command then devolved upon Sir William Johnson, who repulsed a relieving force and captured the fort, thus destroying the French power in the west. The hard-fought path to Canada by Lake Champlain had been confided to Amherst, who started in July, and the French fell back before his cautious advance from Ticonderoga to Crown Point, and from Crown Point to Isle-aux-Noix, where they prepared to make a stand. There the English were compelled to build a fleet, time was consumed, and Amherst was obliged to go into winter-quar-

1759.

ters, where he occupied himself in making every arrangement for the next year.

New York, greatly exposed, and deeply interested in the result, continued to make every effort in her power for the support **1760.** of the war; but in July she had the misfortune to lose her Lieutenant-governor, James Delancey, who had ruled wisely and well, and shown that it was possible for a Governor and Assembly to act unitedly in support of the war, and raise large sums of money by taxation. He was succeeded by Cadwallader Colden, an old friend of Clinton, unpopular, and allied to the Episcopalian and British party, so that the hostility between Governor and Assembly which had slept so long was at once awakened in full vigor. Meantime the war went on ; the arrangements of Amherst were complete ; and while Haviland moved up the line of Lake Champlain, the main body, under the commander-in-chief, made their way to the north up Lake Ontario and down the St. Lawrence. The French fell back everywhere, surrendering their posts ; and the armies from Quebec and Albany met at last before Montreal. There was no escape ; Vaudreuil capitulated, Canada was conquered, and the French empire in America effaced. One legacy of the conquest was the general rising of the Indian tribes under Pontiac ; but they were checked at Detroit and Niagara by the soldiers of Amherst, and beaten by Bouquet in Pennsylvania. Hostilities still went on until 1764 along the frontiers, although the colonies did not suffer severely.

Colden was superseded by General Monckton, who went away to capture Martinique, and soon after resigned New York entire- **1761-** ly, so that he interfered but little, on the whole, with the Lieu- **1762.** tenant-governor. The Assembly continued to meet the requisitions of England, but they also began to wrangle with Colden, and were much occupied with the contest in regard to the territory of Vermont. Peace was hailed with delight ; but the fair prospects which seemed to open with the removal of the dreaded enemy on the north were soon overclouded by the development of the ministerial policy of taxing America. The first step was the enforcement of the Navigation Act, and bore very hardly on New York, which was largely engaged in illicit trade, long connived at by England, with the French and Spanish possessions ; and thus the way was prepared for the universal burst of indignation which greeted the news of the Stamp Act. Parties had always been bitter in New York, and the old lines were rapidly drawn on the new question. New York responded readily

to the invitation of Massachusetts for a Congress; and in New York
that Congress was held, comprising twenty-eight delegates
from nine colonies, presided over by Timothy Ruggles, and
led by James Otis, of Massachusetts, and Gadsden, of South Carolina.
Thus in New York the resolutions were passed denying the right of
taxation without representation, and demanding a repeal of the Stamp
Act; and there, by that Congress, the union of the English colonies
in America was founded.

1765.

Chapter XVII.

NEW YORK IN 1765.

The American colonies were not only governed and controlled by the English, but in every case, except New York and Delaware, that race laid the foundations of the future State. New York was established, built up, and ruled for fifty years by people of a different nationality, although of a kindred origin; and this circumstance had a marked effect not only upon the history of the colony, but upon the social and political system which was gradually developed on the banks of the Hudson.

At the time of the Revolution the population of New York amounted to about one hundred and seventy thousand, of whom twenty thousand were negroes.[1] The larger portion of the whites were still descendants of the original possessors of the province, although the Dutch immigration had almost entirely ceased after the English conquest. The invaders from New England and the mother country, besides holding their original settlements on Long Island, spread themselves over the colony, and, with a continually strengthening minority, were here, as elsewhere, the ruling and dominant race. There was also a large and most excellent element of French Huguenots, gathered chiefly in the city of New York, which, as early even as the year 1652, had become so numerous that the Consistory was

---

[1] Population, Smyth, p. 394, 1776, 200,000; Brissot, p. 128, 1773, 148,000; 1786, 219,000: Burnaby, 1759, 100,000; 15,000 to 20,000 capable of bearing arms: Doc. relating to Col. History of New York, iv., 1698, 18,000 whites, 2000 blacks; 1712, 27,000; vi., Census by Clinton, 1746, 51,000 whites, 10,000 blacks; Doc. History, i., Table for years from 1703 to 1771, when population given as 148,000 whites and 19,000 blacks; for Board of Trade, 1755, 55,000 whites; blacks, 11,000—see Bancroft, iv., 127 and ff.; New York Hist. Soc. Coll., iv., 274, Smith's History, 1762, 100,000. There was in the beginning of the century a superstition which interfered with obtaining a census, because it was believed to bring sickness; see Doc. relating to Col. History, iv., 1712.

obliged to make special religious provision for them. Persecution brought also to the settlements of the Hudson the thrifty and industrious Palatines, and in the city were found a small number of Jews. But the foreign immigration, as a whole, was not important; the bulk of it drifted away into Pennsylvania, and left New York to the Dutch and English.[1] The settlements of the people thus united began with the little towns on the western end of Long Island, and with the city of New York, the New Amsterdam of early days, and the villages of the neighborhood. Thence they followed the Hudson, with its picturesque beauty of mountain, cliff, and meadow, until Albany was reached, where they turned to the west, and were pushed out into the wilderness, along the beautiful valley of the Mohawk, and into the domains of the famous Six Nations. This brief and irregular line of towns, villages, and farms skirting the edge of the forests was all that then gave promise of the great State of the future. Indeed at that period the province was poorly inhabited, in proportion to its opportunities and capacities, labor was dear and development slow.[2]

The two great interests here, as in Pennsylvania, were agriculture and trade; but in New York the latter was the ruling and controlling interest, even if it did not actually engage the larger number of the people. The great staples were farm products, especially wheat, to which attention was chiefly given; and the fur trade was also in New York of first importance. Albany was one of the centres of this traffic; and a usual way for a young man to begin life was to venture to the west to deal in furs—an occupation which, owing to the presence of French competitors, was one of no slight danger, but which was at the same time extremely profitable. The successful adventurer, returning with his furs, would make up a cargo at Albany of skins and timber, float down the river to New York, and dispose of his investment at a great advance. The return cargo was light, consisting chiefly of rum, which was not only used for barter, but to make the Indians drunk when they met, and thus facilitate cheating.

The statistics of trade in New York are so wild that it is out of the question to attempt an exact estimate. The imports and exports were probably worth nearly a million pounds, and employed, including

[1] American Lady, Mrs. Grant, i., 42, 200; ii., 231; Smyth, ii., 378; Kalm, i., 245; Virginia Hist. Reg., ii., 108, 1685, Byrd's Letters; Hist. Soc. Coll., iv., 274; Ruttenber's History of Newburg; Reed's Amenia; Mag. Amer. History, i., 90; Huguenot Family in Virginia, p. 297; Mandeville, History of Flushing; Wood's Long Island.
[2] Hist. Soc. Coll., iv., Smith's History, p. 274 and ff.

coasters and small river craft, about five hundred vessels. The Dutch spirit of enterprise in foreign trade was conspicuous in New York, and the products of the province were carried to the West Indies, to Lisbon, England, and Madeira; while even the little sloops from Albany made long voyages. It was one of these—of eighty tons burden—that in the year 1785 made the voyage to China successfully. There was also a great deal of smuggling; smuggled tea was largely used, and an extensive illicit trade was kept up with the French possessions in the West Indies. There were scarcely any manufactures. The thrifty Dutch appear to have made sufficient progress to have alarmed their English conquerors; but the advance was lost in the eighteenth century; and although there was a considerable domestic manufacture of coarse materials for home use, almost everything else was imported. Feeble attempts at encouragement were made by the Assembly, but they resulted in little. The iron industry was almost wholly neglected; there was some manufacture of glass, and felt hats were made, but neither so well nor so cheaply as in England; and, in fact, the imports so predominated over the exports that it was often difficult to find a return cargo. The trade of New York, however, equalled, if it did not exceed, that of either Boston or Philadelphia, and the town was already a distributing point for the other colonies. Tradesmen and mechanics, especially among the Germans and Dutch, were more common than elsewhere; and we hear of itinerant weavers who went from house to house to finish work. But industries, except those of the grist and saw mills, built in the picturesque Dutch fashion, with wide-spread sails, could not attain any vigorous growth where land was so plenty and so cheap. Servants, imported especially to work at trades, betook themselves to farms as soon as they obtained their liberty; and the great fertility of the soil made the farmers careless in their methods. Agriculture was low, as in the other colonies; yet the province, as a whole, was flourishing and prosperous, and the active trade and energetic merchants brought much wealth to the country.[1]

---

[1] For trade and industry, see Huguenot Family in Virginia, p. 297; American Lady, i., 77, 79, 87; Smyth, ii., 394; Brissot, p. 125; Kalm, i., 253 and ff.; ii., 240, 257; Burnaby, p. 109; Pennsylvania Hist. Coll., i., Hare's Journey; Denton's Account of New York; Hist. Soc. Coll., iv., Smith, p. 274; Munsell's Annals of Albany, i., iv.; Doc. relating to Col. Hist. of New York, iv., 1708; v., 273; vi., Cosby and Moore to Lords of Trade, Clinton's Census, 1744; Doc. History, i., 1720 and 1723; iv., 1737; Acts of Assembly, 1712, 1760; Rochefoucauld, ii., 233, 235; Historic Tales of the Olden Time, Watson, 1685.

After many vicissitudes, beginning with the commercial despotism of the Dutch and the oppressive rule of James II., the political system of New York had finally settled down to the common form of the royal provinces; but, owing to the events of the past, the government was more corrupt, the administration more inefficient and arbitrary, and the power of the popular representatives feebler than anywhere else. The Governor was appointed by the Crown, had a salary of fifteen hundred pounds a year, and perquisites amounting to as much more, which made him the best-paid Crown officer on the continent; and his political power was, moreover, very great. The Council of twelve members was appointed by him at pleasure, sat as an Upper House, and had a negative on legislation. The Assembly, convened by the Governor, consisted of twenty-seven members elected by the freeholders of the counties, with three from the Rensselaer, Livingston, and Courtland Manors respectively. Before Clarke's time the duration of the Assembly was indefinite; but it was then fixed at three years, and, later, at seven, on the English model. The Assembly was ill-managed, and greatly under the influence of the Governor, who gave patents for lands to his supporters at low quit-rents; thus keeping down small holders, and creating, to his own advantage, a class who fomented the dissensions between the English and Dutch. The whole government, says William Smith, the historian and judge, who had had a full experience in the matter, was nothing more than that of a small corporation.[1]

New York was by no means in so good a condition financially as the other colonies; having not only the usual depreciated currency, and a debt of three hundred thousand pounds, incurred chiefly in the French war, but suffering also from burdensome taxation as compared with that of the other provinces. Taxes were raised by duties on negroes and other imported articles, and by direct levies on real and personal estate; and as their amount was considerable, this clumsy method was unjust and oppressive. Such a condition of affairs was due not only to an ill-managed, expensive, and sometimes corrupt government, but to the exposed situation of the colony, which made the frontiers the scene of battle in every war, and necessitated constant expenditures for defence. In the early days each man contributed to stockade the towns; outlying houses were built to resist attacks, the town gates were shut at night, and every citizen took part in watch duty

---

[1] Burnaby, p. 111; Hist. Coll., iv., Smith's History, p. 274 and ff.

and military service; for the Dutch West India Company had always kept troops at New York, and the English followed their example. At the time of the French war severe and elaborate militia laws were passed, requiring the enlistment of every able-bodied man between sixteen and sixty, and exacting a penalty, in case of failure to obey, of forty shillings for every three months. At the close of the French war the militia was computed to amount to over fifteen thousand men, and there were twenty-six hundred regular provincial troops; but although all this was costly enough, the army never rose to the dignity of a profession.[1]

The bench and bar both suffered from the character of the government and the power of the governors, although they were beginning to improve at the time of the Revolution. The arrangement was that familiar in the other colonies. The lowest courts were those of the justices competent to try cases under five pounds, and appointed by the Governor, who gave these places to political favorites, generally men of no character, and some of whom could not even read or write. Above these were the courts of sessions and common pleas, composed of three judges, who sat twice a year, and were appointed by the Governor during his pleasure. The supreme court of the province consisted of a chief-justice and two associate justices, who sat four times a year, and were appointed by the Governor, but held during good behavior. They had jurisdiction as king's bench and common pleas, and claimed that of equity and the exchequer; but these last were discontinued on account of the general opposition. There was a vice-admiralty court, with one judge, also appointed by the Governor. Over three hundred pounds, an appeal lay from the supreme court to the Governor and Council, and equity was with the Governor as chancellor, but this court was so much disliked that its business was very small. Probate carried on by delegates was one of the Governor's many perquisites, and its administration in this way was exceedingly unpopular. At the beginning of the eighteenth century the condition of both bench and bar was very bad. The chief-justice was a good soldier, but no jurist; and the lawyers so called were often of scandalous character. "One of them," says a contemporary, "was a dancing-master; another, a glover by trade; a third, which is Mr. Jamison, was con-

[1] Taxation and Militia, Munsell's Annals of Albany, i.; Watson, Historic Tales of the Olden Times; Acts of Assembly, 1755, 1756, 1761; Burnaby, pp. 108, 109, 115.

demned in Scotland for burning the Bible and blasphemy ;" and nearly all were violent demagogues. Matters improved somewhat as time
went on; but at the period of the Revolution, although three years at
college or seven years in an office were required, the Governor licensed
everybody, and there were many practitioners, therefore, who possessed neither character nor learning. The profession, of course, in an
active business community was both popular and profitable, and the
fees were high, so that it attracted the best as well as the worst elements. The trouble lay in the non-enforcement of the law, and in
the bad government which admitted unfit men as freely as trained lawyers of good standing.[1]

Until after the French war the profession of medicine was worse
than that of law, and practised almost exclusively by a much lower
class. The only attempt to regulate it was a clause in the Duke's
Laws of the year 1665, to prevent violence on the part of doctors toward patients. Quacks abounded; there was no protection from mal-
practice, and any one that saw fit set up as a physician, surgeon, or
apothecary, to prey on the ills of his fellows, which, thanks to the general good health, were neither many nor frequent. In the year 1753,
there were in the town of New York alone forty of these unlicensed
practitioners. Just before that time the first gleam of improvement
was perceptible in an attempt to give instruction from dissection,
then came the demand for army surgeons; and in the year 1760
the Assembly passed an act to prevent bad physicians, and ordered
that no one should practise without a certificate from three members
of the Council and the supreme court. This was a step in the right
direction. Seven years later a medical school was founded in connection with the college, and two years after that a medical society was
established, and the profession began to assume a suitable position,
and attract men of ability and character.[2]

The third and last of the learned professions, that of divinity, stood
much higher than either law or medicine. The province was established by members of the Dutch-Lutheran and Dutch-Reformed Churches, and by English Independents and Presbyterians; and these remained
always the leading, although not the ruling, sects. Both the Dutch and

---

[1] For full accounts of bench and bar, see Hist. Coll., iv., Smith's History, p. 274
and ff.; Doc. relating to Col. Hist., iv., vi., 1767; compare also Brissot, p. 130; and
Zenger's trial for Hamilton's speech, and state of law and lawyers.

[2] Brissot, p. 130; Hist. Coll., iv., Smith's History, p. 274 and ff.; Acts of Assembly, 1760; Wickes, History of Medicine in New Jersey, pp. 37, 52.

English dissenting clergy were men of good character, and for a long
period were the only learned class in the colony. In the Long Island
towns the same system and the same forms prevailed as in New England. Down to the eighteenth century the people were summoned to
church by beat of drum, and constables searched the village, and especially the taverns, for profaners of the Sabbath and truants from divine service, and punished them with fines and the lash. Amusements
were discountenanced, and Puritan strictness reigned. The same theory prevailed in the Dutch congregations, but was much less rigidly
carried out. The clergy, with a few exceptions, were zealous and upright men ; and the pastor was always the chief personage in the little Dutch villages. They were generally jolly companions and free
livers, and not infrequently rough in their dealings; but they preached good morals to their congregations with perfect directness, and not
a little personality. One parishioner, severely reprimanded in the sermon, ventured to expostulate in church, and the pastor replied, "You,
Philip, if you can preach gospel better than I, come up here and try."
Church manners, indeed, among the Dutch, do not seem to have been
of the best. In the little church in Albany, with its pyramidal belfry,
the men sat with their high-crowned hats and muffs on, out of respect
to the climate. The deacons went about during the sermon with a
little black bag and bell to take up contributions, but were obliged to
resort to plates, for the shrewd traders of the congregation, when their
gift could not be seen, contented themselves with dropping anything
that had a chinking sound into the bag. The tendency to strict observances in the Reformed churches is indicated by a proclamation
forbidding sports on Shrove-Tuesday ; but it is evident that the Dutch
were too stolid and good-natured to indulge in any great severity in
this respect.

The general policy under the Dutch rule was one of toleration, to
which the luckless Quakers formed the only exception. These people, who arrived in New York in the year 1657, and preached in the
streets, were at once arrested, and driven from the colony ; and when
at a later time they reappeared in Long Island, the Dutch imprisoned and maltreated them, closed their conventicles, chained them to
wheelbarrows, punished those persons married in the Quaker fashion
for adultery, and had them beaten with tarred ropes until they faint-
ed, while the English whipped them through the streets for sedition. This persecution was as ineffective as it was exceptional. There
were, writes Colonel Byrd, of Virginia, as many sects in New York as

in Amsterdam, and all tolerated; but when the English supremacy was assured, all this was changed. In the year 1692 an act was passed to maintain Protestant ministers in each town and county, and vestries and church-wardens were established to lay rates, and call clergymen to officiate. Thus the English Church began its career, and, ill-advised as its policy was in most of the colonies, it was peculiarly foolish and unwise in New York. They continued the persecution of the Quakers with fine, imprisonment, and harsh treatment in the courts, and extended this intolerance to the dissenters of other sects. This policy reached its height under Cornbury, who forced the Established Church upon English and Dutch alike, taxed all for its support, seized on the churches, glebes, and parsonages of the other sects, enforced the Test Act, and carried matters everywhere with a high hand. Makemie, the famous Virginian minister, was arrested for preaching and thrown into prison, but was acquitted by the jury. A reaction ensued, and favor was shown to the dissenters by Hunter and others, although Cornbury's policy remained substantially the policy of the province. Persecution, it is true, was abandoned; but taxes were laid for the English Church, to which all favors of government were given, and to which charters, refused to other sects, were freely granted. This harsh and narrow policy could have but one result. The English Church, supported by government favor, attracted a certain number of worshippers, and was wealthy and influential; but yet before the Revolution it comprised only about a fifteenth of the population, and every sort of dissent, besides the predominant Dutch Reformed and English Presbyterian Churches, grew and flourished. "Freethinking," wrote Samuel Johnson, the New England convert, to the Archbishop of Canterbury— "freethinking spreads as fast as the Church." The clever young men of the day set up a journal, called the *Independent Reflector*, supported by William Smith, educated at that "nursery of sedition, Yale College," William Livingston, John Morin Scott, and others, who vigorously opposed the Establishment. As late as the year 1773 petitions came up from the Long Island towns against taxation for the Church; and "No Bishops" was a favorite and constant election cry. The Church was indeed a principal grievance against the mother country, and did more in New York than anything else to cool the loyalty and alienate the feelings of the inhabitants. Politics diminished the affection of the people for the Church, while their respect was lowered by the "laudable" lotteries for church building, and by the free-living of divines, like Dr. Cooper, who left five pounds' worth of books in his library, and one hundred and fifty pounds' worth of wine in his cellar.[1]

There was one sect which met with no mercy at the hands of either churchman or dissenter. The power of France—close on the borders of New York, with its wide-spreading net-work of Jesuit influence and political intrigue, always ready, and at short intervals letting hordes of savages loose upon the settlements—combined with the natural Protestant prejudices to raise a spirit of dread and fierce hatred toward the Roman Catholics. In the year 1700 an act was passed against Jesuits and Popish priests, "because they labored to destroy and seduce the Indians;" and all such priests were, after a certain time, if they escaped death, to be imprisoned for life. The spirit which produced this law—a wholly natural one under the circumstances—never seems to have died out, and became the germ of one of the most terrible incidents which occurred in the history of the American colonies. In the year 1741 public feeling was aroused against Spain, and consequently against Rome. In every slave-holding province there is a normal suspicion and dread of the servile class; for the sense of awful wrong inflicted can never be separated from the lurking fear that retribution is at hand. These feelings were now combined; and several fires, which strongly suggested premeditation, led to the discovery of the so-called negro plot. Into its details it is not necessary to enter. A wretched and ignorant woman, employed in a public-house of the lowest kind where negroes resorted, actuated probably by revenge, denounced her landlord, his wife and maid, and one Ury, a Roman Catholic, besides some slaves, as concerned in a plot to burn the city. In the excited state of the public feeling, much less than this would have created a panic; as it was, the whole town

---

[1] For church and clergy in New York, see Huguenot Family in Virginia, p. 297; American Lady, i., 42, 294; ii., 23; Anderson's Hist. of Col. Church, ii., 439; Kalm, i., 250; Burnaby, p. 107; Virginia Hist. Reg., Byrd's Letters, p. 108; Foote, Sketches of Virginia, i., 63; Hist. Coll., iv., Smith's History, p. 274; iii., N. S., 1774; Mandeville, History of Flushing; Life and Travels of Samuel Bownas; Onderdonk's Hempstead; Ruttenber's Newburg; Riker's Newtown; Munsell's Annals of Albany, i., iii.; Stiles, History of Brooklyn; Doc. relating to Col. Hist., iii., iv., vi.; Historic Tales of Olden Time; Doc. History, iv.; Acts of Assembly, 1692, 1695, 1714, 1761; Wood's Long Island; Thompson's Long Island; Furman's Antiquities of Long Island; Long Island Hist. Coll., i., Labadists' Journal; Tyler's American Literature; Massachusetts Hist. Coll., i., 2, 150; Jones's Hist. of New York in the Revolution.

went mad. On the most insufficient evidence—chiefly that of ignorant wretches half dead with fear—a perfect slaughter ensued. One
hundred and fifty-four negroes and twenty whites were arrested and
committed to jail. Four whites were hanged, seventy negroes transported, eighteen hung, and thirteen burnt at the stake. Thirty-five
lives in all were sacrificed, and a large proportion suffered the most
cruel form of death. The dominant motive was the dread of the Papists and Spaniards; for even at the most excited moment no one
supposed that the miserable blacks were aught but tools. Oglethorpe
wrote from Georgia that Spanish priests were to be introduced into
families as physicians and dancing-masters, who would burn every town
in America; and at a later time Governor Clarke wrote that he was
convinced it was Popery, and it was generally believed that Spain was
preparing to send troops to support the conspiracy. The Roman Catholics, at no time more than a handful of the population, were generally arrested, and Catholic priests were in danger of their lives. These
wild stories were firmly believed, and only too thoroughly acted on.
The negro plot belongs to the same class of popular madness as the
Salem witchcraft and the Popish plot of the time of Charles II. Such
outbursts seem to have all the qualities of an epidemic disease, like
cholera or yellow-fever, except that they are moral and mental, instead
of physical. The Salem witchcraft has been used for generations to
brand with the stain of bloody deeds the people of New England.
It occurred at the close of the seventeenth century; it appealed to a
strong and generally accepted superstition; it was concerned with su-
pernatural agencies, was recognized by law, and the best evidence at-
tainable under the circumstances was introduced. The New York
negro plot happened in the middle of the eighteenth century. It was
concerned with a crime perfectly within the range of ordinary tests
and common evidence. The accused were little more than savages,
as incapable of combination as children. In Massachusetts nineteen
persons were hanged, and one, refusing to plead, pressed to death. In
New York, half a century later, twenty-two persons were hanged, and
thirteen burnt at the stake. This comparison is worthless if it shows
merely that the people of New York were no better than those of Massachusetts. What it really proves is that all communities are liable to
mental disease, which, under favorable circumstances, becomes a wild
panic and convulsion, and leads to indiscriminate bloodshed. Such
events are among the miseries incident to humanity under certain
conditions, and as such should be recorded by history; but there is

nothing more shallow or contemptible than to use them as a reproach and to affix a stigma. They are not crimes; they are misfortunes, and only by regarding them in this way can their lessons be learned.[1]

The unhappy race that chiefly suffered in this outbreak was not in New York an important element of the population, although negroes were more numerous than would naturally be supposed when the climate and productions of the province are considered. Under the Dutch, and especially at the beginning of the eighteenth century, large cargoes of slaves, despite the risks from pirates, were brought into the province. The negroes thus became very numerous, and were so riotous that Cornbury issued a proclamation ordering every one to fire upon them if they did not obey. A few years later there was a savage outbreak, with fire and riot, in which several whites were killed, and of twenty-seven negroes seized and condemned, twenty-one were executed. Some were burned, some hanged; one was broken on the wheel, and one hung alive in chains. The lingering recollection of this riot was a principal element in the causes which led to the negro plot of 1741, which had no real existence, and produced so much worse results. The numbers and disposition of the negroes caused objections to them as servants, efforts to replace them with whites, and attempts to check their importation. The result was that at the period of the Revolution they did not comprise more than a sixth of the population. They were employed almost exclusively as domestic servants, and only very rarely as field hands; but almost every family of any consequence had some of them in their household. The laws in regard to them were on the Virginia model, but much less severe. They could be punished by their masters at a discretion not extending to life or limb; and the same limitation was placed on the power of the justices before whom they were brought for striking a white person. They could not be witnesses except against each other in certain specified cases, were usually handed over to a common whipper for punishment, and for ordinary criminal offences they were whipped where a white person was fined. For felonies they were condemned to death in such form as the enormity of the crime warranted; and, instead of being hung in all cases, were not infrequently burned at the stake. The severest laws were with reference to acts which might

---

[1] Horsmanden's Negro Plot; Historic Tales of the Olden Time, Watson; Acts of Assembly, 1700; Valentine's History of New York, Negro Plot; Stone, Life of Johnson, ditto; Doc. relating to Col. History of New York, ditto, vi., 1741.

lead to a general rising; and here the dread of the community found full expression. If more than three slaves met together they were to receive forty lashes; and any slave out after nightfall was liable to be declared a rogue and runaway, and treated accordingly. Flight to Canada, while in possession of the French, was expiated by death; and heavy penalties were laid on all who harbored or received these fugitives. They were in every-day practice well and kindly treated, and properly clothed and fed. They formed part of the family, and it was customary to give, with some ceremony, to each child of the master a negro child of the same age as a servant. Their religious and secular education was but little attended to, although even here there was a marked difference from the southern colonies. The Assembly passed an act to encourage their baptism, which, however, effected no change in their status; and efforts were made by charitable societies in England to provide schools for the blacks, where they might learn to read and sew. The physical prejudice was much stronger, both as to negroes and Indians, than in the south, and there was very little mixture of races; but, on the whole, slavery in New York was as mild as it could well be made. There was very little hard usage, and bad slaves, instead of being punished on the spot, were usually sold at the coffee-houses for the West Indian market. There were also in New York, as in the other colonies, indented servants; but they do not appear to have been very important, except from their bad character as convicts, whose importation was encouraged by both Dutch and English rulers, and strenuously resisted by the colonists.[1]

From the negroes, the free blacks, peculiarly numerous here on account of those formerly belonging to the Dutch West India Company, from transported convicts, and from the dregs of a trading and seafaring community, the criminal classes in New York were recruited. But crime was rare, and robbery, murder, and suicide—the index of misery—were alike uncommon. Life and limb and property

---

[1] Slaves and servants, American Lady, i., 51, 58, 171, 294, 304; Kalm, ii., 267; Hist. Coll., iv., Smith, p. 274 and ff.; Ibid., iii., N. S., Extracts from Newspapers; Riker's History of Newtown; Munsell's Annals of Albany, i., 1691: iv., 1702; x., 1733, 1737; Stiles, History of Brooklyn, i.; De Voe's Markets of New York; Doc. relating to Col. History, iv., v.; Hist. Tales of Olden Time, Watson; Acts of Assembly, 1702, 1705, 1706, 1709, 1714, 1753; Furman's Antiquities of Long Island; Valentine's History of New York; Thompson's History of Long Island; Rochefoucauld, i., 376; ii., 233, 449; Hist. Coll. of Long Island, i., Labadists' Journal.

were safe throughout the province, where every one had too good an opportunity for honest success to make crime either tempting or profitable. In early times the colony suffered from pirates, and to a much greater degree than elsewhere on account of the characteristic corruption of the government. Pirates harbored in the little Long Island ports, and bought immunity from Governor Fletcher, at whose house the Jacobite Club met, by gifts of ships and presents to his wife and daughter. Protections were openly sold in New York, and the gain was so great from this nefarious traffic that Lord Bellomont, in suppressing it, encountered a general resistance and much unpopularity; and his success against the pirates, it was generally said, cost the province one hundred thousand pounds a year. The abolition of piracy was succeeded by much smuggling and illicit trade; and the opposition in New York to the English navigation laws was exceptionally bitter. Crime in general was dealt with in the usual rough and ready fashion. There were many capital crimes expiated at the stake and the gallows, and the lash and the pillory were the favorite penalties for lesser offences; while in the Long Island towns the odd New England customs prevailed. Criminals were there obliged to stand in the market-place, or sit in the stocks on court day, with placards on their breasts, or bridles in their mouths and rods under their arms— a spectacle and warning to the crowd. A specific case brings up before us, better than any general statement, a picture of the time when the stocks, the pillory, and the whipping-post were in vogue, and when criminals were not looked upon as an oppressed class. In the year 1756 two women, for grand larceny, were carted down Broadway and Maiden Lane to the whipping-post, where they each received thirty-nine lashes. They were then sent to jail for a week, and, after their liberation, banished from the city. Crowds flocked to see such sights, and the attendance was especially numerous at an execution, as at Poughkeepsie, before the Revolution, where a white man and a negro were both burned at the stake for incendiarism.[1]

There was probably even less pauperism than crime, and such

---

[1] Crime, Hist. Coll., iv., Smith, p. 274 and ff.; Ibid., iii., N. S., Extracts from Newspapers; Mandeville, Hist. of Flushing; Furman's Brooklyn; Munsell, Annals, iv., 1701; x., 1737; Stiles, Hist. of Brooklyn, ii.; De Voe's Markets of New York; Moulton's New York 170 years ago; Doc. relating to Col. Hist., iv., 1698, Bellomont to Lords of Trade; Hist. Tales of Olden Time, Watson; Acts of Assembly, 1708; Smith's Hist. of Dutchess County; Bolton's Westchester, i., 436, Ballad of Captain Kidd.

as existed was dealt with, so far as any one concerned themselves about it at all, in the New England fashion. An act of Assembly, in the year 1691, ordered the towns to make provision for the poor, and obliged all persons without visible means of support to give surety that they would not come on the parish. In the towns paupers were sold at auction for terms of years, and their children were sold as apprentices. A characteristic example of the methods in vogue occurs in the records of Brooklyn, where it is ordered that "Mad James" be kept by Kings County generally, and that the deacons settle the proportions of the towns for the expense.[1] The colonists, it must be remembered, were in these matters quite as advanced as the rest of the world, and they had an important advantage over Europe, in the fact that neither crime nor pauperism were troublesome or pressing questions.

It is a matter of surprise, when the state of popular education in the colonies generally is considered, that there should have been comparatively little crime or pauperism in any of them. In this matter of education New York was probably as well provided as any of the middle provinces, and much better than those of the south; and yet education was neither widely diffused nor of good quality. Under the Dutch, schools of fair character, sufficiently good to attract pupils from Virginia and the south, were established at a very early period, and supported in large measure by government. The instruction was simple, and the school-master in New Amsterdam was clerk, chorister, and visitor of the sick; in the little villages, sexton and chorister; and always a personage of local importance. Under the English education seems to have fallen off. The Assembly did nothing except to pass an act for the establishment of grammar-schools in the town of New York; and at a much later date appropriate the proceeds of divers lotteries to the use and benefit of the college. The best schools—carried on generally for nine months in the year by itinerant masters, who were boarded among the inhabitants and paid by fees—were to be found in the Long Island towns, where they had been founded and maintained by the English settlers, and in New York and its immediate neighborhood. There, about the middle of the eighteenth century, King's College was established through the exertions of Samuel Johnson, and in connection with the Episcopal interest. The college gave a good course of instruction in the higher branches, and tuition

---

[1] Stiles, Hist. of Brooklyn, i.; Acts of Assembly, 1691; Eager's Hist. of Orange.

fees amounted to only twenty-five shillings a quarter; but it did not
grow rapidly; and at the commencement held in Trinity Church in
1773, and attended by a fashionable audience, only five students received degrees. One great obstacle in the way of the college was its
establishment on a narrow Episcopal basis, which aroused the hostility
of the dissenters, who opposed the charter, and subsequently attacked
the college and its administration. A similar difficulty, indeed, attended the schools. The Dutch stubbornly opposed an English education,
although at the cost of ignorance; and as late even as 1755 the Dutch
Reformed Church imported a master from Holland, who, however, failed, and was obliged to add English branches. Education on the whole,
and throughout the province, was bad and insufficient, and there was
a lamentable amount of ignorance among the poor and in the interior.
The sons of rich men, after such an education as the province afforded, and which out of the city of New York consisted of field sports
rather than books, were usually sent either to the New England colleges, to Princeton, or to an English university; while the daughters
of the household remained at home, read little, and studied less.[1]

In another point closely connected with education the conflict of
races peculiar to New York was strongly manifested. The English
speech made its way slowly but surely from the time of the seizure
of New Netherlands. The trading habits of the Dutch drew men of
all nations to the colony, so that even in the seventeenth century sixteen languages were said to be spoken in the province; but one and
all gave way before the English. The Dutch adhered closely to their
mother tongue, and in the inland towns and villages clung to their
preachers and school-masters; yet before the middle of the eighteenth century the change had begun, and the young people not only
spoke English, but went to the English churches, and wished to be
considered Englishmen. The result of this mixture of speech among
the people generally was great corruption of language everywhere.

[1] American Lady, i., 42, 67; Burnaby, p. 106; Hist. Soc. Coll., iv., Smith, 274
and ff.; Ibid., iii., N. S., Extracts from Newspapers; Stone's Life of Sir William
Johnson; Onderdonk's Hempstead; Ibid., Jamaica; Ruttenber's History of New-
burgh; Riker's History of Newtown; Furman's History of Brooklyn; Barnard's
Life of S. Van Rensselaer; Stiles, i., 1656, and iii.; Watson, Historic Tales of the
Olden Time; Doc. relating to Col. History, vi., 1753; Doc. History; Acts of As-
sembly, 1702, 1756; Furman's Antiquities of Long Island; Long Island Hist. Soc.
Coll., i., Journal of Labadists; Bolton's History of Westchester; Tyler's American
Literature; Massachusetts Hist. Soc. Coll., i., 2, 150.

English prevailed; but in some counties there were so many Dutch that it was difficult to find jurors who understood the language of the government. The foreign tongues, however, were doomed, and the corrupt English of the years preceding the Revolution was a sure sign of their ultimate disappearance.[1]

The great mass of the people, as has already been said, were either farmers or traders, and most of these were of the middle class of small landholders and shopkeepers. But, besides the social distinctions caused by wealth, there existed in New York an upper class, stronger and better defined than in any northern province. Slavery gave, of course, as in all the colonies, an aristocratic cast to the whole social and political system; but there was also an aristocracy quite different from anything in Pennsylvania or New England, and closely allied to the ruling class in Virginia. They did not have the great element of support afforded by a pure slave system, but they had the equally important foundation of large landed estates, and were invested with prerogatives of practical value unknown to the south. This class was composed almost entirely of followers of the system, or of the actual descendants of the great Dutch proprietors, who had received when the colony was founded land grants of almost unlimited extent from the West India Company; and they formed a very striking and important element in the community, both socially and politically. The most famous of these great estates was that of the Van Rensselaers, comprising all the territory in the neighborhood of Albany, peopled by farmers, and containing the thriving village of Rensselaerswyck. This manor, and those of the Cortlands and Livingstons, were each entitled to a representative in the Assembly. Besides these thus endowed with political privileges, there was the hardly less celebrated and extensive Philipse manor; and many leading families, principally of Dutch origin—such as the Schuylers and Cuylers—owned or rented great tracts of land which they leased out to small farmers. The proprietor of a manor was invested with many feudal privileges, and held a position more akin to that of the Old-World nobility than any one else in the American colonies.

The Philipse manor-house at Yonkers was a large stone building, with a high-pitched roof surmounted by a balustrade, and an interior at once luxurious and spacious. The walls were wainscoted, the

---

[1] Kalm, i., 235, 269; ii., 261; Tyler's Amer. Literature; Brodhead, i., 748; ii., 287; Rochefoucauld, ii., 233, 447.

ceilings decorated with arabesques, the chimney-pieces of carved marble, and the great open fireplaces panelled with Dutch tiles; while out-doors and near the house was a handsome formal garden, with walks edged with box, where the ladies of the family diverted themselves by gardening.   On this estate there were two rent-days—one at Philipsburgh and one at Sleepy Hollow—and on these occasions the tenants, after paying their rent in money and kind, gathered at the manor-house and were feasted by the landlord, who maintained thirty white and twenty colored servants in his household.   In the neighboring village the lord of the manor held, once a year, court-leet and court-baron, and meted out justice, sometimes in early days, extending even to capital punishment.   The other manors with their privileges, and in a more general way all the great landed estates, resembled more or less closely that of the Philipses.   All had large, well-built houses of brick or stone, and were handsomely decorated and fitted up within-doors.   They all had, too, their retinues of servants, great barns, abundance of horses and cattle, large, old-fashioned gardens, and great orchards sweeping away from the house; and in all reigned hospitality and good cheer.   Stained glass, bearing their arms, adorned the little church in Albany, and everywhere the sense of a strong and acknowledged aristocracy was felt.   But the New York manors and estates had their bad as well as their good side.   Lord Bellomont, as early as the year 1698, wrote to the Lords of Trade that the province was not popular, because people would not come as bare tenants of the large proprietors, when they could have land in fee-simple in New Jersey or Pennsylvania for the asking; and there can be no doubt that the great estates and land to be held, even for as long a time as " while water ran and grass grew," but still on the payment of rent, did not attract settlers.   The relations, too, between landlord and tenants became more and more unpleasant.   There was wrong on both sides, and complaints of violence and extortion.   Just before the Revolution riots broke out on some of the manors; the landlords were attacked, the sheriff fired on, and finally the rising had to be suppressed by troops.   In the war for Independence the great Philipse manor was forfeited, and the privileges of the others were swept away.   The great land-owners, although they resided for the most part in New York, and only in summer on their estates, were fully alive to the advantages of their position, and took care to maintain it.   The manor of the Rensselaers descended without a will to the eldest son; and in other cases the Dutch habit of division among the children was essentially modified.   Small portions were given to the daughters, and the younger sons each received a larger and equal share, while to the eldest went not only the lion's share of the property but the paternal and family homestead; and in this way the families were kept together and strengthened by what was practically primogeniture.   The influence of these great families in the counties and outside of the town of New York was immense.   The Schuylers and Van Rensselaers were intermarried and irresistible, the Duke of Rochefoucauld tells us; and he adds that the former furnished the brains, and the latter the money. The power of some of these great families was marked out for destruction in the northern atmosphere, and in the progress of American democracy; but it survived and was still vigorous, even after the nineteenth century had fairly begun.[1]

The manors were the most striking feature in the country life of New York, and yet formed but a small part of it.   From the mouth of the Hudson to Albany, and far up the Mohawk Valley, were scattered the settlements of the Dutch, who were the prevailing race among the farmers.   In the southern region they were more mixed with other races, and are said to have been of a character superior to those in the northern and western settlements, where in the early days the convicts and vagabonds sent out by the government had found a resting-place; but everywhere, with tenacious and stolid conservatism, they adhered to the manners and habits of their nation.   In the early days they did all in their power to keep off their restless English neighbors, who could only procure bad titles to land, but who, nevertheless, pushed on, came in companies, got patents from the Governors, and built up towns on Long Island and in the neighborhood of New York.   After the conquest the Dutch clung still closer to their land, refused to sell to the English, kept their large estates, and obliged the intruders to remain in the southern part of the province, and engage in trade rather than agriculture.[2]   This vigorous prejudice and

[1] Huguenot Family in Virginia, p. 296; Amer. Lady, i., 13, 41, 42, 92, 148, 165, 173; ii., 292; Hist. Coll., iv., Smith, Hist., p. 274 and ff.; Woolley's Two Years' Journal in New York; Barber's Hist. Coll.; Mandeville, Hist. of Flushing Old Wills; Barnard's S. Van Rensselaer; Munsell's Annals, i.; Doc. relating to Col. Hist., 1698; Furman's Antiquities of Long Island, Livingston House; Bolton's Hist. of Westchester, ii., Philipse Manor; Smith's Hist. of Dutchess County; Rochefoucauld, i., 369, 376.
[2] Dutch hostility and conservatism, see Journal of Claude Blanchard, p. 115; Kalm, i., 272; ii., 264; Pennsylvania Hist. Coll., i., 363; Denton's Description, 1670.

strong spirit of exclusiveness gave to the country life of New York along the Hudson and Mohawk an almost pure Dutch cast. In the interior villages the utmost simplicity prevailed, and the drowsy life of the little hamlets, where almost every one was a farmer, with here and there a few mechanics, flowed on in peaceful uneventfulness. The farm buildings were usually near the rivers and on the hill-sides, surrounded with gardens and orchards. The houses were generally of wood, sometimes of wood filled in with yellow Holland brick, with an overhanging second story, and the interiors were neat and comfortable, with low rooms—the heavy beams showing overhead—and great fireplaces lined with pictured tiles. The Dutch used no carpets before the Revolution, except a drugget beneath the table on grand occasions, preferring the traditional scrubbed and sanded floor. The furniture was plain and solid, from the great Holland beds to the sideboards and cupboards, filled with wine, and glittering with glasses ranged round a rack bearing a generous supply of pipes. The table was excellent and plentiful, and good living was the rule upon the farms. Wood and pewter were ordinarily used until the middle of the eighteenth century, when the china hitherto kept for company began to come into daily use. Both men and women were comfortably dressed in homespun, and knew little of the imported fashions of the towns. These farmers, as a class, were intent on gain, slow of mind and body, and usually pretty ignorant. They had their comfortable superstitions of a mild character, and believed in ghosts, witchcraft, and witches, who in the early days were now and then brought to trial and found guilty; but they were also sober, industrious, thrifty, and prosperous. To the southward, and especially on Long Island, the English element was more marked; and the towns established there, and for years at war with Stuyvesant and his predecessors, maintained themselves as independent autonomies with the paternal New England form of municipal government, and much strife and litigation among themselves, until the advent of English rulers, when they were swept in with the rest of the towns, and lost their separate standing. The condition of the farmers of all races, however, did not vary much. They were, as a class, remarkably well off, the only drawback being the monotony and narrowness of their lives. They saw little of each other except when harvest or wood-cutting called for mutual assistance; and the only amusements were an occasional picnic in the woods, a corn-husking, or a spinning-bee, and in winter skating and coasting; while in the south and on Long

Island there were the additional entertainments of tavern parties, turtle feasts, and weekly bull-baitings, with an occasional horse-race. Thus they lived on among the peaceful hills of the Hudson, sleepy and contented and comfortable, marking the passage of time with hour-glasses instead of clocks; and on Long Island in like fashion, but with a little more activity. They were simple and unaffected, bringing up their sons to trades, and their daughters to household arts, until after the Revolution, when the untiring Yankees poured in from New England in ever-increasing numbers, and proceeded to develop the country and obliterate the slumberous and picturesque society of the little Dutch villages, over which an enduring halo has been cast by the genius of Washington Irving.[1] There was, in truth, nothing from without to disturb them. Men rode into Albany or the neighboring towns to barter country produce at the variety store, or to attend church, with their women-folk on a cushion behind them, over very rough and stony roads. Saddle-horses, farm wagons, and two-wheeled chaises were the only modes of locomotion; and news from abroad reached them slowly and at long intervals from the towns. An effort was made in Dongan's time for an extensive continental postal service, in the interest of the Duke of York; but it came to nothing, and the mails to Philadelphia were carried by a boy in saddle-bags, which no one thought of robbing, while in the opposite direction they crept slowly up the Hudson on board the sluggish river craft. The first stage line was opened to the south in the year 1756; but not until after the Revolution were they established between New York and the inland villages to the north.[2]

The trading habits of the people outside the agricultural interests tended, of course, to build up towns. Albany owed its existence to the fur trade, of which it was the great centre for the northern colonies; and Schenectady grew up from the same traffic. In the earliest times each dwelling in Albany was also a trading-house, with store-rooms

---

[1] Smyth, ii., 378; American Lady, i., 95, 100, 104, 108; ii., 23; Kalm, i., 235; ii., 284; Hist. Coll., iv., Smith's Hist., p. 274 and ff.; Weise, Hist. of Troy; Onderdonk's Hempstead; Riker's Newtown; Reed's Amenia; Stiles's Brooklyn; Watson, Hist. Tales of Olden Time; Wood's Long Island; Jones's Lecture on Long Island; Bolton's Westchester; Smith's Hist. of Dutchess; Memoirs of Elkanah Watson; Tyler's American Literature.

[2] Weise, Hist. of Troy; Huguenot Family in Virginia, p. 296; Munsell's Annals, i.; Stiles's Brooklyn, i.; Doc. relating to Col. Hist., i.; Watson, Historic Tales; Acts of Assembly, 1708.

for furs in the second story; and the worthy burghers, in the good
Dutch fashion, made the little town a sort of close corporation, kept
the trades to themselves, had apprenticeship carefully regulated by
law, and maintained themselves so successfully, that even as late as
the year 1790 a stranger wishing to transact business had to pay five
pounds for admission as a freeman of the town. Albany was founded by the Dutch, and remained their stronghold down to the Revolution long after they had lost control of the sister city at the mouth
of the river; and there the Dutch commercial spirit, selfish and often
cunning, ruled unchecked, and the Dutch peculiarities of life and manners appeared in full perfection. At the period of the Revolution Albany was a town of about five thousand inhabitants, with one long ill-
paved street, where cattle wandered unrestrained, straggling along the
river's edge. The houses, with gable-ends to the street, low and picturesque, with peaked roofs and long projecting spouts, were solidly built
of brick or stone, and each stood by itself, with a garden and little green
about it. Some of the houses were handsome for the time, with spacious low rooms heavily wainscoted, the date of construction in iron
figures let into the yellow imported brick, and surmounted by elaborate gilded weather-cocks. In the door-ways of their dwellings the old
Dutchmen passed much of their time, peacefully smoking, and watching the oscillations of their own and their neighbor's vanes. These
porches were the only places of social meeting, and every one who
passed had to pause and greet the occupants of the long benches on
each side of the door. They were a reserved people, shy of strangers,
showing great disfavor in the eighteenth century to those who wore
their own hair in a queue like the dreaded Frenchmen, but withal
hospitable and kindly. The rich lived in great comfort; the poor
not so well as their country brethren. Life was quiet and uneventt-
ful. The only diversions were in strolling about and sitting in the
taverns, where the men played billiards, cards, or chess; but the absence of amusements did not weigh upon them. They regarded with
almost Puritanic disgust the festivities and theatricals of the British
officers at the time of the French war, and even as late as the year
1786 strongly opposed a public theatre. Everything about them was
simple and unaffected. The women worked hard, rose early, went to
bed late, were notable housewives, and neat almost to a fault. Their
worst defect, as a people, was their grasping spirit in trade; to illustrate which it was said that not even a Jew could hope to get a living among them; and there is no doubt that travellers complained ve-

hemently of their extortionate prices and love of money. They kept on in their own way, however, contentedly and prosperously until after the Revolution, and then the Yankee appeared in Albany, as he did elsewhere, and improved the city and developed business, and cut off the long projecting spouts which had dripped for a hundred years on the passers-by, and ended by overwhelming the Dutchmen, and absorbing them in his own pushing, driving race.[1]

In the city of New York the original possessors had lost their hold at a much earlier period than in Albany, socially as well as politically; but the town from the beginning, and under every rule, was the centre of provincial life, and the scene of constant activity. Trade brought the Dutch adventurers to the end of Manhattan Island, where the West India Company built its five great storehouses, and trade built up the city, and continued to be the ruling and guiding interest. As early as the year 1648 a weekly market was held between the Company's storehouses and the fort, and the Dutch "kermis" took place every year for the sale of home productions. Ten years later the Broadway shambles came into being, with butchers holding great and small burgher's rights; and the cattle-market of the province was on the strand, where the farmers' boats landed. The narrow and careful but enterprising Dutch spirit was manifested for years in the strict regulations for trade and in the exclusion from handicrafts of strangers, who were not freemen of the city, which they made the distributing point not only for their own, but the neighboring provinces, and thus gave a strong impulse and direction to the whole course of development. New York became at an early day, and has remained, a great centre for trade from all parts of the world, and this gave in colonial days a cosmopolitan tone to the community, which contrasts strongly with anything that can be found in the other provinces. At the period of the Revolution the town rose gradually from the quays which had been built at the southern extremity of the island, and extended inland for nearly a mile with an average width of perhaps half that distance. The streets were paved, except on the high ground, fairly clean, and drained by wide gutters in the middle of the highway, to which rows of tall trees on each side gave a pleasant look. Many years before the Revolution the streets were lighted and watched, al-

---

[1] Kalm, ii., 256, 261, 262, 264, 267; American Lady, i., 44, 95; ii., 23; Smyth, ii., 293; Brissot, p. 127; Pennsylvania Hist. Coll., i. 363; Barnes, Early Hist. of Albany; Worth, Random Recollections of Albany; Munsell, i., vii.; Memoirs of Elkanah Watson.

though the uncertain supply of oil rendered the former benefit for a long time a precarious one. The old Dutch houses—which were all built of brick or stone, commonly of the former, yellow in color, and adorned with checker-work patterns—stood with gable ends toward the street, thus distinguishing themselves from their more modern neighbors, built in much the same style but turning a full face to the road. Almost all the houses were gabled, with high pitched roofs of shingles or variegated tiles surmounted by a balcony railing, within which the occupants of the mansion were wont to sit on summer evenings and enjoy the view of the harbor. The interiors were neat and comfortable, with low rooms, alcoves, and window-seats, high wainscots of painted wood-work, and whitewashed walls. The furniture was solid, usually of mahogany; no carpets covered the sanded floors; pewter and copper were generally used; and china was rare, although every family of standing had a certain amount of massive silver. Hangings were seldom seen; but the influence of trade and travel could be observed in the drawings and pictures which adorned the walls of most of the houses. The public edifices by no means equalled the private houses, and were for the most part insignificant; the college was hardly finished; and the only buildings for the purposes of charity were the hospital for seamen and the pest-houses on the harbor islands. Trade was better supplied, for there were coffee-houses, and an exchange with a spreading arcade where merchants met daily. At the time of the Revolution the town, although said to be less populous than either Boston or Philadelphia, numbered about fifteen to eighteen thousand inhabitants, and had the greatest trade in America.

New York, moreover, was not only the business centre of the province, but that of law and government as well; besides being, until revolution impended, the only military post on the continent, with English troops and officers who added much to the bustle and variety of the place. In addition also to the community which had grown up on the soil, there was a strong foreign element; and the result was a mixed and polished society, as hospitable and much gayer and more entertaining than any other in the English possessions in America.[1]

---

[1] Description of New York, see Huguenot Family in Virginia, p. 296; American Lady, i., 42; Smyth's Tour, ii., 375; Raynal, 1766; Kalm, i., 248, 250, 258; Burnaby, pp. 106, 108, 113; Wansey, pp. 73, 226; Denton, 1670; Stiles's Brooklyn, i.; De Voe's Markets; Watson, Historic Tales; Doc. relating to Col. History of New York, 1744; Acts of Assembly, 1692, 1753, 1761; Elkanah Watson's Memoirs, 1784; Mad. Knight's Journal.

Some of the inhabitants were the great proprietors who came to town for the winter, and in spring went up the Hudson to their estates; while others, of the more wealthy class, had handsome country-seats on Long Island, renowned in the colonies for its fine farms and high cultivation. But the great majority of the New York population of all classes remained in the pleasant town all the year round. They were all, with few exceptions, tradesmen of one sort or another, from the great merchant whose ships sailed to Europe, down through the retail dealers and shopkeepers, to the young adventurer, who started off with his pack of beads and knives to truck and barter with the Indians. Most of them belonged to the middle class, who rose early, breakfasted at daylight, dined at twelve, and worked hard at their shops, which they had the good-sense to close early in order to go forth for amusement and exercise. The wealthiest society was very fashionable in dress and manners, and devoted to the last London novelties. The women wore silks and velvets, the men displayed great luxury at their tables, and the tone of conversation aimed to be witty, sentimental, and refined. This society had its balls, concerts, and private theatricals; and the gentlemen evening clubs at the taverns. The active social life of New York is strongly shown in this matter of clubs. As early as the beginning of the century there was a Jacobite, an Irish, and a French club; and later a convivial club of professional men; but nowhere does there appear to have been much indulgence in the fashionable vice of extravagant gaming. Besides in-door amusements there were in winter sleighing-parties to the neighboring country tavern, and the road was covered in the evening with rapidly driven sleighs, which in fine weather were replaced by picnics and fishing-parties, or turtle-feasts at some favorite inn, when the participants drove out in couples in the chaises universally used, and returned after supper by way of the well-known kissing-bridge.

The amusements of the mass of the people did not differ much from those of the upper class, but the tone of society was strongly aristocratic, and the distinctions of dress were carefully observed. The ladies and gentlemen of fashion wore silks and velvets, powder and wigs, and the latter carried a sword. The wealthy tradesman appeared in broadcloth coat, with spreading skirts and wide cuffs; the shopkeeper in simple homespun, except on festivals; and the workmen in leather aprons, which were never replaced by a long coat. The habits and amusements of the middle and lower classes were simple and wholesome. They strolled in the mall after the day's work, or went, gayly dressed, on a holiday or Sunday afternoon, to see an ox roasted whole on the Battery, in the presence of the Governor and Council, or to the customary bull-baiting, or to the local Ranelagh and Vauxhall, where they saw fire-works and drank beer, and then danced, and had a supper of chocolate and bread, until Dr. Laidlie saw fit to preach down these last harmless pleasures. There was, indeed, no lack of public amusements. The American theatre began its career in New York about the middle of the eighteenth century in a house in Nassau Street, and from that time had a successful existence and not much opposition, until it finally became thoroughly domesticated. The Dutch had also a fortunate liking for holidays, and these they kept, and gradually induced their unresting English neighbors to do the same. There were five great festivals—Christmas, New-year's, Passover, Whitsuntide, and San Claas, or St. Nicholas-day. Besides these there were the "Vrouwen-dagh," or St. Valentine's-day, when young girls went about the streets striking the young men with knotted cords; Easter, May-day, with the classic poles, and Pinkster, early in June, when there was a general exodus to the woods. Then there were the official English celebrations of the Gunpowder Plot, the birthday and the coronation, when great bonfires were lighted on the common, and there was much rejoicing and feasting at the expense of the city. New-year's-day began with firing salutes, and parties then went about the town, stopping at every house to fire guns and drink punch, with much indiscriminate burning of gunpowder, forbidden by the Assembly in the year 1773. "Pinkster" was a day of especial liberty for the negroes, who had great picnics, followed by dancing, sometimes of a most indecent character, which was witnessed by all the people of the town. On all holidays, and indeed at other times, a good deal of rough fun was enjoyed by the boys of different parts of the town, who indulged in factious fights in the streets.[1]

The social life of New York was, as may be seen, gay and pleasant,

---

[1] Amusements and habits, see Huguenot Family in Virginia, p. 296 ; Brissot, pp. 122, 128, 140 ; Wansey, pp. 74, 228 ; Kalm, i., 245 ; Smyth, ii., 376 ; Hist. Coll., iv., Smith's History, p. 274 and ff. ; Ibid., iii., N. S., Extracts from Newspapers ; De Voe's Markets of New York, 1735 ; Watson, Historic Tales of the Olden Time ; Francis, Old New York ; Mad. Knight's Journal ; Furman's Antiquities of Long Island ; Long Island Hist. Soc. Coll., i., Journal of Labadists ; Valentine's History of New York ; Duer, New York as it Was ; Burnaby, p. 115 ; Rochefoucauld, ii., 465.

with no lack of amusements of all sorts—from bull-baiting to concerts; but the intellectual life was by no means equally strong. Indeed, literature in New York had a feebler existence than in any of the
northern colonies. There was none deserving of remembrance outside
the work of Colden—a talented and versatile man—on the Five Nations,
and William Smith's History of New York. With these exceptions,
the only efforts at authorship were those of a knot of clever young
men who wrote verses and essays for the newspapers, mostly of a
political nature, and of a perfectly ephemeral character. In the year
1740 there was only one press in New York, and two or three weekly
gazettes alone possessed the field prior to the Revolution. Albany
had no newspaper until the year 1771, and there was none on Long
Island before the Revolution. In most houses there was no literature
except of a religious kind; and the booksellers had little besides Bibles,
prayer-books, and spelling-books in their stock. Some of the leading
men, like Sir William Johnson, imported many books and periodicals
from England, and good private libraries were not uncommon; but,
as a rule, there was little reading and less writing done in the province.[1]

In regard to two of the three great events in each human life, the
customs of town and country were not essentially different. Marriages were, as a rule, very young, very fruitful, and apparently very
happy. Breach-of-promise suits were rare, and before the year 1786
there is said to have been only one case of divorce. Marriages were
at first by the publication of banns; but this practice fell into disuse,
and was replaced by the Governor's license, which formed a fruitful
source of official revenue. The ceremony was not accompanied by
much parade, and only the immediate friends were present; but the
following day it was the custom for the groom to give a collation in
the morning, which was kept up all day, and concluded with a good
deal of hard drinking.[2] The simplicity of the customs in relation to
marriage, however, were more than made up for by the pomp and circumstance attending funerals, which form a very striking, and, from the

[1] Kalm, i., 266; Stone's Life of Johnson; Furman's History of Brooklyn; Wansey, pp. 75, 284, 288; Munsell's Annals of Albany, i.; Stiles, History of Brooklyn,
i.; Furman's Antiquities of Long Island; Long Island Hist. Soc. Coll., i., Journal
of Labadists; Tyler's American Literature.

[2] American Lady, i., 74, 92; Onderdonk's Hempstead; Furman's Brooklyn;
Munsell's Annals, i.; Furman's Antiquities of Long Island; Watson, Historic
Tales.

excess to which they were carried, a peculiar feature of New York provincial life. When a man married he laid down always some fine Madeira to be drunk at his funeral; and when a death occurred special invitations were sent out, the friends gathered at the house, scarfs and gloves were distributed, and the mourners sat solemnly about the coffin drinking and smoking. After a prayer, the bier was borne to the grave, a long procession following; and the invited guests then returned to the house, where a generous feast was spread. In the country only men went to the grave, but in New York ladies went also, and sometimes acted as pall-bearers. One or two examples bring home this characteristic feature of a past time far better than any general description. In the year 1756 one Lucas Wyngaard, an old bachelor, and the last of his race, died in Albany. After the burial, the mourners assembled at the house of the deceased to make a night of it. They consumed a pipe of wine and an endless quantity of tobacco, kept up their revels until morning, broke all the glasses and decanters, and wound up by making a bonfire of their scarfs on the hearth. Such an instance shows the excesses which these funeral feasts sometimes caused; but all were deeply marked by pomp and expense. A funeral often cost three or four thousand dollars. The first wife of the patroon, Stephen Van Rensselaer, was buried at a cost of twenty thousand dollars; two thousand scarfs were distributed, and all the tenants of the manor came into Albany, where they were entertained for three or four days at the expense of their landlord. On the death of any prominent man or person of wealth, a general invitation to the obsequies was given from the pulpit, and cakes and Madeira were provided for the crowds that came to partake of them. At an official funeral the parade was even greater; as in the case of James De Lancey, who died in 1760. Minute-guns were fired from the forts and shipping while the procession, half a mile in length, moved slowly from the house to Trinity Church. First came the clerks of the church, the rector, and the clergy of the Protestant denominations, in the inevitable chaises; then the hearse, drawn by white horses, with the coffin, covered with a velvet pall emblazoned with gold escutcheons; and finally the relatives, members of the Assembly, magistrates, and gentlemen of the law. The body was carried from the hearse on men's shoulders into the church, which was illuminated. A similar display was made at the funeral of Sir Henry Moore, who died in the year 1768. It is not to be wondered at that such lavish expenditure produced a reaction, and combined efforts for reform. In all the col-

onies pompous funerals were the custom, and the reform movement
seems to have met with a general acceptance; but in New York it
had apparently little effect, and the custom died by the slow process
of changing manners. The peculiar and extreme extravagance of
New York, and the endurance of the custom, are due to the Dutch,
who went far beyond the English in this matter, and to whom such
an excess of cost and parade was indeed peculiar.[1]

It only remains to describe briefly the character of New York politics, which differed very much in some respects from those of any
other colony. Local politics were carried on with great zeal, and a
good deal of bitter feeling and popular excitement; so much so that
elections for the Assembly caused a general stoppage of business. For
a week the candidates kept open house and feasted their supporters,
and on election day bands of drunken electors patrolled the city, and
stopped at every house to demand votes. The character of the provincial politics was but a part of the broader questions connected with
the relations to the mother country. These were discussed and fought
over with a degree of virulence peculiar to New York, and due not
only to the bad quality of the administration, but still more to the fact
that here, and here alone, the territory had been settled and possessed
by one nation and conquered by another. From the time of Andros
and Cornbury, and their oppressive rule, there was always a vigorous
resistance to the imperial government; and there were also, of course,
the usual grievances against England here as elsewhere. In Bellomont's time the sheriffs could not be depended upon to seize smuggled
goods, and the English navigation laws caused intense ill-feeling among
a people so absorbed in foreign commerce. Impressment was another
sore point; and in the year 1744 fishermen, who had suffered from
the press-gang, burnt the boats of an English man-of-war on the
beach. These particular grievances were, however, merely indications
of a general feeling. The ill-advised Church policy caused a continuous struggle between the dissenting sects and the government; and
in the years preceding the Revolution the letters of the Governors are
filled with complaints of the opposition — invariably styled a "faction." Clinton wrote to the Duke of Newcastle that the people
caught at everything to lessen the prerogative; and again, in 1747,

---

[1] Hist. Soc. Coll., iv., Smith, p. 278 and ff., De Lancey Funeral; History of Troy,
Weise; Munsell's Annals, i., Judge Benson's Address; Stiles's Brooklyn; Watson,
Historic Tales; Furman's Antiquities of Long Island.

that the Stamp Act proposed by Clarke was an unwise measure, and would encounter universal resistance. There were in reality three parties. The English officials and the wealthy Dutch merchants in New York were very loyal; they drank the King's health on all occasions, listened to sermons, draped their churches in mourning when the Prince of Wales died, and, in 1770, had great feasting and grand processions in honor of the erection of George the Third's statue, destined at an early day to be run into Revolutionary bullets. At the other extreme were the young men of English race, who published the *Independent Reflector*, and founded the Whig Club, where, in the words of the Tory historian, the New England spirit was rampant, Cromwell and Hampden were toasted, hatred sworn to kings and bishops, and a constant agitation kept up against the government. Between these two extreme parties was the great mass of the people, the Dutch farmers and foreign settlers, and some of the great manorial proprietors, who returned popular candidates to the Assembly. This third party was either lukewarm in their loyalty or positively indifferent, and could offer no opposition to any active faction ready to take a decisive and aggressive attitude.[1] With these factious and bitter politics and strong party feelings, New York was swept easily into the Revolutionary current, and at the same time produced a Tory party of almost unequalled violence and activity.

Thus we come to the end of the middle group. In the south is found the Virginian influence acting upon Delaware and Pennsylvania, and gradually disappearing until it vanishes entirely, and New York is reached wholly free from Virginian ideas, but strongly tinged with those of the compact and strongly marked English communities to the eastward. From New York we pass out of the region which held the balance of power, and come in contact with the other great social and political force which battled with that of Virginia for mastery in the coming nation.

---

[1] American Lady, ii., 231 and ff.; Kalm, i., 264; Hist. Coll., iii., Extracts from Newspapers; Munsell's Annals, x., 1742; De Voe's Markets of New York; Doc. relating to Col. Hist. of New York, iv., vi., Letters of Governors; Watson, Historic Tales; Jones, Hist. of New York in Revolution.

Chapter XVIII.

MASSACHUSETTS FROM 1620 TO 1765.

FROM the Norsemen to John Smith none of the early and daring discoverers and adventurers, if we except the remnants of the Popham colonists, succeeded in gaining a permanent foothold on the repellent shores of New England. The history of Massachusetts begins in an obscure Lincolnshire village, among a company of plain farmers and simple rustics, who had separated from the Church of England, and paid for their temerity by bitter and unceasing persecution. Life became intolerable, and they resolved to fly.

1608. Hunted even to the water's edge, they at last assembled at Amsterdam, where they were free and safe, and could worship God as they pleased. From Amsterdam they removed to Leyden, supporting themselves in both cities by the work of their own hands; but though they had religious freedom, the race feeling and the love of England was strong within them. They could not bear to live under foreign rule, and watch their children grow up and enter foreign service, and fall away from the faith of their fathers; so their thoughts turned to the New World, where surely there would be room, perhaps even an obscure corner of the vast possessions of the British Crown in which they could find rest and peace. After prolonged negotiations and many disappointments, a patent was at last obtained; money was raised by London merchants, who acquired a mortgage in this way on the colony and its inhabitants, and a chosen

1620. band sailed from Delfthaven in the *Speedwell*, and joined the *Mayflower* at Southampton. Twice they started and twice they put back, first to Dartmouth and then to Plymouth; and at last the *Mayflower* sailed alone, with one hundred and two colonists. These men and women were simple rustics, farmers or workmen. The leaders even were not, with one or two exceptions, men of any marked social position. They were poor and friendless, separatists from the Church and exiles from England; but they bore with them the seeds of a

great nation and of a great system of government. They landed
at Cape Cod, and there founded a democratic republic by
Nov. 21, the famous compact of the *Mayflower*. A few weeks later
1620. they landed at Plymouth, the vanguard of a great column,
bearing a civilization and a system of government which was to confront that other system founded far away to the south on the
Dec. 21, rivers of Virginia, and which, after a conflict of two centu-
1620. ries and a half, was destined to prevail throughout the length
and breadth of a continent.

I do not propose to rehearse the history of that memorable settlement at Plymouth. "It has all been told and painted," and the smallest details of the whole story have become household words. There
is no need again to draw the picture of that awful winter of cold, famine, and disease ; and of the little company slowly perishing on the
sandy shores of Massachusetts Bay. There is no need to repeat the
history of their hopes returning with the spring, of the successful dealings with the Indians, of the difficulties at Weymouth, of the contentions with the genial and worthless Morton, and of the dangers from
Gorges and from England. All is familiar, all are details trivial in
themselves, but made grand by after results, and set down at the time
with minute care by men like Bradford, who seemed to have an instinct that a nation would one day long to know their struggles for
existence, and that he and his friends were laying one of the corner-
stones of a great empire. Clinging with marvellous tenacity to the
barren coast, a mere handful of persistent Englishmen, the Plymouth
people held together. They bore up against nature and the savage,
and against their fellow-countrymen. They held out against the harassing complaints of the London traders who had bought their labor,
and, freeing themselves from this tyranny, took up a load of debt
which they honestly labored to discharge. They threw out trading-
posts, hunted, farmed, fished, worked, stayed, and struck root. The colony grew slowly, and its humble fortunes prospered in a small fashion ; but it did its work, and opened the way and marked the spot
for that great emigration which was to build up the powerful Puritan
commonwealths of New England.

While the people of Plymouth were struggling to establish their
colony, some of the English Puritans, restless under the growing despotism of Charles, began to turn their eyes to New England.
1623. Under the lead of the Rev. John White, the Dorchester Company was formed for trading and fishing, and a station was established

at Cape Ann; but the enterprise did not prosper, the colonists were disorderly, and the Company made an arrangement for Roger Conant and others, driven from Plymouth by the rigid principles of the Separatists to come to Cape Ann. Still matters did not improve, and **1626.** the Company was dissolved; but White held to his purpose, and Conant and a few others moved to Naumkeag, and determined to settle there. Conant induced his companions to persevere, and matters in England led to a fresh attempt, for discontent grew rapidly as Charles proceeded in his policy. A second Dorchester Company, not this time a small affair for fishing and trading, but one backed by men of wealth and influence, was formed, and a large grant **1628.** of lands was made by the Council for New England to Sir Henry Roswell and five others. One of the six patentees, John Endicott, went out during the following summer with a small company, assumed the government at Naumkeag, which was now called Salem, and sent out exploring parties. The Company thus formed in England was merely a voluntary partnership, but it paved the way for another and much larger scheme. Disaffection had become wide-spread. The Puritans began to fear that religious and political liberty alike were not only in danger but were doomed to destruction, and a large portion of the party resolved to combine for the preservation of all **1629.** that was dearest to them by removal to the New World. The Dorchester Company was enlarged, and a royal charter was obtained incorporating the Governor and Company of Massachusetts Bay. The freemen of the Company were to meet four times in every year; they could choose a Governor, deputy, and eighteen assistants, who were to meet every month; they were authorized to administer oaths of supremacy and allegiance, admit new associates, defend themselves by arms, transport settlers, and manage in every way their own affairs. Nothing was said of religious liberty; for this famous instrument was as shrewdly as it was loosely drawn. Omit the word Company, and we have the constitution of an independent state with very ill-defined powers.

The new scheme once started, organization proceeded rapidly. Endicott was made local Governor, and Matthew Cradock Governor of the Company; money was freely subscribed, and six vessels with emigrants, supplies, and cattle, under the charge of eminent and "godly" ministers, were despatched at once to Massachusetts. They settled at Salem, established a church by mutual covenant, with Skelton as pastor and Higginson as teacher, and sent out men to prepare for another settlement at Charlestown.   Everything seems to have been preconcerted.   There was no obstruction or discussion, and at every step, and especially in the matter of the Church, we see the development of a well-matured plan.   But these men were not separatists like those of Plymouth.   They were members of the Church of England, Puritans, and Reformers, representing a large, powerful, and ever-increasing element in the English race, and they had behind them religious, social, and political forces unknown in the foundation of other colonies.   They established an independent Church at Salem, not because they wished to break from the English Church, but because they desired a purified Church, and under the circumstances of a new country they were compelled to construct one upon a new and self-sustaining model.   To this course of action two of the counsellors at Salem objected; whereupon Endicott ordered them away, and they betook themselves to England with their complaints of separatism. The Company acted cautiously, but it was clear that they meant to exercise absolute control, and exclude opponents from their domain. Meanwhile events moved fast in England.   Charles was determined to rule arbitrarily and alone, and the Puritans took the next step in their plan of colonization by resolving to remove the Company and its government to New England.   Winthrop was chosen Governor, and Humphrey deputy.   The leaders were country gentlemen, merchants, and soldiers, men of wealth and position—while the bulk of the emigration was, as a rule, from the farmers and yeomanry, who were people of substance.   It was the migration of a people, not the mere setting forth of colonists and adventurers.   The trading purposes of the corporation soon disappear, we can see the whole broad scheme of the Puritan leaders, and how, under the disguise of a trading company and a commercial charter, they went forth to found a State, and erect an independent government.   Those of the Company who did not go to America remained in England to enter the Long Parliament, and fight in the civil wars.   If we run over the names of those connected with the Massachusetts Company we find nearly all the leaders of the Puritan party, the magnitude of the scheme becomes apparent, and we see that if all had been lost in England, there would in a few years have sprung up in America a great Puritan State, powerful enough to have defied the mother country, and stood out as her equal at the very outset.   As it was, a great work was accomplished, and the party which raised up the commonwealths of New England with one hand tore down the Stuart throne with the other.

In the spring of 1630 Winthrop and the other officers and leaders,
1630. having published an address to their brethren in England, sailed with a fleet of eleven vessels; and before the next winter
set in a thousand colonists had arrived. Winthrop found the colony
at Salem languishing from hunger and sickness, while disease and exposure carried off some of his own company. Attention was given
at once to choosing a new site, and the first attempt was made at
Charlestown, where a church was formed on the independent model
of Salem, and courts of assistants were held to punish misdemeanors,
and provide for order and police in the various plantations. The lack
of good water drove many of the people across the river to Boston,
and there the first general court of the Company was held, by which
almost all power was conferred upon the assistants; but as there were
many applications for admission to the Company, it was evident that
the freemen would before long have to be still further consulted. It
was resolved soon after to build a fort at Boston, and then Newtown,
afterward Cambridge, was selected for the capital, where the Govern-
or and assistants agreed to build houses. The winter passed heavily
in wretched and imperfect shelters, and with much suffering.

At the next meeting of the general court, when the first elections
1631. were held, it was enacted that no one should be admitted a
freeman, and so have the right to vote, unless he was a member of one of the churches within the limits of the colony. Thus
the great Puritan theory of Church and State united in one organization was fairly put in practice. One hundred and eighteen persons
were admitted to the franchise, a general court was ordered to be held
every year, and the assistants were to hold from year to year unless
removed, thus concentrating the power still more in the hands of the
magistrates. Winthrop and Dudley were continued as Governor and
Deputy, the capital was soon after finally fixed at Boston, and the
government was carried on in practice wholly by the magistrates; an
absorption which, even in those early days of battle for existence,
1632. soon provoked opposition. A tax was laid for fortification, and
the people of Watertown refused to pay their share for fear
of "bringing themselves and posterity into bondage." They were pac-
ified by Winthrop, who told them the government was in the nature
of a parliament, and that all the assistants were elected. This opposition, however, bore fruit at the next general court, where the freemen resumed the right of electing Governor and Deputy, choosing
Winthrop and Dudley again to those positions; and they also deter-

mined that two delegates should be chosen from every plantation to confer with the assistants about raising a public stock. Thus the foundation of a Lower House was laid, and true representative and parliamentary government begun. Meantime, a church had been started at Boston, where the cabins of the settlers were increasing, and new plantations began to spring up on the shore and in the interior, unmolested by savages, who had been swept from the coast by disease. The chief enemy was in poor crops and scarcity of supplies, and against these evils the colonists battled manfully. Forts were erected to protect the town against French attacks from the north, and the strongly-planted settlement was firmly rooted in the new soil.

The accession of Laud to the primacy gave a fresh start to the tide of emigration, which brought out this year Hooker, who settled at Newtown, and the famous John Cotton, who remained at Boston. This renewed emigration, indeed, assumed such proportions as to attract attention in England, for in the previous year the various persons who had been driven from the colony, backed by Gorges and Mason, who were jealous of their eastern grants, had accused the people of Massachusetts of intending rebellion and independence. The first attack was warded off; but when suspicion was again awakened, the detention of emigrant ships was ordered, and Cradock was commanded to appear and produce the charter. Then it was known that the charter had gone to America, and the royal government was aroused to a sense of what had happened. While danger was preparing at home the colony had grown to three or four thousand inhabitants, distributed in sixteen towns. All the freemen could not assemble, but their representatives did, and proceeded to do much more than advise as to "raising public stock." They took all power into their hands, chose Dudley Governor, to show that no office was a freehold, rebuked the assistants, admitted freemen, passed laws, and administered oaths of allegiance, not to the king but to the government of the colony; and so after three days quietly adjourned, making provision for the future choice of deputies from the towns. Representative democracy was fairly established, and the Puritan system of a united Church and State was on trial.

Trade began, and adventurers made their way to the Connecticut and sailed along the Sound to New York, while farms were opened and tilled, cattle raised, and population rapidly increased. The State was created, and it was now necessary to maintain it against attacks

1633.

1634.

in England and dissensions at home. The latter they had guarded against by banishing disaffected persons; the former they met boldly and wisely. Mr. Cradock sent a copy of the order requiring a production of the patent, and the assistants laid it on the table, and declined to act without authority from the general court. When the court met it was known that a royal commission for the case of the colonies had been organized, and that a Governor-general was to be appointed. The court ordered new forts to be built, and the people to be trained in arms; while Dudley, Winthrop, and three others were appointed to manage any war that might befall; and the ministers soon after were called to advise with the assistants, when it was resolved that they would not accept a general Governor, but defend their lawful possessions. At the next general court farther steps were taken

1635. to fortify the towns, erect beacons, arm and discipline soldiers, and a military commission was appointed with extraordinary powers. This was the answer of Massachusetts to the demands of England. Emigration was prohibited by the royal commission, the Council for New England divided its property among twelve associates, and resigned its charter, and a *quo warranto* was brought by the attorney-general against the Massachusetts Company. Judgment was given against Sir Henry Roswell and others of the original patentees, and it looked as if the end, so far as the law could go, was near; but Massachusetts disregarded all this, and events favored the colony, for ship-money and "prelatizing" absorbed public attention in England, and their most energetic opponent, Mason, died. While thus facing this perilous attack from abroad, the colony had also to confront their first serious opposition at home. Some years before Roger Williams had come to the colony, and got into trouble by refusing to join the congregation at Boston, because they would not publicly repent having had communion with the English Church, and he also denied the right of magistrates to punish for breaches of the Sabbath, and of the first table of the Decalogue. Despite the remonstrances of the assistants, he was chosen teacher of the Salem Church; and then for a time he lived at Plymouth, where he published a treatise impugning the right of Massachusetts to her land under the King's grant. This was laid before the magistrates; Williams made submission, and the treatise was burned. This was after his return to Salem, where he soon raised a ferment by denouncing women for going unveiled, and by inciting Endicott to cut the cross from the flag; but he was nevertheless chosen preacher in spite of the protests of the magistrate. He was soon in trouble again for preaching against the King's patent, and yet again for denying the right to administer an oath to the unregenerate. He was heard before the ministers, the quarrel extended to Salem and the Salem Church, and at last the general court took hold of it, and ordered Williams to leave the colony within six weeks. The time was extended to the fol-

1636. lowing spring; but Williams kept up the disturbance at Salem, and the magistrates determined to send him to England. He heard of the danger, and fled into the wilderness. The whole matter was a mere question of policy, and not at all of religious liberty. Williams attacked the right of the colonists to their land; he denied the powers of the magistrate to enforce the laws; he struck at allegiance to the government; he strove to encourage a policy which would still further inflame the King, and embitter their relations with England; he stirred up disorder and dissension—and all this was done in a time of trial and extreme danger from abroad. That at this day he could have done and said all he did unmolested, is probable; but even now in time of war such a man would be regarded with suspicion. Under the circumstances of the time and place, he was dangerous to the State; the magistrates had the right to turn him out, and they acted strongly and wisely in doing so. Others were wiser than he, submitted to punishment, and gave way. Endicott was called to account for cutting the cross, was relegated to private life, and finally disfranchised for a year; while Israel Stoughton was disabled from office for denying the power of the magistrates.

The commonwealth, for such it had come to be, was growing and strengthening. Courts had been established, and churches and towns ordered and regulated on a uniform model; and in the memorable year which opened with conflict at home and abroad the Puritans founded Harvard College. The previous year had brought to the colony, besides an increasing emigration, the younger Winthrop, bearing a commission from Lord Say-and-Sele, Lord Brooke, and their associates, patentees of Connecticut. A movement had been begun in that direction some two years before, and had been thwarted by the persistent opposition of the magistrates; but, after much controversy, it was found impossible to check the migration, and Hooker had gone thither with a large company. Arrangements were made with these settlers, and with those from Plymouth who preceded them, the new colonies were fairly started, and soon freed themselves from the protecting rule of Massachusetts.

With the younger Winthrop came two men who played a great

part in the troubled times of the Rebellion—the younger Vane and Hugh Peter—who at once mixed themselves up in politics, undertook to revise the administration, heal the feud between the elder Winthrop and Dudley, and, in concurrence with the ministers, enforce greater strictness in every department of the State. Carried away by the glamour of his position and by the brilliancy of his talents, the freemen chose Vane Governor at the next general court, thus doing all in their power to increase the confusion of the stormiest and most perilous year in the early history of the colony. Vane's first act was to get a royal flag from one of the ships, which, with his assent, was displayed at the fort. A committee was raised, also, to revise the laws. But graver matters than these pressed upon the colony; trouble was brewing with the Indians, there were fights with traders, and murders, and, finally, Endicott was sent out with three ships and a body of soldiers. He ravaged Block Island, which only enraged the Pequods without terrifying them; so they began to destroy outlying settlements, and Connecticut seemed doomed to destruction. But the little settlements raised men, and applied to Massachusetts and Plymouth for aid. Soldiers came, and the united forces, under Mason and Underhill, surrounded the chief Pequod town, stormed the ramparts, fired the wigwams, and put to the sword, without regard to age or sex, some seven hundred of the savages. The rest of the tribe were attacked on their retreat, and only a handful finally escaped to New York. The work was done in true Puritan fashion; the Pequod tribe was literally exterminated, and the "land had rest forty years." But while the strain of savage war was upon them, while their soldiers were marching southward to join the men of Connecticut, troubles had broken out at Boston, which arose from the actions and sayings of Mrs. Hutchinson, an active, energetic, uneasy woman, who had followed Cotton to America some years before. Her brother-in-law, Wheelwright, soon settled at Mount Wollaston, was her chief ally, and Mrs. Hutchinson herself propounded various doctrines which were at variance with those generally accepted. She held lectures for women, and assailed the ministers—especially Wilson, of the Boston church — accusing them of being under a covenant of works, not of grace, and satirizing their sermons. Loud and bitter controversies sprang up. Mrs. Hutchinson obtained the powerful support of Vane, and of Dummer and Coddington; and, to a certain extent, of Cotton. Boston was in a ferment of excitement. Wilson, the pastor of the Boston church, where the Hutchinsonians were in the majority, was attacked and censured; and at the next meeting of the court the ministers also assembled, and a fast was ordered. The ministers decided in conclave that for heresy and error the court might proceed without tarrying for the Church; and thereupon Wheelwright, for a sermon preached during the fast, was adjudged guilty of sedition by the court, although the Governor, some members of the House, and the people of Boston protested. The next court for general elections was held in the open air at Newtown, where Winthrop and Dudley were chosen Governor and Deputy, and the Hutchinsonians were left off the board of assistants. After a scene of great violence, the old party, backed by the ministers and the country members, prevailed. Vane behaved petulantly and angrily, and, after some further controversy with Winthrop, left the country forever. The sentence of Wheelwright was deferred; a synod of ministers was held, eighty-two points of doctrine held by members of the Hutchinsonian party were condemned, and it looked as if peace would return without resort to stronger measures. But in the autumn the controversy broke out once more; Wheelwright's sermon was again called in question, and, as its author was contumacious, he was disfranchised and banished, and soon after betook himself to the Piscataqua. Mrs. Hutchinson was then sent for, and, after a stormy trial and fierce altercations, was likewise sentenced to banishment, and during the winter confined in her house, where she was visited by the clergy, and gradually retracted her doctrines, but asserted that much had been falsely attributed to her. This led to fresh controversy; the government finally interfered, a warrant was issued for her expulsion from the jurisdiction, and she departed to Rhode Island. Some of her sympathizers followed her, some were disarmed and banished, but most of them recanted and made submission. The case of Roger Williams was political; that of Mrs. Hutchinson was both political and religious. Her peculiar doctrines and her sharp criticisms aroused the undying hostility of the clergy, the most powerful class in the community; while the action of Vane and his friends associated her with the opposition to the old leaders. An attack upon the Church, in a community where Church and State were identical, was an attack upon the State; and the fierce dissension which she caused was a source of danger to a colony in perpetual peril from English foes. The government drove her from their jurisdiction—as they had a perfect right to do—because the clergy hated her, and because they believed the safety of the State required it. There is no doubt that it was a vigorous

1638.

and arbitrary suppression of freedom of speech and opinion, and the only question is whether, politically, and as a matter of expediency, the government's high-handed measures were justified by circumstances. No one who looks at the matter from the point of view of the year 1637, and not from that of the nineteenth century, can hesitate in answering the question in the affirmative. The strong policy of repression, at all events, answered its purpose, and peace, quiet, and safety were restored. The colony prospered, legislation was improved, and courts extended; while three thousand additional settlers arrived. Another demand for the charter was made in peremptory terms, and, after a long pause, the court sent to the Commissioners of Trade a firm although diplomatic refusal by the hand of Winthrop; but the Scots were arming, and the matter rested for the time.

Events in England had now reached a crisis, and the Puritan party, **1640.** rising rapidly into power, no longer looked to America for a refuge. The great tide of emigration ceased to flow; but the government of Massachusetts went on wisely and strongly under the alternating rule of Winthrop, Dudley, and Bellingham. The English troubles crippled the holders of the Mason and Gorges grants, and the settlements in New Hampshire—whither Wheelwright had gone, and where turbulence had reigned—were gradually added to the jurisdiction of Massachusetts. In domestic matters everything went **1642.** smoothly. There was some trouble with Bellingham, and Winthrop was again made Governor. The oath of allegiance to the King taken by the magistrates was abandoned, because Charles violated the privileges of Parliament, and the last vestige of dependence vanished. Massachusetts was divided into counties; and out of a ludicrous contest about a stray pig, in which deputies and magistrates took different sides, grew a very important controversy as to **1644.** the powers of deputies and assistants, which resulted in the division of the legislature into two branches, and a consequent improvement in the symmetry and solidity of the political system. A short time before a far more important event had occurred, when the first attempt was made at the Federal system, which more than a century later became the central principle in the formation of the United States. Dangers from the Dutch and the Indians had almost at the outset convinced Connecticut and New Haven that some union of the English was necessary. Massachusetts was lukewarm; but at last commissioners from Connecticut, Plymouth, and New Haven came to Boston, and a New England Confederation was formed. This con-

federacy, which excluded Rhode Island and the Gorges settlements in
Maine, and was styled the United Colonies of New England, provided
for little more than an alliance offensive and defensive, with powers
to make war and peace; but it had a marked effect on the people
of New England—greatly increased their power, and showed even in
those early days the path by which a great nation was to be formed
from jarring States.

The confederacy thus established had at once enough to do. They
remonstrated with the Swedes on the Delaware, who had interfered
with traders from New Haven, and checked the Dutch disposition to
interfere in Connecticut; while Massachusetts herself dealt with the
troubles arising between D'Aulnay and La Tour in their conflict for
the governorship of Acadia. The Bay colonists would not interfere
actively, but they took advantage of the situation to open trade with
the French settlements, and suffered La Tour to enlist men in Boston.
This led to serious political differences, the commissioners of the confederacy thought Massachusetts had gone too far, and at the next
election Winthrop was displaced, and Endicott chosen in his stead.
The opposition to Winthrop and his party took a still more marked
form in Essex County, where a combined effort was made to get control of the government, and break down the power of the magistrates,
an attempt which resulted in failure. Massachusetts carried the same
independence into her dealings with King and Parliament as with the
conflicting Frenchmen. She forbade any attempt to draw together a
party for the King, and although she permitted a commissioned ship
to make a prize in the harbor, she stopped privateering there in the
interest of Parliament. The people were also called upon to deal
with an attempt to introduce Presbyterianism, and break down the
religious franchise. A synod was called, but nothing was done;
1646. and soon after the general court, finding that the petitioners
were about to carry their cause to England, arrested them, seized their
papers, and fined them. When the remonstrants did reach England
the Presbyterians were no longer all-powerful, and a second synod
firmly established in Massachusetts the Congregational system
1648. of independent churches. At the same time a strong effort
was made for the work of converting the Indians, and aid obtained in
England, although the colonists proceeded in all other matters with
their customary independence. Meantime, the confederacy concluded
a treaty with D'Aulnay, who had finally got the upperhand in Acadia,
brought Stuyvesant to terms by threatening retaliation for his seizures

of vessels in English waters, and, after much trouble, reduced to obedience the Narragansetts, who had been restless and dangerous. In the
confederacy itself everything did not proceed harmoniously. The attempt of Connecticut to levy a duty on ships at Saybrook was supported by Plymouth and New Haven, and warmly contested by Mas-
1645. sachusetts even to the point of retaliation and a demand for
the revision of the articles. In Massachusetts itself the party
of Winthrop and Dudley again became supreme, the laws were revised, the revenue adjusted, and a system of common schools estab-
1647. lished at the expense of the towns. Two years afterward
Winthrop died, and was succeeded by Endicott, who, with
two intervals of a year each, held the office of Governor for the next
fifteen years.

The years immediately succeeding the death of Winthrop were
years of growth and prosperity, and of a still further development of
1652. independence. Massachusetts spread her jurisdiction to the
south, and, in the north-east, obtained possession of Maine,
while her population and trade alike increased. With the new powers in England she pursued the same wary and firm policy that she
had employed with Charles. After much deliberation she denied the
right of Parliament to meddle with her charter, and took upon herself
another attribute of sovereignty by coining money. She refused to
enter into Cromwell's scheme of transporting the colonists to Ireland,
and, later still, a similar and more cherished plan in regard to Jamaica.
In the confederacy a like cautious policy was adopted. An alliance
with New France was declined; but in the relations with the Dutch
there was more difficulty and grave dissensions; for after protracted
negotiations the other colonies pressed eagerly for war against their
neighbors, and Massachusetts as steadily refused. The contest came
near causing a rupture of the confederation, and there can be no
doubt that Massachusetts dominated the confederacy by her superior
strength without much regard to the articles of union. She succeeded in her wishes, however, and prevented a resort to force; and, in a
similar fashion, stopped a war which was much urged with the Nyantics. Even Cromwell's fleet could not tempt them, and peace finally
removed the danger before hostilities actually occurred. With Cromwell himself Massachusetts practically maintained the relations of an
independent State. She did not proclaim him; and when a letter
came from the Council of State ordering them to proclaim his son
Richard, it was passed by without notice. In a like manner they

23

remained for three months silent as to the restoration of Charles,
and then news came from their agent that their affairs had
1660. been brought before the King, and that complaints had been
made against them; whereupon a special court was convened, and addresses to the King and Parliament, full of compliment, and praying
for favor, were despatched.

The complaints against the colony came from two sources — the
eastern proprietors, whose territory had been absorbed, and from the
Quakers. The wild fanatics of this famous sect had selected New
England as a promising field, and some of them appeared in 1656 at
Boston, where they were seized, and at once sent back on the ships
which brought them. Then came sharp laws providing for whipping,
mutilation, banishment, and death if they returned after being driven
away. The Quakers were drunk with religious zeal, and came a few
at a time, but did little in the way of conversion. They appeared
naked in the streets and churches, hideous with grease and lamp-black
—breaking bottles, and raising a riot and disturbance everywhere.
The magistrates began with whipping and mutilation. Then the
Quakers were banished, and came back to test the law. Two men
were hung in Boston, and a woman and a man not long after; and
then the rising popular indignation prevailed, the law was modified,
and, although the Quakers were punished from time to time, they
had won their victory. The magistrates, headed by the fiery Endicott and by Bellingham, and backed by the Federal commissioners,
had taken the ground that Massachusetts belonged absolutely to its
people, and that they had the right now, as in the early days, to
put down opposition and banish all malcontents. This policy had
already been successful with Williams, Gorton, and Mrs. Hutchinson,
as well as with smaller offenders. The theory was correct enough;
the difficulty was that times had changed, and the people no longer
were ready to put the theory into practice. Absolute intolerance, sustained by capital punishment, was no longer possible in New England; and the first desperate fanatic who was eager to die was able
to put it down. The Quakers made their way into Massachusetts;
and the Baptists, who were at first arrested and dispersed, not long
after obtained a tacit recognition; while the question of baptism became a subject of heated controversy in the churches of the colony.

It is not to be wondered at that the Quakers complained against
Massachusetts as soon as they found any one to listen; but
1661. the King's answer to the address of the general court was,

nevertheless, very gracious. It came, however, in company with an order to apprehend the exiles Whalley and Goffe, who had fled from England, and had been kindly received at Boston. The magistrates did their duty in the premises so far as they were obliged to, and the royal messengers scoured New England, but never reached the regicides. The government then proceeded to take such wary steps as they could to win favor by condemning the doctrines of the Fifth Monarchy men, ordering the Governor to take bonds of ships under the Navigation Act never before enforced, and by appointing a committee who reported on the rights of the colony, and admitted the duty of allegiance to Charles. Then, after fifteen months' delay, Charles was proclaimed. They disregarded the royal mandamus that Quak-

1662. ers should be sent to England for trial, but modified the laws, and still inflicted corporal punishment. They further sent Bradstreet and Norton with an address to England, where they were well received, and whence they returned with another royal and gracious answer, which, however, demanded the oath of allegiance; that all laws in derogation of royal authority should be repealed; that the Book of Common Prayer should be permitted to all desiring to use it; that the religious test for suffrage should be abolished, and the administration of justice be in the King's name. With the last of the requirements the court complied, despite much opposition, but did nothing toward obeying the other commands, which all ex-

1663. cited bitter discontent. A year later the new court considered the royal commands again, and again did nothing except regulate navigation bonds and appoint a committee to consider the

1664. King's letter. When they next met the committee was not ready to report; but, in the mean time, news had come that royal commissioners were on their way to New England; so a fast was ordered, measures were taken for the safety of the charter, the train-bands were organized, and the defences looked after. Thus prepared, the government of Massachusetts awaited their unwelcome visitors, who presently arrived with four men-of-war and troops for the conquest of New York.

The royal commissioners, Nicolls, Carr, Cartwright, and Maverick, brought a letter to the Governor setting forth that they were to look into the affairs of the colony and their relations with the Dutch and Indians, settle boundaries, and inquire as to the former letter from the King. The commission empowered them to hear and decide all complaints and appeals, military and civil; and there were besides two sets of instructions: one public, requiring maps and a report; and one secret, ordering the commissioners to find out about public feeling, sound the leading men, endeavor to found a revenue or tribute, and obtain for the King the nomination of the Governor and of the officer at the head of the militia. When the general court came together, they passed a resolution of loyalty to the King and adherence to the patent; and they followed this with an order for two hundred volunteers for the New York expedition. They also repealed the religious test for the franchise, and substituted as a qualification that the voters should have certificates of good character from their ministers, and be free-holders rated at ten shillings; and they finally appointed a commit-tee, which, after two months, reported a petition to the King, remon-strating against the powers of the commissioners, and begging in moving terms that their charter, laws, and liberties might not be in-vaded.

While this committee was at work the commissioners and their forces sailed away to New York. The business of settling the affairs of the easily conquered territory, and their dealings with the other New England colonies, occupied them nearly two years; but at last all was **1666.** done, and they assembled in Boston for the final and decisive struggle. Endicott was dead, and Bellingham at the helm. One by one the commissioners laid their instructions before the court, which sometimes received them in silence and sometimes met them with argument. Slowly and with increasing acrimony the commis-sioners went over the failures of Massachusetts to comply with the King's letter. They objected to the new test for suffrage, and to the ingeniously qualified oath of allegiance devised by the magistrates; referred constantly to the independence assumed by the colony; and at last gave notice that they would hear an appeal against the Gov-ernor and Company, and set a day. The time for delay and negotia-tion was past, and when the day for the trial arrived a messenger of the court proclaimed in the street that the appeal to the commission-ers was an infringement of the Company's patent, and would not be permitted. The commissioners were helpless and beaten; so they sent in a list of amendments to existing laws, and dispersed. Cartwright, to whom the papers were intrusted, was captured at sea; and while he waited in England for copies indignation had time to cool, and other events and political changes pushed Massachusetts aside. A let-ter came from the King, during the contest with the commissioners, reproaching the court with contempt for his jurisdiction, and requir-

ing some of the leaders to come to England; but for some months
the court went on with military defences against the Dutch, and then
replied that they had given their reasons for not submitting to the
commissioners before, and had nothing to add. Not long after they
sent to England a present of masts for the royal navy, and prepared
1667. to aid in the war concluded by the peace of Breda. In the
following year, after a long interval, the Federal commissioners met again; but New Haven was gone, and the vigor of the old
organization seemed to have departed. Massachusetts, however, resumed her sway in Maine, which the royal commissioners had meddled with, and faced England with apparently undiminished strength.

For eight years after her victory, Massachusetts was employed in
nothing more important than questions of religious doctrines and the
affairs of the college. It was well for her that she had this period of
rest and prosperity, for misfortunes were at hand, which came thick
and fast when they once began to come, and which racked the body
politic, and put the direst strain upon the strength and resources of
the people. For more than the lifetime of a generation there had
been no trouble with the savages more serious than a trivial quarrel,
which had been speedily allayed. But while New England was occupied with the royal commission, and during the succeeding years
of peace, rumors of Indian plots came thicker and thicker, and seemed to have their origin with Philip, who had succeeded his father
Massasoit, the chief of the Pokanokets, and the old friend of Plymouth. Philip was called to account, and made submission several
times; but at last sure information was received that he was plotting, and the murder of the informer, and the conviction and death
1675. of the murderers, brought matters to a crisis. In June, 1675,
the town of Swanzey was twice attacked, the houses burned,
and the people slain; and this was the beginning of the fiercest and
most prolonged of the many Indian wars in which the English colonies engaged. It lasted for two years, and is one long story of
burning and massacre. The outlying farms were broken up, and
their owners shot down by hidden savages; while the smaller settlements were ravaged and destroyed, and on several bloody fields
the troops were surprised, caught in an ambush, and slaughtered.
Beginning in Rhode Island, the war rapidly spread through the west
and north, and then to the eastward, until all New England was engaged in a desperate struggle against desolation and death. At the
lose of the first year the Narragansetts broke their treaty, but before

they could move the combined forces of the colonies were on the march. The great Narragansett fort was stormed with heavy loss of life, and after a terrible fight the wigwams were fired, the Indians cut down without mercy, and the military strength of this formidable tribe forever broken. After this success the fighting drifted away to the west, and the Connecticut Valley and all the frontier towns were assailed, the war raging with greater ferocity than ever, and with varying success. Gradually, however, the tide turned in favor of the English, the Indians were hunted and attacked in large bodies, and slain by hundreds, for the day of mercy had passed, and the fighting spirit of the Puritans had reached its highest pitch. In the summer, Philip, who had wandered back, with disaster, defeat, and submission on every side, was tracked to his lair at Mount Hope, and **1676.** killed by the forces under the command of Church, the most daring and jovial of Indian fighters. In the south and west the war was now nearly over; but for more than a year it continued in the east, and the settlements in that region were in large measure ruined.

1677. Troops were sent from Massachusetts, and, after much sanguinary fighting, the Indians were finally brought to terms, and the war ended; but this long and desperate conflict fell upon New England with crushing effect. A vast amount of property had been destroyed, and there was mourning in every household. The colonies were loaded with debt, while the enormous expenditure of men and money had crippled the public resources, weakened the government, and depressed the spirit of the people. It was the evil hour of Massachusetts, and the opportunity of her enemies, who were not slow to take advantage of it.

The claims of Mason and Gorges, and the hostility of the London merchants to New England, for her evasion of the navigation laws, were the moving causes of this renewed attack. The opinion of the solicitor-general was favorable to the claims; the Lords of Trade decided that the time had come to regulate New England affairs, and Edward Randolph was sent out as agent. He arrived in the midst of the Indian war, and at once laid before the Governor and assistants a royal letter, requiring them to send agents to answer the claims of Mason and Gorges. He was told that an answer should be sent, and then devoted himself to stirring up a party for the Crown in Boston, working on the fears of the smaller colonies, and preparing complaints of the infractions of the Navigation Act. He finally returned to England full of accusations of all sorts, from coining money to not observing Christmas, and on no good terms with the magistrates. He was soon followed by Stoughton and Bulkeley as agents of the general court, and the last struggle was fairly opened. Into the details of that prolonged contest, covering nearly eight years, it is impossible here to enter. Massachusetts temporized, procrastinated, and resisted at all points, yielding here and there, but rarely in essentials, postponing the evil day as long as possible, and buying off Gorges quietly, to the intense disgust of the King. In England matters went steadily against the colony. Mason was sustained, and royal reproofs came with increasing severity, while, worst of all, Randolph succeeded in building up a party of submission to the Crown, led by Joseph Dudley, and comprising some of the foremost men in the colony. There was no mistaking the issue. The independence of the commonwealth was at stake, and the contest was desperate. At last

1681. Charles sent a peremptory letter, requiring agents to be despatched to give in unqualified submission. The court had to yield, and sent Dudley and Richards, the former unpopular at home, but representing the party of the Crown. They carried with them, however, a letter so unyielding in tone that the King's patience gave way,

1683. and a writ of *quo warranto* was issued against the Company. This writ Randolph took to Massachusetts, where he had worked so well that the magistrates voted to give way, and let the King regulate their charter and their laws; but the deputies stood firm,

1684. and resolved to defend themselves to the last. Their case, however, was hopeless, and the charter was annulled; but before the official announcement reached them Charles was dead, and

1685. James was proclaimed at Boston. By the advice of Randolph a provisional government by commission, with the now hated Dudley as president, was formed, against which the general court protested, and relapsed into helpless silence. Colonel Kirke, who had been chosen by Charles, and confirmed by James as the ruler of New England, was detained by Monmouth's rebellion; and the provi-

1686. sional government went on for a year, doing little, and hated much, until the long-dreaded Governor-general arrived in the person of Sir Edmund Andros.

With the charter were swept away representative government, and every right and every political institution reared during half a century of conflict. The rule of Andros was on the model dear to the heart of his royal master—a harsh despotism, but neither strong nor wise; it was wretched misgovernment, and stupid, blundering oppression, and this arbitrary and miserable system Andros undertook to force upon a people of English race, who had been independent and self-governing for fifty years. He laid taxes at his own pleasure, and not even according to previous rates, as he had promised; he denied the *Habeas Corpus* to John Wise, the intrepid minister of Ipswich, arrested for preaching against taxation without representation, and he awakened a like resistance in all directions. He instituted fees, was believed to pack juries, and made Randolph licenser of the press. Worst of all, he struck at property, demanded the examination of the old titles, declared them worthless, extorted quit-rents for renewal, and issued writs of intrusion against those who resisted; while, not content with attacking political liberty and the rights of property, he excited religious animosity by forbidding civil marriages, seizing the old South church for the Episcopal service, and introducing swearing by the Book in courts of justice. He left **1688.** nothing undone to enrage the people and prepare for revolution; and when he returned from unsuccessful Indian warfare in the east, the storm was ready to burst. News came of the **1689.** landing of the Prince of Orange. Andros arrested the bearer of the tidings, and issued a proclamation against the Prince; but the act was vain. Without apparent concert or preparation Boston rose in arms, the signal-fire blazed on Beacon Hill, and the country people poured in, hot for revenge. Some of the old magistrates met at the town-house, and read a "declaration of the gentlemen, merchants, and inhabitants," setting forth the misdeeds of Andros, the illegality of the Dudley government by commission, and the wrongful suppression of the charter. Andros and Dudley were arrested and thrown into prison, together with the captain of the *Rose* frigate, which lay helpless beneath the guns of the fort, and a provisional government was established, with Bradstreet at its head. William and Mary were proclaimed, the revolution was complete, and Andros soon went back a prisoner to England.

Affairs went on quietly under the provisional government. Increase Mather was in England as agent for the colony, and Cooke and Oakes were associated with him by the general court. In the first burst of joy on the success of the revolution it seemed as if the colonists would regain their old charter, but time passed, the active opposition of Randolph and Andros gathered strength, the King had no mind to give more than was necessary, or to treat the colonies like English towns in a similar condition, and the agents finally had to be content

with a new provincial charter. The absolute independence of the old
1691. charter was lost, but the frame of government was far more
liberal than that of most of the royal provinces. The Crown
was to appoint the Governor, deputy, and secretary, who in turn appointed the judiciary ; the Governor's assent was now necessary to legislation, and he could summon, dissolve, and prorogue the deputies.
The Council, however, was to be chosen by the House, subject to the
approval of the Governor, and the whole power of the purse was given
to the representatives of the people. The religious test for the franchise was replaced by a property qualification, so that religious liberty
was assured. Plymouth, which had grown slowly since its settlement,
but remained weak and unprotected, was refused a charter, and incorporated with Massachusetts, as well as the district of Maine and Nova
Scotia, while New Hampshire became finally a separate government.
Other royal officers, in the shape of a surveyor of woods, collector of
customs, and admiralty judge, were to appear and perform their unwelcome duties in Massachusetts.

The selection of officers for the new government was left to Mather,
who picked out Sir William Phips for the place of Governor, probably
as a man whom he could control. Phips was a native of Maine ; he had
made his fortune by raising a Spanish galleon, his reputation and title
by his capture of Port Royal and conquest of Nova Scotia in 1690, and
his popularity by his payment of the soldiers after the failure of the
attempt on Canada in the same year. He was a hot-headed, energetic,
vain man of slight political capacity, and his administration was neither successful nor important. The opening years of his term were
clouded by the terrible tragedies of the witchcraft delusion, which I
have discussed elsewhere ; while in public affairs a strong opposition
was formed against him by the friends of the old charter, which checked his movements and irritated his temper. He failed in an Indian
expedition, and quarrelled violently and openly with the royal officers.
His political strength was in the country, and he succeeded in breaking the power of Boston by a law requiring deputies to reside in the
town they represented—a pernicious principle of local political residence which has become embedded in the political systems of the
1695. United States. His lack of wisdom and his violent quarrels
finally led to his recall, to answer the charges made against him
in London, where he died in the following year. Under Phips the
current of Massachusetts history changes, and becomes like that of
other royal provinces. The great Puritan experiment of Church and

State united had failed, and was at an end, and the strength of the once all-powerful clergy was rapidly declining. The political struggle was no longer that of Massachusetts against England, but of the people of Massachusetts against the royal Governors, and this contest is one familiar to us in all the colonies.

The withdrawal and death of Phips left the government in the hands of the Lieutenant-governor, William Stoughton, bitterly unpopular as one of the party of the Crown in the dark days when the life of the old charter was at stake. He was chiefly occupied during his term of office with the Indian wars, bequeathed to him by Phips, in the north and east, a part of the great struggle between France and England, and instigated by the French Jesuits in Maine, among whom Stephen Rasle now assumes an evil prominence. After a gloomy but not unsuccessful administration of nearly five years, Stoughton was superseded by Lord Bellomont, who, appointed some time before, had been delayed upon his journey, and then by his government in New York. Bellomont was well received, and the Legislature made him a generous allowance, about which he grumbled after the fashion of his kind, but they refused to fix a permanent salary; and they succeeded also in establishing a judiciary, their former efforts in this direction having been defeated in England. Bellomont favored the popular party in Massachusetts as in New York, and carefully investigated the affairs of the province, occupying himself principally with the suppression of piracy and with bringing Kidd to justice.

1699.

1701.

He appears to have been much liked, but he only remained in the province a little more than a year, and soon after died in New York, when the government once more devolved upon Stoughton, who died a few months later; and in the following year Joseph Dudley attained the summit of his ambition, and came out with a royal commission to govern his native province and that of New Hampshire. Joseph Dudley, untrue to his country and to the honored name he bore, had been the principal leader of the Crown party against the old charter. Rewarded by the presidency of the government by commission and by the chief-justiceship of New York, he had gone to England and been made Governor of the Isle of Wight, and chosen a member of Parliament. Defeated in his hopes by the appointment of Bellomont, the death of his successful rival left the field open before him, and he received a commission from Anne, and came out to rule over his fellow-citizens, who for the most part thoroughly disliked him. Dudley was, however, a man of force and ability, and had certain advantages as a Puritan and dissenter, so that he gradually built up a party bound together by ties of self-interest, but he failed to gain political supremacy, and the people never forgot his past career. At the outset he demanded a permanent salary, which was refused, and he immediately exercised his power of rejecting counsellors, thus opening a fresh and bitter source of controversy. In this same way his administration went on to the end, with constant wrangles about salaries, appropriations, and counsellors, and upon every point on which a difference could arise. Dudley was proud and overbearing, strongly suspected of dealings which savored of fraud and treason, and for which his supposed accomplices suffered, and became more unpopular as time went on, while in every essential point he was baffled by the shrewd, persistent, popular opposition led principally by Elisha Cooke, but perfectly capable of dealing with the Governor without leaders. Cotton Mather, who had helped Dudley to his appointment, found he could not rule him, and the pair soon fell out. The clergy generally joined the opposition, but, headed by the two Mathers, they were defeated in regard to the college, and thus lost their last stronghold. The principal events of Dudley's term of office were connected with the war between France and England, renewed on the accession of Anne to the throne.

1702. In New England this war meant Indian atrocities. Instigated and led by the French, the savages broke in upon the settlements of Maine and the Connecticut valley, pillaging, slaying, and burning in the usual manner, and once more ruining many of the already blood-stained settlements of the east. Colonel Church was sent to the relief of these settlements, but effected little, and the war went on for years with savage reprisals on both sides, but little result, and with the balance of suffering against the English. At last Dudley raised

1707. a force of a thousand men in New England for an expedition against Port Royal; but the campaign was a failure, and the army wasted away with disease. Three years later, with English aid,

1710. obtained by Schuyler and Nicholson, the combined forces of the colonies reduced Port Royal, a success which was overbalanced by the disaster in the next year of Hill and Walker, in which Massachusetts suffered heavy losses both of men and money. The peace of Utrecht finally brought the much needed relief; and after three years more of domestic quarrel George I. came to the throne, the Whigs were again supreme, the complaints of Massachusetts were attended to, and Dudley was refused a new commission.

The government devolved upon Tailer, the Lieutenant-governor, dis-

tinguished at Port Royal, and under whom the popular party had things
pretty much their own way. The principal political question
grew out of the financial difficulties, the debt and the paper-
money of the colony. Colonel Burgess, who received the appointment of Governor, was understood to favor the "private bank" scheme,
and was therefore bought off for a thousand pounds by the agents of
Massachusetts, through whose influence new appointments were made,
and Samuel Shute, a soldier, and William Dummer, a native of
Massachusetts, came out as Governor and Lieutenant. Shute
was an honest man, but with a rigid military sense of obedience to instructions, and of the sacredness of order and discipline; and his throwing himself upon Dudley's party for support, though perhaps inevitable, did not help him. He was not, in fact, fitted to rule over a wary
and astute set of popular politicians, and his whole administration was
made up of a series of quarrels on a variety of points, some new and
some old. One of the new questions was in regard to the forests and
the trees marked by the royal surveyor with the broad arrow for the
King's use. The back settlers, who had won their land by hard fighting from nature and from the savages, had no mind to submit to this
loss of their most valuable export; so while the surveyor, John Bridges,
marked trees, the farmers cut them down, and the whole frontier was in
a ferment. Complaints came to Boston of the action of the surveyor;
Cooke supported them, and the Governor turned him out of the Council, whereupon the general court remonstrated, and printed their remonstrance despite the prohibition of the Governor. They further
elected Cooke Speaker, but Shute refused to confirm him, claiming
that right as part of his prerogative, and dissolved the court, thus
opening a new source of controversy and dispute. The Legislature
had, however, much the best of the Governor in the chronic quarrel
about salaries, and they used this power to hamper him in every
new difference. They not only adhered firmly to their refusal to
grant a permanent salary, but, to emphasize their displeasure, they
cut down the annual allowance year by year, until the Lieutenant-
governor's became so small that Dummer refused to accept it. A
matter of much more serious interest to the welfare of the colony
was the long-standing financial trouble growing out of the expenditures in the French and Indian wars, which bore fruit in debts and
depreciated bills of credit. One party favored resumption in gold
and silver; another desired a private bank and unlimited paper; a
third urged a public bank, with careful limitation and regulation of

1715.

1716.

bills of credit. In regard to all these schemes public feeling ran high. Burgess had been bought off because he favored the private bank, and Shute incurred the enmity of this faction by supporting the public

1721. bank, which was far better, and was at last established, but nothing, however, could check the heedless issues of more and more paper currency, until even the small token-money consisted of ragged bits of paper, and a depreciation set in which was really frightful.

Another source of dispute grew out of renewed troubles with the eastern Indians, who were continually incited to hostilities by the French rulers and the Jesuit priests. Shute urged the establishment of public trading-posts, to stop the sharp dealings of private traders; but his scheme was frustrated by the never-ceasing political dissensions. He also endeavored, unsuccessfully, to negotiate with the tribes, and to send a Puritan minister among them; but they would not make peace, and would not desert the Jesuits, so that at last war broke out, with the usual surprises and slaughtering in the outlying settlements, and bringing in its train a fresh political quarrel. The general court, dissatisfied with the conduct of the campaigns, undertook to get control of the troops, appoint the officers, and coerce and punish them by withholding their pay. They had no possible right under the charter to seize military control; but they crippled the operations

1723. of the war, and finally drove the harassed Governor to England in search of relief. William Dummer, upon whom the government devolved, was a temperate and intelligent man; but he was assailed, as his predecessor had been, in regard to military matters, and found that he could expect no mercy in this respect. He, however, stood his ground firmly, and, after much wrangling, the general court gave way, the contest was allayed, and the war prosecuted with some vigor. In the following year an expedition was sent out, directed against the centre of intrigue and hostility. Rasle's settlement was surprised and destroyed, and Rasle himself, the prime mover of all the burning and murdering, was righteously shot by a Massachusetts soldier. The war went on in guerilla fashion for nearly two years more,

1726. with its usual accompaniments of ambuscades, massacres, and bloody fighting, until at last the Indians, worn out and deprived of their guide and counsellor, made peace.

Shute, meantime, had been at work in London, whither the court also sent agents — Jeremiah Dummer and Cooke — to oppose him. Shute's complaints, however, in many respects only too well founded, prevailed; and first came a remonstrance, and then an explanatory charter, which the court was forced to accept, and which, denying them the right to adjourn themselves for more than two days, also gave the Governor the power to confirm the Speaker. While Shute was preparing to return to the colony, which was well satisfied with Dummer, George I. died, Shute was put aside, and Massachusetts and New Hampshire conferred upon William Burnet, who arrived in the following year, and whose brief administration was one continuous and bitter fight over the salary question, to which the court added the claim to audit the accounts, and forbid the Governor to draw from a general appropriation by his simple warrant. Burnet's instructions were peremptory to obtain a fixed salary, and he was not a man to yield a jot. He combatted the court earnestly and angrily, dissolved and prorogued them, adjourned them to Salem and Cambridge—a new and bitter grievance—and lectured and scolded them unceasingly. The court met argument with argument, were to the full as stubborn as the Governor, and could not be moved. When the conflict was at its height, Burnet died suddenly of a fever, and the court, which had received him lavishly and thwarted him steadily, gave him a sumptuous funeral.

1727.

1728.

1729.

Dummer, again at the head of affairs, refused to accept anything except a permanent salary; and the court, although unyielding here, gave way for the time on the matter of auditing accounts, and supplied the treasury. Burnet's successor soon came out in the person of Jonathan Belcher—a native of Massachusetts—an adroit and not over-sensitive politician, who had of late years taken the popular side, and a good manager, but a man of narrow mind and contracted views. He brought with him instructions as to the salary as decided as those given to Burnet, accompanied with a threat to bring the whole matter before Parliament. The House, however, was not in the least disturbed, but stood their ground without flinching, and refused all compromises urged by the Council, until at last, as everything was at a stand, they sent a memorial to the King, asking that Belcher be allowed to accept their temporary grants. For three years this assent was accorded, and then the Privy Council gave way, and the House triumphed, for they had fairly won the power to keep the Governor in order by an annual allowance. Belcher had undertaken to build up a party devoted to himself by a redistribution of the offices—a proceeding very distasteful to the people—and he had broken the power of Cooke, the popular lead-

1730.

1735.

er, by getting him into a judgeship; but, despite the ill-feeling thus aroused, and the defeat on the salary, he gained a substantial victory over the House as to their right to audit accounts. The Governor was not distressed by an empty treasury, unpaid officials, and neglected public business, but the people were; so the House had to give way, and allow the Governor to draw by his warrant without special act. This contest was revived when war came with Spain, and prevented Massachusetts from taking much part in that struggle; but the victory, on the whole, was unquestionably with the Governor. The chief troubles of Belcher's administration were, of course, connected with the wretched financial condition of the colony, now made worse by floods of bills from Rhode Island; and fresh issues and deeper depreciation make up the history of the currency. In the midst of this a wild scheme of a land-bank was proposed, which was very popular, but did not receive the sanction of Parliament, so that the Company was dissolved. Against this land-bank scheme Belcher set his face, removed officers right and left, and disallowed the elections of those interested in the project, a course which stirred up a host of active enemies; while another source of hostility came from the settlement of the New Hampshire boundary, in which the Governor was said to be dishonestly interested, and where he certainly **1741.** offended many persons. His popularity did not increase, and his combined opponents finally obtained his removal; so that long before he could vindicate himself, his successor, William Shirley, who had lived some years in the province, was appointed.

Shirley found himself face to face with the financial difficulties, enhanced by the land-bank scheme and by the approaching day of redemption, after which time he was forbidden to allow the continuance of bills of credit; but, in deference to the wishes of the court and the popular dread of severe taxation, he boldly violated his instructions, and allowed the bills to be continued. He also succeeded in securing the confidence of the deputies, and in establishing for the first time harmony between the various branches of the government. When political matters were quiet, the province was shaken by the religious revival, and by the work of Edwards and Whitefield, which produced much excitement and some controversy, but did not enter **1744.** into politics. While Massachusetts was thus engaged, the storm of war was slowly gathering between France and England, and broke at last, threatening the colonies, as usual, with the terrors of savage hordes from the north. Shirley, who, although bred a lawyer, was not without boldness and imagination as a soldier, formed an extensive plan for the capture of the great stronghold of Louisburg by New England, aided by the English fleet. The general court, doubting and amazed, fell in with the Governor's plan; an army was raised of twenty-two hundred men from Massachusetts, and some eight hundred from Connecticut and New Hampshire, while the co-operation of the English fleet under Warren was secured. William Pepperell commanded the provincial troops, who were safely landed at Louisburg, where the outlying batteries were stormed and taken, the town **1745.** invested, the English fleet blocked the harbor, and the French, worn down by hunger and fighting, surrendered. It was a gallant exploit—almost the only glory of an unsuccessful war. Pepperell was made a baronet, and he and Shirley were both made colonels. The further expedition against Canada, in planning which Shirley took a conspicuous part, came to nothing, and the truce or peace of Aix-la-Chapelle put an end to a conflict in which New England had suffered much and gained little. Her expenditures were reimbursed; and Massachusetts, to whom the lion's share fell, received her payment in silver and copper, thanks to the exertions of Bollan and Hutchinson. The depreciated currency was called in and replaced by coin thus obtained, laws were passed excluding the paper of other colonies, and the finances of the province were at last upon a sure and strong foundation; but beyond this Massachusetts gained nothing. Peace gave Louisburg back to France, the prize-money was entirely absorbed by the English navy, and Commodore Knowles came with his fleet to Boston, where, as a mark of respect, he sent his press-gangs on shore and seized men for his vessels. A fierce riot broke out in Boston; Shirley withdrew to the Castle, English officers were seized, and Knowles threatened to bombard the town; but the general court restored order, the officers were given up, and the impressed seamen returned. There can be no doubt that the whole movement, though apparently a riot, was managed by shrewd and leading men; and the affair did not tend to increase the popular affection for England.

After the peace, Shirley went to England, leaving his government in the hands of Spencer Phips, in order to urge the fortification of Crown Point; and while there, he was one of a **1749-1753.** commission to settle boundaries with France, which proved futile, so that he returned to Massachusetts eager for a renewal of the conflict between the French and English, and full of schemes of conquest. War was, in fact, on the verge of breaking out, and hostilities which are associated with the name of Washington were already beginning in the valley of the Ohio. The death-struggle of the two great powers striving for a continent was at hand, and into this conflict Shirley, inflamed by his success at Louisburg, eagerly threw himself. He was the most distinguished of colonial governors—sanguine, high-spirited, adroit, and popular in Massachusetts. He took a leading part in the Congress of Governors at Albany, and warmly supported the abortive scheme of union proposed by Franklin. He also had a large share in the campaigns of the following year, **1755.** heading in person the expedition against Fort Niagara, which went no farther than Oswego, and planning that under Johnson, which resulted in the defeat of Dieskau. In all he was sustained by Massachusetts, whose troops bore a prominent part in every expedition. The principal event of the year was the conquest of Acadia, planned in Massachusetts, and carried out by New England troops under the lead of Winslow, who reduced the country and captured the forts. The conquest was marked by the expulsion of the simple and inoffensive Acadians, in accordance with instructions from England, and was due to a policy in which Shirley had an important part; but the terrible scenes accompanying the removal of these harmless people from their homes are dark stains upon the English in the conduct of this great war.

The conquest of Acadia and the defeat of Dieskau, however, did **1756.** little more than balance the awful disaster of Braddock. Shirley, who had now reached his highest point, was commander-in-chief of all the forces, and, at a meeting of Governors, in his usual grand manner proposed three expeditions—against Fort Du Quesne, Fort Frontenac, and Ticonderoga, respectively. His plans were accepted; but confidence in his ability had begun to wane in Massachusetts, where he only succeeded in getting men by advancing to the colony money received from England. The truth was that Shirley's success at Louisburg had created the impression that he was a man of military genius, which was far from being the case. He was brilliant, fertile, and plausible; but engaged in war on a large scale his real incapacity was soon revealed; his enemies, too, were active, and he had hardly begun to use his powers as general-in-chief when he was recalled. Lord Loudon came out to take command of the army, and **1757.** on the death of Phips, the Lieutenant-governor, Thomas Pownall, one of Shirley's opponents, appeared in Boston as Governor. While these changes were in progress, Massachusetts contin-

ued to raise men, and take an active part in the war; but under Lord Loudon matters went rapidly from bad to worse. Shirley's brilliant schemes were abandoned, a weak policy of defence was assumed, Montcalm swept down upon Oswego, and in the following year appeared on the lakes and took Fort William Henry. By subjecting provincial to royal officers Loudon bred ill-feeling in all directions, and this, combined with his wretched mismanagement and overbearing ways, led to quarrels with the colonial assemblies, and consequent refusal of men. The colonies began to look out for themselves without a thought of union, and the frontiers were defenceless. At this juncture Pitt again came to the head of affairs, provincial officers were given proper standing, and twenty thousand men responded to his summons for troops. Ships and men and money, and, above all, good generals, came from England, and the war took on a new **1758.** appearance. Three great expeditions were planned—against Du Quesne, Ticonderoga, and Louisburg. Forbes took Fort Du Quesne, and Wolfe and Amherst carried Louisburg; but the grand army, directed against Ticonderoga, in which were five thousand men from Massachusetts, was repulsed with heavy losses, including Lord Howe, to whom the province raised a monument in Westminster Abbey. The only relief to this misfortune was the capture of Fort Frontenac by the brave Bradstreet, the defender of Oswego, and the most distinguished of the Massachusetts soldiers. Undeterred, however, by the defeat of Abercrombie, Pitt urged on still more ex-
1759. tensive plans for the following year. Parliament, under his guidance, gave money freely to the colonies, and Massachusetts alone raised seven thousand men. The campaign was one of unbroken triumph. Wolfe, at Quebec; Stanwix, on the Ohio; Johnson, at Fort Niagara—all won great victories; while on the lakes, where the interest of New England centred, the French were driven back from Ticonderoga to the Isle aux Noix. The next year Amherst
1760. reduced Montreal, and the empire of France in America fell forever.

Pownall, who had been prudent and popular, was in this same year transferred to South Carolina, and was succeeded by Francis Bernard, the Governor of New Jersey. Relieved from the stress of war, public attention was again turned to home politics, and causes of difference were not wanting. Shirley and others of his stamp had in their schemes of conquest eagerly urged union, taxation of the colonies, and a stronger exercise of the prerogative; while, on the other hand, the attitude of the colonies under Lord Loudon had shown how quickly they would resent such doctrines. The broad views of Pitt, and the enthusiasm he excited, had pushed aside all these subjects of contest; but with the conquest of Canada they began once more to come to the surface. England had already begun to meddle. The iron industry had been checked, and the Sugar Act, raising a revenue on that staple, and thus striking at the chief commercial interest of New England, was revived. Under this act there had been many seizures and much ill-feeling, until at last suit was brought against the officers, and decided in their favor. They then asked for writs of assist-

1761. ance to enable them to search for contraband goods. When the case came to trial, Thomas Hutchinson, the native leader of the Crown party, was on the bench as chief-justice, and James Otis at the bar. In arguing against the writs, Oxenbridge Thacher took the technical position that the writs were beyond the power of the court; but Otis, going outside of this, took up in a speech of fiery eloquence the broad ground that such writs were an invasion of the rights of Englishmen. He triumphed at the moment, but Hutchinson succeeded in having the case continued, and got authority from England to issue the writs. The next struggle was with the Governor, who, by provisions for the payment of the crews of ships, was accused by the House of striking at the right of taxation; but these controversies were only the forerunners of the gathering tempest, and simply show a greater watchfulness and a more ready opposition in Massachusetts than elsewhere.

Far more serious measures were, indeed, preparing in England, where

1763. a new King had come to the throne, and small men occupied the place once filled by William Pitt. Peace, which gave such joy to the colonists, was merely the opportunity for the new policy. A resolution was passed to raise a revenue from America, and the ships of war were ordered to assist officers of the customs. When Grenville came to the head of affairs he turned his attention to the extension of the stamp duties to the colonies; and it cannot be doubted that behind all this was a far-reaching purpose to entirely reorgan-

1764. ize the colonial governments and make them mere provinces. Massachusetts was alive to the danger which threatened her, and the House instructed their agent to protest against the Sugar Act, as well as any other forms of taxation. Still the ministry pushed on. Notice was given of the coming Stamp Act, and a bill raising revenue from sugar and other foreign products was introduced. Excite ment in Massachusetts rose rapidly. Otis used both pen and voice to arouse the people; a committee of correspondence was established; and at last the Governor, after much delay, was compelled to summon the House. After much opposition in the Council, a very moderate address to the King was agreed upon, and the representatives were greatly encouraged by the still stronger resolution of Virginia and New York. Early in the following year came tidings of the passage of the Stamp Act, under the pressure of which public feeling

1765. rapidly rose, and the popular determination to resist became more and more apparent. When the general court assembled the House voted that there ought to be a meeting of colonial delegates; and, despite the opposition of Hutchinson and Bernard, a circular letter of invitation went forth to all the colonies. All sympathized, and eight responded by sending delegates, who met with those of Massachusetts, headed by James Otis, at New York in October. This call was the first formal summons to union, and with that great act the history of Massachusetts is joined to that of her sister colonies.

Chapter XIX.

CONNECTICUT FROM 1635 TO 1765.

THE history of Massachusetts, in its main features and in all external matters—as in the condition and form of its society—is the history of the other three New England colonies, which were offshoots of the great colony of the Bay, and peopled by men and women of the same hardy stock. This was especially true of Connecticut. The Plymouth people and the Dutch set up trading-posts, and contended for the dominion of the Connecticut valley; but the future possessors of that pleasant region came from Massachusetts. Even in the earliest days emigration was discussed in the towns near Boston; and, although the magistrates frowned upon the scheme, settlers pushed out and made their way to the river valley. Two **1635.** years later John Winthrop, the younger, came out as Governor of Connecticut under the patent of Lord Brooke and Lord Say-and-Sele, and, taking formal possession of the country, tore down the Dutch arms and built a fort at Saybrook. Emigration now increased rapidly; and a year later Hooker, the great rival of Cotton in the clergy of Massachusetts—at the head of the whole congregation **1636.** of the Newtown church—journeyed through the woods and settled at Hartford. For a year the little towns thus founded were governed under a commission from Massachusetts, Winthrop's settlement being little more than a military post; but when the time of **1638.** the commission expired the towns chose representatives, and held a general court at Hartford. While the feeble colony was thus struggling for existence, it was suddenly threatened with all the horrors of Indian war. The trouble with the Pequods belonged to Massachusetts and Plymouth; but while it was a peril to those colonies, it meant extermination and death to the settlers of Connecticut, where the savages were already murdering and burning on the outlying farms. The colonists faced the danger with stern Puritan courage. Their fighting men were mustered, and put under the command of John

Mason, who led them against the stronghold of the Indians; and in the desperate assault upon the Pequod fort the men of Connecticut bore the heaviest share, and did more than any others to break the power of their formidable enemies, and give the land the peace of forty years. The order for the Pequod war came from the general court at Hartford; and its results bore heavily upon the settlers, burdened them with debts, and entailed serious losses by the interruption of agriculture. But the men who had overthrown the Pequods were able to cope with any difficulties. They levied taxes, toiled at their farms, and in a short time established a government with the first written constitution in America. The form of government was purely democratic and wholly independent; all power being vested in **1639.** the freemen, who chose the general court, the assistants, and Governor. The first Governor was John Haynes, who had already held the same office in Massachusetts; the second was Edward Hopkins; and these two men were elected alternately to the Governorship for many years.

During the Pequod war another settlement was made in Connecticut still farther to the south. A body of emigrants of property and respectability — under the leadership of John Davenport, a minister, and Theophilus Eaton, a wealthy London merchant — came to Massachusetts. Deterred either by the heated religious conflicts, or desiring to try plans of their own undisturbed, these new colonists did not remain in Massachusetts, but sailed away to the south, and settled at Quinnipiack, on the Sound, thirty miles west of the Connecticut river, where they lived for a year, under no rule other than a compact to obey the Scriptures. They then met in a barn, and, in accordance with the Bible phrase, chose seven men as the "seven pillars," who formed a Church, which, in this most intensely religious of all the New England colonies, was the State, and church membership and citizenship were of course identical. Two months later they again met, and formed a civil government — another independent religious democracy like that of Connecticut — with Theophilus Eaton as Governor. The tide of immigration now flowed steadily; other churches were gathered on the New Haven model, and other towns sprang up. Some fell within the Connecticut jurisdiction, and sent representatives to Hartford; while others for years governed themselves each in its own way. Springfield was resigned to Massachusetts; but the towns of Connecticut steadily increased, and the Puritans spread themselves through the river valley and along the shores of the Sound and of Long Island. Slowly and surely the English, who had come to stay, drove out the Dutch, who merely came to trade; and they even began to encroach upon Dutch territory. Despite their growth and prosperity, however, the situation of these scattered settlements was precarious, for they were surrounded by savages, and next door to the Dutch; so that they felt strong-

1643. ly the need of union, and their efforts finally resulted in the formation of the New England Confederacy, which greatly strengthened the position of Connecticut and New Haven. It enabled the latter to look after her traders in the Delaware, with whom the Swedes had meddled, and it gave both colonies great weight in their difficulties with the Dutch, which now came thick and fast, involving questions of boundary jurisdiction and payment of duties on ships. In domestic affairs the Connecticut people prospered steadily. Both settlements increased, the laws were codified, and government was administered in the most rigid Puritan fashion, and by constantly reelected magistrates.

Notwithstanding the advantages of the confederacy, however, everything did not go smoothly. Connecticut undertook to lay a duty

**1647-
1649.** upon the Springfield vessels passing Saybrook; Massachusetts remonstrated, and the quarrel, which threatened to break up the confederacy, was protracted for nearly two years. The preponderating influence of Massachusetts could not be overcome, and the smaller colonies had to sacrifice their pride, and submit, as a rule, to her dictation. In the year following Stuyvesant came to Hartford,

1650. and soon after a boundary was settled, which was much to the advantage of the English; but still, Connecticut and New Haven remained uneasy and suspicious, and rumors of Indian conspira-

1653. cies, instigated by the Dutch, together with the war in Europe, moved them to put their defences in order, and urge upon the confederacy the necessity of war. Massachusetts held back; her people were disinclined to fight unless the need was very clear, and the proofs of Dutch hostility and Indian conspiracy were by no means indisputable. The commissioners, however, with the exception of Bradstreet, voted for war, and assigned the quotas of the colonies; but Massachusetts refused to be bound, and, with Connecticut and New Haven clamoring for war, it seemed, after a prolonged controversy, as if the union must be dissolved. A similar policy was pursued then, and later, by Massachusetts, in regard to the Nyantics, when the smaller colonies were again compelled to give way. So long as the confederacy acted in accordance with the wishes of Massachusetts, all went well; but when she differed from the others, she was ready to dissolve the union rather than yield.   Despairing of aid from Massachusetts, Connecticut and New Haven at an early day appealed to England for help, and received with great joy the news of the setting forth of Leverett and Sedgewick with ships and men.   Both colonies eagerly prepared for the expedition against New Netherlands, and raised troops and voted money; but peace in Europe came in season to prevent the expedition, and saved the Dutch from the colonists of Connecticut, to the great chagrin of the latter.   In the tranquillity brought by peace, domestic affairs were ordered and regulated, and both colonies continued to thrive as before, and increase in population and wealth.   This was particularly true of Connecticut, who spread her settlements in all directions, and further strengthened herself by choosing John Winthrop, the younger, Governor.

1654.

1657.

The wisdom of this choice was soon shown.   At the Restoration, New Haven and Connecticut found themselves confronted by a Stuart king, and utterly unprotected by a charter, as was the case with Massachusetts.   New Haven hesitated, and only acknowledged and proclaimed Charles after much delay; but Connecticut acted at once.   An address, in flattering language, was drawn up and given to Winthrop, who was despatched to London to present it to the King, and was further empowered to obtain a confirmation of the Say-and-Sele patent, or, if possible, a royal charter.   Winthrop was admirably adapted for the work.   He was graceful, courteous, diplomatic; he not only engaged the assistance of all sympathizers with the Puritans, but by his own address and by his scientific tastes he had won many friends, especially among the members of the Royal Society, just then in high favor with Charles.   By his own skill, and aided by the ministerial desire to break the confederacy, raise up a rival to Massachusetts, and extinguish the intense Puritanism of New Haven, with its religious franchise, he obtained in a few months a charter of the most liberal kind.   Nineteen patentees, and such as they should associate with themselves, were constituted a corporation, under the title of the Governor and Company of Connecticut.   All power was given to the freemen of the towns, who were to choose a governor, deputy, assistants, and representatives, and the only restriction was the very vague one that the laws should not be contrary to those of England. To this corporation was given all the territory from Narragansett Bay

1660.

1662.

to the Pacific, thus including land from Massachusetts, Rhode Island, and New Netherlands, and the whole of New Haven. Winthrop had promised that New Haven should have the liberty of choice; but the people of Connecticut, who received the charter with great joy, had no such views, and set to work at once to incorporate towns and territory in all directions, and to unite New Haven without delay or concession. New Haven stubbornly resisted, and was supported at the meeting of the Federal commissioners by Massachusetts and Plymouth; but Connecticut went on its way, despite the remonstrances of Winthrop, and rapidly drew in the southern towns. New Haven held out through all with like obstinacy, as town after town fell away

1664. from her jurisdiction, until the arrival of the royal commissioners, and their subsequent conquest of New York. Only three towns then remained outside the Connecticut government, and it was obvious that the whole of southern Connecticut, and New Haven as well, would be absorbed in New York, unless the controversy was quickly ended. A consolidation was the only hope of escape, and New Haven, with grief and bitterness, gave way; her government was dissolved, her towns sent representatives to Hartford, and her separate existence came to an end. The union greatly strengthened their position, but they still had to deal with the royal commission-

1665. ers, who, having settled affairs in New York, then visited the smaller New England colonies, reserving Massachusetts to the last. They made the same demands of Connecticut which had been made and complied with in Plymouth, asking that all householders should take the oath of allegiance, and that justice should be administered in the King's name; that all men of competent estate should be admitted as freemen, and to office; that all persons of orthodox opinions and decent lives should be admitted to communion, and that all laws derogatory to the King should be repealed. These requests were not in conflict either with the practice or policy of Connecticut, and were at once obeyed; but they were a bitter infliction to the recently annexed New Haven towns, where a system of Church and State had prevailed even more rigid than that of Massachusetts. But as Connecticut was in the ascendant, her policy had to be followed, and New Haven was left to make the best of it.

Quiet and prosperity reigned after the departure of the royal commissioners, and Winthrop was continued from year to year in the office of Governor. The Federal commissioners resumed their meetings; but the confederacy, shorn of one member by the annexation

of New Haven, seemed to have lost not only its balance, but its activity as well.   The most exciting subjects of public interest during
these years were a prolonged discussion about baptism, which led to
a synod, and a proposition from Nicolls to join in his expedition
against Canada, which met with a very cold reception.   The tranquillity of the colony was at last broken by the reappearance
1673.   of their former foes—the Dutch—and the reconquest of New
York.   The old spirit was again awakened in Connecticut.   She interfered for the protection of the Long Island towns, sent defiant
messages to the Dutch—who treated them contemptuously—raised
troops, and appealed to the Federal commissioners.   Massachusetts,
as of yore, held back, but finally began to arm ; and the Connecticut
forces had already repulsed the Dutch on Long Island, when
1674.   news came of peace, and of the transfer of New York to the
English, followed very shortly by the appearance of Major Edmund
Andros as Governor of New York, which, under the new patent taken
out by the duke, extended to the Connecticut river.   Andros at once
raised his claim to western Connecticut, and sent copies of the
1675.   patent to Hartford.   The court replied that the boundaries
had been settled by the royal commission, and denied that Andros
had any rights.   Hearing of Indian troubles, however, Andros announced that he must attend to the defence of the duke's property,
and accordingly appeared at Saybrook, whither Connecticut troops had
been sent with instructions to receive him civilly, but prevent his passage up the river by force if necessary.   Andros landed, read the patent and his commission, heard a protest read, and then departed, utterly unable to effect anything.

The rumors of Indian wars, which had furnished an excuse for the
visit of Andros, were the first mutterings of the terrible storm of Philip's war.   In that fierce conflict Connecticut did her share of gallant
fighting, although, from her position, she suffered but little from Indian attack, except on her northern frontier, and the current of her
prosperous growth was not seriously checked.   In the first year
1676.   of the war she lost by death her excellent Governor, the younger Winthrop ; but the government went on as successfully and quietly
as ever; agriculture improved, and trade grew and extended.   The only
serious trouble arose from the complications in regard to the Rhode
Island boundary, a tangled dispute which was mixed up with various
other claims by the Atherton Company and by Massachusetts, and
which was carried hither and thither from colony to colony, and from

the Federal commissioners to the Privy Council. Feeling at last ran so high against the Rhode Island people, who continued to come upon

1680. the disputed lands, that Connecticut began to arm to repel the intruders. This induced a pause, and two years later colonial commissioners, appointed by the King, heard the case, and set aside

1683. the claims of Rhode Island, who refused to appear. During all these years Connecticut had constantly given expression to the loyalty which distinguished her from the other New England colonies; and Randolph, then in the midst of his warfare upon Massachusetts, not only left Connecticut alone, but even cultivated her goodwill. At the meeting of the boundary commission, he started an old claim of the Duke of Hamilton against the colony for lands; and though the commission would only transmit the papers, and the case

1684. finally went against the claimants, it remained open, and annoyed Connecticut for many years. Not long after, the confederation, which had been languishing, held its last meeting, and the

1685. death of Charles II. left Connecticut to deal with the difficulties of Stuart rule, which she had hitherto so prudently and successfully avoided.

James II. was at once proclaimed, and loyal addresses of condolence, and congratulation, and beseeching favor were sent to England, where they arrived about the same time as a list of charges from Randolph, who was now giving attention to Connecticut. His accusations involved the crimes of independent government, laws contrary to those of England, hostility to the Established Church, and more of the same sort, with which long practice had made Randolph familiar. The charges were referred to the attorney-general, with orders to pre-

1686. pare a writ of *quo warranto*, and in the following year Randolph sent word from Boston that he was the bearer of the writ. He omitted to state that the time for appearance to contest the writ had passed; but he demanded that the colony should yield up its charter without more ado and submit. Two weeks later he appeared in person at Hartford to urge his demands, and the court replied by a humble address to the King, and by appointing an agent to represent them and employ counsel. They likewise declined to come under the government of Dudley, even at the risk of annexation to New York, and they judiciously tried to keep on good terms with Dongan; but their hearts were heavy, they had slight expectations of justice from the English courts, and the arrival of Andros as Governor-general seemed to put an end to all hopes. Andros sent imme-

diate notice to the colony that he expected the surrender of the charter, and Randolph in insolent terms informed them that an-
1687. other writ had been issued. The government congratulated
Andros upon his arrival, and sent a letter couched in ambiguous language to the Secretary of State, Lord Sunderland, who construed it
as a submission ; but beyond this they would not go. They met
and transacted no business, while Andros pushed intrigues for surrender in all directions, and their agent Whiting, in London, although
with slight hope, succeeded in putting off the dreaded trial of the
quo warranto. At last Andros resolved to go in person to Connecticut, and with a large escort proceeded to Hartford, where he met
the Governor and Council, to whom the court had intrusted the sole
management of their desperate affairs. In the evening a conference
was held, and tradition asserts that the lights were suddenly extinguished, and the charter carried off and concealed. Either the original or a duplicate was safely preserved ; and it is also certain that
the next day Andros took possession, was acknowledged, and appointed counsellors, and that the free-charter government of Connecticut
was, in appearance at least, finally overthrown. Andros interfered but
little with Connecticut, which remained quiet, and bided its time
without murmuring. When the news arrived of the deposi-
1690. tion of Andros, that time had come. The principal men of
the towns came together, the old government with the same officers
was re-established, the courts were opened, the military organization
was confirmed, and a month later the general court again convened,
and joyfully proclaimed William and Mary. The shrewd and conciliatory policy of Connecticut, which Massachusetts had been too strong
and too proud to adopt, had postponed Randolph's attacks until the
accession of James. By this delay Connecticut saved her charter ;
while Massachusetts, where every inch of ground was contested, lost
hers. After the attack was made the same yielding policy was pursued, and fortune also favored Connecticut. Her apparent submission, and the delays of the law encouraged by her agent, resulted in
leaving her charter untouched when the Revolution came. Connecticut, by addresses and through her agent, begged for a formal confirmation, which was never given ; but Increase Mather obtained from
the law-officers of the Crown the opinion, that as the surrender had
not been under the common seal, nor enrolled, nor recorded, and as
there was no judgment of record against it, the charter was intact.
Efforts were made to destroy it, and at one time to annex Connecti-

cut to New York, but all proved futile. The free charter government was safe.

From the accession of William and Mary until the Revolution, the affairs of Connecticut were conducted in the old, simple, and quiet fashion. With the exception of Rhode Island, it was the only one of all the colonies which was wholly free from the contests over salaries, fees, prerogatives, rights, and privileges which form so marked a feature in the colonial history of the eighteenth century. Having a government chosen by the freemen throughout, there was no representative of the Crown to fight with, and no liberties to be jealously guarded, while the dangers of outside interference practically disappeared with the Stuarts. Connecticut readily took part in aiding her neighbors in their difficulties; helping Massachusetts in the east with men and money, and sustaining Leisler by sending soldiers. In the luckless Canadian expedition, which was to have met Phips at Montreal, Connecticut had a leading part, and sharp quarrels with Leisler. She successfully kept at arm's-length the right of appeal from her courts to England, and in the matter of military control resisted the efforts to **1693.** give it to Phips and Fletcher; sending the latter home from a visit to Hartford, helpless and grumbling at the curt refusal of the Puritan magistrates. Free from harassing Indian wars and from the religious troubles of Rhode Island, with an independent government, Connecticut was the most peaceful, the most prosperous, and the happiest of the colonies. Her schools flourished, her towns throve, the franchise was extended, legislation improved, debt avoided, faithful magistrates continued long in office, and great attention paid to everything calculated to improve the welfare of the people. The only troublesome question was that of boundaries on the north and east, which remained open for many years, and gave rise to much heart-burning; until finally, on the east, the Rhode Island construction was accepted.

Connecticut took little part in Queen Anne's war during its early **1707.** years, and refused to help Dudley, for whom she had no love, in his expedition against Port Royal; but that same year, Fitz-John Winthrop, who had been Governor for ten years, died, and was succeeded by Gurdon Saltonstall, who induced the adoption of a more energetic war policy. For the Canadian expedition of 1709, which never even reached the border, Connecticut raised men and money; the next year she sent three hundred men and five transports to share in the capture of Port Royal, and again she sent men under the lead of Saltonstall as far as Albany, to support the disastrous ex-

pedition attempted by Walker and Hill in the St. Lawrence.   Money
1711. for these campaigns was obtained by bills of credit; but the
financial arrangements were so sound that the bills hardly
depreciated at all, and the debt was slowly and surely extinguished.
1713. Not long after the end of the war the northern boundary was
finally settled, and Connecticut gained over a hundred thousand acres.   During this period Dudley was at work against the charter, and a bill was introduced in Parliament to vacate all charters;
but despite this, and trouble with the Mohegan claims, all attacks
were warded off.   During the war, too, the ecclesiastical system was
reorganized, with provision for association, and for a closer union
than had hitherto been the custom in New England; while more important than any other event in the domestic history of the time was
the foundation and development of Yale College.

In the years which followed the accession of the House of Brunswick, there is the same quiet growth, thrift, and prosperity, and the
same uneventful history to be recorded of Connecticut.   Sporadic attacks of varying danger were made against the charter, principally instigated by merchants annoyed at the disregard of the laws of trade;
but they were all defeated by the exertions of Ashurst, and, above
all, of Jeremiah Dummer, the great defender of the charters.   Outside of this there was little to break the repose of the colony.   Connecticut took no part in the wars stirred up by Rasle, and the most
serious affairs were those of the college, the Mohegan claims, the fanaticism of the Rogerenes, and the final running of the Rhode Island
line.   After sixteen years of wise, strong rule, and of great influence
1724. during a period of transition, and often of difficulty, Gurdon
Saltonstall died, and was succeeded by Joseph Talcott, who for
a like period continued in office, until he, too, was removed by death.
During Talcott's long term, the happy period of the *quieta non mo-
vere* policy of Robert Walpole, Connecticut history offers nothing for
record except the more rapid growth of the colony in trade, population, and prosperity, and the quick increase of towns.   The general
courts came and went year after year, made necessary and wholesome
laws, kept the finances sound and pure, and free from the paper con-
tagion, encouraged their college, looked after their rights in England,
and carried on a steady, frugal government, which was probably one
1741. of the best the world has ever seen, and offers no material for
history.   When Talcott died, his lieutenant, Jonathan Law, was
promoted, and Roger Wolcott was put in the place of Law—a change

of magistrates which made no alteration whatever in the conduct of public affairs, but was very nearly coincident with the close of the period of profound peace and the outbreak of the wretched war with Spain, to which Connecticut freely gave both money and men, most of whom never returned from Vernon's expedition. The war dragged along, until at last France entered the field; and the dread of their old enemy, with the still fresh recollection of his terrible raids from the north, roused all New England. When Shirley's plan was **1745.** proposed, Governor Law called a special court, and Connecticut readily sent five hundred men, under the command of Lieutenant-governor Roger Wolcott, to take part in the capture and defence of Louisburg, which reflected so much glory on New England. In the expedition of the following year, which was one of the many fruitless attempts to conquer Canada, Connecticut again took an active part, and raised a thousand men; but peace soon put an end to her exertions, which had burdened the colony with a heavy debt, a source of trouble previously unknown, and one which weighed upon the people for many years. In the great French war to which that of 1744 was but a preliminary, the conduct of Connecticut continued the same. With an independent and united government she was spared political wrangles, and from beginning to end poured forth men and money against England's enemies and her own. The part taken by Connecticut in the French war corresponded with that of Massachusetts, and there is no need to rehearse again the events of that great struggle. It left no mark upon Connecticut except in the loss of life and treasure, and in the benefit less important to her than to others of the removal of the constant peril at the north.

Connecticut was one of the first among the colonies to raise opposition to the policy of taxation, which soon succeeded the victories of the war; and when the news of the coming Stamp Act reached Hartford, able arguments and defences of the chartered rights, and of the illegality of such taxation, were sent to England in charge of the agent, Jared Ingersoll. After this prompt action the condition of public feeling seemed to become apathetic, probably from long years of uninterrupted independence, and from a disbelief in the reality of the danger; so that when the news arrived that the Stamp Act had become law, it seemed as if in the independent colony of Connecticut it was about **1765.** to find its strongest support. Governor Fitch, and many of the leading men and ministers, counselled submission; but they had strangely mistaken the people among whom they lived. The cautious, yielding policy of the previous century had long since ceased to be possible. Articles began to appear in the newspapers, resistance began to crop up here and there, the feeling of hostility, the dread of oppression spread rapidly, and Sons of Liberty were soon numerous and active. When Governor Fitch proposed to the Council to take the oath, Colonel Trumbull left the room, followed by a majority of the assistants; and the arrival of Ingersoll with a commission as Stamp Collector was the signal for a general rising in all the towns. The Sons of Liberty began to gather. Ingersoll was met on the road by large bodies of armed men, and forced to resign his office. His captors rode with him to Hartford, where the ceremony was repeated, and where the timid Governor was instructed in his duty by Colonel Putnam, one of the popular leaders. This event occurred in September, very early in the contest, for Connecticut had no one to thwart the will of the people; and in the following month delegates, chosen by the general court, met with those of the other colonies in Congress at New York.

CHAPTER XX.

RHODE ISLAND FROM 1636 TO 1765.

VERY different from the strong, well-equipped bands of prosperous Englishmen who left Massachusetts to win the region of the Connecticut were those who founded the little colony of Rhode Island. Roger Williams, fleeing from banishment, and from a government to which he would not submit, passed a dreary winter among the **1636.** Indians, was warned off by the Plymouth people, and finally, with five companions, established at the head of Narragansett Bay a little settlement to which he gave the name of Providence. For ten years scarcely anything is known of the fortunes of this small and struggling community. They formed a township where the majority of householders, and such as they chose to admit, ruled; while Williams's relations with the Indians, and knowledge of their language, served to protect them from the savages; and two years after their arrival, another fierce conflict in Massachusetts brought fresh exiles to Rhode Island. Mrs. Hutchinson and her **1638.** friends, acting on the advice of Williams, bought from the Indians the Island of Aquetnet, and formed a settlement at Portsmouth. There they organized a government, with Coddington as judge, and Aspinwall as secretary; but they brought faction and dissension with them, and before the year was out Coddington was displaced, and Aspinwall formally accused of seditious practices. Cod-**1639.** dington and his friends thereupon went farther south, and founded Newport. Emigrants came in small numbers; they acknowledged their allegiance to the King, and wrote to Vane to get a patent. In another year the divided settlements were united, the offices were shared between them, and Coddington was once more chosen Governor. These loosely organized communities went on in this way for two years quarrelling among themselves, until the general court of Rhode Island appointed a committee to take steps to procure a patent. The people of Providence had a similar desire, and

Roger Williams was finally selected, and sent to England to act for
them all.   He sailed from New Amsterdam, and on his arrival
1643.   was well received in London, where his views as to freedom of
conscience were just then in favor.

The first settlers of both Providence and Newport were the extreme fanatics who always come to the surface in a period of intense religious fervor.   They were men and women who could not
submit to a strong and well-ordered government—the factious and
turbulent elements of the rigid, order-loving, and strong communities
of Connecticut and Massachusetts.   Roger Williams, the ablest and
most imaginative among them, had been driven out not because he
believed in freedom of conscience, but because his acts were politically dangerous.   To a man of his liberal but loose mind, the treatment
he had received nourished the belief in religious toleration, and he
engrafted that principle on the settlements he founded, and then de-
viated from it in various ways when he came to face the task of
government.   The other settlers of Rhode Island, less highly endowed than Williams, were far more factious and turbulent; and when
they were driven from Massachusetts, and had no government to resist, they fell to quarrelling among themselves, and kept up their
wrangles for a long series of years.   The disorderly character of
these settlements shut them out from the confederacy, checked their
growth, and produced endless disputes, of which the detailed history
is neither instructive nor profitable.   For the present purpose it is
sufficient to sketch them in the barest outline, and there is no need
to follow them out or attempt to unravel the tangled skein of their
history.

The first serious disturbance involved Massachusetts.   One of Williams's settlements was much annoyed by the presence of a lawless
and disorderly set of men under the lead of Gorton, Holden, and
Greene, who had all been in trouble, and been punished and driven
out of Massachusetts and Plymouth, and who, after figuring in Newport and elsewhere, had finally settled down near Providence, where
they became a curse to the neighboring country.   The settlers on the
Pawtuxet appealed to Massachusetts for protection, and were told that
nothing could be done unless they acknowledged some jurisdiction.
They accordingly came under the government of Massachusetts, while
the affair was further complicated by conflicting Indian claims, and by
a war between the Narragansetts and Mohegans, in which Miantonomo
was captured by Uncas and killed.   At last Massachusetts warned off

Gorton and his followers. Holden returned an insulting answer; and then commissioners came with soldiers, the settlement was broken up, and Gorton and his followers brought as prisoners to Boston, where they were sentenced to jail and hard labor for blasphemy—Massachu-

1644. setts not caring to deal with them for appeals to the King and meddling with the Indians. After a few months they were released, returned to Rhode Island, regained their old influence with the Narragansetts—who were persuaded to put themselves and their land under the dominion of the King—and then proceeded to excite them against Massachusetts. For a time it seemed as if there would be a great Indian war; but the Narragansetts were finally brought to terms, a truce was concluded, the danger was avoided for the moment, and the kindly efforts of Gorton and his friends were frustrated. Gorton, however, who was full of energy, carried his grievances to England, where he got from the commissioners of Parliament an order that his people should be undisturbed, and should be allowed to pass peaceably to their settlements. His further attempts were checked as soon as Winslow arrived as agent of Massachusetts; and when Gorton went out he was arrested at Boston, and released only in consideration of a letter from the Earl of Warwick. He then betook himself to Shawo-

1648. met, which received the name of Warwick; and the turbulent settlement finally gave up quarrelling, and became orderly and decent. The whole of the Gorton affair is typical of the class of people who gathered in Rhode Island. Gorton and his friends were perhaps the worst of their kind, but they were nevertheless representative. They were as sturdy, pertinacious, and bold as the Puritans of Massachusetts, but had none of the love of rigid order or of the strong conservatism which reigned in the Bay colony and in Connecticut. It is not to be wondered at that such people were sharp thorns in the side of New England, were excluded from the confederacy, and led a political existence in which their hand was against every man's, and every man's hand against them.

Before Gorton left America, Williams had obtained through the influence of Vane a patent for the Providence plantations, which permitted the erection of any government desired by the inhabitants.

1644. With this liberal instrument Williams returned, and was received at Providence with great enthusiasm. But neither this generous charter, nor the pressure of outside danger from Massachusetts and Plymouth—claiming all the territory both of Providence and Newport—could unite the factious settlements, which obstinately held aloof from each other, and carried on internal conflict with undiminished zeal. Williams withdrew to the Narragansett country, and was returned as a deputy from Providence, when, after a struggle of three years, a government was finally formed under the patent by a convention of the Narragansett settlements. Coggeshall was elected President, and Williams and Coddington were two of the assistants; but in three years more the crazy structure fell to pieces. Williams strove to promote harmony, but in vain. There were bitter attacks on Coddington and other leaders; it was impossible to get a President, there were frauds in the elections, and men were sent as deputies so unfit that the court vacated their seats. At last everything came to a standstill, and there were renewed efforts to send Williams to England to do over again the work of obtaining a charter. The fanaticism and extreme independence of the settlers rendered them unfit for organized government; and the strong confederacy of the other colonies let them severely alone—content to have a place whither all the disorderly characters who were dangerous to settled government could find a refuge with those of a like way of thinking, and could quarrel with each other as much as they liked.

Coddington, disgusted at his deposition, and at the attacks upon him, went to England, whence he returned with a commission making him Governor of Rhode Island for life, with a board of six assistants to be chosen by the freeholders. This, of course, aroused a strong opposition, especially among the Baptists, who had gradually risen to great importance in Rhode Island, much to the dissatisfaction of Massachusetts, where severe laws were passed against them. This new party, headed by John Clarke, determined to overthrow Coddington, who leaned strongly to the confederacy, and a consequent alliance with the hated colony of the Bay. Clarke and two friends—Holmes and Crandall—at once set out for Massachusetts, to show, probably, the tendency of Coddington's policy. If they wanted persecution, they got it in the form of whippings, fines, and imprisonment; and so supplied with grievances, Clarke started for England, where he was joined by Williams, sent out as agent by Providence and Warwick. Coddington meantime set up and carried on with some success his rather arbitrary government. Providence and Warwick, thus cut off, went on with a burlesque of government under the patent; and when Gorton was chosen president, and felt the responsibilities of office, he proceeded to lay a heavy hand upon his enemies, and degrade and punish them. Coddington by this time was, of course, thoroughly embroiled; and it looked so much like complete dissolution that, with the news from England of the revocation of Coddington's commission through the influence of Clarke and Williams, an attempt was made to again unite the four towns. The scheme not only failed, but produced still wider estrangement, and two hostile governments at Providence and Newport; while, with affairs in this wretched condition, Rhode Island entered into war with the Dutch, commissioned privateers, and erected an admiralty court. This led to fresh wrangles at home, and to piracy at sea—the Rhode Island cruisers preying on French, Dutch, and English, and making endless trouble for her neighbors of the confederacy—until the disorders, indeed, be-

1654. came so bad that they drew forth an angry letter from Vane, the friend and protector of the colony. Armed with this letter, Williams returned to the scene of dissension, and by strenuous efforts brought about a meeting of commissioners and a reunion of the towns under the patent government, in which he was chosen president. Not long after there was a riot at Providence, growing out of differences

1655. of religious opinion, and this produced laws to maintain the peace, and send disturbers to England. Coddington was again fiercely attacked, and with difficulty allowed to sit as a deputy, although he submitted entirely; while a fresh agitation was soon after aroused by William Harris, one of Williams's old associates and admirers, who was a great believer in freedom of conscience, and so hot an agitator that Williams, cooled in his feeling for universal toleration

1657. by the cares of office, had him arraigned for high-treason, and put under bonds for good behavior. This effort to preserve order led to Williams's defeat at the next election, and to the choice of Benedict Arnold as president. The only substantial gain since the reunion was in the annexation of the little Pawtuxet settlement, owing to the withdrawal of Massachusetts and Plymouth.

Clarke remained in England after the departure of Williams, and looked after the affairs of the colony. Through him was transmitted

1660. the congratulatory address to Richard Cromwell; and when Charles was restored, Rhode Island instantly proclaimed him, ordered writs to run in his name, and sent a formal commission to Clarke to act as their agent. Clarke was an adroit and able man; and when the younger Winthrop thought he had settled everything, he found that Clarke had obtained promises which, if carried out in the Rhode Island charter, would greatly curtail the territory of Connecticut. The whole matter of boundary was also complicated by the lands of the Atherton Company, who gained royal favor, and desired to be within the Connecticut jurisdiction. The conflict, in fact, endangered both charters, and was finally patched up by Winthrop and Clarke in ambiguous and impossible terms, which avoided present trouble, and laid the foundation for half a century of tedious, bitter, and ill-tempered dispute. Clarke's charter soon after passed the seals, and the Governor and Company of Rhode Island and Providence Plantations were fairly incorporated. This charter, like that given to Connecticut, was drawn in the most liberal terms possible— establishing a purely popular elective government—while it bore the mark of its authors in the provision that no one should be molested for any religious opinion if the peace was kept. No oath of allegiance was demanded, and free passage through the other colonies was secured to the inhabitants of Rhode Island. The ministry of Clarendon was glad and ready enough to favor the colony excluded from the confederacy of the suspected Puritan commonwealths.

1663.

The charter was received in Rhode Island with great joy, and a government immediately constituted, with Arnold as Governor, and Williams among the assistants. Thus compacted at last into some sort of political system, Rhode Island turned her attention to dispossessing the settlers on the land of the Atherton Company, which had selected the jurisdiction of Connecticut, and to beginning with the same colony and with Massachusetts the interminable boundary disputes. But these little matters of domestic interest were soon overshadowed by the arrival of the royal commission, with general powers to regulate all the New England colonies. The disfavor with which Rhode Island was regarded by her neighbors had been of great service to her as a suitor in England, where she had invariably received generous treatment; so she had little to fear, apparently, from the commissioners, to whom she was perfectly ready to grant all that they wished. Their first act, on their return from New York, was to take the whole Narragansett country —including the Atherton lands—away from all the colonies, on the ground of the cession made by the Indians in Gorton's time to the Crown, and then convert it into the "King's Province," under the temporary management of Rhode Island. In Rhode Island itself all their demands met with prompt compliance, and they were allowed without a murmur to hear appeals in various causes; so that, as may be supposed, their report was, of course, most favorable, and

1664.

1665.

1666.

the colony backed it up with a loyal and flattering address, in which the commissioners were highly complimented.

In the years following this event, Rhode Island went on under the charter government, not very successfully, it is true, but still so much better than before that a great step was made, for any government at all was a gain, even if it was weak and disorderly. The interest in the new system soon abated, and it became necessary to impose heavy fines in order to persuade men to attend to their duties. There was a bitter quarrel over Clarke's accounts, and threats of armed resistance to the assessment laid to meet them, while to all forms of taxation there was a steady and determined opposition. Harris again came to the surface, agitated more violently than ever, nearly raised an insurrection, and was finally arrested on information from Williams, upon **1672.** a charge of traitorous correspondence with Connecticut. During this period, also, a new element came into Rhode Island, in the shape of the Quakers, who rapidly increased, and gained a controlling influence; so much so that Easton, one of their number, soon rose to be Governor. During his administration George Fox appeared in Rhode Island, where he was well received, and was a guest of the Governor; but while he was at Newport, Roger Williams came down from Providence and challenged him to public discussion. The challenge was accepted, and an angry debate of three days ensued, raising to white-heat the old religious discord, and resulting in thick volumes on both sides, filled with the direst invective. In the midst of all this dissension and disorder at home, Rhode Island did not forget her external affairs. She strove to stir up the other colonies against the Dutch when they reconquered New York, and with unwearying pertinacity labored to regain the Narragansett country and push back the boundaries of Connecticut—a vital struggle, in which defeat meant territorial insignificance.

In Philip's war, Rhode Island was the scene of many massacres and **1675-** much hard fighting, for in that region the war broke out, there **1676.** the great fort of the Narragansetts was taken, and there Philip was tracked to his lair and killed. The war was carried on by the forces of the strong confederate colonies; but although Rhode Island sent no troops, her sufferings were by no means slight. Warwick was destroyed entirely, Providence partially, and great difficulty and expense were incurred in guarding the island settlements. In the quickly following struggle with England, Rhode Island fared better, as she was not disturbed by Randolph, and her government and

society were beginning slowly to improve. Clarke, Williams, Coddington, and others of the old leaders died, and the younger generation
was more inclined to order and quiet, and less violent in matters affecting religious belief. The old policy of entire submission and loyalty was steadily pursued, and King James was proclaimed and pro-
pitiated with a humble address; but even this could not save them.
Randolph had neglected, but had not forgotten them; and when Massachusetts was overthrown, he brought charges of illegal impositions,
denial of appeals, disloyalty, and evasions of the Navigation Act in the
usual form against Rhode Island, and obtained a writ of *quo warranto*,
1686. which he served soon after his arrival with Dudley's commission. The Assembly, on receiving the writ, determined not to
stand suit with his Majesty, but sent an address petitioning for a continuance of the rights and privileges of the charter; a course of action which it is hardly necessary to say caused deep dissensions. The
Quakers sent an address of their own, and still another party sent one
in favor of a fuller submission than had been made by the government. The Narragansett country was promptly absorbed by Dudley's
government, while the address to the King served to bring Rhode Isl-
and at once within the commission of Andros, to whom the colony
submitted without a murmur. The charter was given up, counsellors
who never attended were appointed, and Rhode Island sank into a
new and complete quiet under Andros, who devoted himself to obtaining for the Crown complete possession of the Narragansett country to the exclusion of all others interested. When the news was re-
1690. ceived of the fall of the Governor-general, delegates from the
towns assembled, and re-established the old charter government under the old officers, with the exception of Walter Clarke, the
Governor, who had been superseded and now refused to serve, so that
Rhode Island went on for some time without a chief magistrate.

The change effected by the Revolution was by no means so welcome in Rhode Island as elsewhere, for the despotism of Andros had
been wholesome, and had given the colony more rest and quiet than
it had ever before known. But as the charter had never been vacated, the old government, which had been revived by the Revolution,
went on in a lame and impotent fashion, some governors declining to
1697. serve, others serving weakly and unprofitably for short terms,
until at last Samuel Cranston was elected, and continued to be
chosen annually for the next thirty years. Although Rhode Island
was so submissive to the Crown, she retained plenty of her old fight-

ing qualities in other directions. The commission of Phips to command her militia aroused a determined opposition, sharpened by the old and lasting hatred of Massachusetts; so an agent was sent to England, and a compromise effected by which the colony retained practical control of her soldiers. The weak and unsettled condition of her government, however, at last brought Rhode Island into deep disrepute in England, which was especially due to Lord Bellomont, who, full of the business of extirpating pirates, had his attention strongly **1699.** drawn to Narragansett Bay, where the buccaneers constantly resorted. Lord Bellomont went in person to Rhode Island to investigate their affairs, and sent home a report full of charges against the colonists for ignorance, corruption, connivance with the pirates, poor public officers, and evasions of laws of trade. The Governor and **1700-** Council deprecated his action, after some difficulty got an agent **1701.** in England, and passed an act to show an ostensible compliance with the Navigation Act. Rhode Island was at last reaping the fruits of her early follies. Dudley also, who was resisted in his efforts to command the militia, and to check the unlicensed privateer- **1702.** ing in which Rhode Island indulged, sent home, after a visit to that colony, reports as dark as those of Bellomont, calling the province a "receptacle of rogues and pirates." The Massachusetts Governor no doubt exaggerated, but the condition of affairs was wretched enough, and came very near bringing a royal Governor upon them. In the protracted war of Anne's time, Rhode Island, under much pressure, took at first a spasmodic part, and finally sent men regularly for the Canadian expeditions; but this public spirit resulted in the issue of bills of credit, which became a pest to the other colonies, and in a financial condition worse, more hopeless, and more prolonged, than was to be found anywhere else.

Nothing, in fact, could have been more unfavorable to successful colonization than the whole course of events in Rhode Island. Yet, with all this disorder and disturbance, in addition to the unavoidable difficulties of settlement, such was the vigor of the race that Rhode Island grew slowly but steadily; her government very gradually gained permanency and consistency, and an extensive trade in all directions bore witness to an enterprise and persistence which nothing could quench. The colony had its troubles abroad, and its selfish **1722.** policy, moreover, and inherited dislike of its neighbors, did not help it. When George I. ascended the throne, and again seven years later, their charter was menaced, and was saved, like that of

Connecticut, by the exertions of Dummer. Their situation protected them from Indian wars; so that when Shute appealed for aid they considered the matter for two years, and decided to do nothing except inform Vaudreuil, the Governor of Canada, that if he did not desist from his intrigues with the Indians he would incur the heavy penalty of their hostility. Their laws were loose, conflicting, and uncertain, the finances were ruinous, taxation was difficult and slight, and the administration of justice was very poor. The complete religious license which prevailed made the colony a fertile soil for fanatical and peculiar sects, which sprang up, disturbed the community, hurt its reputation, checked its prosperity for the moment, and then disappeared. Nevertheless, there was a steady growth and improvement, sometimes creeping **1724.** and imperceptible, sometimes more marked, as in the franchise which was finally limited to freeholders worth one hundred pounds; and again in the case of the chaotic militia, when, after a **1730.** protracted and for a long time uncertain conflict, elected officers were done away with. Thus the colony went on prospering, developing, and showing the best proof of progress under the circumstances by an uneventful history, broken only by a violent **1727-1734.** dispute between Jenckes, the successor of Cranston, and the Assembly, on the question of paper-money, about which the Governor held sound and courageous views, which cost him his office.

The war with Spain offered a fine field for Rhode Island privateering, and a small body of Rhode Island troops suffered with Vernon at Carthagena. When war with France came, the Assembly took prompt measures for strengthening their defences and improving and increasing their forces. When Shirley's invitation was received for the attack on Louisburg, the Assembly voted one hundred and fifty men, who arrived too late to take part in the siege, and a sloop-of-**1745.** war, which went with the Connecticut transports, and had an indecisive engagement with a French frigate. But now, as at the beginning of the Spanish war, the chief services of Rhode Island were in the risky but profitable work of privateering; and in the next year the colony contributed to the Canadian expedition, and anxiously prepared to defend itself against the expected French fleet.

1747. The year following the long contested northern boundary— although there were quarrels and even riots before the line was finally run—was settled, giving a large addition of territory, and leaving the colony at last with undisputed jurisdiction, and free from harassing controversy. Rhode Island did not reap from the war the great benefit derived by Massachusetts from the indemnity-money devoted to redemption of the currency. Neither Connecticut nor Rhode Island followed this wise policy; the old financial troubles went on unchecked, trade was severely injured by the failure to grasp **1478.** the opportunity, and there was a good deal of distress among the people when the peace of Aix-la-Chapelle was made. The currency, rendered more worthless by exclusion from Massachusetts, went on increasing and depreciating, and the colony plunged deeper and deeper into the inflation policy, which finally brought on widespread distress and many heavy failures among merchants. **1753-1763.** This bad condition of affairs was of course much enhanced by the great war with France. Rhode Island from the beginning to the end contributed freely, giving both soldiers and sailors to the full extent of her power; but all the increased expenditure was met by fresh issues of vast amounts of nearly worthless bills. Insolvency became so common that a general insolvent law was passed; and toward the end of the struggle taxation became a subject of bitter political feeling, which was always familiar in Rhode Island, and which ran very high at this time in the determined personal contest, carried on with varying success, between Ward and Hopkins for political supremacy.

While the peace gave the colony opportunity to regulate in some **1763.** degree its wretched finances, the new policy of colonial rule was begun in England. The first symptom was the increased activity and vigilance in the collection of the revenue, which came home to Rhode Island—wholly dependent on trade, and entirely used to constant evasions of the Navigation Act—with peculiar sharpness. The cruisers ordered to enforce the revenue laws were especially obnoxious, and troubles began with their officers, which increased rapidly in frequency and violence, from threats to open fire from the forts, **1764.** to riots and burning the boats of the men-of-war. By her agent, too, Rhode Island protested vigorously against the revival of the Sugar Act; and when it was known that that act had passed, a committee of correspondence was appointed, and the agent was instructed to oppose both that and other measures to raise a **1765.** revenue. The public mind was fully prepared, therefore, for a vigorous resistance to the Stamp Act when the news of its passage was received. Strong resolutions were passed in response to the circular of Massachusetts; and the stamp-collector, who was also the attorney-general, resigned his new office at once because it was against the will of the people. Riots broke out in Newport, the revenue officers took flight, and an attack upon the royal cruiser *Cygnet* was planned. When the General Assembly came together, steps were taken to preserve order, a committee was appointed to consider the proper course to be pursued in regard to the Stamp Act, and delegates were chosen, who met those from the other colonies at the October Congress in New York.

CHAPTER XXI.

NEW HAMPSHIRE FROM 1623 TO 1765.

WHEN the Colony of Plymouth was struggling into existence, two companies of settlers came out under the auspices of Mason and Gorges, to whom the eastern region of New England had been granted, and planted settlements at Portsmouth and Dover. There they struggled on for many years, hunting, fishing, and trading with the Indians, but making little progress, for Mason and Gorges were filled with the wild ideas common at that period, and believed that gold would be discovered; so that their colonists were mere adventurers, for the most part, who looked to England for support.

1629. When Mason and Gorges divided their property, Maine fell to the latter, and New Hampshire to the former, including the two little settlements, which were each ruled by a separate agent, and which quarrelled heartily on slight provocation. Under these circumstances, the settlements, naturally enough, did not flourish, but exhausted the resources of their founders, who made every exertion to sustain them. The death of Mason, and the surrender of the charter of the Company of New England, left the colonists to themselves; for the

1635. heirs, weary of the expense of the undertaking, withdrew their settlers, and were left with only a claim to a vast extent of wilderness. In the mean time, Wiggin, the superintendent, brought over some puritan families to Dover, where a church was built, and a government erected which was at once torn with controversies between the new-comers and the old settlers. At Portsmouth, a handful of settlers, under the Mason grant, still remained; and in a few

1638. years the Antinomians, under the lead of Wheelwright, fleeing from the stern rule of the Bay Company, settled at Exeter; while in the same year men from Massachusetts, and emigrants from England, founded a colony at Hampton. Thus were formed four independent churches, and four little republics, on the familiar New England model. They were very disorderly little republics too,

1623.

with many hostile, jarring elements, and so turbulent that, after a few years of violent and petty controversy, they came willingly un-**1641.** der the strong jurisdiction of Massachusetts, within which they continued for thirty-eight years. During that time the history of the two colonies is one and the same in all respects, and has already been told. The first warning of a change came with the Restora-**1660.** tion, when Robert Tufton, who took the name of Mason, re-vived the dormant Mason claim. This claim was one ostensible cause of the movement immediately set on foot against Massachusetts, was thwarted by that colony when the royal commissioners retired dis-comfited from Boston, and was warded off for many years. It again became prominent during Philip's war, in which, as in all Indian wars, both then and for many years afterward, the frontier settlements of New Hampshire suffered severely. The Mason claim was again made the first ground of attack against Massachusetts by Randolph, and on **1676.** the report of the law-officers of the Crown that Mason had a good title, Massachusetts was summoned to answer the com-plaints. The court decided that Massachusetts had no jurisdiction **1677.** over the New Hampshire towns, but they also decided that Mason had no claim to the government; and under these cir-cumstances, the King took the matter into his own hands, a commis-sion passed the great seal separating the two colonies, and New **1679.** Hampshire was turned into a royal province, with a govern-ment of President and Council appointed by the Crown, and an Assembly to be chosen by the people.

Of the new government thus established, John Cutts was made **1680.** president, and almost the first act of the province after the arrival of the royal commission, and the formation of the government, was to address a letter of gratitude and regret to Mas-sachusetts, to which the enforced separation was not more grievous than it was to them. Laws were adopted, regulations made, and the militia organized quietly and thoroughly in the manner to which the people had long been accustomed; while a firm and vigorous op-position was at once begun against the meddling of Randolph, who was now collector of customs, and against his deputy, Barefoot. Ma-son also appeared on the scene as counsellor to look after his inter-ests, and proceeded to demand leases for his lands. He was order-**1681.** ed to desist by the Council, defied them, and then a warrant being issued for his arrest, escaped to England. Soon after Cutts died, and was succeeded by the deputy, Major Waldron, who in turn was replaced by Edward Cranfield as royal Governor, whose appointment was obtained through the influence of Mason, and by his surrender of one-fifth of his quit-rents for the Governor's support. Cranfield was one of the typical men of the day—one of the greedy, arbitrary fortune-hunters, of whom there were always plenty about Charles II. His commission gave him power to remove counsellors, and thus incapacitate them from serving as deputies, of convoking, dissolving, and proroguing the legislature, of vetoing bills, erecting courts, and appointing all officers, from the Deputy-governor down. Almost his first act was to remove Waldron and Martyn from the Council, in order to pack that body and all other offices with his own and Randolph's henchmen; but the poverty of the province so annoyed him that he speedily quarrelled with Mason as well, and the Assembly, pleased at this turn of affairs, voted him a gratuity. Cranfield, however, went back at once to his old position, and, as the Assembly differed with him, dissolved them and gave the charge of the fort to Barefoot. This dissolution, a proceeding hitherto unknown, was regarded as so tyrannous that an insurrection broke out at Hampton; but the rising was quelled, and Gove, the ringleader, was arrested, convicted of high-treason, and sent to England, where he was ultimately pardoned. Thus strengthened, Cranfield gave notice that all the inhabitants must take leases from Mason, under pain of forfeiture, which produced, of course, general resistance. The first suit was against Waldron. The jury was packed, Mason had been made Chancellor, and Waldron, not being allowed to challenge jurors, withdrew, and lost judgment by default. The same course was pursued with others; but it had no effect except to excite bitter hatred, for no one would buy the forfeited lands. In all the misgovernment to which the colonies were at various times subject, there is no instance of more unmitigated tyranny and oppression than was used by Cranfield, and that, too, against a people who for nearly half a century had possessed complete self-government. Cranfield and his associates, not content with attacking property, prosecuted Martyn, the former treasurer, excluded Massachusetts vessels from the river, altered the value of coin, changed town boundaries, and would not permit the towns to levy taxes until those of the province had been paid. The burden at last became so heavy that the people secretly raised money, and sent Nathaniel Weare to England to plead with the King. Soon after Cranfield, compelled by necessity and impending war, called the Assembly together; but they would not

1682.

1683.

1684.

do his bidding, and were dissolved. Not satisfied with what he had accomplished thus far, he now struck at religion, demanding that Mr. Moody, the Portsmouth minister, should give the Communion to him in the Episcopal form. Moody refused, was convicted under the Act of Uniformity, sentenced to prison for six months, and his "benefice" forfeited, while the magistrates who dissented from the decision were deposed, and the clergyman at Hampton, upon whom the same demand had been made, fled to Boston. Not long after Cranfield took the last step in his course of oppression by levying taxes without the consent of the Assembly. Meantime Weare had gained a hearing from the Privy Council, who sent word to Cranfield that he must not attempt to crush the presentation of the case against him. Disgusted with his failure to make money, Cranfield had already asked leave to withdraw, and this order in Council was not an agreeable addition. Worst of all, the illegal taxes led to a general revolt, the collectors were assaulted, abused, and beaten, and the troops refused to turn out. Permission to retire came when this turbulence was **1685.** at its height, and Cranfield hastily departed to the West Indies, leaving Barefoot as deputy at the head of the government; a change which was no improvement, and the disturbance went on until New Hampshire was again united to Massachusetts, under the government of Dudley and the commission. The old union, renewed under such different and unhappy circumstances, continued unbroken through the tyranny of Andros, and was cemented by the re-establishment of the old and beloved charter government, when New **1690.** Hampshire, asking to again be incorporated, was admitted as before, and everything went on in the old fashion.

This popular arrangement was not destined to long continuance, for the new government in England refused to include New Hampshire within the jurisdiction of Massachusetts. It was determined **1692.** to erect a separate government, and Samuel Allen, who had bought up the Mason claims, was made Governor, and his son-in-law, John Usher, his lieutenant, to act in his absence. Usher at once entered upon his government, which was upon the model common in the royal provinces. His administration was disturbed and unprofitable. The long Indian wars of the east had begun, and they fell with terrible force upon the exposed New Hampshire towns. The people were poor, and the growth of the colony slow. The iron courage and persistence of the settlers alone kept them up against the enduring warfare of the savages. They took land where they desired, won it from the wilderness, and paid for it with hard fighting, so that they naturally resisted stoutly all the attempts of Usher to assert proprietary rights in the soil. Usher was active in providing for defence; but he was in conflict with the people about lands, and most unwisely became embroiled with Phips when the strength of Massachusetts alone could avail against the Indians. His position was certainly not attractive. The people were very poor, the revenue was very slender—not enough to pay for defences—the Assembly would give him nothing; and as his father-in-law, Allen, was equally obdurate, Usher asked to be

1697. relieved. A successor, William Partridge, the treasurer of the province, was, however, already on the way; but when he arrived Usher found his dislike of office vanish, disputed Partridge's credentials, and resumed control of the province. A letter from the Lords of Trade confirming Partridge drove Usher into retirement, and soon

1699. after Lord Bellomont appeared as Governor, and was formally proclaimed, with Partridge as his lieutenant. Bellomont was popular in New Hampshire as elsewhere, and the Assembly gave liberally from their scanty resources, but were absolutely unable to take the measures of defence which their Governor thought proper. They were further troubled by Allen and his land claims, which made but

1702. slow progress among the sturdy frontiersmen; and, after much discussion, the question was taken to England shortly after the death of Bellomont, Usher going to represent Allen, and Vaughan the province.

The policy of confiding New Hampshire to the Governor of Massachusetts, which was begun with Bellomont, was continued in England. Dudley, although disliked in Massachusetts, was not unpopular in the smaller colony, where the Assembly gave five hundred pounds for

1703. fortifications, and voted further a fixed annual salary of one hundred and sixty pounds. This secured the Governor's goodwill, although he complained on other points; for New Hampshire, while yielding on the salary question, was as ill-behaved as Massachusetts and other colonies in her disregard of the laws of trade. Par

1704. tridge was replaced by Usher as Lieutenant-governor, which was in practice the executive office of the province. The troublesome question of the Mason claims continued to be the most important matter in public affairs, while Queen Anne's war kept alive the normal and distressing hostilities of the Indians. The province was too poor to lend aid to the Canadian expeditions; but the settlers fought on doggedly in defence of their homes, supported by Massachusetts, and no part of New England suffered more than New Hampshire through all those trying years. The Allen claim, sent back by the Privy Council to the provincial courts, was decided there adversely to the claimants; and, in order to avoid another appeal, the province offered to concede all the wild lands, to give five thousand acres in the settled districts for a quit-claim deed of the rest, and, in addition, they agreed to pay two thousand pounds. Allen died before he could accept this generous offer, and the litigation was inherited by his son, who obtained a royal order for a new trial, with instructions for a special verdict. Again Waldron's title, which made the test case, was tried, and once more the jury, disregarding orders, refused a special verdict, and gave a general one in favor of the defendant. Before another appeal could be taken, Allen's son died; his heirs were minors, who did not push the controversy, and the claim sank out of sight, **1715.** to the great relief of the New Hampshire people, whose right to their homes had been so long in contest.

The second administration of Usher closely resembled the first. He carried on the Indian wars with energy and activity; but he soon quarrelled with the people, and also with Dudley, by whom he had at the outset been favored. The personal controversy became very bitter, and Dudley forced Waldron, Usher's principal opponent, into the council. Attacked on all sides, Usher fell from power with Dudley, whom the province had steadily supported after the death of Anne, and, being replaced by George Vaughan, retired to his home in Massachusetts. Vaughan was popular in the province, but he got on no better with his superior officer, Governor Shute, than Usher had with Dudley. Shute had early difficulties with the Assembly in regard to money, and Vaughan, carried away by the apparent strength of his position, refused to obey Shute's orders unless he was actually present in the province; going so far in his disobedience and opposition that he even lost his hold partially upon the people, while the com- **1717.** plaints of Shute were listened to in England and caused his removal. He was succeeded by John Wentworth, a native of the province, and a wealthy merchant, who administered his trust well for thirteen years, and desisted from opposition to his superior officer. The respite at this period from Indian wars gave the colony opportunity for growth and improvement, and the hardy settlers were not slow to take advantage of the first opening thus afforded by peace. Trade was rapidly developed, farms and settlements extended, and population increased. A company of Irish Presbyterians came out, and Wentworth, brushing aside the old claims which seemed about to revive, gave them lands on the Merrimac, where they founded the thriving town of Londonderry. With increase of strength there was an increase of the natural opposition to the royal government; and the conflict in regard to the surveyor of woods was especially fierce in New Hampshire, where they never ceased from their attacks upon these officers of the Crown. They remonstrated with Shute for not

1722. calling a new Assembly for five years; and when the new Assembly met, they opened the question of a fixed salary, taking the ground of Massachusetts. On Shute's departure, Wentworth was left at the head of the administration, and for six years he conducted the affairs of the province as a separate government. The war incited by Rasle in the east fell, as usual, most heavily upon New Hampshire, whose history for half a century, indeed, was little more than that of a life-and-death struggle with the savages. The death of Rasle brought relief and comparative quiet, which was assured by the treaty

1725. made by Dummer at Falmouth, and the Assembly then continued their contest over the salary, insisting on the principle of an annual allowance, and subsequently passed an act limiting the

1727. life of an Assembly to three years, and made a fruitless struggle over the Governor's power to negative the choice of a speaker, a point settled by the Explanatory Charter of Massachusetts.

1728. The contest thus begun went on with increasing vehemence and obstructions on both sides, until the House voted an address to the King, praying for annexation to Massachusetts; and it was while matters were in this condition that the arrival of Burnet again brought the two provinces under one head. Burnet had the same instructions in regard to New Hampshire as to Massachusetts touching the salary question, but he encountered no opposition with the Assembly of the former, who voted him an annual salary of two hundred pounds while he remained in office.

Belcher's administration, which followed that of Burnet, was a period of violent political controversy. The Governor, after his man-

1730. ner, went to work at once to build up a party in his own interest, a project in which he was largely successful. He quarrelled with Wentworth, whom he wished to reduce to insignificance and dependence; but Wentworth's death, instead of clearing his path, only made way for a much more obnoxious and combative man — one David Dunbar, an Irishman — who had been appointed surveyor of woods, and was already cordially disliked in Massachusetts on account of attempted settlements and land speculations to the eastward, and through efforts to disturb the Massachusetts post at Pemaquid. His schemes had been frustrated, and Belcher had worked against his appointment, **1731.** so that he took office with strong feelings of enmity toward his superior. He at once set up the old claim to independent action, when the Governor was not in the province, and succeeded in getting a following which was strong enough to control the House. Belcher's party desired annexation to Massachusetts, a scheme not liked in England, where an unchartered royal province was highly prized; while, on the other hand, Dunbar's party wished that there should be a complete separation of the provinces, and that New Hampshire should have a Governor of her own. The principal objection to separation lay in the poverty of the smaller colony. Governor and Lieutenant worked incessantly for each other's removal, and Dunbar, by his control of the Assembly, kept the treasury empty, and hampered Belcher at all points. The final settlement by the royal commission of the eastern boundary dispute with Massachusetts in favor of New Hampshire, and a series of defeats by Belcher's use of his higher powers, **1737.** drove Dunbar to Pemaquid to surveys of the woods, and more difficulties, and finally to England to seek promotion. He there renewed his fight against the Governor, and it was largely through **1741.** his exertions that Belcher, who had become unpopular in both provinces, was at last removed.

The favorable decision of the King in the previous year in regard to the boundaries added territory to New Hampshire, and strengthened the province. Dunbar's policy, backed by the popular party, prevailed, and Benning Wentworth, the true leader of that party, returned from England as royal Governor, and was welcomed with enthusiasm at Portsmouth. The long political battle was at an end, and the colony had an opportunity for quiet and for rapid progress, which en- **1745.** abled her to send three hundred men to take an active and conspicuous part in the siege of Louisburg. Encouraged by this success, the province readily voted men and money for the abortive expedition against Canada; but her strength was fully employed in preparing to repel the French fleet, and in meeting the inevitable Indian war which then and for some years longer devastated the frontier. In the midst of the conflict the Mason claim was **1749.** bought up by a company which at once released the already settled lands, and that vexed question was, after more than a century of dispute, disposed of. The return of peace gave room for controversies between the Governor and Assembly, which had been suspended by the exigencies of war. The Governor, desiring money for fortification which the Assembly would not give, undertook to enlarge the representation and pack the House, a proceeding which the Assembly stubbornly resisted. No more vital point of attack could have been chosen; and, unjust as the Governor's claim undoubtedly was, it had a practical force from the unfortunate fact that the right of representation rested only on his commission and instructions. After a deadlock of three years, during which public business was para-

1752. lyzed, the treasury empty, and the soldiers unpaid, a new Assembly met, the matter of representation was adjusted, and quiet was restored. Despite the political struggle, which, indeed, showed the increasing strength of the colony, and of a popular party, the province rapidly gained ground; the population increased to thirty thousand, new settlements sprang up, and Wentworth began to make lavish grants in Vermont, already claimed by New York, and which were a fruitful source of future difficulty.

In the French war New Hampshire took an active part, contributing freely both men and money, although the Indians broke out at once on her frontiers, and renewed the familiar scenes of massacre and pillage. No colony sent better troops into the field; and her "Rangers," inured to savage warfare, gained a continental reputation. Peace brought a fresh rush of immigration, and a renewal of grants, a source of great emolument to the Governor, who contended stoutly with the Governor of New York for the profits from the Vermont lands, which were fast bringing on a conflict in which an actual resort to force seemed probable. But while the colony was thus rapidly prospering the new policy of taxation was begun, and feeling rose in New Hampshise as in the other colonies. Less secure in her rights than her neighbors, and with an able and experienced Govern-

1765. or, the action of the people was crippled, and Wentworth succeeded in preventing the choice of delegates in response to the Massachusetts circular. New Hampshire was not represented at New York; but the excitement against the Stamp Act could not be checked; there were outbreaks at Portsmouth, and Meserve, the collector, was forced to resign. Thus New Hamshire drifted into the movement and the general policy which united the colonies, and prepared the way for the overthrow of the English power in America.

Chapter XXII.

NEW ENGLAND IN 1765.

The last group of English colonies in America were those whose political history has been briefly traced in the preceding chapters, known collectively as New England, and comprising, at the time of the Revolution, Massachusetts, New Hampshire, Rhode Island, and Connecticut. Massachusetts then included what is now the State of Maine, and New Hampshire had claims to what afterward became part of Vermont. These colonies, in the same latitude as New York, occupied until the conquest of Canada, the most eastern portion of the British dominion in America. In Vermont and the valley of the Connecticut river were farming lands of fair quality, and scattered here and there through New England were tracts of more or less fertility; but the soil generally was thin and poor. Great rock formations, lying near the surface, were everywhere predominant. North of Cape Cod the shore was rugged and forbidding; while to the southward sand ran from the beaches many miles inland, and treacherous shoals infested the approaches to the coast. There were vast and noble forests, affording a generous supply of timber, fine rivers with plenty of undeveloped water-power, and ample and safe harbors; but there was nothing else. The climate was one of violent extremes, with magnificent summers and autumns, terrible winters, and harsh, inclement springs. Nature gave almost nothing; and all that man obtained in New England had to be won by unflinching and incessant toil. Not wealth and prosperity merely, but even a bare subsistence had to be wrung from a niggardly soil, and from the cold and stormy sea which washed the coasts and lashed the jagged cliffs.

In this region Englishmen made their homes, founded and built up rich and powerful States, and covered the land with prosperous villages, and the coasts with thriving towns. The people who did this were of pure English race. Between the years 1629 and 1639— during the period of Strafford and Laud's supremacy—twenty thousand Puritans came to America; and from these twenty thousand, and from a small but steady immigration of exactly the same kind during the seventeenth century, sprang the people of New England. There came also a few Normans from the Channel Islands, some Huguenots from France, and some Scotch-Irish to New Hampshire— all excellent elements, sturdy and vigorous, but so trifling in amount that they produced no effect upon the general character of the population. At the time of the Revolution the people of New England were pure Englishmen, the purest part of the race, perhaps; for during a century and a half they had lived in a New World, and received no infusion of fresh blood from any race but their own. This purity of race, free from any admixture, was something unknown in the middle provinces, and was by no means equalled in the south, even in Virginia, where the foreign elements were practically unimportant. It formed a conspicuous characteristic of the New England people, and was fully recognized in the other provinces, where it was one cause of the dislike not uncommonly felt toward the inhabitants of the eastern colonies.[1]

Purity of race simplifies in one important point the difficulty of any attempt to revive the New England of the past; but there is also uniformity in many other ways, which not only enables us to treat the New England colonies as one province, but which makes easy the effort to understand and appreciate their social and political condition in the last century. Race, language, religious belief, manners, customs, and habits of mind and thought were the same from the forests of Maine to the shores of Long Island Sound. In some respects the people of the large coast towns differed from those of the inland villages, as city always differs from country, and there was still further difference between the old settlements and those of the northern frontier; but these differences were of degree only, and not essential. Other variations may be discovered on close investigation, but they are so slight as to be of no practical value, and do not affect the general proposition. The only important exception to the predominant uniformity was in the case of Rhode Island, where in early times not only the more liberal in religious matters, but the radical, disorderly, restless elements of the Puritan communities to the north and west, had found an abiding place. The result was, that this little colony was for many years the scene of faction and turbulence; a

---

[1] Crévecœur, The American Farmer, p. 48; Rochefoucauld, ii., 214.

sharp thorn in the sides of its neighbors; a constant source of trouble, and of little comfort or value to itself or anybody else. But the stock was good, and Rhode Island gradually settled down into a thriving and prosperous community. The old spirit of faction and pettiness broke out from time to time, notably under the confederation, and in the refusal to accede to the Constitution; but the best trait of the early differences, that of religious toleration, was the longest lived and the most prominent, as was shown in the diversity of belief, and in the many sects which flourished in Rhode Island. Except in this particular, it did not at the time of the Revolution differ materially from the rest of New England.

At the outbreak of the Revolution, the total population of New England did not fall far short of seven hundred thousand. Massachusetts and the district of Maine had over three hundred thousand inhabitants, Connecticut two hundred, New Hampshire seventy-five, and Rhode Island over fifty thousand. In New Hampshire there were some seven hundred slaves, in Massachusetts about five thousand, in Connecticut about six thousand, and in Rhode Island perhaps half that number. Here too, therefore, was an important variation from the other colonies in the insignificance of a servile and inferior race.[1]

Community of race was strengthened, and its effects increased by community of class. The settlers of New England were drawn from the country gentlemen, small farmers, and yeomanry of the mother country. In England they formed the famous "country party" which sent Hampden, Pym, and Cromwell to the House of Commons, and fought afterward the battles of the Long Parliament in the field. Many of the emigrants were men of wealth, as the old lists show, and all of them, with few exceptions, were men of property and good

[1] Some of the best estimates and most exact statistics of the population of New England are as follows: New Hampshire, Burnaby, p. 151, 1759—40,000; Census of 1774, Prov. Paper, x., 636—72,000 whites, 674 blacks; Massachusetts, Burnaby, 136—200,000, 40,000 bear arms; 1763, Barry's Hist., ii., 272—245,000 whites, 5000 blacks; Rhode Island Col. Records, 1749, v., 270—28,000 whites, 3000 blacks; Memoirs of Elkanah Watson, 1778—60,000; Burnaby, p. 121, 1759—35,000 whites, several hundred blacks; Connecticut, Mass. Hist. Soc. I., vii., 1773—191,000 whites, 6000 blacks; Hinman, Conn. Antiq., p. 362, Governor to Lords of Trade, 70,000 whites, 1000 blacks, militia 10,000; Fowler's Hist. of Durham, Governor's letter, 1774, to Lords of Trade, 191,000 whites, 6000 blacks; New Hampshire Hist. Coll., i., 227, 1730—10,000 whites, 200 blacks; Mass. Hist. Coll., I., iv., 196, 1763—5000 slaves, 45 whites to 1 black.

standing. They did not belong to the classes from which emigration is usually supplied, for they all had a stake in the country they left behind them. This apparent anomaly was due to the causes which led to their emigration. /They left England not for the sake of adventure, discovery, or trade, but solely from political and religious motives; and in this fact is to be found the reason of the high average and even quality of the Puritan emigration to New England./ They felt this strongly themselves, and were encouraged in their notions by their peculiar religious views. "God sifted a whole nation," said stern old Governor Stoughton, "that he might send choice grain over into this wilderness." Such was the rooted belief of the people of New England, and there was in it a large element of truth, for there has never been in modern times such an emigration from one country to another. This strong pride of race and origin has been one reason for the unpopularity of the people of New England in later as well as in colonial times; but it was then, as in Virginia, and in all parts of the world, one of the characteristics of a superior and dominant race, and is one important secret of their success.[1]

Such were the people who sought to found States in New England. Material success was more difficult of attainment than political, and had to be extorted from an unfriendly soil and a stormy ocean. The first resort of the colonists was agriculture, which they soon supplemented by trade; and from the latter, wholly the result of their own skill and energy, they derived their wealth. The interests of the population were pretty evenly divided between these two branches of industry. In New Hampshire the colonists were for the most part farmers; in Maine and Massachusetts the people were divided; in Rhode Island trade predominated; and in Connecticut agriculture. Except in the latter colony, the farms produced little more than a comfortable subsistence for their owners, and the methods of cultivation, on account of the poor character of the soil, were superior to those in use elsewhere. In the valley of the Connecticut and in the province of the same name, land was better, and farming much ruder and more profitable than to the north. The chief products were hay, grain, and cattle, which were exported to New York, Philadelphia,

---

[1] As to the wealth, position, and character of the Puritan emigrants, proofs abound; but see, *e. g.*, Hollister's History of Connecticut, i., 419, and New England Genealogical Register, vol. xxx., 155.

and the West Indies, and which found an outlet through Boston, Rhode Island, and New York, and sometimes by small craft, which ascended the rivers and took ventures from the farmers, to the West Indies, bringing back slaves or casks of sugar. In this way a frugal and hard-working population derived a subsistence from the soil of New England, while their wealth came from the sea. The principal source of profit was in the whale and cod fisheries. The homes of the fishermen lined the coast of New England, and they ventured in the severest weather to the dangerous regions of the Great Bank. The fisheries of Massachusetts alone were estimated to be worth two hundred and fifty thousand pounds a year. The fish thus caught were dried, and exported in vast quantities—the best to Spain and Portugal, the poorer to the West Indies—and formed the principal article of export; but there were besides fish-oil, timber, and ships built in the ports of Maine and Massachusetts. Wines were brought back in return from Madeira and Malaga, and sugar and molasses from the West Indies, to be distilled into rum, some of which was consumed in New England and some re-exported. The bulk of the return cargoes, however, consisted of manufactures, and the balance was heavily against the colonists. The exports of New England in the year 1770 were only one hundred and fifty thousand pounds, while the imports were nearly four hundred thousand; a great gap which was filled up by the carrying-trade, developed entirely by the native energy of the people. They not only carried for the other colonies, especially for those to the south, but for Europe as well. The New England captain would take his cargo of fish to the West Indies, load with the products of the island, carry them to Europe, and after selling not only the cargo, but frequently his vessel, would charter an English ship and come home with British manufactures. The foreign commerce of Boston alone employed six hundred vessels, and more than a thousand were engaged in the fisheries and coast trade. The little colony of Rhode Island, with narrow limits and sterile soil, offered the best example of this untiring energy. By carrying the products of her neighbors and of foreign countries, she became a prosperous State, although it is to be feared that the traffic was not always as honest as it was profitable; for, in addition to slave-carrying to and from the West Indies and the southern provinces, there was a great deal of smuggling and privateering. Newport was stigmatized at one time with more force, perhaps, than justice, as a nest of corsairs, and the famous Godfrey Malbone was said to have gained his great wealth from illicit trade. This, however, was exceptional. The trade of New England was, as a rule, honest and fairly earned, and is the greatest proof of the enterprise and sagacity of the people.

The hard struggle for existence which nature had forced upon New England led to the development of other fields. Every man almost was of necessity a mechanic, and learned to work with poor and coarse tools with a remarkable degree of success. The result of this was remarked by foreign travellers, to whom the New England villages recalled Europe, and who noted the streets lined with shops where every form of trade was busily plied. In this intensity of industry the germs of the great manufacturing interests of New England may be readily traced; but at the time of the Revolution, thanks to the policy of the mother country, they amounted to little. There was no mineral wealth, and copper was unprofitable; but iron was mined in Connecticut, and both there and in Massachusetts worked from early times with encouraging success. The rivers turned the wheels of saw and grist mills, which were common everywhere, timber was cut for exportation, and corn ground not only for the native farmers, but for the inhabitants of other colonies. Other industries were in their infancy. Paper was made in small quantities, and beaver hats of coarse quality were manufactured. Linens and coarse woollens were made chiefly by Scotch-Irish in Massachusetts and New Hampshire; leather was prepared by tanners and curriers, who did a thriving business; and there were several large distilleries of New England rum. Domestic manufactures were, however, the most important, and were so large as to make New England far more independent and self-supporting than any of the other colonies, and to such an extent that the conflict with the mother country told less severely upon her resources than on those of her neighbors. Common furniture, implements, and utensils were almost always made by the farmer and his sons, who needed them; and almost all the clothing, from dressing the flax to cutting the cloth, was made by the women of the family. In every household the spinning-wheel was conspicuous, and homespun and coarse linen, and on the frontier dressed deer-skin, were universally worn. This simplicity of dress was due in large measure to the evenness of social condition, which made it possible; but it was part also of the general result of a struggle for existence and material prosperity so hard that nothing was too trifling to be passed over, and in which every opportunity was turned to the best account. To this struggle, too, is due the versatility and quickness of mind and body, well exemplified in the trade and man-ufactures of colonial New England, which became and has continued to be during a century a national characteristic.[1]

The governments of the New England provinces differed among themselves, and still more from those of the other colonies. When New Hampshire was taken from Massachusetts a royal government was erected, which conformed to that ordinarily found in the Anglo-American dominions. The Governor and Council were appointed by the Crown, constituted the Executive department, and formed the Up-per House; while the Lower House was composed of representatives elected by the freemen. In Massachusetts, after the loss of the old charter, a new charter was obtained, which established a form of gov-ernment more closely resembling its predecessor than the common provincial government from which some features were taken. Under the old system the charter of a trading corporation, drawn with in-tentional vagueness, had, without color of law, been converted into the foundation of an independent State. The tests of citizenship were religious profession and property; but once within the pale, the sys-tem was that of a pure democracy. The Governor, the Assistants, or Upper House, and the Lower House were all chosen annually by the freemen; but by the new charter the appointment of the Governor was given to the Crown, the assistants or Council were chosen by the Assembly, subject to the Governor's approval, and the representatives still continued to be elected by the people, while under an earlier pressure the religious test had been removed. The Governor was de-pendent for his salary upon the votes of the representatives, and his

---

[1] Trade, Agriculture, and Industry in New England, Hildreth, ii., 559, General Table of Exports, etc.—Massachusetts, Brissot, p. 101; Abbé Robin, pp. 17, 19, 23; Burnaby, pp. 131, 136, 137; Pennsylvania Hist. Soc. Coll., i., 376, Hare's Jour-ney; Long Island Hist. Coll., i., Journal of the Labadists; Proc. Massachusetts Hist. Soc., iii., 109, Bennet's MS. Hist. of New England; New England Hist. Gen. Register, Early Ship-building, vi., 255; xiii., 23, 38; Byrd MSS., i., 8; Rochefou-cauld, i., 398, 417, 427, 481; Voyages and Travels of Capt. Nath. Uring, 1709, p. 110; Massachusetts Hist. Soc. Coll., I., viii., 202; III., vii., 199—New Hampshire, Prov. Papers, vi., 8, 1750; Bouton's Hist. of Concord, p. 521; Brissot, 387; New Hamp-shire Soc. Hist. Coll., i., 227, Answer to Lords of Trade; Burnaby, p. 151—Rhode Island, Abbé Robin, p. 33; Burnaby, p. 172; Memoirs of Elkanah Watson; Roche-foucauld, i., 496, 504; Chastellux, i., 19—Connecticut, Massachusetts Hist. Coll., I., vii., 234, and ff.; Rochefoucauld, i., 510; ii., 13; Chastellux, i., 30; Hinman, Con-necticut Antiq., p. 362, 1749; Barber's Hist. Coll., p. 204; Hist. of Glastenbury, p. 130; Hist. of New London, p. 267; Litchfield County Centennial, p. 36, Iron; Hist. of Norwich, Caulkins, p. 367; Fowler's Hist. of Durham, p. 156.

appointments required the assent of the Council; so that, besides the ordinary points of dispute, the charter of Massachusetts offered special opportunities for conflict between the executive and the people. Massachusetts occupied a half-way position between the common form of royal provincial government and the free-charter governments of Connecticut and Rhode Island, where the early charters, drawn as if for corporations simply, partly by the insignificance of the provinces, partly by adroit management, and in some measure by good fortune, escaped the storm which overwhelmed the Company of the Bay, and floated safely into the calmer political waters of the Protestant Succession. In Connecticut and Rhode Island, although the religious test for the suffrage had ceased in the one case and was never enforced in the other, the early Puritan democracy survived in all its purity, and endured down even to the middle of the nineteenth century. In both these colonies the Governor, Deputy, Assistants, and House were elected annually by all the freemen voting under a property qualification, no act was valid without the consent of both Houses, and all appointments were made by Governor, Council, and Houses in general court assembled. Year after year the same men were chosen to office, and the sovereignty was wholly with the people. The omission of the King's name in certain public documents was the only mark of the Revolution; and the inherent conservatism and toughness of these simple systems were so great that they withstood not only the shock of war, but for more than half a century the even greater strain of new and changing principles of society and politics. The great features of the New England governments were the extent of the popular power, the almost entire independence of the mother country, and the simplicity and conservatism of practical administration. In all the colonies of the east taxes were low, and salaries very small. The royal Governor of New Hampshire received six hundred pounds a year, but the Governor of Connecticut only half as much, and in all cases assistants and representatives received a few shillings a day. The revenue, except a small amount from excise in New Hampshire, was raised by a tax on land, on polls, and on personal property, or "faculty," as it was commonly called. The theory of taxation was simple and democratic—to levy on all property without distinction; and although a system suited to the condition of a colony has long been outgrown, it still prevails not only in New England, but in many parts of the United States, a monument of Puritan policy and of conservatism of thought and habit.

There is one other feature of the New England governments wholly distinctive, although now extended far beyond its original limits, and upon which the whole system rested. This was the principle of town government. The town was the political unit, and as such was represented in the legislature. The Puritan emigrants, reproduced in the New World, unconsciously, of course, but in all essential features the village community which the Saxons, Angles, and Jutes brought to England more than a thousand years before from the forests of Germany. In other provinces settlers slowly gathered, until they built up a town or formed a county; but in New England, as a rule, entire communities settled down from the beginning in certain places, and erected at once a township, which was not merely an aggregation of human beings nor a mere municipal organization, but a well-defined and represented political entity. Each member of this community had his due share in the land of the town, a home lot in the village, a farm lot and certain rights in the common belonging to the whole community. To this day these commons, with their cattle, sheep, and other rights, may be found in different parts of New England, a direct survival among direct descendants of the same and kindred races, of customs which flourished before Julius Cæsar founded the Roman Empire. These communal organizations were born of circumstances, and of the doctrines which found their first expression in the compact made on board the *Mayflower;* and like all thoroughly wholesome political institutions, they were the creatures of time, place, and necessity, modified by the political habits of thought of their creators. The communal system, in its fullest extent as attempted at Plymouth, soon died out; but from the germ thus planted sprang the municipal organizations known as towns, which present the fullest and most perfect example of local self-government either then or now in existence. These village communities, besides their right of representation in the General Assembly, had charge of every local interest; providing for religion, for roads and bridges, for levying taxes, for the poor, for police, and for every municipal want. In the town meeting all the freemen gathered, and every one took part in the proceedings and the debates. The State might fall to pieces, and the towns would still supply all the wants of every-day government. The next step was to federation, to form the State; the next to a union of States, which composed the New England confederacy; and then, at last, to the constitution of 1789, which found its strongest support among the descendants of the Puritans. On the towns rested the whole political structure, and from them came the capacity for practical self-government, the readiness for federation, and the keen sense of local rights. Among all the institutions of the Puritans the town government is pre-eminent, not only as a distinctive mark, but for its strength, usefulness, intrinsic sense, and political importance.[1]

Second in importance, of course, only to the system of government and administration, was the judicial system of New England, which did not, however, differ materially from that of the other colonies. In Massachusetts, under the original charter, the power of establishing courts of justice was without any warrant assumed, like many other powers, by the colonists. At first the general court exercised the whole judicial as well as legislative authority, and decided cases by a majority of votes; but owing to the pressure of business, inferior courts were established in the year 1639, the general court retaining only an appellate jurisdiction in certain specified cases. The highest of the inferior tribunals was the court of assistants, or "great quarter court," composed of the Governor, Deputy-governor, and assistants. They had general appellate jurisdiction, and heard all capital cases and cases of divorce; were held to combine all the powers of the King's Bench, Common Pleas, and other English courts; exercised admiralty jurisdiction; and in the year 1673 were empowered to try certain causes without a jury, which was a great innovation in New England. Below the court of assistants came the county courts, with jurisdiction extending to all causes, civil and criminal, except capital cases and cases of divorce, and analogous to the English courts of quarter sessions. They were composed of an assistant, or magistrate, residing in the county, or of one specially appointed by the general court, aided by commissioners, nominated by the freemen, and appointed by the general court. These county courts, besides their purely legal powers, had authority to lay out highways, license public-houses, see that an able ministry was supported, admit freemen, exercise probate,

---

[1] The New England systems of government and the town systems are described in many histories, notably Palfrey and Bancroft, and, among foreign writers, Tocqueville. For special descriptions, and for such points as salaries, taxes, offices, etc., see Burnaby, pp. 121, 139; Proc. Massachusetts Hist. Soc., iii., 109, Bennet's MS. History; New Hampshire Hist. Soc., i., 227, Answer to Lords of Trade; Rochefoucauld, ii., 144, 190; Massachusetts Hist. Soc. Coll., 1, vii., Description of Connecticut; Hinman, Connecticut Antiquities, p. 362; New England Gen. Hist. Reg., vii., Case of Common Rights at Marblehead; Parker, Origin of Towns, in Massachusetts Hist. Soc. Proc., vii., 14.

and grant administration, while their clerks were *ex officio* recorders. Below the county courts were the local tribunals, corresponding to those of justices of the peace or magistrates in the other colonies. They were held by an assistant or magistrate, if such a person lived in the town, by "commissioners of small causes," elected by the people, and sometimes by the select-men of the town. These courts tried small cases, and punished for petty offences. Outside this general system, there was a "strangers' or merchants' court," held by the Governor or Deputy, and two magistrates, for the benefit of strangers trading to the colony, and with an appeal to the court of assistants. Chancery jurisdiction, so far as it was required, was retained and exercised by the general court until the year 1685, when they erected a court composed of the magistrates of the county courts, chosen by the freemen to hear causes "containing matters of apparent equity," and with an appeal to the court of assistants. The old Puritan system, as a whole, fully and sufficiently met the needs of the society for which it was formed. It was administered admirably, and substantial justice was obtained through men of no special legal training, but with the natural aptitude and respect for law and its traditions which are such striking features of the early New England character.

The judicial system, as finally established under the provincial charter, was simplified and separated from the executive and legislative departments, but did not in other respects differ essentially from that of the colony which had preceded it. The lowest courts were those of the justices competent to try all causes under forty shillings, when land was not concerned, and to punish for petty offences. The business of the old county courts was divided under the new system. A court of quarter sessions, or general sessions of the peace, composed of the justices of the peace of the county, was established, and held quarterly. They had the care of roads, bridges, inns, etc., and the criminal jurisdiction of the old county courts, while the whole civil jurisdiction was given to courts of common pleas, composed of four judges specially appointed for each county. The highest court in the province, replacing that of the assistants and the general court, was the superior court, consisting of a chief-justice and four associate justices, who were appointed by the Governor at pleasure, but were, until the year 1772, dependent upon the Legislature for their salaries. Their jurisdiction extended to all actions, civil or criminal, with general appellate jurisdiction, including appeals, reviews, and writs of er ror, "as fully and amply to all intents and purposes whatsoever as the courts of King's Bench, Common Pleas, and Exchequer, within his Majesty's kingdom of England." To the judges of the superior court was given the power to issue the writ of *Habeas Corpus;* and after the failure to establish a court of chancery by the act of 1692 they exercised all the equitable jurisdiction required in the colony. The Governor and Council formed the supreme court of probate, and, by the right of substitution as a civil law court, appointed judges of probate for each county, a system which was loosely administered; but not, apparently, in such a way as to do harm, or fail in the performance of its duties. There was also a vice-admiralty court, with a judge appointed by the Crown, which was in Massachusetts, as elsewhere, generally unpopular, and came not infrequently into collision with the superior court of the province.

This provincial system too, as a whole, worked well; the law was properly administered, and justice done. The bench—filled at first by men of social and political eminence, and of high character, but of no special training, except in some instances for the ministry—gradually changed its character during the eighteenth century, as the legal profession became an important pursuit, and drew to itself much of the best ability in the province. At the period of the Revolution some of the judges were thoroughly trained lawyers; and a picture of the court, as it appeared at the time of the writs of assistance, has come down to us in a letter from John Adams: "The scene is the Council-chamber in the old Town-house in Boston. The date is in the month of February, 1761. The Council-chamber was as respectable an apartment as the House of Commons or the House of Lords in Great Britain, in proportion, or that in the State-house in Philadelphia, in which the Declaration of Independence was signed in 1776. In this chamber, round a great fire, were seated five judges, with Lieutenant-governor Hutchinson at their head as chief-justice, all arrayed in their new, fresh, rich robes of scarlet English broadcloth, in their large cambric bands and immense judicial wigs. In this chamber were seated, at a long table, all the barristers-at-law of Boston, and of the neighboring County of Middlesex, in gowns, bands, and tie-wigs. They were not seated on ivory chairs, but their dress was more solemn and more pompous than that of the Roman Senate when the Gauls broke in upon them. Two portraits, at more than full length, of King Charles the Second and King James the Second, in splendid gold frames, were hung up on the most conspicuous sides of the apartment."[1] The bench and bar of Massachusetts, as they appear before us in that celebrated trial, are both a respectable and imposing body. In the other New England colonies the judicial system did not differ materially from that of Massachusetts. New Hampshire as a royal province had its highest court of appeals in the Council of twelve members, but there was the same stubborn and effective popular resistance to a court of chancery as in Massachusetts. In Connecticut there was one supreme court, with a chief-justice and four associate justices, sitting twice a year in each county; while the county courts consisted of one judge and two or more justices of the quorum. There were eighteen probate districts, with a judge for each, justices' courts in every town, and a sheriff and King's attorney in every county. The Rhode Island system was substantially the same.[2]

The bar in New England, as in the other American provinces, did not come into prominence until the generation which carried through the Revolution was upon the stage. The first barrister, in the strict sense of the word, does not appear in Massachusetts before the year 1688. This was owing undoubtedly to the absence of any opportunities for study, to the attractions offered to men of intellectual tastes by the ministry, and to the fact that legal training was not necessary to obtain a seat on the Bench. Attorneys were plenty, and laymen were ready to argue their own causes; but there was no lack of business, for the people were very litigious, especially in Connecticut, and rejoiced greatly in the sturdy and frequent contests between towns for tracts of land. The only wonder is that a field so promising, and offering such an opening for men with special training, should have been so long neglected by a people who were ready to seize on every opportunity to earn a living. The change came before the middle of the eighteenth century in the towns, and somewhat later in the country districts, in proportion as the claims of the Church weakened, and the importance of the judiciary and of the business of the law increased. Many of the ablest graduates of the colleges, particularly those who were the architects of their own fortunes, turned to the law for support and advancement; and at the period of the writs of as-

---

[1] Works of John Adams, x., 244; see also Tudor's Life of James Otis, pp. 60, 61.

[2] As to courts, jurisdiction, etc., see Charters of Rhode Island and Connecticut; Washburn's Judicial History of Massachusetts; Massachusetts Hist. Soc. Coll., I., vii., Description of Connecticut; Hinman, Connecticut Antiquities, p. 362; New Hampshire Prov. Papers, iv., 479; Hildreth, ii., 355.

sistance the bar of Boston was composed of such men as James Otis, John Adams, Samuel Gridley, Samuel Quincy, Oxenbridge Thacher, Robert Auchmuty, and others; some destined to great places in the world's history, and all sound and good lawyers. A similar improvement took place throughout New England; and at the time of the Revolution, and afterward, the lawyers had become a powerful and influential class in the community, and one conspicuous in politics; the profession was eagerly sought, and chiefly filled by men of social position and marked abilities. By the description just quoted from the letter of John Adams, it may be seen that the dress and appearance traditional in the English courts was preserved not only by the bench, but by the members of the bar as well, who came into court in silken gowns, bands, and tie-wigs. The opportunities for study continued to be very meagre, and had to be supplemented by zeal and perseverance, especially as the crude system in vogue required a practitioner to be equally well versed in every branch of the law. Practice was very loose, but was for actual use an improvement on the technicalities which held sway in England. Litigation was easy and cheap, so far as the courts were concerned, but the amount of business and good fees made the profession lucrative. The counsel read the complaint, explained the nature of the evidence, and then put it in; and the plaintiff and defendant were always heard if, as often happened, they wanted to address the court. The oratory at first was very bad, but gradually improved with the development of the profession. No record of causes was kept, and appeals were frequent. A jury considered several cases at once, and were allowed while in session to wander freely about. Special pleadings and demurrers were not admitted; the general issue was always pleaded, and defects in form were not suffered to abate the writ. There were, of course, no suits in equity, but the judges, not being bound by strict law, could give equitable construction; and it cannot be doubted that substantial justice was obtained, or that the system, on the whole, worked satisfactorily. In the year 1761 the distinction between barristers and attorneys was introduced, and three years' practice in the inferior court demanded before admission could be obtained to the superior court. Five years later, three years' study was required to be an attorney, two more to be a counsellor, and two more to become a barrister. The law was the common law of England, and the statutes of the realm and of the province. At the period of the Revolution the bar of Massachusetts was, in point of learning, practice, and general standing—with the exception, perhaps, of Virginia—the best in America.[1]

The compact population and extensive mercantile interests which did so much to push forward the legal profession when it once began to assume its proper place, assisted also the development of the practice of medicine, which, however, was never in the hands of such dubious characters as was the case at first in the other colonies. Many of the emigrant clergy studied medicine before they embarked, while others were brought up to both professions; so that even in the seventeenth century most of the physicians were learned men, possessed of more or less special training. Sometimes the school-master was the village doctor, and much more rarely the healing art was found in combination with some trade, like mending shoes. The first medical work which appeared in America was Thacher's "Brief Rule to guide the People in Small-pox," published in 1677. Early in the following century the profession had many men exclusively devoted to its pursuit, and a general interest was felt in it, and in questions connected with it, as is shown by the character of the controversy which raged in Boston about the year 1720 in regard to inoculation. To Zabdiel Boylston belongs the credit of its introduction; but the conflict spread to all classes, and especially interested the clergy, perhaps on account of their earlier connection with medicine. The great champion of inoculation was Cotton Mather, who appeared at this time in a better light than at any other period of his life; but his enlightened advocacy of the new theory called out the bitterest attacks. Inoculation was opposed on both religious and economical grounds, because it anticipated the action of the Almighty, and because it was very expensive. Cotton Mather writes, in the year 1721, of a "spiteful town and poisoned country," and of his "sufferings from a barbarous and bloody people," and gives thanks for his "late miraculous escape" from a "granado" which some friend of old-fashioned small-pox threw in at his window. Although inoculation slowly made its way, the opposition was stubborn and long-lived; and as late as the year 1774 the hospital on Cat Island was burned, because it was feared that it would be turned into an inoculating hospital, and the mob

[1] Brissot, p. 90; Upham's Salem Witchcraft, i., Introduction; Proc. Massachusetts Hist. Soc., iii., 109, Bennet's MS. History; New England Hist. Gen. Reg., xxx., 206; New Hampshire Hist. Soc. Coll., iv., 38; History of New Boston, p. 201; Bouton, History of Concord—Rhode Island, Greene's History of East Greenwich, p. 166 —Connecticut, Rochefoucauld, p. 536.

protected the incendiaries against the officers of the law. At the beginning of this controversy the clergy had abandoned medicine, and trained men had not yet taken it up. Doctors were primarily druggists, but they were well paid, and in the towns had a large practice, owing to the strangers brought thither by trade. Special education, however, was even then appreciated, and had its reward; and the physicians rose rapidly in the social scale, became a learned and respectable body, and at the time of the Revolution more numerous than either lawyers or clergy. In Maine and the outlying districts there were few or no physicians or surgeons, and the people were much at the mercy of quacks; but, on the whole, the profession was made up of excellent men, who were looked up to by the community, and held in high consideration. Little was done for the public health. A hospital on Rainsford Island, in Boston harbor, seems to have been almost the only effort in this direction, and here New England fell behind Pennsylvania. Nor was so much done for medical education as in the middle provinces. The first course of lectures in America were those on anatomy, delivered in Newport by William Hunter, one of the famous Scotch family of that name, about the year 1754; but this was exceptional. There was no organized system of study even at the seats of learning, and medical associations were not established until just before the Revolution, and then only in a few places.[1]

The army and navy, strictly speaking, had no more existence as professions in New England than in the other colonies, but the material for both was more abundant and better trained than anywhere else, while the sea gave careers to a large portion of the boldest and most enterprising part of the population. The English Puritan was essentially a fighting man, and excelled in the art of war. Many of the early leaders had seen service in Europe, and others of a later time had followed Cromwell to battle, and been trained in the harsh school of the civil wars. Dangers from the Indians kept this war-

---

[1] Rochefoucauld, i., 427; Brissot, p. 89; Dunton's Letters (Bullivant and Oakes), p. 37; Wickes, History of Med. in New Jersey, pp. 14, 32, 37; Massachusetts Hist. Soc. Coll., II., i., 81, 105, Medicine in Massachusetts; II., vii., 71, Letter from Franklin; IV., ii., Douglass to Colden; V., vi., 133, Sewall Diary; IV., vii., Mather Papers, 1721; New Hampshire Hist. Soc. Coll., i., 157; iv., 38; v., 135; History of New Boston, p. 201; History of Chester; History of Rindge—Rhode Island, Greene's History of East Greenwich—Connecticut, Litchfield County Centennial, p. 61; History of Norwich, Caulkins, pp. 193, 426.

like habit in full exercise, and the Puritan at the very outset dealt
with the Pequods with an effectiveness and completeness unequalled
in the annals of the time. In the seventeenth century all men went
armed; even the farmers wore swords, and the military spirit was
wide-spread and ardent. All adults were in the militia, and the
training-day, when the soldiery went out to drill with pike and mus-
ket, was the great break in the dark monotony of daily life. This
custom and the military tradition endured until the Revolution, when
the militia appear under the famous name of Minute-men. In
Connecticut alone there were eighteen regiments of foot, and troops
of horse. The train-bands of each town turned out four times a
year, and the muster was always full. The training opened with
prayer; then came drill, shooting at a mark, feasting, and great consumption of cakes, ale, and cider. The soldiers armed themselves,
and chose their own officers, and although they had not the discipline of a regular army, they furnished the best material for one.
Fort William, in Boston harbor, was heavily armed, and garrisoned
in time of peace by one hundred men; and on the appearance of an
enemy, the signal was flashed from the light-house to the fort, thence
to the town, and thence throughout the country. The lighting of
the beacon on Beacon Hill, in Boston, would, when the revolutionary troubles began, bring forty thousand armed men to the town
within twenty-four hours. From Virginia to New Hampshire, says
Chastellux, all men had seen service, and the experiences of the old
French war were still fresh in the minds of every one.[1] The fighting capacity of New England, however, may be best judged from a
report made to Congress in the year 1790, by which it appears that
Massachusetts alone had furnished more men in the war for Independence than all the colonies south of Delaware together.[2]

The sea offered a livelihood to many of the New England people.
Every port on the rugged coast had its little town from whose harbor issued the fishermen and coasters, who faced the storms of the
North Atlantic, and did as much as any single class to build up the
fortunes of the Eastern provinces. Besides these, many large vessels

---

[1] Abbé Robin, p. 16; Journal of Labadists, Long Island Hist. Soc. Coll., i.;
Upham, Salem Witchcraft, i., Introduction; Proc. Massachusetts Hist. Soc., iii.,
Bennet's MS. Hist., p. 109; Letters of John Dunton—Connecticut, Massachusetts
Hist. Soc., I., vii., 234 and ff.; History of New London, p. 406; Westerly and its
Witnesses, p. 142; Chastellux's Travels, i., 19.

[2] American State Papers, Military Affairs, i., 14.

sailed from New England to trade to all parts of the world, giving great opportunities to men of courage and sagacity. The crews of the coasters and the fishermen were a rough but hardy race, who combined the tenacious and combative qualities of the English seaman with an intelligence and quickness peculiarly their own. They manned the innumerable privateers of the Revolution, which inflicted such terrible injuries on the commerce of England, and largely contributed to the brilliant success of our little navy in the war of 1812. In the merchant-service men of a superior class, and often of the best standing and condition, found the path of fortune and advancement, and many of those who then reached the quarter-deck, a highly-respected position in New England, afterward attained the highest rank both in public and private life, and became leaders in the state and nation.[1]

The last profession which remains to be considered is that of the clergy, who not only occupied in New England a wholly exceptional position, but drew to their ranks a large proportion of the ability and strength of the community. The Puritan theory of a system where Church and State were one and the same, was tried fairly and fully nowhere except in New England; and one result of the experiment was to produce a government which was largely theocratic, and which gave to the priesthood a social and political power rare at any period or in any nation, but unknown in modern times in a free state. The failure of the Puritan theory, carried out as it was with rigid completeness, may be traced in the decline of the theocracy, and in its ultimate breakdown as the controlling force in the state. But although the system came to an end politically in a little more than fifty years, the class which it had welded and built up endured, with all its traditions and much of its influence, for nearly two centuries.

The ministers of the Puritan emigration were men of birth, education, and breeding. Many of them had been driven from the pulpits of the English Church, and all possessed the sternest courage and deepest convictions. They were without exception leaders in every way among the people, formed the strongest class in the community, and were bold, vigorous, intolerant, able men, who set their mark indelibly upon the early institutions of New England. In accordance with their views the laws were framed; by their opinions much

---

[1] As to the seamen and fishermen of such towns as Portsmouth and Marblehead, see Drake's Nooks and Corners of the New England Coast.

of the public policy was directed; for them the college was founded, and they alone were thought worthy of the highest education. To them the people looked up with a voluntary reverence and with profound awe; while from their pulpits they wielded an authority and exercised a power which was simply overwhelming. The vigor and force of the damnatory passages in the sermons of Hooker, who led his flock into the wilderness of Connecticut, are marvellous, and Hooker was simply a conspicuous example of his class. "I love to sweeten my mouth with a piece of Calvin before I sleep," said John Cotton; and the awful doctrines of the Swiss reformer lost none of their effect in the hands of the New England clergy. But the Puritan ministers did not rule over congregations of ignorant and superstitious peasants. They had to deal with hard-headed, educated, and thinking English farmers and country gentlemen. They had to prove their right to their high office not only by strong and irreproachable character, but by the breadth and depth of their acquirements. Their sermons were monuments of learning, and they were without exception profound scholars. Chauncy, the President of Harvard College, had the Hebrew Bible read in the morning, the Greek Testament in the afternoon, and commented upon them extempore in Latin. They were all versed in ancient languages, and perfect masters of them, and sometimes of modern tongues as well. The same deep learning characterized the Mathers, Willard, and all the leaders, and in a greater or less degree the whole body of the clergy.

The affection and veneration in which they were held is shown by the account given in a journal, toward the end of the seventeenth century, of the proceedings on the occasion of the illness of a prominent clergyman, when a day of fasting and prayer was appointed to be held in the church. First came a prayer of two hours, then a sermon of an hour, then more prayers and psalm singing, the whole occupying about four hours, and the services being conducted by three ministers. Even when the Puritan system gave way, and the indifference and worldliness of the eighteenth century were strongly felt in New England, the zeal and power of the clergy suffered little abatement. One of the early resolutions of Jonathan Edwards was, "to live with all my might while I do live;" and with such a spirit as this among the clergy, it is not to be wondered at that they remained a strong influential class, comprising many of the best minds and strongest characters in the community. In colonial times the country pastors had a glebe, and a fixed salary raised by collections; while in the towns they were paid wholly by the contributions of the parishioners. After the Revolution and the adoption of the new constitution, they still continued to form a compact and energetic body, supported by state laws and by state taxation. They were the heads of all colleges, admitted only teachers of their own persuasion, and controlled the higher education of the state. The latitudinarian movement of the eighteenth century begun by Jeremiah Dummer, the political writer and friend of Harley and St. John, did much in Massachusetts to modify their opinions and liberalize their sentiments, thus prolonging in a milder form their influence and position. In Connecticut they had greater power, and used it more unsparingly; so that they continued to be not only the strongest class in the community, but to possess an almost unlimited authority until they were overthrown in the conflict with the Episcopalians in the year 1818.[1]

The position and character of the clergy, however, is but an introduction to the great subject of religion, which was for many years the ruling force in New England, was always a predominant interest, and which left a peculiar and enduring imprint on every form of social and political life. In any community religion is an important element if we wish to understand the people, but in New England it was so essential, and filled so great a space in life and thought, that without a full knowledge of its forms and conditions it would be futile to hope for even the slenderest appreciation of the society in which it was at first the all-absorbing and at every period a prevailing interest. This applies not so much to the doctrinal points as to the religious habits and observances, and to the part which religion played in common every-day existence. Of the former it is sufficient to say that the generally accepted tenets were those of Calvin, and that their discussion and development formed during the seventeenth century the only intellectual excitement of the people. Points of doctrine and questions of interpretation were argued with a zeal which equalled that of the preachers of Crusades, and with a subtlety and learning which would have done honor to the schoolmen. The history of this side of New England religion comes out strongly in their literature, which will afford a better opportunity for its description. At present it will suffice to confine ourselves to the broad field

---

[1] Proc. Massachusetts Hist. Soc., iii., 109 and ff., Bennet's MS. Hist.; Brissot, p. 78; Journal of the Labadists, Long Island Hist. Soc. Coll., i.; Tyler's Am. Literature, i., 189; Rochefoucauld, ii., 214; John Dunton's Letters; Hollister's History of Connecticut, i., 424.

of the forms, observances, and effects of religion in the ordinary life
of the people.

The organization of the churches was that known at the time of the
Great Rebellion as the Independent form. Each church was a self-
sustaining, independent body, and the sovereign power rested with the
congregation. The officers consisted of the pastor, lecturers, teaching
elders, and deacons, who were chosen by and were dependent upon the
congregation. Synods were held from time to time; but they gradually fell into comparative disuse, and never exercised great influence
as such among the clergy or laity, nor were they invested with any
very extensive authority. The vigorous intolerance of the early Church
in New England is one of the most familiar facts in our history; but
this softened greatly toward the close of the seventeenth century, when
John Eliot sadly bewailed the decline of religion; and in the eighteenth century it had almost wholly disappeared. "The present generation in New England," says Douglass, in his summary in the year
1749, "are of an extensive charity to all Protestants, though differing
in some peculiar but not essential modes or ways of worship;" and
again the same writer says, "At present the Congregationalists of New
England may be esteemed among the most moderate and charitable
of Christian professions." At a much later period Brissot stated that
the ministers of Boston rarely preached dogmatically, and that the
American principle of universal toleration was then strong in Massachusetts. The contrast, indeed, between the conduct of the men who
drove out Williams and Anne Hutchinson, and that of their successors
of the eighteenth century, is very striking. Intolerance at that time
still lingered in customs and observances, but in public policy a perfect religious toleration prevailed. A peculiar hatred had been developed in New England toward the Church which they had left, and
many of whose rites and ceremonies they had abandoned. There was
long and stubborn resistance to the introduction by government of
worship in the forms of the English Church; and it was a bitter trial
to Boston when Andros took possession of the Old South Meeting-
house for that purpose. At an earlier period there was strenuous opposition to the use of the Prayer-book anywhere in New England,
and the sound of its noble sentences, when permitted, caused the
most thorough disgust and anger. The diary of Judge Sewall—that
wonderful picture of declining Puritanism—strongly reflects this same
feeling. The worthy magistrate notes every year with pleasure that
Christmas is not yet observed except in official circles, but that the peo-

ple go about their business as usual upon that day; while on another occasion he records his disgust at the crosses worn and the healths drunk on April 23d in honor of the "fictitious St. George." This feeling was deep and wide-spread, unquestionably, but it found no practical expression, although, as the province and town grew, and official society and importance grew with them, the Episcopal Church, countenanced and approved, of course, by the executive government, had in Boston a rapid increase. It met with no bitter opposition, however, even in society, although fervent ministers had days for private fasting and prayer for those who turned to the Church of England, and against its being set up here. The clergy in Massachusetts generally wrote and declaimed against the Church of England, and inveighed against the Connecticut ministers, who went over to the Episcopalians, as they did against Jonathan Edwards, and then against Whitefield and the itinerant preachers of the great revival, and finally against the Reverend East Apthorp, sent out to Cambridge by the Society for the Propagation of the Gospel; but words were the worst that came of all this. With a royal Governor strong measures could not have been taken against the Church of England, and it is not apparent that they were desired, for nothing was done to suppress the New Lights. Even Apthorp, much as he was written down, was—as we are informed by no less a person than the Archbishop of Canterbury—well treated by the very heathen he was sent to convert. But Episcopalianism had, on the whole, little success in the two northern provinces outside of Boston and Portsmouth, never spreading into the country, nor obtaining any hold upon the mass of the people. The feeling in this matter was, therefore, milder in New England than elsewhere, and less of a grievance at the revolutionary period, for no attempt had been made to force the English Church upon the Puritan polity, but merely to obtain for it a foothold. On the subject of a colonial bishop alone — an innovation of which there was a keen dread—did religious matters tend to embitter the colonists against the mother country, although difference of creed had in an imperceptible fashion done much to alienate them.

In Connecticut, where the old charter government still endured, there was rather less toleration than in Massachusetts. When the first attempt was made in New Haven, in the year 1736, to found an Episcopal church, only one churchman was discovered in the town, and the would-be founder was driven off by the people; but by the middle of the century, the numbers of churchmen increased, and Episcopal churches were started in various places. At the same time several clergymen, headed by Samuel Johnson, seceded from the church of their fathers, and were driven out of the colony by the bitter hostility of the Congregational ministers, who were still all-powerful, and who controlled the college and the education of the state. At the time of the great revival under Whitefield the Congregational party went even further, procured legislation against the "New Lights," and suspended several pastors for heresy. Thus the ancient authority was preserved intact; but in the year 1818 it finally broke down completely under the strain which had unwisely been put upon it in a time when the old theories no longer appealed to the public sympathy.

In Rhode Island the whole history and position of religion was utterly different from that common to her sister provinces. The settlement was formed by men in opposition to the accepted Puritan policy, the founders belonged to the class of extremists generated in a period of intense religious excitement, and all the radical, lawless, and adventurous spirits flocked to the new colony. Inability to conform to any settled system was the characteristic of the early settlers of Rhode Island, and the principle of toleration which they advocated resulted for many years in nothing but faction, turbulence, and loose government, which left a lasting mark upon the community. Perfect toleration was established, and finally bore good fruit; and members of every despised sect found a resting-place and recognition in Rhode Island. The charter of Brown College, which divided the trustees among the Baptists—the predominant sect—the Friends, Episcopalians, and Congregationalists, is a good illustration of the Rhode Island policy. But the religious conflicts and varying creeds which had given birth to the colony bore fruit also in numerous religious fanatics and crazy sects, such as the Beldenites, Wilkinsonians, and Morseites, which sprang up and flourished in the congenial soil, and produced more or less commotion and disorder.[1]

---

[1] As to religion in Massachusetts, see Anderson's Colonial Church, iii., 407; Douglass, Summary, i., 432, 441; Brissot, p. 74; Burnaby, p. 134; Wansey, pp. 31, 43; Long Island Hist. Soc., i., Journal of Labadists; Nason's Life of Frankland; New England Gen. Hist. Reg., x., 322; xiv., 204; John Dunton's Letters, p. 66; Doc. relating to Col. History of New York, vi., Johnson to Secker, etc., 1753, 1759; Uring's Voyages, p. 110; Massachusetts Hist. Soc. Coll., II., ii., S. Johnson, etc.; II., viii., 72; IV., iv., 421; New Hampshire Hist. Soc., iv., 37; Brewster, Rambles about Portsmouth, Second Series, p. 357; Prov. Papers, iv., 650—Rhode Island, Burnaby,

Such were the general aspects of religion in the New England provinces in the eighteenth century; but its real character, and its effect upon life and society, require more detail for a complete understanding. The most striking part of New England religion, and one which presents a vivid picture of New England daily life, is to be found in the forms of worship, in the observance of Sunday, and in its laws and customs. The Puritan Sabbath was observed with strict uniformity throughout New England; and although its stern features soften as we approach the Revolution, it is still essentially the same as during the old charter government. The Sabbath laws formed an important part of the Puritan legislation; they were rigidly enforced by the early immigrants, and produced a day of rest which was absolutely terrible in its grimness. The Sabbath began at six o'clock in the evening on Saturday, and lasted until sunset on Sunday. All work of every description was suspended; while amusements and sports, rare enough on week-days, were absolutely prohibited. There was no travelling, no movement in the streets, nothing but religious exercises at home and in church. No traveller could be entertained, and the constables made the rounds of the town on Saturday evening to see that all taverns were closed; and if any one was absent from church for more than one Sunday, the tything-men sought the offender out, and he was obliged to offer sufficient defence or be fined, set in the stocks or in a wooden cage, or whipped. The order maintained in church was of the severest kind. A luckless maid-servant of Plymouth, who in the early days smiled in church, was threatened with banishment as a vagabond. Sunday was no day for smiling in the Puritan theory, and such it remained for more than a century. These principles began to relax at the close of the seventeenth century, and were modified a great deal during that which followed; but this was not the case with their customs. Toward the end of the seventeenth century Robert Pike, the sturdy opponent of witchcraft, had one Sunday urgent business which called him from home. He waited impatiently for the close of the day, and as the sun sank into a bank of clouds, he mounted his horse and rode away. As he passed the door of an unfriendly neighbor, the treacherous sun gleamed out through a rift in the clouds upon horse and rider; and

---

p. 117; Rochefoucauld, i., 496; Cahoon, Sketches of Newport, p. 43, 136; Greene's East Greenwich, p. 161—Connecticut, New Haven Hist. Soc., i., 53; History of New London, p. 442; Hollister's History of Connecticut, i., 469.

next day Robert Pike was fined for travelling on Sunday. Increase Mather, in a sermon, attributed the terrible conflagration in Boston, in the year 1711, to carrying burdens and practising servile employments, such as baking, upon the Sabbath ; and his son, Cotton Mather, said it was a warning from the Holy One for non-attendance on the Thursday lecture. This spirit suffered little diminution. In the middle of the eighteenth century no one was allowed in Boston to go in or out of town ; the gates were shut, the ferry guarded, and men were seized in the country. There was no trading, no walking to the water's edge, or even in summer on the common. No barber could ply his trade, no public-house was open, two or three people talking in the street were likely to be dispersed or arrested, and justices went about with constables to enforce the laws. At the period of the Revolution everything stopped on Sunday ; the streets were deserted, except between services, for every one was either in his own house or at church. The most innocent amusements were forbidden, and a young Frenchman, one of our allies, venturing to dispel the *ennui* of the day by playing on the flute, an angry mob gathered about the house, and he was compelled by his host to desist. Even at that time men were arrested for carrying bundles in the street, and the select-men of the country towns stopped all travellers who came within their reach. There have been great changes since then ; but in no respect has the strength of the Puritan character, and the depth of the impression they left on their race, been more forcibly shown than in the fact that it is their Sabbath which in all essentials endures to this day among the English-speaking race throughout Great Britain and the United States.[1]

The church services corresponded to the general character of the day. Long prayers and longer sermons were the predominant features, the sermon alone often occupying two hours, with the prayers in proportion. After the regular services all the members took the

[1] Sunday Observances, Massachusetts, Abbé Robin, pp. 10, 11 ; Journal of Claude Blanchard, p. 183 ; Life of Robert Pike, p. 94 ; Journal of the Labadists, Long Island Hist. Soc., i. ; Tyler's Amer. Literature, i., 104,189 ; Proc. Massachusetts Hist. Soc., iii., Bennet's MS. Hist., 109 and ff. ; Rochefoucauld, i., 427 ; Anburey, ii., 58 ; Massachusetts Hist. Soc. Coll., i.–v., 53 ; Ibid., V., vi., Sewall's Diary, ii., 323—New Hampshire, Rochefoucauld, ii., 190 ; Wilton Centenary, Peabody, p. 61; History of Rindge, p. 383 — Connecticut, Fowler's History of Durham, p. 171 ; History of Meriden and Wallingford, p. 402 ; Abbé Robin, p. 41 ; Rochefoucauld, i., 527.

sacrament, and those who were not yet admitted looked on; but the spectators were few, for every boy and girl on coming to a fit age was required or induced to take the covenant.[1] A curious and characteristic trait, strongly illustrative of the studied indifference, or, perhaps, dislike, of anything agreeable, and of the tenacious conservatism of the Puritan character, is exhibited in the matter of church music. During almost the whole of the colonial and provincial periods this music consisted wholly of congregational singing. The hymns of the Bay Psalm-book, for a long time the only ones in vogue, have a roughness of language and versification which is appalling, and these verses were given out by leaders, a line at a time, and chanted by the whole congregation, who did not at the outside know more than five tunes. This singing "by rule" sounded, says one of its opponents, "like five hundred different tunes roared out at the same time," an effect which must have been greatly heightened by the pause after each line, while the leader or precentor gave out the next. Early in the eighteenth century this organized discord produced resistance, and a reform was begun with a view to substituting singing by note for singing by rule, which led to a prolonged struggle all over New England, and particularly in Massachusetts, the contest being carried on with an interest and a bitterness which are almost inconceivable, and which display vividly the intense feeling in regard to all religious customs. Singing by note prevailed in the course of fifty years in the large towns, and the Abbé Robin speaks of the majestic and impressive manner of chanting the Psalms in the Boston churches. But in the country the old style held its own much better, enduring into the present century, and yielding very slowly. "Leaders and lining" did not disappear from New Hampshire until after the Revolution. In the little town of Harwinton, in Connecticut, when the new singing was introduced, in the year 1773, one of the deacons rose and left the church, crying, "Popery! popery!" an objection apparently very common among the lovers of the old fashions.[2]

In the church buildings there was a change similar in character to

---

[1] John Dunton's Letters; Sibley's Harvard Graduates, p. 566; Tyler's Amer. Literature, i., 189; Upham's Salem Witchcraft, i.

[2] Hood's History of Music in New England; Abbé Robin, p. 11; New England Gen. Hist. Reg., viii., 272; Ibid., xx., 122—New Hampshire, Bouton's History of Concord—Connecticut, History of Glastenbury, p. 77; History of Harwinton, p. 113; Timlow's Sketches of Southington, p. 192; History of Meriden and Wallingford, p. 403; Claude Blanchard's Journal, p. 112.

that in the singing; but it does not appear to have met with opposition, nor to have been carried very far. The earliest churches were simply barns of rude construction; then came those with the square tunnel roof, improved in the middle of the eighteenth century by the addition of a steeple, which continued down almost to the present day the typical country meeting-house, although further changes were made in the churches of the principal towns during the provincial period. The architecture of Queen Anne's time was adopted somewhat for exteriors and much more for interiors, and many of the latter had a good deal of simple and grave beauty, despite the inferior style to which they belong. As a rule, however, the characteristic quality of the New England church, within and without, was unrelieved bareness. The walls of the houses of God were as devoid of ornament as the forms of worship were of pomp or ceremony.[1]

Changes there were, too, in the appearance of the congregation. The meetings on Sunday among the early Puritans are impressive pictures, even as we look at them through the mists of more than two centuries. In a rude building of logs, perhaps in a barn, the settlers gathered at the beat of a drum or the sound of a horn; and more than three generations passed away before bells were in general use. For many dreary years the savages lurked near the villages; and Sunday, when all were gathered in church, was a time of especial danger. The minister at the desk was armed, all the men were armed, sentinels were posted at the door, and others kept watch outside. Thus the early Puritans worshipped God; and cases like the famous attack on Hadley, when the war-whoop rose above the voice of prayer, and men rushed from church to fight for their homes, were not lacking to show the need of such precautions. Gradually the danger, receding from the coast, died away, and the congregation could gather undisturbed; but the mere physical discomfort was still great enough to require a good deal of fortitude and religious zeal. There were no means of heating the church except to open the doors to the sun. In early times men drew bags over their feet and women carried heated stones in their muffs, and later little hand-stoves. Seated on hard benches, and exposed to the cold, they listened for hours to the exhortations of their pastor; and after the service they filed up the aisle, each contributing his portion to the support of the church and the salary

---

[1] Drake's Nooks and Corners of the New England Coast; Rochefoucauld, i., 400; Abbé Robin, p. 15.

of the clergyman. As time went on, matters somewhat improved; the churches were better built, and pews took the place of hard benches. Strict discipline was always observed, and any tendency to fall asleep was promptly checked. Below the pulpit sat the elders and deacons; in the body of the church were ranged the congregation, the men on one side, the women on the other, according to age, rank, and social condition. In the back seats or in the gallery were placed the children and negroes, and behind all, the tithing-men with long staves tipped with brass, with which they rapped unmercifully the heads of slumbering or disorderly boys or men; while for delinquents of the fair sex they contented themselves with brushing their faces with a hare's foot appended to the rod.

In the country there was an element in going to church which gave it a pleasanter side than was to be found in the towns; and it must be remembered that in every village there was a church and pastor, except in some of the wild districts of Maine, where they depended on itinerant preachers, for the first thing done by every band of settlers was to build a church. The Sunday services were in the country for many years the only occasion for social intercourse. Every one went; families from a distance came for the whole day, bringing their dinner with them, and leaving one child at home to watch the house and prepare the supper. The elders rode, carrying their wives on pillions; and long sheds, where a hundred horses might often be seen, became the invariable accompaniment of the meeting-house. The young people walked to church, sometimes many miles; and were wont, with a thrifty regard for appearances, to stop and change their shoes and stockings just before they reached the church. Between services was the great occasion of the week. Then all the news and gossip of the neighborhood were interchanged, and formed, with the sermon, the topics of discussion. This brief interval of friendly meeting is the one gleam of enjoyment which relieves the New England Sabbath. The Puritans effaced from Sunday every trace of its holiday character, such as it has in Europe, as a mark of popery, and they fastened upon their race the Sabbath with which English-speaking people are familiar at the present day.[1]

---

[1] Tyler's Amer. Literature, i., 189 ; Claude Blanchard, p.112 ; Massachusetts Hist. Soc. Coll., III., iii., 331 ; Upham's Salem Witchcraft, i., 20,122 ; New England Hist. Gen. Reg., pp. 28, 243 ; John Dunton's Letters ; Rochefoucauld, i., 400, 427—New Hampshire, Wilton Centennial, p. 61 ; Bouton's History of Concord, p. 528 ; Parker's

But the observance of Sunday, although a chief part of New England religious life, was still only a part, for religion, among the Puritans, was never absent from their thoughts, and entered into all their daily life. The custom of private fasts was common, with days spent in prayer for the family, for politics, for the Church, and for the state of England. Morning and evening, and every meal, were occasions for prayer, and every religious obligation was fulfilled with rigid severity. Children were taken within a week after their birth to be baptized, no matter what the weather might be; and at weddings and burials, on private and public occurrences, the resort of the Puritan was to his Bible, and to immediate communion with an ever-present God. In a society where religion was so deeply felt, and where so much importance was attached to its practice, it cannot be doubted that there was more or less hypocrisy; but it is equally certain that the great mass of the people had a deep and profound sincerity. In nothing is the decline of Puritanism so marked as in the gradual and sluggish disappearance of religious rites from every-day life during the eighteenth century.[1]

Another trait of the New England religion, which gradually disappeared in the last century, was the element of superstition. The most striking example of this, and one which has acquired a world-wide renown, and given rise to an almost proportionate amount of misunderstanding, is, of course, the Salem witchcraft. Volumes have been written upon this famous subject, and it is only necessary to refer to it here as an illustration of one side of the New England religious character. The Salem witchcraft was a virulent case of mental disease, marked, as such epidemics always are, by contagious panic, and having its origin in many co-operating circumstances. The general causes are to be found in the gloom of nature which beset the early settlers, in the hard toil in cultivating the sterile soil, the desolate and unending forests, the dread of Indian attacks, and constant losses from them; all of which, combined with a severe and terrible religious faith, gave a dark tinge and brooding melancholy cast to the minds of the people. With these general causes, special ones were united toward

Londonderry, p. 138; History of Hollis—Connecticut, Fowler's History of Durham, p. 168; Bouton's History of Norwalk, p. 32; Caulkins's History of Norwich, p. 121.
[1] Massachusetts Hist. Coll., V., v., vi., Sewall's Diary generally, and, e. g., p. 216; John Dunton's Letters; Wilton Centennial, Reminiscences of Abiel Abbot; Parker's Londonderry, p. 70.

the close of the seventeenth century. Pirates had begun to infest the coast, commerce had declined, the old charter, dearly beloved and almost sacred in the eyes of the people, had been taken away; there was universal, political, and financial depression, and the scourge of Indian warfare had just swept over the land, leaving a heavy legacy of debts and taxes. The natural gloom of Puritan society had thus deepened until it had become morbid, and wild beliefs needed only a spark to set them into a blaze of fanatical and blood-thirsty fear. To a people of this sort, who were familiar to a high degree with Biblical theories, witchcraft and the intervention of Satan came as terrible but natural afflictions; while the course of the clergy, striving at that period to retain their power, and urged on by the fanaticism of Cotton Mather, fanned the flame. The belief in witches was then general and unquestioned in all parts of the civilized world; and when the delusion became active anywhere, with favorable influences, it went to awful lengths; for, the possibility of witchcraft being once admitted, overwhelming evidence could always be produced. The panic spread, the people of Salem and its neighborhood went mad, and nineteen persons, including Giles Corey, who was pressed to death, were executed on the gallows. Two more died in prison, and hundreds were committed. The tempest raged furiously, spent its force, and then the reaction followed, and nothing more was heard of witchcraft in New England. This panic has already been contrasted with that which occurred more than fifty years later in New York. Both the Salem witchcraft and the negro plot belong to the same class of popular mental disease; both were awful in their results, but neither is a fit subject for reproach. In one case the disease took a religious, in the other a secular form, owing to the difference in the two communities; but both may be traced to specific causes which it is important to understand for the sake of science and truth; but neither is a fit theme for abuse or a ground to revile the people who were so unfortunate as to be afflicted with them.

Elsewhere and at other times in New England there were sporadic cases of witchcraft, such as we find in all the English colonies in America; but they have no special or peculiar significance. The superstition of New England took another form, very Biblical, but neither very practical nor very ignorant. The Puritans were men who dreamed dreams and saw visions; and they pondered deeply on these occurrences as being, perhaps, communications from the Almighty. Every portentous and monstrous birth, every extraordinary and inexplicable event, was ascribed to the immediate intervention of God. Manifestations of Satan were expected and found, noises were heard in the air, and signs seen in the heavens; and all became subjects of interpretation and conjecture. In the diary of Noadiah Russell, a tutor at Cambridge toward the close of the seventeenth century, we find entries recording the appearance of figures in the heavens—one of a ship, another of the devil; and, also, an account of a man in Connecticut who prophesied four dreadful judgments on New England. Then comes the inevitable New England shrewdness after this solemn record; we must pay heed to these revelations, says the worthy tutor, but not accept them as oracles. The one fact, however, which comes out strongly in a consideration of New England superstition is the small amount of it. Everything tended to its development. Intense religious zeal and absorption, a life of deadly monotony, a constant struggle with Indians and with nature for existence, and a morbid habit of introspection, would seem to make extreme and violent superstition almost a necessity. That there was so very little of it, is the strongest testimony possible of the hard sense, robust character, and sharp intelligence of the New England people.[1]

With a religious life so strong and so peculiar, it becomes of great importance to learn its effect upon the closely connected subject of general morality; for it is not only necessary to have a general idea of the state of public and private morals, but of the results produced by a faith so dark in its tenets, so intense, and so absorbing. Among the early Puritans the belief that they were a chosen people was very strong, and every affliction which visited the community was regarded as the direct action of God, to punish the people because the churches had become worldly, or for neglect of religious observances, or for sin of one sort or another. With such opinions, and guided largely in practice by the Old Testament, the Puritans not only made religion a test of citizenship, and enforced to the last point the performance of religious duties, but they legislated in the most parental and sumptuary fashion about everything, no matter how trifling, which they conceived could in any way affect morals. The representatives and the magistrates dealt by law with what men and women thought, said, or did in public or private affairs; and they strove to regulate

---

[1] Upham's Salem Witchcraft, i., ii., generally; New England Hist. Gen. Reg., vii., Diary of Noadiah Russell; Massachusetts Hist. Coll., V., v., vi., Sewall's Diary; New Hampshire Hist. Soc., i., 255; iii., Journal of John Pike—Rhode Island, Greene's History of East Greenwich, p. 161.

what they should eat and drink and wear, and how they should de-
mean themselves under all circumstances. They exacted in the most
stringent manner respect for parents; and for misconduct in this respect, in strict law, the penalty was death. One John Porter, of Salem, for abusing his father was made to stand on the gallows with a
rope round his neck, was soundly whipped, fined, and imprisoned, and
only saved from death by the intercession of his mother. The son of
Major Waldron, of New Hampshire, for drinking, disorderly conduct,
and abuse of his father, was, on the latter's complaint, arrested, chained to a post, whipped if he did not work, and his labor sold for the
benefit of the public. Duelling was strongly condemned, and participants in the few combats which occurred in Boston were forced to
flee the country. The strictest and most perfect order was maintained in the towns and villages. The constables made the rounds every evening, arrested all loose characters, and followed strangers into
taverns, in order to be satisfied as to their conduct and purposes.
Two specific examples will give better than anything else an idea of
the extent to which the civil power dealt with private morals and individual opinion. In the year 1662 John Spofford, of Boston, cursed
certain merchants because they refused to sell corn in a time of scarcity, and for this offence was brought before the court and tried for a
misdemeanor. He was acquitted, however, on pleading from Prov-
erbs,[1] "He that withholdeth corn, the people shall curse him; but
blessing shall be upon the head of him that selleth it." The quota-
tion was certainly in point, and Solomon, although not an authority
known to the common law, was fully recognized as a learned judge in
New England. In New Haven, a few years earlier, one John Meigs, a
currier and tanner, fell under the displeasure of the town for the quality of his leather and shoes, and was brought into court, where he had
apparently been before on a like charge, to be punished for his offences. In delivering judgment, the court said, "In a single pair of
shoes several evils appear: such as contempt of court, continued un-
righteousness, and other similar evils; and how many shoes he had
made and sold of such faulty materials, and so loaded with evils, the
court say they know not." The offending cobbler was soon after
obliged to leave the colony. Besides the action of the civil power,
the Church and the community itself sometimes undertook to regulate
morals and manners, the ministers, of course, taking the lead. John

---

[1] xi., 26.

Cotton and Elder Cushing petitioned to have the taverns closed to check drunkenness; and a minister's wife, at the same period, who was thought to dress too finely, was denounced for "carnal-mindedness." Dress was a fruitful topic for reproof, as it was a fertile occasion for the exhibition of a worldly spirit. The mode of wearing the hair was especially disquieting. Among the early Puritans long hair, or love-locks—recalling the Cavaliers, those sons of Belial—came to be regarded with particular abhorrence, and an association, headed by John Endicott, was formed for its suppression; while at a later time it was strongly denounced by Wigglesworth, eminent among New England divines, as effeminate, vicious, and indicative of pride. The introduction of wigs was another subject of sore trouble and anxiety to the strict members of the Church; and Sewall, "the judge of the great assize," who felt deeply the evil of this new fashion, expostulated with those who adopted it, and filled his diary with lamentations over this grievous sin.

Such, in mere outline, was the general character of Puritan morality, sharply watched and guarded by both Church and State; and such, in all essential points, it remained down to the Revolution. Here, as elsewhere, the only change was in a gradual softening and modification of the original system. Puritan austerity slowly relaxed everywhere, but more rapidly in Boston, from the effects of the society formed by the officers of the Crown. Yet, despite this relaxation, when the fact was known that Sir Harry Frankland kept Agnes Surriage in his house as his mistress, the popular indignation was so great that, although Frankland was the most important Crown officer, next to the Governor, he was obliged to withdraw into the country, taking the fair but erring Agnes with him. There was a still further relaxation during and after the French war; but, as a rule, the morality of New England remained of a very rigid quality. There were, of course, outbreaks against so severe a system, even in the earliest times; and when the stringency diminished, there was a general lowering of the standard. The two failings to which there was always the greatest inclination were intemperance and incontinence—the latter increased, no doubt, by the curious practice of "bundling or tarrying," which must have produced a good deal of trouble from its very nature, although the balance of evidence is in favor of the general innocence of the habit. But even in these respects the laxity of morals was anything but extreme, and probably less than in most communities; while in other directions the public and private morals were very high, and it is not a little curious that there was no violent reaction and no outburst of vice when the old iron system gave way.[1]

Passing from general morality to the more specific question of crime and its close ally, pauperism, we find but trifling differences between New England and the other colonies. Crime, especially of an aggravated sort, was somewhat rarer in the eastern even than in the middle or southern provinces; and after the dread of savages had passed away, doors and windows were always left unbarred in the country. The roads were perfectly safe. Young girls not only travelled alone in public conveyances, where they were universally well treated and protected, but rode through lonely woods after nightfall, unguarded and without fear or molestation. The early penal codes were, perhaps, severer than those elsewhere, but at a later time the practice did not vary much from the common standard of the eighteenth century. The law affixed the extreme penalty to many offences. Not only murder, but arson, blasphemy, rape, adultery, abuse of parents by a child over sixteen years of age, and repetitions of theft or highway-robbery, were punished with death, although the sentence was not often carried out, except for the first two mentioned. The ordinary mode of inflicting death was by hanging; but there were a few instances after 1681 of negroes, male and female, burned at the stake for murder or arson. The peculiar feature of the Puritan criminal system was the extreme publicity which they aimed to give it. Murderers were always brought into church on the Sunday before their execution, and preached to by some learned divine for nearly two hours. To this were added lengthy prayers at the scaffold, set up in some public place, where the people flocked to see the punishment inflicted. The suppression of the pirates afforded great opportunities in this respect, and on several occasions they were marshalled in small squads in one of the principal Boston churches, to serve as an edifying text for a long discourse. One of them balked this proceeding by refusing to go to church, and by jumping into the cart with a nosegay in his button-hole, and going smiling and bowing to the gallows in true London fashion, instead of

---

[1] Brissot, p. 71; Nason's Life of Frankland; Upham's Salem Witchcraft, i.; Tyler's American Literature, i., 104; Proc. Massachusetts Hist. Soc., iii., 165; Massachusetts Hist. Soc. Coll., IV., v., 56, 269; New England Hist. Gen. Reg., i., Wigglesworth; ix., 318; John Dunton's Letters; Anburey, ii., 39; Coll. Massachusetts Hist. Soc., III., iii., 326—New Hampshire, Massachusetts Hist. Soc. Proc., 1878, Waldron; Parker's Londonderry—Connecticut, Peters's General History; New Haven Hist. Soc., i., 39; History of Glastenbury; History of Durham, p. 171.

in a state of horror-stricken gloom. But, as a rule, criminals of this sort not only suffered death, but endured many fervent delineations, both of their earthly crimes and of the eternal torture which awaited them. The Puritan theory was that sin, public or private, must be repented of, and expiated, if necessary, in all its deformity and with the utmost publicity. From Charles Stuart to the meanest malefactor, all sinners and criminals were not only to receive punishment in the full glare of noonday, but were to be held up and expatiated upon for the benefit and solemn warning of the people. The same theory ran through their whole system of dealing with petty offences and misdemeanors. Jails, of course, they had—dark, mean, repulsive places, and usually in conspicuous positions, like the gallows and whipping-post; and at the time of the Revolution convicts were sent to Castle Island, near Boston, and put to hard labor at making nails; but even then their prison system was very rude, and far behind that of Pennsylvania. There was no faith in confinement, labor, or prison discipline, as a punishment or remedy for crime, and it was long before this doctrine was eradicated. Fines were the mildest form of penalty, and the punishments commonly in vogue were whipping, branding, cropping, mutilation, the pillory, or the stocks. All were arranged in such a way as to make the culprit's offence as conspicuous and public as possible, and call attention to it in every conceivable way, great ingenuity being manifested in accomplishing these purposes in both serious and light cases. The burned scar was the worst mark, but letters of brilliant color, worn for a term of years and indicative of certain crimes, were a favorite device to at once brand and punish. Scolds were gagged and set at their own doors, subjects of contemplation for the passers-by, and many offences were expiated not only by stripes, but by sitting on the gallows or on a raised platform, with a placard on the breast, on market-days. There was but little change in the manner of dealing with crime during the eighteenth century. Some of the odd Puritan fancies disappeared; but the lash, the branding-iron, and the pillory continued in general use in New England, as in all the other dominions of Great Britain, down to the Revolution.[1]

---

[1] Claude Blanchard, p. 185; Long Island Hist. Soc., i., Journal of the Labadists; Drake, Nooks and Corners of the New England Coast—Jails, Pirates; Proc. Massachusetts Hist. Soc., i., 320; iii., Bennet's MS. Hist., p. 109; New England Hist. Gen. Reg., ix., 45; John Dunton's Letters; Rochefoucauld, i., 405; Massachusetts Hist. Soc. Coll., I., v., 53; II., i., 1769, 1797; V., vi., 111—New Hampshire, Proc. Massachusetts Hist. Soc., 1878; Rochefoucauld, ii., 190; Hist. of Barnstead, Court Rec

Travellers at the period of the war and shortly after, assert that neither poor persons nor strolling beggars were ever seen in New England. There was, in fact, comparatively little pauperism in the country, in many places none at all prior to the Revolution; but there was always more or less of it in the large towns, although it did not appear on the surface. The settlement laws, which gave a residence after three months, were very strict, and rigidly enforced. A stranger coming to any town or village, was at once sought out by the officers, and compelled to satisfy them that he could support himself and family. If this assurance was not furnished, the new-comer was forthwith "warned off," and if he did not heed the warning, he received twenty lashes and was driven from the town. Such paupers as there were were treated on a simple and practical system characteristic of New England, but which spread far beyond its original limits. Paupers were set up at auction, and sold to the lowest bidder for their support, who took them for such work as he thought he could get out of them. Debtors occasionally made an assignment of all their property, and were then supported directly by the town, but the ordinary way was by auction. In Boston, as in all towns of any size, and possessing commerce, there was a considerable number of poor persons, who received much charity both private and public, and were kindly dealt with; and there, too, there were from a comparatively early time both workhouses and almshouses, which were very rare in the country and smaller towns. The usual method was that just described, by which the pauper was rendered as self-supporting as possible, and which, although harsh, and probably abused in some cases, was thoroughly carried out, did much toward checking pauperism, and, although rough, was certainly effective and economical.[1]

One cause of the greater rarity of crime and pauperism in New England than in the other colonies is to be found in the fact that the servile classes were numerically very small. For a long time convicts and indented servants were unknown, and when the latter began to

---

ord—Connecticut, Abbé Robin, p. 42; Brissot, p. 109; Rochefoucauld, i., 527; Barber's Hist. Coll., p. 56; Hollister's History of Connecticut, i., 428—Rhode Island, Greene's East Greenwich, p. 19.

[1] Proc. Massachusetts Hist. Soc., iii., Bennet's MS. Hist., p. 109; Coll. Massachusetts Hist. Soc., V., vi., Sewall, p. 8—New Hampshire, Chase, Hist. of Chester, p. 253; Hist. of Rindge, p. 385; Hist. of Dumbarton, p. 138—Connecticut, Wansey, p. 61; Hist. of New London, p. 474; Hist. of Durham, p. 165—Rhode Island, Westerly and its Witnesses, p. 139.

come they were well treated, the laws for their government were mild, and their rights were protected. There were "redemptioners" in the eighteenth century, and down to the Revolution advertisements "of parcels of Irish servants for sale" are found in the newspapers; but they were so few, and their opportunities for advancement were so good in a region where labor was not a disgrace, that they rapidly merged themselves in the body of the people, and were as a class perfectly insignificant.[1] The same, as may be seen from the estimates of population, held true in large measure of the negro slaves. Slaves there were in Massachusetts and elsewhere in New England from the earliest times, but the general drift of public opinion was against slavery; and such a man as Samuel Sewall published a tract against it at the very beginning of the eighteenth century. Their intermarriage with whites was forbidden under heavy penalties, but marriages among themselves were authorized and guarded. The laws, as a rule, were mild in regard to them, and punishment was carefully limited. They were easily manumitted, and soon after the Revolution were slaves only in name. They were most numerous in Boston and Connecticut, and were invariably employed as domestic servants, kindly treated, and instructed in reading, and in the Bible. So great, indeed, was the apparent equality of master and slave in Connecticut that a Boston lady, early in the eighteenth century, speaks of it with surprise and dislike, having seen negroes eat at their owner's table, and having heard of a case of arbitration between a master and his slave. Slaves, in fact, as a class, were wholly unimportant, and as a domestic institution had little or no effect.[2]

Feeble, however, as slavery undoubtedly was in New England, its mere existence, carrying with it the principle of a servile class, had some influence probably in the maintenance of strong social distinctions. An aristocracy unquestionably existed in New England from the beginning, always possessing great power, and fully recognized; but it rested neither on great landed estates nor on a system of primogeniture, and flourished in the midst of a society which was in theory democratic. The foundations of rank were birth, ances-

---

[1] Barber's Hist. Coll. of Conn., p. 166; Westerly and its Witnesses, p. 143.

[2] Upham's Salem Witchcraft, i., Introduction; Proc. Massachusetts Hist. Soc., iii., Bennet, p. 109; Massachusetts Hist. Soc. Coll., V., v., 163, Sewall's Tract against Slavery; V., vi., Sewall, 16, 143; Ibid., I., iv., 196; II., i., 81 — New Hampshire, Rochefoucauld, ii., 190—Connecticut, Rochefoucauld, i., 530; Mad. Knight's Journal; Fowler's History of Durham, p. 161.

tral or individual service to the state, ability, education, and, to some extent, wealth. The aristocracy thus produced was respected and acknowledged, but its existence was uncertain and precarious, without the usual, essential, and only enduring supports of great estates and of primogeniture. There were some large landed estates in New England; but they were neither numerous nor important, and carried nothing with them. Sir William Pepperell, it was said, could ride from Portsmouth to Saco without leaving his own acres, and in the other New England colonies there were a few large domains, but they had no real hold upon either the social or political system. They were not congenial either to the character, habits, or pursuits of the people, or to the climate and nature of the soil and country. The New England aristocracy was to be found chiefly in the larger towns, although every village had its local "Squire," who stood at the head of society. This absence of landed estates had a strong tendency to discourage any system of entail, even if the people had been inclined to it. The method of descent was that familiar to the English law as gavelkind, land being held under the charter in free and common socage of the manor of East Greenwich and according to the custom of Kent. There was always perfect freedom of bequest throughout New England, and although the Biblical double portion to the eldest son was recognized in the "Body of Liberties," and continued down to the year 1789 in the distribution of intestate estates, besides being always common in wills, yet law and custom united in giving ample provision both to the younger sons and the daughters. The tendency, therefore, was in favor of the division of property, and against the preservation and establishment of large estates and wealthy families. The main supports of an aristocracy were, therefore, wanting, and when other causes ceased to operate, the aristocratic system fell rapidly to pieces in a society which was in fact and theory democratic. But down to the Revolution, and, indeed, for many years subsequently, these other causes were vigorous, and aristocracy flourished and was strong. The robust conservatism of their race led the people of New England to regard with great respect their public officers and magistrates. Birth, wealth, and social position were almost necessary qualities for the attainment of high office, and simplicity and dignity characterized the rulers elected by the people. Bradstreet, the last of the colonial governors, lived in a house of ordinary appearance, and not one of the most costly. He dressed in black silk, but not sumptuously, and his manner was quiet and grave. Trumbull, the war-governor of Connecticut, impressed Chastellux as the great magistrate of a small republic; and this was the type of the rulers of New England. They respected their office, but regarded it as a position to which they were in a measure entitled by their standing in the community. The weight of social position in such matters is aptly illustrated by an incident which occurred in Boston in the year 1759. The removal of a certain Mr. Phelps from the commission of the peace was urged because he was the son of a bricklayer, and not of a magistrate. The ground of objection was admitted without question to be perfectly sufficient, and the only effort was to disprove the fact. Social distinctions were fully recognized and carefully observed in matters relating to public office; but in every-day life and in common affairs they were carried even further.

At the very outset, in the letters in answer to the proposals of Lord Say and Lord Brooke—which aimed at the establishment of nobility—classes were recognized, and the practice thus begun was never abandoned in the provinces. All the leaders of the great emigration, and many of their followers, were drawn from the English gentry, were men of property and position, and proud of their descent. The difference thus established between gentlemen, yeomen, merchants, and mechanics was never lost sight of, although the lines were not drawn quite so sharply as in the mother country. The first named were the best educated men, and of the best families in the community, who sometimes farmed large estates, but as a rule filled the pulpit, the bar, the magistracy, the bench, and the profession of medicine. Titles were sparingly but carefully used. Honorable was applied only to governors, esquire was at first rarely used except of men in high office, and master and mistress belonged to those alone who had birth, education, and position. Among the mass of the people the ordinary prefix was merely good-man or good-wife, or, still more simply, neighbor. These distinctions had great importance in the churches and colleges. In the former the seats were " dignified," and the congregation was arranged " according to the places they are in, the age they bear, the estates they enjoy;" or, in another formula, according to " authority, age, wealth, house-lots." The business of thus distributing the pews and seating people according to rank was a work of great delicacy, and an event of deep interest in every village. It gave rise to many heart-burnings, quarrels, and complaints, but it was none the less enforced, and scrupulously carried out. In the college the lists of students drawn up during the freshman year were made out on the same system, and excited great interest. It was easy to fix on the students for the top and bottom of the list, but the intermediate places roused much contention. When the list was completed it was hung up in the college buttery, and every student retained throughout the course the place thus assigned, unless he was degraded. Besides the social recognition thus conveyed, the students at the top of the list had most influence and the best rooms. Yale abolished the system in 1768, and Harvard five years later, substituting an alphabetical arrangement; but the classes of provincial times still appear in the catalogues, graded according to social position, a puzzle to their democratic posterity. In Boston and some of the larger towns the aristocracy, influenced by the presence and society of the Crown officials, made more display of their rank than their predecessors, or than their country brethren. They had fine houses, estates in the country, and many slaves; they put their coats-of-arms upon their coaches, and wore cloth, velvet, and lace, while the mass of the people dressed in homespun. But the great body of the New England aristocracy adhered to the ways of their fathers. No matter what their social and official rank might be, they were all brought up to work with their hands; the children were expected to earn their living by professions or otherwise, and no drones were permitted in the hive.

The most striking and most important feature, and the one showing most clearly the existence and strength of the aristocracy, was connected with the franchise, for which religion was one test, property in land the other. When the former was abolished, the latter was continued, and survived even the Revolution. A conversation which has been preserved, and which occurred at the very end of the eighteenth century, between Increase Sumner—afterward Governor of Massachusetts—and Fisher Ames, affords an excellent illustration of this point. A law was before the legislature to modify the qualification for voting, and Ames said it would give any man who earned sixty pounds a year, but had no property, the right to vote. "Why," replied Judge Sumner, "that construction never entered any man's head. It amounts almost to universal suffrage. It never will prevail; but if it does, Brother Ames, my confidence in it (the government) is very much diminished." Yet the spirit of equality reigned even then, and French dukes remarked with surprise that the rich shook hands with the poor.

In every department of life, in fact, the aristocratic system prevailed; and, maintained as it was solely by the conservative instincts of the people, and the ability of its defenders, it is surprising that it lasted so long, and held such complete sway. The aristocracy of New England did not have at bottom any of the great strength of that in Virginia, but its existence was as real, and its power almost as great and unquestioned.[1]

Although great estates were few, large and costly houses were numerous, and afforded an opportunity, readily taken advantage of, for comfort and display. From the earliest times the magistrates and the wealthy citizens had dwellings of a superior kind, while to the clergy were given the best houses the people could afford. Handsome houses were most numerous in the seaport and larger inland towns, and their neighborhood. They lined the roads for twenty miles about Boston, and a few were found scattered through the country districts. On many of them sums of money were expended which in those days amounted to a large fortune. The Lee house, at Marblehead, which was said to have cost ten thousand pounds, was built of stone, handsomely fitted up with pictures set as panels, and wainscoted walls hung with tapestry. Twenty thousand pounds of the doubtfully-acquired fortune of Godfrey Malbone were sunk in his house in Newport, and the same gentleman had, besides, a beautiful villa outside the town. In Portsmouth were the Cutts and Pepperell houses, of a similar character, and the more famous Wentworth house, the home of the Governors, a great, rambling mansion, with fifty-two rooms, endless panelling, carved mantel-pieces, and every architectural extravagance of the time. In Boston and its immediate neighborhood there were many such houses, built generally of stone or brick, and sometimes of wood, with large, low rooms, broad, easy staircases, and great fireplaces. All were wainscoted with hard wood, sometimes with mahogany from the West Indies, and were adorned with tapestries, until the fashion of plaster and wall-papers began to come in just before the Revolution. Numerous as these houses, the sure marks

---

[1] Long Island Hist. Soc. Coll., i., Journal of Labadists; Hazard's State Papers, i., 377; Nason's Life of Frankland; Proc. Massachusetts Hist. Soc., VI., p. 32; VII., 118; New England Hist. Soc. Reg., ii., Old Wills; viii., 115; xi., 79; xx., 122; xxiii., 38; Mag. Amer. History, i., 260; Rochefoucauld, i., 405; ii., 214—New Hampshire, ibid., ii., 190—Connecticut, Wansey, p. 61; Massachusetts Hist. Soc. Coll., I., x., 99; Chastellux, p. 30; Peters's General History, p. 220; History of Windham County, p. 93; History of New London, p. 380; Bouton, Hist. Discourse of Norwalk, p. 52; Caulkins, History of Norwich, p. 122; Timlow, Sketches of Southington, p. 181; Hollister's History of Connecticut, i., 421—Rhode Island, Claude Blanchard, p. 78.

of solid fortunes, were, they were still only the houses of the aristocracy, and the homes of the body of the people were of much simpler
construction. When the villages were first settled, the church and the
block-house, with its overhanging upper story, rose side by side, and
the latter remained conspicuous for generations, long after its loop-
holed walls had ceased to have any practical significance. Around
this building clustered the rude dwellings of the pioneers. Gradually the log hut was replaced by the "lean-to," a frame house with
steep pitched roof, and of the simplest construction; and this in its
turn was succeeded by the gambrel or hipped-roofed houses, of which
many still remain in undisturbed corners. These frame houses, with
gambrelled and gabled roofs, were universal throughout New England,
varying in size with the wealth and position of the possessor. Both
they and their ruder predecessor, the "lean-to," were very solidly built,
with low-studded rooms, heavy hewn-oak timbers, almost as enduring
as stone, great fireplaces, masses of heavy stone chimneys, and diamond
panes in the windows. The chief characteristics of the New England
country houses, even of those, and they were many, which had but one
story and an attic, were simplicity, solidity, and neatness. Occasionally there was found in some quiet village a house like that to which
Sir Harry Frankland and Agnes Surriage retreated to find shelter from
the virtuous indignation of Boston. The Frankland house, at Hopkin-
ton, stood in the midst of gardens, laid out in the old style with box
hedges and terraces. The house itself was a spacious, comfortable
building, rising picturesquely among the trees, with dormer-windows,
great chimneys, and an interior hung throughout with tapestry and
decorated with carving and painting. Such a house, however, was exceptional. Almost all were of the kind just described, and were the
dwellings which, with orchards and gardens, gave the air of thrift,
prosperity, and comfort which every traveller remarked in the New
England villages, and even on the outlying farms, for agriculture was
then the great interest, and the homestead was a source of pride as
it descended from generation to generation of permanent families.[1]

---

[1] Brissot, p. 101; Nason's Life of Frankland, p. 41; Drake, Nooks and Corners
of the New England Coast; Upham's Salem Witchcraft, i., Introduction; Rochefoucauld, i., 400, 473; ii., 202; New England Hist. Gen. Reg., xxv., 37—New Hampshire, Drake, ibid.; New Hampshire Hist. Soc. Coll., i., 157; Parker's Londonderry,
pp. 76, 94—Connecticut, Abbé Robin, p. 40; History of Durham, p. 165; Norwalk,
Bouton, p. 39; Hollister's History of Connecticut, i., 428—Rhode Island, Elkanah
Watson's Memoirs; Chastellux, i., 107; Greene's East Greenwich, p. 158.

The general similarity in the matter of houses was but part of the wider uniformity in manners, customs, and habits of thought which has been already alluded to.   In all these respects the people of New England, from Maine to the western border of Connecticut, were substantially the same.   On one side only did they have neighbors ; but while there was a strong infusion of New England manners in New York, Dutch influence had produced no effect upon New England. Such differences as there were among the people of the eastern group of provinces were simply those differences of degree which always subsist between town and country, and which in this case might almost be still more narrowly limited, as those between Boston and the rest of the provinces ; for in the smaller towns the distinction was by no means strongly marked.

In the country, therefore, it is necessary to look for the type of New England life and manners, since only a small portion of the population was gathered in the large towns.   Yet, at the same time, it must be remembered that one strong characteristic of the New England civilization, as contrasted with that of Virginia, was the fact that the country was settled and occupied not by individuals but by groups of persons, or communities famous in history as the township, the organization of which has already been described.   There were, of course, on the frontiers, and here and there in remote places, isolated farms ; but these were marked exceptions, and the country was covered with little towns.   In these villages the church, the block-house, the town-house, the school, and the variety store, well stocked to supply everything needed by the farmers and their families, were built near together, and formed a central point.   Around them, and in close proximity, were the homes of the minister and of the teacher, and the houses and shops of those who plied the various trades, always well conducted and well represented in every New England village.   Beyond and around this little nucleus of houses were scattered the homes of the farmers, some very near, others at a considerable distance alone on outlying tracts.   In this arrangement there was always a point where the life of the neighborhood centered, where some social intercourse could be obtained ; and circumscribed as this life was, it was nevertheless far removed from the absolute solitude so common in Virginia, and was not without marked effect upon the character of the population.   The striking features of this New England society were general well - being, increasing industry, and equality of condition.   There was neither indigence nor wealth, neither very rich nor very poor, but an entire community of men and women in good cir- cumstances, and maintained there by unrelenting toil. In Rhode Island the standard was somewhat lower, owing to the manner of settlement; the people were poorer, agriculture was ruder, there was more idleness and litigiousness, the towns were less well ordered, and the roads and bridges less well kept up than in the adjoining prov- inces. But with this exception, which did not go very deep, hard- earned and deserved but moderate prosperity prevailed. Every one worked, both men and women, all day and every day, except Sunday, the former on the farms, the latter in-doors at household affairs, and with the unceasing spinning-wheel, and sometimes in the fields. All the sons and daughters were taught trades, besides learning to man- age the farm. In that climate, and with that soil, man could never let go his hold of nature, and that he did not do so is one of the great- est proofs that we have of the iron persistence of the English race. Thus the struggle, not only to make advances, but even to retain that which had been already won from earth and air, was constant and severe, leaving a deep impression upon those who fought the battle. The conflict marked them both physically and mentally, although they were still conspicuous for purity of blood and fineness of race. The round, red look of the Englishman had gone, and the New Englander was a tall, sinewy, powerful but spare man, with rather a gaunt look, and a face in which all the lines and contours had been sharpened and strengthened. The women were noted for their beauty, which was remarked by travellers from other colonies, and from the Old World; but these same observers also record the fact that this beauty faded early, and that the delicate tints disappeared, which they attribute to immoderate indulgence in hot tea and hotter bread, with consequent indigestion, prosaic reasons which accounted also for the loss and de- cay of teeth noticeable in both sexes.

As the features of the men had grown sharp, and those of the women more delicate in the New World, so did their minds grow more acute. The people of New England were very shrewd, quick, and inquisitive. A Virginia gentleman, who travelled a good deal in the eastern provinces, said that on arriving at an inn he always, in order to avoid the delay caused by inevitable questions, made a brief statement as to himself and his business, told those about that he knew no more, and then asked for supper for himself and his horse. Yet, with all their queries, they were at bottom kind and hospitable, although they were very formal, stiff, and reserved with strangers after the fashion of their race and creed. Their failing was in pushing too far their natural acuteness. They were great adepts at bargains and trade; and although they adhered to the letter of the law with scrupulous fidelity, they were far too ready to infringe its spirit. Necessity, working on strong intelligence, had made them an ingenious, enterprising, and inventive people, with a readiness and capacity to do any work in life with fair success, a quality which has grown into a national attribute. They were almost universally frugal, hardworking, thrifty, intelligent, and honest; but they were also hard, often narrow, averse to spending money, and not generous either in their conception or mode of life. They had a rigid sense of duty and of religion, and a lurking inherited distrust of enjoyment, for which they made up in some measure by keen perceptions, a strong sense of the ridiculous, and a dry, caustic wit mingling with an odd sort of humor, which is of a fine and peculiar sort, and which was possible only in a community where the whole body of the people was at once shrewd and educated.

In every way they were a simple, unpretentious race. Everything about them and their houses was neat and clean, and of good quality, but not showy. The men wore homespun, and in many places moosehide or sheepskin breeches, while the women's dresses were of coarse, strong linen. On Sunday, partly from the immense importance attached to the day, and partly from the love of finery innate in human nature, there was much dressing in every little town, and even in the wild border settlements of Maine. The men put on their cloth coats and black beaver hats, the women their carefully preserved silk or brocade, and then dressed and powdered their hair, usually worn in a simple braid, but now built up and decorated in the fashion of the day, and thus they went to church, reminding the soldiers of Louis XVI. of thrifty French burghers.

The houses were cold, so cold that ink and wine froze often in the rooms where a generous wood-fire blazed upon the hearth. This was the only method in general use both for heating and cooking, and around the great kitchen fireplace with its projecting crane, the whole family were wont to gather in the evening. The furniture was plain, strong, and sufficient, but rarely handsome. Sundials served usually instead of clocks, which were scarce and dear; while pewter and wood took the place of china, which was kept for state occasions, and the table, though plentiful, was extremely simple. The people were much addicted to a vegetable diet, and to the consumption of Indian meal in every form, particularly with molasses, which was a staple article in every household. Meat was abundant, except in remote districts, where its daily appearance was a mark of wealth; and fruits, both wild and cultivated, were very plentiful. Tea was extensively used, coffee rarely, and the ancestral beer was entirely replaced by cider, which was drunk everywhere, and, if something stronger was desired, New England rum was always produced.

In the matter of furniture and dress a curious trait of the New England character was manifested. Almost every respectable family had more or less handsome silver, which appears in the inventories attached to wills, and seems to have been hoarded and kept out of sight, together with rich suits of velvet, handsome arms, and costly stuffs. All these articles, indicative of prosperity, seem to have been prized merely for the sense of ownership and the love of heirlooms, and never to have been put to practical use until their possessor turned them over to his descendants, to retire again into the recesses of cupboards and chests. The farms were in comparatively high cultivation, and presented a good appearance, and to them the men of the family devoted their lives, while their sons were generally content to come after them, although the movement to new regions went on with steady increase. The women were constantly employed within-doors; the girls were free, not bashful, but never licentious, and the matrons virtuous and prudish. They were rarely accomplished, but not infrequently possessed of a heavy learning in Latin and Greek, derived from the minister, and with a taste for theological controversy.[1]

The manners and customs of the people in the larger towns differed but little from those of the country. Almost all the towns, other than Boston, of any importance, were scattered along the coast,

---

[1] Brissot, p. 101; Pennsylvania Hist. Coll., i., 376, Hare's Journey, 1774; Baron Riedesel, i., 226; Life of Robert Pike, p. 224; Drake's Nooks and Corners; Upham's Salem Witchcraft, i., Introduction; Uring's Voyages, p. 110; Rochefoucauld, i., 427; ii., 202; Anburey, ii., 46—New Hampshire, Drake; Uring, p. 113; Wilton Centennial, p. 61; Parker's Londonderry, p. 128; Chase, History of Chester, p. 413; History of Bedford, p. 133; Bouton, History of Concord, pp. 520, 521, 524—Connecticut, Abbé Robin, pp. 39, 43; Claude Blanchard, p. 112; Journal of Mad. Knight; Rochefoucauld, i., 536; Chastellux, pp. 30, 41, 48; Peters's General History, p. 224; History of New London, p. 267; Litchfield County Centennial, pp. 44, 112; History of Durham, pp. 157, 167; History of Norwich, p. 76; Hollister's History of Connecticut, i., 428, 433—Rhode Island, Claude Blanchard, pp. 44, 52, 78; Burnaby, p. 126; Memoirs of Count Fersen, i., 40, 51; Rochefoucauld, i., 496; Chastellux, i., 19.

Worcester and Hartford, which were the most important of the inland towns, being little more than large villages. The houses were chiefly of wood, and the streets broad and shaded with handsome trees; more trades were carried on than in the purely country districts, and the immediate neighborhood of both was covered with farms in a state of comparatively high cultivation. On the seaboard, to the north of Boston, were Salem and Portsmouth, both supported by trade, and both well built, with many houses of brick and stone; and the former even threatened to become the rival of Boston. Portsmouth was the capital of New Hampshire, and, therefore, the centre of government and the home of the Crown officials. To the southward were Providence and Newport. The former was a flourishing town of some five thousand inhabitants, and growing rapidly; but the latter was already in great measure eclipsed, and had sunk into a pretty quiet town, built almost entirely of wood, and already, from the appearance of Southern planters in summer, giving promise of the watering-place of the future. New Haven was the chief town of Connecticut, an important point of trade, and the seat of learning. All these towns were characterized by neatness of appearance, good order, and prosperity; but the life of their inhabitants did not vary much from that led by the people of the country villages. There was more wealth, handsomer dressing, larger and better houses, more china, silver, and tapestry, and an important class of wealthy and successful merchants; but the essentials of life and the modes of thought were the same as in the country. The general simplicity of manners and distrust of innovations, is, perhaps, as well illustrated by the fact that the owner of the first chaise in Norwich in the middle of the eighteenth century was fined for riding in it to church, as by anything else. Greater opportunities for social intercourse, and a closer connection with the outside world, tended to liberalize the population of the seaports, but this was the most marked distinction. Where society in the towns differed from that in the country it approached that of Boston, which requires a separate description; and in a general way it may be said of New England that, while it was made up of towns, there were hardly any large ones.[1]

---

[1] Wansey, p. 52; Pennsylvania Hist. Soc. Coll., i., 376, Hare's Journey; E. Watson's Memoirs; New England Hist. Gen. Reg., xx., 122 — New Hampshire, Burnaby, p. 150; New Hampshire Hist. Soc. Coll., v., 83; Rambles about Portsmouth, Second Series, pp. 76, 90—Connecticut, Abbé Robin, pp. 39, 66; Brissot, pp. 106, 111; Litchfield County, p. 44; Caulkins's History of Norwich, pp. 325, 332—

The general aspect of life, even in the larger towns, was sober in the extreme. There was great precision required in every way, and the monotony of existence must have been intense. The Puritan system frowned severely on amusements, for enjoyment was no part of their theory of earthly existence. Against this doctrine human nature rebelled, even under the strictest dispensation of the early times. Neighbors would gather about the great fireplaces to shell nuts and make brooms, or chat and tell stories, and sometimes simple games were started, and, in moments of great conviviality, a dance. The shovel-board of Shakspeare's time was almost the only game not expressly prohibited, and was much in vogue; but even this was regarded with disfavor, and the minister of Salem was urged to refuse the communion to Bridget Bishop, one of the victims of the later witchcraft delusion, because she kept her public-house open at a late hour, and permitted shovel-board to be played on her premises. This impossible system of restraint, however, gradually gave way before the absolute necessity of some slight relaxation, and certain amusements came into fashion, and gained a firm foothold. Besides the weekly gathering between services on Sunday, and the monthly meeting at the county-town when the court was in session, there was a great deal of visiting done by the women in the country, who would go constantly to each other's houses, taking their children and their work with them, and spend an hour or two in cheerful gossip. A more marked occasion was the house-raising, which grew out of the readiness of the people to assist each other, and in which every one bore a part. After the house was up, there was feasting, dancing, and drinking, but very rarely intoxication, although New England rum was the common drink. Besides this, there were quiltings, huskings, and spinning-bees, all concluding with a simple supper and a dance. As time went on, sleigh-rides, picnics, tea-parties, supper-parties, and dancing-parties became common; and on great occasions—such as the ordination of a new minister—there was a grand ball, got up by the young men, to which the whole country-side was invited. Holidays were few, but were highly prized. Two were religious—thanksgiving and fast day—and two civil—election, and training which occurred four times yearly. Fast-day was wholly given up to religious exer-

---

Rhode Island, Abbé Robin, p. 33; Claude Blanchard, pp. 41, 78, 151; Burnaby, 117; E. Watson's Memoirs; Rochefoucauld, i., 496; Chastellux, i., 19; Channing's Early Recollections of Newport, p. 22; Old Times in Connecticut, by Leonard Bacon, New Englander, Jan., 1882.

cises; but on the others, after the sermon, the voting, or the drill, all the young men of the neighborhood gathered on the green, and indulged in every kind of athletic sports, which were very popular in New England, the favorites being running, wrestling, boxing, pitching quoits, and sometimes shooting at a mark. The day always concluded with feasting and a dance, in which all participated. In the larger towns the amusements were of a very similar character, supplemented by hunting, fishing, and riding, and by a boisterous celebration of the fifth of November, which it was found necessary to suppress by law. Outside the towns were often inns, with gardens and bowling-greens, where people resorted in fine weather to drink tea or play games; and after the middle of the eighteenth century, we hear of horse-races and bull-baitings, but these were very exceptional; and as late as the year 1762 stage-plays were prohibited by law in Rhode Island. There were in the towns more balls and parties of a very simple kind, and more good eating and drinking than in the country; but everything was plain and primitive, even among the wealthiest, and was kept within very narrow bounds of decorum.[1]

If it had not been for the town system, and the social intercourse afforded by it, life in New England, as in the other colonies, would have been isolated and solitary in the extreme. There was no regular connection with the outer world except on the seaboard, and means of communication in the interior were very limited. The postal service for the colonies was consolidated, soon after the act of union with Scotland, with the chief offices at New York, Boston, and Philadelphia. The letters were brought by ship captains, who were required, under a penalty, to deliver them to the deputy post-master. A large proportion of the mails, therefore, passed through the New England towns, and all the principal seaports were in the line of the post, which ran regularly from Portsmouth to Philadelphia, along the seaboard; and thence, when sufficient letters were collected, at uncertain intervals, to Williamsburg. Thus, news came earlier, oftener, and in greater

[1] Upham's Salem Witchcraft, i.; New England Hist. Gen. Reg., xiv., 164; Anburey, ii., 87—New Hampshire, Wilton Centennial, p. 61; Parker's Londonderry, p. 77; Rambles about Portsmouth, Second Series, p. 171; Bouton, History of Concord, p. 534 — Connecticut, Abbè Robin, p. 40; Peters's General History, p. 221; History of New London, pp. 406, 481; Litchfield County, p. 35; History of Durham, pp. 157, 168, 170; Norwalk, Bouton's Hist. Discourse, p. 39; Caulkins, History of Norwich, p. 331; Hollister's History of Connecticut, i., 433, 438—Rhode Island, Claude Blanchard, p. 56; Col. Records, vi., 325.

abundance to New England, and at more points, than elsewhere, and the roads and bridges north and south from Boston were exceptionally good; but in the interior the case was quite different. No post seems to have run to the inland towns before the Revolution, and the people depended on chance visits to the seaports for news. The roads, although better, usually, than in the other colonies, were often neglected, as in Rhode Island, and were of very rude construction in the outlying districts. No public conveyances made their appearance until shortly before the Revolution, and one of the first was a curricle carrying three persons, which ran from Portsmouth to Boston in two days; while the stages to New York were four days on the way, even after the Revolution. In the large towns, and on the coast, coaches were somewhat used, while in Boston cabs had been for some time common; but chaises became, during the eighteenth century, the almost universal vehicle. No wheeled carriages, however, appeared in the interior much before the Revolution. Produce and supplies were carried on sleds in winter, and ox-carts in summer; and all journeys, whether for business or pleasure, to church or to court, were made on horseback or on foot. Every one who could afford it rode, and the women and little children sat behind on the pillion. The roads were not only of fair quality, but the forest was constantly broken, not by solitary plantations, as in the South, but by thriving villages of considerable extent.

The inns of the large towns were exactly like their prototypes in the mother country, and we find in Boston that they had characteristic English names, such as the "Bunch of Grapes," the "Cromwell Head," the "Anchor," and the "Cross-keys." In the country the inns, which were none of the best, although better than those in the other colonies, were in some ways peculiar. The early Puritan policy had been to regulate public-houses with great severity, and licenses were issued only to thoroughly responsible persons; the result of which was that the country innkeeper was generally one of the leading men of the neighborhood, a colonel of militia, and a person of wide acquaintance and much influence. They often received travellers in their own homes, and there was in every village at least one house of this sort—half tavern and half private dwelling. The lodging thus obtained was good, and the prices reasonable; but the fare consisted too much of ill-baked bread, had too little variety, and the wines were generally of inferior quality. The character and position of these landlords made them excessively indifferent to their guests.

whom they regarded frequently as a source of trouble rather than of profit. The mixture of privacy and publicity, and the eagerness for gain, produced another peculiarity in the custom of expecting to be paid by every stranger, whether the host kept an inn or not. Chastellux mentions several cases where he brought letters of introduction to his hosts, who received him kindly and treated him well, and then charged him as if he had been at a tavern, neither excessively nor very moderately, but exactly what seemed just for the trouble and expense to which they had been put. These customs gave a peculiar stamp to travelling in New England, and explain also the prominence of inn-keepers, as a class, in all public affairs. On the whole, however, travelling was easier, and communication more frequent in New England than in any other part of the British dominions in America.[1]

In this general survey of New England everything has been included except Boston, the seat of Puritan government, the capital of Massachusetts, and the chief city of the eastern provinces. At the close of the seventeenth century Boston was by far the largest, wealthiest, busiest, and most important town in America. There was the seat of government for Massachusetts, and the centre of trade, learning, and society for all the New England provinces. Boston continued to stand at the head of the American cities until after the middle of the eighteenth century, when Philadelphia caught up with her in point of population, extent, and wealth. At the period of the Revolution, the population of Boston was about the same as that of the Quaker City, and was apparently in the neighborhood of twenty-five thousand.[2]

---

[1] Claude Blanchard, p. 48; Douglass, Summary, p. 457, full account of Post-office, and p. 471; Brissot, pp. 97, 98, 384; Wansey, pp. 38, 41, 42, 52; Pennsylvania Hist. Coll., i., 376, Hare's Journey; Upham's Salem Witchcraft; Proc. Massachusetts Hist. Soc., iii., Bennet's MS. History, p. 109 and ff.; John Dunton's Letters; Uring's Voyages, p. 110—New Hampshire, Hist. Soc. Coll., iii., 190; v., 83; Parker's Londonderry, p. 127; Adams, Annals of Portsmouth, p. 204; Rambles about Portsmouth, Second Series, p. 362; Chase, History of Chester, p. 429; History of Rindge, p. 358; Bouton, History of Concord, p. 513—Connecticut, Claude Blanchard, p. 112; Rochefoucauld, i., 510; Chastellux, i., 30; Peters's General History, p. 220; Hinman, Connecticut Antiquities, 1674, 1693, p. 193, Post-offices; Litchfield County Centennial, p. 35; History of Norwich, p. 100—Rhode Island, Claude Blanchard, p. 42.

[2] Small as these numbers appear now, they were, as has been said with reference to Philadelphia, very large for the time. Boston was then one of the most considerable towns in the British empire, and we find it compared with Liverpool and Bristol. The estimates of population vary, of course, widely and wildly, and the

As seen from the harbor, Boston was formed of an amphitheatre of houses, rising gradually one above the other from the water's edge. There were many wharves, built out with much industry; and conspicuous among them was the "Long" wharf, esteemed a prodigious work at the time, which was two thousand feet in length, and covered with handsome warehouses. From Long wharf ran King Street, then the principal business street, through the heart of the town, and at its head was the Town-house, where the state government in all its branches met, and beneath which the merchants held their exchange and booksellers their stalls. The streets were sufficiently wide, but crooked and irregular, paved with cobble-stones, with gutters in the middle, and sidewalks marked off by a line of posts and chains. The streets were clean and well kept, and although they were not lighted with any sufficiency before the year 1773, were quiet and orderly. In the daytime the streets and squares swarmed with the bustling life of a driving, trading community; and there were many fine and well-stocked shops, as well as two fairs, one at each end of the town, which were held daily for ordinary traffic. To the south of the town there was a small but pleasant common, where, even at the end of the seventeenth century, John Dunton writes that "gallants were wont to walk with their marmalet madams as we do in Moorfield." Besides the Townhouse there were some very respectable public buildings, such as Faneuil Hall, and the Province House, where the royal Governor lived. There were also some twenty churches, all of which were solidly built, and many with handsome interiors, in the style of Queen Anne's time. The houses were at first of wood, and the consequence was the occurrence of disastrous fires, accompanied with considerable loss of life, in 1679, 1711, and 1761. The first produced sharp legislation in regard to building materials, and by the middle of the eighteenth cen-

figures in the text are simply the best approximates possible. See Abbé Robin, p. 9, 6000 houses and 30,000 population, 1783; Byrd MSS., i., 8, middle of eighteenth century, 8000 houses, 40,000 population; Raynal, i., 85, 1766, population from bills of mortality, 30,000; Anderson's Colonial Church, iii., 407, 1723, population 20,000; Burnaby, pp. 133, 134, 3000 houses, 18,000 to 20,000 population, 1759; Wansey, 1794, after decline caused by war, p. 39, population 18,000; Watson, population, 1778, 25,000; Nason's Frankland, 1741, population 16,000, 1500 negroes; Coll. Hist. Soc. of Massachusetts, I., iii., 152, 1742, population 16,000, 1200 houses, 1300 negroes; Uring's Voyages, p. 110, 1709, 4000 houses, 18,000 population; Drake's Old Landmarks of Boston, p. 20—estimates of population from 1639 to Census of 1870, Drake gives 16,000 in 1765. The estimate in the text is, I think, rather under than over.

tury a large proportion of the private houses were of stone or brick. The new ones at first resembled those of London after the great fire, and continued to be erected by wealthy persons on the outskirts of the town, where they had space for fine gardens. The old houses which fire had spared were heavily built of wood after the country fashion, with gambrel roofs and gables, and balustrades around the top. The general appearance of Boston was that of an old English country town, while the business streets strongly recalled to travellers those of London.[1]

For many years the manners and habits of society in Boston differed in no respect from those of the country towns, which were all founded upon the same principles as the capital; but changes came, and considerable and inevitable alterations were effected by the growth of trade, wealth, and population. Elements wholly unknown in the simple villages of the interior were furnished by the officers of the Crown, who were for the most part Englishmen, together with the set which associated with them and copied their manners, and by the rich merchants who, like John Dunton's friend, Mr. White, of an earlier period, "crossed both the torrid and the frozen zone midst rocks and swallowing gulfs for gainful trade." The families of the English officials set the fashion, and were implicitly followed by those who made up society in the technical sense, although there was a large class, possessing both birth and property, who adhered steadily to the sober habits of their ancestors. This official society attended the Episcopal Church, and figured conspicuously on all public occasions. They introduced a great deal of gayety into the old town, and stood out in bright relief against the darkly tinted background of the Puritan past, affecting more or less even those who clung to traditions and held aloof from the more modern ways. The change, however, came chiefly from the fact that Boston became a rich commercial town, and commerce brought in its train liberality and luxury.

The houses were large, spacious, and well furnished. Their owners suffered from cold, for the only method of heating was by wood-fires,

---

[1] Abbé Robin, pp. 8, 9 ; Brissot, pp. 70, 87 ; Burnaby, pp. 133, 134 ; Wansey, pp. 38, 39 ; Long Island Hist. Soc. Coll., i., Journal of the Labadists ; Memoirs of E. Watson ; Nason's Life of Frankland ; Proc. Massachusetts Hist. Soc., iii., Bennet's MS. History, p. 109 and ff.; Ibid., vi., 322 ; New England Gen. Hist. Reg., xvi., Laws on Building ; xxiv., Goellet's Diary ; Coll. Massachusetts Hist. Soc., V., v., vi., Sewall's Diary ; John Dunton's Letters, p. 66 ; Rochefoucauld, i., 406 ; Uring's Voyages, p. 110 ; Massachusetts Hist. Soc. Coll., I., iv., 188 ; I., ii., 81 ; III., iii., 319.

and these were insufficient for the climate. " 'Tis dreadful cold," writes Cotton Mather, in the year 1720, with his wonted simplicity of expression; "my ink-glass in my standish is froze and splitt in my very stove. My ink in my very pen suffers a congelation." This probably continued to be the case down to the Revolution; but in all other respects the well-to-do people of Boston had every comfort that money could purchase. In every house there was abundance of handsome furniture, and a good deal of decoration. Many had large estates in the country, whither they went in summer; and there was a strong tendency, especially among the merchants, toward the life of a country gentleman. Every family of position had stores of silver, glass, china, and tapestry. The markets were well stocked, food cheap, and the tables were well supplied and well served; while good wines, especially those of Spain and Madeira, were found in every cellar, and were freely used. There was a great deal of handsome and even extravagant dressing. Men wore broadcloth and velvet, lace ruffles, silk stockings, and diamond shoe-buckles, powdered their hair, and carried swords. The women, who were pale and faded early, but were also well made and handsome in youth, dressed even more richly and extravagantly, in silks and brocades, with high head-dresses and ostrich feathers, although it must be confessed that such good judges as the Prince de Broglie thought their magnificence of a very tasteless sort. Ladies rarely went abroad except in a chaise accompanied by a negro servant; while the gentlemen generally rode, and they, too, always had a black in attendance. The first coaches were those of the Governors, who, early in the eighteenth century, drove in them with six horses richly harnessed; but at the period of the Revolution coaches and four were also used by the wealthiest among the private citizens. The mass of the inhabitants lived more soberly and dressed more quietly, and mechanics wore the dress of their trade; but the general effect was one of wealth and good living. The people of Boston were kindly and hospitable, with more readiness to receive strangers, who found the town and its inhabitants very agreeable, than was common in the smaller towns. They knew more of the world, and had more of its habits than their brethren in the country; but they could not shake off their inheritances, and underneath the exterior which wealth and foreign commerce gave they were the same race, and the peculiarities cropped out with unfailing certainty. They were sharp in trade and quick at bargains. The men were stiff and formal, the women cold and reserved. Riches, official society, and intercourse with the world softened them and modified their character ; but at bottom they were the true descendants of the Puritans, stern, hard, strong, and acute ; and a plain simplicity of thought and life was remarked beneath the surface by every careful observer.[1]

Amusements in Boston, after the Puritan austerity disappeared, were of course more varied and less simple than in the country. Besides the universal athletic sports, and riding, hunting, fishing, shooting, and skating, there were sleigh-rides in winter to some neighboring tavern, followed by a supper and dance, and, in summer, excursions down the harbor, picnics on the islands, and little parties into the country to drink tea and drive home by moonlight. Theatres were strongly resisted, and do not seem to have been fairly established and accepted until after the Revolution. In the year 1767 Andrew Eliot writes to Hollis : " I am no enemy of innocent amusements, but I have long thought our modern theatre the *bane of virtue*. I had such an opinion of their pernicious tendency, especially in a young country, that I had exerted myself to procure an act to prohibit them when introduced some years ago. This does not wholly prevent them, but so many are engaged to prevent them that they will not soon be tolerated." This was probably a fair expression of Boston opinion at the time, but the ultimate result was very different from that anticipated by the letter-writer. There were no coffee-houses except the one at the Merchants' Exchange, but there were numerous clubs, which met at private houses or at taverns, and which were well attended and much enjoyed. On a coronation or royal birthday, or on great public occasions—such as the taking of Louisburg—there were extensive celebrations ; the town was illuminated, bonfires were lighted, and the streets were filled with people.

Entertainment of a quieter and more every-day kind was found by ladies and gentlemen in walking in the mall every fine afternoon, and then going to each other's houses to pass the evening, unless they went to lecture, which was possible on six nights out of seven. These were narrow limits, for not only were plays and music-houses discountenanced, but dancing-parties and balls were by no means encouraged.

[1] Abbé Robin, p. 14 ; Brissot, pp. 70, 73, 80 ; Nason's Life of Frankland ; Proc. Massachusetts Hist. Soc., iii., Bennet's MS. History, p. 109 and ff. ; New England Gen. Hist. Reg., II., vi., Wills ; Mag. Amer. History, Prince de Broglie, p. 379 ; John Dunton's Letters ; Rochefoucauld, i., 406 ; ii., 175, 214 ; Anburey, ii., 61, 62 ; Uring's Voyages, p. 110 ; Coll. Massachusetts Hist. Soc., IV., vii., Mather Papers ; V., v., vi., Sewall's Diary, and, *e. g.*, ii., 59.

"Of late," says one writer, in the year 1740, "they have set up an assembly, to which some of the ladies resort. But they are looked upon to be none the nicest in regard to their reputation, and it is thought it will soon be suppressed, for it is much taken notice of and exploded by the religious and sober part of the people." Yet they did not seem dispirited or moping for lack of amusement; and the same writer says elsewhere: "The ladies here visit, drink tea, and indulge in every little piece of gentility to the height of the mode, and neglect the affairs of their family with as good a grace as the finest ladies in London." The old system, in fact, was giving way before the presence of an energetic and pleasure-loving social element, and balls and parties soon became an unquestioned part of social life. After the troops were quartered in Boston, an attempt was even made to infringe upon the Sabbath. "We have had an innovation here never known before," writes a worthy citizen, in the year 1773. "A drum or rout given by the admiral last Saturday evening, which did not break up till two or three o'clock on Sunday morning, their chief amusement being playing cards." This innovation was a step too far, and disappeared with the English soldiers; but, nevertheless, at the time of the Revolution, the old abhorrence of amusements was nearly gone, and social life in Boston was by no means sombre or depressing; so that those who found time in the midst of an active life for relaxation had no lack of opportunities.[1]

In social habits nothing now remains to be described but the two important, although very common, incidents of marriage and death, and the observances connected with them, which were substantially the same in town and country throughout New England. On every institution, public and private, the Puritan laid his hand, and dealt with each after his own fashion. They determined that marriage was simply a civil contract; hardly any weddings were solemnized by ministers before the eighteenth century, and clergymen were even obliged to get a special commission in order to officiate. "We do not wish to introduce here," said John Winthrop, "the English custom of solemnities at a marriage. If any minister is present, he might bestow an exhortation; but we adhere to the strict Protestant principle that marriage is purely a civil right." To this doctrine there was rigid adher-

---

[1] Brissot, p. 80; Wansey, p. 42; Nason's Life of Frankland; Proc. Massachusetts Hist. Soc., iii., Bennet, p. 109 and ff., 1740; Ibid., vi., 322; John Dunton's Letters; Coll. Massachusetts Hist. Soc., I., i., 49; IV., iv., Eliot to Hollis.

ence for nearly a century. Weddings were usually celebrated very quietly at the home of the bride, in the presence of a few friends, and by a justice of the peace; but the extreme simplicity thus enforced led gradually to the overthrow of the system. The religious theory of marriage never reached great importance, but the severe abstinence from any form of celebration gave way entirely. Marriages took place usually at a very early period of life, many girls becoming wives at sixteen or seventeen. John Dunton speaks of a Miss Wilkins, an old maid of twenty-six, looked on in Boston as " a dismal spectacle ;" and John Higginson writes of some young ladies that they " are like to continue ancient maids, Sarah being twenty-five or twenty-six years old." This was at the close of the seventeenth century; but the custom not only of young, but of repeated marriages, continued down to the Revolution ; and as these marriages were very fruitful, families were large, and thus the population was supplied which overflowed New England, and pushed out to the fertile lands of the north and west. Marriage wrought a marked change in the position of a woman. Young girls were allowed an amount of liberty which would now be inconceivable if remnants of it did not still survive; but when they married all freedom was at an end. The wives and mothers were not only very domestic, but extremely prudish ; anything but the simplest dress was looked upon with marked disfavor, and intrigue, gallantry, or adultery were so rare as to be almost unknown. As has just been said, the extreme privacy and quiet of the early marriages wholly disappeared. At first feasting was added to singing psalms and prayer, and then weddings became occasions for much social festivity. All the friends were entertained at the bride's home with a collation or supper, and afterward a dance ; while in the country they were the most important social events. The banns were proclaimed in church, and all the neighbors were invited from the pulpit to attend the ceremony. On the day of the wedding muskets were fired, a procession was formed, and marched to the bride's house, where the marriage took place ; and then came a dinner, a dance, and great merry-making. Usually these wedding-feasts lasted through the day and evening, but they were sometimes kept up for two or three days. On one occasion at New London there was a great wedding dance on the day after the marriage, when ninety-two ladies and gentlemen assembled and proceeded to dance ninety-two jigs, fifty-two contra-dances, forty-five minuets, and seventeen hornpipes. This was probably an extreme case ; but all over New England weddings were great occasions, and were celebrated with much pomp and rejoicing.[1]

With the same unsparing hand the early Puritans strove to cut down to the last point the final offices of respect to the dead, and the first settlers carried their dead from the house on their shoulders after a brief prayer, and silently laid them in the earth. But death was too grand a theme for moralizing to be passed over so simply. The Puritans became dissatisfied with their own experiment on this point, and long before the seventeenth century closed funerals had become important and observed occasions. The religious rites continued to be very simple; but great state and pomp were introduced into the last obsequies. At the funeral of Governor Leverett the hearse came first, with four gentlemen carrying banner rolls, then four more carrying the armor and sword of the dead man, then two leading the horse, and again four with banners, and finally a long train of citizens. In a less degree this came to be the practice at every funeral. There were always pall-bearers from among the leading men of the community, a long procession to the grave, great distribution of scarfs, gloves, and rings, and, to close the day, baked meats and drinking. A list of charges at a private funeral in Boston in the middle of the eighteenth century includes twelve pounds for scarfs and gloves, nine pounds for a barrel of wine, and three shillings for tobacco. At the funeral of Governor Belcher's wife one thousand scarfs and pairs of gloves were given away, and it was even customary for the towns to supply scarfs and gloves on the burial of a pauper. The fashion of expensive funerals was carried to such extremes, and the extravagance was so great, especially in Massachusetts, that it was found necessary in that province to regulate these ceremonies by law, in order to make them less costly. In the country the system was substantially the same. If a death occurred in the night the bell was tolled at sunrise; if in the daytime, at sunset, once for a child, twice for a woman, thrice for a man. The funeral was somewhat simpler than in the capital, but its

[1] Brissot, p. 72; Proc. Massachusetts Hist. Soc., ii., 283; Ibid., iii., Bennet, p. 109 and ff.; Proc. Massachusetts Hist. Soc., vi., 322; New England Hist. Gen. Reg., vi.; xi., 253; xx., 122; John Dunton's Letters; Anburey, ii., 88; Massachusetts Hist. Soc. Coll., III., vii., 199; V., vi., 24—New Hampshire, Hist. Soc. Coll., iii., 190; Parker's Londonderry, p. 74—Connecticut, Rochefoucauld, i., 536; Chastellux, i., 79; History of New London, pp. 194, 406; History of Norwich, Caulkins, pp. 177, 332; History of Meriden and Wallingford, p. 408; Hollister's History of Connecticut, i., 438—Rhode Island, Westerly and its Witnesses, p. 142.

main features were the same. All work was suspended, and every one in the village gathered at the house of mourning, whence the coffin was borne to the grave on men's shoulders, followed by a long procession. When the burial was over all returned to the house, and feasting and drinking ensued. This celebration of funerals was, as has been seen, common to all the northern and middle colonies, and was carried to strange extremes, borrowed originally from English customs.[1]

In many respects, for one reason or another, New England differed, sometimes for better and sometimes for worse, from the other colonies, often very slightly, and then again very widely; but there was one point on which the dissimilarity was more marked than on any other. This was education. The Puritan theory of a direct personal communion between each human being and his Maker, and the consequent interest in divine precepts, made the Bible and the capacity to read it an essential part of their system of society. The tradition of a time when the Bible was chained up in churches, when it was the privilege of the priesthood and denied to the people, was still fresh in their thoughts. Ignorance, slavery, and papacy were to their minds inseparable, and to unbar the gates of knowledge and keep them open for all and each was one of their chief political and religious doctrines. With strong, unflinching narrowness they strove to regulate every detail of human life, with rigid intolerance they persisted in attempts to bind opinions and check their utterance unless they accorded with certain well-defined principles; yet, even while they did this, they made it one of their cardinal doctrines to strike off the shackles from the mind, and put knowledge within the reach of every one. The two policies thus inevitably united were, of course, hopelessly inconsistent. The Puritans held down liberty of thought and action with one hand, and raised up intellectual freedom with the other. From their race, and from the conditions of their development, they could not do otherwise, and this contradictory policy could have but one result. They freed the human mind, and then tried to limit it in a new fashion. The effort was vain. The liberated intelligence broke the bonds of Calvin as it had those of Rome; and the spirit of inquiry proved as fatal to

---

[1] New England Hist. Gen. Reg., viii., 212 · Coll. Massachusetts Hist. Soc., II., viii., 44; Ibid., V., v., vi., Sewall's Diary generally—New Hampshire, Parker's Londonderry, p. 76; Rambles about Portsmouth, Second Series, p. 334; Bouton, History of Concord, p. 512—Connecticut, History of New London, p. 267; History of Meriden, and Wallingford, p. 380; Hollister's History of Connecticut, i., 438.

the peculiar political and social system of the Puritans as it had to the tyranny of the Popish hierarchy. On one side the Puritan was the dark, unrelenting, religious enthusiast, fierce of spirit and gloomy in creed; on the other, he was the champion of education, and rendered unequalled services to the enlightenment of the human race.

Thus it was that one of the earliest acts of the settlers of New England was to found a system of public schools. A certain number of families were required by law to maintain a grammar-school, and free Latin schools were sometimes established in county towns by general law, and sometimes in the principal city by special act, as at Portsmouth and Boston. In many cases in Massachusetts the towns and the schools were founded apparently almost together, and date back to the early years of the Puritan immigration. By the year 1649 education was compulsory everywhere in New England except in Rhode Island. Throughout New England the school-house followed hard upon the church and block-house, which were the first buildings erected when a new community was organized. At first, of course, teachers were not plentiful, and there was home instruction, the children of every family being taught the rudiments by their parents until they were able to go to the nearest grammar-school; and this continued to be the case in New Hampshire and in outlying districts down to the time of the Revolution. The home instruction of the first settlers was followed by dames' schools, itinerant teachers, and sometimes by settled masters who were officers of the town. The instruction in these schools was of course very simple and rudimentary, but it served as a beginning, and growing steadily developed into a universal system of public common schools. These were supplemented by Latin schools; and where the latter were not established boys were fitted for college by private instruction from the clergyman of the parish. The result was that at the time of the Revolution everybody could read from one end of New England to the other, and illiteracy, except on the wild frontiers of Maine, was almost wholly unknown. The children of the very poorest parents had all some education, so that they cannot be compared with the ignorant classes of Europe, and those of more prosperous families were as well educated as in England. The boys when they left school were sent to college, the girls were taught fine work, music, and dancing. There was no need to send children abroad for an education, as was so much the practice in the southern provinces, and it was very rarely done.

More remarkable even than the foundation of the public school sys-

30

tem was the establishment of a college for the cultivation of the highest learning by the general court of Massachusetts, within seven years from the time when Endicott and his followers landed at Salem. There is no need to trace the history of Harvard College, thus founded to train up "learned and godly ministers," for it is part of the history of the colony itself. It was sustained and carried through many long years of discouragement by the energy of a powerful clergy, and the support of an intelligent and far-sighted people. The learning of the New England clergy was very great, and so was that of the college they administered. At the period of the Revolution the college probably afforded in theology, philosophy, and the classics as good an education as could be obtained in Europe, for the professors were men of character and learning, and some of them eminent. The college had some goodly brick buildings, a library of five thousand volumes, and good sets of astronomical and philosophical apparatus. The education of the common schools and the higher education went hand in hand in Massachusetts, and by the grants of the legislature, by the gifts of towns, and by the legacies of individuals, can be seen the deep and wide-spread popular interest felt in these subjects.

In Connecticut, Yale College was founded at the very beginning of the eighteenth century, and entered on a career of usefulness and success which fell little short of that of the older university. At a later period Dartmouth College was founded in New Hampshire, and well managed; and, still later, Brown College in Rhode Island. In this last colony education was not so good as in the other New England provinces. There were, of course, public schools, but of less high quality, and for the best and final education the children of those who could afford it were usually sent to Massachusetts or Connecticut. The striking fact about New England education was the high average. Every one could read, write, and cipher, and ignorance was even more uncommon than pauperism.[1]

---

[1] Abbé Robin, p. 24; Upham's Salem Witchcraft, i.; Proc. Massachusetts Hist. Soc., iii., Bennet's MS. Hist., p. 109 and ff.; New England Hist. Gen. Reg., vi., School in Ipswich; Rochefoucauld, ii., 214; Tyler's American Literature, i., 98; Coll. Massachusetts Hist. Soc., II., iv., Schools in Plymouth — New Hampshire, Rochefoucauld, ii., 196; Hist. Soc. Coll., i., 157; iv., 15; Prov. Papers, iii., 364; History of Rindge, p. 273—Connecticut, Abbé Robin, p. 41; Wansey, p. 67; Rochefoucauld, i., 527; Barber's Hist. Coll., p. 146; History of Glastenbury, p. 110; History of New London, p. 395; Litchfield County Centennial, p. 48; History of Norwich, p. 92—Rhode Island, Claude Blanchard, p. 43; Rochefoucauld, i., 496, 504; Cahoon, Sketches of Newport, pp. 43, 56; Col. Records, vi., 385.

Where education both in school and college was so general and wide-spread, the atmosphere was much more favorable to literature and other purely intellectual pursuits than in the other colonies. The Puritan leaders and the Puritan clergy brought with them a strong love of letters, and even in the very infancy of the colony, in the midst of the hard struggle for existence in the wilderness, they did not neglect them. Through the dark period of settlement and isolation the Puritan clergy carried the light of literature undimmed. They sedulously maintained their connection with their brethren in England, and the chain of thought was never broken, nor was the attachment to the learning and scholarship of the Old World ever lessened. In this way there grew up in New England a native literature, strengthened by its connection with Europe, but bearing the deep impression of the peculiarities and characteristics of the people, among whom it had developed. The proportion of learned men, including the clergy, among the early settlers was very large. It has been computed that there was one Cambridge graduate to every two hundred and fifty immigrants; and the result of this and of the maintenance of learning in the provinces was a great literary activity in the seventeenth century, which was continued, with some abatement and slight changes, through the eighteenth down to the Revolutionary epoch. As the chief purely intellectual interest was religion, so the principal part of New England literature was polemical divinity; but there was also a literature of politics, memoirs, poetry, and history, all deeply tinged with religious thought, a quality which gradually fades away as the eighteenth century advances.

The political and religious beliefs which led to the Puritan immigration impressed the participants in that movement with a deep sense of the vastness of their undertaking, and the importance of preserving personal records of events. This feeling gave us the diary of Bradford, of Plymouth; the diary of Governor Winthrop, the most interesting of all, and of considerable literary merit; the journal of Francis Higginson; and a number of others of less importance. Then comes a second period of native diarists, among whom Samuel Sewall is conspicuous, covering the close of the colonial and the first thirty years of the provincial period. In all these diaries the marked quality is the introspection and constant religious and moral questionings of the writers, accompanied by a minute record of public and private events, with appropriate reflections exhibiting a great deal of penetration and shrewd observation. These memoirs reflect the thought, and are literary examples of the period in which they were composed, but their publication was left, of course, to a late posterity.

Social and political tracts made their appearance in the earliest days of the settlement, and continued to be published by both laymen and ministers until the period of the Revolution. The clergy predominated among the writers at first very largely, but early in the seventeenth century they began to lose their leadership. Sewall, among others, published an able attack on slavery; and Jeremiah Dummer's Defence of the Charters was, perhaps, the most powerful of the New England political tracts. At the beginning of the troubles with England the change had gone still farther, and political writing passed into the hands of the laity, and particularly of the lawyers. In the early days, also, there was a good deal of verse written, chiefly by clergymen; but the best and most conspicuous of the verse writers was Anne Bradstreet, the daughter of the elder Dudley. She was a follower of Quarles and Withers, and the euphuists—a pernicious style very popular in New England; but some of her shorter and simpler poems are not without merit. The literary development of New England can, however, be best traced in the writings of the clergy, who were the great repositories of learning, and the real exponents of New England literature. The line of clerical writers is a long and famous one, and their activity extended into every field. Besides an unbroken and immense series of published sermons, they produced many more extensive and ambitious works in theology, doctrinal controversy, history, politics, and poetry, of which even the most purely secular were strongly tinged with the religious feeling. Descriptions of the country were among the earliest writings; but the most successful of these first efforts was the fierce satire of Nathaniel Ward, the "simple cobbler of Agawam," brimming over with attacks upon manners in New and Old England, and full of bitter intolerance and invective against such matters as long hair and woman's dress. All the clergy had a great fancy for versifying. The fearful verse of the Bay Psalm-book was the work of eminent ministers like Weld, Eliot, and the first Mather. Cotton and Wilson, the first ministers of the Boston church, both indulged in bad verse; John Norton and John Rogers were followers of Anne Bradstreet; and Urian Oakes, the President of Harvard College, attempted an elegy on Shepard. In all alike there is a dire struggle for the expression of genuine feeling in harsh and stilted lines. The most prolific poet was of a later time, Michael Wigglesworth, who embodied in interminable verses the dogmas of Calvinism. His masterpiece was the "Day of Doom," redolent with the fire and smoke of the Calvinistic hell. The elaborate account of the fate of the wicked concludes as follows:

> "Die fain they would, if die they could,
> But death will not be had;
> God's direful wrath their bodies hath
> Forever immortal made.
> They live to lie in misery
> And bear eternal woe;
> And live they must whilst God is just,
> That he may plague them so."

Then follows a description of the happiness of the saints, "who rejoice to see judgment executed upon the wicked world." The passage just quoted is very mild in tone, but shows the utter failure of the stiff New England mind to deal with poetry. The subject, it is true, was an impossible one to anything short of the genius of Milton, but nevertheless Wigglesworth, although master of a good vocabulary, was clearly painfully deficient as a poet; yet his works had an immense sale, and were read by every one in New England, and reprinted in London. Wigglesworth was, however, much the best of the verse-makers. After his time the wretched school of the euphuists gradually died out, and was followed by equally poor ballad-makers, and by bad imitators of Pope, such as the eminent divines Colman and Byles. Poetry continued to be cultivated, however, and in the year 1762, a series of adulatory poems, on the accession of George III., entitled "Pietas et Gratulatio," emanated from the college. They were written in faultless Latin, and were fully up to the level of the English universities, but they evinced nothing but learning.

In other fields the clergy appeared to better advantage. The profound learning of the early clergy has already been alluded to, and its tradition was never lost. Conspicuous among them was the Mather family, eminent for four generations. Increase Mather, second in the succession, was not only a foremost man in politics, but was a prodigy of learning. He could read and write Hebrew and Greek with perfect ease, and speak Latin fluently when he graduated; and his published works, including a history of the Indian wars, numbered ninety-two. In the way of literary productions, however, he was far surpassed by his son, Cotton Mather, aptly styled by the historian of American literature "the literary behemoth" of New England. Cotton Mather published three hundred and eighty-three books and pamphlets, which comprised many sermons, treatises on every possible topic, and the great folio of the " Magnalia Christi." Cotton Mather was a man of undoubted ability and vast erudition, and much of his work may still be read with curiosity and interest; but as a historian he was untrustworthy, and his style, overcharged and involved, was the worst, as it was the last, in the fantastic fashion of the seventeenth century. Besides the Mathers, there were many who attained reputation by their writings. Samuel Willard gained fame by a massive folio, entitled the " Complete Body of Divinity," a posthumous publication. Benjamin Colman, for many years the first preacher in Boston, was a graceful and eloquent man, familiar with English society, and master of the polished Addisonian style. Mather Byles, " aristocrat and apostle," the last of the long line — although driven from his pulpit as a Tory by the storm of the Revolution—was a courtly, elegant, refined man, very witty in society, and very eloquent as a preacher—a curious contrast to the men of 1629, whom he succeeded, and a strange witness to the process of development. A famous contemporary and champion of the patriot side was Jonathan Mayhew, a forcible and influential controversialist. The wide range of pulpit subjects gave great scope at every period to the talents of the ministers; but the clergy of the eighteenth century included in their ranks one man who, with the exception of Franklin, was the greatest of the New England minds during the colonial period. Jonathan Edwards, like Franklin, achieved a European reputation, and his powerful reasoning was renowned wherever the doctrines of Calvin were revered. When a mere child, he could read Greek, Latin, and Hebrew, and the most abstruse English. He wrote on metaphysics while still in college, and subsequently achieved distinction as a philosopher, and by his acquirements in physical science. He was the leader of a great party in the Church, and as a reasoner upon doctrinal questions he displayed a mental vigor and severity of logic which has seldom been surpassed; while his work upon the " Freedom of the Will " is still a masterpiece in its particular field.

The clergy at first monopolized the department of history, as they did most others, and Hubbard and Increase Mather were the leaders in this branch; but in the eighteenth century the historians increased in number, and included many of the laity. To this second period belong Calef, Scottow, Penhallow, Church, Douglass, Prince, and Hutchinson, all of whom produced valuable and important books; while some of them—such as Hutchinson, the last of the series—had real literary merit, and others—like Church—besides possessing this quality, narrate personal experiences with a strong dash of quaint humor, and much originality.

The literary activity of New England, and the intellectual tastes of the people, find abundant evidence in other ways. The first printing-press in America was started in Cambridge, in the year 1639, just ten years after the settlement, and its career was never checked or broken. In 1662 heresy was thought to be about, and the press was put under the charge of official licensers, a restraint which was not removed until 1755; but the work of this early press—its effects and its results —were of vast importance, and show conclusively the vigor of intellectual life in New England. The earliest form of current literature was the Almanac, a species of publication of great importance, and widely read throughout the English colonies. The first was issued from the Cambridge press in 1639; and the next colony to have one was Pennsylvania, in 1686. They gradually appeared in all the colonies, and were crowned finally by "Poor Richard," who has gained a world-wide fame. The first newspaper, too, appeared in Boston in 1690. It was entitled *Public Occurrences*, and was promptly suppressed for "uttering reflections of a very high nature." The next newspaper, and the first permanent one in the colonies, was the *Boston News-letter*, which appeared in 1704; and in 1754 there were four newspapers in New England, all published in Boston. The following year, the *Connecticut Gazette* was started in New Haven, and three years later the *Summary* appeared at New London. In 1775 Boston had five newspapers, and Salem, Newburyport, and Portsmouth one each. These journals were universally read, and could be found in the remotest farm-houses, where they were regularly taken. They formed, however, but a small part of the reading of the people. The best literature of the day, and the English classics, were always in the hands of the educated classes. Even so strict a Puritan as Samuel Sewall records in his diary that he read Ben Jonson; and the *Spectator* and its successors, and the novels of Richardson, found their way regularly to the homes of Boston merchants. A simple mechanic like Franklin's father had a good library of polemical divinity, and hardly any New England family was so poor as not to possess a number of books, commonly of a religious character. Besides this private effort, book companies were formed—some as early as 1737 —for the importation of books; and at the time of the Revolution there was a subscription library in almost every township.

Science was never carried far, and the appliances for its study were almost wholly wanting, except at Cambridge. Yet from the time of John Winthrop, of Connecticut, one of the early members of the Royal Society, and a man of broad learning, there were always in New England a few men zealously engaged in scientific investigation. The arts can hardly be said to have existed. There was neither the opportunity nor the wealth so essential to their development. Sewall speaks of the death of "Tom Child, the Painter," and there was a succession of portrait-painters in Boston during the eighteenth century, including Pelham and Smibert, and concluding with the famous Copley. There were a few portraits in Faneuil Hall and in the college, and here and there fine pictures bought in Europe could be found in the homes of wealthy merchants; but art was wholly exotic and very limited, and entered in no perceptible degree into the life of the people. The first faint indications could be discerned, but that was all. Yet, as we survey the whole field of literature, science, and art, the vigorous, intellectual life of the people is very marked, of much greater strength, and far more widely diffused and desired, than in any other part of the English possessions.[1]

The only intellectual interest which entered at all into competition with religion among the New England people was that of politics. Not only was the pure religion to find a refuge in the New World, but there the Puritan state was to be built up if Charles succeeded in establishing a despotism in the mother country. The trading charter of the Bay Company was but a thin veil concealing the really independent state which grew up in Massachusetts. The system was in theory thoroughly democratic, and political equality was one of the corner-stones of the structure. In a similar fashion the settlements of Connecticut and Rhode Island developed into independent communities, and so continued down to and beyond the Revolution. The old charter in Massachusetts was lost, and New Hampshire

---

[1] Brissot, p. 86; Tyler's History of American Literature, ii., 98 and ff.; Wansey, p. 47; Nason's Life of Frankland; Thomas's History of Printing; Mag. Amer. History, ii., 247; Rochefoucauld, ii., 214; Coll. Massachusetts Hist. Soc., V., vi., 167, 170, Sewall; Works of Franklin, i., 15; Coll. Massachusetts Hist. Soc., IV., ii., Douglas, Letters to Colden; Ibid., IV., vii., Mather Papers—New Hampshire, Farmer's Hist. Coll., ii., 174, 176; Annals of Portsmouth, Adams, p. 189 — Connecticut, Barber's Hist. Coll., p. 164; New Haven, Hist. Coll., i., 147; History of New London, p. 472; History of Durham, p. 104—Rhode Island, Chastellux, p. 19; Cahoon, Sketches of Newport, p. 56.

became a royal province, but the spirit of the people was unchanged. Constant conflicts with successive governors were carried on unceasingly, and with rare ability, so that not only did prerogative fail to make any advance, but it was steadily pushed back. The jealousy of external power never slept. Sewall knew of no power, he said, to take pirates out of the colony for trial in England, and the seizure of sailors for men-of-war was steadily opposed and openly resisted. A little incident, early in the eighteenth century, shows the underlying sense of equality before God and the law which reigned in New England, despite the conservative recognition of ranks and distinction. The Governor's coach in winter met some carts in a narrow road, and the teamsters not getting quickly out of the way, Governor Dudley and his son alighted, ordered the men aside, and drew their swords upon them. Blows followed. " I am as good flesh and blood as you !" said the carter, closing with the Governor, and breaking his sword. The carters were soon after arrested and sent to prison, pursued by the Governor with a bitter spirit of revenge, but when they came before the court and the evidence was all in, they were discharged. The Governor was powerless, for public sentiment sustained the men who had been dealt with as if they were inferiors and entitled to no rights.

Another feature of the New England character which helped to increase the love of political independence and self-government, was the keen dislike of foreigners and great pride of race. Except the few French Huguenots of the seventeenth century, who were gladly welcomed in New England, no foreigners came among them. They hated Papists, and Irish, and Frenchmen with a bitter hatred. Even the Scotch Presbyterians of Londonderry were distrusted and disliked, because papacy was suspected in all who came from Ireland ; and even the timely help of France in the Revolution could not obliterate the sense of inherited enmity and deep suspicion. The process of naturalization was slow, difficult, and very rare, and the practice was utterly discouraged. As soon as England put herself in the position of an external and foreign power this deep-rooted dislike of foreigners extended to her, and combined with the strong spirit of liberty and hatred of interference to bring on the resort to arms.

Yet with all this there were few grievances, and the people were thoroughly loyal. Apart from an angry dread of a colonial bishop, there was none of the Church oppression which did so much to alienate the other colonies. The laws of trade bore hardly upon New England ; but they were so generally evaded and disregarded, either by the venality of the collectors, a post highly valued on this account, or by open and unpunished violation, that in practice they were not felt. When the British ministry began to enforce them, the first sense of oppression was given to the New England people. The genuine loyalty of the people was unquestioned. All the best evidence of the time concurs on this point, and we have the direct opinion of such a man as John Adams as to its truth. The deepest interest was felt in every public event in England, and the Protestant succession was very dear to the descendants of the Puritans. They rejoiced publicly on every victory of the English arms; they celebrated royal births, marriages, and coronations with all the pomp they could muster. They mourned formally and carefully on the occasion of every death in the royal family, and these outward manifestations were not tainted with hypocrisy. They still looked back to England as the home of their race, and her glory was theirs. But everybody in New England was a politician. "They are all politicians down to the house-maids," says Rochefoucauld, "and read two newspapers a day." Politics always ran high, and parties were strong and active. There was no need of an elaborate warning to such people that their rights were invaded. They all knew it by instinct, and, once aroused, the old spirit of independent government and the hatred of outside interference broke out and could not be quenched. Thus it was that, when England began to meddle with the colonies which Sir Robert Walpole had so wisely neglected, the opposition began, and the war opened on the soil of New England. There were no special grievances, there was no peculiar disloyalty; but there was a thoroughly homogeneous people, pure of race, wedded to independence, all educated, all keen politicians, hating external power, and still imbued with the traditions of their fathers, who had fought the great Rebellion and brought a king to execution. Such a people could not be governed except as seemed right in their own eyes; and when an attempt was made to rule them in other ways the war for independence began.[1]

---

[1] Abbé Robin, pp. 22, 26, 28; Claude Blanchard, p. 48; Brissot, p. 87; Journal of Labadists, Long Island Hist. Soc. Coll., i.; Nason's Life of Frankland; Proc. Massachusetts Hist. Soc., ii., 337, Naturalization; New England Hist. Gen. Reg., xiii., 328; xxx., 328, Letters of Jay and Adams on Loyalty of Colonies; Rochefoucauld, i., 398; Coll. Massachusetts Hist. Soc., III., ii., 26; IV., ii., Douglass to Colden; V., vi., 4, 144, 317, 327—New Hampshire Hist. Soc., i., 155; vii., 35; Parker's Londonderry, pp. 70, 77; Connecticut, History of New London, p. 406; Rhode Island, Fersen, p. 40; Rochefoucauld, i., 496.

New England is the last of the three groups of colonies. It is easy to see the qualities which were peculiar to her people, and the great divergence between their system and that of the South. The former were pure in race, simple and frugal in their lives, thrifty, prosperous, and enterprising, a population of small freeholders, with slight inequalities of condition, and a wide-spread and high average of education and intelligence. Their system was democratic, with a voluntary recognition of aristocracy. From this strong and vigorous race came many great leaders, eminent in civil and military life; but the great strength was in the body of the people. They were all imbued with the same principles, they all had the same unyielding tenacity of purpose, reckless audacity, shrewdness, and force. They carried their principles into the new national government of the United Colonies. Between them and Virginia was the contest for supremacy, while the great middle colonies held the balance; and the history of that conflict of ideas is the history of the United States.

Chapter XXIII.

PREPARING FOR REVOLUTION: FROM 1765 TO 1776.

1765. In October, 1765, the representatives of nine colonies met in Congress at New York and founded the American Union, for the example of federation once given was not forgotten, and was quickly followed. Timothy Ruggles, of Massachusetts, was chosen President; but the leaders on the floor were Gadsden and Rutledge, of South Carolina, and Otis, of Massachusetts. Under the lead of South Carolina, the arguments founded on chartered privileges were laid aside, and the broad doctrines of inalienable rights and liberties were adopted. In a series of resolutions and memorials to both Houses of Parliament the Congress asserted the right to trial by jury against an extended admiralty jurisdiction, the right to freedom from taxation, except by the colonial assemblies, as the people could not be represented in Parliament, and, therefore, that Parliament could not constitutionally tax them. They complained of the acts of trade, admitted a due submission to King and Parliament, and the right of Parliament to legislate generally and to regulate trade; but beyond this they would not go. Ruggles, of Massachusetts, and Ogden, of New Jersey, alone refused to sign, and the latter was hung in effigy for his pains. Meantime the current of popular resistance flowed on stronger and fuller than ever. Agreements not to import English manufactures were rapidly formed. Everywhere there was a general opposition to the Stamp Act, and mobs forced the collectors to resign. On the first day of November, when the act was to take effect, bells were tolled, processions formed, and the goddess of liberty buried. No one would use the stamps. In Connecticut the newspapers appeared without them. In Boston there was a fierce mob, which, after compelling Oliver to resign his office in the presence of a great crowd, ran riot, and sacked the house of Hutchinson, the Lieutenant-governor. In New York the "Sons of Liberty," guided by Isaac Sears, the popular leader of the town, boldly faced Colden, who had prepared to use the English troops, burnt him in effigy, sacked the house of a British officer, and finally obliged the reluctant Governor to yield the stamps into the keeping of the city government. They followed this up by seizing the stamped paper intended for Connecticut, and burning it in the streets. The Maryland distributor fled to New York, only to be arrested there by the watchful Sons of Liberty, and forced to resign. In Charleston the act was burnt, and the bells of the city tolled. The Stamp Act was annulled in America.

While the storm raged in the colonies, the Rockingham ministry met Parliament. They were not prepared then to deal with the American question, and when they met again after the recess they had reached no agreement. The matter, however, could not be post-

1766. poned, and the debate opened on the address to the King.

On that memorable night Pitt took the floor, and, while upholding the power of Parliament to legislate generally and to control trade, denied their right to lay internal taxes on the colonies. Grenville ably defended the act of which he was the author; and then Pitt spoke again, contrary to rule, and uttered the famous sentence which rang through two continents: " Sir, I rejoice that America has resisted." At last the ministry had a policy, the one pointed out by the great commoner. They brought in two acts, one declaring the power of Parliament to be supreme over the colonies in every respect, and another repealing the Stamp Act. A month passed in the examination of witnesses by the Commons, and in debates by the Lords. Camden defended with splendid eloquence the position that taxation without representation was unconstitutional, and put the matter further on the broad and statesman-like ground that, however the law might be, the great principles of justice demanded that the Americans should be allowed to tax themselves. He was answered by Mansfield in a speech of consummate ability, and was hopelessly defeated on a division. Parliament would not accept the doctrine of Pitt. On the seventeenth of February, Conway, who had never faltered or changed in his opposition to the Stamp Act, brought in a resolution for its repeal; there was another great debate, and the resolution passed. The conflict was protracted still longer, but at last both the repeal and the act declaratory of the supreme power of Parliament passed both Houses. The theory was maintained, but the practice was abandoned, for the pressure in England had become too great to be borne. The non-importation agreements of the colonies had struck home to the pockets of the English manufacturers, and eager crowds had filled the lobbies, and hailed with shouts the appearance of Conway, after his memorable victory of the seventeenth of February. The news of the repeal filled America with rejoicing and happiness. Portraits and statues of Pitt and Conway, of Barré and of the King, were ordered by the grateful assemblies; and celebrations of the great event were held everywhere, and the defenders of American liberty were toasted and applauded.

All this rejoicing was as natural as it was unfounded. The Stamp Act had been repealed, the immediate grievance had been remedied; but the new policy of taxation was checked, not defeated; the principle of the supreme power of Parliament had been strongly asserted, and was more full of vitality and meaning than ever before. The great debate, in which all the eloquence and reason of England's statesmen had been employed, had resulted in the establishment of the principle and the defeat of a particular measure. Pitt's position was that of a great statesman, of a broad and liberal-minded man, but his theory was untenable. There was no middle ground between the doctrine of Mansfield that Parliament was everywhere supreme, and that of some of the Americans that internal and external taxation were alike unconstitutional. If Pitt's theory had been adopted and acted upon as he himself would have acted upon it, all would have gone well. It would have been neither the first nor the last impossible compromise in the history of the English race to have met with success. But Parliament was logical, if nothing else, and it believed its own power to be supreme and complete, and so declared it. That it would soon put its theory in practice, and that America would soon take up the opposite and equally logical position, was certain; the only question was one of time, and events moved rapidly.

The sound of the rejoicings called forth by the repeal of the Stamp Act had hardly died away before it was seen how little had really been gained beyond immediate and temporary relief. The Stamp Act was gone, but the Declaratory Act, and the Sugar Act, and the Mutiny Act, requiring quarters to be provided for English troops, and recently extended to the colonies, remained unmodified and unchanged. The Rockingham ministry was dissolved; Pitt came again to the helm, and was made the Earl of Chatham. The clouds of his strange illness gathered about the prime-minister, and the conduct of affairs fell into the hands of Charles Townshend, a believer in the Stamp Act, and with no faith in Pitt's distinction between internal and external taxation. He was determined to pursue the policy of

Grenville, and laid his plans to quarter garrisons in the large towns of America, and have them supported by the colonial assemblies, and to exact a revenue from the colonies. The trouble had, indeed, already begun in New York, where the Assembly, which had passed a limited act for the supply of two regiments in December, 1766, refused to provide for quartering troops, and stood firm through a long controversy with Sir Henry Moore. In the following spring, Parliament, under the lead of Townshend, suspended the legislative powers

1767. of New York, as a punishment for their disobedience. This was a warning which could not be mistaken. In the other colonies, even when requisitions were complied with, there was careful evasion of obedience to the terms of the act, and sympathy with New York spread far and wide, carrying with it deep disquiet and indignation. Not content with beginning to enforce the Mutiny Act, Townshend carried measures to impose port duties on wine, oil, and fruit from Spain and Portugal, and on glass, paper, lead, colors, and tea. The revenue thus raised was to be used for the payment of the Crown officers, and for the establishment of a civil list. This was a blow at the most vital rights of the colonies, for it took from them the control of their governments. The new policy, unchecked by the death of Townshend in the autumn of 1767, excited the utmost apprehension in America, and fanned into flame the smouldering embers of the opposition to the Stamp Act. Again non-importation agreements were discussed, but without combination or effect; and Massachusetts, thoroughly alarmed at the prospect of independent Crown officers, determined on stronger measures. The Assembly resolved to

1768. send a petition to the King, and letters to the statesmen of England. In the petition drawn, probably, by Samuel Adams, the Assembly set forth the conditions of their settlement, argued against taxation without representation, and protested against the presence of a standing army, and the project of rendering the judicial and executive officers independent of the people. They followed this action by a resolve inviting the other colonies to unite with them in petitions to the King against the new taxation. At every step Bernard and Hutchinson resisted the Assembly, which moved forward steadily, cautiously, and firmly, making no mistakes, and giving no openings. Bernard and the Crown officers met the action of the Assembly by a counter-memorial, inveighing against the freedom and independent temper of the colonists, and advising the immediate presence of fleets and armies; supporting their requests with tales of projected riots, for the people had begun to be restless, although there was really no danger of any serious outbreak.

Hillsborough, the new Secretary of State, and the King's friends were indignant at the action of Massachusetts, and letters were sent to the other colonies denouncing the Massachusetts circular, and to Bernard, instructing him to order the House to rescind their resolve, and, if they refused, to dissolve them. Meantime, the excitement increased. John Hancock's sloop, *Liberty*, was seized, on the ground of evasion of the customs. There was a slight disturbance, and revenue officers, in pretended fear of their lives, took refuge on the *Romney* man-of-war, while the town and the Governor quarrelled about the affair. When the general court met, strengthened by the sympathy of Connecticut and New Jersey, and by the letter of Virginia, where their principles had been sustained by resolutions of the Burgesses, Hillsborough's letter was presented. The House, by an overwhelming vote, refused to rescind; the court was dissolved, and Massachusetts was left without a legislature. Boston town-meeting took into its hands the power which Hillsborough and Bernard sought to crush. They called a convention of delegates from the towns of the province while troops were on their way to Massachusetts; and this convention came together, demanded in vain a general court, passed strong resolutions against taxation and a standing army, and adjourned, while the Council refused to make provision for the expected soldiers until the barracks were filled, and the old beacon was prepared as in the days of Andros. Soon after the convention dissolved, two regiments, presently increased to four, and artillery, landed and marched into the town. The Council refused quarters until the barracks were occupied; and, after camping for some time in the open air, the troops were finally quartered and supplied at the expense of the Crown. No measure could possibly have been taken better calculated to produce civil war. The troops were sent to overawe, and they merely irritated the people. Into a peaceful town, into a province which had simply remonstrated and petitioned legally and properly in defence of their rights, were suddenly thrust royal regiments. The strong feeling of independence in a country where garrisons were absolutely unknown was outraged, while the bad character and licentious habits of the soldiery incensed a rigid, austere, and sober people. Attempts at military coercion and the presence of troops were sure to breed trouble; and, worse than this, they not only awakened the sympathy of the other colonies, but alarmed them for their own safety. It was outside pressure and peril in its strongest form, and nothing tended so strongly to produce that union which alone could be fatal to English rule.

In Virginia, when the Burgesses met, resolutions were passed declaring against taxation, and asserting the right to trial by a jury of the vicinage, and to combination among the colonies. Botetourt dissolved the Assembly, and the Burgesses met in convention and formed a stringent non-importation agreement. Virginia carried with her the southern colonies, her example was followed in Delaware and Pennsylvania, and when the general court came together again in Massachusetts they promptly adopted the resolutions. Some of the troops had been withdrawn; but two regiments were kept on Bernard's request, and he and the legislature were in no good-humor when they met at Cambridge, whither the Governor adjourned them. The House refused flatly to provide for troops, or to give a salary for the year to Bernard, who was recalled, and who soon after, having prorogued the refractory Assembly, departed from Boston, amid the noisy rejoicings of the populace, leaving Hutchinson to rule in his stead. While Massachusetts and Virginia were thus coming together, and preparing the American union, the ministry in England, halting and undecided, rather frightened at the results of their energetic policy, and desperately embroiled with Wilkes, decided to recede. They sent a circular to the colonies, promising to lay no more taxes, and to repeal the duties on glass, paper, and colors, retaining only that on tea. Their action was that of well-meaning, narrow, and weak men. They should either then and there have enforced their policy at the point of the bayonet, or they should have fully and frankly given way on every point. To save their pride, maintain their doctrines, and please the King, they retained one paltry tax, yielding, perhaps, three hundred pounds a year, but which carried the vital principle with it as surely and clearly as revenue involving millions. The course of the ministry had slowly brought the conflict to the point at which complete victory on one side or the other was alone possible. The colonies were fully alive to the situation, and saw that while one tax remained nothing had been gained. The non-importation agreements spread everywhere, and were strongly enforced, and all society was drawn into a refusal to use tea. Conflicts with the revenue officers in Rhode Island and elsewhere grew more and more frequent, and the relations of the people with the soldiery in New York and Boston more and more strained. In New York there were violent affrays between the soldiers and the

1769.

1770.

31

people over the erection of the liberty-pole, and there was fighting in the streets. These outbreaks heightened feeling in Boston, where the soldiers were taunted and insulted, and where recurring fights between populace and redcoats showed that a crisis was at hand. On the third of March there was an ugly brawl, and on the evening of the fifth there was another fray and trouble with the sentry. Before quiet was restored there was renewed fighting, and a crowd gathered round the sentry in King Street. Alarmed and angry, the man called out the guard; the mob rapidly increased; insults were followed by missiles; one soldier discharged his gun; there was a scattering fire from the troops, and three of the citizens were killed and two mortally wounded. Blood had been shed, and it looked as if civil war had begun. The regiments were turned out, the people poured into the streets; it was a mere chance that the American Revolution was not then to open. But Hutchinson appeared in the balcony of the State-house, promised an investigation, and besought peace. The people dispersed, and war was for the moment averted; yet nothing could efface the memory of this affray. Regular troops had fired upon the citizens, human life had been sacrificed, and the exaggerated title of the " Boston Massacre " showed the importance attached to this event, which served for years to keep alive and develop resistance to England.

The morning after the massacre the select-men waited on Hutchinson, and urged the removal of the soldiers. At eleven the town meeting came together, and chose a committee, with Samuel Adams at its head, to wait upon the Governor, and demand the withdrawal of the troops. Hutchinson wished to delay and postpone. He offered to have the Twenty-ninth Regiment, which had fired on the people, removed to the castle, and the other put under proper restraint. The committee went back through thronged streets, and made its report, which was pronounced unsatisfactory, and a new committee, again headed by Adams, went back to the Governor. The interview which followed in the Council-chamber, as the daylight slowly faded, was one of the great dramatic scenes of the American Revolution. In that moment Samuel Adams was pre-eminent, and all the greatness and force of his mind and character concentrated to raise him up as the great tribune of the people. The incarnation of right and justice, the true champion of the people, he stood before the fit representative of a weak, vacillating, proud, and stupid ministry, and made that representative quail before him. " If you can remove one, you can remove both," he said to Hutchinson; "there are three thousand people in yonder town-meeting; the country is rising; night is falling, and we must have an answer." Hutchinson hesitated a moment, trembled, and gave way. Before a week elapsed, all the troops were withdrawn; and meantime they had watched the funerals of their victims, seen their companions arrested for murder, beheld a town-meeting called to hurry their departure, and had been kept under strict guard by the militia of the town they went forth to garrison. Staying and going were alike full of humiliation and defeat. It was a great triumph; and as the news spread of the events at Boston, a strong sense of relief filled the colonies.

While the colonies were thus engaged the Duke of Grafton had fallen from power, and the "King's friends," led by Lord North, were at the head of affairs. With the full concurrence of Parliament, they repealed the obnoxious taxes, but succeeded by a slender majority in retaining the fatal duty on tea. The mitigated policy of England and the victory at Boston tended to sow dissension among the colonies. Virginia and other southern provinces began to slacken in the enforcement of the non-importation agreement; and New York, where enforcement had been most stringent, after chafing under this relaxation elsewhere, finally, though not without much opposition from Sears and his followers, abandoned the agreement, except so far as it related to tea. It looked as if the temporizing policy of the ministry would work its natural result in dividing the colonies and appeasing resentment, and that the troubled waters would subside, and flow quietly in their old channels. All this would have come to pass if the English ministers had not insisted on emphasizing the declarations of the powers of Parliament by retaining a nominal tax on tea, and if they had let the refractory province of Massachusetts alone; but they would neither give up the one nor refrain from the other.

In the town of Boston the conflict, which was fast dying out in the other colonies, was sedulously kept up by the representatives of the Crown. Hutchinson again summoned the general court at Cambridge, an act as unnecessary as it was ill-advised; and, while the House remonstrated, all legislation stood still. Hutchinson reproached them with their disregard of the rescinding order; and, in obedience to Hillsborough's instructions, gave up to Colonel Dalrymple the possession of the fort, reserved by the charter to the Governor. While Boston was thus being converted into a military station, and the Governor of Massachusetts was urging the destruction of her charter, the general court elected Benjamin Franklin their agent to plead their

cause in England. The overthrow of the regulators in North Carolina strengthened the Crown in the south, and Lord North's ministry
gained stability and votes enough to assure working majorities. To
men like Samuel Adams, who had begun to feel that the true solution
of all difficulties was to be found in independence, the outlook was
very dark. The next year Hutchinson again called the general court at
Cambridge, and again the House protested against this unre-
1771. strained use of the prerogative. Hutchinson vetoed the supply
bill because the incomes of the commissioners of revenue were not exempted, and the House remonstrated strongly, taking the ground that
such exemption struck at the very root of free government, and tended to vacate the charter. The power of King and Parliament was
fairly drawn into the discussion, and the Governor and Assembly
parted in no good-humor. The apparent tranquillity of the southern
states, which encouraged Hillsborough to urge Hutchinson forward in
his arbitrary course, began to show signs of disturbance. The
1772. Governors of Georgia and North Carolina were at odds with
their Assemblies; and the petition of Virginia—warmly supported in
the northern colonies—that the slave-trade might be checked was disregarded and overruled. In Rhode Island there was much bitter feeling against the officers of customs, and especially against Duddington,
the commander of the cruiser *Gaspee,* who insulted and abused the
inhabitants and fired on their boats. In June Duddington gave chase
to the Providence packet, and ran his vessel aground. Boats came
off from Providence in the night, manned by colonists, who boarded
the hated cruiser, wounded Duddington in the scuffle, took him and
his crew prisoners, and then, setting fire to the *Gaspee,* burnt her to
the water's edge. Civil war was not far distant when the people
were ripe for acts like these.

In Massachusetts, Hutchinson, for the fourth time, convened the
general court at Cambridge, but at last gave way on this point of useless offence, and adjourned them to Boston. There the House gave
its attention to the danger to their constitutional rights from the payment of Crown officers by warrant from a fund established by Parliament, and adopted a report which hinted in plain terms that such a
course relieved them from their dependence. Even while the storm
was slowly gathering, and while its mutterings could be heard in all
parts of the continent, Hillsborough hastened to announce that the
King had made provision for the support of the law officers in Massachusetts. The drift of this measure was plainly seen by Adams, and

he began at once to move against it. At the October town-meeting a committee was raised to inquire of the Governor if the judges were to be paid, and to ask that the Assembly meet on the day to which it had been prorogued. The Governor refused to answer the question, and denied to the town the right of demanding a meeting of the general court. At the next town-meeting the committee reported, reciting their grievances, and declaring that the right to life, liberty, and property must be defended, if necessary, by arms. Then Samuel Adams moved for a new committee to correspond with those to be raised in other towns, and the union of the American colonies was founded. Beginning in the hamlets of New England, it was destined to cover a continent. The towns rapidly fell in, and the spirit of opposition spread, excited by the news that orders had come to send the destroyers of the *Gaspee* to England for trial.

When the general court of Massachusetts came together at the opening of the new year, Hutchinson saw fit in his speech to renew **1773.** the discussion of the supremacy of Parliament, arguing that there was no middle ground between submission and independence, but the Governor was dealing with abler men than himself. Adams and Hawley eagerly embraced the issue, and the House replied to the Governor that the source of trouble was clearly in taxation, and deduced from his own premises the right to independence. In Rhode Island the royal commission met to inquire into the affair of the *Gaspee;* but the chief-justice refused to allow the offenders to be arrested for trial in England, and the royal commission adjourned without acting. The news of these events spread southward, and met with warm approval when the Burgesses of Virginia came together; and Dabney Carr, supported by Patrick Henry and Richard Henry Lee, introduced and carried through a series of resolutions in favor of a system of correspondence among the colonies. Union was far advanced when it received the adhesion of the great colony of Virginia, whose resolutions were warmly received everywhere, but above all in Massachusetts; the other New England colonies came at once into line, and the northern and southern groups were firmly united. The action of Virginia was more ominous to British rule than anything that had yet happened; and in Massachusetts fuel was added to the fire of popular resistance by the publication of the letters of Hutchinson and Oliver to the ministry. These documents, which Franklin, by means even now not fully known, had succeeded in obtaining, were full of deadly hostility to the province and its chartered liberties, and led to a petition for the removal of their authors, and to an outburst of anger before which Hutchinson quailed and desired to resign.

While these events were transpiring, the untiring efforts of Samuel Adams to bring about a Congress and cement union received a fresh stimulus from the action of the ministry. The East India Company was in difficulties, and Lord North authorized them to export tea to America, agreeing to allow a drawback equal to the whole duty. The news of this determination aroused the deepest indignation in the colonies; for not only was the principle of taxation to be maintained, but the tea which carried the principle with it was to be forced upon them. The consignments were already on their way, when the citizens of Philadelphia came together, denied the right of Parliament to tax them, condemned the duty on tea, declared all who took part in its importation enemies of the country, and forced the agents of the East India Company to resign. In Charleston there was a like spirit manifested, and in New York the Sons of Liberty made every disposition to resist the landing of the tea, and the agents resigned. But the question was to be decided in Boston, where the opposition had begun, and where the consignees, more stubborn than elsewhere, refused to yield. They were handed over by the town-meetings to the committees of correspondence, and in the midst of the excitement the tea-ships arrived. The other towns began to move, the men from the country poured into Boston, and town-meeting succeeded town-meeting. The Council refused to support the Governor, who talked of retiring to the fort, while every hour brought tidings of the support of other towns. The consignees began to lose heart. They offered to store the teas, and await instructions, but said they could not send them back. The offer was refused. In vain Hutchinson strove to disperse the meetings; the whole province was fast rising in arms. At last Rotch, the owner of the *Dartmouth*, gave way, and applied for a clearance, which the officers of the customs refused. There lay the ships, guarded night and day, and no tea was landed. The time was running out; in a few days the tea would be forfeit to the Crown, and would be landed by the officers of customs. Men-of-war were stationed to prevent their departure, and they could not pass the fort except with the Governor's permit. On the sixteenth of December the crisis was reached. Seven thousand men were gathered in town-meeting, and Rotch was sent to Milton to ask Hutchinson for a pass. While he was gone the meeting voted that the tea should not be landed. The day wore slowly away, and when Rotch returned to announce that the

Governor refused the pass, night had fallen. It was another of the dramatic scenes in American history—another turning-point in the preparation for revolution, and again Samuel Adams was the central figure. Rising slowly in the dimly lighted church, he said, simply and solemnly, " This meeting can do nothing more to save the country." There was a wild war-whoop outside, and a band of men disguised as Indians rushed through the streets, boarded the ships, and in three hours the tea was floating in Boston harbor. The American Revolution had begun. In every colony the destruction of the tea at Boston met with warm approval. In Philadelphia the tea-ship was compelled to return with her cargo intact; and in Charleston, where it became forfeit to the government and was landed, it mouldered in damp cellars.

When the news of the sixteenth of December reached England, the **1744.** ministry were engaged in severing another link in the chain which bound the colonies to the parent country. If there was any one man who could have checked the course of revolution, it was Benjamin Franklin, wise, famous, and popular. He was not as yet an enemy to England, but still hoped for peace and reconciliation. It became his duty to present the petition of Massachusetts for the removal of Hutchinson and Oliver on account of their misconduct, and of the letters which Franklin had obtained and published. The appearance of those letters had led to a duel, and had caused great anger against Franklin; so that when the petition came up for hearing before the Council, he was made the target of a violent attack by Wedderburn, who appeared for the accused, and acted as if Franklin was on trial. The great American was abused, and the petition contemptuously rejected. The English ministry esteemed it wise to insult and outrage the strongest man in the colonies, and receive with hearty applause the coarse and powerful invective which helped to dismember the empire. It was part and parcel of the ignorant arrogance which began with Grenville, and ended in the loss of thirteen colonies. In this condition of the public temper the resistance of Boston was not likely to be pardoned. It was not too late to retreat and retain the colonies; but there was no one in England who had the power and the desire for such a course. King and people were thoroughly in sympathy, and determined to punish the rebellious colonists. A series of measures ingeniously adapted to cause civil war were rapidly passed through Parliament, and were in part opposed only by a few far-seeing men, and by some of the old Whig party of Rockingham. While the people of Massachusetts, well knowing the desperate struggle in which they were engaged, impeached Chief-justice Oliver for taking his salary from the Crown ; and while, by the hand of Samuel Adams, they sent their last instructions to Franklin, Lord North introduced and carried through without objection the Boston Port Bill, which closed the port of Boston until the East India Company was indemnified, and the King satisfied of the submission of the rebellious town. General Gage was appointed civil Governor, and sent with four regiments to carry out the provisions of the bill, and arrest and bring to judgment the patriot leaders, among whom Adams was foremost. The next in the series of measures was far graver than the Port Bill, and struck at the political life of every colony alike, for this second act altered by will of Parliament alone the charter of Massachusetts, and it provided for the destruction of town-meetings, for the appointment of the Council, and also of the Sheriffs, into whose hands was given the selection of the juries. To the credit of England it can be said that this witless piece of revengeful oppression did not pass unchallenged. It was opposed by Burke, Fox, and Conway, and by most of the Rockingham Whigs, and was only carried through after long and strenuous debates in both Houses. Such opposition can hardly be wondered at, for the English Parliament has passed but few measures which were the direct cause of such mighty results. The act to alter the charter of Massachusetts firmly united the American colonies, and divided the empire of England. The third measure of the ministry transferred the trial of any soldier or Crown officer indicted for murder or other capital offence in Massachusetts to Nova Scotia or England. A few bold men raised their voices against a bill which gave immunity to soldiers in a defenceless colony ; but their warning was unheeded, and the act passed rapidly with large majorities. A fourth act provided for quartering troops in Boston ; and a fifth, known as the Quebec Act, dealt with the recent conquests of England, gave toleration to the Roman Catholics, erected an arbitrary government, and extended the bounds of the new province to the Ohio, absorbing the territory of the old colonies, and threatening the possessions of Virginia and Pennsylvania. Something had been done to anger every colony ; but the weight of the blow fell upon Massachusetts, in whose fate every province beheld what might with equal fitness come to them.

Massachusetts received the news in ominous silence, but with no signs of yielding. Samuel Adams and his friends saw what was coming, but they devoted themselves to renewing the non-importation agreements, and sent messengers forth to ask for a general suspension of trade. The Port Bill and the Charter Act roused the continent in support of Massachusetts. New York moved first, and the Sons of Liberty wrote to Massachusetts and proposed a general congress. The old committee dissolved, and a new one was formed with many Tories among the members, but controlled by the moderate men, who finally came forward under the lead of John Jay. Connecticut adopted a declaration of rights; Rhode Island demanded a general congress. In Pennsylvania the moderate party, under the guidance of John Dickinson, had the upper hand. They had little sympathy for Massachusetts; they dreaded to become involved in her fate, but they favored a congress, and opposed a suspension of trade. In the absence of Franklin, Mifflin and the patriot party made slight headway. In Virginia, when the Burgesses met, a day of fasting was appointed when the Port Bill went into operation. Whereupon Dunmore dissolved the Assembly, and the Burgesses met in convention, voted for an annual congress, and elected a committee of correspondence. The action of the great southern province was decisive, and the other colonies fell quickly into line, demanding in most cases, from South Carolina to New Jersey, a suspension of trade and a general congress. The effect of the penal measures in suddenly advancing the conflict with England is strongly shown by the rapid development of parties. Many of the aristocracy and of the wealthy, and all timid, conservative, or interested persons began to range themselves on the side of the Crown. Hitherto there had been substantial unanimity, but men were now compelled to choose their side; the dread of disturbance and of war began to be felt, and party lines were sharply drawn. In New York the Tories fought for possession of the committee, and the contest was bitter and doubtful. In Pennsylvania the Crown party had the upper hand, and were supported by the moderate patriots. In Virginia the patriot party was in complete control, for the ruling aristocracy was of one mind with the people in opposition to England, and the same held true of the other southern colonies, although there was a vigorous opposition. The New England colonies were wholly on the patriotic side, except in Massachusetts, where the Crown party rallied in the coast towns, and sent addresses to Hutchinson on his departure. But this was all they could do. The power rested with Adams, Warren, Hancock, and the rest, and in Massachusetts the decisive steps had to be taken. The conflict had opened there, and there the revolution was to begin.

Gage was already at odds with the town of Boston and the com mittees when the general court came together in Salem, where, after a quarrel over the address, in which Hutchinson was censured, the House, which had been worked up to the required point by Adams, met on the seventeenth of June—a day soon to be made memorable in history. The doors were locked, as they had been in a more famous but not more momentous Parliament by the forefathers of these men who now came together in the little New England seaport. While Gage's messenger knocked vainly at the door and read to the crowd a proclamation dissolving the Assembly, the representatives of Massachusetts fixed the first of September as the day, and Philadelphia as the place for the general congress, and then chose Bowdoin, Cushing, Paine, and John and Samuel Adams as delegates. While they were thus taking the last decisive step toward union, the people of Boston gathered in town-meeting, with John Adams in the chair, and voted not to indemnify the East India Company. Lord North's coercive measures, backed by fleets and armies, had failed miserably, and Boston in her hour of trial received sympathy and generous aid from all parts of the continent; but the material and pecuniary suffering was not the worst that befell the town and province. The mandamus councillors and the salaried judges were no longer a fear, they were a terrible reality, and holding office. The regulating act was being enforced in their midst. In all directions there were meetings, and thousands gathered to force the councillors from their places and to close the courts. Some of the councillors resigned, and those who held out dared not leave Boston and the protection of the troops. The courts were at a standstill, and the militia began to drill, while in every village companies of Minute-men were formed, and county conventions were held, and resolutions passed breathing independence and resistance. Gage began to clamor for more troops to fortify Boston, and to seize provincial stores and gunpowder, while threats were heard of letting loose the Indians upon the rebellious colonists. The storm clouds were coming very near in Massachusetts.

Meanwhile the other colonies had rapidly responded to the call of Massachusetts, and chosen delegates to the Congress. In New York and Pennsylvania the moderate party and the Tories prevailed in the choice of delegates, but elsewhere the patriots carried the day. The journey of the delegates of Massachusetts was very like a triumphal progress, and when they met their brethren in Carpenter's Hall on the fifth of September, the representatives of eleven provinces answered to their names. Peyton Randolph, of Virginia, was chosen President, and

Charles Thomson, Secretary. Among the delegates on the floor were George Washington and Patrick Henry, John and Samuel Adams, Jay, Gadsden, and Rutledge. It was a gathering of able and sober-minded men, and England would have done well to heed what they said. At the outset, in the very dawn of American union, the standard of State rights and separatism was raised, and firmly planted. After much debate, and despite the eloquence of Henry, it was agreed that the voting should be by colonies; and the principle found practical expression in the exemption of rice from the non-exportation agreement, out of deference to South Carolina. True to the traditions and habits of their race, the Congress decided to rest their case upon historic, and not upon natural rights. In October they voted to sustain Massachusetts in her resistance; they signed agreements to neither import nor export; they passed a resolve against the slave-trade, appointed a second congress, to which Nova Scotia and Canada were invited; and finally gave to the world the fruits of their deliberations in a declaration of rights, an address to the people of Great Britain, drawn by Jay, and an address to the King, drawn by Dickinson. These remarkable State papers were eminently moderate, fair, and conciliatory. The recital of grievances went back no farther than the year 1763, and the concession of the right to regulate external trade was introduced and defended by such an ardent patriot as John Adams. The tone of the addresses, drawn as they were by two conspicuously moderate men, was manly and direct, but thoroughly and honestly loyal and eager for reconciliation. The issues involving the right of taxation and the right to preserve their governments unchanged were firmly and strongly met, and the Congress opened the way for an adjustment, which would have removed every difficulty. Warning was not wanting elsewhere. The general court of Massachusetts became a provincial congress, Connecticut began to arm, the Marylanders burned a tea-ship, the close corporation known as an assembly in New York refused to consider the doings of the first Congress, or choose delegates to the next, and the people, filled with indignation, were thrown on their own resources. Everywhere the Congress received full support and approbation, and even in Georgia, weak and divided, the spirit of resistance broke out, and a delegate was chosen in one parish. The suspension of trade was rigidly enforced. The royal governments were dropping to pieces, the colonies were arming, and with the flame of revolution flashing in their eyes the new Parliament of England came together.

The English people fully sustained the King and his ministers, who met Parliament with stronger majorities than ever before. The proposals of the Congress were rejected, the broad and statesman-like measures of Chatham for adjustment and conciliation were cast aside **1775.** with contempt, New England was shut out from the fisheries, Massachusetts was declared to be in rebellion, and preparations were made for war. Lord Howe was sent out in command of a fleet, and with offers of compromise, which Lord North, in weak good-nature, wished to make. He proposed that if the colonies would tax themselves to the satisfaction of Parliament, Parliament would be content to regulate trade, forgetting that to people whose governments were being swept away, such a proposition was childish. But while England made ready to crush out opposition by force, revolution with hurrying steps came nearer and nearer. Gage made an abortive attempt to seize stores at Salem; but the prize was removed, and the troops came back discomfited. Dunmore seized powder in Virginia, and was forced by the people, headed by Henry, to give it up. Sooner or later such attempts as these would lead to fighting. The day of battle could not be long deferred, and it came at last in Massachusetts. The events of the famous nineteenth of April have been told again and again. They have employed the art of the poet and the historian, they are commemorated by the pencil and the chisel. To every American all the hurrying scenes rise up in sharp distinctness. The lights flash from the steeple of the Old North Church, the horsemen spur out into the darkness and ride through the Middlesex villages calling the farmers to arms, while fast behind them come the British soldiers. In the gray dawn they were at Lexington faced by some seventy Minute-men, hastily summoned to the field. Some one fired, no matter who; the troops poured in a close and deadly volley, there was a scattering return, and, as the smoke rolled away, it disclosed seven killed and nine wounded among the Americans. The colonists had faced the troops, and blood had been shed. The fatal step had been taken, and civil war had begun. On the troops pushed to Concord, whence the stores had been removed, and where but little damage was done. A party of soldiers advanced to the bridge, and were met by the Minute-men of Acton and Concord. The British fired with effect; there was a moment's hesitation, and the Americans returned the fire. Two of the English fell, others were wounded, and they fell back, leaving the Americans in possession of the bridge. The battle of Concord had been fought. Not only had blood been shed, but the colonists had resisted. There was a pause while the British moved out of the village, and then the Minute-men began to pour in and attack them on their march. The fire of the Americans along the road was scattering, but galling and deadly, so that the retreat was quickened, and was almost a rout, when the tired men met Lord Percy with re-enforcements and artillery at Lexington. Then the chase began once more; faster and faster came the militia, and more and more soldiers fell beneath their shots. It was after sunset when Lord Percy's hunted and beaten army crossed Charlestown Neck and reached a place of safety.

The news spread like wildfire. From all New England the militia hastened to Boston, and the King's army was soon besieged by twenty thousand men. The clash of arms and the blood shed in battle startled the colonies north and south, and everywhere the people rose ready for war. In May, the hardy and untamed settlers of the Green Mountains, under the lead of Ethan Allen, captured by surprise Ticonderoga and Crown Point. In June, the leaders of the scattered forces around Boston, where there had been some slight skirmishing, resolved to anticipate the plans of the British by taking sudden possession of the high ground near Charlestown, and thus commanding the town and shipping. On the night of the sixteenth, Colonel Prescott, with about a thousand men, crossed Charlestown Neck, and in the few hours between midnight and sunrise threw up an earthwork on Breed's Hill. At daybreak the men-of-war opened fire on the redoubt, and the batteries on Copp's Hill followed. At noon over two thousand English were on their way to take the hill. Prescott's forces were reduced, and he received neither aid nor re-enforcements until the arrival of Stark with the New Hampshire men, who joined those from Connecticut, posted by Prescott at a rail fence heaped with hay to defend the flank. Setting fire to Charlestown, and under cover of a heavy cannonade, the British advanced against the intrenchments. Twice they were driven back with slaughter from the redoubt and the rail fence, mowed down by the heavy and concentrated fire of the Americans. The third time they were rallied with difficulty, and came on in silence. They were received with another deadly volley, but they still pressed on. The powder of the Americans was exhausted, and their fire slackened and ceased. Without bayonets, the provincials fought with clubbed muskets, yielding inch by inch, until at last Prescott gave the word to retreat; and then slowly, and in good order, covered by the brave band at the rail fence, the Americans fell back and left the British in possession of the hard-fought field. At the last moment, Joseph Warren, eminent as a patriot leader, and present only as a volunteer, was killed at the redoubt. The British won the victory and gained a hill. They lost over a thousand men in killed and wounded, of whom no less than eighty-three were officers, while the American loss did not reach five hundred. Covered by wretched intrenchments, the colonists had twice repulsed with slaughter the best English troops, fully equipped and perfectly disciplined. They had completely crippled Gage, and the British had merely the ground they stood on to show as a trophy of the bloody battle. The delusion that Americans would not fight was at an end; and this made the defeat at Bunker Hill of more value than many victories.

Nearly a month had passed after the fight at Lexington and Concord, when the second Continental Congress assembled in Philadelphia on the tenth of May. There were the same leaders, but the strength of the moderate and Tory parties had declined, and at the same time the attitude of Congress was one of indecision. They found themselves confronted by the gravest issue, for the choice between war and submission had become imperative. They would not yield; they dreaded to advance. With reluctance they permitted the retention of Ticonderoga, and they advised New York not to oppose the landing of troops, but to prevent the erection of fortifications. Jay moved a second petition to the King, and long debates ensued. Slowly the Congress was drawn along by the current of events; hanging back at every step, they advised Massachusetts not to set up an independent government, and they would do nothing for the other colonies, where the Crown governments were rapidly falling to pieces. They were gradually forced into a policy of defensive warfare, inasmuch as war was a hard reality which could not be overlooked, for the skirmishing went on outside, and there were continual affrays between Americans and British both by land and sea. In one breath the Congress, which had just placed at its head the proscribed traitor, John Hancock, advised the colonies to prepare for defence, and in the next voted a second petition to the King. The Governor of Virginia took refuge on board a man-of-war, and royal government was at an end. Massachusetts asked for a commander-in-chief, and John Adams urged the appointment of Washington. Still, Congress, full of loyalty, eager to avert war, and dreading rebellion, hesitated; but the pressure of events could not be resisted. It was voted to raise money to buy gunpowder, the organization of the Continental army was begun, and on

June fifteenth George Washington was elected commander-in-chief. On the following day he appeared in Congress, and, with a modesty as fine as it was simple and sincere, accepted the heavy burden imposed upon him. Even while the delegates were pledging themselves to sustain Washington, Prescott was preparing for his march to Breed's Hill, and the clouds of war were gathering very fast about the hesitating Congress, who went on with half measures, published an address justifying their taking up arms, sent another petition to the King, and on the first of August adjourned for five weeks.

On the third of July Washington took command of the army. He found himself at the head of a horde of militia, brave and patriotic, but ill-armed, undisciplined, unorganized, and wanting in almost everything necessary for successful war. As the summer wore away, and autumn and winter followed, Washington slowly, and in the face of almost inconceivable difficulties, brought order out of chaos, and gave strength and unity to his raw and scattered forces. Gunpowder failed, large bodies of the militia went back to their homes, winter set in with its usual severity, but still Washington moved steadfastly onward, drawing his lines closer and closer about the besieged city. Frequent skirmishes accustomed the men to war; Knox brought the cannon of Ticonderoga over the snow to Boston before the spring opened, and then Washington was ready to strike. The works had been brought nearer and nearer to the town, until at last, from Dorchester Heights, the bombardment was begun. The British, who had come to conquer, were helpless, and word came to Washington that, if Howe was permitted to embark unmolested, the town would be spared. The proposal **1776.** was agreed to; the British took to their ships, and sailed to Halifax; and on the seventeenth of March the American forces entered the town, and the siege of Boston was at an end. While Washington was slowly and surely investing Boston, and forcing the British from the soil of New England, other movements were in progress, promising more brilliant results, as developed by the capture of Ticonderoga, and by the successful partisan warfare of Allen and Arnold in the region of the lakes. An expedition for the conquest of Canada, under the command of Schuyler, started from Ticonderoga. Schuyler's ill-health soon left General Montgomery at the head of the army, and for two months he persisted in the siege of the fort at St. John's, contending with every possible difficulty, from lack of supplies to insubordination and inefficiency among the soldiers and officers. Allen made a foolhardy attempt upon Montreal, and was taken prisoner; but Montgomery's gallantry and persistence finally prevailed over every obstacle. The forts of Chambly and St. John's were taken, and the Americans pushed northward and took Montreal, whence Carleton had retreated to Quebec. Soon after Montgomery started from Ticonderoga, another expedition, also aimed against Quebec, left Boston in the early days of autumn. Commanded by Arnold, this force was to make its way through the wilderness of Maine, surprise Quebec, and join Montgomery. After two months of terrible privation and suffering by cold, hunger, and disease, Arnold, with sadly depleted forces, reached the St. Lawrence. Precious time had been wasted, and a surprise attempted by Arnold with his weakened forces came to nothing. Carleton reached Quebec with his troops from Montreal, and soon after Montgomery joined Arnold. In the dead waste of a Canadian winter, with the ground deeply frozen, regular approaches were out of the question; and an assault was therefore agreed upon, which was made in the midst of a storm, just as the year was closing. Desperate as it was, it came within a hair's-breadth of success, and failed only through the death of Montgomery, who was killed at the head of his advancing men. Arnold, with another column, penetrated Quebec, but was wounded, and carried from the field. Morgan, of Virginia, pushed on with the men, and, after a night of fierce street-fighting, was compelled to surrender, being cooped up in the narrow streets, and with no aid from without. After this, the winter wore slowly and uneventfully away, until in March General Wooster arrived with troops, and took command. He effected nothing, and factious disorder heightened the difficulties of the disheartened army; so that, when General Thomas took the command, he was forced to retreat to the Sorel, suffering heavy losses inflicted by the garrison of Quebec. At all other points the Americans were beaten as the spring advanced, and Sullivan, who succeeded Thomas, was just in time to encourage an expedition which was badly beaten at Point du Lac, and then fall back to Ticonderoga. The Canada campaign just missed success. Full of bright hope and brilliant promise, and marked with the utmost gallantry on the part of the leaders, it resulted in nothing but ruinous disaster; and the only gain to the colonists was the hard experience of unsuccessful war.

Meanwhile Parliament, in full accord with the King, was ready to push hostilities. The army was raised to forty thousand men, the fleets were increased, large bodies of mercenaries were bought of the miserable princes of Germany, extensive campaigns were planned, and preparations were made to strike the colonies at various points. The value of New York as a military position was obvious to both English and Americans, and the latter made haste to prevent its falling into the hands of their enemies. Domestic dissensions were already running high, and the conflict between Tories and patriots, fomented by the new Governor, Tryon, became more and more bitter. The Tories controlled the government, and struggled for the committee; but the patriots were backed by the people, and under the lead of Sears destroyed the Tory press, and brought many of the supporters of the Crown to reason by no gentle means. But all this led to nothing, until the arrival of General Charles Lee, who went energetically to work to fortify the city, a course vigorously pursued by his successor, Lord Stirling; and as soon as Washington was released by the evacuation of Boston, he pushed his army forward, arriving in New York himself, with all his forces, by the middle of April, when the city rapidly assumed the appearance of a fortified camp.

In the south, meantime, Dunmore had failed to excite servile insurrection, and had lost his hold upon Virginia; while in North Carolina, Martin strove to stir up civil war, and in a proclamation denounced the rebels, and summoned the inhabitants to rally about the standard of the King. The Highlanders of the province, and many of the Regulators, who had been conciliated by Martin, responded to the call, and marched to the coast with nearly a thousand men. But the proclamation had brought the patriot party also into the field. They met the royalists at a bridge near Wilmington, where they repulsed and dispersed them, making many prisoners. Martin had already fled, and the cause of the King was broken in North Carolina, and not revived for four years. Against South Carolina more formidable preparations were made, and the King sent seven regiments under Clinton and Cornwallis, and a fleet under Admiral Parker, to reduce Charleston. Lee, who was in charge of the southern department, worked with his usual energy, but the glory belongs to the patriot leaders. A fort was hastily constructed on Sullivan's Island, in the harbor, and put in charge of Colonel Moultrie; Gadsden, on James Island, defended the approach by land, while the city itself was hastily fortified. On the twenty-eighth of June the British fleet moved up the channel, and for twelve hours poured shot and shell upon Moultrie's fort. The tough palmetto resisted their shot; the Americans stood their ground unflinchingly, and returned a heavy and well-directed fire, while the land-forces were repulsed and prevented from reaching the island.

32

After a prolonged contest the British withdrew. Their losses had been severe, and, giving up their plans of capture, they returned to New York. The south was safe.

But while the South Carolinians were driving off the British the great crisis in the existence of the colonies was drawing on. **1775-** All through the autumn, winter, and spring, with offensive and **1776.** defensive war raging around them, the Continental Congress had been hesitating and moving forward with reluctant pace. It is easy to see how much might have been gained by prompt, decisive action, by throwing off at once the bonds of the mother country, organizing government, and adopting a vigorous war policy. But the Congress of the colonies was a body of law-abiding, conservative men, longing to bring back harmony, and not plotting independence. They did not advance a step until England had gone beyond in wrong-doing, and they acted only under the strongest outside pressure. With the outbreak of hostilities the spirit of independence began to grow rapidly, finding expression in the resolutions of towns, and then of counties, while it was boldly advocated by Paine in his famous pamphlet, " Common Sense." The colonies began to form governments of their own, and declare for independence. There was no mistaking the drift of public sentiment, which every day grew stronger and more imperative. In Congress a party in favor of independence was developed, and began to push for energetic action and for a declared rupture with England, while the measures necessitated by war urged them on in the same direction. Bills of credit were issued, the army was regulated, negotiations were opened with Canada, and plans for a general government were discussed, so that in the spring the independent movement had become almost irresistible, although Pennsylvania hung back, and New York was divided. The strength of the moderate party was in the middle colonies; but Virginia and Massachusetts, the two representative provinces, the strongholds of the opposing political forces of the country, were for the first and last time in our history thoroughly united; and before their combined strength the timid and backward conservatism of Pennsylvania was powerless. One colony after another was brought into line and joined in the cry for independence; even in Pennsylvania the popular party gained the control; and Maryland and New York, the latter still sadly divided, were swept along in the current. On the seventh of June, while the various colonies were still moving on the great question, Richard Henry Lee, seconded by John Adams, introduced three resolutions—one for independence, one for foreign alliance, and one for confederation. Action was postponed, and a committee appointed to draft a declaration. There was long debate and deliberation, John Adams leading for the independent party, John Dickinson for the party of conciliation. On the second of July the resolution declaring the colonies independent was passed, and on the fourth the declaration of independence, drafted by Jefferson and somewhat amended by the committee and by Congress, was adopted and ordered to be printed. Four days later, it was given to the world. The English colonies in America had ceased to exist, and a new nation was born.

The most significant fact in regard to the declaration of independence was the delay in making it. Two years had elapsed since the Continental Congress first assembled; and for more than a year the colonies had been engaged in desperate hostilities, and had an army in the field. Yet they lingered and hesitated. There was in truth, so far as the colonies themselves were concerned, nothing inevitable about the American Revolution. There was no irresistible cause for its coming then or later, nothing which was not wholly within human control. No old system was breaking down and forcing the rise of a new one. The people in the English colonies were thoroughly and sincerely loyal. Here and there might be found a man like Samuel Adams, who felt that independence ought to come; but such men were rare exceptions. The colonies had lived for years under their own governments, which were free and simple; and if the wise policy of Walpole, of letting them severely alone, had been continued, the connection between the colonies and the parent country need never have been severed. The American Revolution was wholly due, from the very outset, to the condition of England and of English politics, and to the gross and arrogant stupidity of the King and his ministers, supported by the mass of the people. From the very inception of Grenville's scheme of taxation to the declaration of independence, the course of the English government was a tissue of ignorant mistakes. They found that taxation without representation was firmly resisted in the colonies; and instead of quietly abandoning the principle, they enforced it. This aroused a conflict in one province, and they then made the cause of that colony the cause of all, by attempting to inflict the most senseless and arbitrary punishment imaginable. They forced a Continental Congress into existence, and then trampled on its loyalty, scoffed at its measures, and scorned its appeals. They knew that the colonists were almost entirely men of

English race, that they were of fine English stock, and many of them descendants of the men who had fought the great Rebellion. Knowing all this, thick-witted peers announced in the House of Lords that the Americans were cowards; and it was assumed with an imbecile stupidity which passes expression that Americans would not fight. The insults of Lord Sandwich and his fellows were bitterly answered by the shouts of the Minute-men, as the flower of the British army recoiled and fell back from the slopes of Bunker Hill. English officers precipitated bloodshed, and English ministers planned the conquest of three million people of their own race, separated from them by the Atlantic Ocean. Very rarely does history record great events so largely caused by actions as needless as they were avoidable. Ignorance and arrogance have been responsible for many misfortunes, but they never cost any nation more than they did England in 1776. By her own errors and her corrupt politics, and by absolutely nothing else, she drove her great colonies into independence, and dismembered her empire.

Chapter XXIV.

THE WAR FOR INDEPENDENCE: FROM 1776 TO 1782.

1776. WITH the Declaration of Independence colonial existence came to an end; but six dreary years of hard fighting were to pass before the declaration became an admitted fact. The War of Independence is the period in our history which above all others is thoroughly familiar to every one, and it would be useless and superfluous to attempt here to add anything to what has already been written of the war, or to trace its events in detail. So far as the present work is concerned, it comes to an end, strictly speaking, with the action of Congress on the second of July, 1776. But American history is divided into two parts—the history of the colonies and the history of the United States; and between these two portions—between the Declaration and the Treaty of Paris—lie six years of war. In that intervening period, although the colonies had ceased to exist as such, the struggle to build up and develop a great nation had not begun. Everything was absorbed in taking the first step which must precede national life—in securing independence. The English colonies could not begin their career as a nation until they had extorted from England, and from the world, an acknowledgment of their independence. In the fullest sense, the history of the colonies does not end until that of the nation begins—with the Treaty of Paris. For the sake of historical completeness, therefore, it becomes necessary to trace in the barest outline the events of the war which insured national existence. With the close of that war a new era opens, and the forces generated during a century and a half of colonial life begin to play their part, and work out their destiny on the broad stage of national history.

Before Congress had agreed to the Declaration of Independence, the forerunners of a fine English army of over thirty thousand men, including eight thousand Hessians, had already arrived in New York harbor; and by the end of August these well-equipped and thoroughly disciplined forces were ready to move against the American works on Long Island. Thus far the scales of war, despite the ill-fated Canadian expedition, had inclined heavily in favor of the colonists; but they were now about to turn, and the rebellious Americans were soon to feel the full strain of the doubtful conflict in which they had engaged against the great power of England. On the twenty-seventh of August the fighting began on Long Island. The American outposts were driven in, a strong body of British troops advanced by an unguarded pass, and reached the flank of Stirling's command, which was also attacked in front; and finally Stirling was forced to surrender with nearly a thousand men. The Americans were pushed back to their inner defences, and, although strongly re-enforced by Washington, were in great danger. The suspense continued for two days, while the British advanced their works, and prepared to crush the main body of the American army; but on the twenty-ninth it was resolved to retreat; and during the night, in the face of many difficulties and mistakes, the American forces were all safely transported to New York. This abandonment of Long Island, and the safe removal of the army, were all performed under the immediate supervision of Washington, and were the first exhibitions of his genius for sustaining defeat, holding his army together, and escaping from apparently hopeless difficulties. While the British hesitated and lingered for two weeks, the question of evacuating New York was anxiously debated. At first it was decided to hold the city; then Congress left the whole matter to the commander-in-chief; and Washington, fully understanding the faults of his motley and unorganized forces, determined to abandon the city. Howe, anxious to intercept him, sent vessels up the river and landed troops. At Kip's Bay the Connecticut militia gave way in a panic; while Washington, in a towering passion at their flight, rode up and down, and vainly tried to rally them. The other rear divisions, hotly pressed, escaped in safety, and the whole army was brought together on Harlem Heights, having lost through their want of discipline cannon and supplies. Their failings were those of raw troops, for there was no lack of courage and spirit among them. The very day after their disorderly retreat they had a sharp skirmish with the British, and inflicted severe losses upon them. Disorder and discontent still continued; but the fire which destroyed a large part of New York, and the slowness of the British, gave a brief breathing space. On the twelfth of October Howe began to advance again, intending to cut off Washington's retreat; but his movements were so clumsy and deliberate that Washington, who was fully prepared, fell back in good order to White Plains, skirmishing with success, and leaving a garrison in Fort Washington. At White Plains he intrenched himself. The British attacked one of the American positions, and, after a short, sharp fight, the latter retreated, having suffered less than their enemies. Washington soon after again fell back to an unassailable position on Northcastle Heights, while Howe retraced his steps, and carried by assault and with heavy losses Fort Washington. Not long after, Fort Lee, now untenable, was abandoned, and the Hudson was open to the British.

Washington's condition was trying in the extreme. His army was greatly reduced by the return to their homes of large bodies of the militia, and so many more were soon to go that the General seemed on the point of being left without soldiers. He was hampered, too, by the orders of Congress, who believed that their collective wisdom was suited to the conduct of war, and he had not that control over his officers so essential to a commander, but which was not understood in America. With all these difficulties pressing upon him, he was obliged to act; for it was clear that the British would move through New Jersey upon Philadelphia. Leaving Lee and Heath in New York, Washington started for New Jersey, with the British, under Cornwallis, close at his heels. As the Americans went out at one end of a town, the British entered at the other. With an army reduced to three thousand men, Washington continued his retreat, watching for an opportunity to strike a blow; and after him came the soldiers of the King, ravaging, burning, and destroying as they advanced. Washington sent in every direction to raise troops, and appealed strongly and constantly to Congress for the formation of a regular army. Lee, who was ordered to join him, hung back, aiming at a separate command, and was luckily captured by a British scouting party; and then Sullivan, who succeeded Lee, moved rapidly forward, and joined Washington on the twentieth of December. Pennsylvania and New Jersey were wild with panic and fear; Congress had left Philadelphia in alarm, and the loyalists were coming in and accepting the pardon offered by Howe. The curse of jarring councils and colonial jealousies began to make its evil influence strongly felt. It was the supreme moment of the American Revolution, and the fate of the colonies hung trembling in the balance. The great conflict, with all its tremendous issues, was centred in one man, at the head of a small, dispirited, and neglected army. As great a statesman as he was general, Washington felt to the full the gravity of the situation; and he knew that for moral effect, far more than for any military gain, a victory must be won.   He carried the American Revolution in his hands, and saved the cause of the colonies.   Crossing the Delaware on Christmas-night, Washington, despite delays, and the failure of the co-operating columns, swept down upon Trenton.   The Hessians posted there were surprised; their commander, Rahl, was mortally wounded, and, over-whelmed by the fierce charge of the Americans, they surrendered. Nearly a thousand men, with guns, cannon, and flags, were the tro-phies of the victory.   Washington crossed the river, recrossed it, and **1777.** was again at Trenton, gathering re-enforcements, and holding his little army well together, while the startled British made hasty preparations to retrieve the disaster.   Concentrating seven thou-sand men at Princeton, Cornwallis marched to Trenton and confront-ed Washington, who was in position on the other side of Assanpink Creek.   The situation was perilous in the extreme.   Leaving his fires burning, Washington marched back by another road in the very direc-tion by which Cornwallis had just come.   In the morning he was at Princeton, and, after a sharp skirmish, in which General Mercer was killed, he broke into the town, and routed the regiments left there by Cornwallis.   Leaving Princeton, Washington withdrew to winter-quarters at Morristown, and there was a pause in the war.   The forces engaged in these actions were trifling, but the life of a nation was at stake, and this brief campaign, both from a political and military point of view, was, for its length—if the issues involved and all the conditions be considered—as brilliant, and as full of skill and daring, as anything in the annals of modern warfare.   It has all the qualities of Napoleon's last campaign against the Allies in France, and, if Wash-ington had never fought another battle, would entitle him to the place of a great commander.

During the winter there were various small affairs, raids and sur-prises, on both sides, in which the Americans had, on the whole, the advantage; but the most important event was the despatch of sup-plies from France, through the efforts of Beaumarchais, and with the connivance of the French government.   Meantime Washington devoted himself to reorganizing and increasing his army, aided to some extent by Congress at last waking up to the needs of the war.   The work, however, was slow and arduous, the colonies were lax and disorganized, and it was nearly summer before Washington succeeded in getting even seven thousand soldiers together.   He watched Howe closely, but could gather little information as to his movements until the end

of July, when the English fleet and army sailed from New York and
appeared in the Delaware. Washington hastened southward to meet
them, and was joined in his camp on the Neshaminy by Lafayette,
De Kalb, and a few other French officers. A few days later news
came that Howe, who had left the Delaware, was in Chesapeake Bay,
and Washington again pushed forward to check his advance. The
opposing forces met at the river Brandywine. The Americans, confused and misled by uncertain intelligence, suffered their right flank
to be turned; Sullivan fell back in disorder, Wayne was repulsed, and
Washington was forced to retreat. A few days later Wayne's command was surprised at Paoli, and suffered severely. The British pressed on; the news of their advance drove the members of Congress
and the patriots in hasty flight from Philadelphia; and on the twen-
ty-sixth of August Howe was in possession of the city. The English
forces were then somewhat divided. Troops had been sent against
the forts on the Delaware; Cornwallis, with several regiments, was in
Philadelphia; and the main body of the army was encamped at
Germantown, where Washington, undeterred by defeat, determined
to fall suddenly upon the main body of the enemy. His plans
were laid with his wonted skill, but the attack was to be made by
four columns, and he failed through the errors of his subordinates.
Early in the morning, on the fourth of October, the Americans advanced rapidly under cover of a thick mist, driving in the advance
posts, and pushed on, flushed with success, upon the main line. Everything promised success; but some of the British threw themselves
into the Chew House, and thus brought on a sharp engagement in the
rear of the advancing columns. Time was thus lost. In the smoke
and fog, and with firing behind them, the Americans fell into confusion; two of the co-operating columns mistaking each other for the
enemy, became engaged, the English forces concentrated, and Washington was again forced to retreat, with heavy loss. The moral effect
of proving his ability to fight so soon after a defeat was the only
gain in the disaster at Germantown. Howe withdrew his forces to
Philadelphia, and devoted himself to clearing the river; but his first
attempt on Fort Mercer failed completely. Colonel Donop and four
hundred Hessians were killed, and the rest driven back to the city.
With the aid of the fleet the next effort was more successful. Fort
Mifflin was taken, and Fort Mercer soon after was abandoned. Master
of the river, Howe endeavored to draw Washington into a general
battle, but Washington would not leave his position. There was

some heavy skirmishing, in which the advantage was with the Americans; and then Howe went into winter-quarters at Philadelphia, and Washington, with his barefooted, ragged, and suffering soldiers, withdrew to Valley Forge.

While Washington was waging doubtful war, enduring defeat, and solely by skill and constancy holding the enemy in check, the fate of the Revolution was decided in the North. In accordance with a favorite plan of the King, General Burgoyne, with eight thousand men, a large body of Indians, and a heavy train of artillery, came down from St. John's, aiming at Albany, and intending to join Howe and cut off New England from the rest of the colonies. At first all went well. Through the negligence of St. Clair, Ticonderoga had to be abandoned, and the Americans retreating, lost heavily by the attacks of the British, who pursued them closely. Schuyler, who was in command in the northern department, fell back from Fort Anne to Fort Edward, where he joined St. Clair. They could only muster between them about five thousand men, and Schuyler sent for re-enforcements. Washington, straitened as he was, responded, and sent troops, including Morgan and his Virginia riflemen; but the whole country was terror-stricken by Burgoyne's rapid success. In reality the alarm was most fortunate. To form a regular army in the colonies was a task of surpassing difficulty; to call out in defence of their invaded homes men who were brave and skilled in rough fighting, was comparatively easy. The keen sense of danger roused the people to arms. Burgoyne was delayed after his victories by Schuyler's having torn up bridges and obstructed the roads, and in that time the tide turned against him. Burgoyne intended to strike right and left as well as in front, and in pursuance of this plan Colonel St. Leger was sent to the west to capture Fort Schuyler, defended by Colonel Gansevoort, with some seven hundred men. Gansevoort was fully prepared, and refused to surrender; and while St. Leger besieged him the militia of the country turned out under Herkimer, and marched to the relief of the fort. St. Leger met them at Oriskany, and there was a bloody and desperate fight, which gave the soldiers in the fort opportunity for a successful sally, and checked the British completely. St. Leger, alarmed by rumors of the advance of fresh forces, raised the siege and retreated. In the east, Burgoyne sent out five hundred men under Colonel Baum, to capture the supplies stored at Bennington, of which he began to have sore need. Again the militia turned out, composed of the hardy settlers of New Hampshire and Vermont, led by John

Stark. They surrounded the British, stormed their earthworks, captured Baum and all his men, and repulsed with slaughter Colonel Breyman, who had been sent to his relief. These victories inspired all the country with enthusiasm. Men poured into the camp at Bemus's Heights, where Gates had superseded Schuyler, and was ready to reap the fruits of the victories achieved by the people. The British had no choice but to push forward, and on the nineteenth of September they attacked the American position in force. There was a day of hard fighting, little generalship, each corps fighting for itself, and in the evening the Americans withdrew within their lines. It was nominally a drawn battle, but it was disastrous to the British. There was a delay of nearly three weeks, while the British strengthened their defences, and fresh troops came into the American camp. Clinton was burning and ravaging on the Hudson; but he gave no hope to Burgoyne, whose situation was fast becoming desperate. On the seventh of October he again advanced, there was another hard fight, and the British fell back in disorder to their camp. The next day Burgoyne began his retreat, and abandoning almost everything, moved to Saratoga; but his position was hopeless. Every avenue of escape was cut off; his provisions were nearly exhausted; and on the seventeenth of October, after some negotiation, he surrendered, and over five thousand men laid down their arms and were sent as prisoners to Boston.

The battles in New York, which have taken rank among the decisive battles of the world, produced three important results.
1778. The first was a wretched intrigue, known as the Conway Cabal, to supersede Washington and put Gates at the head of the armies. While Washington was struggling through the dreary winter at Valley Forge, overcoming every sort of obstacle, arguing with Congress, and trying to teach them their duty, spending his whole strength of heart, and mind, and body, this miserable faction was at work against him. They were not without hopes of success; for Congress, which had begun to degenerate, was dazzled by the northern victories, and failed to comprehend the greater services rendered by Washington in defeat. The whole business finally came to light, and was ruined at once by the popular support given to Washington. Gates was sent from the board of war to the North, Mifflin was put on trial for mismanagement in the quartermaster's department, and Conway's resignation was accepted, and his place as inspector-general filled by Baron Steuben, who did excellent work in effecting discipline and organiza-

tion among the troops. The second issue of Burgoyne's surrender was the recognition of the colonies by France, and a treaty of alliance with that power, negotiated by Franklin and ratified by Congress in May. The third result was an offer by Lord North to abandon the right of taxation, and recognize Congress. The opposition wished to go farther, and, without yielding independence, to hold that question in abeyance, and make peace at all hazards; but the insane obstinacy of the King thwarted the opposition, and Lord North's propositions, like all the rest of his policy, had the fatal defect of being too late.

The spring of 1778 wore away without any event of importance. The British made an attempt to capture Lafayette, sent out with an army of observation, and were completely foiled. The end of June came before the English army moved, and then it was merely to retreat. Fourteen thousand men, under command of Sir Henry Clinton, who had succeeded Howe, marched from Philadelphia, which they had vainly held all winter, toward New York. Washington broke camp at once and started in pursuit, determined to strike a heavy blow. He came up with the British at Monmouth Court-house, and Lee, in command of the advance, was ordered to attack as soon as the enemy began to move. The opening skirmishes were in favor of the Americans; but Lee gave contradictory orders, the troops became confused, and finally Lee fell back. He was met by Washington, filled with anger at this disregard of his orders, and there was a stormy scene between them, the affair resulting subsequently in Lee's trial by court-martial and suspension. Washington set to work to remedy Lee's mistakes. He stopped the retreat, brought up the main body of his army, and repulsed the British, who had begun to advance; but the opportunity for victory was lost, and the battle was not decisive. Clinton marched on, and reached New York in safety, followed by Washington, who took up his position at White Plains.

The arrival of the French turned every one's attention in a new direction. Philadelphia was saved. D'Estaing, the French admiral, believed there was not sufficient water to admit his entrance at New York, and he therefore sailed to Newport, held by the British, under General Pigot, with six thousand men. The French troops were to co-operate with Sullivan, who was in Rhode Island with some ten thousand soldiers. Sullivan advanced, however, before the time agreed upon, there was a misunderstanding with D'Estaing, and a fatal delay. Lord Howe, with the English fleet, appeared off the harbor, and D'Estaing put to sea to give him battle. The British avoided him, a storm scattered both fleets, and D'Estaing came back with his ships much shattered, and then, despite the prayers and remonstrances of the Americans, departed to Boston to repair and refit. Sullivan, thus left alone, determined to fight at all events, and on the twenty-ninth of August advanced. Although most of his troops were raw levies, they fought well and bravely; but were finally driven back, suffering, however, much less than the enemy. The news of coming re-enforcements from New York obliged Sullivan to retreat to the main-land, a movement which he executed safely and just in time. Thus the first combined attempt of the allies, from which so much was confidently expected, came to nothing, owing mainly to the slackness of the French, and left behind it much heart-burning and discord. Elsewhere little was done. On the western frontier the Indians, incited by the British, broke in upon the settlements and laid them waste, the Wyoming Massacre standing out among these forays with evil prominence. But the gain, on the whole, was with the Americans. Clarke finally made himself master of Vincennes, and the Indians began to desert the British standard. George III. and his ministers had, in fact, little but a long list of failures and defeats to contemplate. They had been driven from New England. For two years they had subjected the middle provinces to all the horrors of war, and the only result was that Clinton controlled the ground upon which his troops were camped, and was held in check by Washington and prevented from making any effective movement. One portion of the colonies had remained unmolested, and it was determined to carry the war, which had failed elsewhere, to the South.

Colonel Campbell, late in the autumn of 1778, landed in Georgia with two thousand men, surprised and defeated Robert Howe, in command of the American forces, and captured Savannah. There he was joined by Prevost from St. Augustine, and soon after the seizure of Augusta restored Georgia to England. These victories were, however, the signal for the outbreak of savage and desperate civil war. The Tories were stronger and more determined in the South than anywhere in the North, except in New York, and they eagerly joined the King's forces and formed regiments. On the other side the patriots formed companies of rangers and guerillas, and the whole country, from Georgia to Virginia, was desolated during the period of the British ascendency by bitter partisan warfare. The success **1779.** of the English alarmed Congress. Lincoln was hastily sent down to take Howe's place, and during the winter and spring neither he nor his enemy accomplished anything of importance. In May Prevost appeared before Charleston, where some of the citizens were for making terms, but Rutledge and the patriots would not yield. Lincoln attacked Prevost and was repulsed, and soon after the British fell back to Savannah. In the North Clinton remained inactive. General Matthews landed with a small force in Virginia, plundered houses and ravaged the country, while Tryon made a second sanguinary raid in Connecticut, burning and destroying, and killing the inhabitants of the villages. Further movements of this sort were checked by Wayne's brilliant assault upon Stony Point, resulting in the capture of the fort, with five hundred men and cannon and supplies, and in the destruction of the works, which kept Clinton quiet and attentive to the defence of New York. There was also an attempt—with land and naval forces—made by Massachusetts against a British post on the Penobscot, which ended in defeat and disaster; and with the coming of autumn both Clinton and Washington went into winter-quarters.

The centre of war had in truth shifted to the south. Soon after Prevost returned to Savannah, D'Estaing, who had been repulsed in the West Indies, appeared there with his fleet. Troops were landed, and Prevost summoned to surrender. While the negotiation halted re-enforcements arrived, the British determined to stand their ground, and Lincoln, hastily collecting the best army he could, pushed south and joined the French. The British, however, still held out, and at last D'Estaing, alarmed by the lateness of the season for the safety of his fleet, resolved to withdraw, and an immediate attack became necessary. On the ninth of October the assault was made, and the French and Americans were repulsed, with heavy slaughter. D'Estaing was wounded, and Pulaski killed. The French took to their ships and sailed for France, while Lincoln, whose army was chiefly made up of militia, and rapidly melted away, retreated as best he could to Charleston. More formidable preparations, however, were making against the South than those of Prevost and Campbell. Late in December Sir Henry Clinton left New York with eight thousand men, and the fleet under Arbuthnot. After suffering severely from storms, and not until the end of January, Clinton found himself in Georgia with a united force of ten thousand men. Sending to New York for Lord Rawdon and three thousand additional soldiers, Clinton began to advance slowly and carefully upon Charleston, where Lincoln was in command of the army, and strongly sustained by the State government. But there was a great deal of fear and disaffection, and the unfortified city was really indefensible. Washington would have had Lincoln withdraw, and not risk so much in defence of the town; but this view was not accepted, and Lincoln devoted all his energies to constructing fortifications. The task was hopeless. Arbuthnot passed Fort Moultrie in safety; Clinton pushed his works forward, and on the twelfth of May Lincoln capitulated, and the town and army fell into the hands of the British. The plundering of Prevost was continued, but in a more organized fashion, and the English soldiers and officers enriched themselves with the spoils of the city. Ten days later confiscation was threatened to all who did not submit; and on the third of June Clinton issued a proclamation requiring all the inhabitants, on pain of being treated as rebels, to take up arms for the King. This was the beginning of a policy of crushing and brutal severity, replete with plundering, confiscation, hanging, ill-treatment of prisoners, and massacres after surrender; which, backed as it was by a large party of native loyalists, gave to the war in the South a character for savage barbarity and bitter feeling unknown elsewhere. Soon after his proclamation was published, Clinton departed for New York, leaving Cornwallis, now the favorite of the ministry and his own rival, in command. The winter in the North had been marked by great suffering in the American army, and by indecisive and trifling actions, with little advantage to either side. On his return from South Carolina, Clinton turned his attention to gaining by treachery what he had failed to win by force; but there is no need to rehearse the familiar story of Arnold's treason. It is the black chapter of the war for Independence. The prize was West Point and the control of the Hudson. The plot failed miserably, and Major André met the merited death of a spy by the hands of the hangman; while the greater criminal, Arnold, took himself and his services over to the British.

But the last scenes in the war were not to be enacted in the northern or middle states. The final decision of the great question was to be made in the South. The fall of Charleston for the moment paralyzed resistance in South Carolina, and the fortified posts of the interior fell one after another into the hands of the British. Tarleton ranged over the country, ravaging, plundering, and dispersing the small parties of militia retreating to the north, while Cornwallis enforced everywhere his policy of harsh severity and brutal punishments. The middle of July had come before the patriots, who had rallied under Sumter, fell upon a party of British raiders and routed them. Sumter followed up this affair by attacking the British unsuccessfully at Rocky Mount, and later defeated some regiments of loyalists at Hanging Rock. Meantime Washington had detached from his little army two thousand men under De Kalb, and Virginia voted as many more. Washington wished to have the southern department confided to Greene, but Congress appointed Gates, who hurried southward, gathering militia on the way, and joined De Kalb at his camp on Deep River. Thence he pushed on, full of confidence, to overwhelm the British under Lord Rawdon at Camden; but his delays at a critical moment gave Rawdon time to intrench, and Cornwallis to come up. The army was weakened by detaching Sumter with eight hundred men to cut off the British convoy and stores. Ignorant of the number of his soldiers, with a bad disposition of his troops, who were strange to each other, and chiefly untrained militia, Gates advanced, and the armies came together near Camden. The militia broke in a panic, and fled from the field, with Gates among them. De Kalb and his Continentals stood their ground for a time, but De Kalb was killed, and his men gave way. The British lost heavily in the battle, but the rout of the Americans was complete. The whole army was scattered; Gates fled two hundred miles to Hillsborough; and Sumter, who had captured the convoy, was by his own carelessness surprised and beaten by Tarleton. The American forces in South Carolina were utterly dispersed.

As in the North after the fall of Ticonderoga, so in the South after Camden, the tide turned in the darkest hour, and again it was a popular movement, the rising of men in defence of their homes. Cornwallis, destroying property and life, and flushed with triumph, looked forward to easy conquest, and a victorious march through North Carolina and Virginia. Major Ferguson was detached with two hundred regulars to raise the loyalists, and he soon succeeded in enrolling a large body. Separated from Cornwallis, he occupied himself with the pursuit of various partisan bands, and learned too late that the rising was becoming serious. Williams raised a strong band in Ninety-six, and, uniting with the backwoodsmen of North Carolina and Virginia under Sevier and Shelby, fell upon Ferguson at King's Mountain. They stormed the heights held by the British, Ferguson fell, and his men were all either killed or made prisoners. The effect of the victory was electric. The loyalist rising in North Carolina was checked, the patriots everywhere began to take arms, the partisans under Sumter and Marion increased in numbers and activity, while Cornwallis was forced to concentrate his army, and move more slowly and less confidently. Meanwhile Congress, taking at last the advice of Washington, sent Greene to take command in the South. Greene hastened to Charlotte, where he found a miscellaneous body of militia gathered by Gates after his defeat, utterly unorganized, and requiring all the weary work which had been expended on the soldiers of the North. With quiet persistence Greene addressed himself to his task of organization and enlistment; and his first act was to shoot deserters, for the militia came and went as they pleased. While thus engaged, Morgan, with a separate command, had advanced into South Carolina, where he was breaking up the roving bands of royal partisans and checking their marauding. Cornwallis, eager to cut him off, sent Tarleton in pursuit, and at the same time moved the main army forward to intercept his **1781.** retreat. Tarleton, eleven hundred strong, and well equipped with artillery, came up with the Americans at the Cowpens. Morgan placed his cavalry in reserve, the Marylanders in the centre, and the famous riflemen on the wings, and threw forward the militia. The latter fell back before the British onset, skirmishing heavily, and the main line came into action. As the British began to gain, Morgan withdrew the Maryland troops, and formed them again, while the enemy, confident of victory, rushed forward. Again the Maryland troops fronted them, the wings pressed forward, and the British found themselves surrounded and exposed to a deadly and converging fire. Colonel Washington and his cavalry, coming from the woods, charged, and the British gave way in hopeless confusion, losing more than half their force in killed, wounded, and prisoners. Destroying their heavy baggage, they fled, leaving arms, cannon, and standards in possession of the Americans. Gathering up his prisoners and spoils, Morgan retreated in leisurely fashion into North Carolina.

The blow was a heavy one to the British; but Cornwallis, full of his scheme of ending the war on the Chesapeake, destroyed his heavy baggage, and pressed on to the north to subjugate North Carolina and Virginia. The forces of Greene and Morgan had united at Guilford, but were too weak to offer battle. The light troops, under Williams, hung upon the British flank, and Cornwallis, resolving to crush the Americans, moved rapidly after them. By a rapid and masterly retreat of two hundred miles from the Catawba to the Dan, Greene saved his army, and the moment the British ceased from pursuit was again in the field. The loyalists who had taken arms in North Carolina were routed and their rising stopped, while Greene, baffling Cornwallis un-

33

til he should receive re-enforcements, refused to fight. At last, by the middle of March, he felt strong enough to risk an engagement, and awaited the enemy at Guilford Court-house, where a sharp battle ensued, in which the British lost over five hundred, and the Americans over three hundred men. The British broke the American line, and Greene, without having used his reserves, retreated in good order to a place of safety; while Cornwallis, crippled by his victory, hurried away closely pursued by Greene, eager and ready to fight again, and succeeded in escaping safely to Wilmington. Instead of seeking to regain Charleston and maintain his hold on the Carolinas, Cornwallis, still inflamed with a sense of his own triumphs, persisted in his plan of uniting with the other English forces on the Chesapeake, and, leaving Wilmington, marched on to Virginia.

Greene, as soon as Cornwallis had departed, turned back to South Carolina. He struck first at Camden, fought with Rawdon at Hobkirk's Hill, was defeated, and retreated in good order with his artillery and baggage, and baffled Rawdon, who pursued him vainly with fresh troops. Marion and Lee in the interval cut the communication between Camden and Charleston, and the British were obliged to abandon the former position, while their outlying posts fell one after another into the hands of Sumter and Marion. The north-western part of South Carolina being cleared, Greene moved against Ninety-six, and, after failing to carry it by storm, was forced to retreat by the advance of Rawdon. The moment the British turned, Greene was on their heels harassing and distressing them. Ninety-six was isolated, and Cruger obliged to abandon it and join Rawdon, who soon after sailed for England. Everywhere the British were beaten in detail, and their posts and forts lost. Coming down from the Santee, Greene gave their united forces battle at Eutaw Springs, where at first he carried all before him; but his advance was checked by a party who threw themselves into a brick house, and he was in a second attack defeated. The total loss to the Americans was over five hundred; to the British, over fifteen hundred men. After this action Greene withdrew to the heights of the Santee to recruit. In a campaign of less than a year, against every conceivable difficulty, with raw troops and no supplies, he had taken two states from the enemy. He had fought, been beaten, and fought again, cleared the country, and shut the British up in Charleston. The campaign was a masterpiece of skill and fortitude, and justly places Greene next to Washington among the soldiers of the Revolution.

While Virginia was generously sending her troops to the south, her own territory was invaded. In January, Arnold, with sixteen hundred men, was on the James, and soon after Phillips arrived with a larger force, and a general plundering and destruction began; for Lafayette, who had been hurried to Virginia with two thousand men, was too weak to offer any effectual resistance. In May, Cornwallis, arriving from the south, relieved Arnold from the command which had devolved upon him through the death of Phillips, and devoted the early summer to harrying Virginia from one end to the other, destroying property to the value, as it was computed, of three millions of pounds. Lafayette and Steuben were obliged to retreat before him, and Wayne, who had also come to the scene of war, was defeated in an action near Jamestown. Cornwallis was checked by orders from Clinton to detach troops to New York, and had begun reluctantly to obey, when fresh instructions came from the ministry, with whom he was in high favor, to continue the Virginia campaign. Clinton was therefore compelled to give way, and Cornwallis, concentrating his troops, took up a strong position at Yorktown.

In the course of events, and in the circumstances of the times, Washington, with unerring sagacity, saw that the supreme moment had come, and that the decisive blow could now be struck, for it was possible to unite at last the allied forces. De Grasse was expected in the Chesapeake, where, in fact, he soon arrived, and landed four thousand men. Graves, the English admiral, was incompetent, and quarrelled with Hood, so that De Barras slipped out from Newport with his fleet and the transports, carrying ordnance, and joined De Grasse. Rochambeau, marching from Rhode Island, effected a junction with Washington, while Clinton, firm in the idea that the siege of New York was intended, suffered them to cross the Hudson without molestation. Early in September the allies were moving rapidly to the south, and by the end of the month they were before Yorktown. With difficulty keeping De Grasse at his important post, Washington pushed the siege with all possible vigor. The British fell back from their outlying works, the allies pushed their trenches rapidly, and on the fifteenth of October the Americans under Hamilton, and the French under Deux Ponts, stormed two advanced redoubts, carried them, and included them in their lines. The position of Cornwallis was now hopeless; his sorties were unavailing, his escape impossible. On the eighteenth the capitulation was signed; on the following day seven thousand British soldiers laid down their arms, and gave up York

town, with ships, cannon, and supplies, to their conquerors. This victory was a fit crown to Washington's military career. To win it he
had to employ every talent both of the statesman and the general.
He had to overcome the difficulties inseparable from allied forces—
to unite in common action not only the French and American armies,
but the French fleet, which was essential to his plans—to move rapidly, and strike hard. The perfection of his work is shown by his
triumph and by its results. For nearly a year more the war
1782. dragged along; nothing was done in the North, but in the
South the fighting went on fitfully. Wayne cleared Georgia, and
forced the British to evacuate Savannah, and the treaty of peace soon
after removed them from New York and their last hold upon the colonies. But the surrender at Yorktown was the real close of the war,
and was recognized as such both in America and Europe. It crushed
the last lingering hope in England of subjugating the rebellious provinces, and led to the Treaty of Paris, by which the independence of
the thirteen colonies was secured and acknowledged, after seven years
of hard and often desperate war.

Chapter XXV.

PEACE: 1782.

WHILE the armies of the colonies were in the field during the six years of war, a rapid political development had gone on side by side with the battles and sieges by which independence was secured. A confederacy, loose and ill-constructed, had been formed by Congress and assented to by the colonies, which had one after another cast off their old governments, adopted constitutions, and became states. The defects of the confederacy had begun to show themselves very clearly; the separatist principle was predominant, and Congress had greatly declined in character and ability. All this political growth and movement, both in the individual states and in the confederacy, belongs not to the history of the colonies but to that of the United States. The great forces of nationality and separatism, of aristocracy and democracy, which have made up the history of the United States, were then just coming into play and beginning to be felt, were laying the foundation of future parties, and drawing the geographical lines on which those parties were formed. The political development of the war period is of deep importance, but it belonged to the future, not to the past; it was national, not colonial.

The struggle for independence has also another side, that of diplomacy, which fought the battle of the colonies among the continental nations of Europe. Thither went some of the ablest men in America. The conspicuous figure is that of Franklin, who turned the scale in our favor at the court of France. To strive vainly for the selfish and useless friendship of Spain, John Jay was sent to Madrid; Henry Laurens, on his way to negotiate for a loan in Holland, fell into British hands, and was sent to the Tower; John Adams, appointed peace commissioner, after a season in France, sustained the failing finances of the colonies by loans which he effected with the Dutch, and obtained their recognition of the young republic. In June, 1781, Congress joined all these distinguished men in a new peace commission, with instructions inspired by Luzerne, requiring them to ask only for independence and the validity of the treaties with France.

In England the slow and unsuccessful war had rapidly developed the strength of the opposition, and the surrender of Cornwallis crushed the last hopes of the ministry. On the twenty-seventh of February, Conway's motion against continuing the war passed by a majority of nineteen; this was followed by an address to the King, declaring all those his enemies who advised a prosecution of the war; a bill was introduced to enable the King to make peace; and on the twentieth of March Lord North resigned. The government passed into the hands of the Rockingham Whigs. Shelburne had the home department, which had always included the colonies, while Fox had the foreign affairs.[1] Shelburne at once sent Mr. Oswald as his representative to Paris, and soon after Fox attacked him, and sent Mr. Grenville to represent his department. Each envoy struggled to get control of the negotiation; and Franklin, who had been occupied in shutting Spain out of the treaty, made the most of both of them. The contest between the secretaries became bitter; Rockingham died, Fox withdrew from the Cabinet, and Shelburne was at the head of the ministry. The new Prime Minister, anxious to keep the cause of the colonies separate from that of France, was eager to come to terms with Franklin; and the negotiation seemed almost concluded, when Jay appeared on the scene at Paris. Jay, disliking and mistrusting Spain, and believing Franklin too ready to yield to France, checked the negotiation, which was prospering so well with Shelburne. Again Franklin got the wheels moving, and a treaty was drafted; but soon after, John Adams, and then Laurens, appeared, and there was more delay. Shelburne's ministry was tottering, the conciliatory spirit was growing weaker, and the fate of the treaty became every day more doubtful. At last, as November was closing, Oswald, who had been re-enforced by two colleagues, concluded a treaty with the American commissioners. By that treaty independence was acknowledged, British debts were to be secured, boundaries were agreed to, a claim was introduced to prevent the carrying away of slaves, and the right to the fisheries was conceded to the Americans. The success of the treaty was chiefly due to Franklin,

[1] I have used these familiar terms which, as nearly as may be, express the jurisdiction of the two secretaries. The Secretaries of State were for the northern and southern departments, both having foreign relations. Efforts had been made to define these offices, but their powers were still confused when Shelburne and Fox took office.

who managed the English envoys, played off his somewhat intractable colleagues against Vergennes, and Vergennes against his colleagues, and, disregarding the instructions of Congress, brought the negotiation to a conclusion before the advantage to be gained from Shelburne was lost by his fall from power.

Thus was the prize for which the colonists had fought won by war and diplomacy. Independence was forced upon America by the condition and policy of England; and when it was achieved colonial history was at an end, and the history of a new nation began. The place obtained in the world by that new nation, in the century which has elapsed since the Treaty of Paris, is known to all men. The thirteen struggling colonies which then fringed the Atlantic coast have become masters of a continent, and a chief factor in the affairs of civilized mankind. They are still working out their uncompleted destiny; but the great forces which have been developed, and which in their conflict have made the history of the United States, are to be found rooted deep down among the people of the colonies who founded the nation. The studies of life, character, social condition, and political habits contained in this volume have been written to little purpose if they do not tell their own story, and disclose the various elements of national history which were bursting into life when the Treaty of Paris was concluded. By the light of colonial history we can see the causes which have influenced that of the United States, and understand the inevitable character of the national development.

We see thirteen colonies, peopled in the main by men of English race, but with a sufficient infusion of other blood to make race prejudices in the end politically impossible. Each colony had a representative government, on the general model of King, Lords, and Commons, and the independent governments—state and federal—were sure to conform to that model. The strongest quality of the predominant English race was its conservatism; and no system was possible which was struck out at white-heat from the brains of theorists, and aimed to be ideally perfect. With strong conservatism and rooted political habits, the men of English race in America used only the materials with which they were familiar, and which had long been tried. They adapted them to new conditions with the least possible change, and in the same spirit they clung to the system of law to which they were accustomed. No one thought of suggesting codes and the introduction of civil law; but the common law of England found a new home and a secure one in America, and with that common law went the strong respect for it and for the courts which administered it. Every form of religious belief found support among the colonists. A state religion was impossible; a free church, in a free and wholly secular state, was the only possible outcome of such conditions, and was accepted in the Constitution of the United States.

So far there was but one opinion—so far all was harmonious; but in the social and economical condition of the colonies, and in the sovereignty which each had assumed, there were to be found the sources of political and social conflict. In every colony there was an aristocracy; but while the system of Virginia was aristocratic, that of New England was democratic, and in the middle states the two systems mingled. The people of the south were agricultural, the leaders were great landholders, the social and political fabric rested on slave labor; in New England the people were traders, mechanics, and small freeholders, and free and honored labor was the leading principle of the community. In the middle states free labor prevailed, and the system was at bottom like that of New England; but the large foreign elements made their politics shifting and uncertain. In all the states the separatist feeling was strong, but especially so in the south, where the aristocracy who controlled the states added class pride to the love of self-government. The pressure of war bound the colonies together; but even then the separatist feeling was dominant, and the members of the confederacy fell speedily apart, while with each succeeding year the bonds of union became weaker, and the interest in the general government diminished. Geographical isolation and community of race and language were the only natural aids to union. Against them were distance, differences of habits and pursuits, local pride, a people accustomed to little or no government, with an exaggerated dislike of anything resembling external power, and habituated for more than a century to incessant contests with those who administered their governments. The very existence of the colonies as a respectable state demanded union, and brought about the adoption of the Constitution. With this beginning, a national sentiment had to be created, and a nation built up. In the contests of parties it was inevitable that the party in power should be a national party, and the party of the minority should fall back on the rights of states. The opposition was assured of a formidable weapon unknown in other countries.

But the political parties which made use of the forces inherent in the form of government grew out of the differences in the social and economical conditions of the colonies. New England represented democracy and progress; Virginia, aristocracy and conservatism, and they contended for the possession of the middle states, which held the balance of power. These two opposing elements go back to Plymouth and Jamestown. From Plymouth went forth one great column of civilization which controlled the States of the West and North; from Jamestown went out the other column to possess the West and South. Population increased rapidly in the North and slowly in the South, and the latter could only maintain itself by dividing the power of its rival. At last this resource failed, and the two hostile and advancing columns met far out on the plains of Kansas. There was a moment's pause, and the battle raged along the whole line. After a bloody civil war of four years the democracy of Plymouth triumphed, and the conservative aristocracy of Virginia was broken in pieces, together with the slave system which supported its power. With the close of the war between the states a new era begins. Down to that time the history of the United States has followed the lines marked out during the period and by the circumstances of colonial development. Whether this will continue to be the case, it is as yet too early to say; but to understand the past history of the United States we must know thoroughly that of the English colonies in America, and be able to appreciate the people who made them the foundation of a great nation.

CHRONOLOGICAL TABLES.

VIRGINIA.

1584. Raleigh's first expedition under Amidas and Barlow lands at Roanoke Island.
1606. London and Plymouth Companies chartered.
1607. January 1st, Captain Newport sails from the Downs with first settlers.
1607. May 13th, Landing at Jamestown.
1609. New charter obtained by Company. Gates and Somers sent out with fleet. Return of Smith. Percy acting Governor.
1610. Lord Delaware Governor.
1611. Sir Thomas Dale Governor, and during presence of Gates deputy.
1616. Dale returns. Yeardley deputy.
1617. Samuel Argall Governor
1619. Sir George Yeardley Governor. June, House of Burgesses meet. August, First slaves landed.
1621. Sir Francis Wyatt Governor.
1622. Great massacre by Indians.
1624. London Company for Virginia dissolved.
1626. Sir George Yeardley Governor.
1627. Francis West elected Governor by the Council.
1628. John Pott elected Governor by the Council.
1629. Sir John Harvey royal Governor.
1632. Trouble with settlers of Maryland.
1639. Harvey recalled, and Sir Francis Wyatt reappointed.
1642. Sir William Berkeley Governor.
1644. Second Indian outbreak suppressed by Berkeley.
1652. Surrender of Virginia to commissioners of Parliament. Richard Bennet chosen Governor by Burgesses.
1655. Edward Digges chosen Governor by burgesses.
1656. Samuel Matthews chosen Governor by burgesses.
1659. Death of Matthews.
1660. Sir William Berkeley elected Governor by the burgesses, and confirmed by Charles II.
1663. Insurrection by the Puritans.
1674. Second insurrection threatened.
1675. Indian war.

1676. Insurrection headed by Nathaniel Bacon, Jr. Death of Bacon, and suppression of rebels by Berkeley.
1677. Berkeley recalled. Sir Herbert Jeffreys Deputy-governor.
1678. Sir Henry Chicheley Deputy-governor.
1680. Lord Culpepper Governor.
1684. Lord Howard of Effingham Governor.
1690. Sir Francis Nicholson Deputy-governor.
1692. William and Mary College founded. Sir Edmund Andros Governor.
1698. Sir Francis Nicholson Governor.
1704. Earl of Orkney titular Governor.
1705. Nicholson succeeded by Edward Nott Lieutenant-governor.
1706. Death of Nott.
1708. Appointment of Robert Hunter as Lieutenant-governor. Never arrives.
1710. Alexander Spotswood Lieutenant-governor.
1716. Spotswood crosses the Blue Ridge.
1722. Hugh Drysdale Lieutenant-governor.
1726. Death of Drysdale.
1727. William Gooch Lieutenant-governor.
1740. Virginia joins in Carthagena expedition.
1749. Resignation of Gooch.
1752. Robert Dinwiddie Lieutenant-governor. Establishment of Ohio Company.
1753. Washington sent to Fort Du Quesne to protest against French encroachments.
1754. Surprise and death of De Jumonville. Washington surrenders at Great Meadows.
1755. Defeat and death of Braddock.
1758. Lord Loudon Governor; never takes office. Francis Fauquier Governor of Virginia. Forbes captures Fort Du Quesne.
1763. The "Parson's cause."
1765. Virginia prevented from sending delegates, but supports action of Stamp Act Congress at New York.

MARYLAND.

1628. George Calvert (Lord Baltimore) visits Virginia.
1632. Charles I. gives charter of Maryland to Cecilius Calvert (Lord Baltimore).
1634. Leonard Calvert and his followers land in Maryland and found St. Mary's.
1635. Clayborne driven from Kent Island.
1638. Assembly refuses to accept Lord Baltimore's laws.
1645. Ingle and Clayborne's rebellion.
1646. Leonard Calvert returns, and re-establishes the government.
1647. Death of Leonard Calvert. Thomas Green Governor.
1648-1649. } William Stone Governor.
1649. Passage of the Toleration Act.
1652. Maryland taken by Parliamentary commissioners.

1655. Stone defeated in battle at Providence by Puritans. Puritan supremacy.
1656. Lord Baltimore commissions Fendall as Governor.
1657. Proprietary government re-established.
1660. Philip Calvert Governor.
1661. Charles Calvert Governor.
1675. Death of Cecilius Calvert (Lord Baltimore).
1676. Thomas Notly Deputy-governor.
1681. Rising under Fendall and Coode quelled by Lord Baltimore.
1684. Government intrusted to Council, and President William Joseph.
1689. Government seized by Coode and the Protestant associators.
1692. Royal government established. Sir Lionel Copley Governor.
1694. Francis Nicholson Governor.
1698. Nicholas Blackiston Governor.
1703. John Seymour Governor.
1709. Death of Seymour. Edward Lloyd President of Council.
1714. John Hart Governor.
1720. Charles Calvert Governor.
1726. Benedict Leonard Calvert Governor.
1731. Samuel Ogle Governor.
1742. Thomas Bladen Governor.
1747. Samuel Ogle Governor.
1751. Death of Charles (Lord Baltimore), and accession of Frederick, sixth and last Lord Baltimore.
1752. Death of Governor Ogle.
1753. Horatio Sharpe Governor.
1765. Delegates from Maryland attend the Stamp Act Congress.

NORTH CAROLINA.

1584. Raleigh's first expedition under Amidas and Barlow.
1629. North Carolina granted by Charles I. to Sir Robert Heath.
1653. Virginians begin to settle on Roanoke and Chowan.
1660-1661. New England men at Cape Fear.
1663. Charles II. grants the Carolinas to Clarendon and others.
1664. Under Sir John Yeamans, men from Barbadoes settle at Cape Fear.
1667. Sayle explores coast. Samuel Stephens Governor of Albemarle.
1669. First Assembly meets. "Fundamental Constitutions" of Locke and Shaftesbury published.
1674. Death of Stephens. Carteret Governor.
1676. Eastchurch appointed Governor.
1678. Culpepper's rebellion.
1683. Seth Sothel Governor.
1688. Rebellion against Sothel, who is driven from the province.
1689. Philip Ludwell Governor.
1693. Ludwell succeeded by Alexander Lillington, and then Thomas Harvey.

1695. Joseph Archdale Governor.

1696. Thomas Harvey Deputy-governor.

1699. Henderson Walker President of the Council.

1704. Death of Walker. Robert Daniel President.

1705. Thomas Cary Deputy - governor. Prolonged struggle between Cary and
       Glover for supremacy.

1710. Edward Hyde Lieutenant-governor.

1711. Indian war breaks out.

1712. Death of Hyde. Thomas Pollock President of the Council.

1714. Charles Eden Governor.

1715. Tuscaroras broken, and peace made with Indians.

1718. Virginia destroys pirates.

1722. Death of Eden.

1724. George Burrington Governor.

1725. Sir Richard Everard Governor.

1727. Virginia line run.

1731. Sale of proprietary government to the Crown. Burrington Governor.

1734. Gabriel Johnston Governor.

1752. Death of Johnston.

1754. Arthur Dobbs Governor.

1760-
1765. } Troubles between Dobbs and Assembly.

1765. Death of Dobbs. William Tryon Governor.

1771. Battle of the Alamance, and suppression of the "Regulators." Josiah Mar
       tin Governor.

1774. North Carolina chooses delegates to the Congress at Philadelphia.

———

SOUTH CAROLINA.

1562. Ribault in South Carolina.

1564. Expedition under Laudonniere.

1565. French settlement destroyed by Menendez. St. Augustine founded.

1568. Massacre of Spaniards by De Gourgues.

1663. South Carolina granted by Charles II. to Clarendon and others.

1667. Sayle explores the coast.

1669. Sayle Governor. Death of Sayle.

1670. Sir John Yeamans Governor.

1674. Joseph West Governor.

1683. Joseph Moreton Governor.

1684-
1686. } Kyle, Moreton, West, Quarry, governors.

1686. James Colleton Governor.

1690. Overthrow of Colleton. Sothel seizes government.

1691. Philip Ludwell Governor.

1692. Thomas Smith Governor.

1694. Introduction of rice.

1695. Joseph Archdale Governor.
1696. Joseph Blake Governor.
1700. James Moore Governor.
1703. Sir Nathaniel Johnson Governor.   Church controversy.
1708. Colonel Edward Tynte Governor.
1710. Death of Tynte.   Robert Gibbes Governor.
1712. Charles Craven Governor.
1715. Successful Indian war closed.
1717. Robert Johnson Governor.
1719. Popular rising against Johnson.   He is deposed, and James Moore chosen Governor by convention.
1721. Sir Francis Nicholson provisional Governor.
1725. Arthur Middleton Governor.
1729. South Carolina sold to the Crown.
1731. Sir Robert Johnson Governor.
1735. Death of Johnson.   Thomas Broughton Governor.
1737. William Bull Lieutenant-governor.
1740. Negro insurrection.   Spanish War.
1742. Repulse of Spaniards at Frederica.
1743. James Glen Governor.
1753. Glen makes treaty with Cherokees.
1756. William Lyttelton Governor.
1760. War with the Cherokees.   William Bull Lieutenant-governor.
1761. Peace with the Cherokees.
1764-}
1767.} Troubles with the "Regulators."
1765. South Carolina chooses delegates to Stamp Act Congress.

GEORGIA.

1732. Georgia granted to Oglethorpe's association.
1733. Oglethorpe arrives with settlers, and founds Savannah.
1734. Oglethorpe returns to England.
1735. Comes out with "grand emigration."
1738. Raises troops in England.
1739. Declares war against Spain.
1740. Invades Florida, and forced to retreat.
1742. Repulses Spaniards at Frederica.
1743. Invades Florida again.   Returns to England.   William Stephens President.
1749. Slaves admitted to Georgia.   Insurrection of Bosomworth.
1751. Henry Parker President.
1752. Trustees surrender Georgia to the Crown.
1754. John Reynolds first royal Governor.
1757. Henry Ellis Lieutenant-governor.
1760. James Wright Governor.

1765. Wright prevents choice of delegates to Stamp Act Congress.
1768. Georgia supports the Massachusetts circular.

DELAWARE.

1623. First post established on the Delaware by the Dutch.
1631. Swaanendael founded.
1632. Swaanendael destroyed by the Indians.
1635. Virginians driven from the Delaware by the Dutch.
1637. Swedes land in Delaware under Minuit.
1641. Hollandaere Governor.   New Englanders driven off.
1643. John Printz Governor.
1646. Troubles with the Dutch.
1651. Stuyvesant builds Fort Casimir.
1653. John Pappegoia Governor.
1654. John Rysingh takes Fort Casimir, and assumes government.
1655. Stuyvesant takes Fort Casimir, and establishes Dutch power in Delaware.
1656. Delaware sold to city of Amsterdam.
1657. Amsterdam sends out settlers.
1663. Dutch West India Company cede all South river to city.   Delaware seized
     by Sir Robert Carr.
1673. Delaware reconquered by the Dutch.
1674. Delaware ceded to England by treaty of Westminster.
1682. Delaware surrendered to Penn.

PENNSYLVANIA.

1681. Charles II. grants Pennsylvania to William Penn.
1682. Penn comes to Pennsylvania.
1684. After organizing government and founding Philadelphia, returns to England.
     Thomas Lloyd President of Council.
1688. Blackwell Governor.   Replaced by Thomas Lloyd.
1691. Troubles caused by George Keith.   Union with Delaware dissolved.
1693. Penn deprived of government of Pennsylvania, and Benjamin Fletcher sent
     out as royal Governor.
1694. Penn recovers his government.   Markham Deputy-governor.
1699. Penn sails for America.
1701. Grants a new charter to Pennsylvania, and returns to England.   Andrew
     Hamilton Deputy-governor.
1703. Death of Hamilton.   John Evans Deputy-governor.
1709. Removal of Evans.   Charles Gookin Deputy-governor.
1712. Penn attempts to sell the province to the Crown; fails through ill-health.
1717. Recall of Gookin.   Sir William Keith Governor.
1718. Death of Penn.

1723. Paper money issued.
1726. Keith removed.   Patrick Gordon Deputy-governor.
1736. Death of Gordon.   James Logan President of the Council.
1738. George Thomas Deputy-governor.
1739. Difficulties from Spanish war between Governor and Assembly.
1746. Resignation of Thomas.   Anthony Palmer President of the Council.
1749. James Hamilton Deputy-governor.
1750. Franklin a leader in the Assembly.
1754. Robert Hunter Morris Deputy-governor.   Continued quarrels with the Assembly.
1756. William Denny Deputy-governor.
1759. Capture of Fort Du Quesne.
1760. James Hamilton Deputy-governor.
1762. Indian war.
1763. Victory of Bouquet and the Paxton Massacre.
1764. Franklin agent in England for Pennsylvania.
1765. Pennsylvania Committee at the Stamp Act Congress.

NEW JERSEY.

1664. Grant of New Jersey to Berkeley and Carteret.
1665. Philip Carteret Governor; comes out with emigrants.
1668. First Assembly.
1672. James Carteret heads insurrection and seizes governorship.
1673. James Carteret deposed.   Lord Berkeley sells his share.   Conquest by the Dutch.
1674. Restored to England.
1675. Philip Carteret returns as Governor.
1676. Andros arrests Fenwick at Salem.
1677. Large Quaker emigration under Byllinge.   Settlement in West Jersey.
1678. Fenwick arrested by Andros at Salem.   Philip Carteret seized by Andros in East Jersey.
1680. Sir William Jones awards West Jersey to the Quakers.
1681. Philip Carteret reinstated.   Repels Brockholst.
1682-
1683. } Sale of Carteret interest (East Jersey) to Penn and others.
1684. Gawen Lawrie Deputy-governor of East Jersey.
1688. Surrender of New Jersey forced by the King.
1689. Andros Governor-general.
1692. Andrew Hamilton Deputy-governor.
1698. Jeremiah Basse Deputy-governor.
1699. Andrew Hamilton reappointed Deputy-governor for West Jersey.
1702. Proprietors surrender New Jersey to the Queen.   Lord Cornbury Governor.
1708. Recall of Lord Cornbury.   Lord Lovelace Governor.
1709. Death of Lovelace.   Richard Ingoldsby Lieutenant-governor.
1710. Robert Hunter Governor.

1720. William Burnet Governor.
1728. John Montgomerie Governor.
1731. Death of Montgomerie. Lewis Morris President of the Council.
1732. William Cosby Governor.
1736. Death of Cosby.
1738. New Jersey separated from government of New York, and Lewis Morris Governor.
1746. Death of Morris. John Hamilton President of the Council.
1747. Death of Hamilton. John Reading President of the Council.
1748. Jonathan Belcher Governor.
1757. Death of Belcher.
1758. Francis Bernard Governor.
1760. Thomas Boone Governor. Josiah Hardy Governor.
1762. William Franklin Governor.
1765. Delegates from convention sent to Stamp Act Congress.

NEW YORK.

1609. Henry Hudson at Sandy Hook.
1614. Fort Nassau built near Albany. Voyages to east and south.
1615. Formation of New Netherland Company with charter for three years.
1621. Dutch West India Company chartered.
1623. Settlers sent out by Company. Cornelis Jacobsen May first Director.
1624. William Verhulst Director.
1626. Peter Minuit Director.
1629. Establishment of Patroons.
1632. Minuit returns to Holland.
1633. Wouter Van Twiller Director.
1637. Van Twiller removed.
1638. William Kieft Director.
1640. The Company opens New Netherlands to free-trade.
1641. Establishment and election of "twelve men."
1643. War with the Indians. "Eight men" chosen.
1644. Underhill defeats Indians with great slaughter in Connecticut.
1645. Peace with Indians. Removal of Kieft. Revision of government.
1647. Arrival of Peter Stuyvesant as Director-general. "Nine men" chosen by representatives of the people.
1649. New board of "nine men" appointed to appeal to Holland.
1650. Treaty and settlement of boundary with New England.
1651. Stuyvesant builds Fort Casimir, on the Delaware.
1652. Burgher government established.
1654. English invasion prevented by peace made between Cromwell and States-general.
1655. Stuyvesant conquers the Swedes, and becomes master of Delaware. Indian war.
1658. Indian war breaks out at Esopus.

1660. Trouble with Lord Baltimore.
1662. Loss of Long Island and northern territory by Connecticut charter.
1664. English conquest of New Netherlands. Richard Nicolls Governor of New York.
1668. Nicolls returns to England. Francis Lovelace Governor.
1673. The Dutch take New York. Anthony Colve Governor.
1674. New York ceded to England by the treaty of Westminster. Edmund Andros Governor.
1680. Andros recalled. Anthony Brockholst Lieutenant-governor.
1683. Thomas Dongan Governor.
1685. James revokes his charter, or " Duke's laws."
1688. New York annexed to New England. Andros Governor-general.
1689. Rising under Leisler. Expulsion of Nicholson.
1690. French war. Destruction of Schenectady.
1691. Henry Sloughter Governor. Leisler surrenders, and is executed. Death of Sloughter. Richard Ingoldsby Lieutenant-governor.
1692. Benjamin Fletcher Governor.
1698. Lord Bellomont Governor.
1701. Death of Bellomont. John Nanfan Lieutenant-governor.
1702. Lord Cornbury Governor.
1708. Removal of Cornbury. Lord Lovelace Governor.
1709. Death of Lovelace. Ingoldsby Lieutenant-governor.
1710. Robert Hunter Governor.
1711. First negro plot.
1713. Peace with France.
1719. Hunter retires.
1720. William Burnet Governor.
1727. Burnet transferred to Massachusetts.
1728. John Montgomerie Governor.
1731. Death of Montgomerie. Rip Van Dam President of the Council.
1732. William Cosby Governor. Zenger prosecuted for libel.
1736. Death of Cosby. Contest between Van Dam and George Clarke for possession of government. Clarke commissioned as Lieutenant-governor.
1741. Second and great negro plot.
1743. Admiral George Clinton Governor.
1746. Indian war.
1748. Peace of Aix-la-Chapelle.
1753. Clinton retires. Sir Danvers Osborn Governor; kills himself. James De Lancey Lieutenant-governor.
1754. Congress of governors at Albany. Franklin's plan of union.
1755. Johnson defeats Baron Dieskau at Fort George. Sir Charles Hardy Governor.
1756. Montcalm takes Oswego.
1757. Hardy retires. De Lancey Lieutenant-governor. Montcalm captures Fort William Henry.
1758. Abercrombie repulsed at Ticonderoga. Bradstreet takes Fort Frontenac.
1759. Johnson takes Fort Niagara. French retreat before Amherst to Isle-aux-Noix.

1760. Death of De Lancey.   Cadwallader Colden Lieutenant-governor.   Amherst
     takes Montreal.
1761. General Monckton Governor.
1762. Monckton resigns.   Colden Lieutenant-governor.   Peace with France.
1765. Stamp Act Congress meets in New York.

MASSACHUSETTS.

1620. Pilgrims sail from Delfthaven.

Nov. 21, 1620. } Pilgrims land at Cape Cod.

Dec. 21, 1620. } Pilgrims land at Plymouth.

1623. Dorchester Company establishes a fishing station at Cape Ann.
1626. Conant and others remove to and settle at Naumkeag.
1628. Land granted to second Dorchester Company.   John Endicott, one of the
     patentees, comes out.
1629. Charter obtained for Governor and Company of Massachusetts Bay.
1630. John Winthrop Governor.   Arrives with his company in Massachusetts.
1631. Second general court.   Only members of churches to have votes.
1634. Troubles begin with England.
1636. Roger Williams banished from Massachusetts.   Harvard College founded.
1636-1637. } Henry Vane Governor.
1638. Expulsion of Mrs. Hutchinson.
1643. Establishment of New England Confederacy.
1647. Establishment of common schools.
1652. Annexation of Maine.
1659. Quakers hung in Boston.
1660. Complimentary address to Charles II.
1664. Arrival of the royal commissioners in Boston.
1666. Royal commissioners baffled, their power denied, and leave Boston.
1675. Outbreak of Philip's war.
1676. Death of Philip.
1677. Peace with eastern Indians, and end of the war.   Edward Randolph sent
     out as agent by Lords of Trade.
1683. *Quo warranto* issued against charter.
1684. Charter vacated.
1685. Provisional government.   Joseph Dudley President.
1686. Sir Edmund Andros Governor-general.
1688. Indian war at the east.
1689. Popular rising.   Andros seized at Boston and imprisoned.   Old charter
     government provisionally re-established.
1691. A new charter granted.
1692. Sir William Phips Governor.
1695. Phips recalled.   Returns to England.   William Stoughton Lieutenant-governor.
1697. Earl of Bellomont appointed Governor.

1699. Bellomont arrives in Boston.
1701. Death of Bellomont. Stoughton Lieutenant-governor. Death of Stoughton.
1702. Joseph Dudley Governor.
1703. Outbreak of Queen Anne's war.
1707. Failure of Dudley's expedition against Port Royal.
1710. Capture of Port Royal.
1711. Failure of Hill and Walker's expedition.
1715. William Tailer Lieutenant - governor. Dudley removed by death of sovereign.
1716. Samuel Shute Governor.
1721. War with eastern Indians under Rasle.
1723. Shute goes to England for aid against general court. William Dummer Lieutenant-governor.
1724. Death of Rasle.
1726. Peace with Indians.
1727. The explanatory charter.
1728. William Burnet Governor.
1729. Death of Burnet. Dummer Lieutenant-governor.
1730. Jonathan Belcher Governor.
1735. House prevails on the salary question.
1741. Recall of Belcher. William Shirley Governor.
1745. Louisburg taken by New England army.
1755. Shirley commands the expedition against Oswego.
1756. Shirley commander-in-chief. Recalled.
1757. Thomas Pownall Governor.
1758. Defeat of Abercrombie at Ticonderoga.
1759. Fall of Quebec.
1760. Montreal taken by Amherst. Francis Bernard Governor.
1761. The writs of assistance.
1765. Massachusetts invites the other colonies to a congress, and sends a delegation to New York

---

CONNECTICUT.

1635. John Winthrop establishes a post at Saybrook.
1636. Emigration from Newtown to Connecticut under Hooker.
1638. Colony of New Haven founded.
1639. Constitutions adopted by Connecticut and New Haven.
1643. New England Confederacy formed.
1650. Boundary treaty with Stuyvesant.
1657. John Winthrop Governor.
1662. Charles II. grants charter to Connecticut.
1664. Consolidation of Connecticut and New Haven.
1665. Visit of the royal commissioners.
1675. Duke's claim repelled.
1686. *Quo warranto* against the charter.
1687. Andros at Hartford takes possession of the government.

1690. Charter government re-established.
1707. Death of Fitz-John Winthrop.   Gurdon Saltonstall Governor.
1713. Settlement of northern boundary.
1724. Death of Saltonstall.   Joseph Talcott Governor.
1741. Death of Talcott.   Jonathan Law Governor.
1745. The Connecticut contingent at Louisburg.
1765. Resistance to Stamp Act, and delegates sent to Congress at New York.

RHODE ISLAND.

1636. Roger Williams founds Providence.
1638. Arrival of Mrs. Hutchinson and her friends.
1639. Coddington founds Newport.
1643. Williams goes to England for a charter.   Gorton taken prisoner to Boston.
1644. Williams returns with patent.   Gorton goes to England.
1647. Government established under patent.
1648. Gorton returns, and names Shawomet Warwick.   End of the Gortonian disturbances.
1651. Coddington obtains a commission in England, and sets up a government. Williams goes to England for a new charter.
1653. Gorton President.
1654. Williams returns with a letter from Vane, and is chosen President under patent.
1657. Defeat of Williams.   Benedict Arnold President.
1663. Agreement between John Clarke and the younger Winthrop.   Clarke obtains a charter for Rhode Island.
1664. Establishment of the charter government.
1665. Visit of royal commissioners.
1672. Visit of George Fox.
1675-
1676. } Philip's war.
1686. *Quo warranto* issued against charter.   Andros Governor-general.
1690. Old charter government re-established.
1697. Samuel Cranston Governor.
1724. Limitation of the franchise.
1727. Opposition of Governor Jenckes to paper money.
1747. Settlement of the northern boundary.
1764. Resistance to Navigation Act.
1765. Delegates sent to Stamp Act Congress.

NEW HAMPSHIRE.

1623. Mason and Gorges found settlements.
1629. Mason and Gorges divide, and Mason obtains New Hampshire.
1635. Death of Mason, and abandonment by his heirs of attempts to establish a colony.

1638. Arrival of Wheelwright and his friends.
1641. New Hampshire united to Massachusetts.
1660. Revival of Mason claim.
1676. Law-officers of the Crown sustain Mason claim.
1677. English courts annul jurisdiction of Massachusetts.
1679. Royal government established.
1680. John Cutts President.
1681. Death of Cutts.
1682. Edward Cranfield royal Governor.
1685. Departure of Cranfield. Barefoot Deputy-governor. United to Massachu setts under Dudley.
1686. Andros Governor-general.
1690. United to Massachusetts under old charter government.
1692. Allen buys up Mason claim. John Usher Lieutenant-governor.
1697. Thomas Partridge Lieutenant-governor.
1699. Bellomont Governor.
1702. Allen's claims carried on appeal to England. Dudley Governor.
1703. Usher Lieutenant-governor. Replaces Partridge.
1715. Death of Allen. Abandonment of suit to establish claim. Shute Governor George Vaughan Lieutenant-governor.
1717. Removal of Vaughan. John Wentworth Lieutenant-governor.
1728. Burnet Governor.
1730. Belcher Governor.
1731. David Dunbar Lieutenant-governor.
1741. New Hampshire finally separated from Massachusetts. Benning Went worth Governor.
1765. Resistance to Stamp Act, but no delegates sent to New York.

THE UNITED COLONIES.

1765. The Stamp Act Congress meets in New York.
1766. Repeal of the Stamp Act.
1767. Suspension of New York Assembly. Townshend's revenue bills.
1768. Massachusetts petitions against the revenue acts. Refuses to rescind her resolution, and the court is dissolved. Boston calls a convention. Arrival of British troops.
1769. Virginia resolutions against taxation.
1770. The Boston massacre, and removal of the regiments. Repeal of all the revenue acts except that laying a duty on tea. Resistance slackens in the colonies.
1771. Hutchinson's controversy with the general court as to the power of Parliament.
1772. Renewal of resistance at the south. Burning of the *Gaspee*.
1773. Hutchinson discusses further the power of Parliament. Committees of correspondence advised by Virginia. Publication of the letters of Hutchinson and Oliver. The East India Company authorized to export tea to the colonies. Destruction of the tea at Boston and elsewhere.

1774. Wedderburn's attack on Franklin. Passage of the Boston Port Bill and other penal acts. General Gage civil Governor of Massachusetts.

June. Massachusetts demands a Congress.

Sept. Congress meets.

1775. Chatham's plan of compromise rejected, and armies sent from England.

April. Lexington and Concord.

May. Allen takes Ticonderoga and Crown Point. Second Congress meets.

June. Battle of Bunker Hill.

July. Washington takes command of the army. Siege of Boston.

  "   The expedition against Canada, and defeat of Americans at Quebec.

1776. Evacuation of Boston. Americans retreat from Canada. Defeat of Loyalists in North Carolina. Repulse of British at Charleston.

July 4. Declaration of Independence adopted and ordered to be printed. Arrival of British army.

Aug. Washington retreats from Long Island, and evacuates New York.

Oct. Battle of White Plains.

Dec. Battle of Trenton.

1777,
Jan. } Battle of Princeton.

Sept. Battle of the Brandywine. Howe takes Philadelphia.

Oct. Battle of Germantown. Surrender of Burgoyne.

Dec. Washington at Valley Forge.

1778. The Conway cabal. Treaty of alliance with France.

June. Battle of Monmouth Court-house.

July. Battle of Newport.

Dec. Defeat of Americans in Georgia, and capture of Savannah.

1779,
May. } Prevost marches to Charleston and retreats.

July. Wayne takes Stony Point.

Oct. Americans and French repulsed at Savannah.

1780,
May. } Charleston surrenders to Clinton.

Aug. Battle of Camden.

Sept. Arnold's treason.

Oct. Battle of King's Mountain.

Dec. Greene takes command in southern department.

1781,
Jan. } Battle of the Cowpens.

March. Battle of Guilford Court-house. Cornwallis marches north.

April. Battle of Hobkirk's Hill.

Sept. Battle of Eutaw.

Oct. Surrender of Cornwallis at Yorktown.

1782,
March. } Resignation of Lord North.

July. Evacuation of Savannah.

Nov. Treaty of peace with Great Britain signed at Paris.

INDEX.

A.

ABERCROMBIE, General, defeated at Ticonderoga, 309, 370.

Acadia, pillaged by Argall, 8. D'Aulnay and La Tour in, 352. Conquest of, 369.

Acadians in Pennsylvania, 234, 235. Expulsion of, 369.

Adams, John, description of trial of writs of assistance, 417. Testimony as to loyalty of New England, 474. Delegate to Congress; presides at Boston town-meeting, 490. Moves election of Washington as commander-in-chief, 494. Seconds resolution for independence, 498. Leads in debate, 499. Mission to Holland, 517. Peace commissioner, 518.

Adams, Samuel, draws petition to King, and resolve for union, 479. Demands withdrawal of troops from Hutchinson, 482. Founds committees of correspondence, 485. Leads in discussion of powers of Parliament with Hutchinson, 486. Delegate to Congress, 490.

Albany, centre of fur-trade, 313. Arms in church, 328. Description of, 331, 332.

Allen, Ethan, captures Ticonderoga, 493. Taken prisoner at Montreal, 495.

Allen, Samuel, buys up Mason claim; Governor of New Hampshire, 400. Land suits; death; claim not pressed by his heirs, 402.

Altham, Lord; indented servant, 242.

Ames, Fisher, conversation with Sumner as to suffrage, 445.

Amherst, Sir Jeffrey, drives French back to Isle-aux-Noix, 309. Captures Montreal, 310, 370.

André, Major, hung as a spy, 511.

Andros, Sir Edmund, Governor of Virginia, 25. Suppresses Fenwick in Delaware, 209. Attempts to gain control of New Jersey, 265. Governor-general of New Jersey, 267. Receives New York from Dutch, 297. Governor of New York, 297, 298. Governor-general of New York; government overthrown, 299. Governor-general in Massachusetts, 359. Deposed, and made prisoner, 360. Dealings with Connecticut as Governor of New York, 378. Governor-general of Connecticut, 379. Visit to Hartford, 380. Governor-general of Rhode Island, 392; of New Hampshire, 400. Seizure of old South Church, 426.

Anglesea Peerage Case, 70.

Annapolis, foundation and description of, 118, 119. Society in, 129, 130.

Annesley, James, case of, 70.

Antinomians in New Hampshire, 397.

Apthorp, East, Rev., Episcopal minister in Cambridge, 427.

Arbuthnot, Admiral, commands British fleet at Charleston, 510.

Archdale, John, Governor of North Carolina, 139, 140; of South Carolina, 162.

Argall, Samuel, history and character of; his administration, 8. Recalled, 9.

Arlington, Lord, grant of Virginia to, 19.

Armstrong, John, defeats Indians at Kittanning, 223.

Arnold, Benedict, President at Providence, 389. Governor of Rhode Island under charter, 390.

Arnold, Benedict, partisan leader on the lakes, 495. Commands eastern expedition against Quebec; repulsed and wounded, 496. Treason of, 511. In Virginia, 515.

Ashurst, Sir Henry, defends New England charter, 382.

Aspinwall, William, secretary at foundation of Portsmouth, Rhode Island, 385.

Assanpink, retreat of Americans from, 504.

Atherton Company, relations of, with Connecticut, 378. With Rhode Island, 390.

Augusta, Georgia, description of, 201. Taken by British, 509.

Curler, Jacob Van, establishes post on Connecticut river, 287.

Cushing, Elder, petitions for closing taverns, 438.

Cutts house at Portsmouth, 446.

Cutts, John, President of New Hampshire; death of, 398.

Cuylers, estates of the, 327.

Cygnet, royal cruiser, attack planned upon, 396.

D.

Dagworthy, Captain, trouble with Washington, 109, 110.

Dale, Sir Thomas, Governor of Virginia; his administration, 7, 8.

Dalrymple, Colonel, takes possession of fort in Boston harbor, 483.

Dam, Rip Van, struggle with Cosby, 304; with Clarke, 305.

Daniel, Robert, Deputy-governor of North Carolina, 140; of South Carolina, 164.

Dartmouth College, 466.

D'Aulnay, relations of, with New England, 352.

Davenant, Sir William, appointed Governor of Maryland by Charles II., 102.

Davenport, John, Rev., founder of New Haven, 374.

De Lancey, James, chief-justice of New York; supports suppression of negro plot; controls Governor Clinton, 305. Commissioned Lieutenant-governor, 306. Acting-Governor, 306, 307. Presides at Albany Congress, and opposes Franklin, 307. Controls Hardy, and again Lieutenant-governor, 308. Funeral of, 338.

Delaware, discovery and settlement of, by Dutch, 205. Settlement of, by Swedes, 206. Growth under Swedes, 206, 207. Contests of Dutch and Swedes, and defeat of latter, 207. Under Dutch, and city of Amsterdam, 208, 294. Conquest by English, 208, 209. Ceded to Penn, 210. United with Pennsylvania, 212. Union dissolved; brought back by Fletcher, 214. Union finally severed, 216. Geographical situation; identity with Pennsylvania, 227. Occupations, 229. Government, 230, 231. Judiciary, 232. Towns, 240. Non-importation agreement, 481.

Delaware, Lord, Governor of Virginia; his administration, 7. Friends of, oppressed by Argall, 8. Re-appointed Governor, and dies on voyage out, 9.

Denny, William, Deputy-governor of Pennsylvania, 223.

Deux Ponts, Viscount de, at Yorktown, 515.

De Vries, D. P., Patroon; arrival in South

river, and loss of his settlers, 205, 287. Troubles with Van Twiller, 287. Comes out with Company to Staten Island, 288. Kindness to Indians; remonstrates with Kieft, 289.

Dickinson, John, opposes attempts to destroy proprietary government in Pennsylvania, 225. Leader of moderate party in Pennsylvania, 489. Draughts address to King, 491. Leads in debate against independence, 499.

Dieskau, Baron, defeated by Johnson at Fort George, and killed, 307.

Digges, Edward, Governor of Virginia, 17.

Dincklagen, Lubbertus Van, schout, quarrel with Van Twiller, 288.

Dinwiddie, Robert, Governor of Virginia, conflicts with Burgesses, 29, 30.

Dobbs, Arthur, Governor of North Carolina, 143–145.

Donck, Adrian Van der, heads opposition to Stuyvesant, 292.

Dongan, Thomas, Governor of New York; interferes with East Jersey, 266. Administration in New York, 298, 299. Efforts to establish a mail service, 331. Relations with Connecticut, 379.

Donop, Colonel, killed at Fort Mercer, 505.

Dorchester Company, 342, 343.

Douglass, William; toleration in New England, 426.

Dover founded, 397.

Drayton, Michael, poem on departure of Virginian expedition, 5.

Drummond, William, leader in Bacon's rebellion, 20. Governor of North Carolina, 135.

Drysdale, Hugh, Governor of Virginia, 28.

Duddington, Lieutenant, commander of *Gaspee*, 484.

Duddy, Richard, prosecuted for damning Duke of Cumberland, 283.

Dudley, Joseph, plots with Cornbury against charter governments, 302, 382. Leader of Crown party; agent of Massachusetts; president of government by commission, 359. Thrown into prison with Andros, 360. Character, career, and administration, 362, 363. Connecticut declines to come under his government, 379. Refuses to help him in Queen Anne's war, 381. Attacks Rhode Island, 393. President of New Hampshire by commission, 400. Governor of New Hampshire; controversy with Usher, 401, 402. Quarrel with the carters, 473.

Dudley, Thomas, Deputy-governor of Massachusetts, 345. Governor, 346. To manage war, 347. Re-chosen Deputy-governor, 350.